Levius est

VOL. 1

STORY & ART BY
Haruhisa Nakata

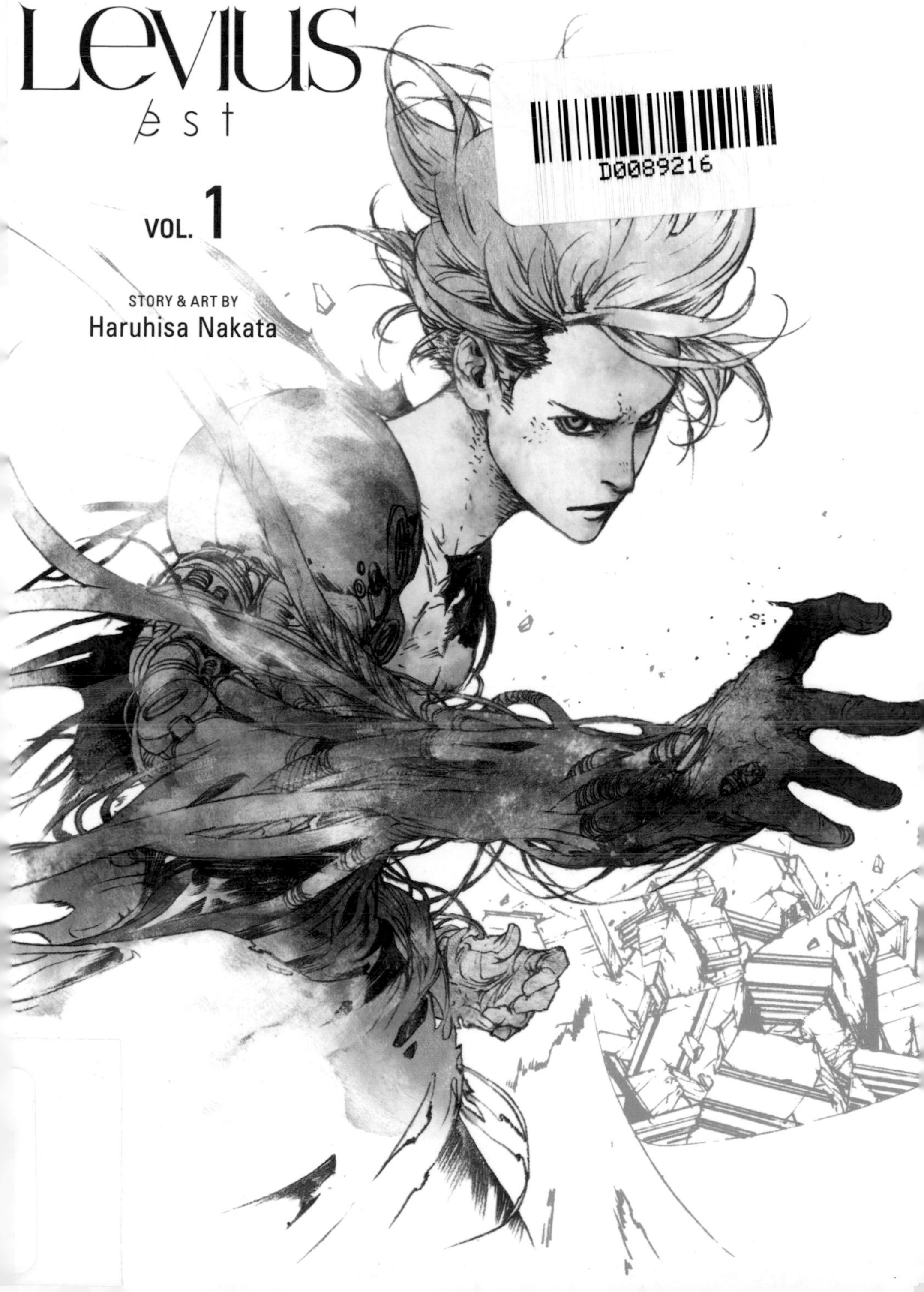

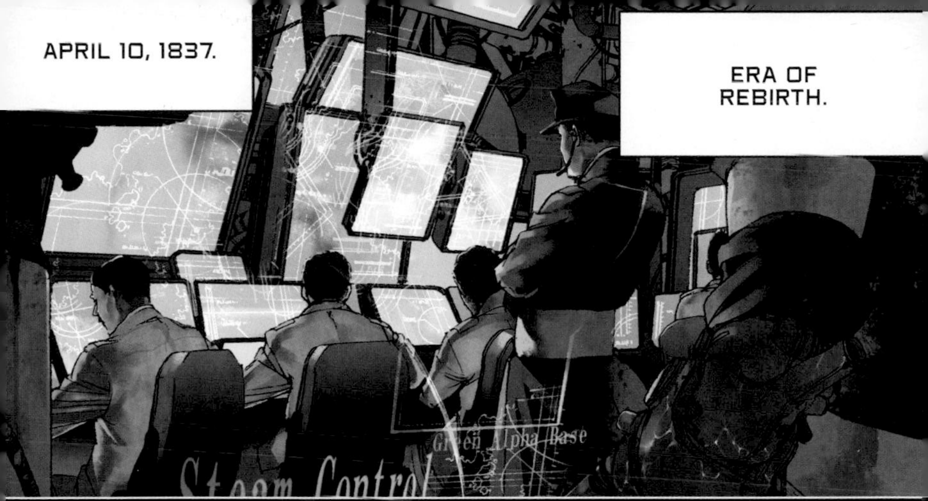
APRIL 10, 1837.
ERA OF REBIRTH.
Green Alpha Base

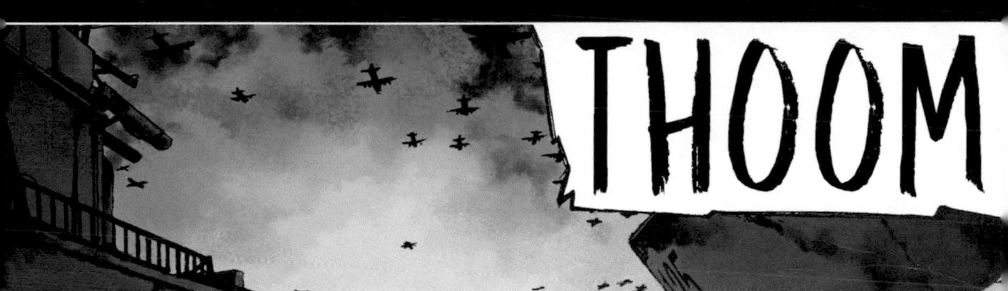
THOOM

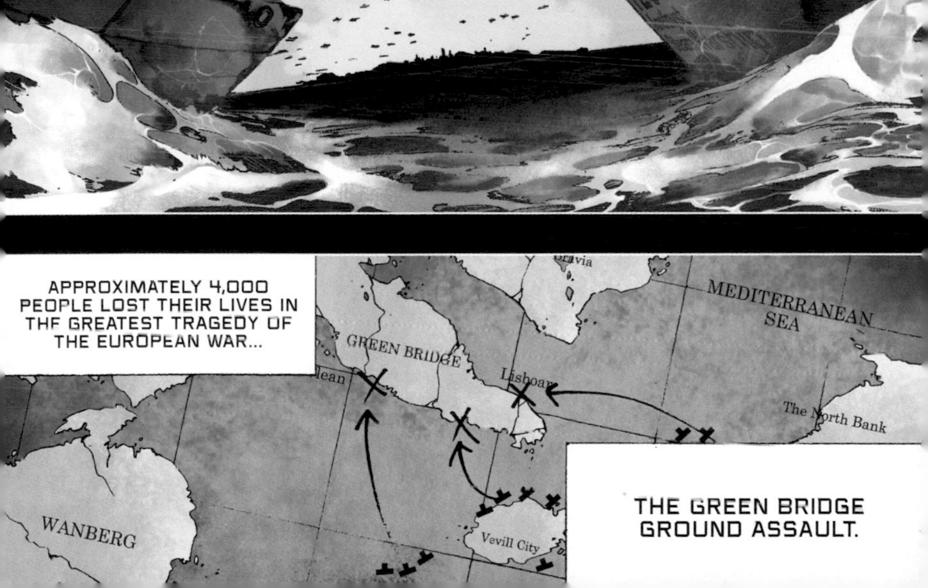
APPROXIMATELY 4,000 PEOPLE LOST THEIR LIVES IN THE GREATEST TRAGEDY OF THE EUROPEAN WAR...
MEDITERRANEAN SEA
GREEN BRIDGE
The North Bank
WANBERG
Vevill City
THE GREEN BRIDGE GROUND ASSAULT.

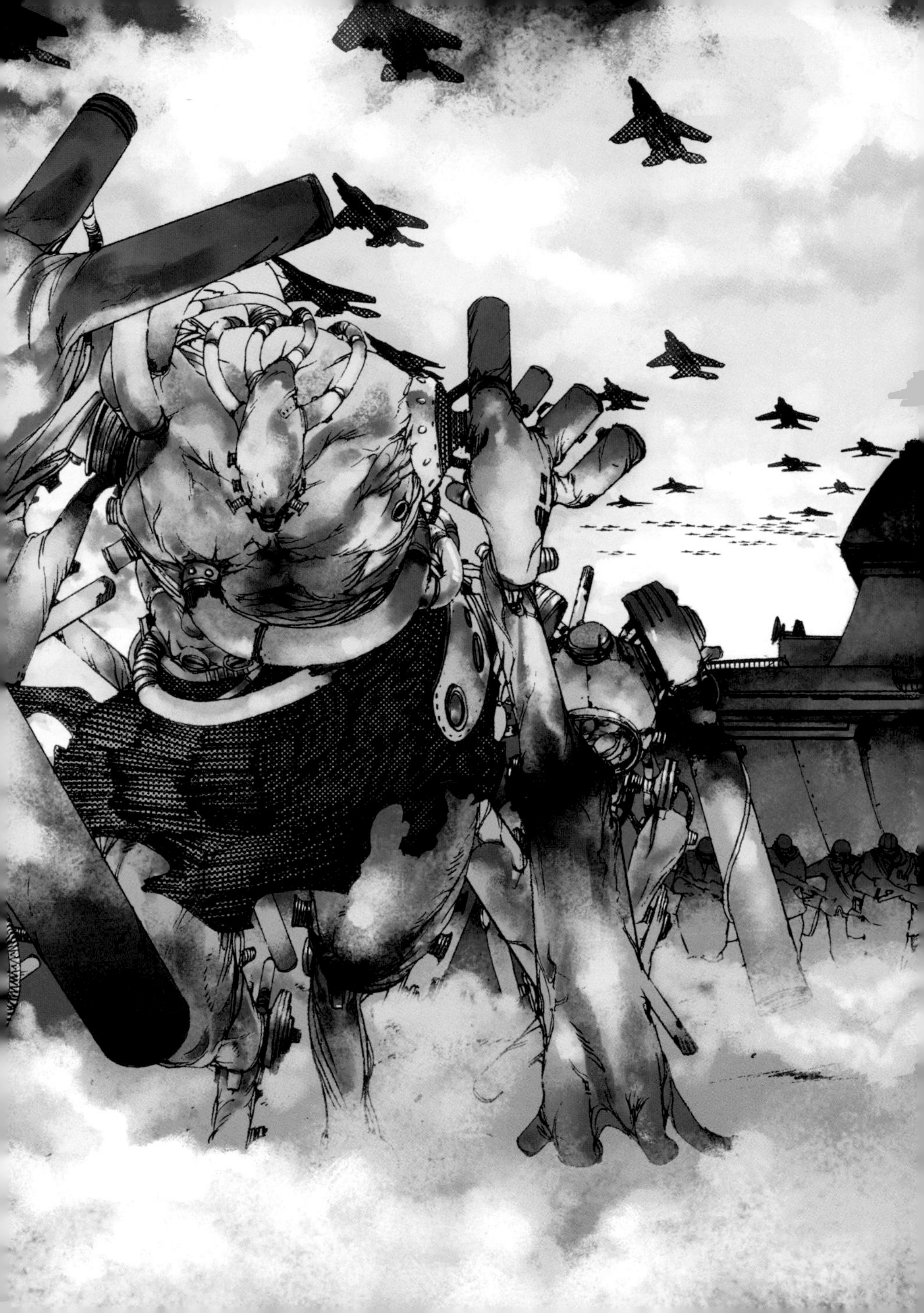

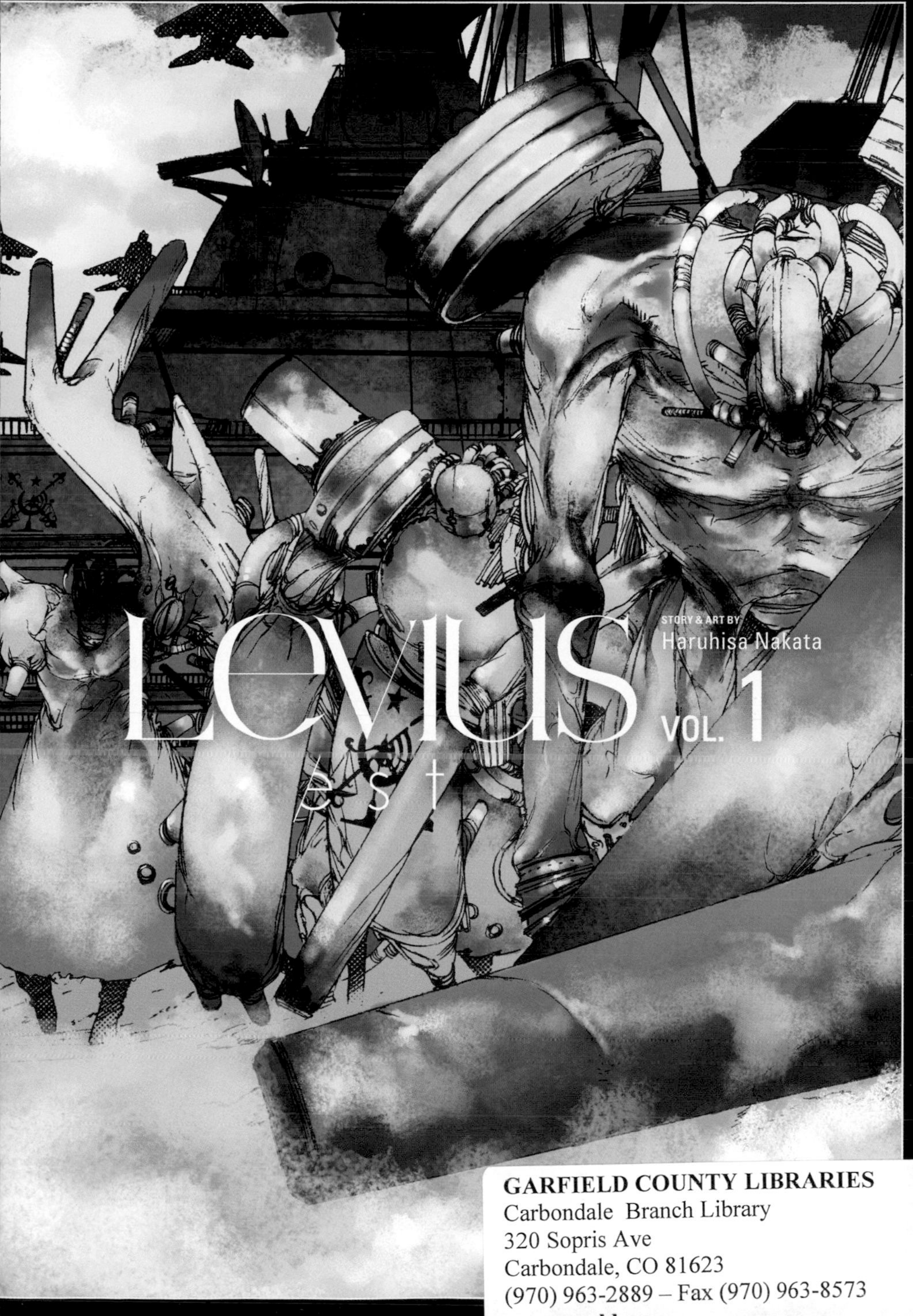
LEVIUS est
VOL. 1
STORY & ART BY
Haruhisa Nakata

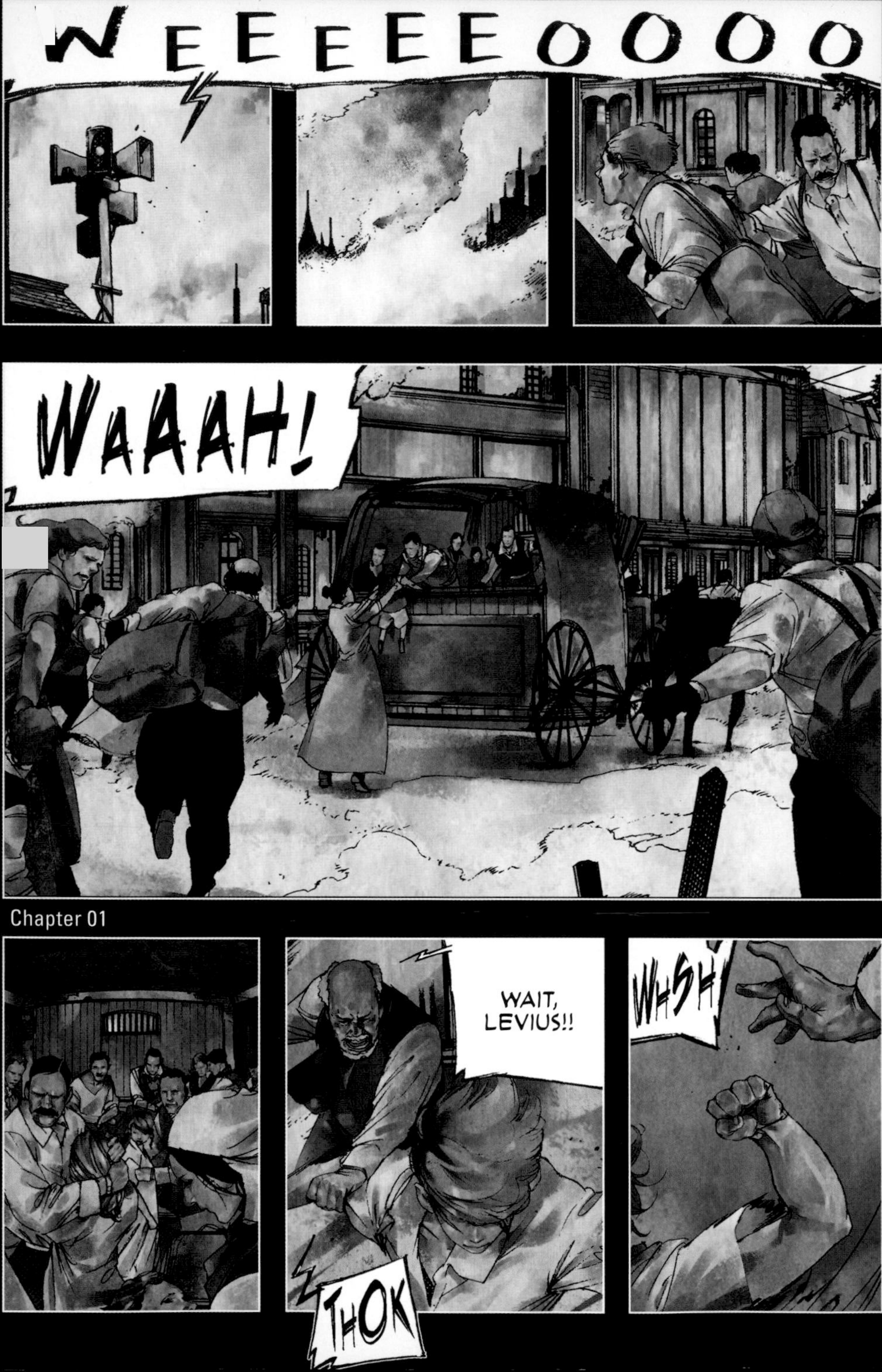
WEEEEOOOO
WAAAH!
Chapter 01
WAIT, LEVIUS!!
THOK
WHSH

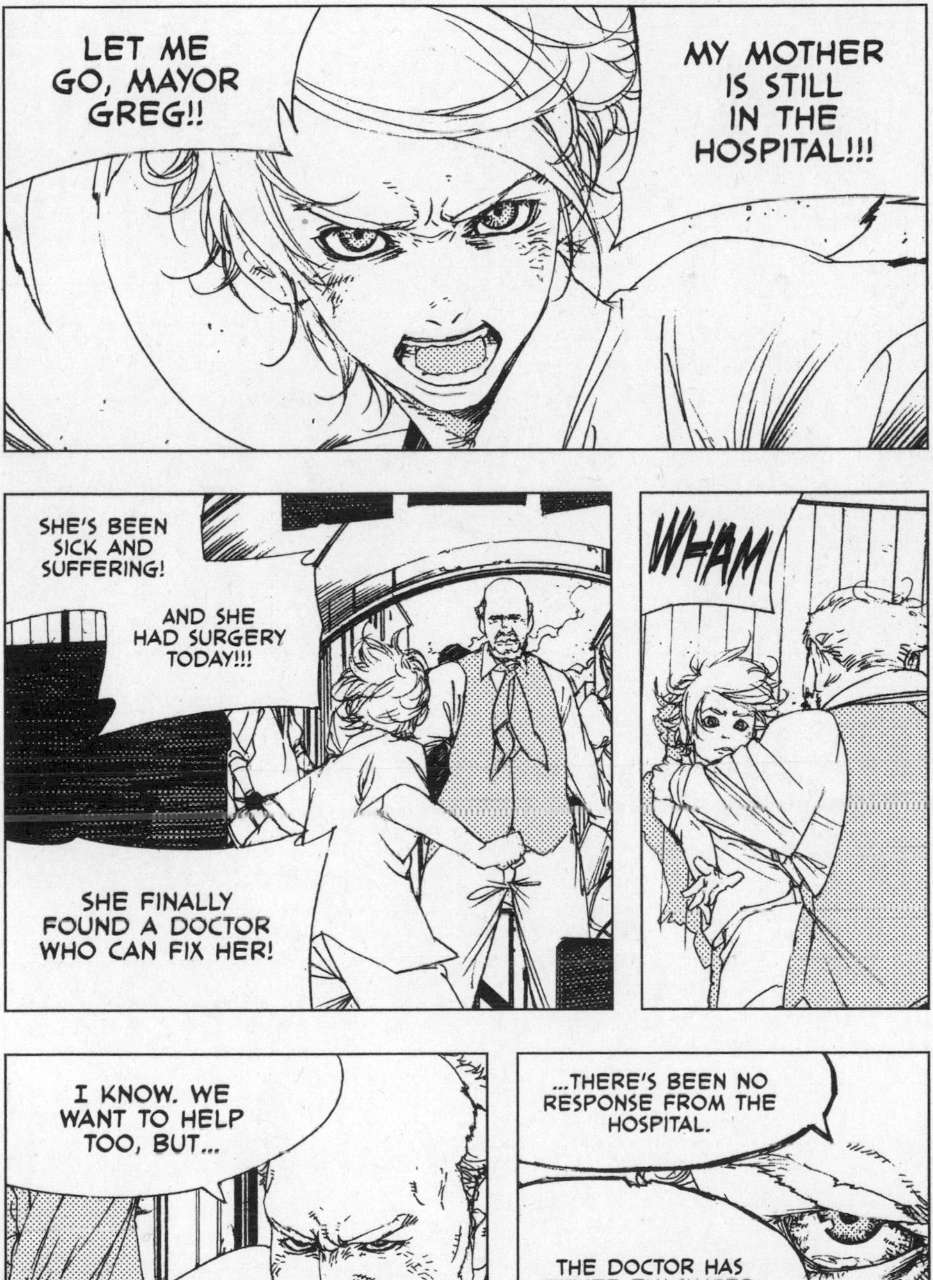
LET ME GO, MAYOR GREG!!
MY MOTHER IS STILL IN THE HOSPITAL!!!
SHE'S BEEN SICK AND SUFFERING!
AND SHE HAD SURGERY TODAY!!!
SHE FINALLY FOUND A DOCTOR WHO CAN FIX HER!
WHAM
I KNOW. WE WANT TO HELP TOO, BUT...
...THERE'S BEEN NO RESPONSE FROM THE HOSPITAL.
THE DOCTOR HAS EITHER EVACUATED OR HE'S DEAD. AND YOUR MOTHER...

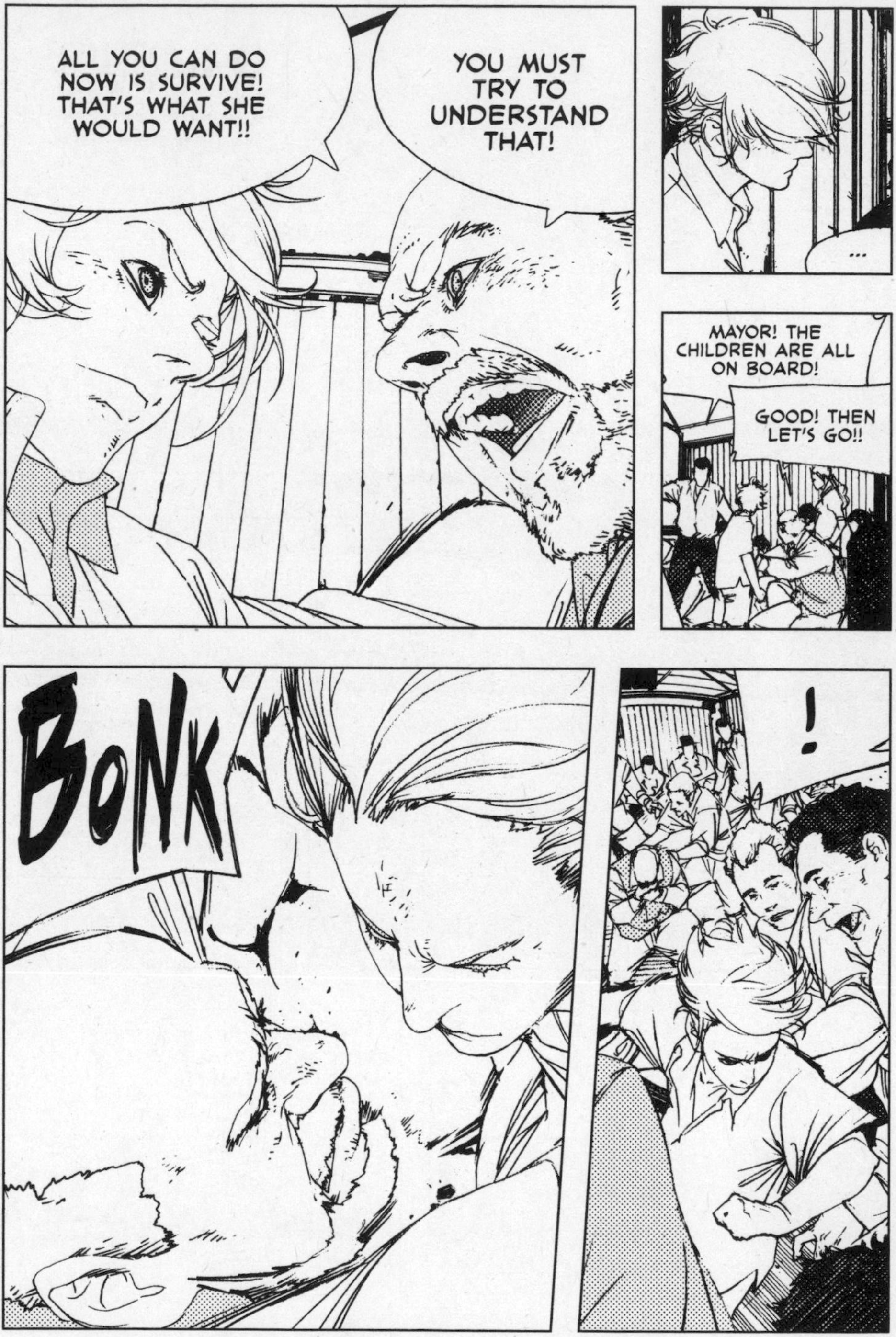
ALL YOU CAN DO NOW IS SURVIVE! THAT'S WHAT SHE WOULD WANT!!
YOU MUST TRY TO UNDERSTAND THAT!
...
MAYOR! THE CHILDREN ARE ALL ON BOARD!
GOOD! THEN LET'S GO!!
BONK
!

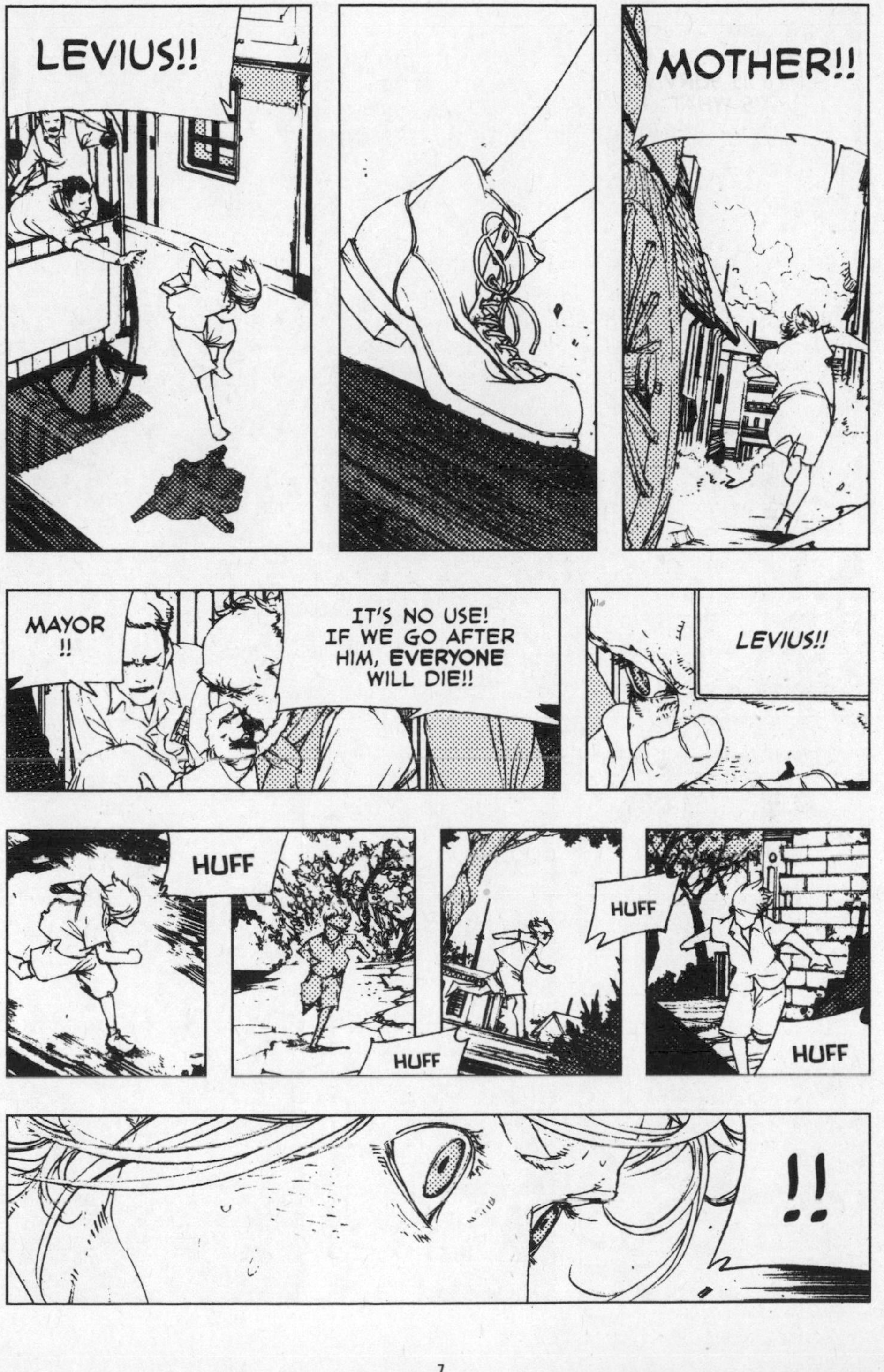
MOTHER!!
LEVIUS!!
LEVIUS!!
IT'S NO USE! IF WE GO AFTER HIM, EVERYONE WILL DIE!!
MAYOR !!
HUFF
HUFF
HUFF
HUFF
!!

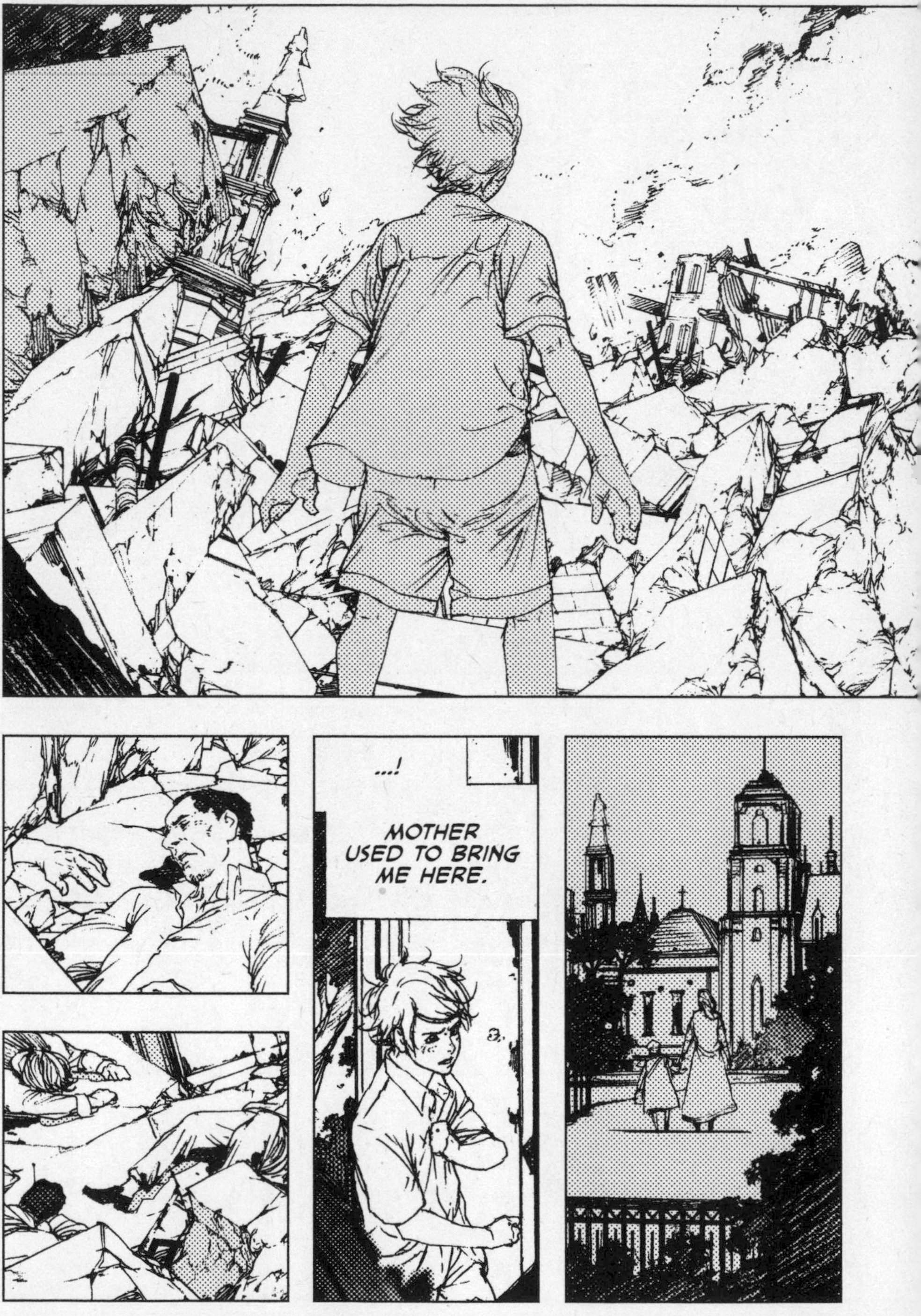
...!
MOTHER USED TO BRING ME HERE.

ARGH!!

PLEASE, BE SAFE!

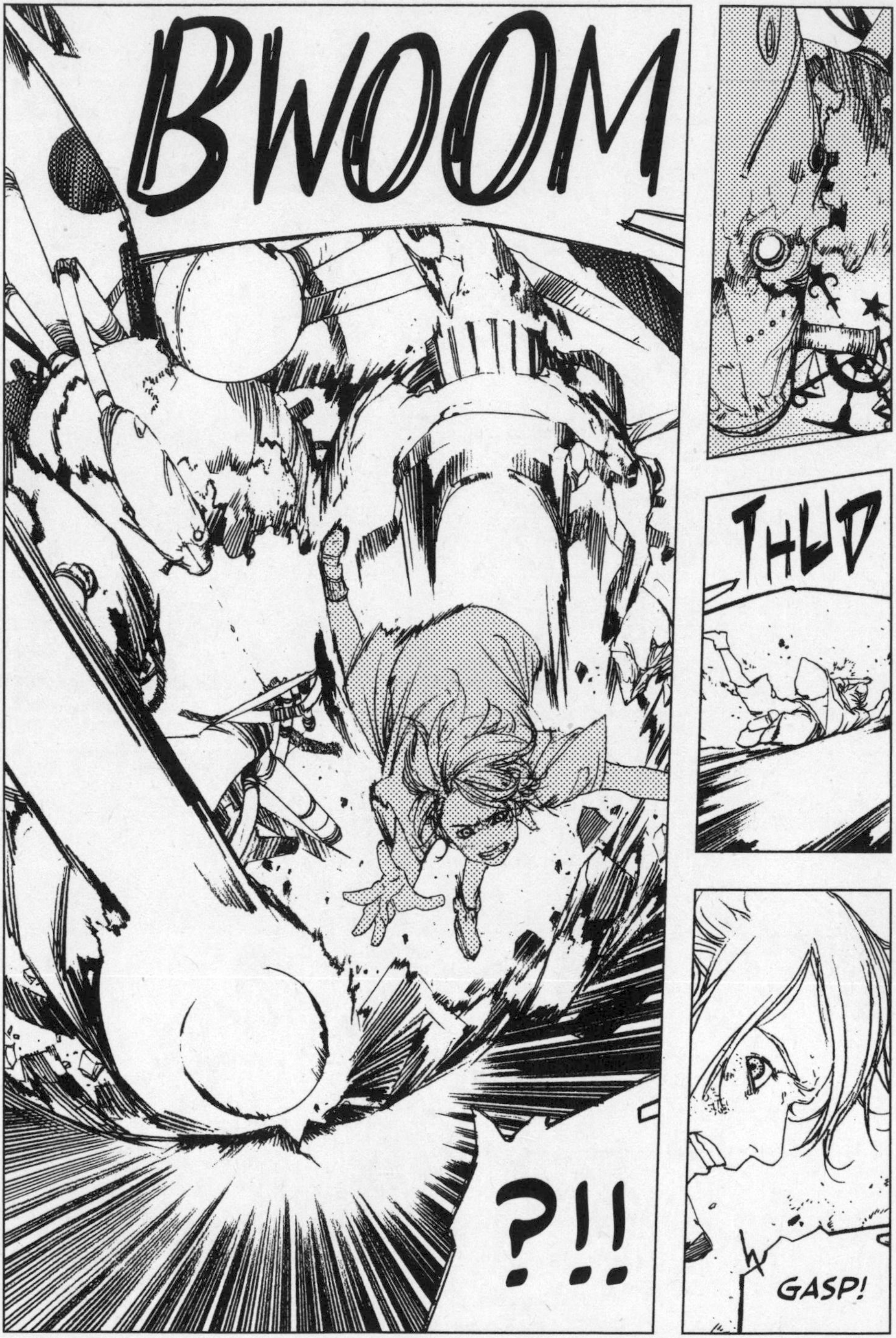
THUD
GASP!
BWOOM
?!!

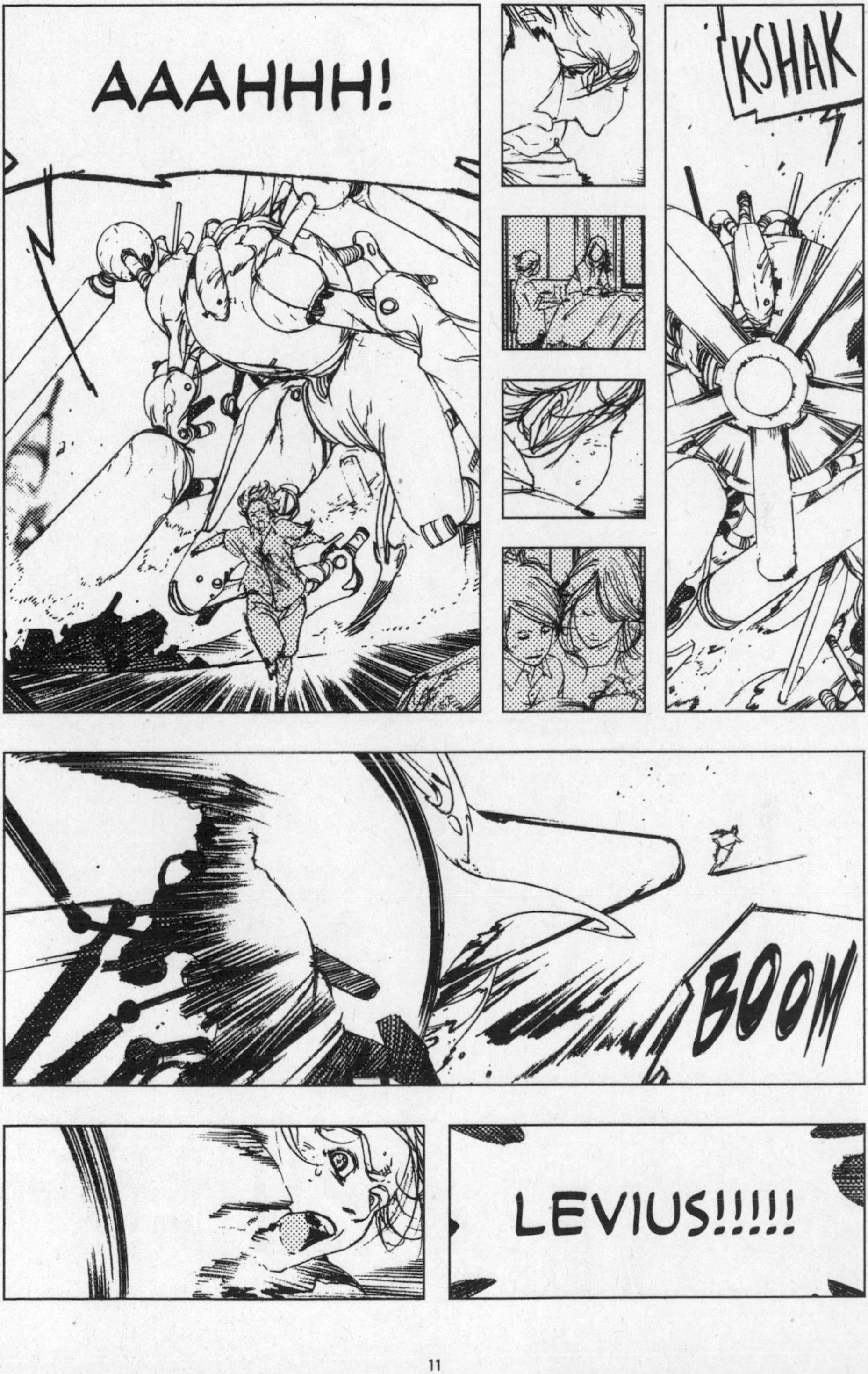
KSHAK
AAAHHH!
BOOM
LEVIUS!!!!!

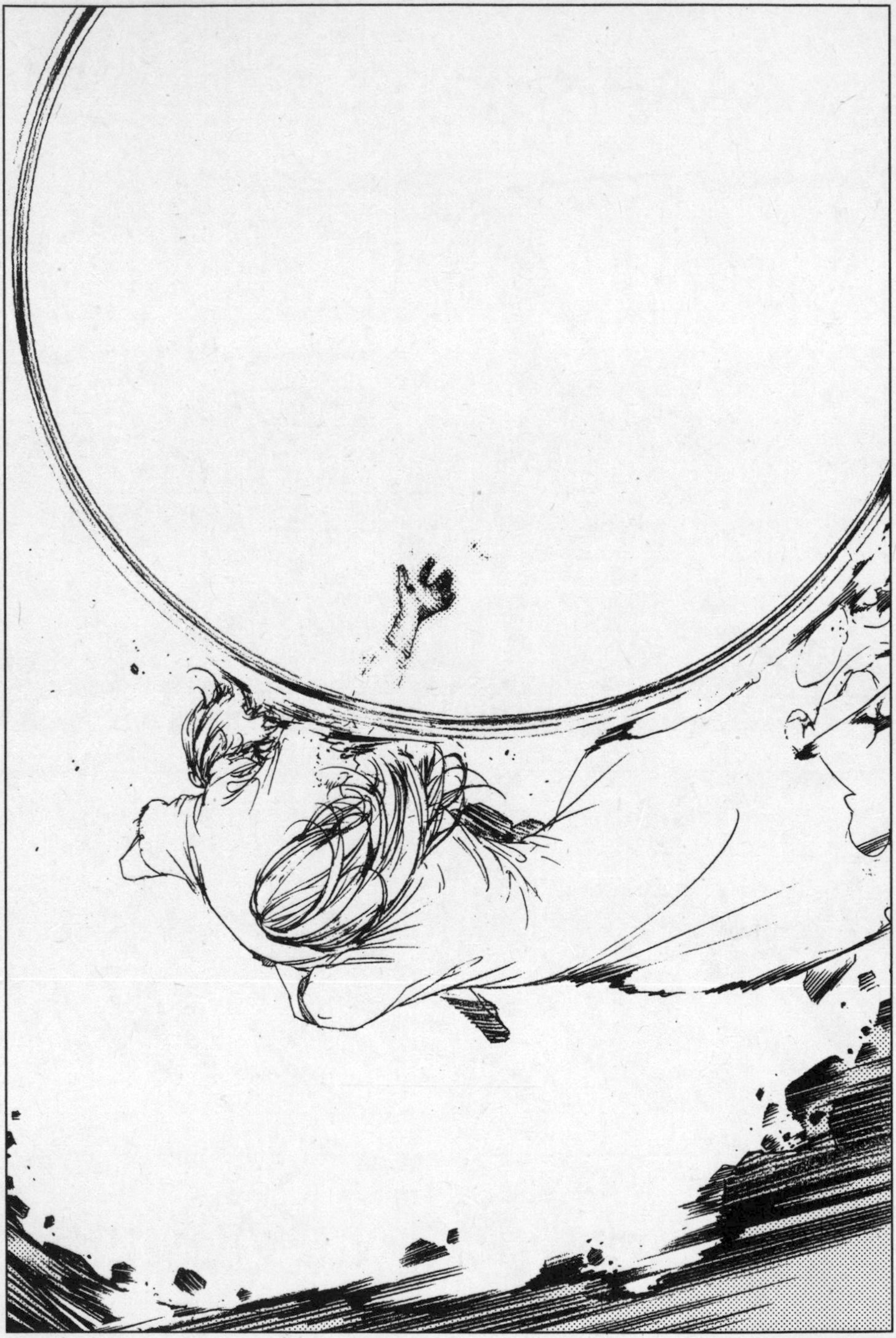

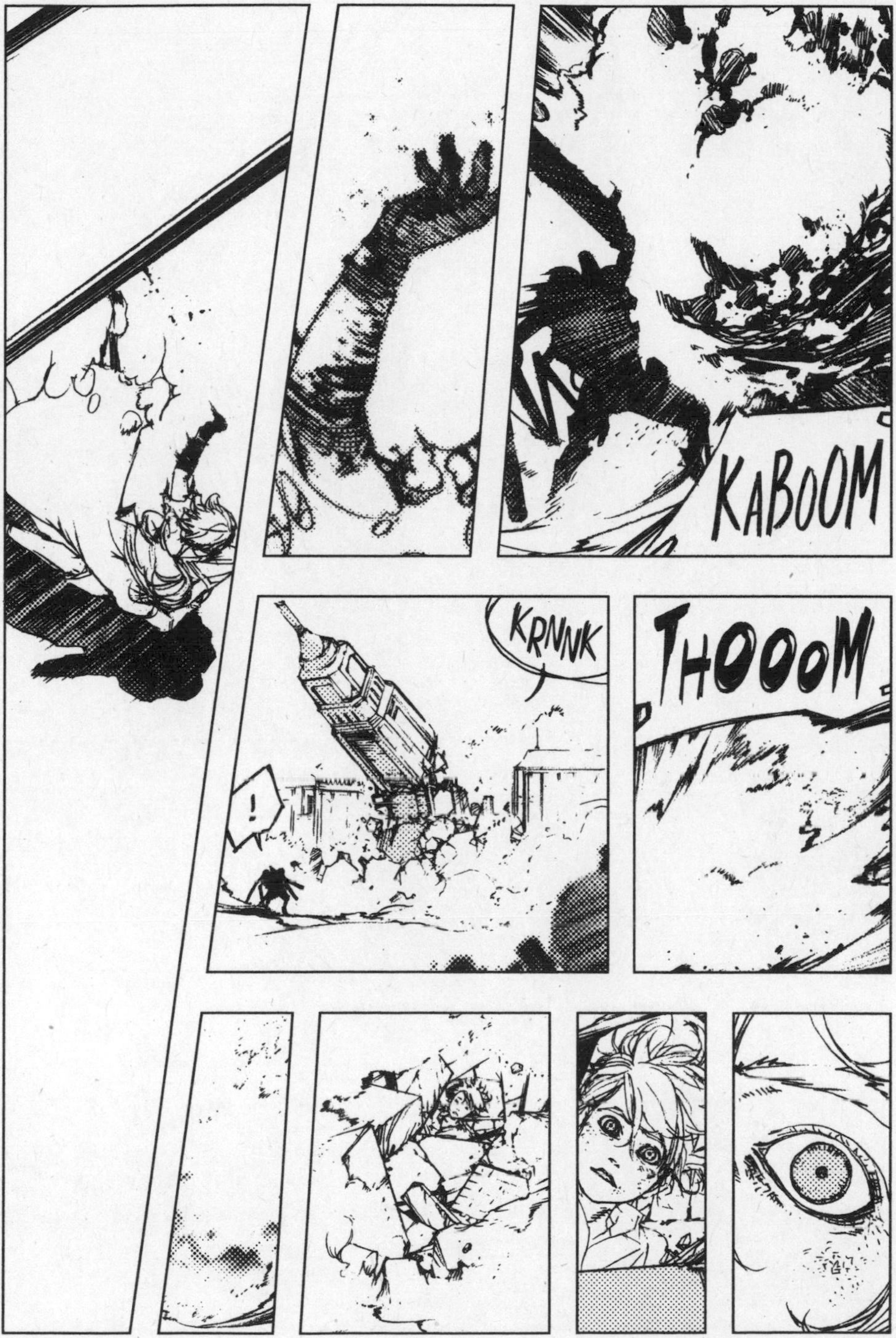
KABOOM
THOOOM
KRNNK
!

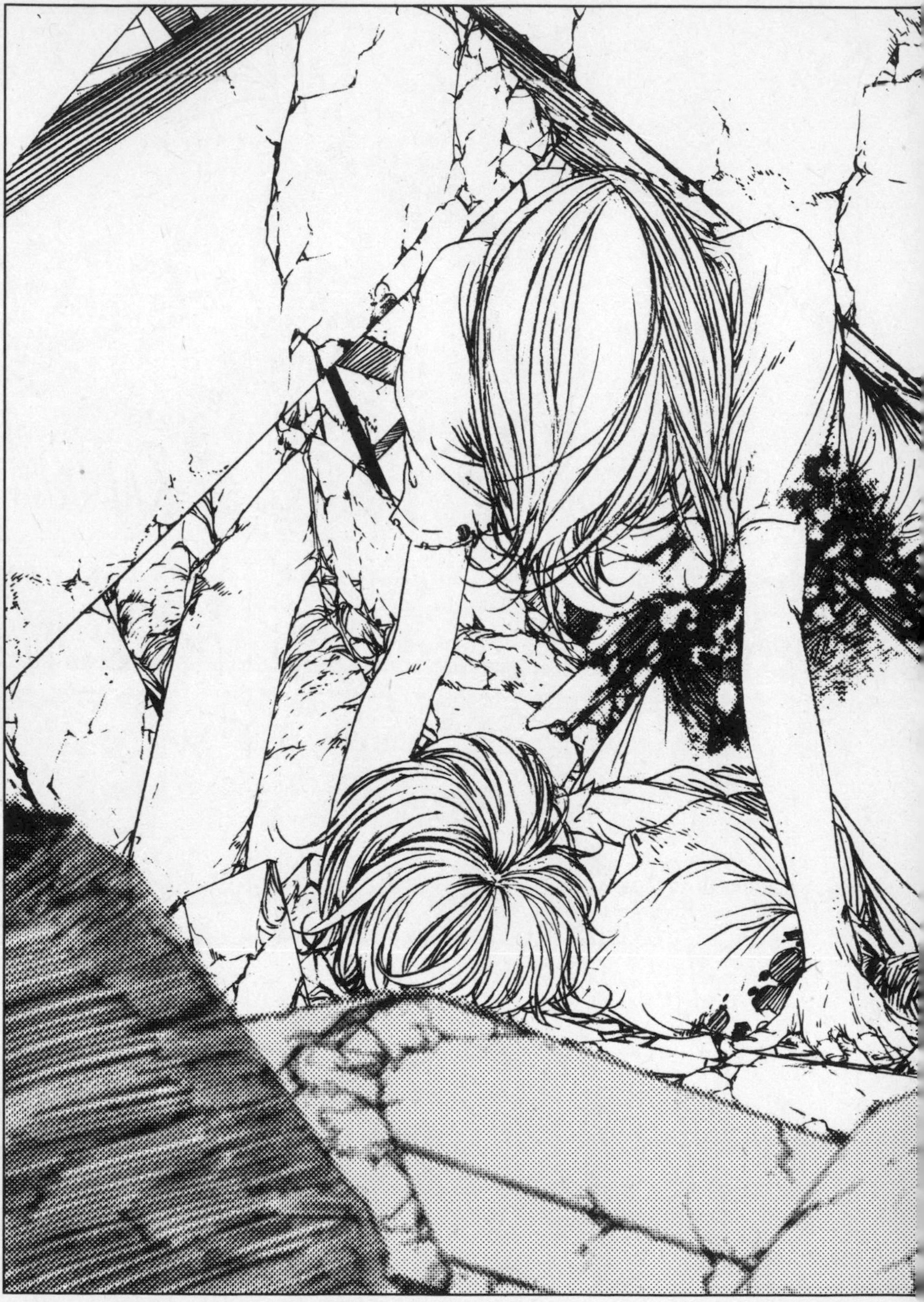

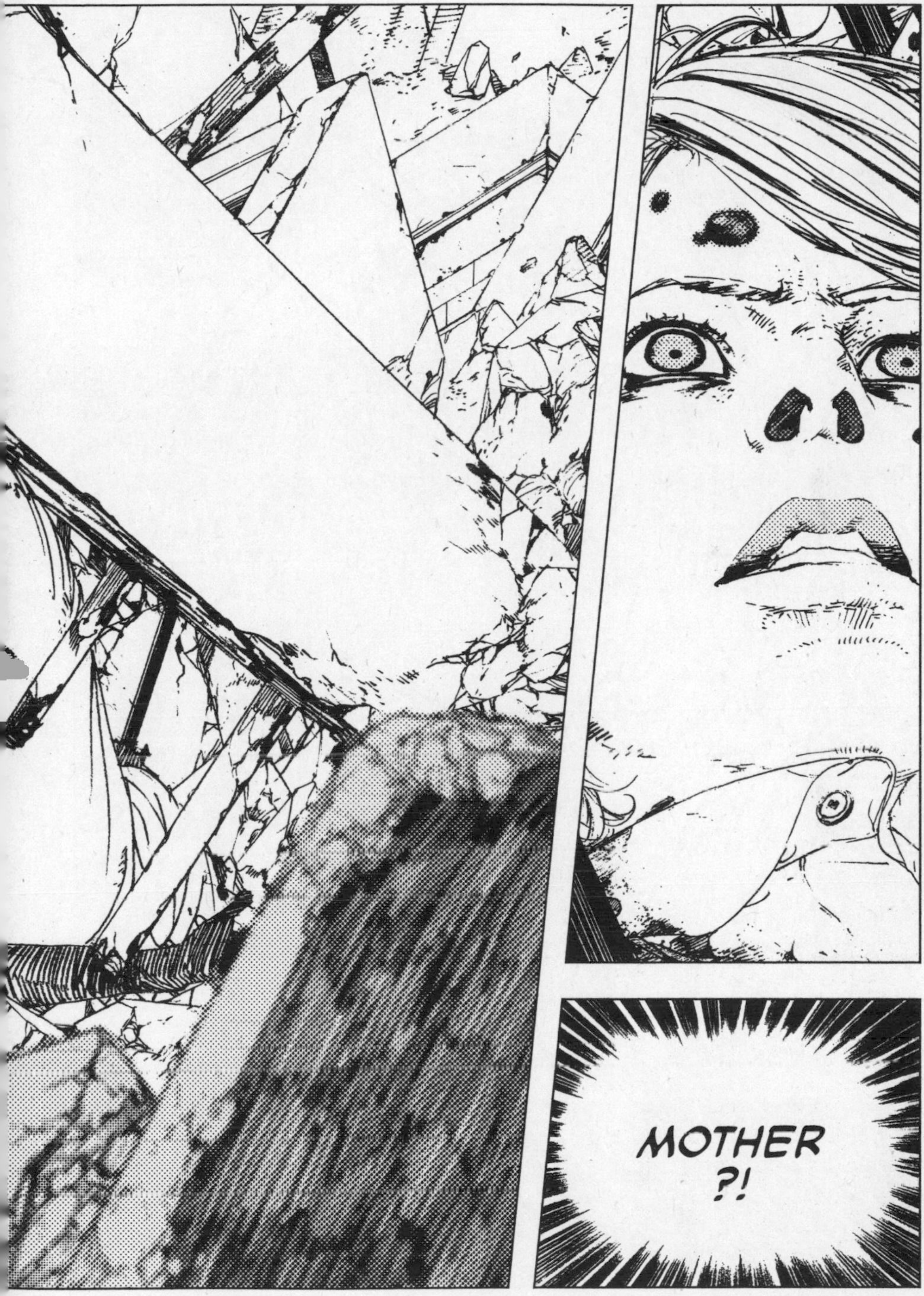
MOTHER
?!

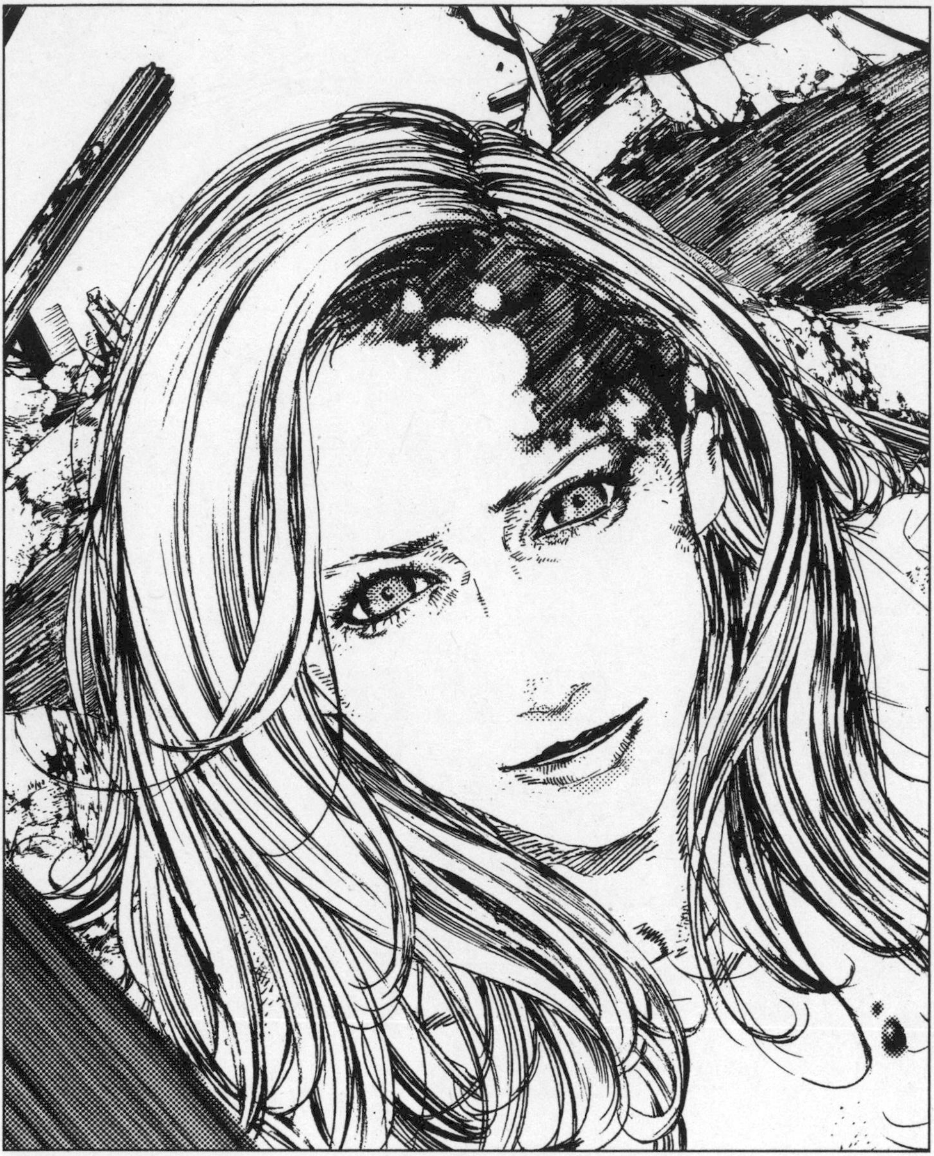

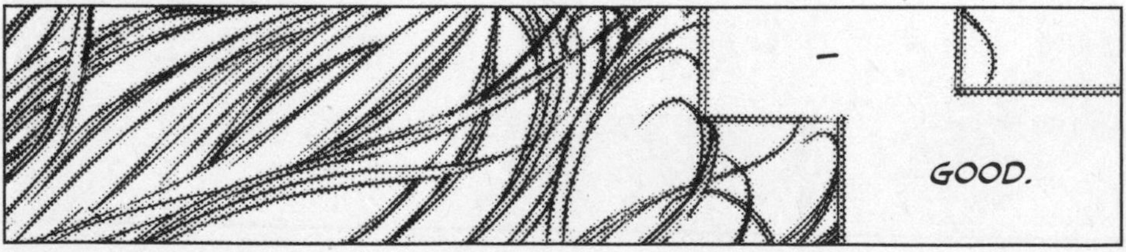
GOOD.

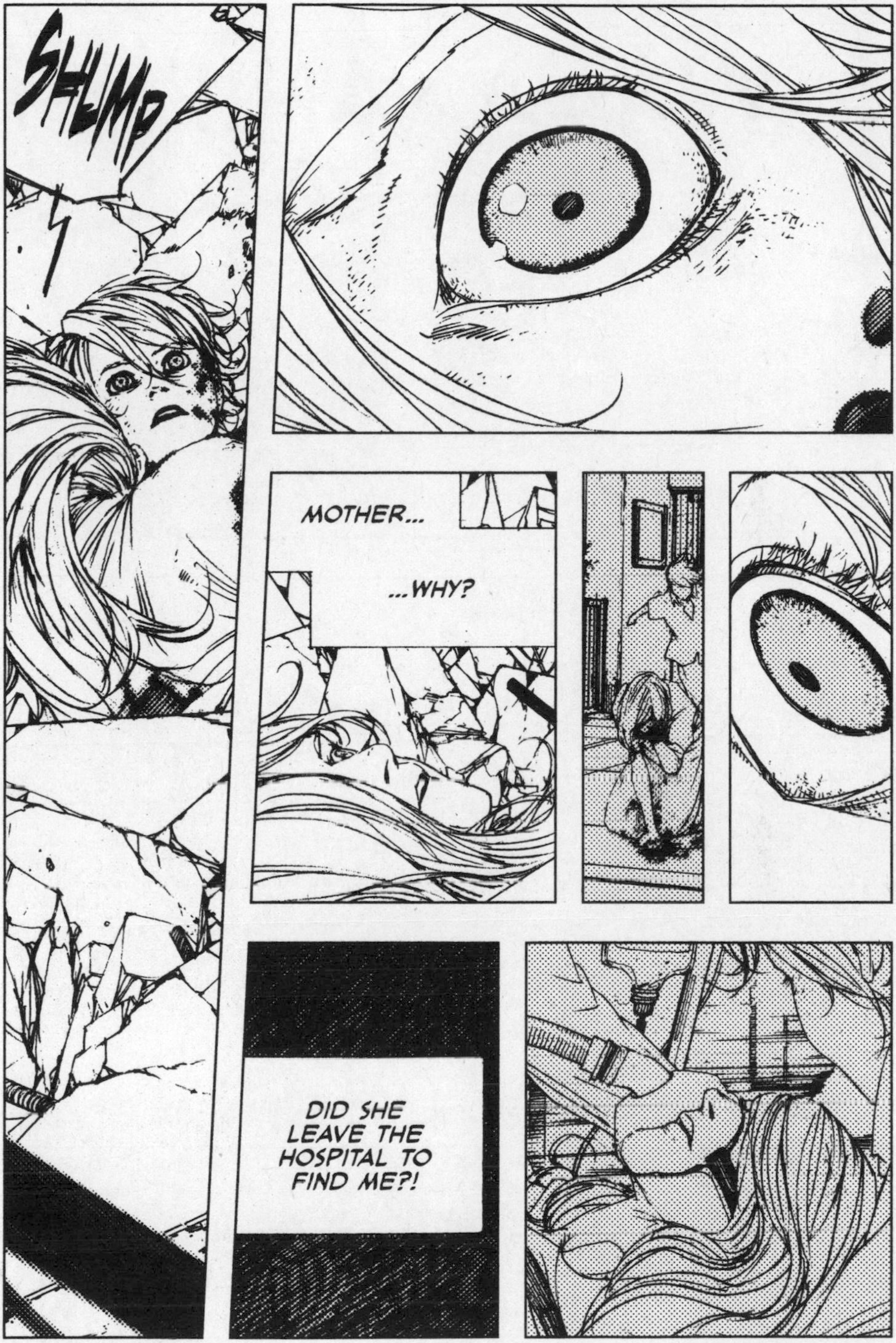
SHLUMP
MOTHER...
...WHY?
DID SHE LEAVE THE HOSPITAL TO FIND ME?!

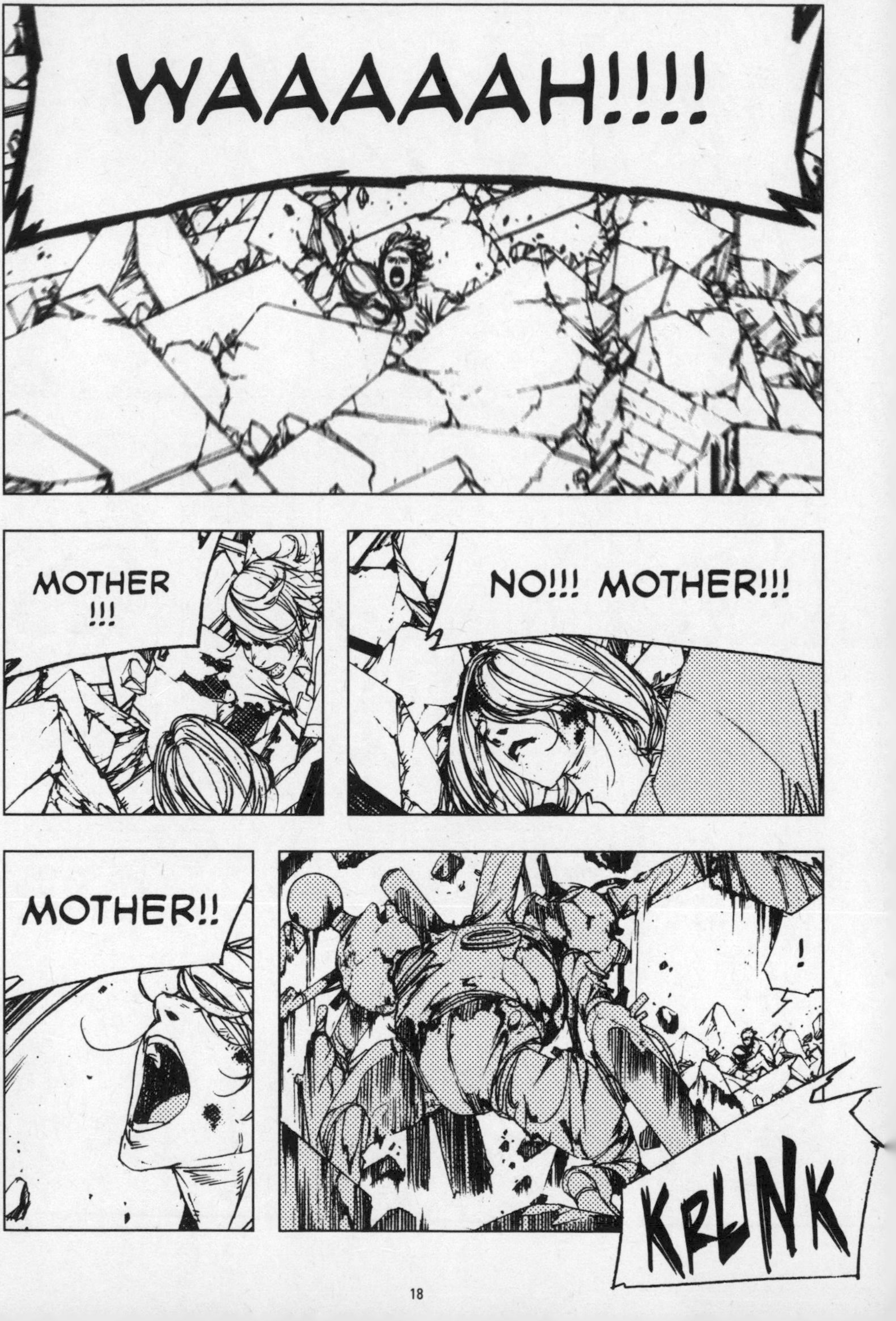
WAAAAAH!!!!
NO!!! MOTHER!!!
MOTHER !!!
!
KRUNK
MOTHER!!

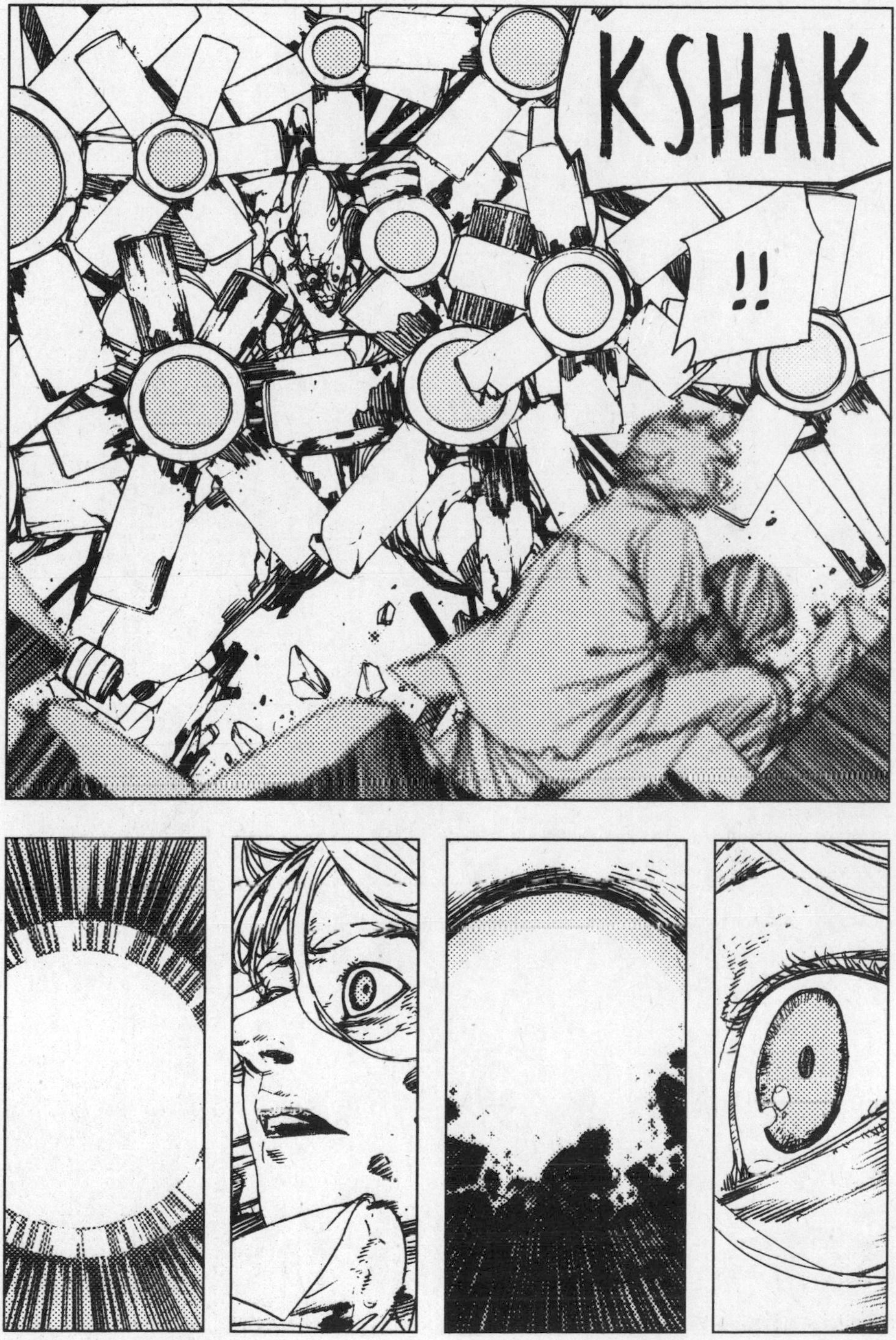
KSHAK
!!

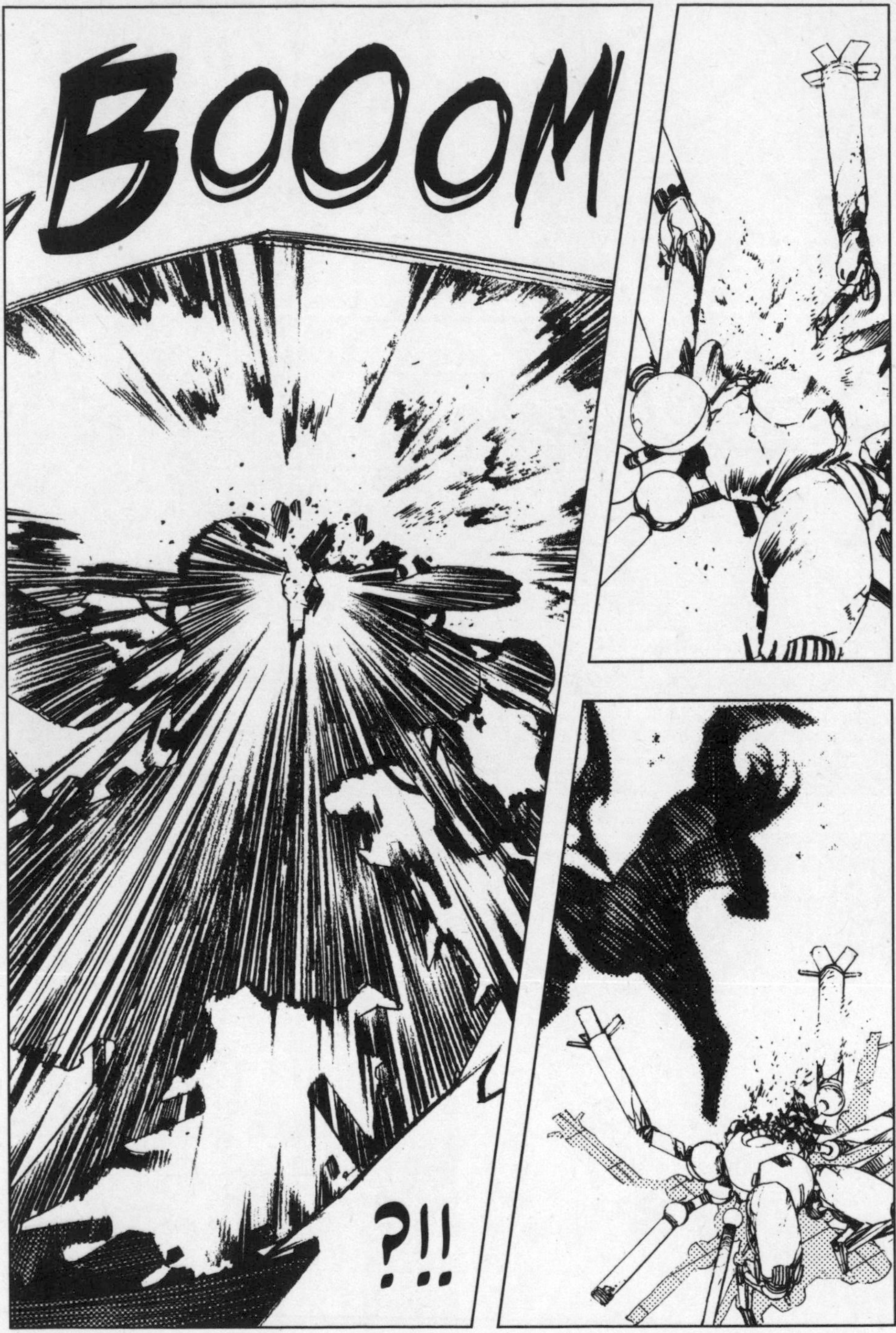
BOOOM
?!!

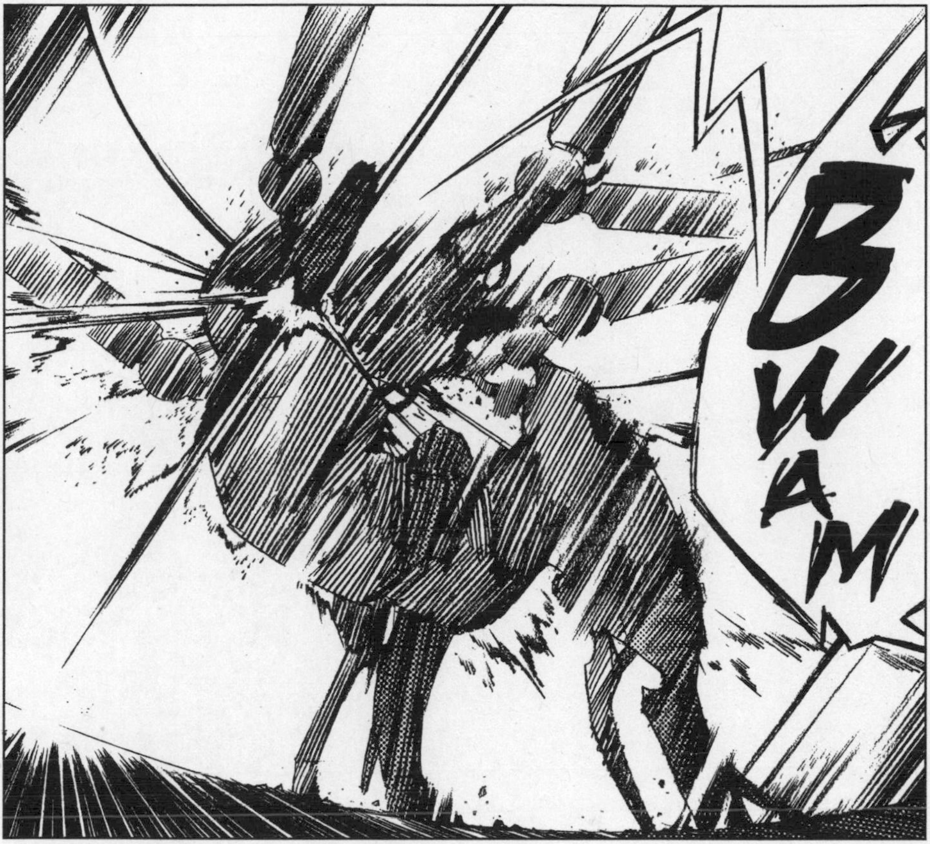
BWAM
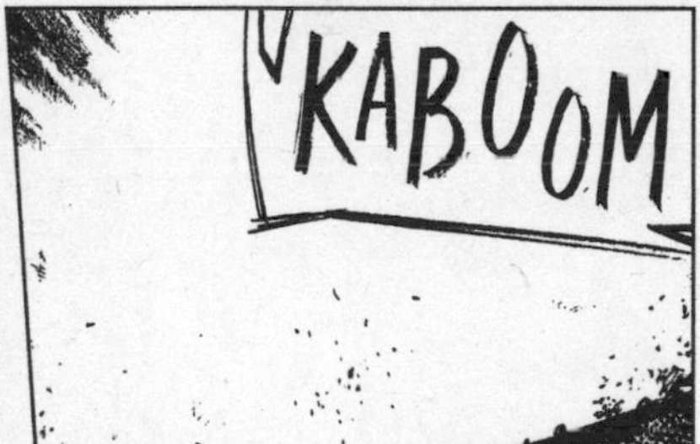
KABOOM
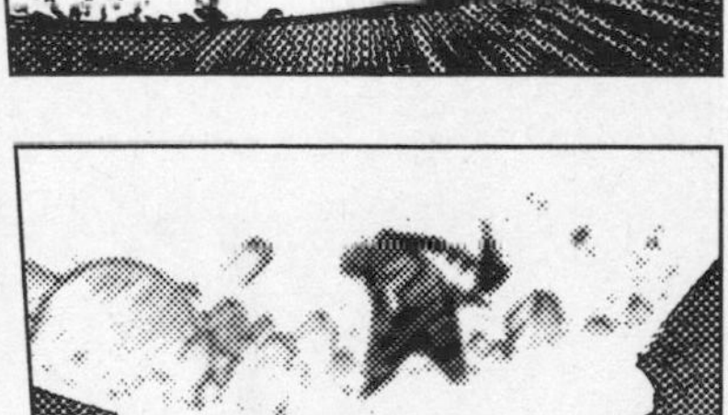
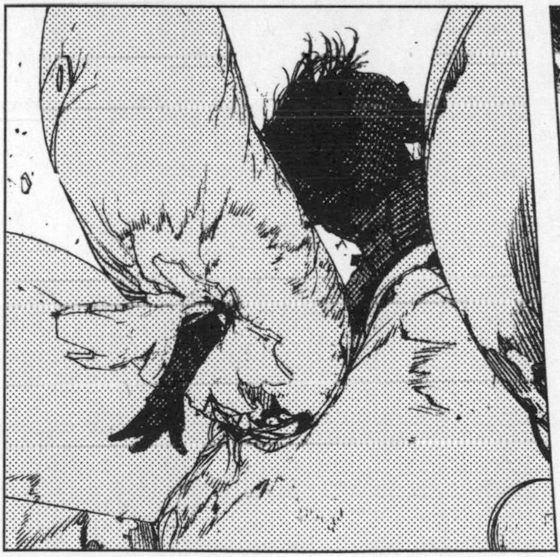

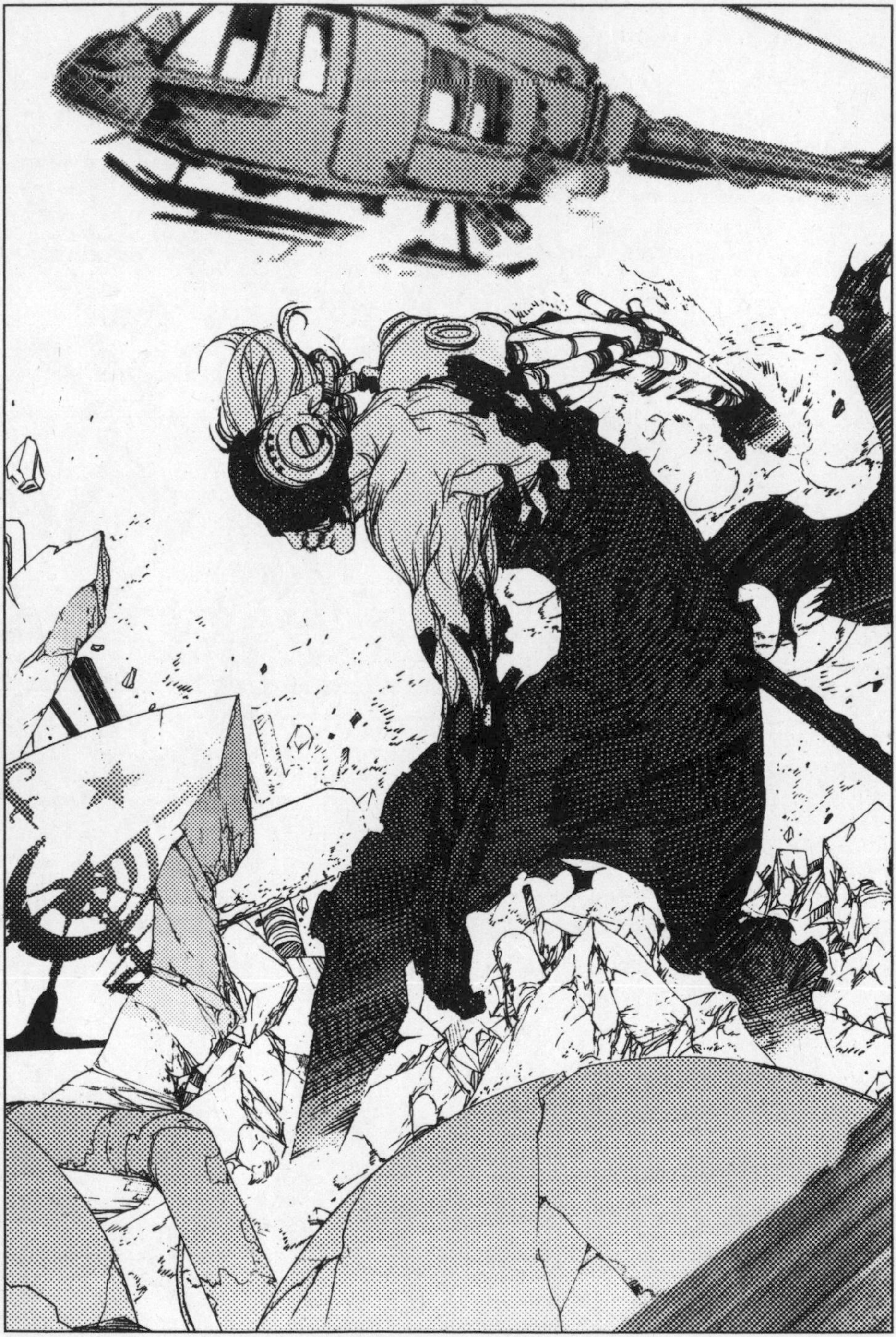

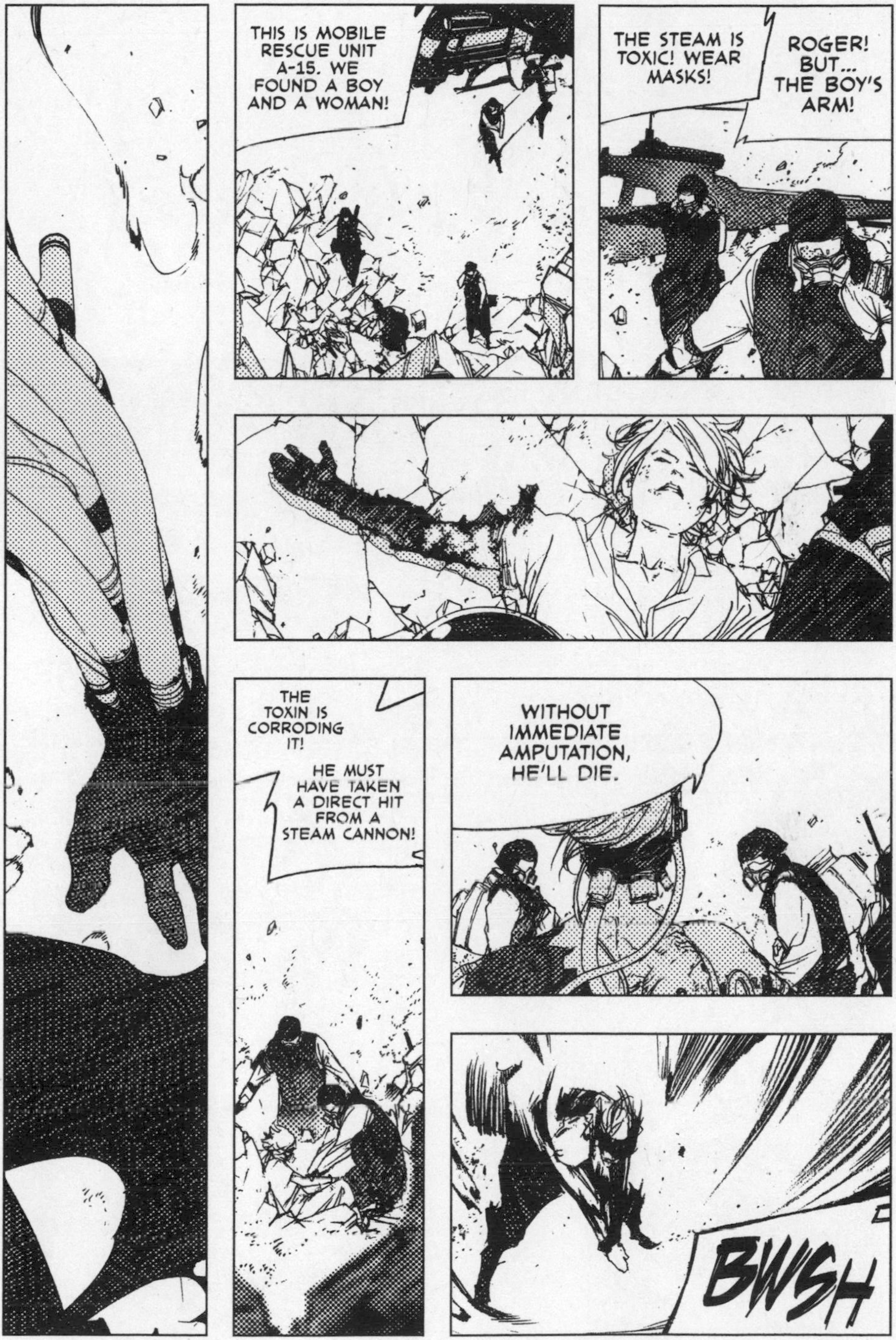
THIS IS MOBILE RESCUE UNIT A-15. WE FOUND A BOY AND A WOMAN!
THE STEAM IS TOXIC! WEAR MASKS!
ROGER! BUT... THE BOY'S ARM!
THE TOXIN IS CORRODING IT!
HE MUST HAVE TAKEN A DIRECT HIT FROM A STEAM CANNON!
WITHOUT IMMEDIATE AMPUTATION, HE'LL DIE.
BWSH

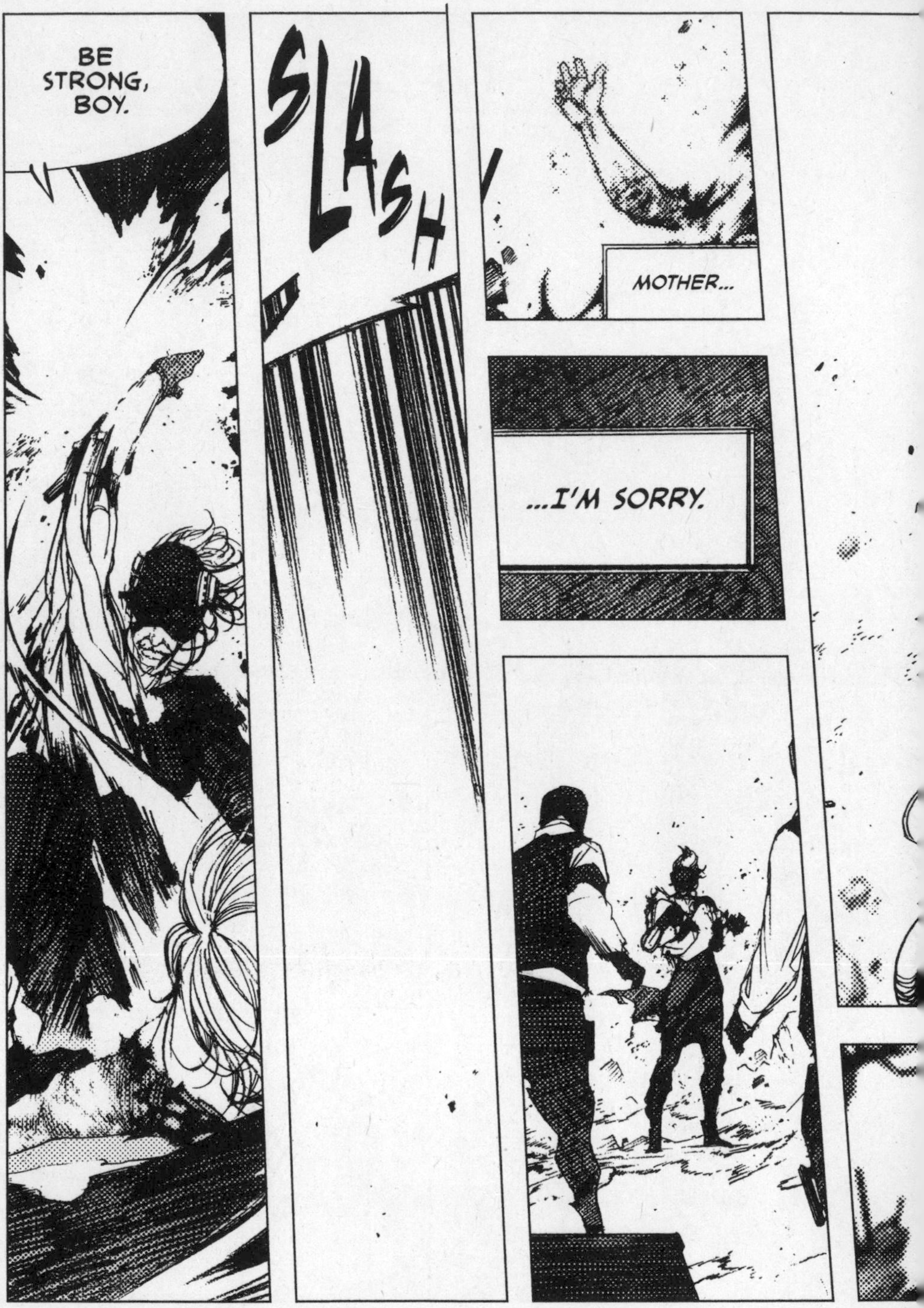
MOTHER...
...I'M SORRY.
SLASH
BE STRONG, BOY.

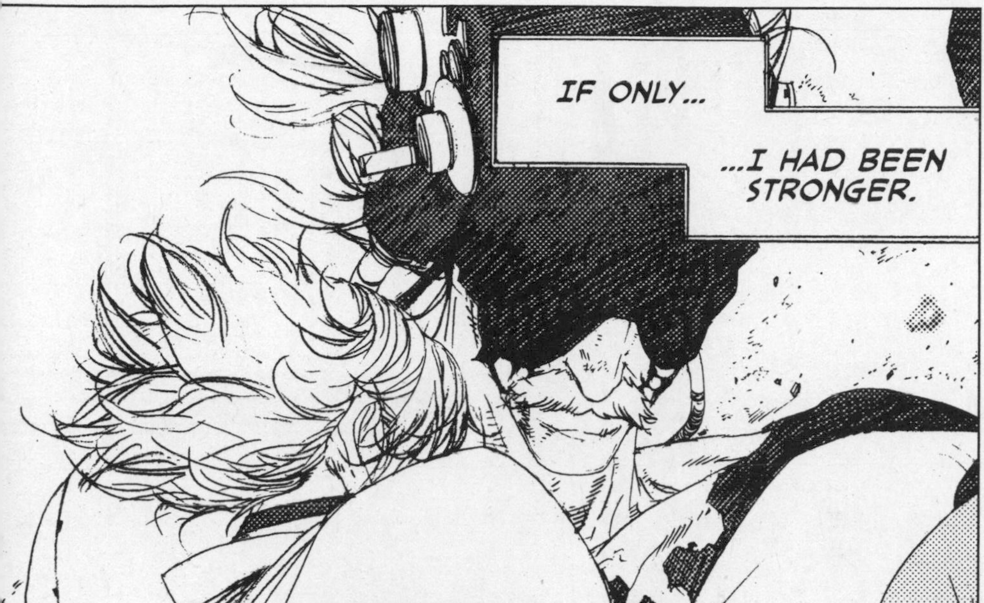
IF ONLY...
...I HAD BEEN STRONGER.
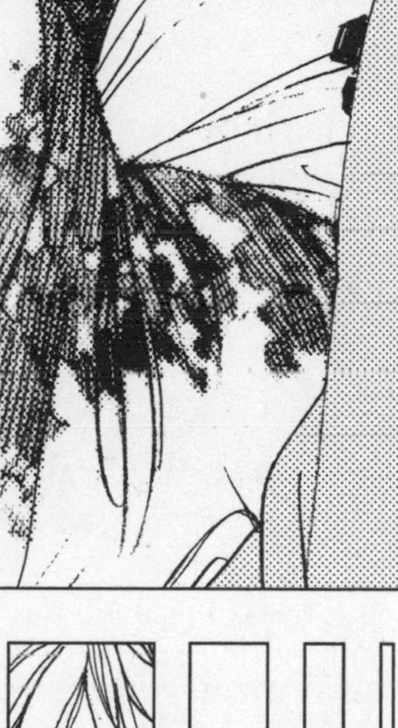
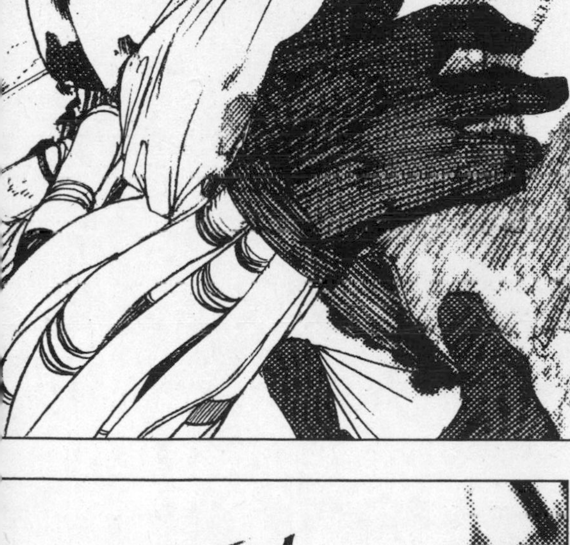

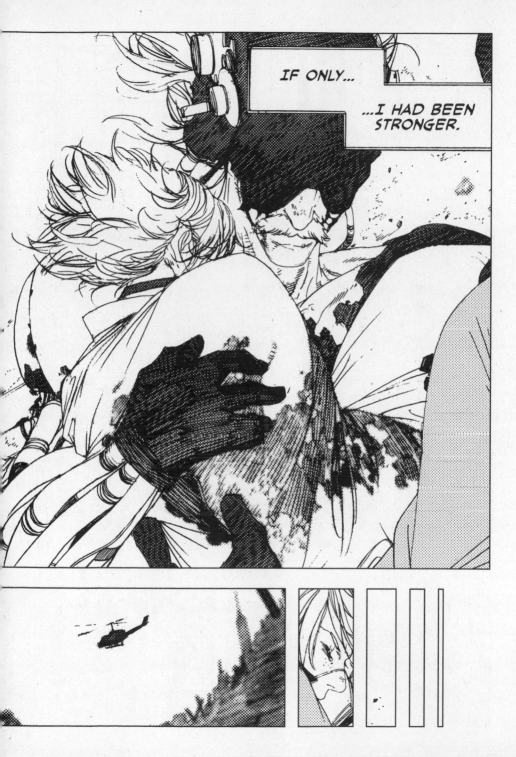

HUFF
HUFF
HUFF
!!

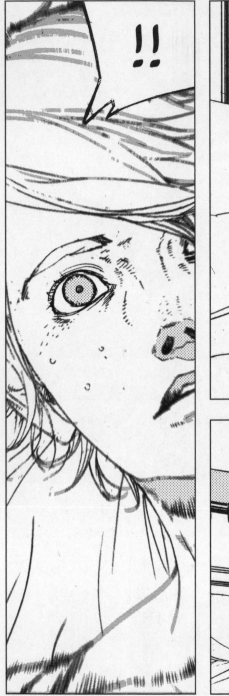

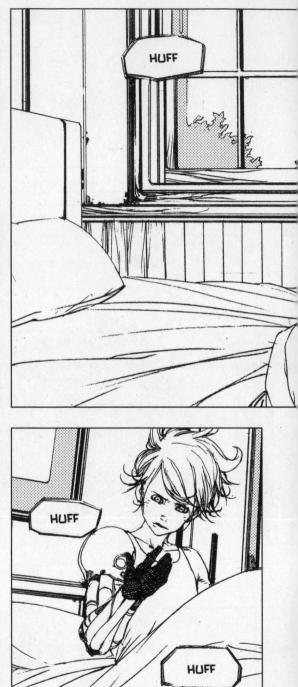

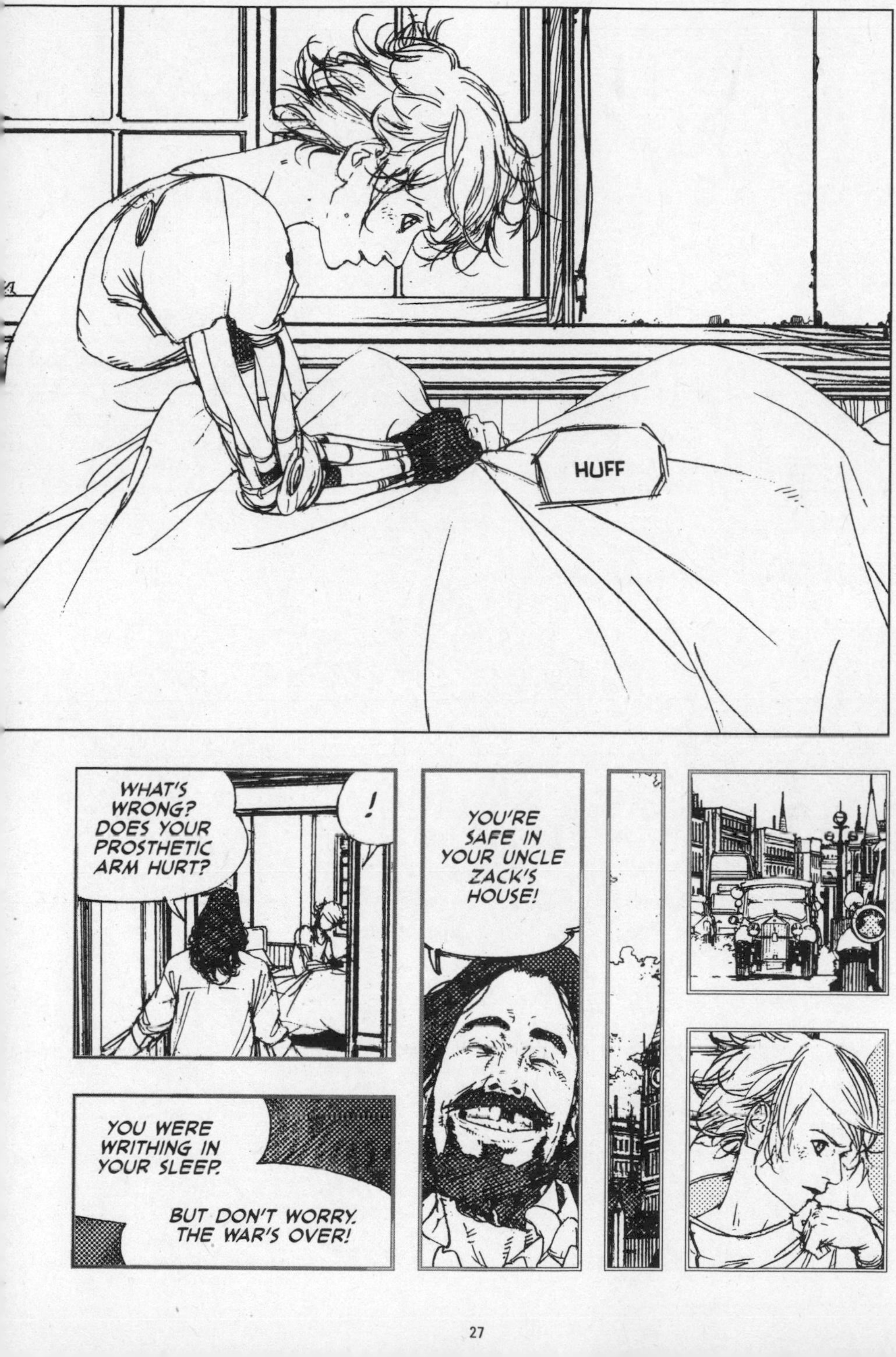
HUFF
WHAT'S WRONG? DOES YOUR PROSTHETIC ARM HURT?
!
YOU WERE WRITHING IN YOUR SLEEP.
BUT DON'T WORRY. THE WAR'S OVER!
YOU'RE SAFE IN YOUR UNCLE ZACK'S HOUSE!

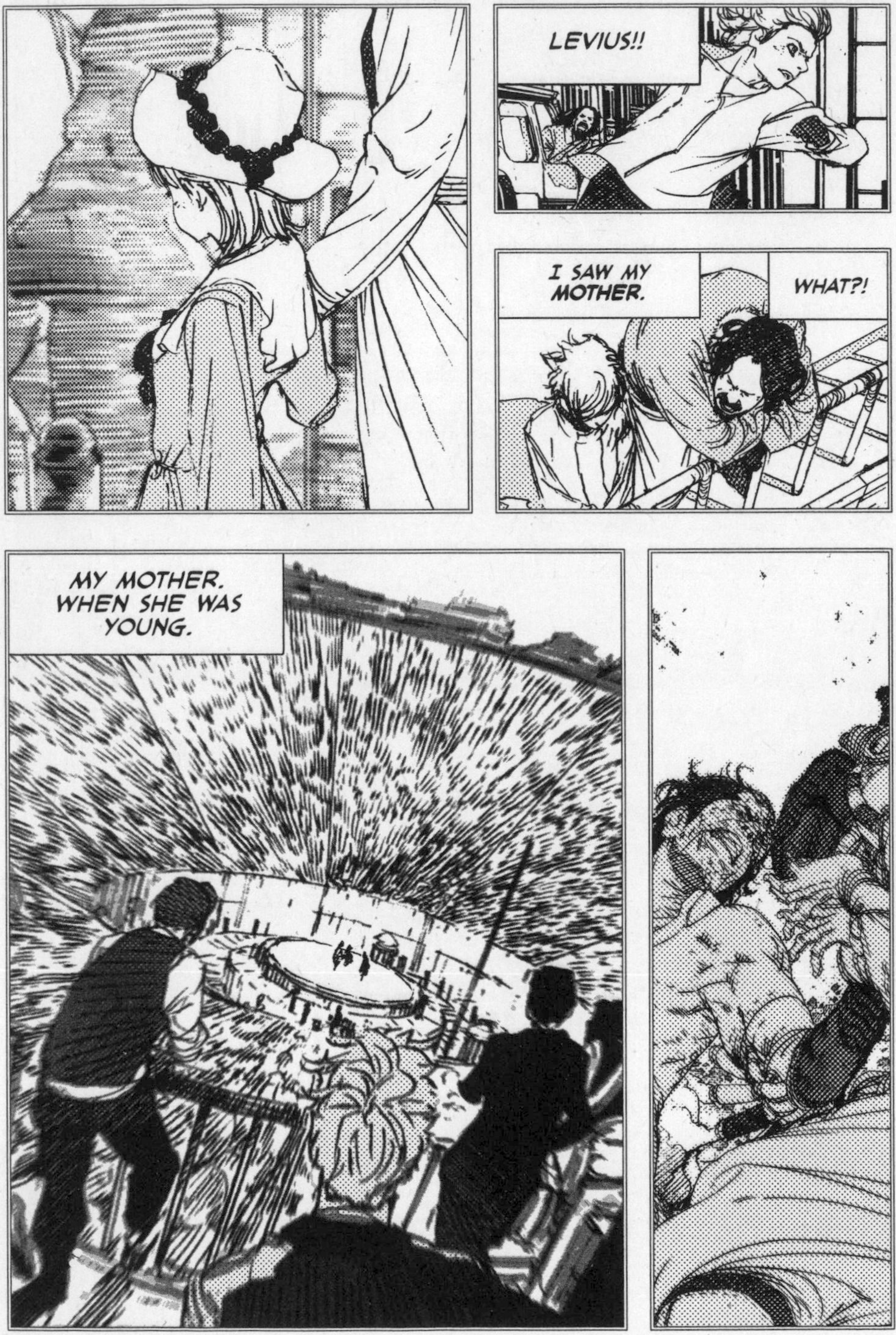
LEVIUS!!
I SAW MY MOTHER.
WHAT?!
MY MOTHER. WHEN SHE WAS YOUNG.

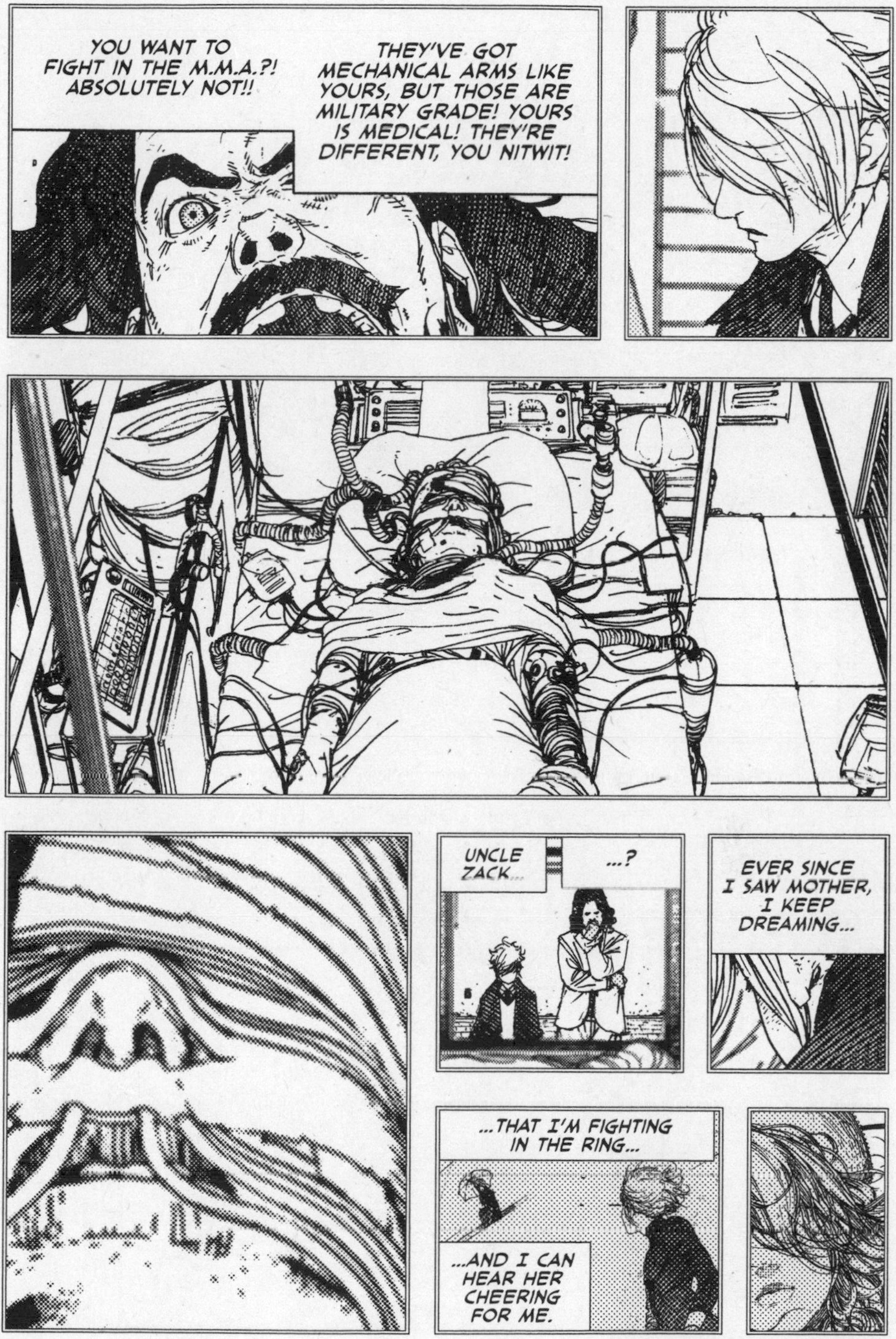
YOU WANT TO FIGHT IN THE M.M.A.?! ABSOLUTELY NOT!!
THEY'VE GOT MECHANICAL ARMS LIKE YOURS, BUT THOSE ARE MILITARY GRADE! YOURS IS MEDICAL! THEY'RE DIFFERENT, YOU NITWIT!
UNCLE ZACK...
...?
EVER SINCE I SAW MOTHER, I KEEP DREAMING...
...THAT I'M FIGHTING IN THE RING...
...AND I CAN HEAR HER CHEERING FOR ME.

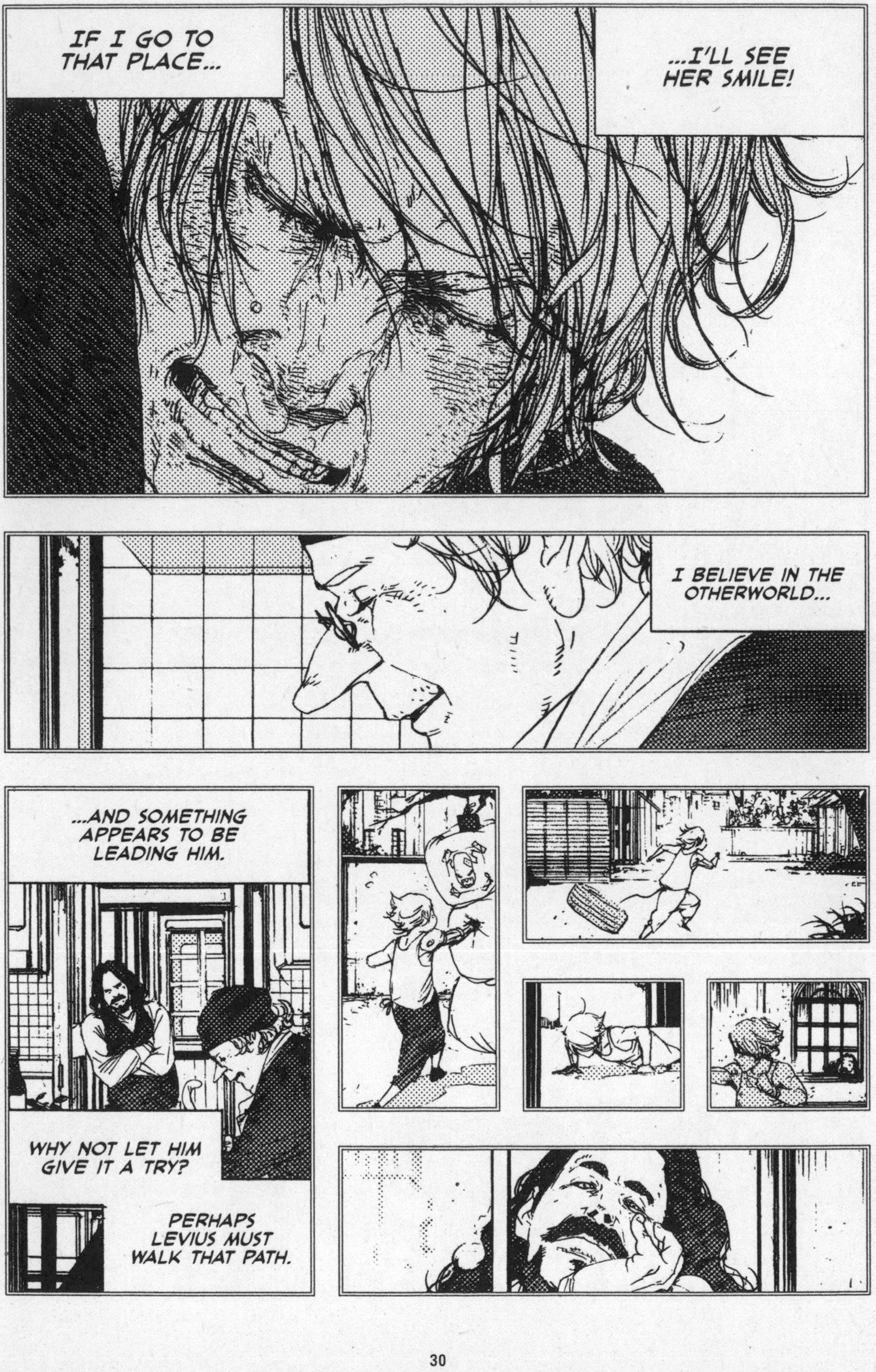
IF I GO TO THAT PLACE...
...I'LL SEE HER SMILE!
I BELIEVE IN THE OTHERWORLD...
...AND SOMETHING APPEARS TO BE LEADING HIM.
WHY NOT LET HIM GIVE IT A TRY?
PERHAPS LEVIUS MUST WALK THAT PATH.

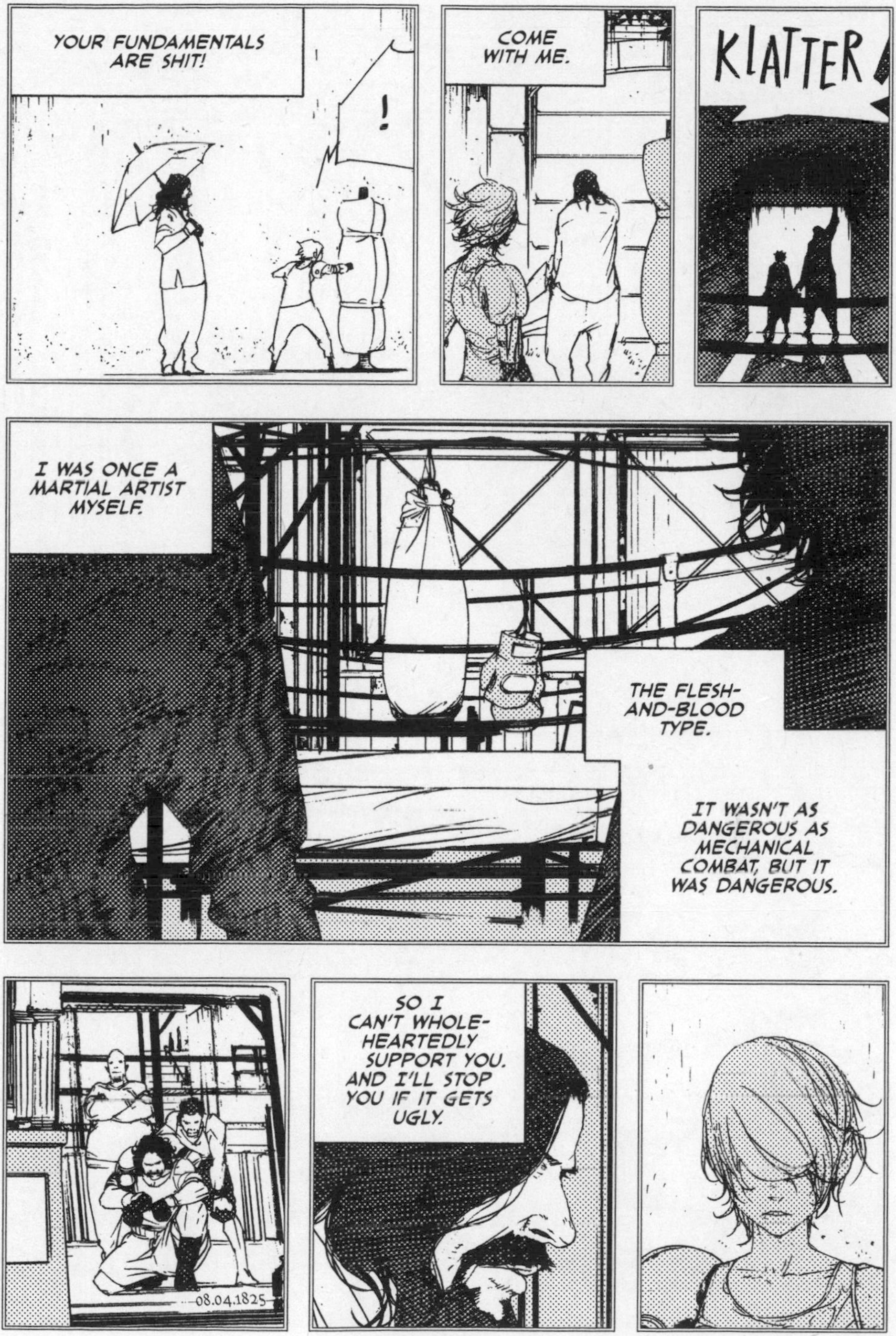
YOUR FUNDAMENTALS ARE SHIT!
!
COME WITH ME.
KLATTER
I WAS ONCE A MARTIAL ARTIST MYSELF.
THE FLESH-AND-BLOOD TYPE.
IT WASN'T AS DANGEROUS AS MECHANICAL COMBAT, BUT IT WAS DANGEROUS.
08.04.1825
SO I CAN'T WHOLE-HEARTEDLY SUPPORT YOU. AND I'LL STOP YOU IF IT GETS UGLY.

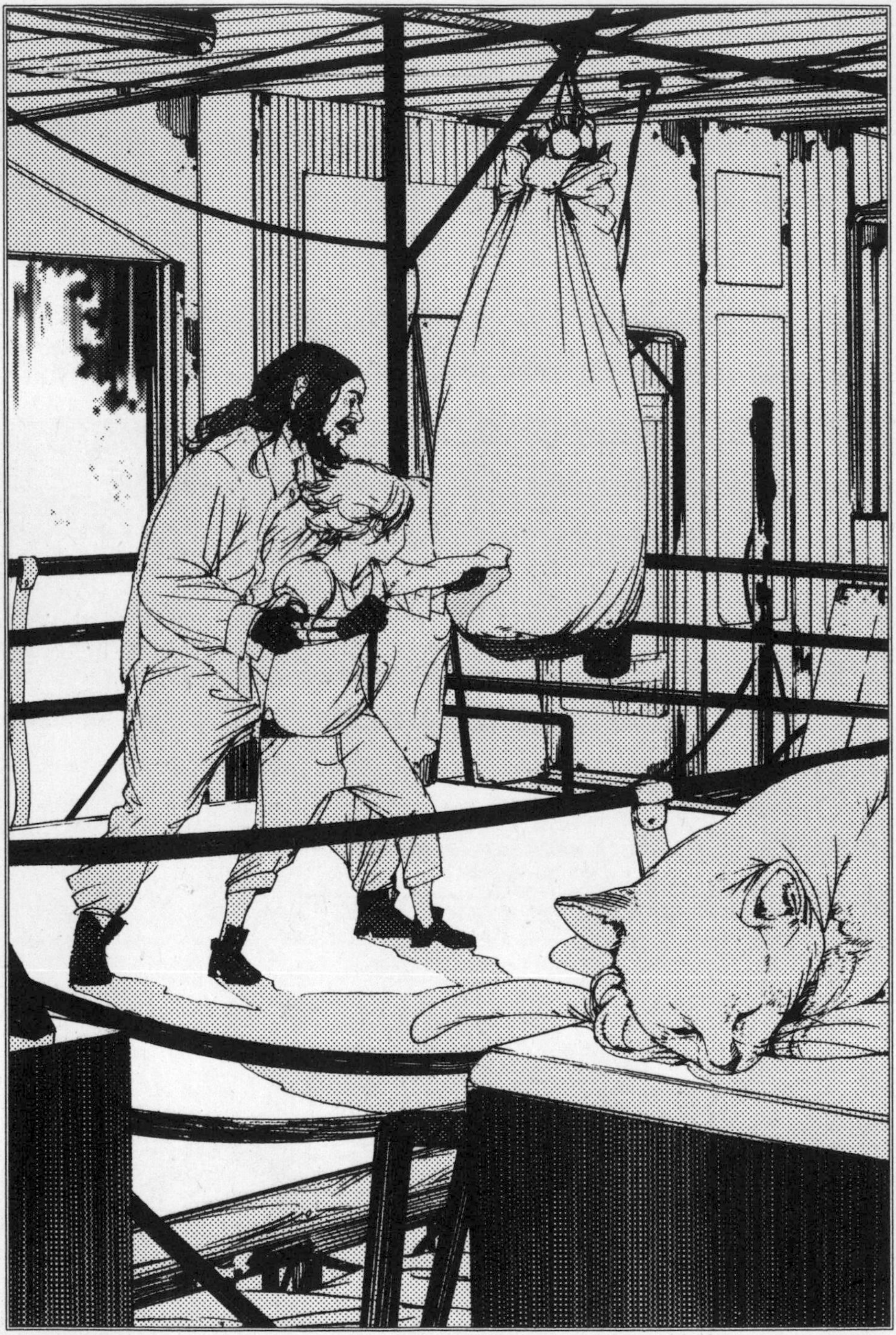

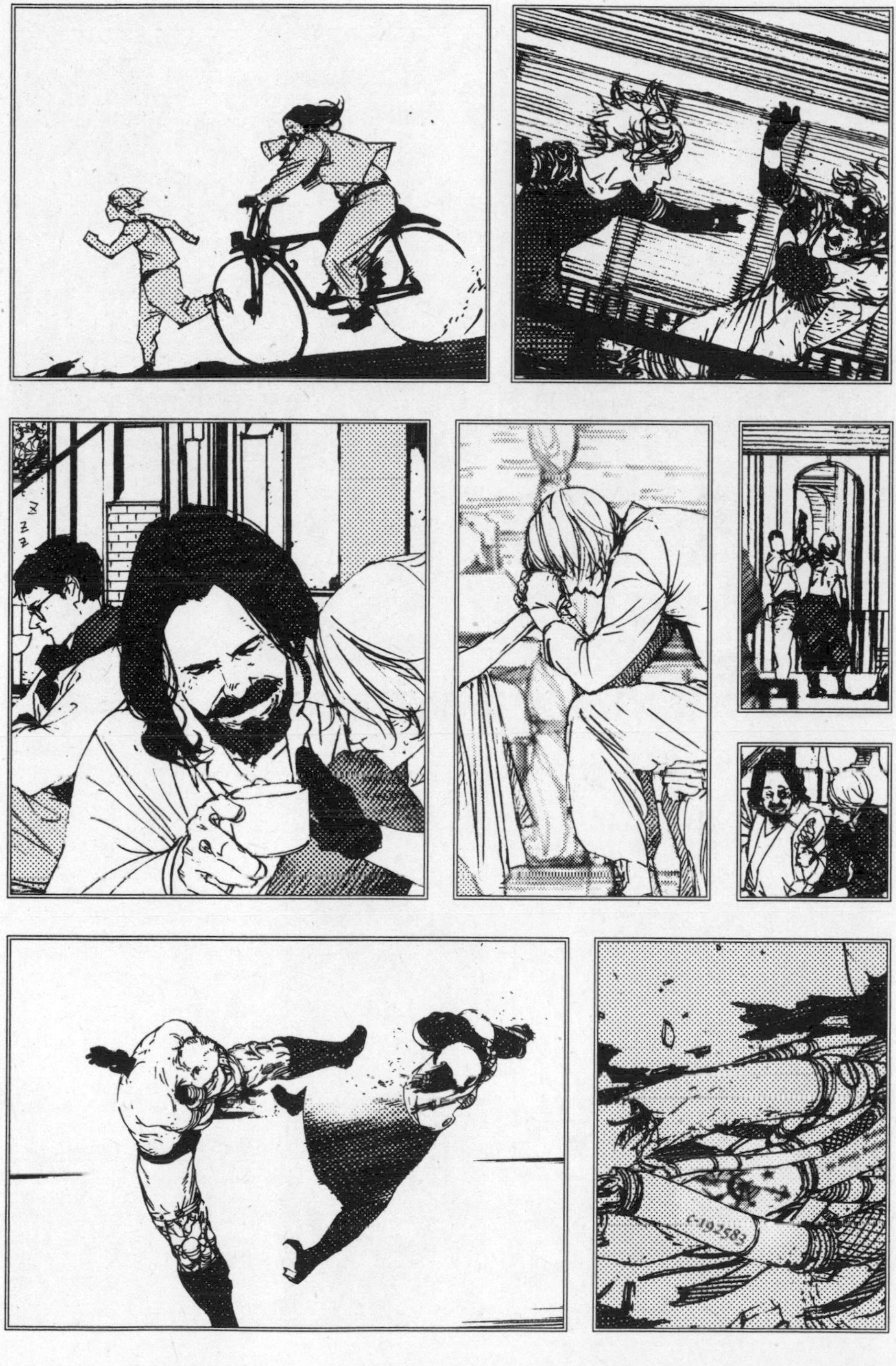
c-192583

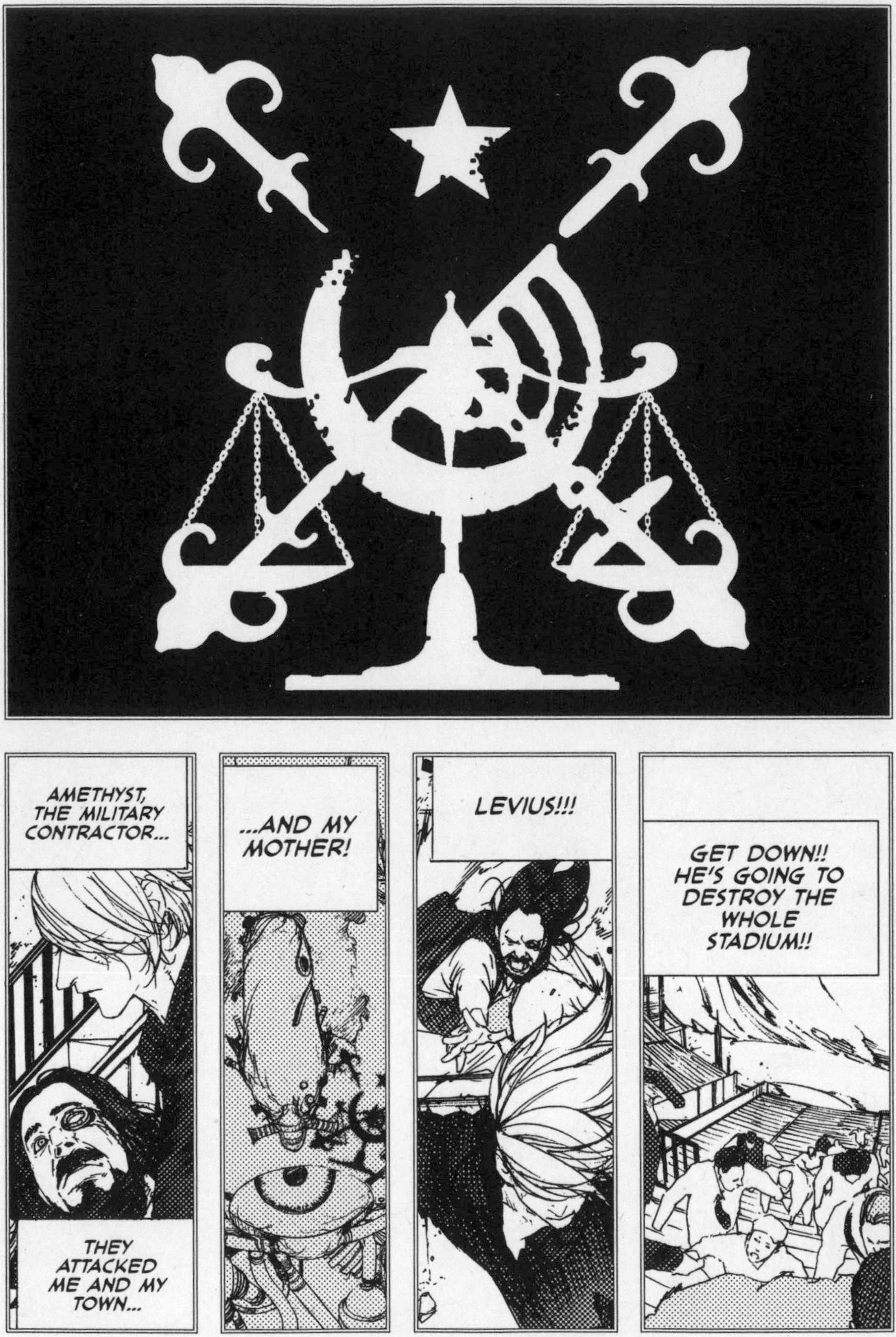
AMETHYST, THE MILITARY CONTRACTOR...
THEY ATTACKED ME AND MY TOWN...
...AND MY MOTHER!
LEVIUS!!!
GET DOWN!! HE'S GOING TO DESTROY THE WHOLE STADIUM!!

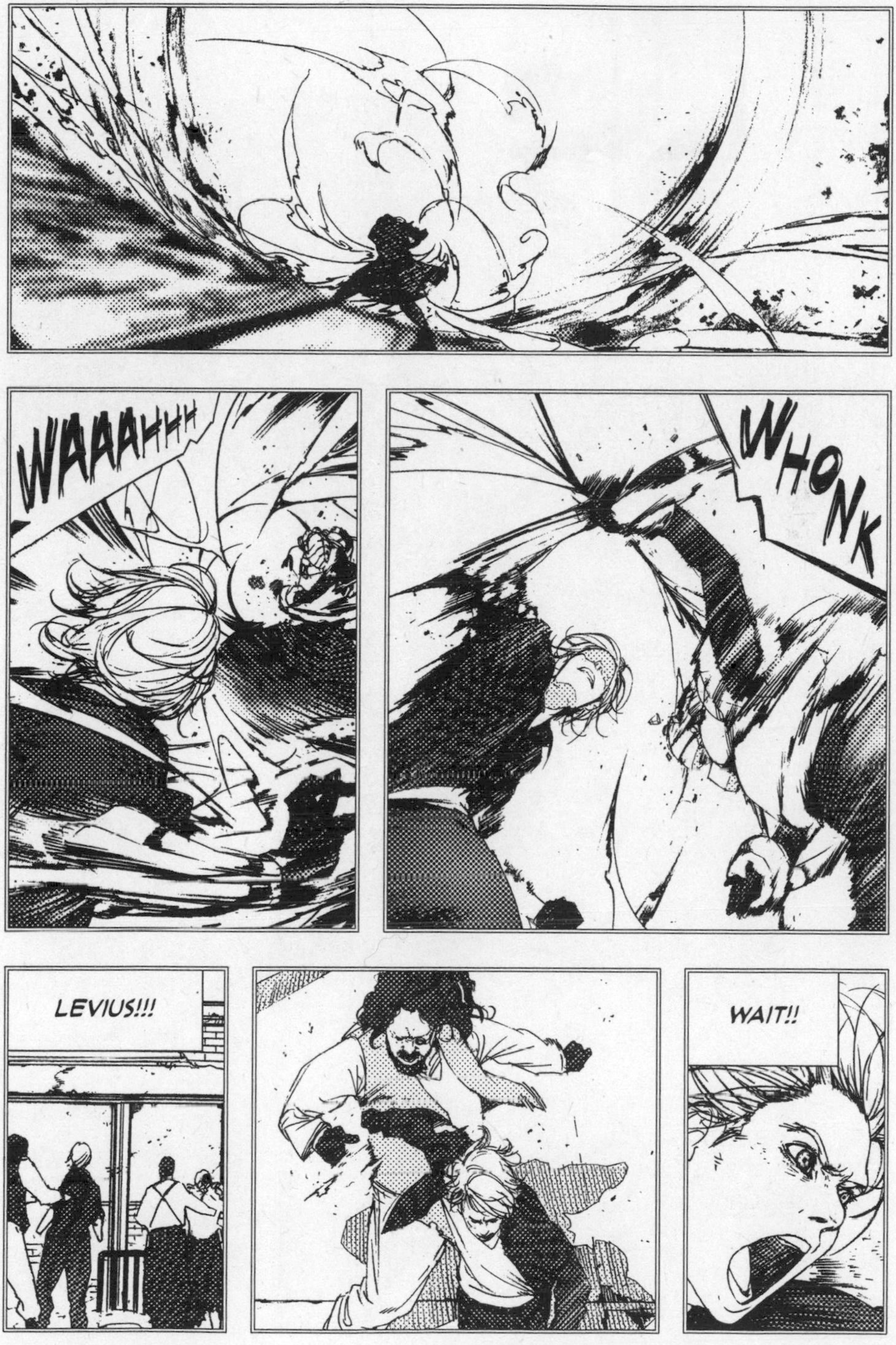
WHONK
WAAAHHH
WAIT!!
LEVIUS!!!

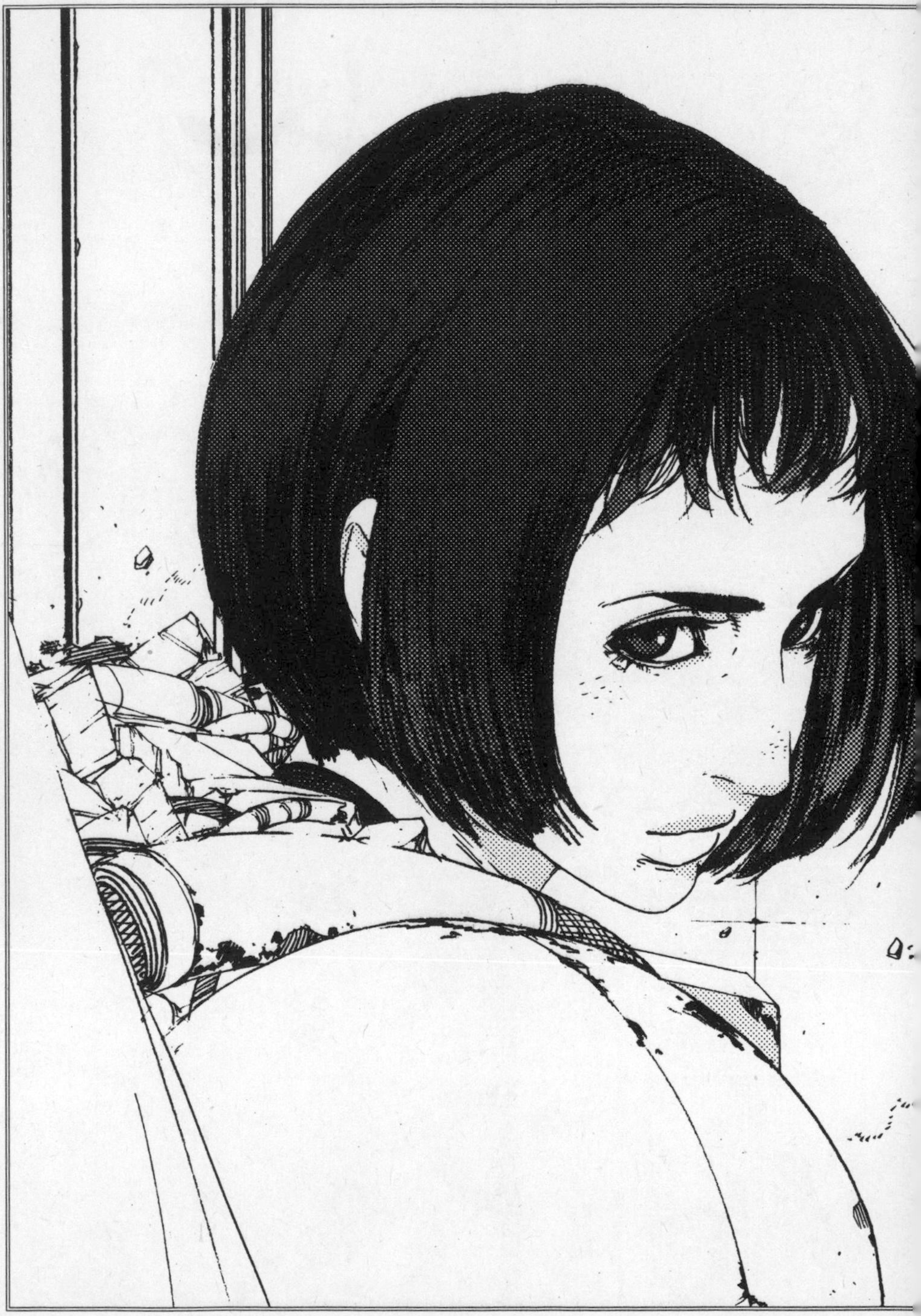

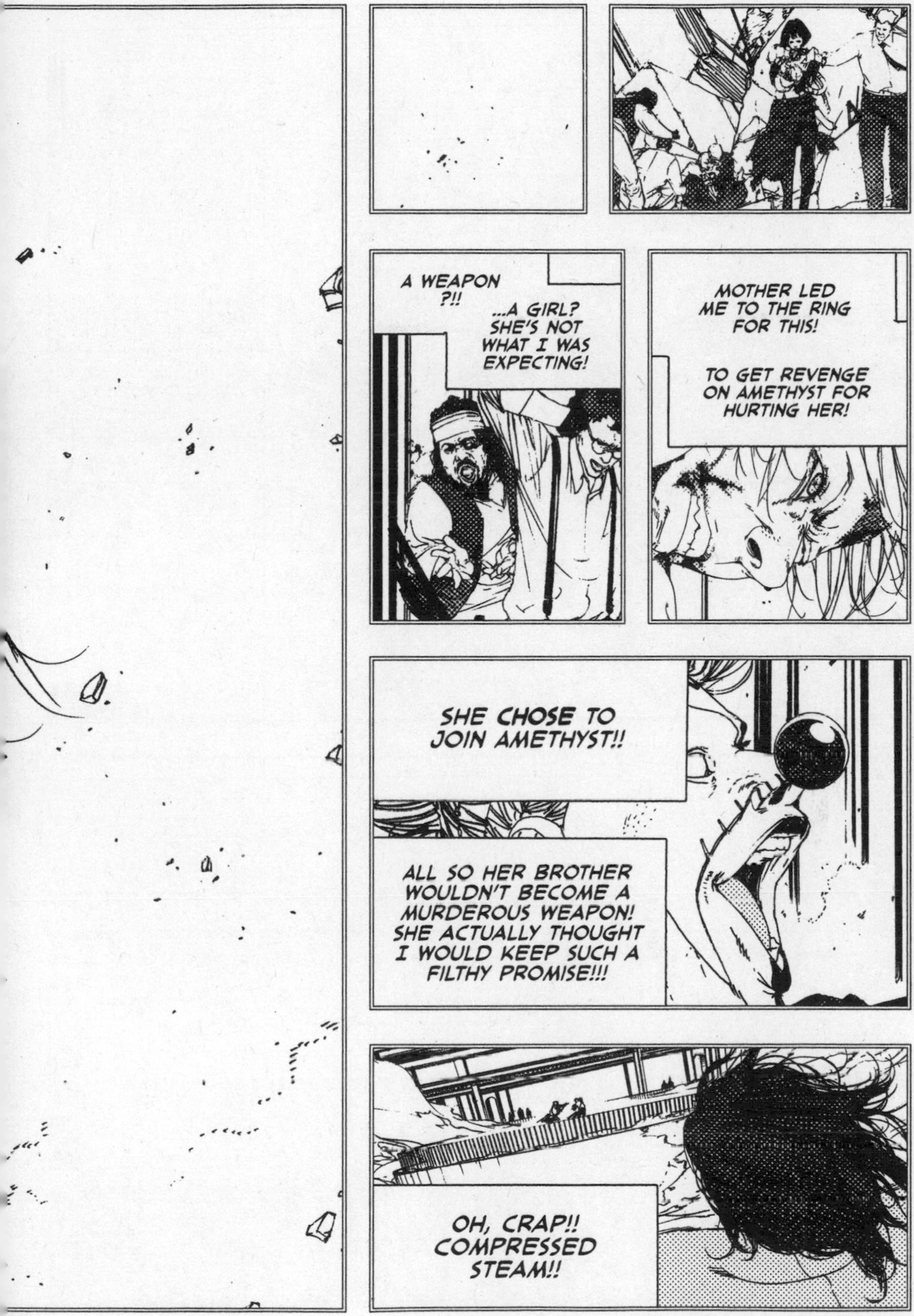
MOTHER LED ME TO THE RING FOR THIS!
TO GET REVENGE ON AMETHYST FOR HURTING HER!
A WEAPON ?!!
...A GIRL? SHE'S NOT WHAT I WAS EXPECTING!
SHE CHOSE TO JOIN AMETHYST!!
ALL SO HER BROTHER WOULDN'T BECOME A MURDEROUS WEAPON! SHE ACTUALLY THOUGHT I WOULD KEEP SUCH A FILTHY PROMISE!!!
OH, CRAP!! COMPRESSED STEAM!!

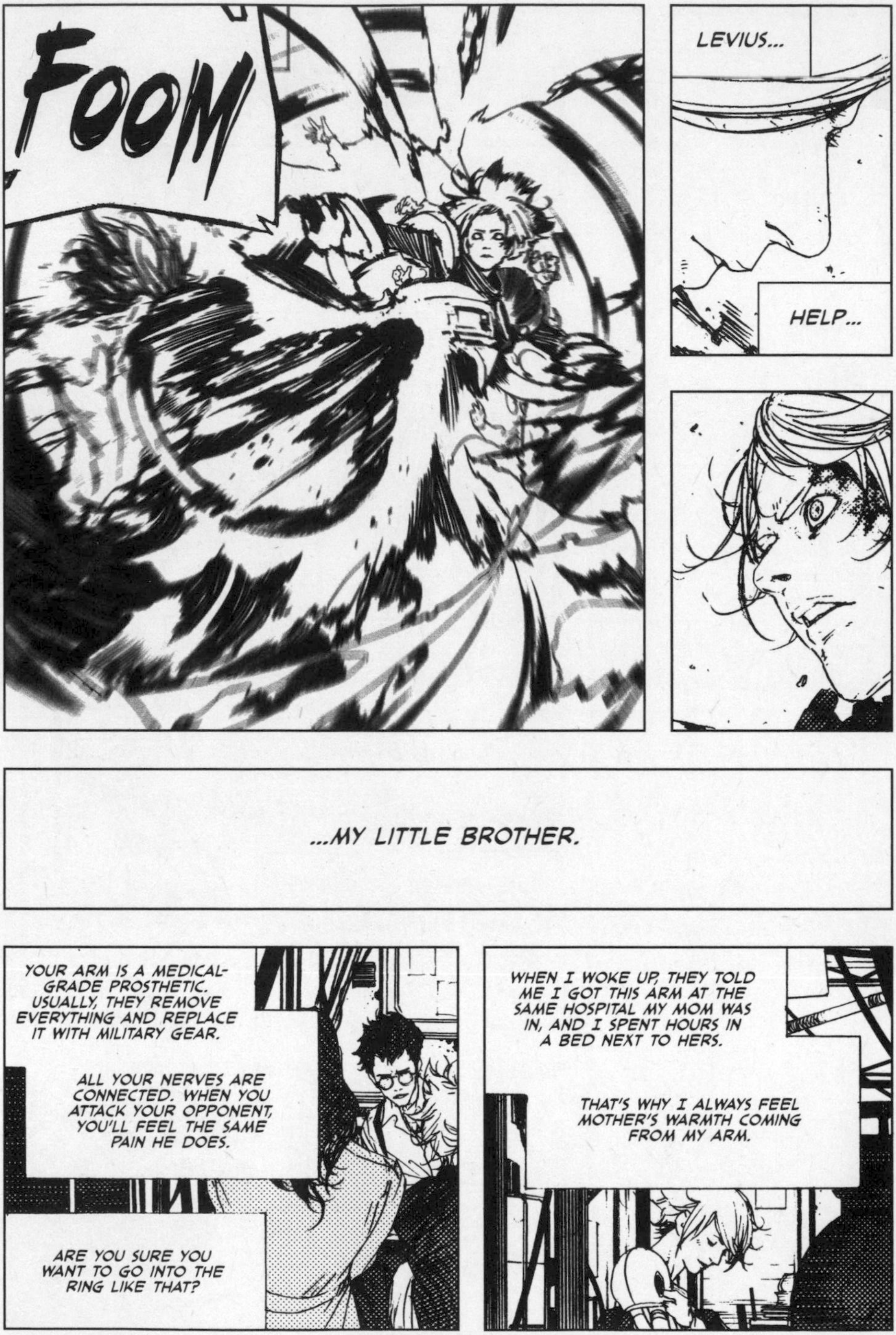
FOOM
LEVIUS...
HELP...
...MY LITTLE BROTHER.
YOUR ARM IS A MEDICAL-GRADE PROSTHETIC. USUALLY, THEY REMOVE EVERYTHING AND REPLACE IT WITH MILITARY GEAR.
ALL YOUR NERVES ARE CONNECTED. WHEN YOU ATTACK YOUR OPPONENT, YOU'LL FEEL THE SAME PAIN HE DOES.
ARE YOU SURE YOU WANT TO GO INTO THE RING LIKE THAT?
WHEN I WOKE UP, THEY TOLD ME I GOT THIS ARM AT THE SAME HOSPITAL MY MOM WAS IN, AND I SPENT HOURS IN A BED NEXT TO HERS.
THAT'S WHY I ALWAYS FEEL MOTHER'S WARMTH COMING FROM MY ARM.

I LIKE FEELING CONNECTED TO HER.

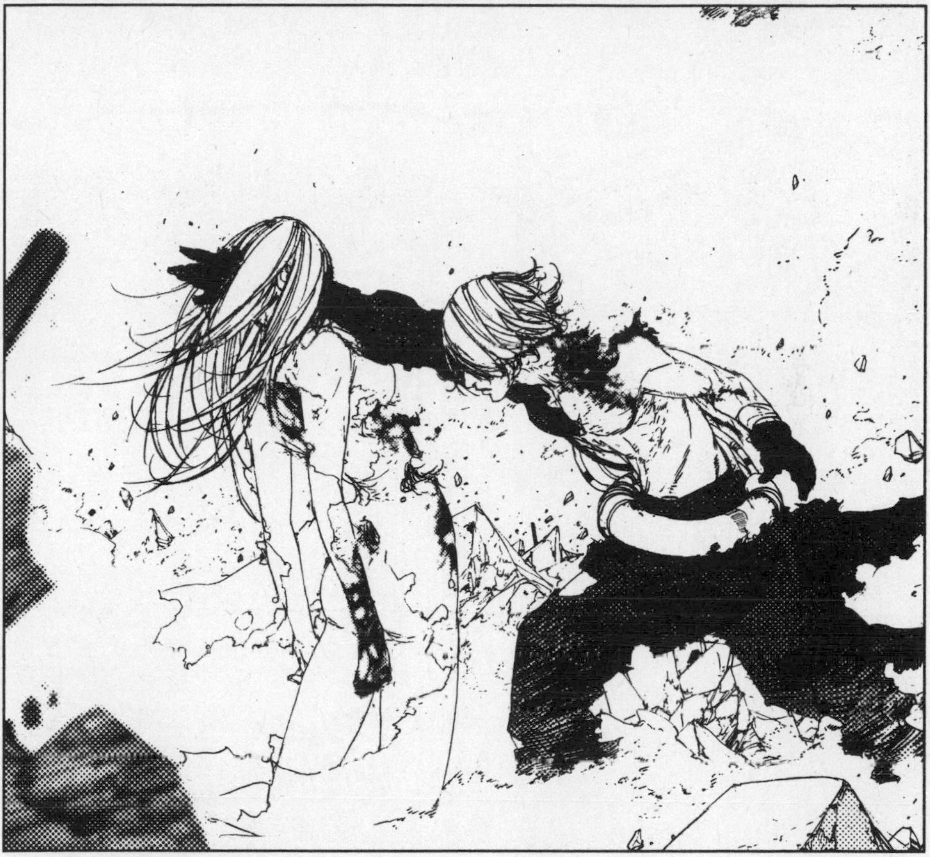

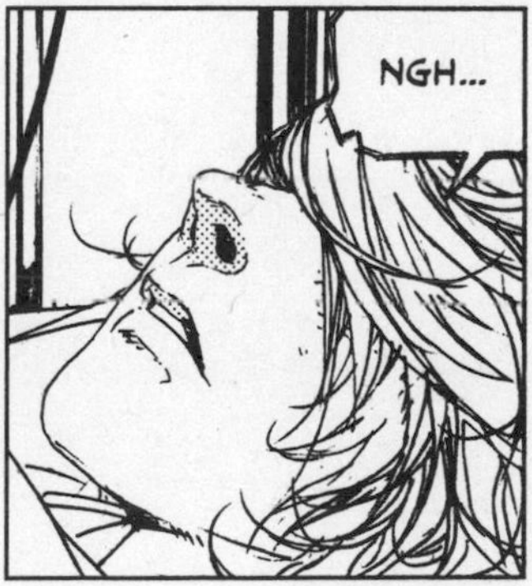
NGH...

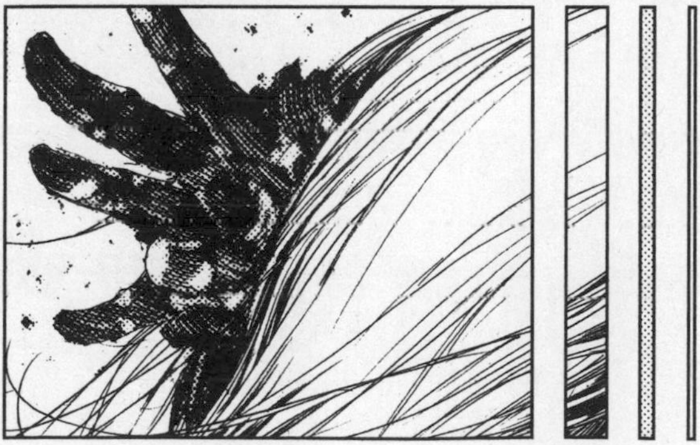

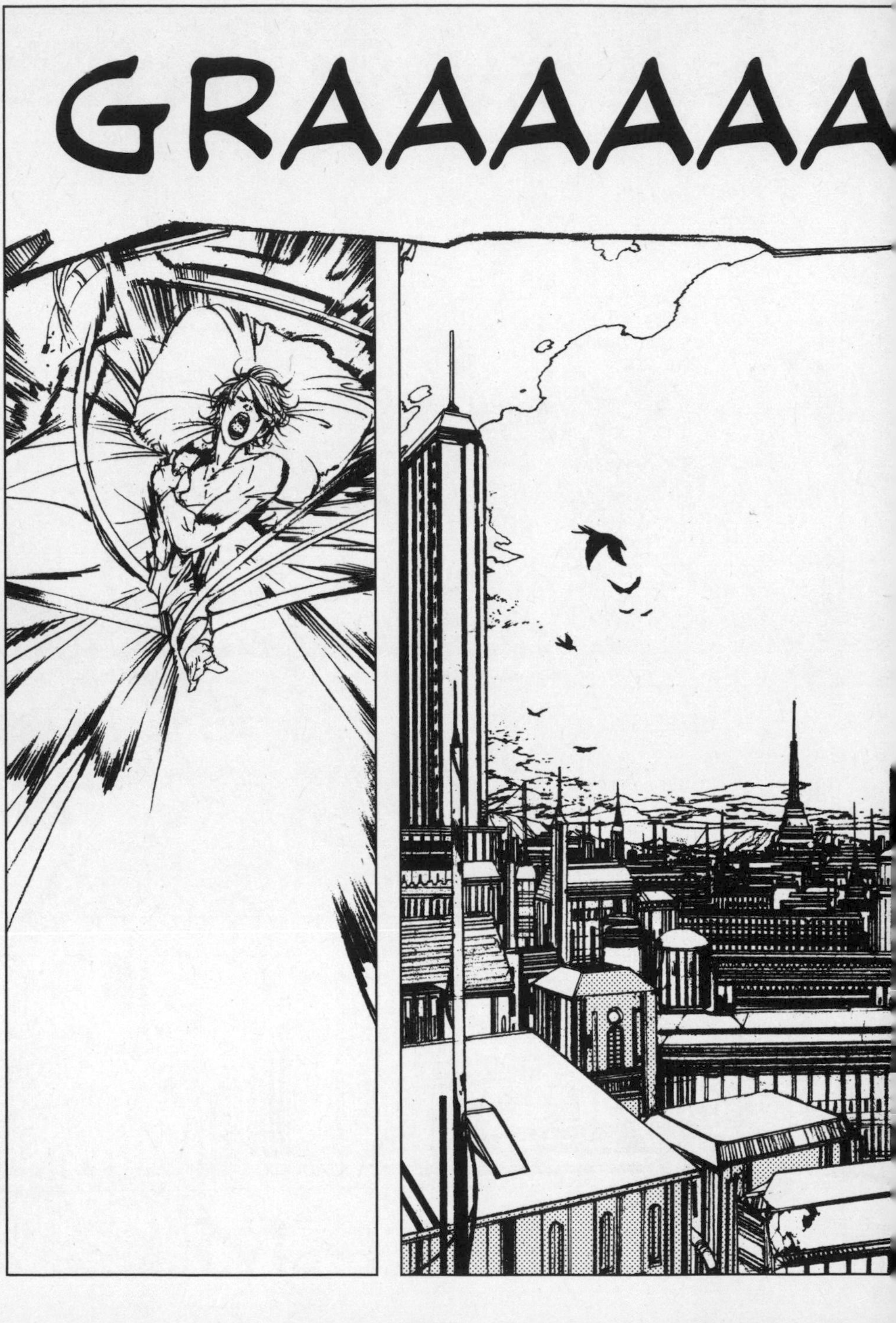
GRAAAAAA

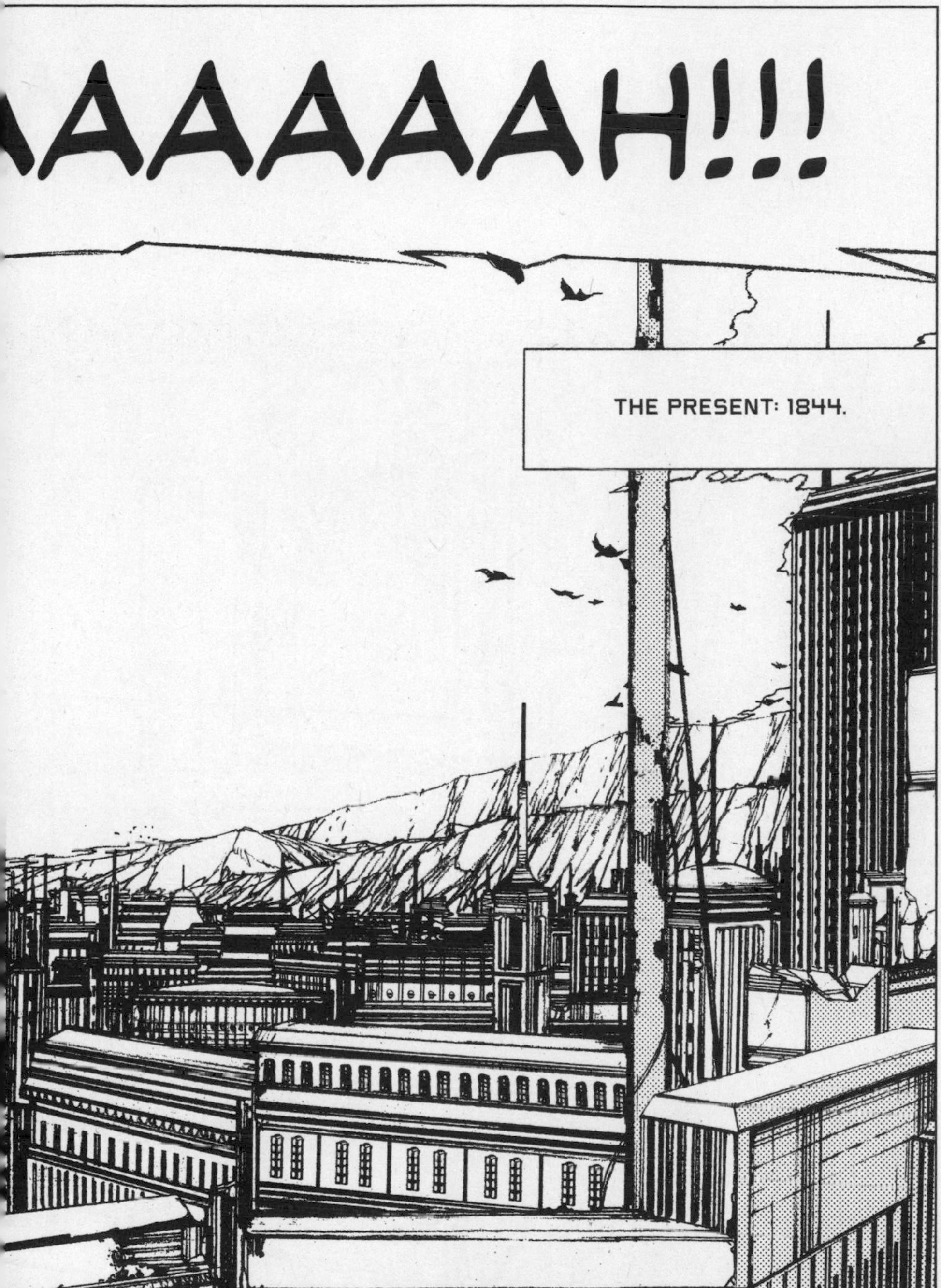
AAAAAAH!!!
THE PRESENT: 1844.

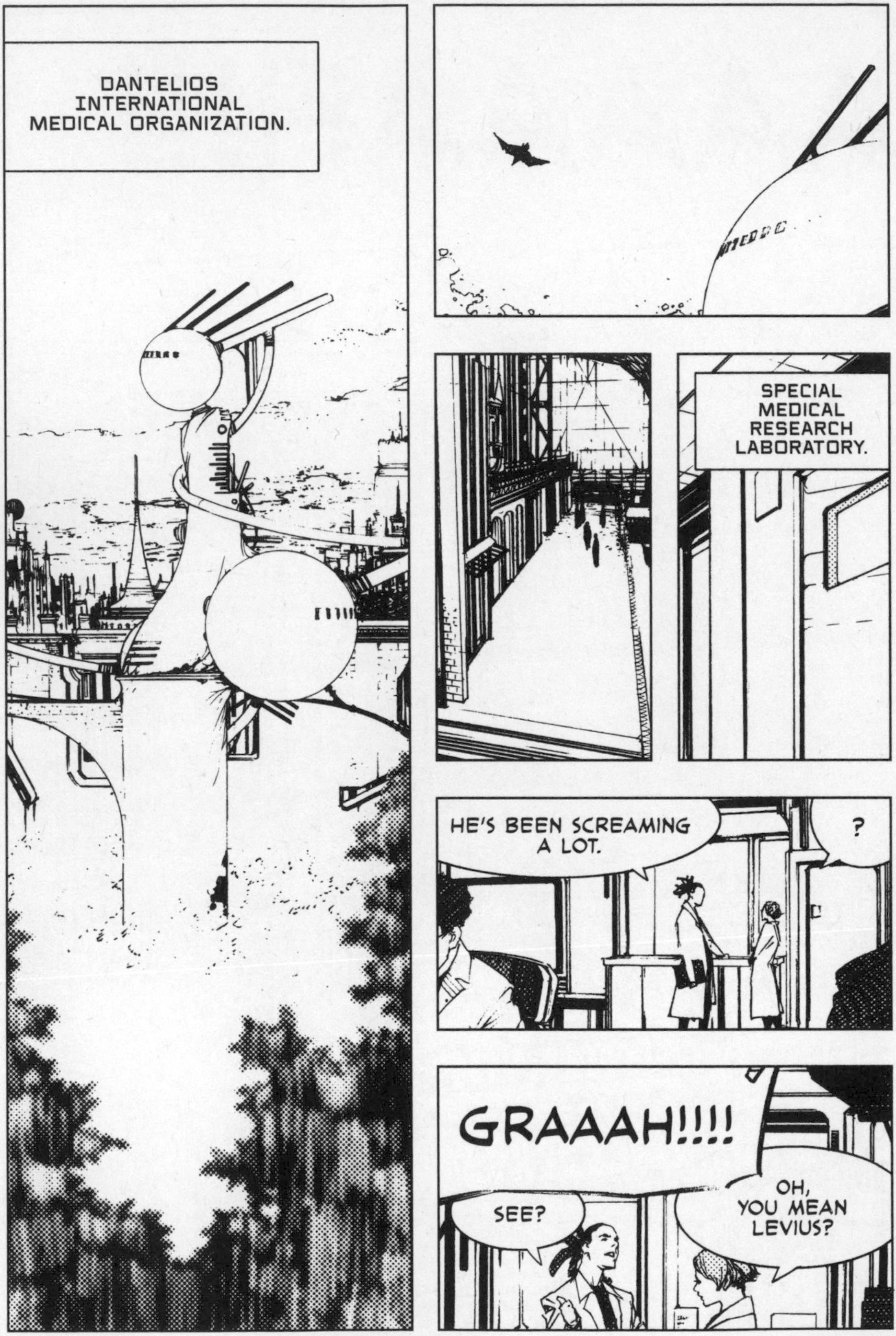
DANTELIOS INTERNATIONAL MEDICAL ORGANIZATION.
SPECIAL MEDICAL RESEARCH LABORATORY.
HE'S BEEN SCREAMING A LOT.
?
GRAAAH!!!!
SEE?
OH, YOU MEAN LEVIUS?

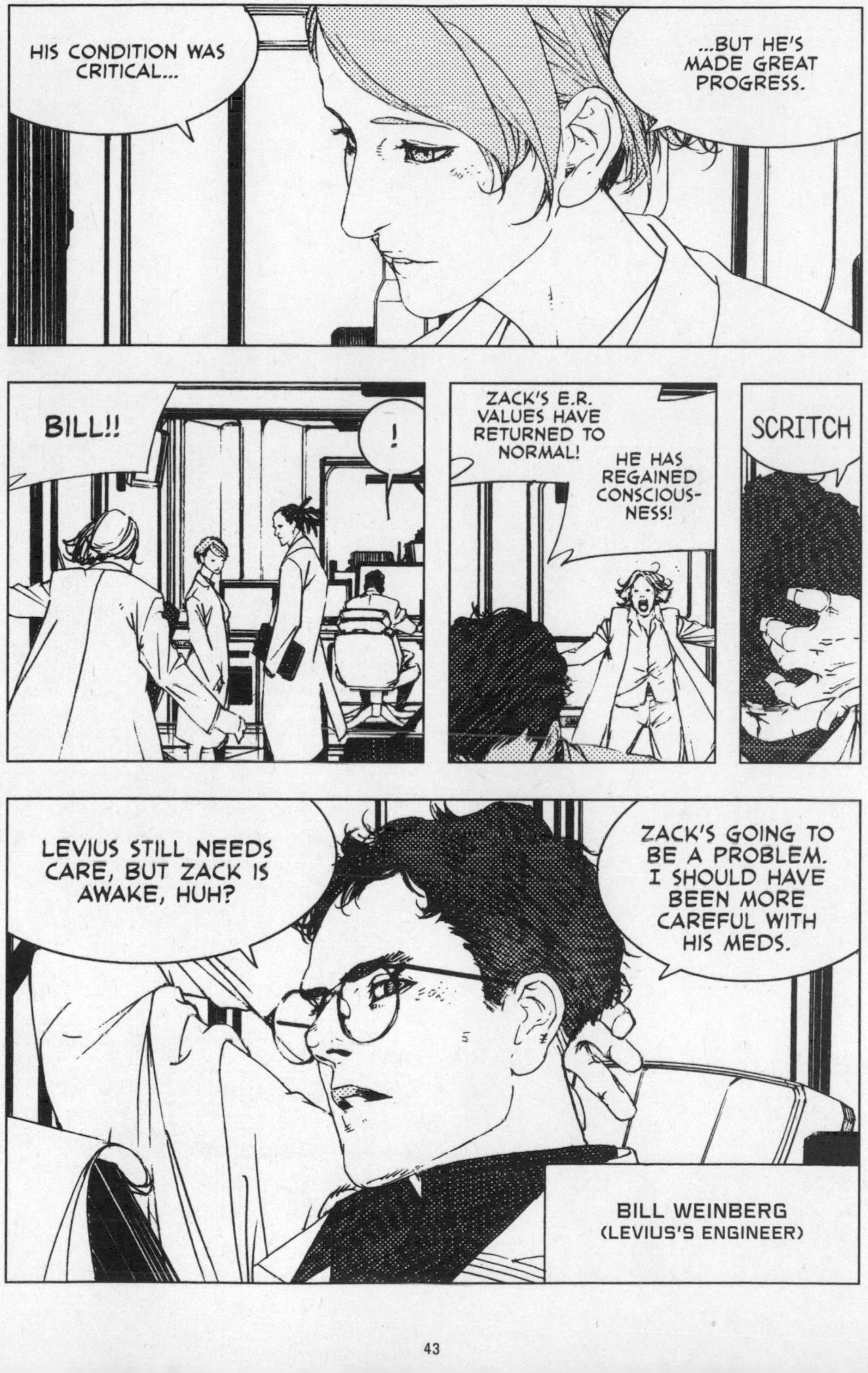
HIS CONDITION WAS CRITICAL...
...BUT HE'S MADE GREAT PROGRESS.
BILL!!
!
ZACK'S E.R. VALUES HAVE RETURNED TO NORMAL!
HE HAS REGAINED CONSCIOUS-NESS!
SCRITCH
LEVIUS STILL NEEDS CARE, BUT ZACK IS AWAKE, HUH?
ZACK'S GOING TO BE A PROBLEM. I SHOULD HAVE BEEN MORE CAREFUL WITH HIS MEDS.
BILL WEINBERG
(LEVIUS'S ENGINEER)

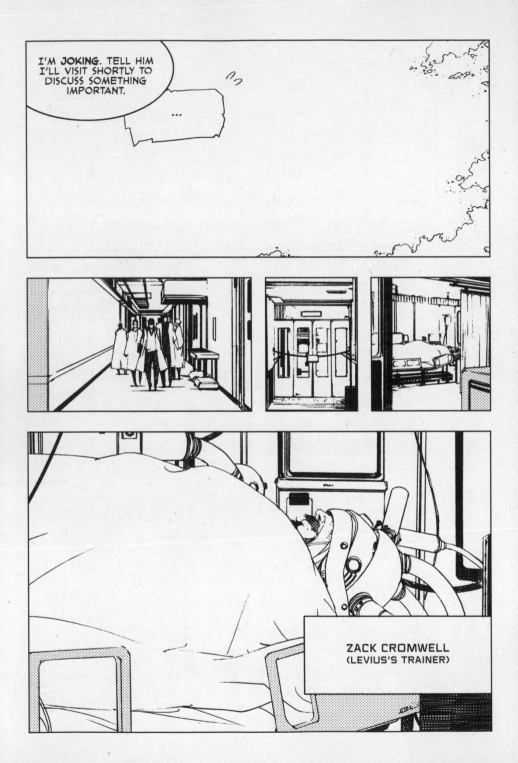

I'M **JOKING**. TELL HIM I'LL VISIT SHORTLY TO DISCUSS SOMETHING IMPORTANT.

...

ZACK CROMWELL
(LEVIUS'S TRAINER)

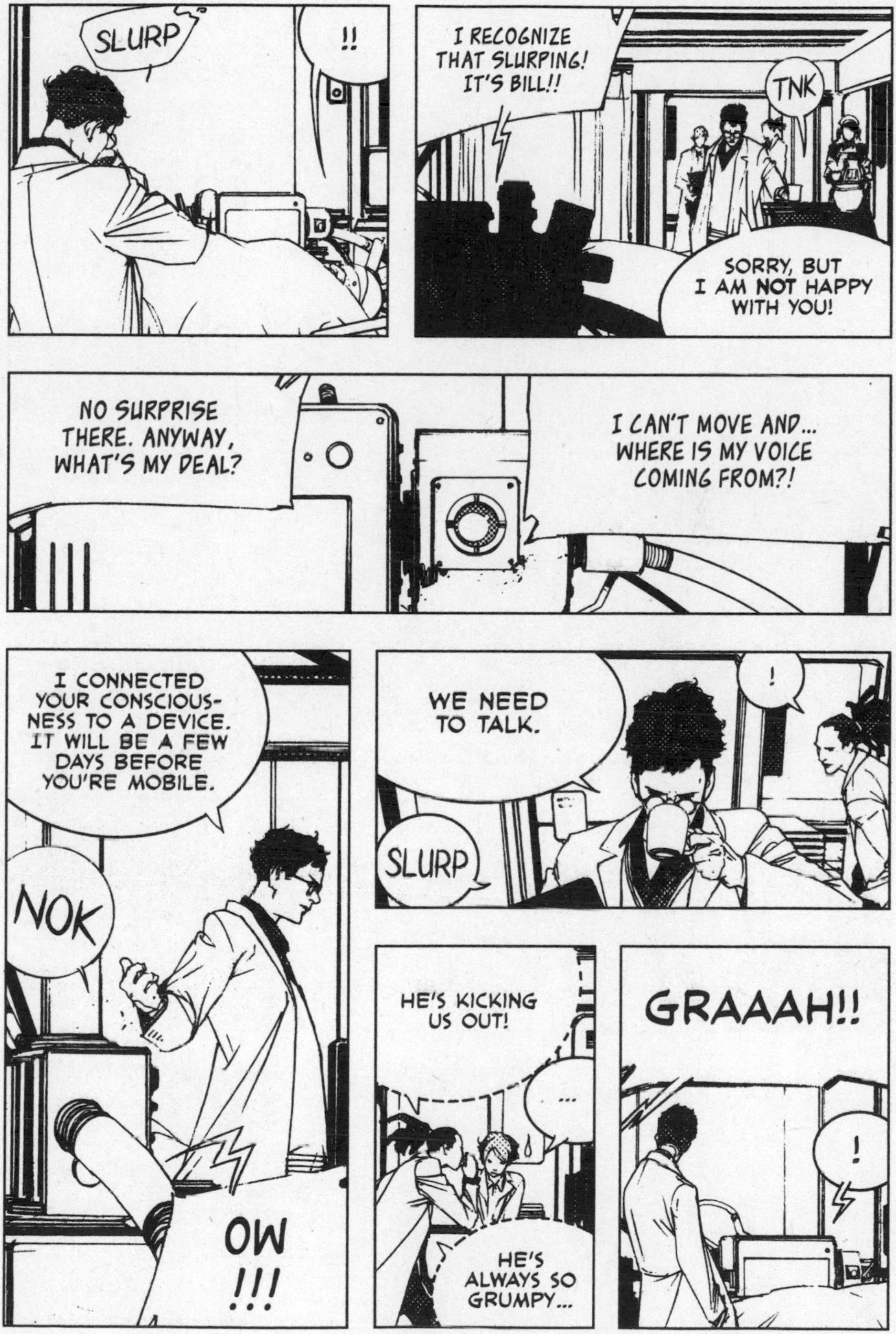
SLURP
!!
I RECOGNIZE THAT SLURPING! IT'S BILL!!
TNK
SORRY, BUT I AM NOT HAPPY WITH YOU!
NO SURPRISE THERE. ANYWAY, WHAT'S MY DEAL?
I CAN'T MOVE AND... WHERE IS MY VOICE COMING FROM?!
I CONNECTED YOUR CONSCIOUS-NESS TO A DEVICE. IT WILL BE A FEW DAYS BEFORE YOU'RE MOBILE.
NOK
OW !!!
WE NEED TO TALK.
!
SLURP
HE'S KICKING US OUT!
...
HE'S ALWAYS SO GRUMPY...
GRAAAH!!
!

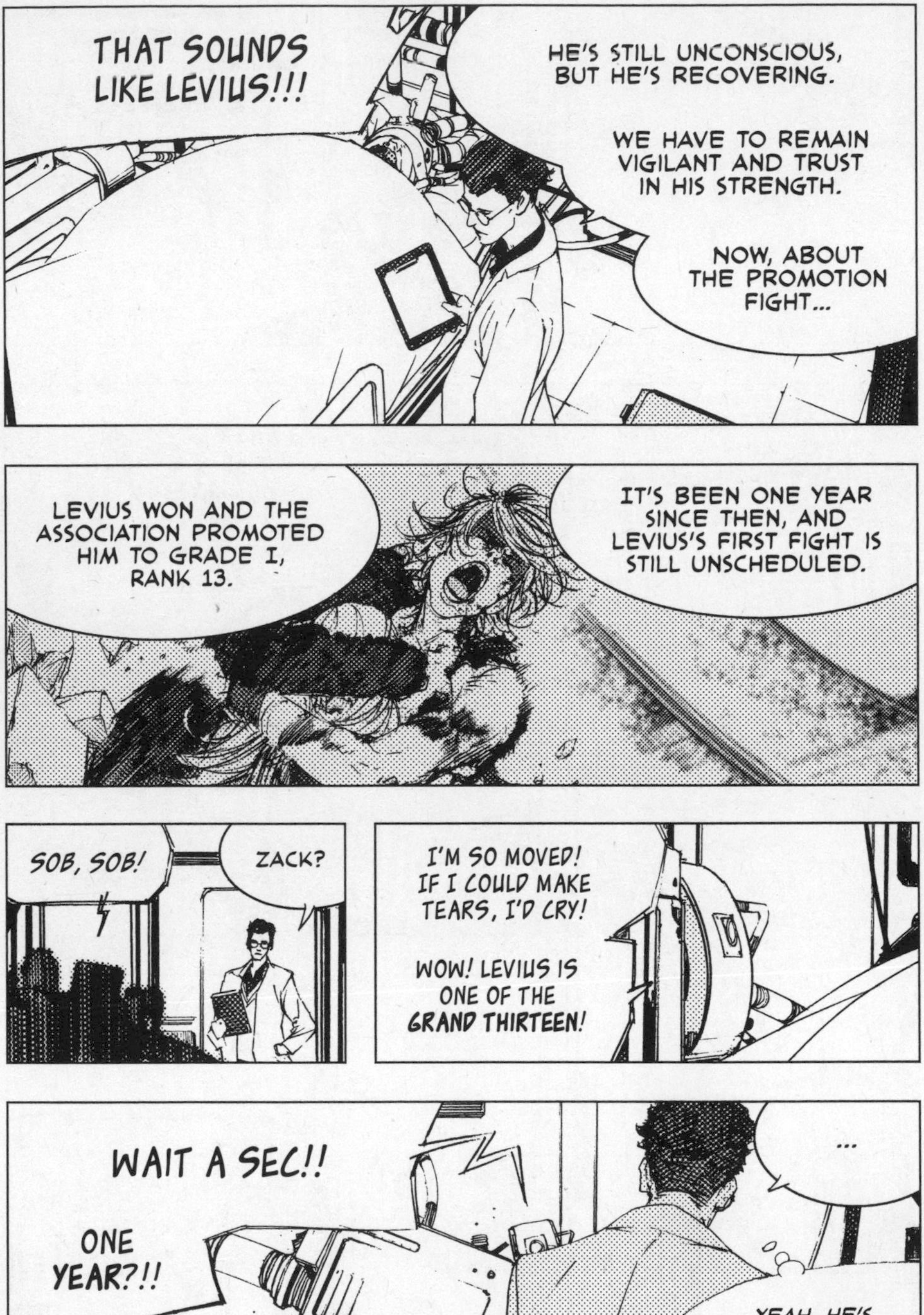
THAT SOUNDS LIKE LEVIUS!!!
HE'S STILL UNCONSCIOUS, BUT HE'S RECOVERING.
WE HAVE TO REMAIN VIGILANT AND TRUST IN HIS STRENGTH.
NOW, ABOUT THE PROMOTION FIGHT...
LEVIUS WON AND THE ASSOCIATION PROMOTED HIM TO GRADE I, RANK 13.
IT'S BEEN ONE YEAR SINCE THEN, AND LEVIUS'S FIRST FIGHT IS STILL UNSCHEDULED.
SOB, SOB!
ZACK?
I'M SO MOVED! IF I COULD MAKE TEARS, I'D CRY!
WOW! LEVIUS IS ONE OF THE GRAND THIRTEEN!
WAIT A SEC!!
ONE YEAR?!!
...
YEAH, HE'S A PAIN...

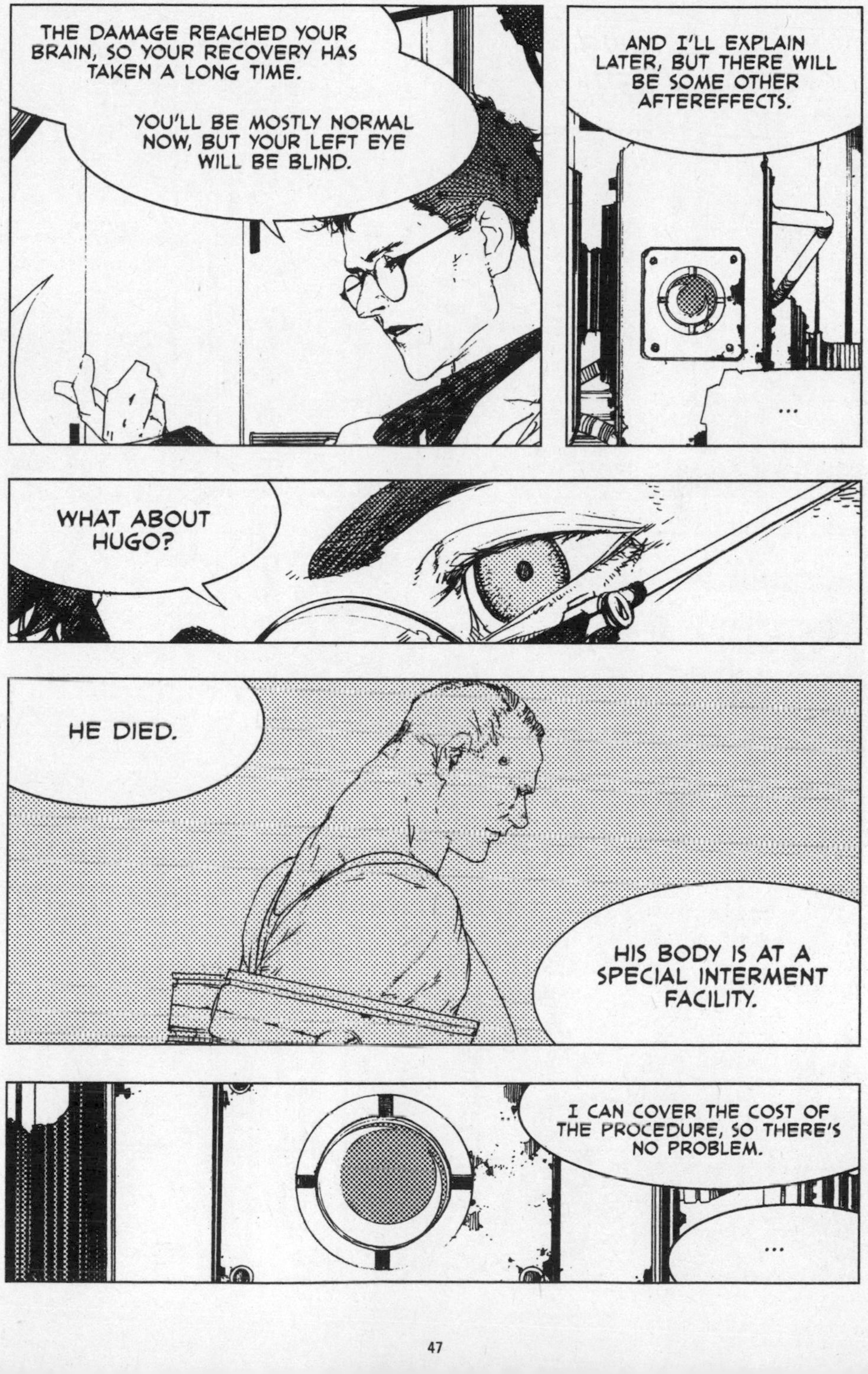
THE DAMAGE REACHED YOUR BRAIN, SO YOUR RECOVERY HAS TAKEN A LONG TIME.
YOU'LL BE MOSTLY NORMAL NOW, BUT YOUR LEFT EYE WILL BE BLIND.
AND I'LL EXPLAIN LATER, BUT THERE WILL BE SOME OTHER AFTEREFFECTS.
...
WHAT ABOUT HUGO?
HE DIED.
HIS BODY IS AT A SPECIAL INTERMENT FACILITY.
I CAN COVER THE COST OF THE PROCEDURE, SO THERE'S NO PROBLEM.
...

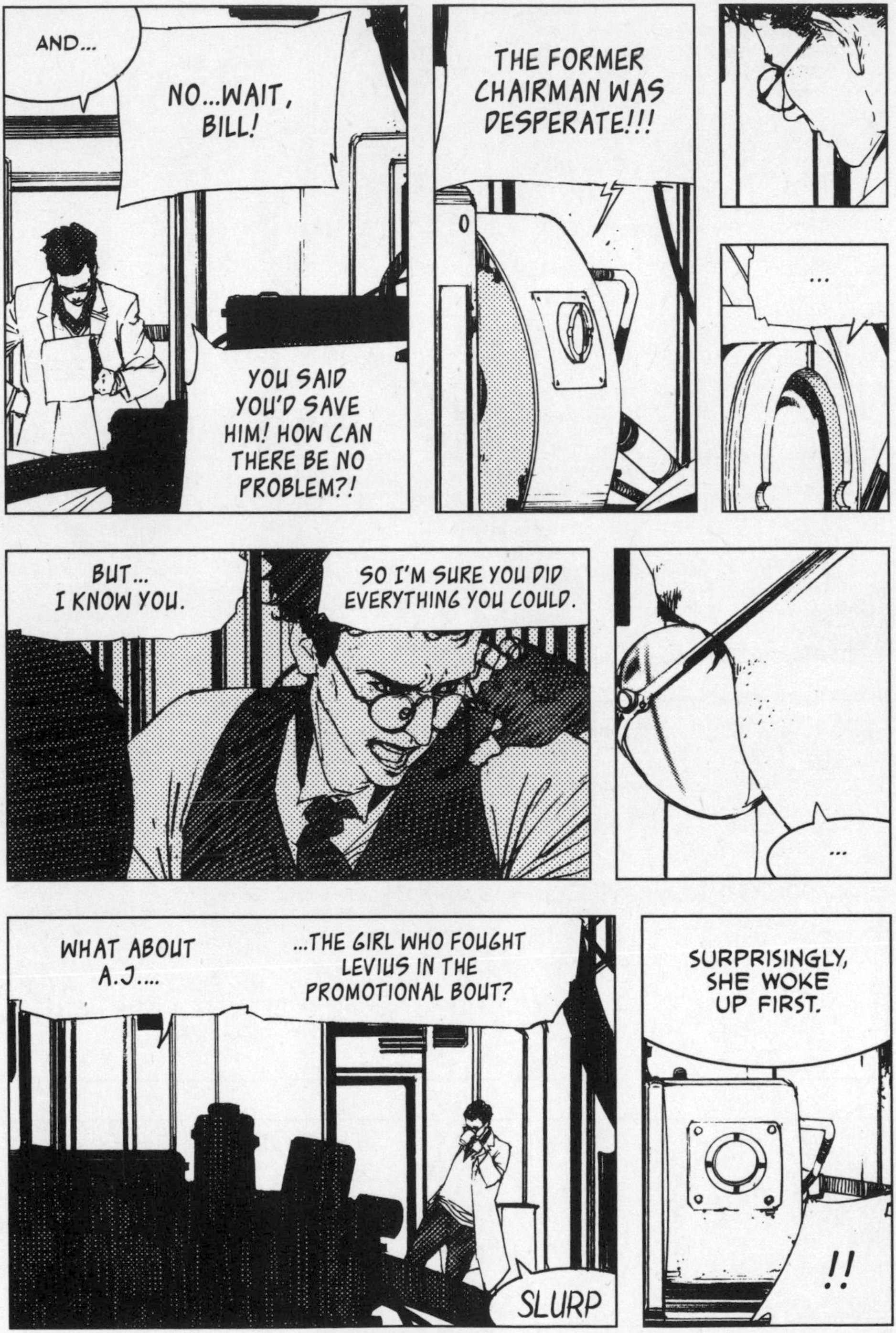
AND...
NO...WAIT, BILL!
YOU SAID YOU'D SAVE HIM! HOW CAN THERE BE NO PROBLEM?!
THE FORMER CHAIRMAN WAS DESPERATE!!!
...
BUT... I KNOW YOU.
SO I'M SURE YOU DID EVERYTHING YOU COULD.
...
WHAT ABOUT A.J....
...THE GIRL WHO FOUGHT LEVIUS IN THE PROMOTIONAL BOUT?
SLURP
SURPRISINGLY, SHE WOKE UP FIRST.
!!

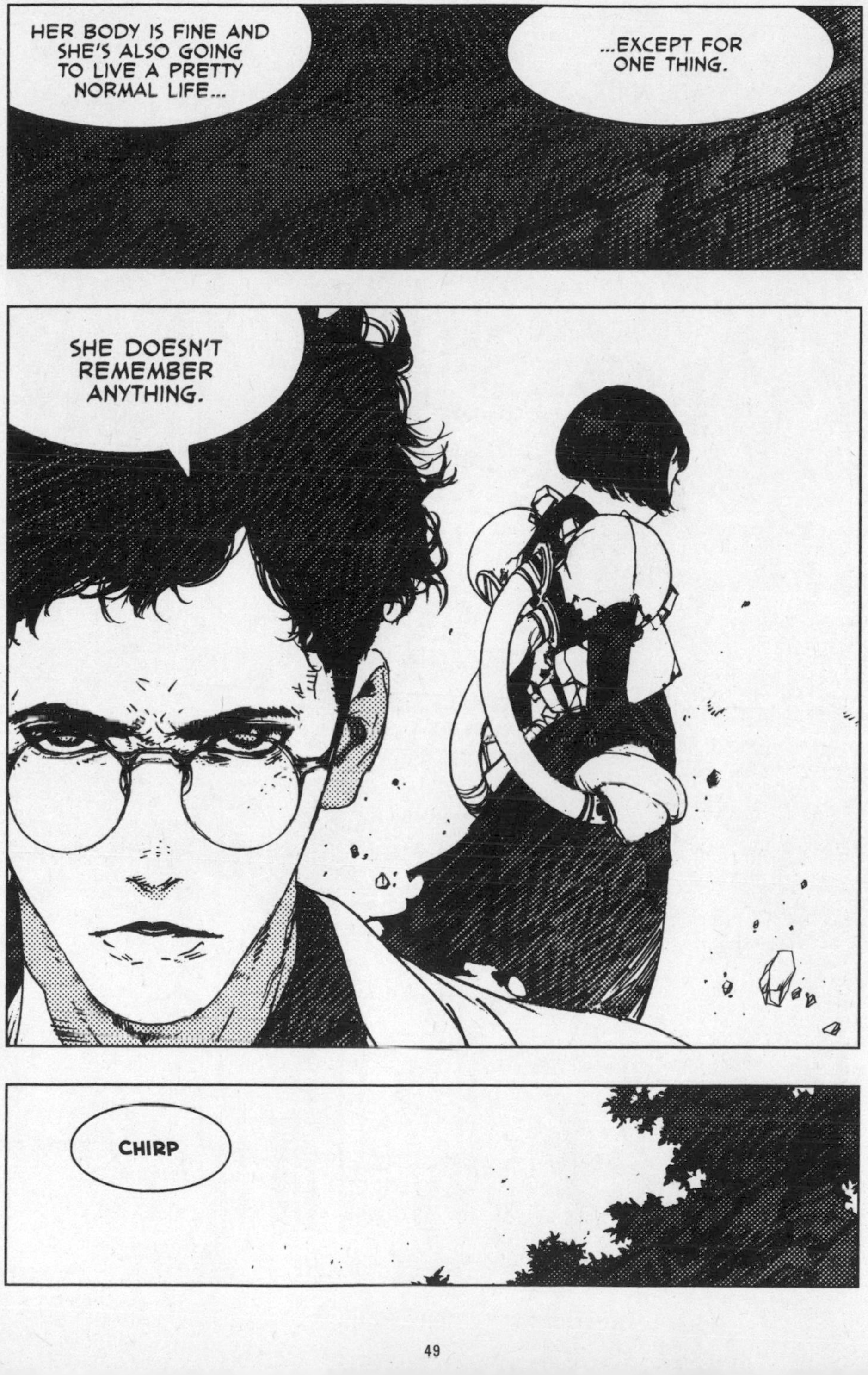
HER BODY IS FINE AND SHE'S ALSO GOING TO LIVE A PRETTY NORMAL LIFE...
...EXCEPT FOR ONE THING.
SHE DOESN'T REMEMBER ANYTHING.
CHIRP

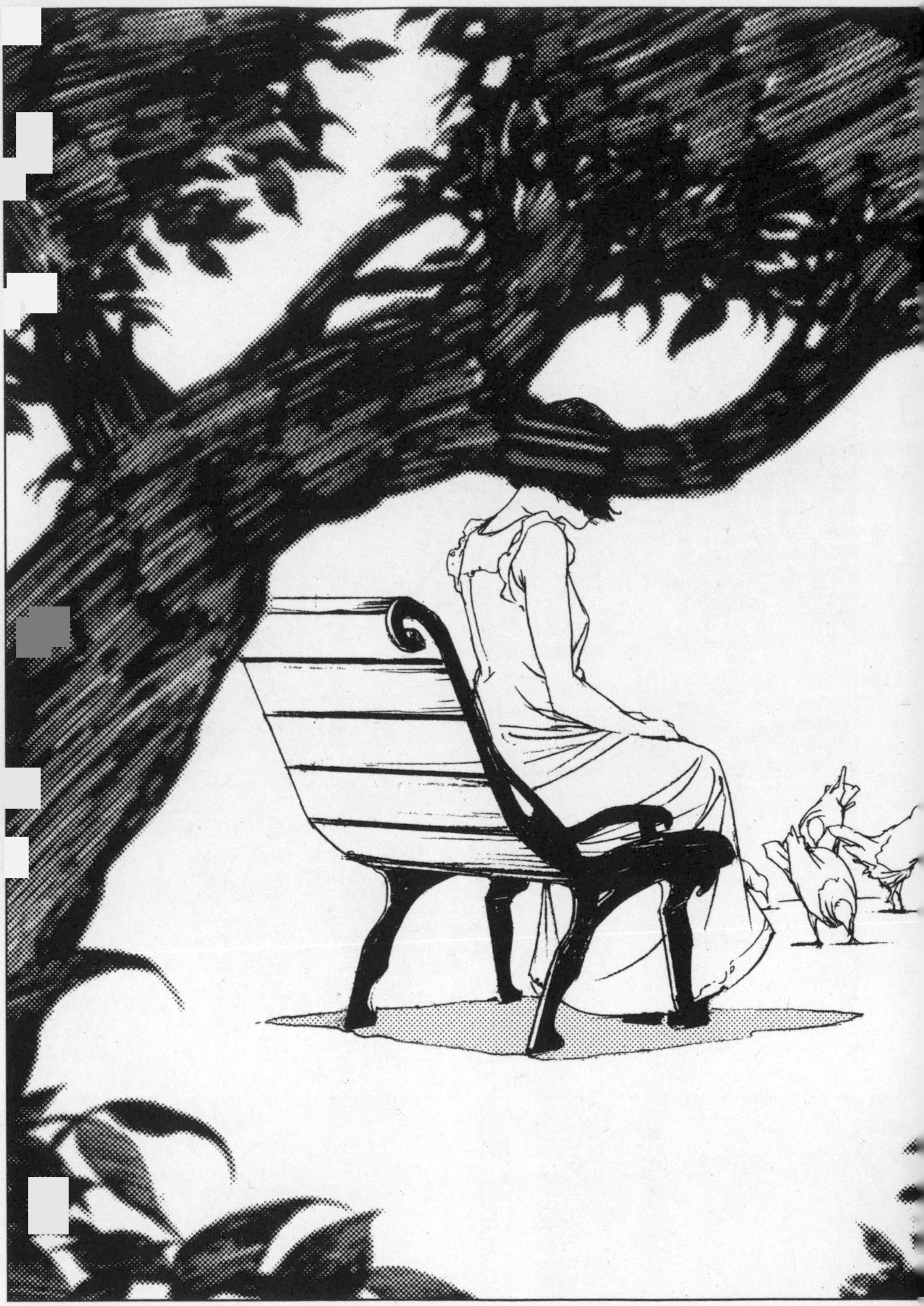

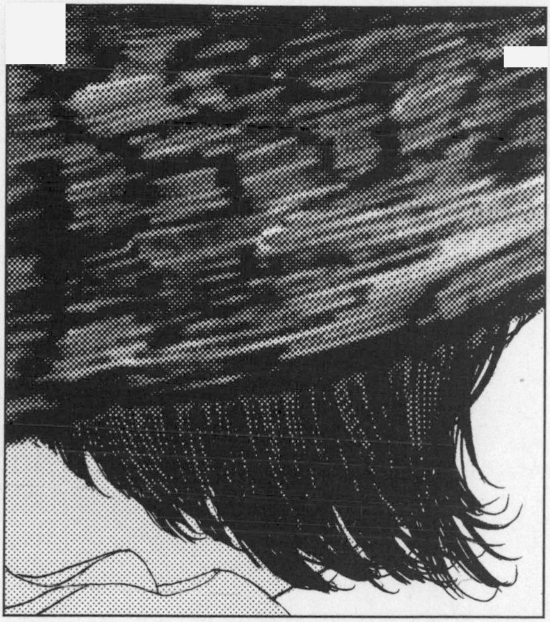

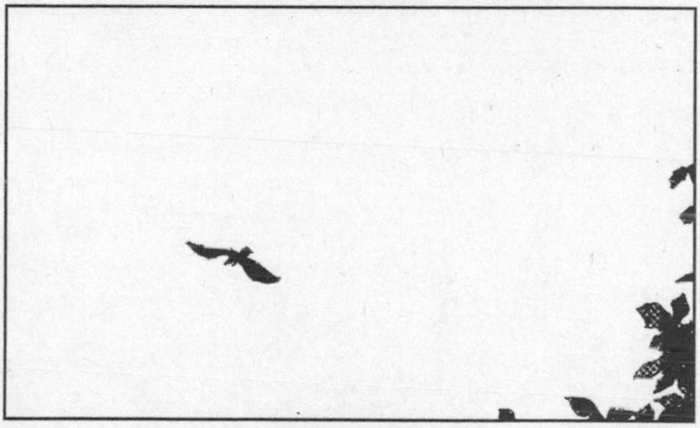

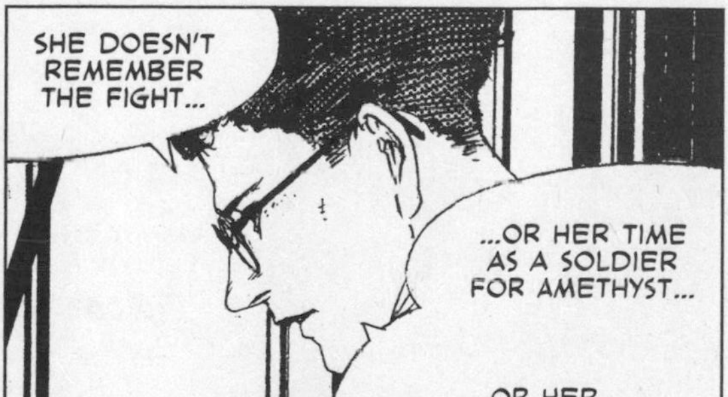
SHE DOESN'T REMEMBER THE FIGHT...
...OR HER TIME AS A SOLDIER FOR AMETHYST...
...OR HER YOUNGER BROTHER.

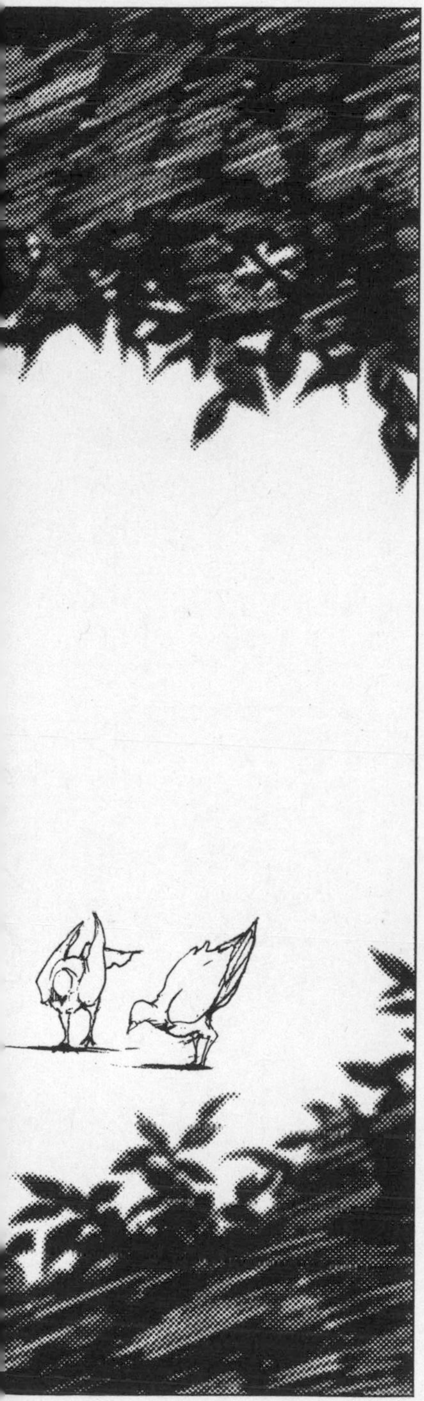

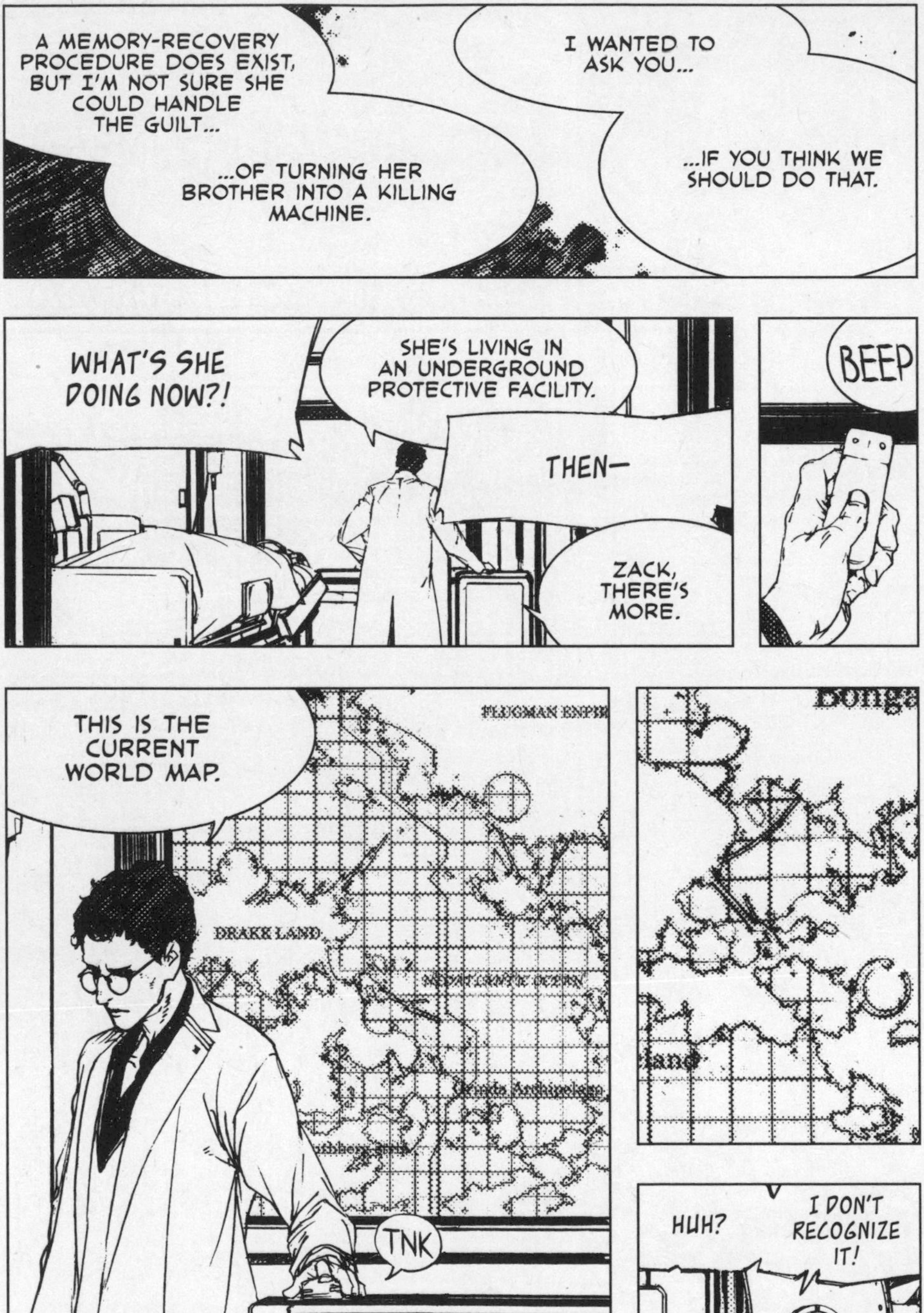
A MEMORY-RECOVERY PROCEDURE DOES EXIST, BUT I'M NOT SURE SHE COULD HANDLE THE GUILT...
...OF TURNING HER BROTHER INTO A KILLING MACHINE.
I WANTED TO ASK YOU...
...IF YOU THINK WE SHOULD DO THAT.
WHAT'S SHE DOING NOW?!
SHE'S LIVING IN AN UNDERGROUND PROTECTIVE FACILITY.
THEN—
ZACK, THERE'S MORE.
BEEP
THIS IS THE CURRENT WORLD MAP.
DRAKE LAND
TNK
HUH?
I DON'T RECOGNIZE IT!

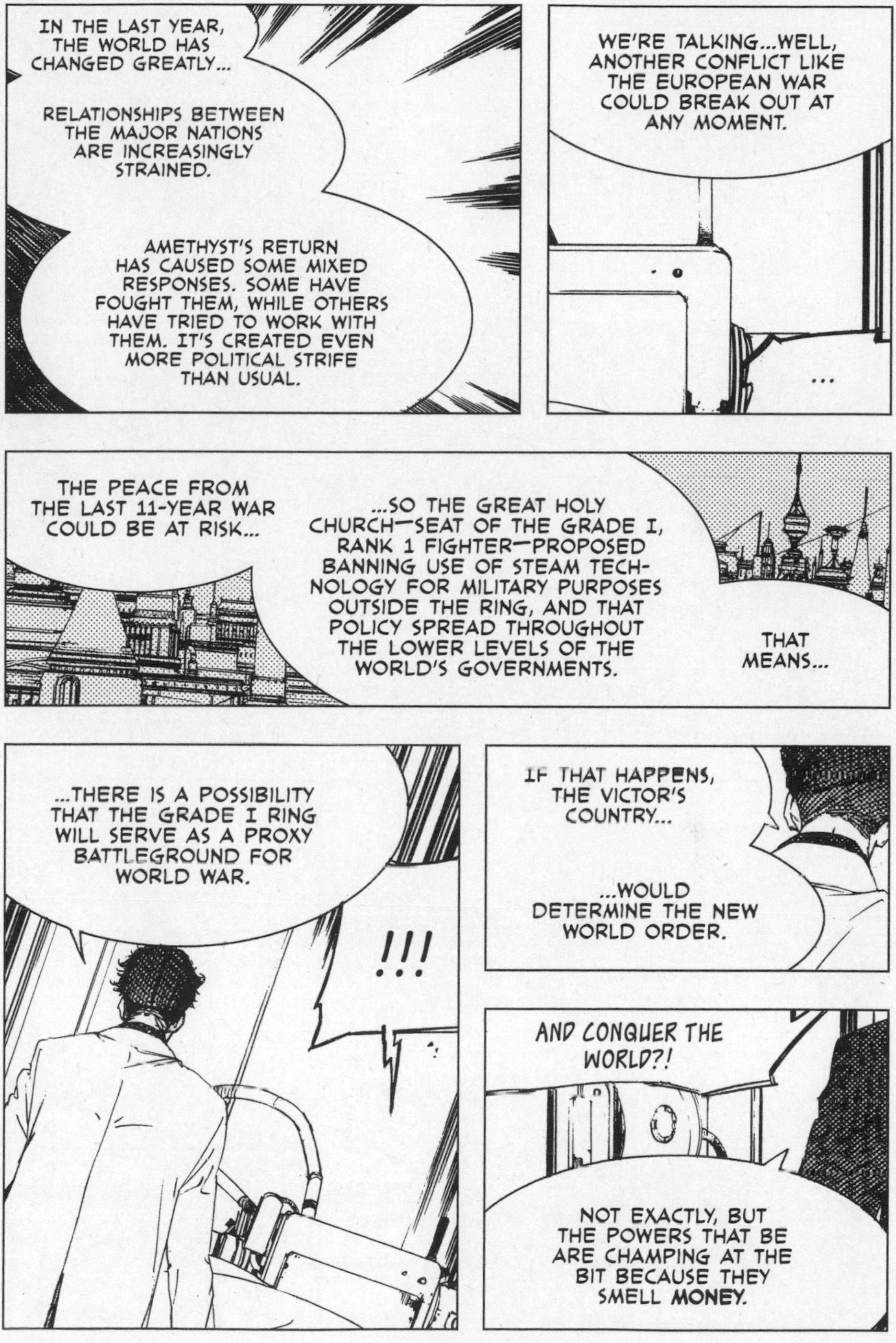
IN THE LAST YEAR, THE WORLD HAS CHANGED GREATLY...
RELATIONSHIPS BETWEEN THE MAJOR NATIONS ARE INCREASINGLY STRAINED.
AMETHYST'S RETURN HAS CAUSED SOME MIXED RESPONSES. SOME HAVE FOUGHT THEM, WHILE OTHERS HAVE TRIED TO WORK WITH THEM. IT'S CREATED EVEN MORE POLITICAL STRIFE THAN USUAL.
WE'RE TALKING...WELL, ANOTHER CONFLICT LIKE THE EUROPEAN WAR COULD BREAK OUT AT ANY MOMENT.
...
THE PEACE FROM THE LAST 11-YEAR WAR COULD BE AT RISK...
...SO THE GREAT HOLY CHURCH—SEAT OF THE GRADE I, RANK 1 FIGHTER—PROPOSED BANNING USE OF STEAM TECHNOLOGY FOR MILITARY PURPOSES OUTSIDE THE RING, AND THAT POLICY SPREAD THROUGHOUT THE LOWER LEVELS OF THE WORLD'S GOVERNMENTS.
THAT MEANS...
...THERE IS A POSSIBILITY THAT THE GRADE I RING WILL SERVE AS A PROXY BATTLEGROUND FOR WORLD WAR.
!!!
IF THAT HAPPENS, THE VICTOR'S COUNTRY...
...WOULD DETERMINE THE NEW WORLD ORDER.
AND CONQUER THE WORLD?!
NOT EXACTLY, BUT THE POWERS THAT BE ARE CHAMPING AT THE BIT BECAUSE THEY SMELL **MONEY**.

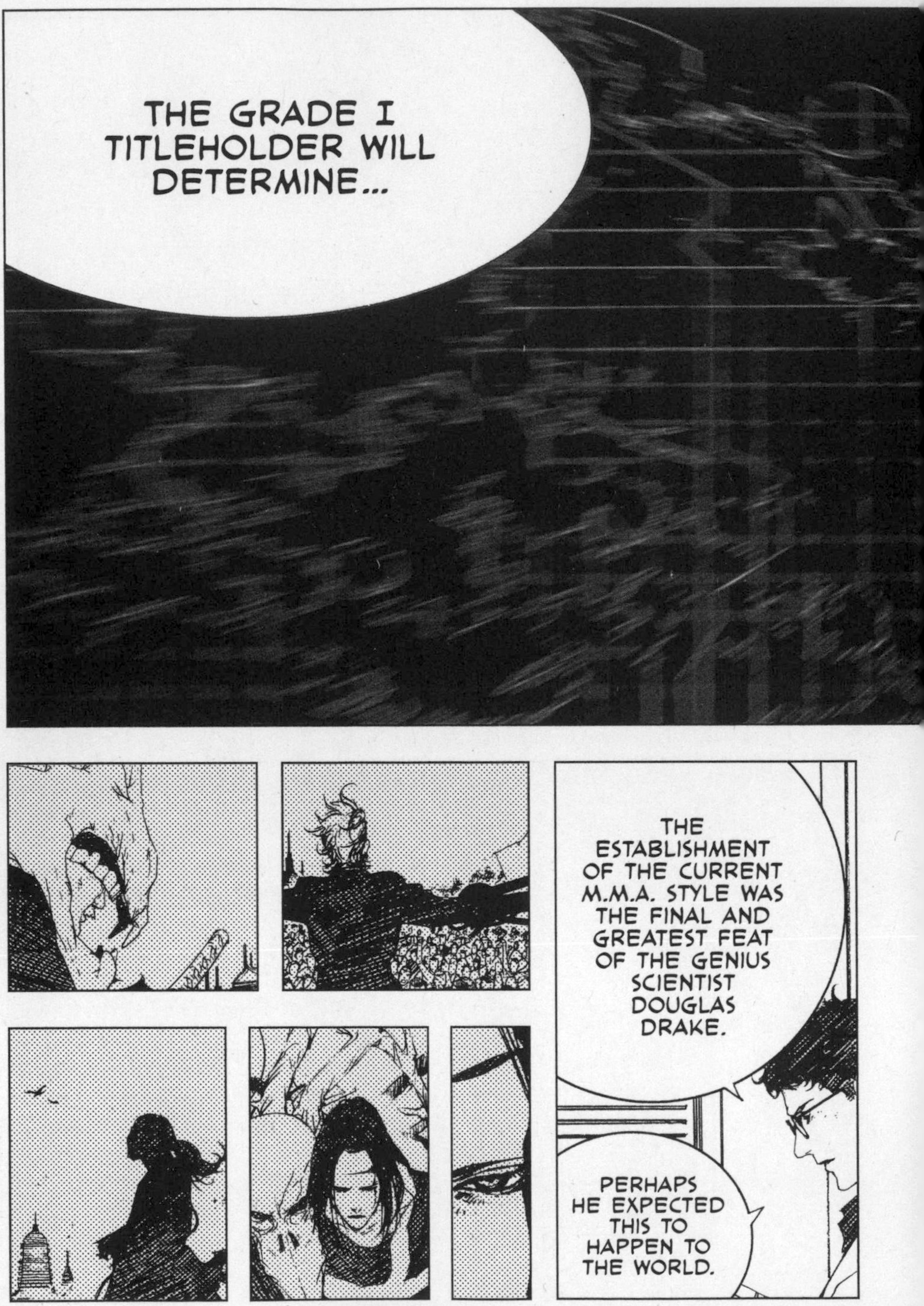
THE GRADE I TITLEHOLDER WILL DETERMINE...
THE ESTABLISHMENT OF THE CURRENT M.M.A. STYLE WAS THE FINAL AND GREATEST FEAT OF THE GENIUS SCIENTIST DOUGLAS DRAKE.
PERHAPS HE EXPECTED THIS TO HAPPEN TO THE WORLD.

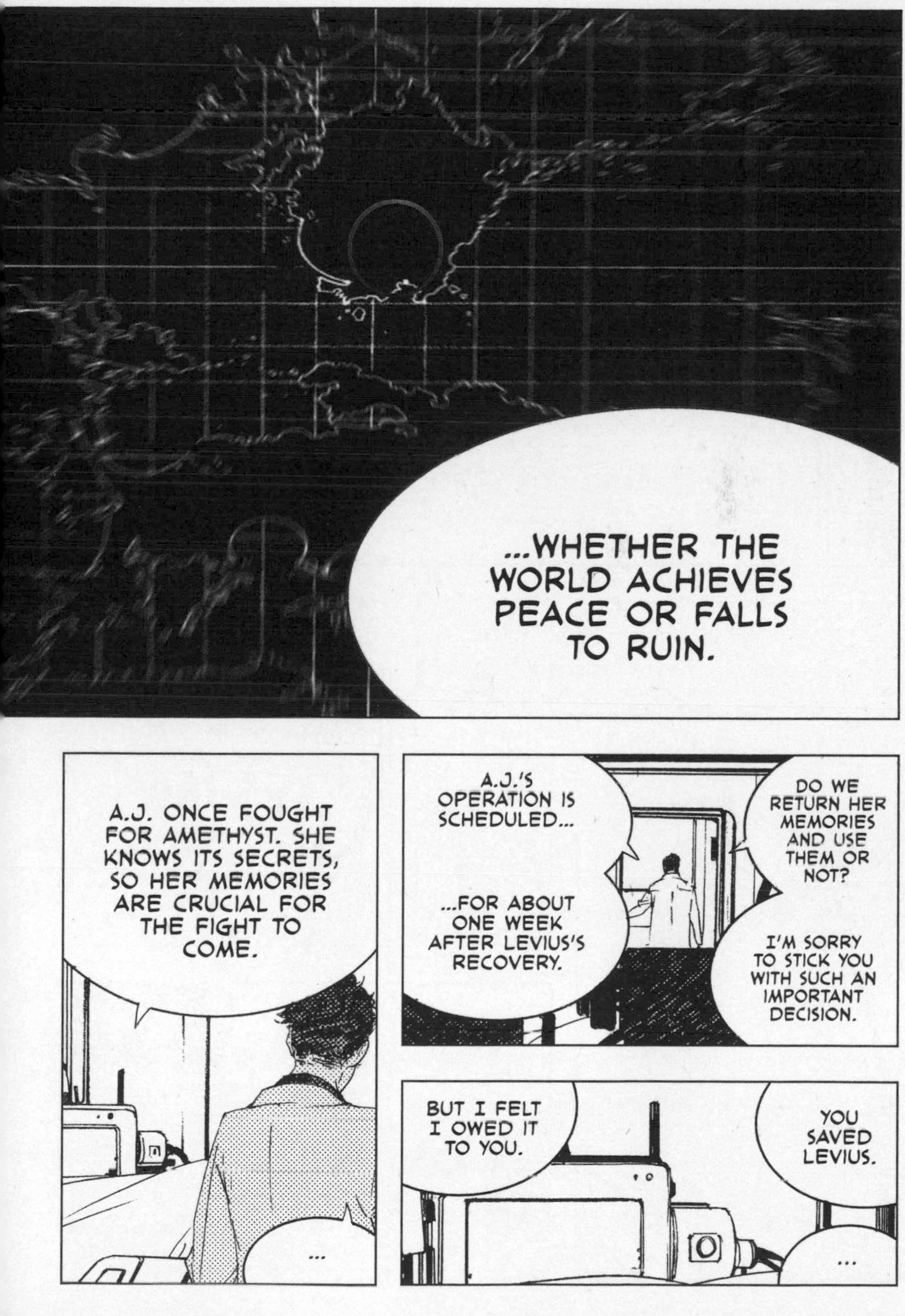
...WHETHER THE WORLD ACHIEVES PEACE OR FALLS TO RUIN.
A.J. ONCE FOUGHT FOR AMETHYST. SHE KNOWS ITS SECRETS, SO HER MEMORIES ARE CRUCIAL FOR THE FIGHT TO COME.
...
A.J.'S OPERATION IS SCHEDULED...
...FOR ABOUT ONE WEEK AFTER LEVIUS'S RECOVERY.
DO WE RETURN HER MEMORIES AND USE THEM OR NOT?
I'M SORRY TO STICK YOU WITH SUCH AN IMPORTANT DECISION.
BUT I FELT I OWED IT TO YOU.
YOU SAVED LEVIUS.
...

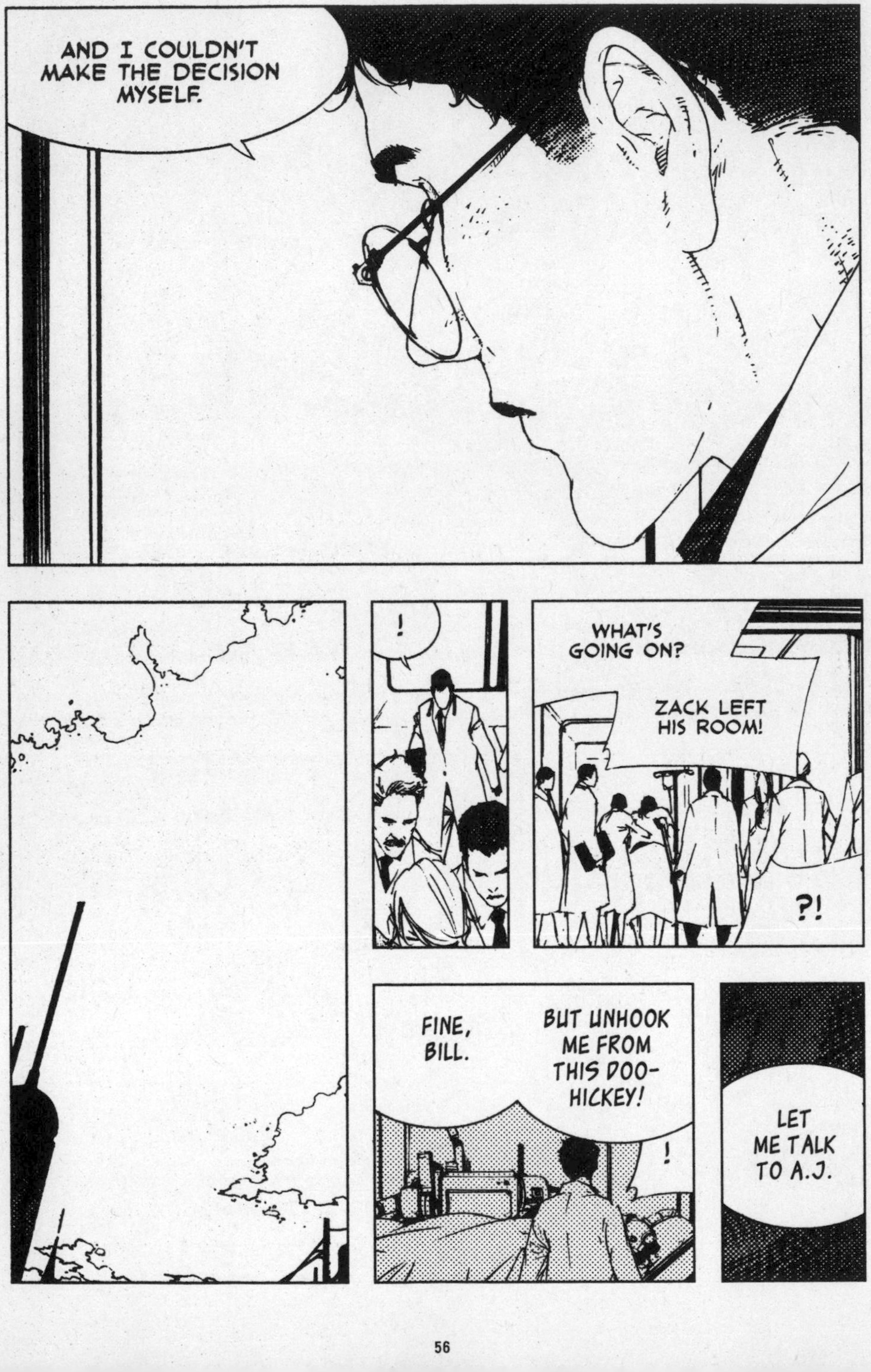
AND I COULDN'T MAKE THE DECISION MYSELF.
WHAT'S GOING ON?
ZACK LEFT HIS ROOM!
?!
!
LET ME TALK TO A.J.
FINE, BILL. BUT UNHOOK ME FROM THIS DOO-HICKEY!
!

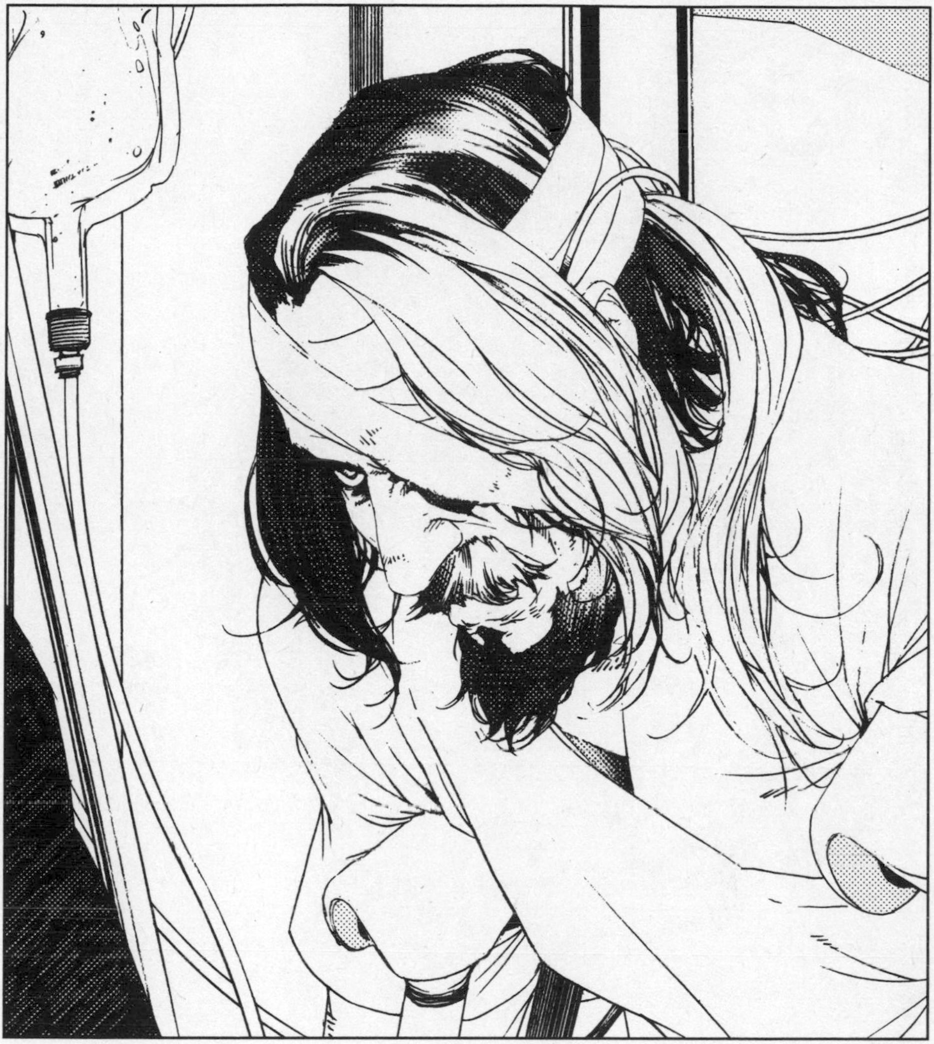

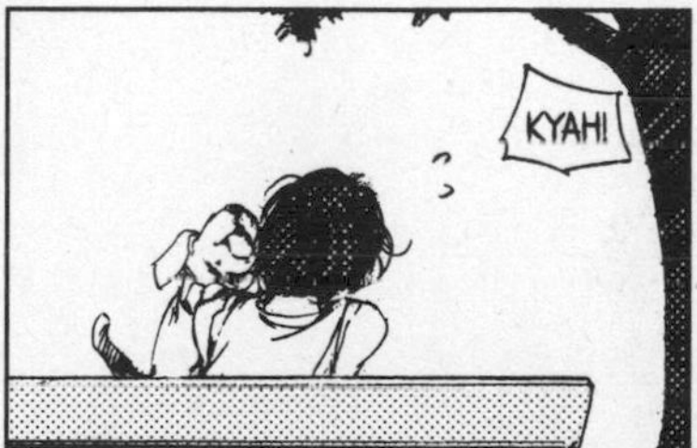
KYAH!

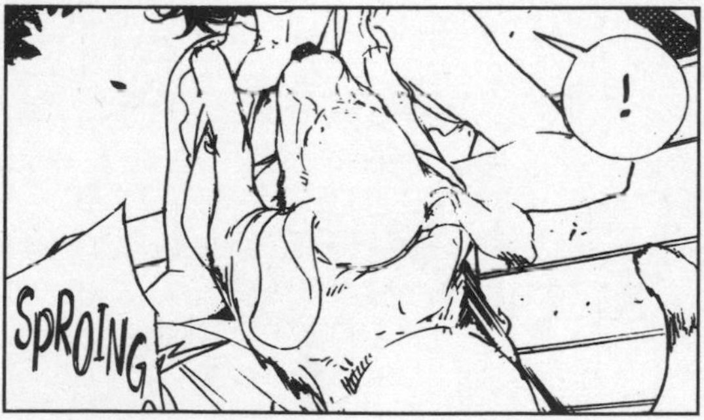
!
SPROING

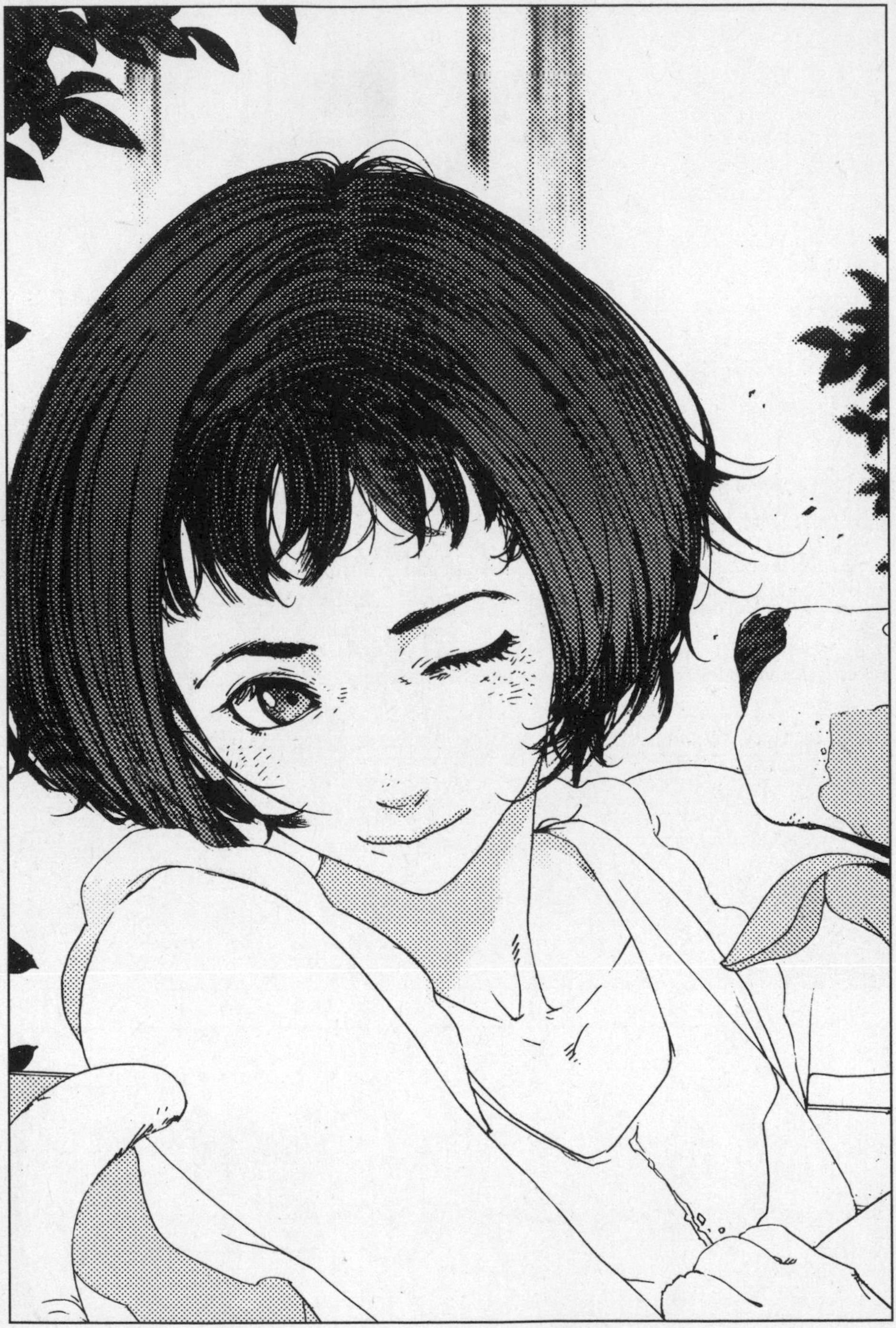

Levius/est
VOL. 1

Chapter 02

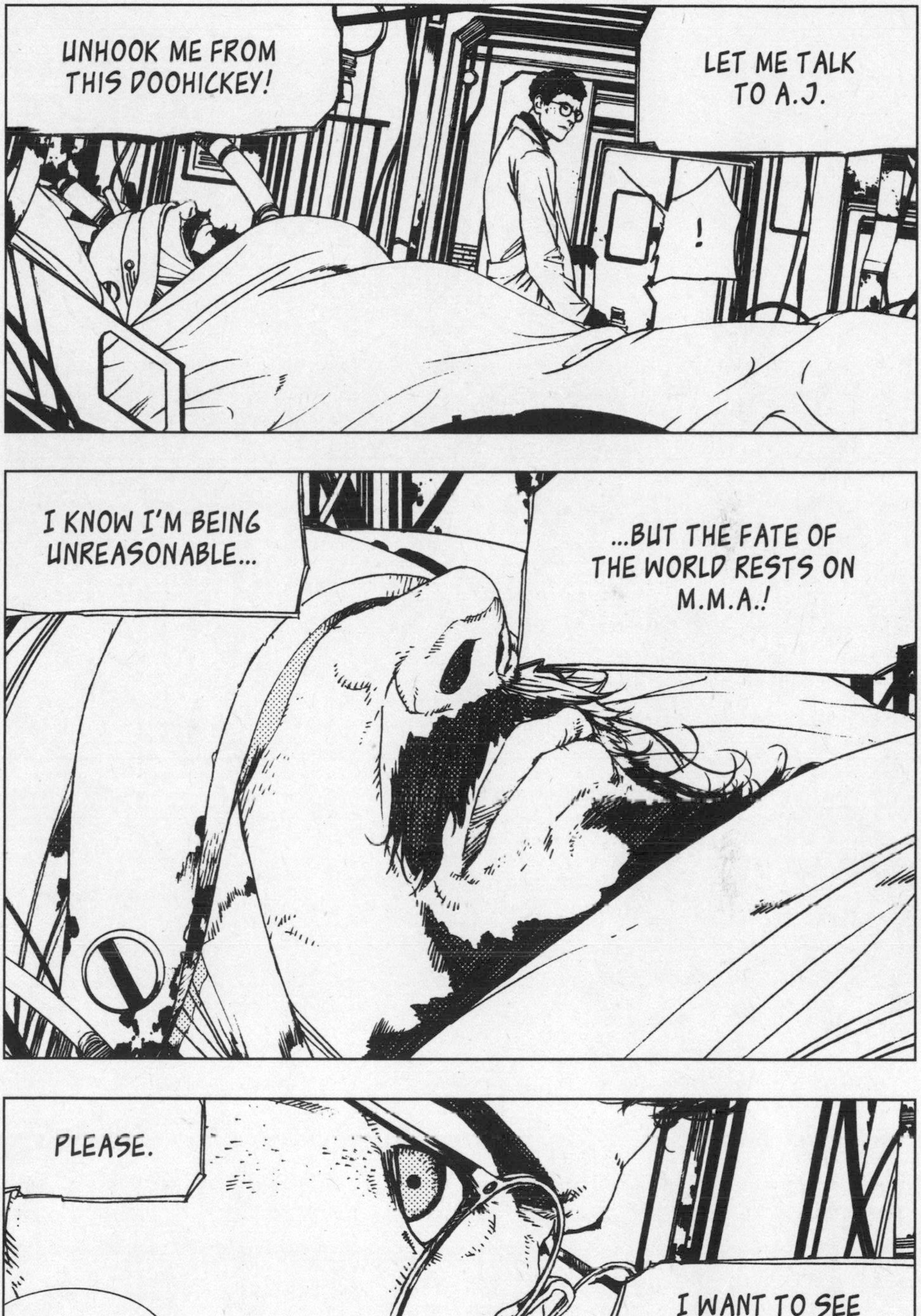
UNHOOK ME FROM THIS DOOHICKEY!
LET ME TALK TO A.J.
!
I KNOW I'M BEING UNREASONABLE...
...BUT THE FATE OF THE WORLD RESTS ON M.M.A.!
PLEASE.
...
I WANT TO SEE FOR MYSELF.

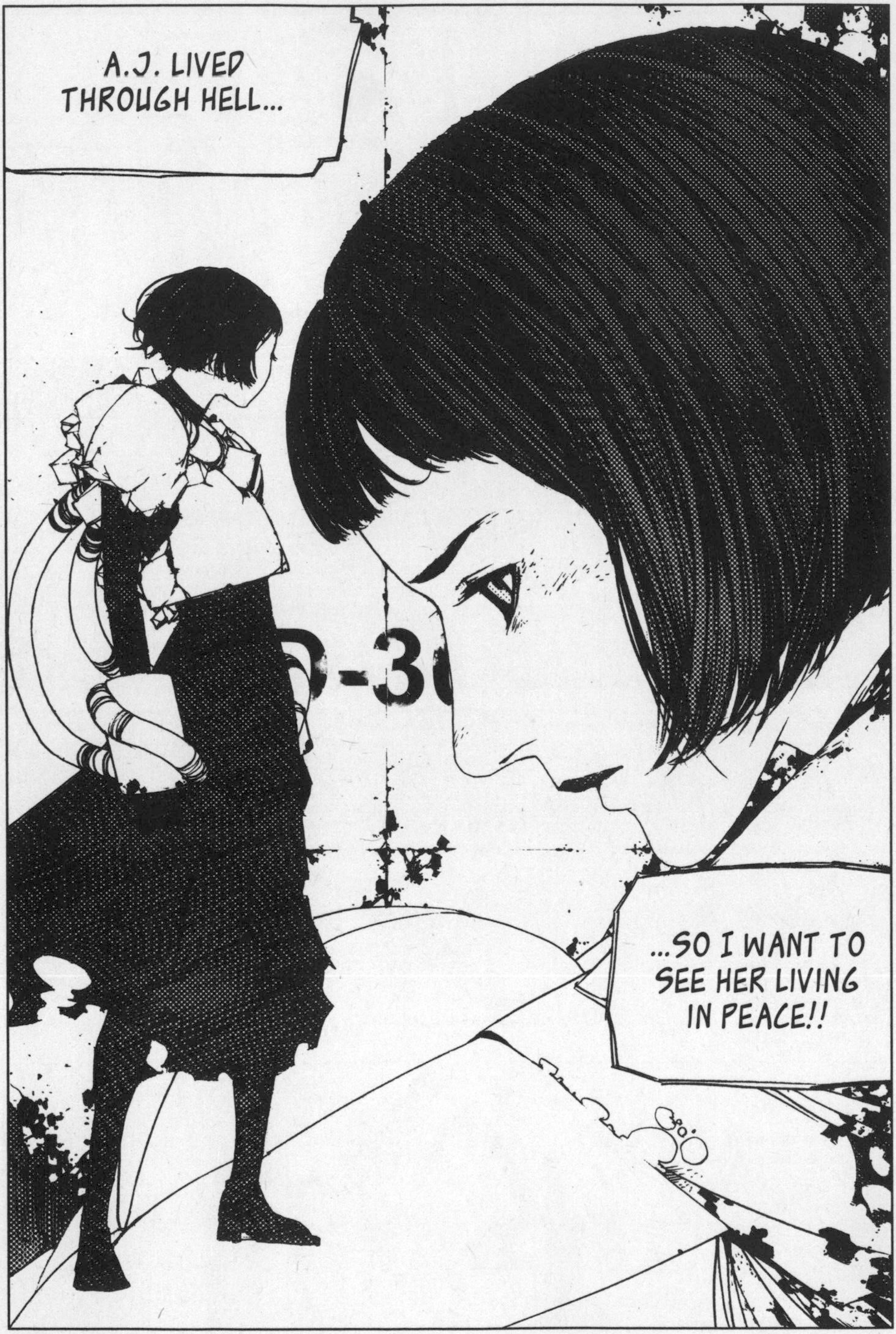
A.J. LIVED THROUGH HELL...
...SO I WANT TO SEE HER LIVING IN PEACE!!

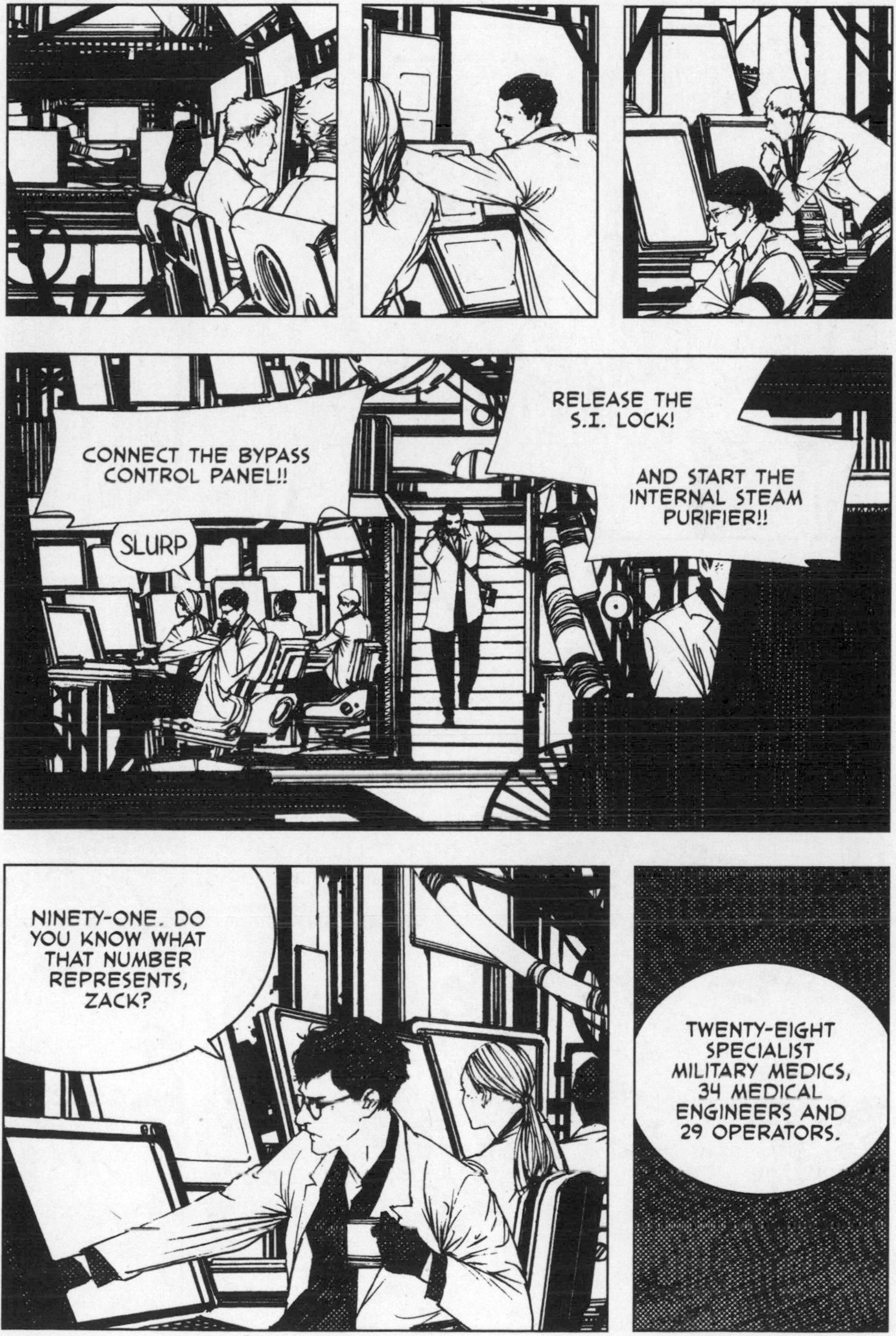
CONNECT THE BYPASS CONTROL PANEL!!
SLURP
RELEASE THE S.I. LOCK!
AND START THE INTERNAL STEAM PURIFIER!!
NINETY-ONE. DO YOU KNOW WHAT THAT NUMBER REPRESENTS, ZACK?
TWENTY-EIGHT SPECIALIST MILITARY MEDICS, 34 MEDICAL ENGINEERS AND 29 OPERATORS.

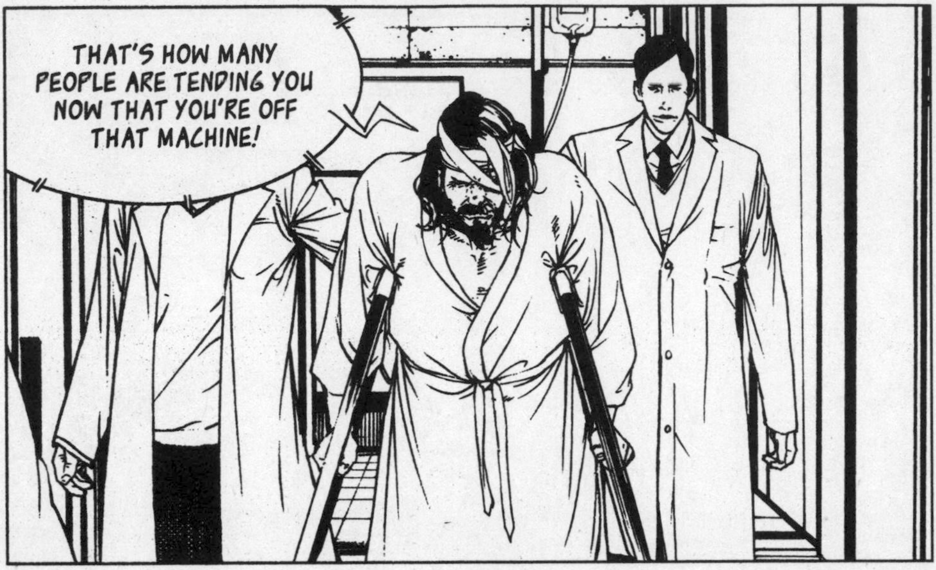
THAT'S HOW MANY PEOPLE ARE TENDING YOU NOW THAT YOU'RE OFF THAT MACHINE!

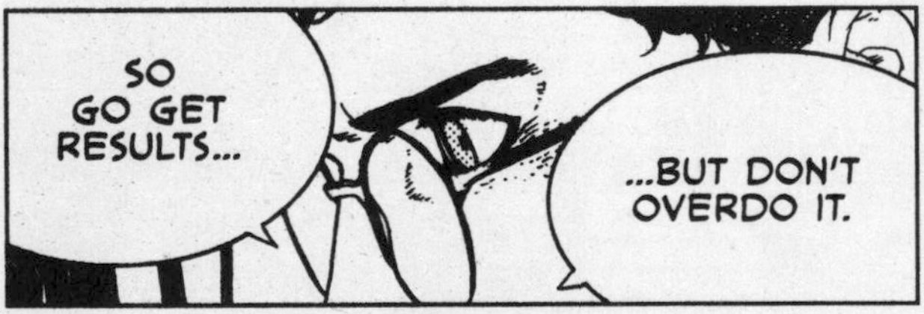
SO GO GET RESULTS...
...BUT DON'T OVERDO IT.

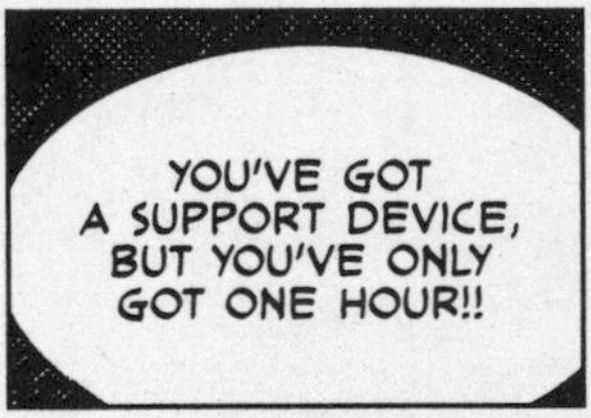
YOU'VE GOT A SUPPORT DEVICE, BUT YOU'VE ONLY GOT ONE HOUR!!

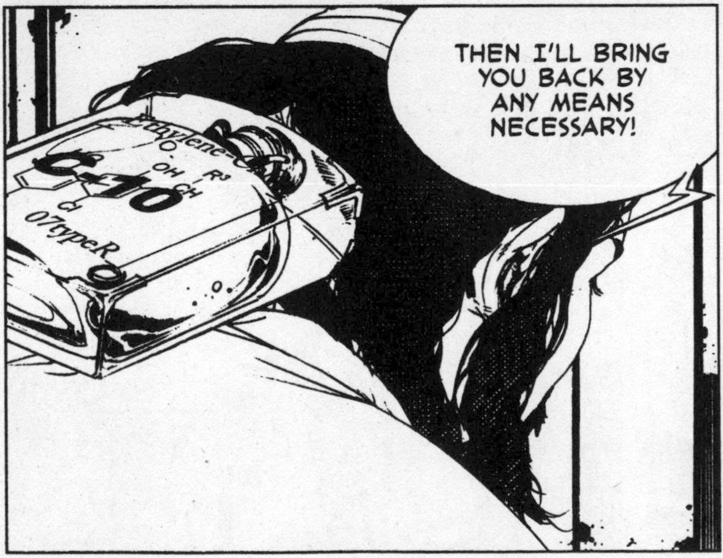
THEN I'LL BRING YOU BACK BY ANY MEANS NECESSARY!

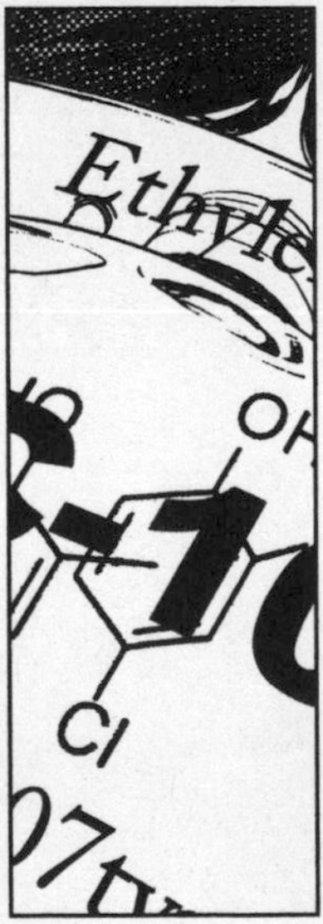

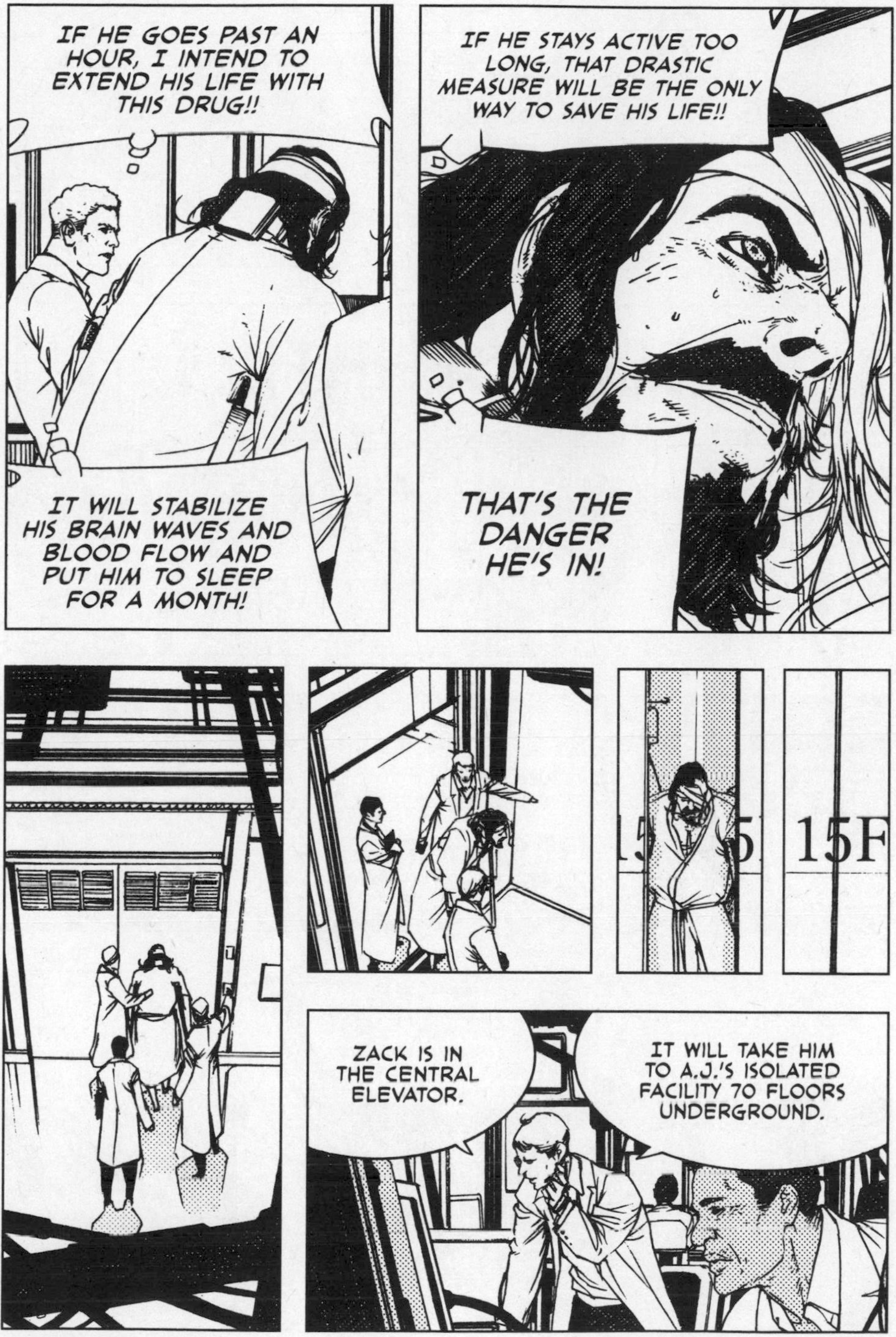
IF HE GOES PAST AN HOUR, I INTEND TO EXTEND HIS LIFE WITH THIS DRUG!!
IT WILL STABILIZE HIS BRAIN WAVES AND BLOOD FLOW AND PUT HIM TO SLEEP FOR A MONTH!
IF HE STAYS ACTIVE TOO LONG, THAT DRASTIC MEASURE WILL BE THE ONLY WAY TO SAVE HIS LIFE!!
THAT'S THE DANGER HE'S IN!
15F
ZACK IS IN THE CENTRAL ELEVATOR.
IT WILL TAKE HIM TO A.J.'S ISOLATED FACILITY 70 FLOORS UNDERGROUND.

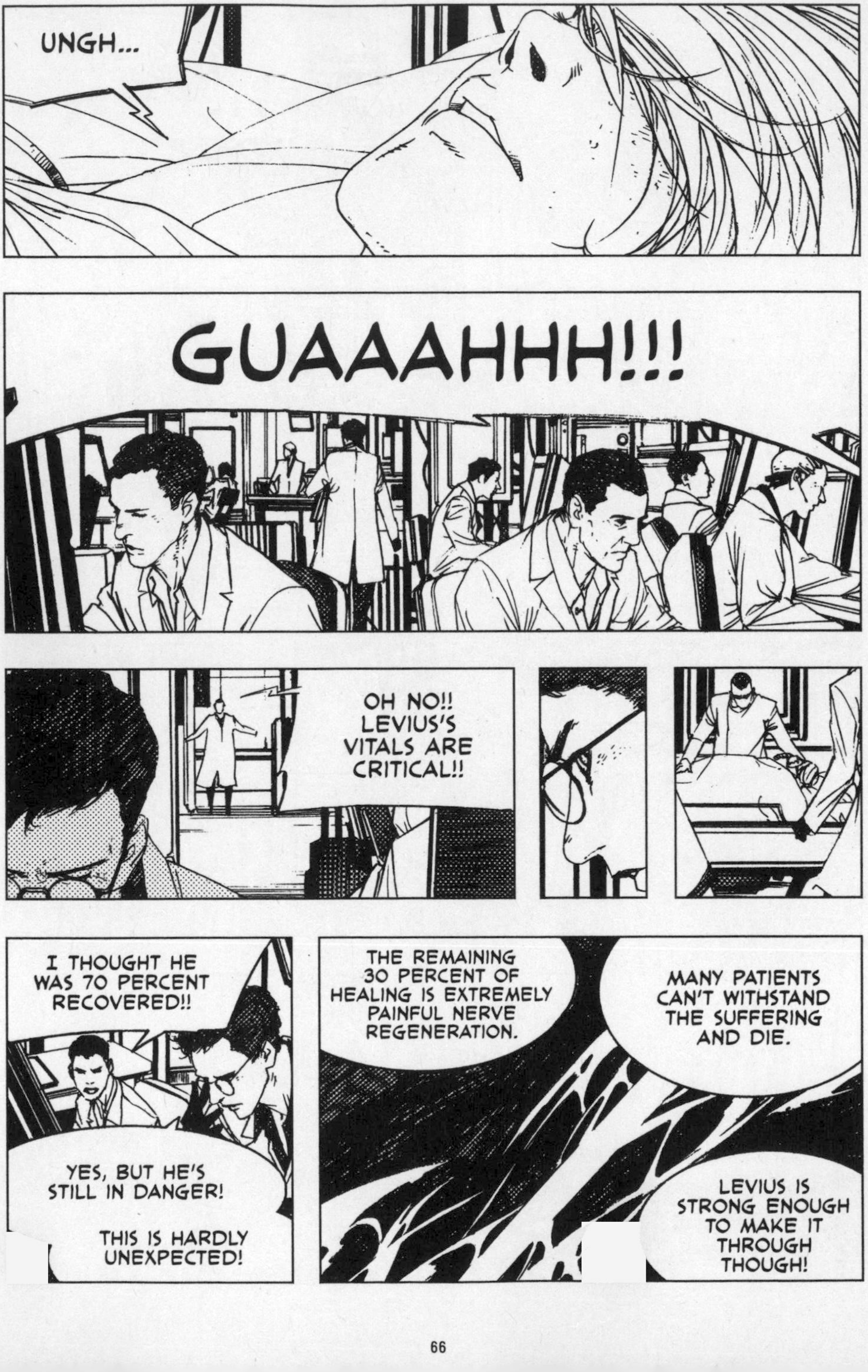
UNGH...
GUAAAHHH!!!
OH NO!! LEVIUS'S VITALS ARE CRITICAL!!
I THOUGHT HE WAS 70 PERCENT RECOVERED!!
YES, BUT HE'S STILL IN DANGER!
THIS IS HARDLY UNEXPECTED!
THE REMAINING 30 PERCENT OF HEALING IS EXTREMELY PAINFUL NERVE REGENERATION.
MANY PATIENTS CAN'T WITHSTAND THE SUFFERING AND DIE.
LEVIUS IS STRONG ENOUGH TO MAKE IT THROUGH THOUGH!

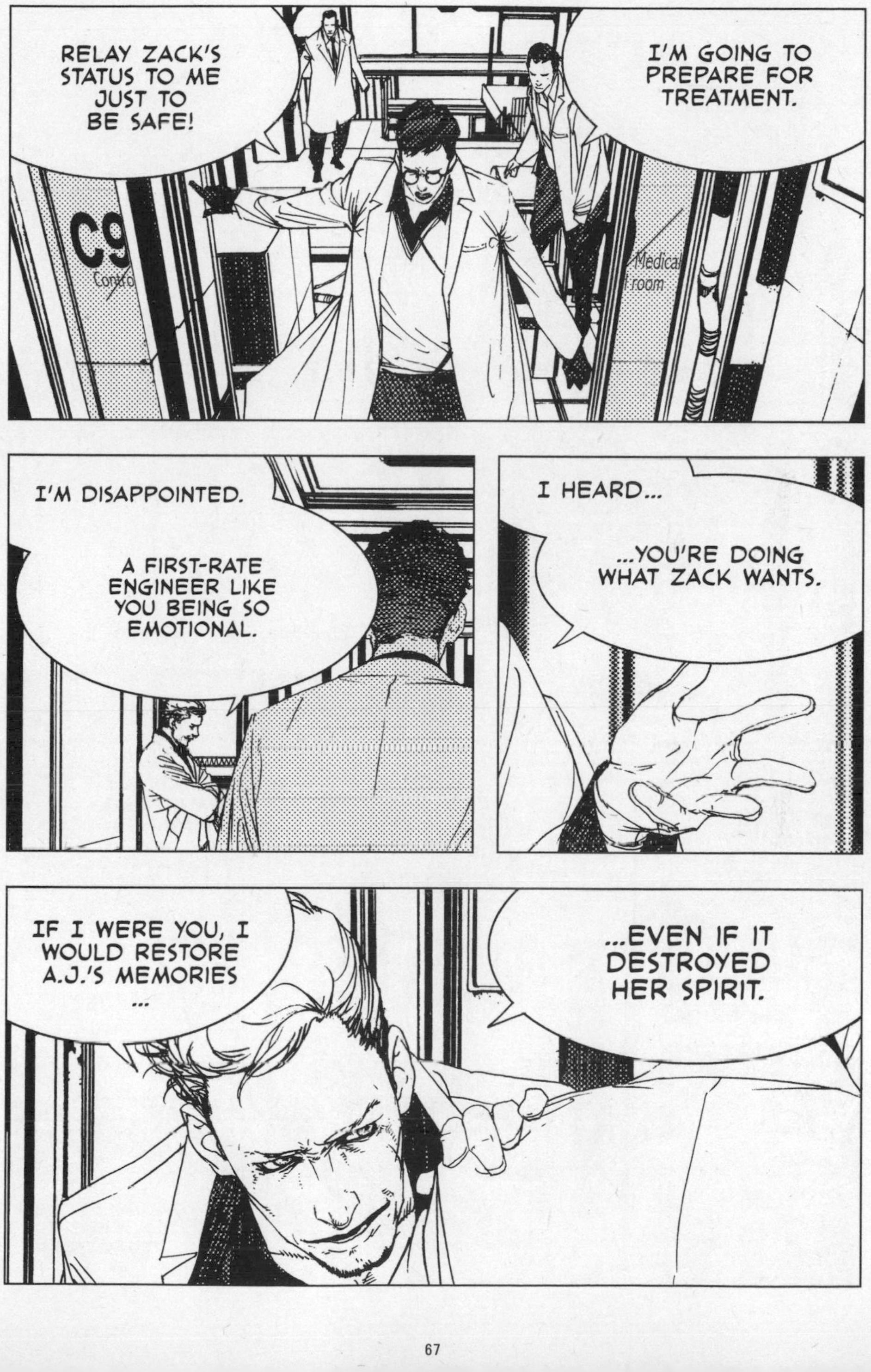
RELAY ZACK'S STATUS TO ME JUST TO BE SAFE!
I'M GOING TO PREPARE FOR TREATMENT.
I'M DISAPPOINTED.
A FIRST-RATE ENGINEER LIKE YOU BEING SO EMOTIONAL.
I HEARD...
...YOU'RE DOING WHAT ZACK WANTS.
IF I WERE YOU, I WOULD RESTORE A.J.'S MEMORIES ...
...EVEN IF IT DESTROYED HER SPIRIT.

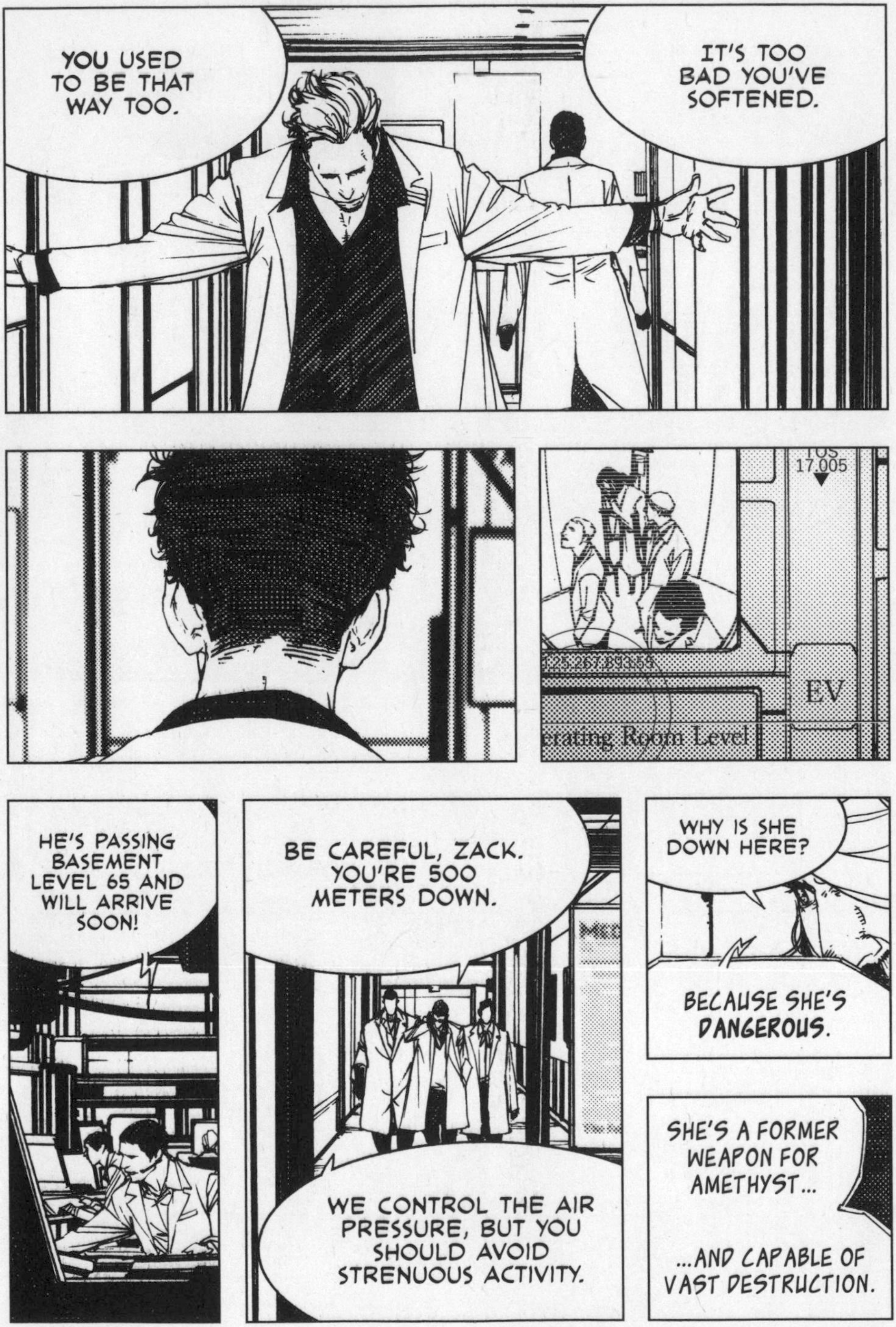
YOU USED TO BE THAT WAY TOO.
IT'S TOO BAD YOU'VE SOFTENED.
17.005
EV
erating Room Level
HE'S PASSING BASEMENT LEVEL 65 AND WILL ARRIVE SOON!
BE CAREFUL, ZACK. YOU'RE 500 METERS DOWN.
WE CONTROL THE AIR PRESSURE, BUT YOU SHOULD AVOID STRENUOUS ACTIVITY.
WHY IS SHE DOWN HERE?
BECAUSE SHE'S **DANGEROUS**.
SHE'S A FORMER WEAPON FOR AMETHYST...
...AND CAPABLE OF VAST DESTRUCTION.

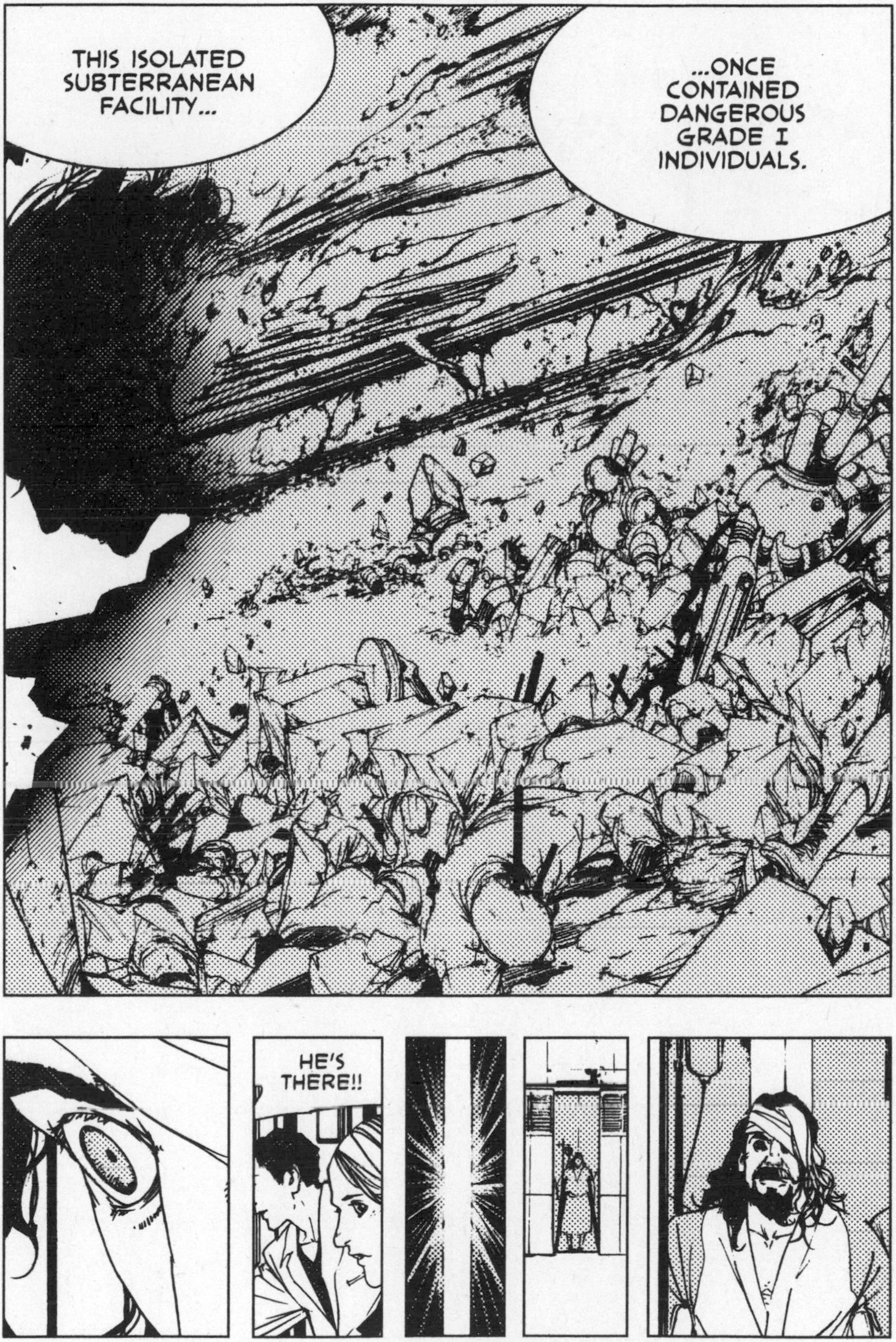
THIS ISOLATED SUBTERRANEAN FACILITY...
...ONCE CONTAINED DANGEROUS GRADE I INDIVIDUALS.
HE'S THERE!!

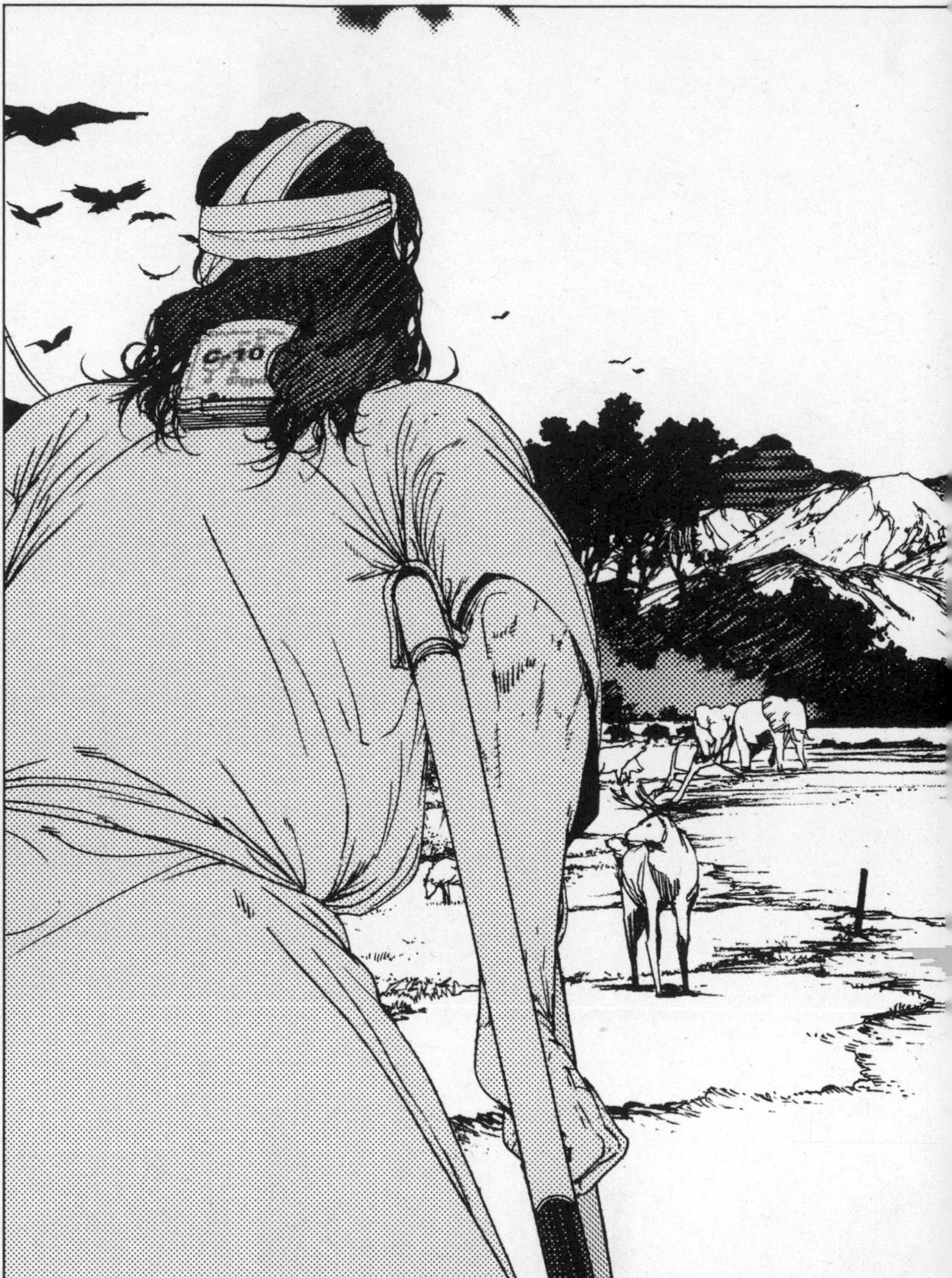
C-10

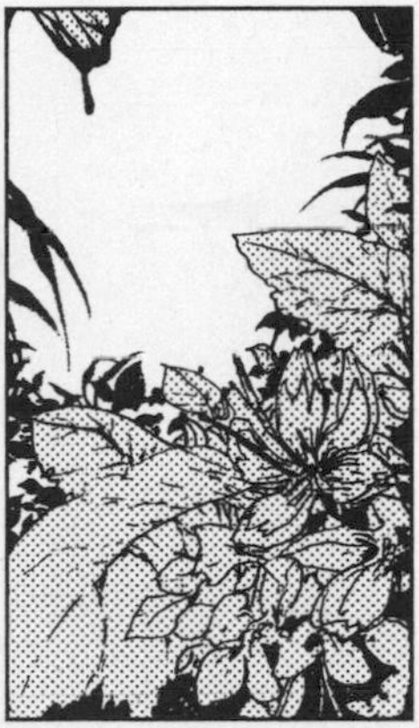
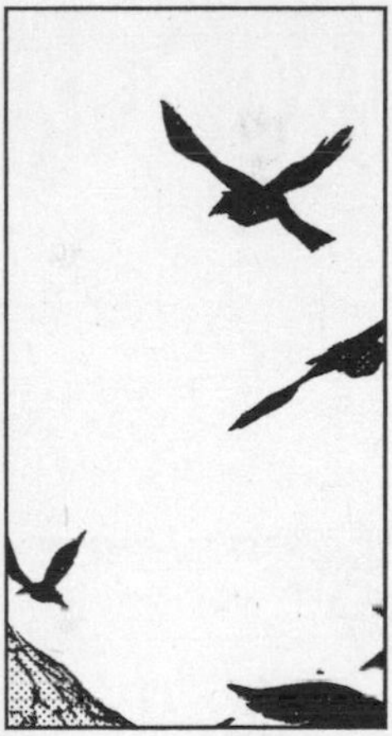
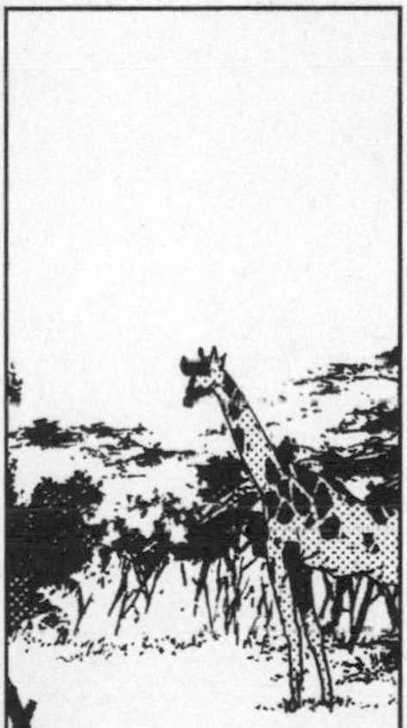
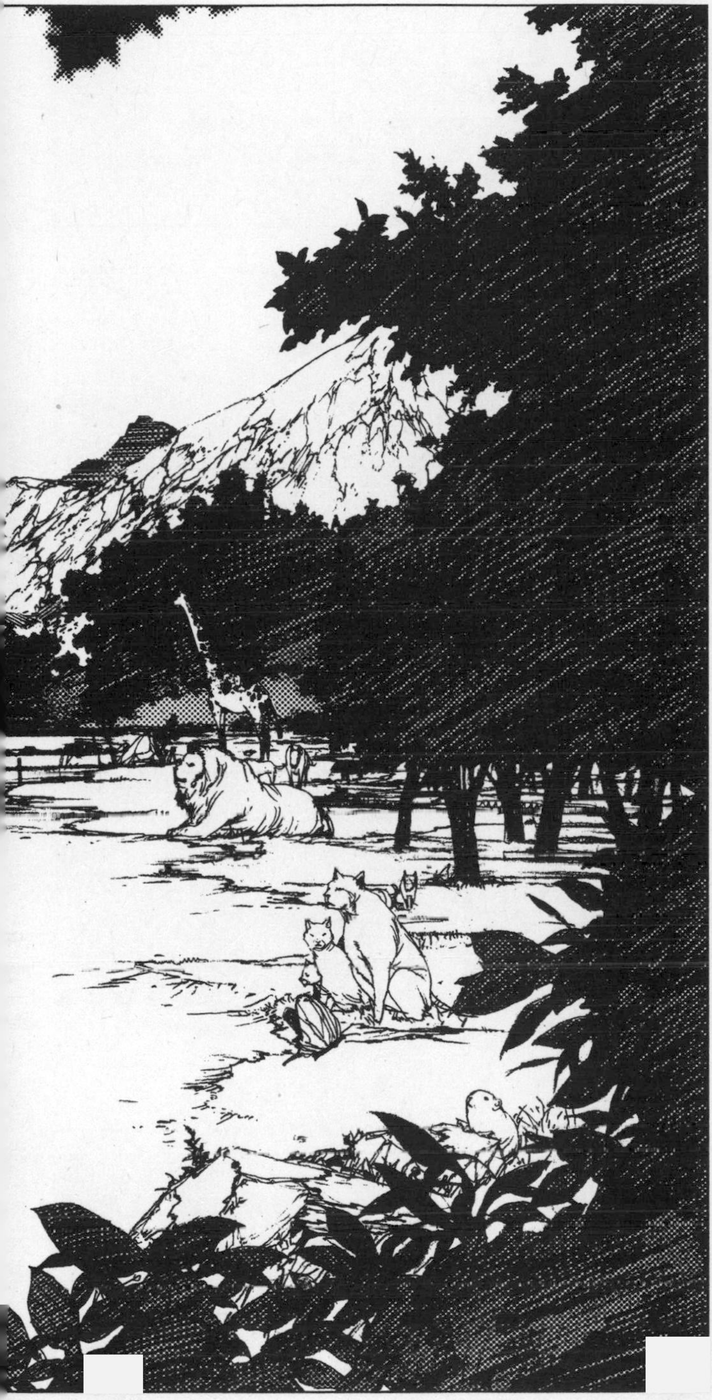

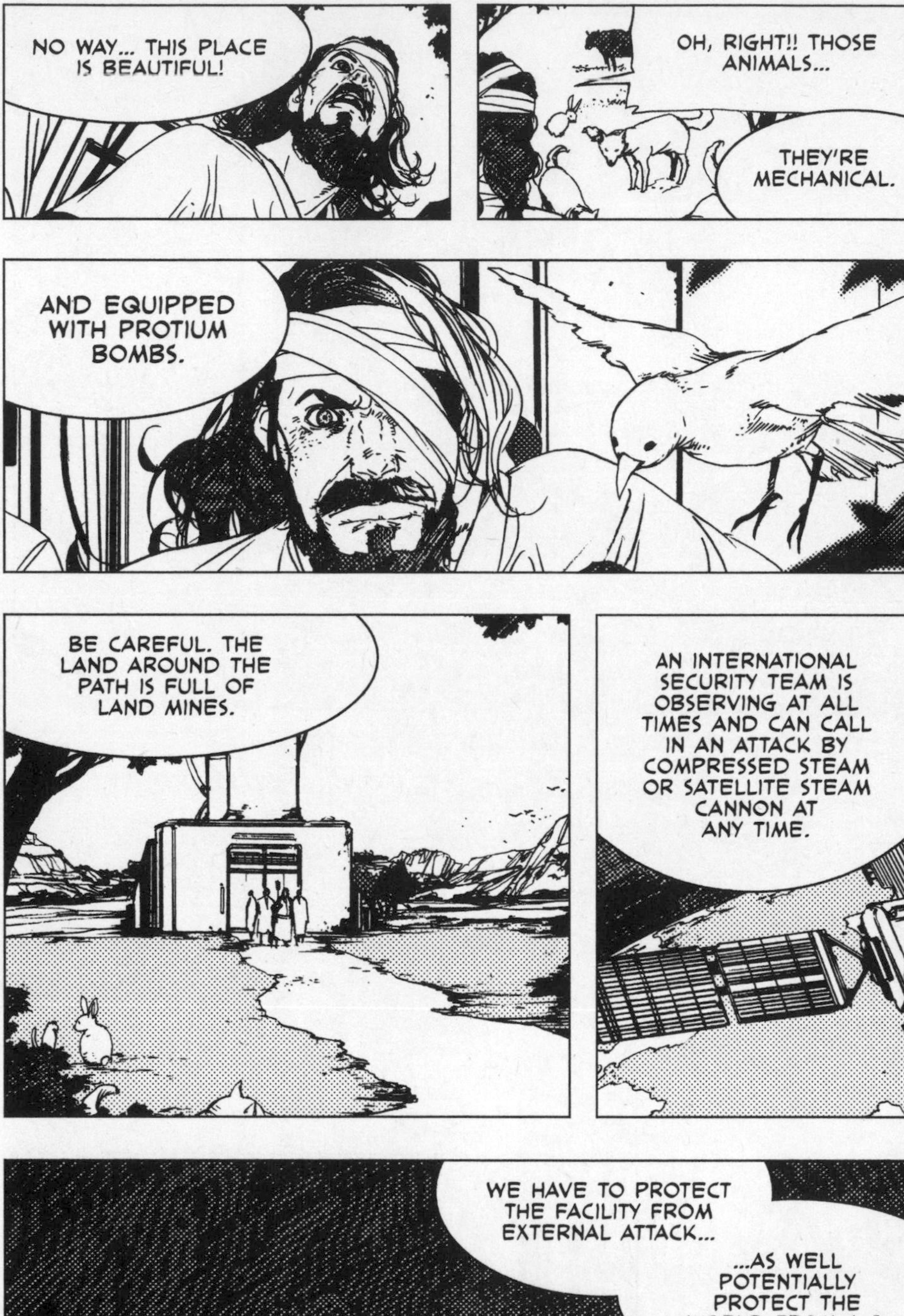
NO WAY... THIS PLACE IS BEAUTIFUL!
OH, RIGHT!! THOSE ANIMALS...
THEY'RE MECHANICAL.
AND EQUIPPED WITH PROTIUM BOMBS.
BE CAREFUL. THE LAND AROUND THE PATH IS FULL OF LAND MINES.
AN INTERNATIONAL SECURITY TEAM IS OBSERVING AT ALL TIMES AND CAN CALL IN AN ATTACK BY COMPRESSED STEAM OR SATELLITE STEAM CANNON AT ANY TIME.
WE HAVE TO PROTECT THE FACILITY FROM EXTERNAL ATTACK...
...AS WELL POTENTIALLY PROTECT THE WORLD FROM A.J.

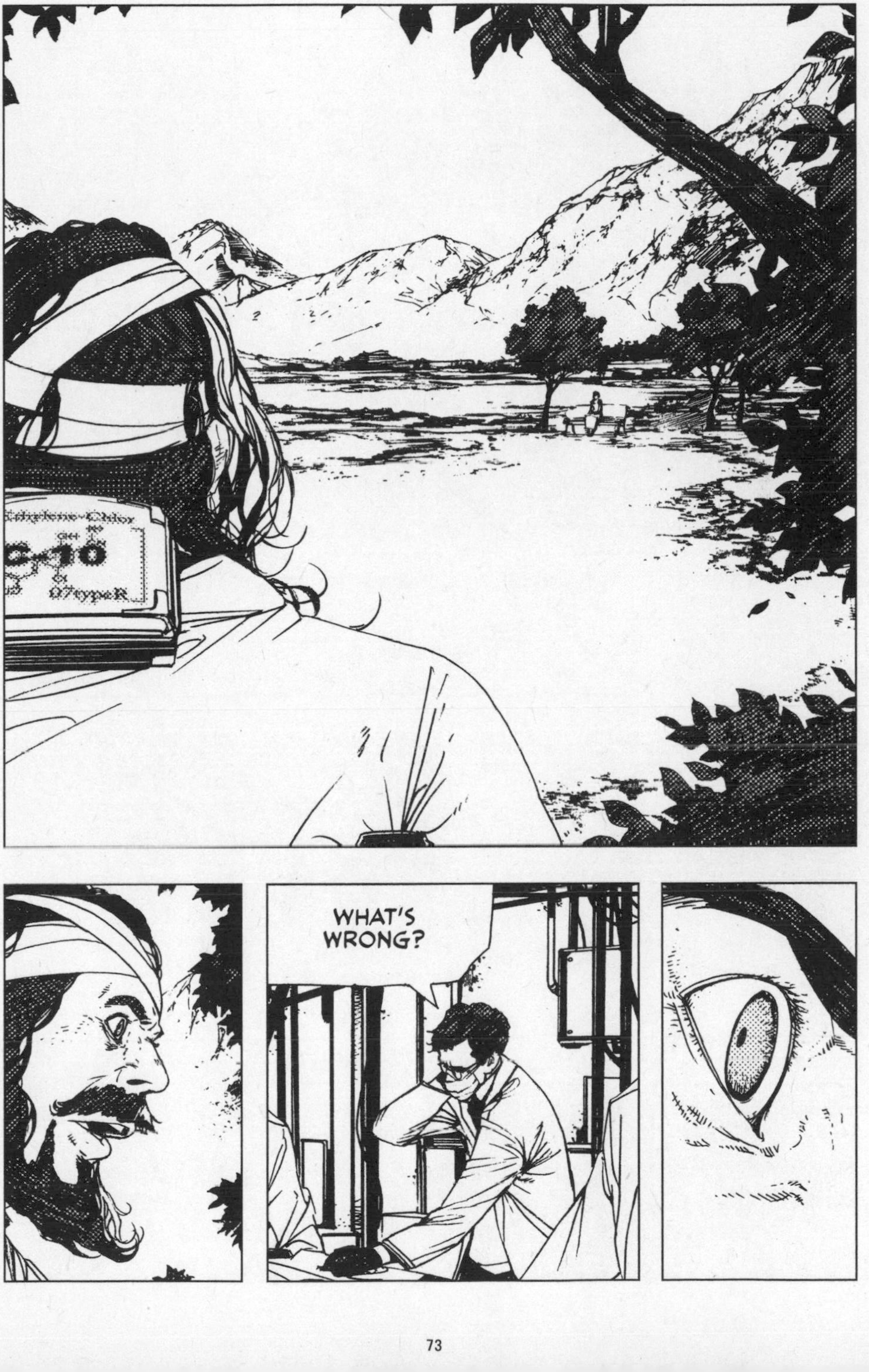
WHAT'S WRONG?

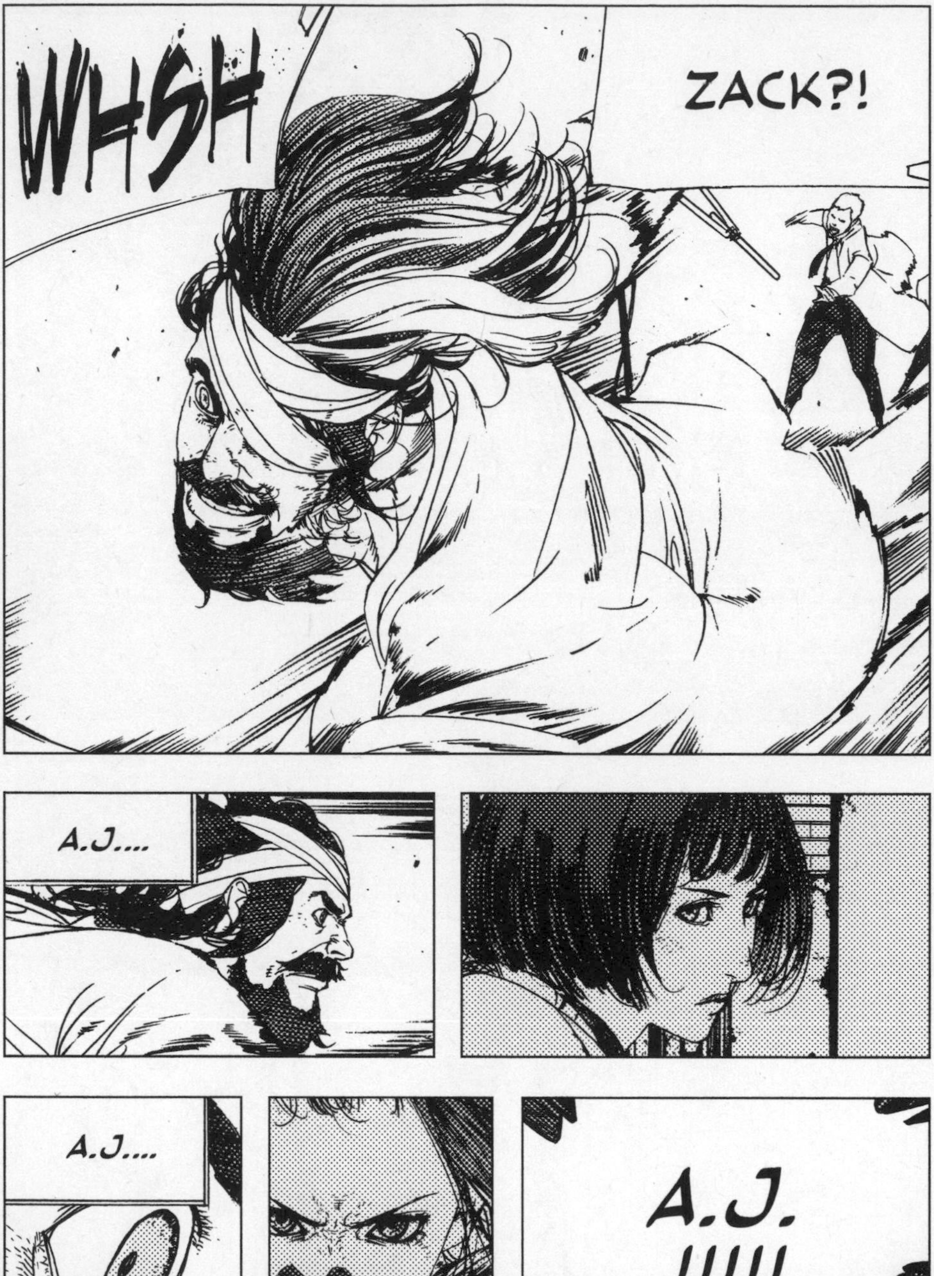
ZACK?!
WHSH
A.J....
A.J.
!!!!!
A.J....

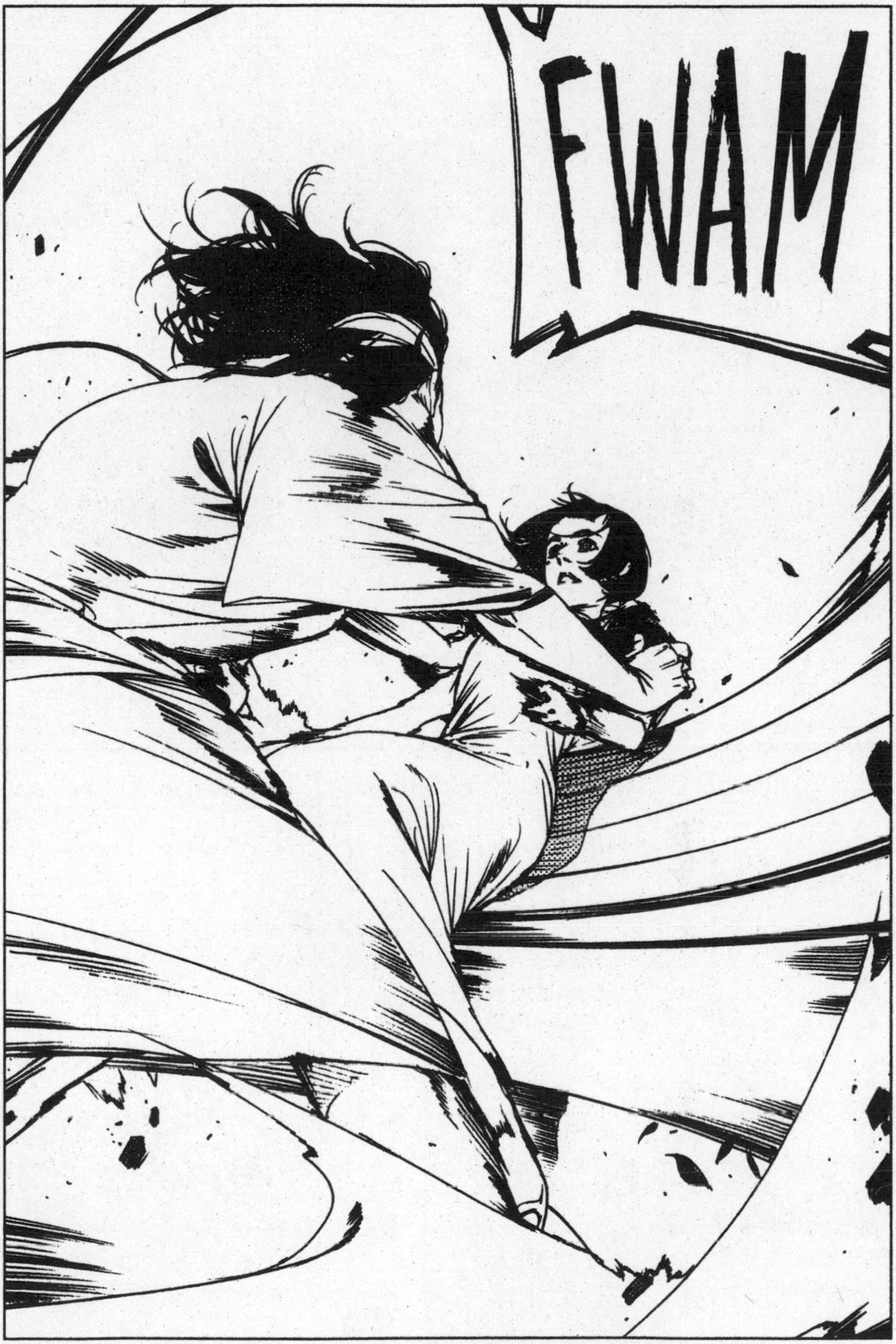
FWAM

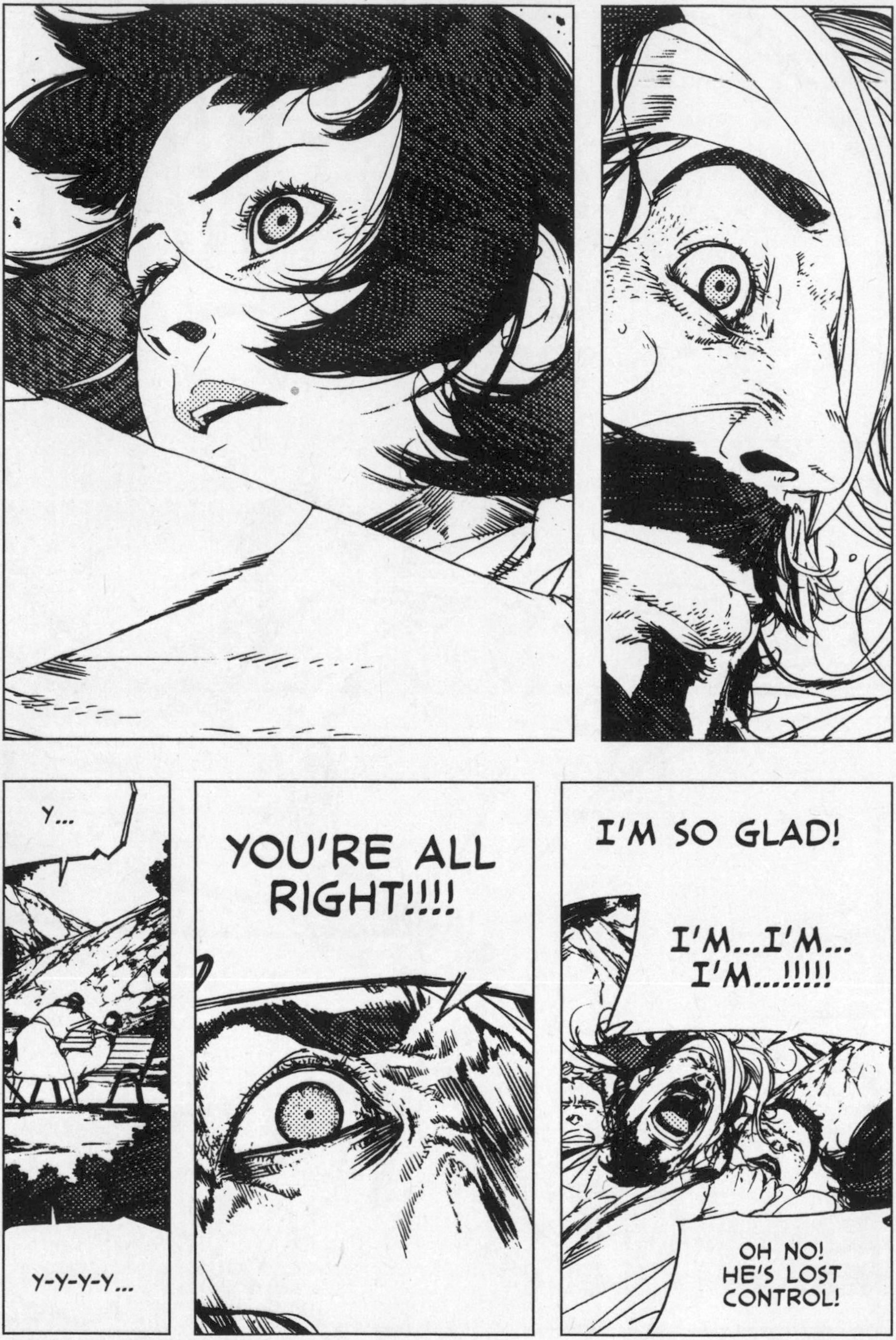
Y...
Y-Y-Y-Y...
YOU'RE ALL RIGHT!!!!
I'M SO GLAD!
I'M...I'M... I'M...!!!!!
OH NO! HE'S LOST CONTROL!

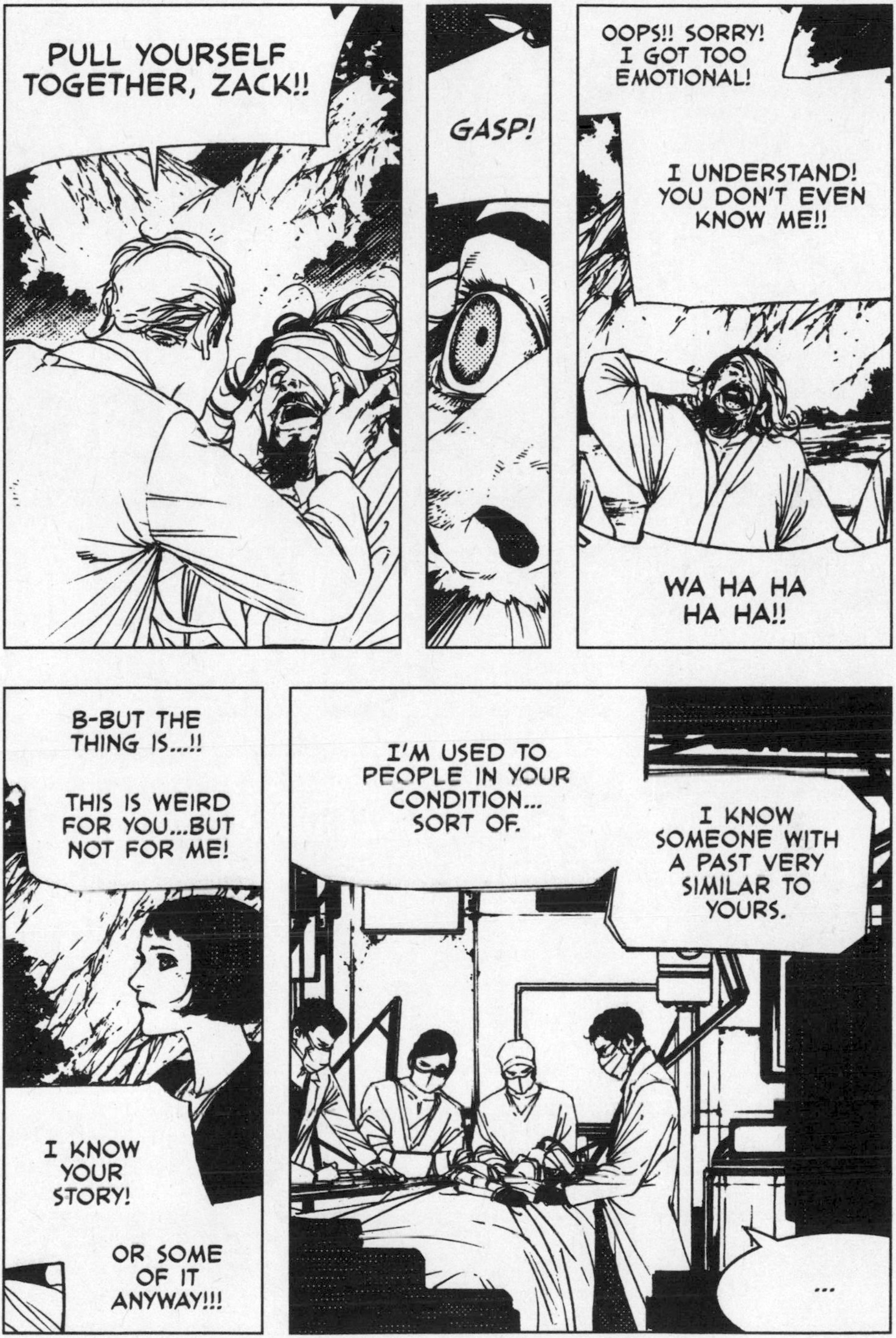
PULL YOURSELF TOGETHER, ZACK!!
GASP!
OOPS!! SORRY! I GOT TOO EMOTIONAL!
I UNDERSTAND! YOU DON'T EVEN KNOW ME!!
WA HA HA HA HA!!
B-BUT THE THING IS...!!
THIS IS WEIRD FOR YOU...BUT NOT FOR ME!
I KNOW YOUR STORY!
OR SOME OF IT ANYWAY!!!
I'M USED TO PEOPLE IN YOUR CONDITION... SORT OF.
I KNOW SOMEONE WITH A PAST VERY SIMILAR TO YOURS.
...

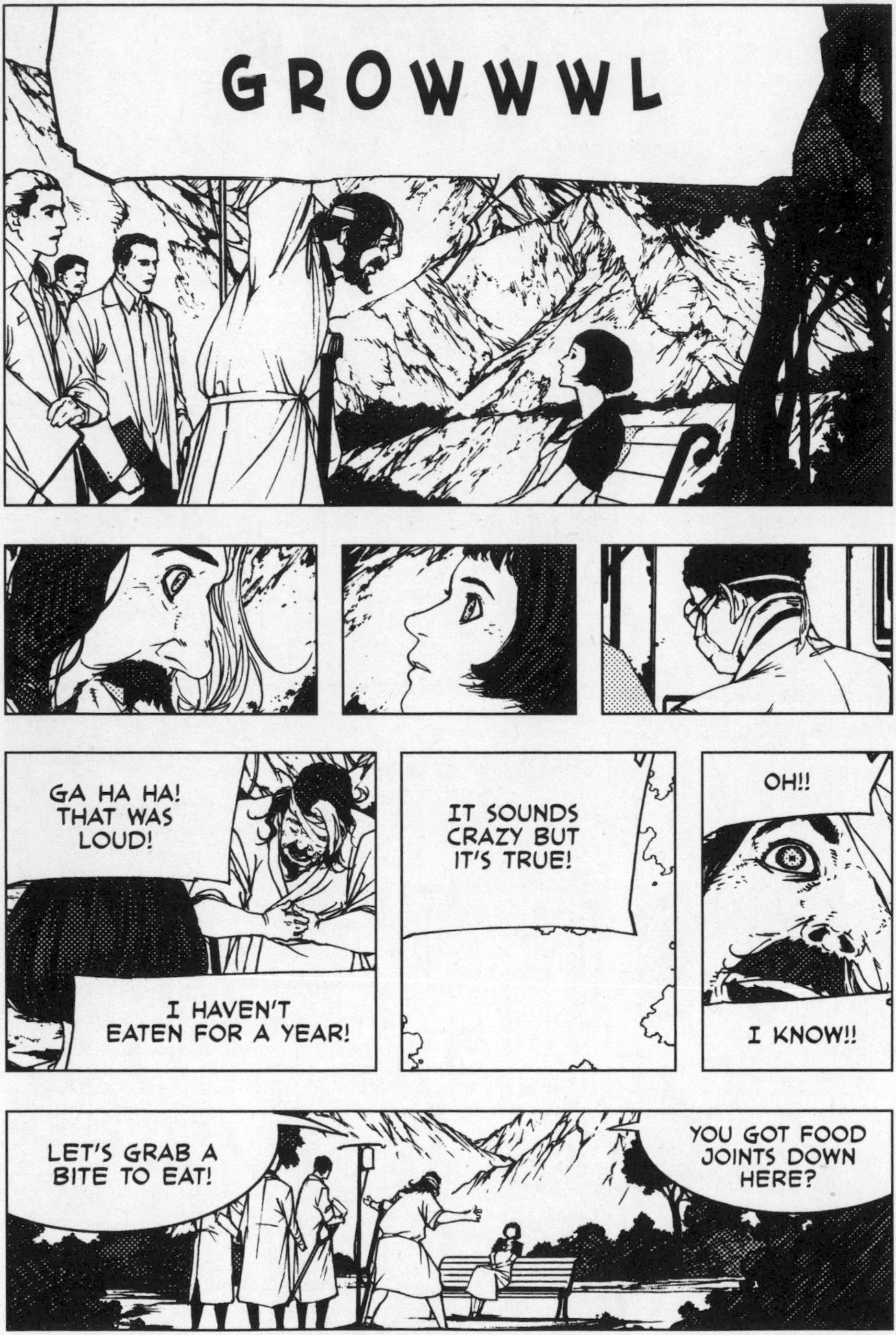
GROWWWL
GA HA HA! THAT WAS LOUD!
I HAVEN'T EATEN FOR A YEAR!
IT SOUNDS CRAZY BUT IT'S TRUE!
OH!!
I KNOW!!
LET'S GRAB A BITE TO EAT!
YOU GOT FOOD JOINTS DOWN HERE?

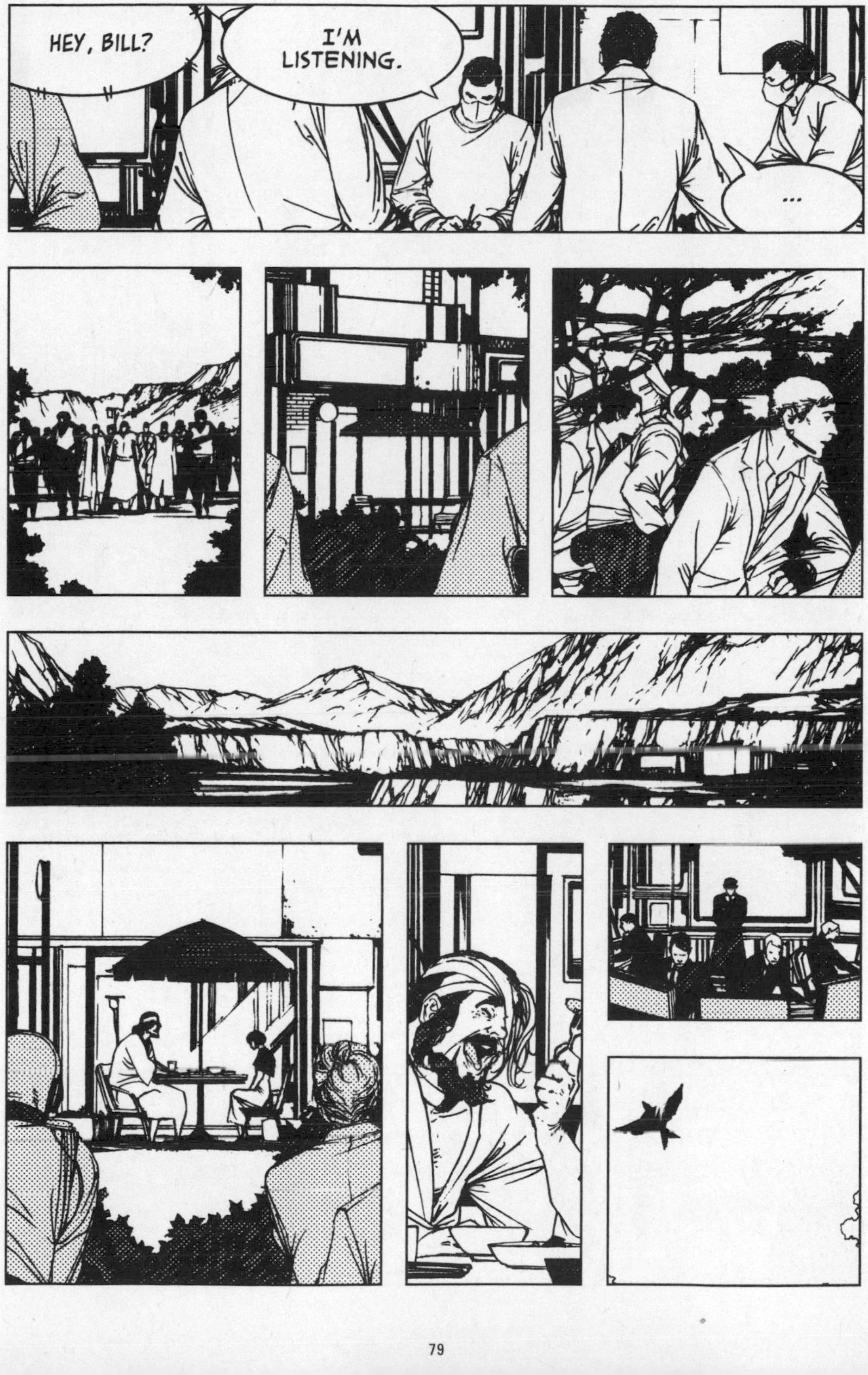
HEY, BILL?
I'M LISTENING.
...

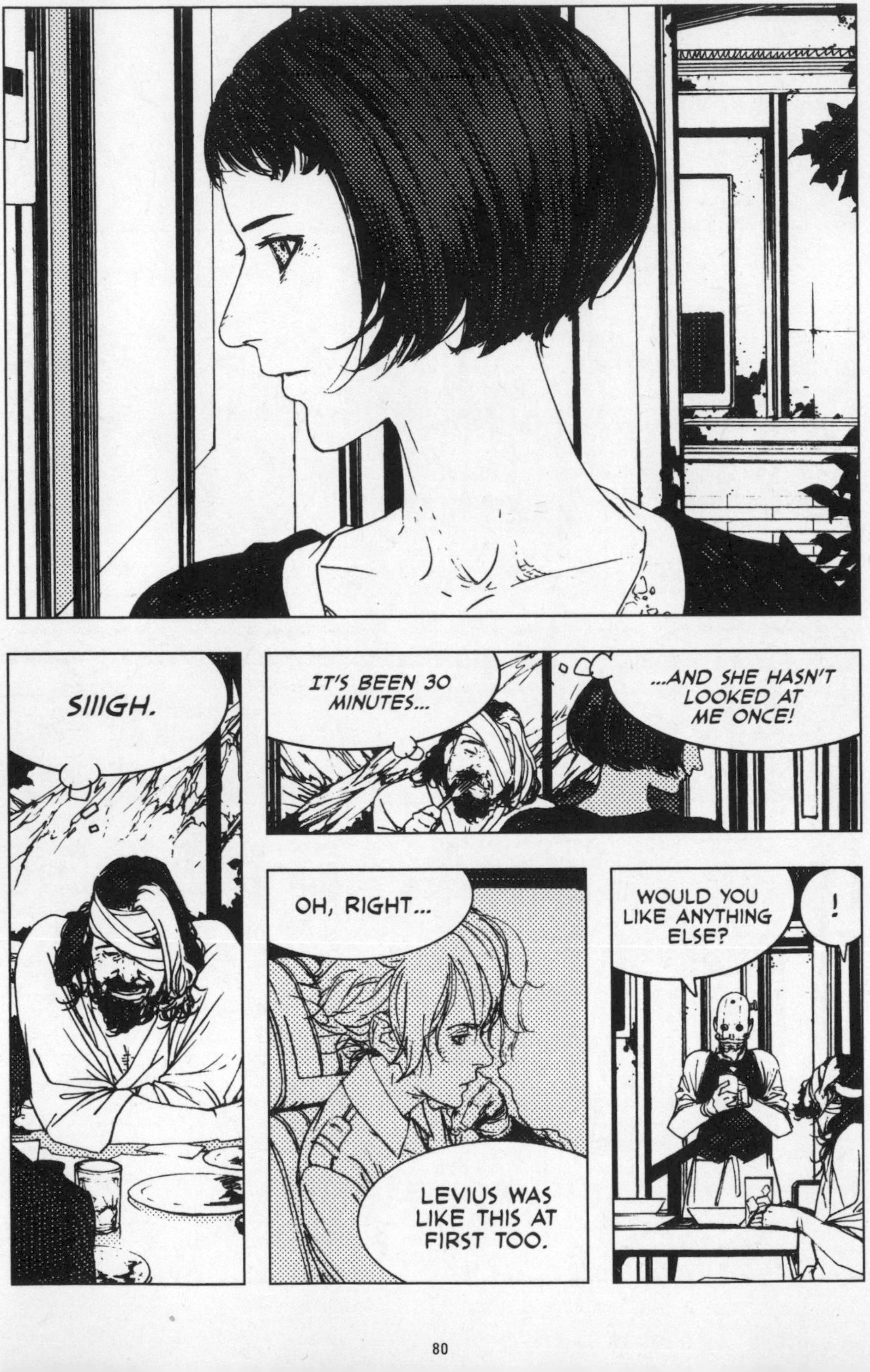
SIIIGH.
IT'S BEEN 30 MINUTES...
...AND SHE HASN'T LOOKED AT ME ONCE!
OH, RIGHT...
LEVIUS WAS LIKE THIS AT FIRST TOO.
WOULD YOU LIKE ANYTHING ELSE?
!

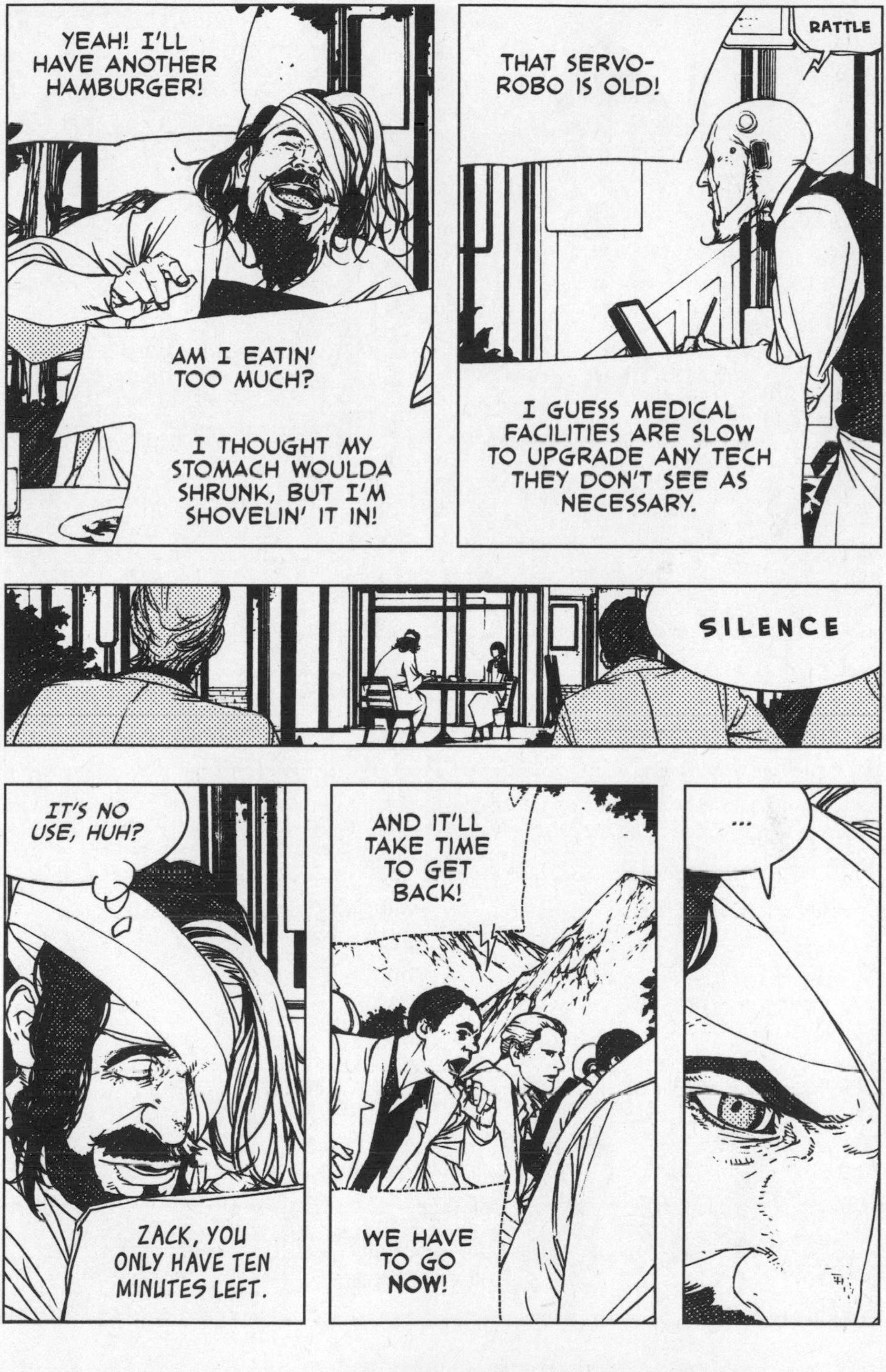
YEAH! I'LL HAVE ANOTHER HAMBURGER!
AM I EATIN' TOO MUCH?
I THOUGHT MY STOMACH WOULDA SHRUNK, BUT I'M SHOVELIN' IT IN!
THAT SERVO-ROBO IS OLD!
RATTLE
I GUESS MEDICAL FACILITIES ARE SLOW TO UPGRADE ANY TECH THEY DON'T SEE AS NECESSARY.
SILENCE
IT'S NO USE, HUH?
ZACK, YOU ONLY HAVE TEN MINUTES LEFT.
AND IT'LL TAKE TIME TO GET BACK!
WE HAVE TO GO NOW!
...

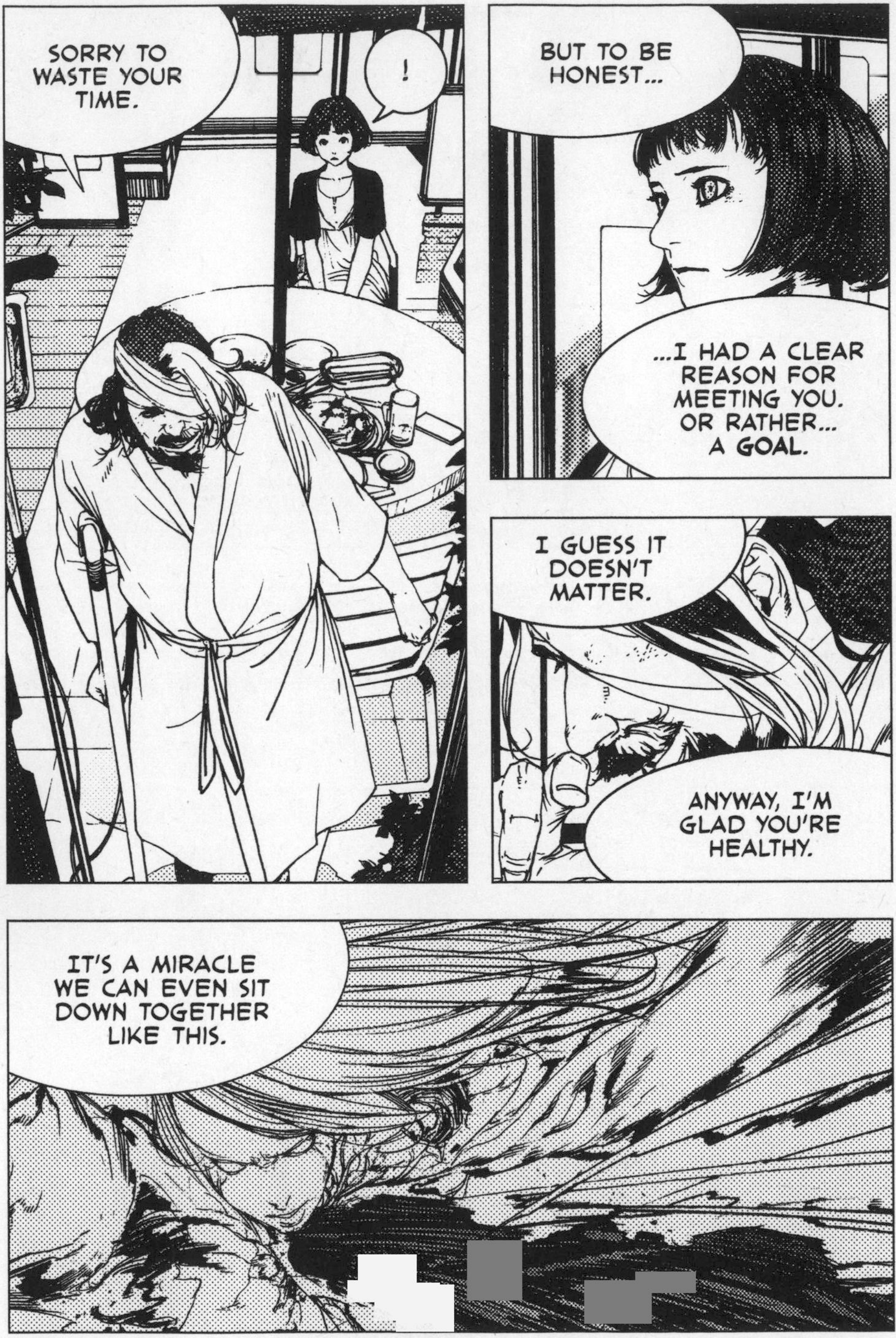
SORRY TO WASTE YOUR TIME.
!
BUT TO BE HONEST...
...I HAD A CLEAR REASON FOR MEETING YOU. OR RATHER... A GOAL.
I GUESS IT DOESN'T MATTER.
ANYWAY, I'M GLAD YOU'RE HEALTHY.
IT'S A MIRACLE WE CAN EVEN SIT DOWN TOGETHER LIKE THIS.

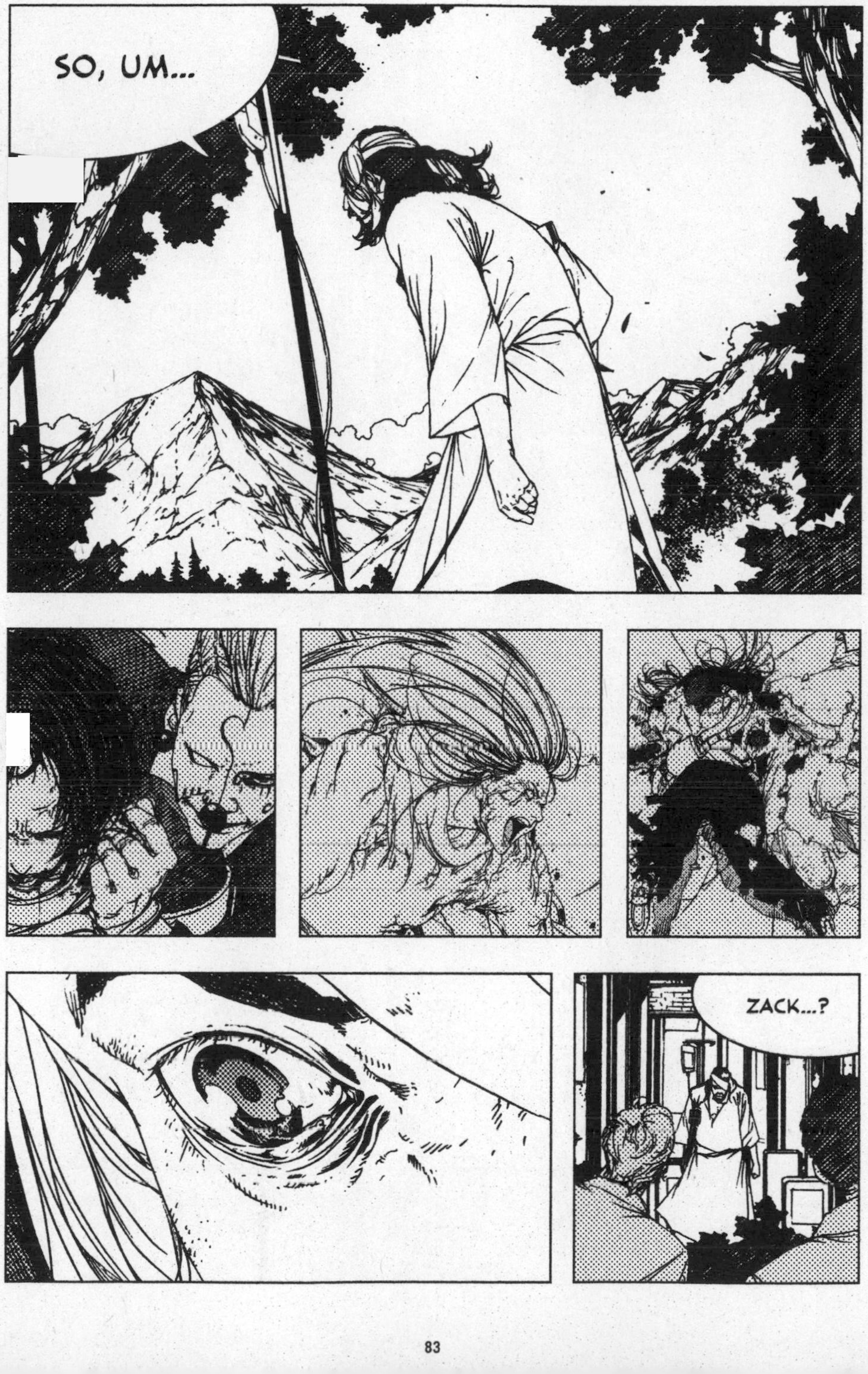
SO, UM...
ZACK...?

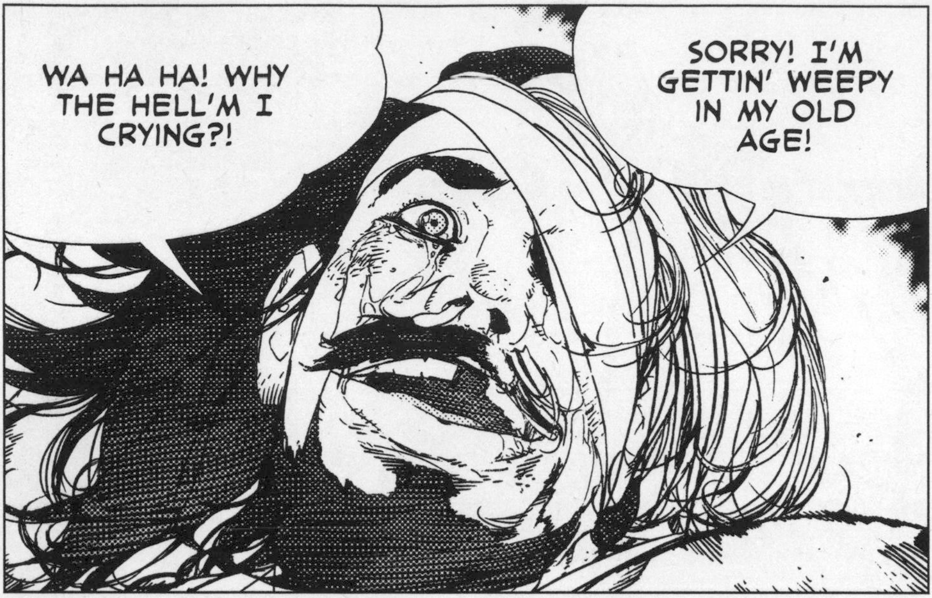
WA HA HA! WHY THE HELL'M I CRYING?!
SORRY! I'M GETTIN' WEEPY IN MY OLD AGE!

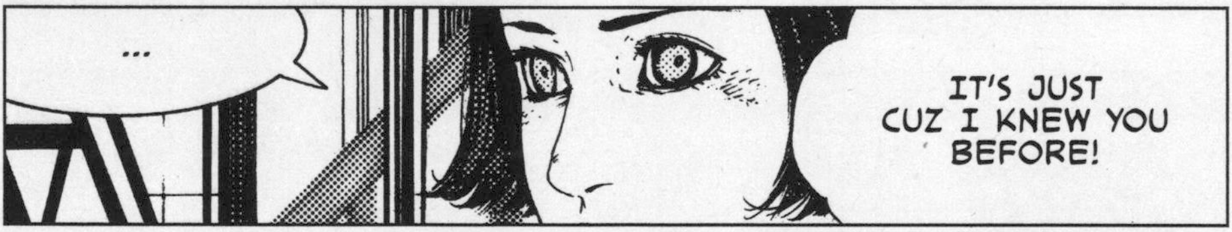
...
IT'S JUST CUZ I KNEW YOU BEFORE!

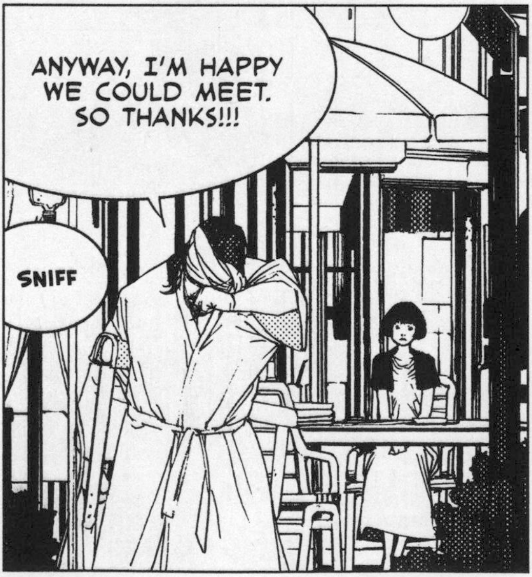
ANYWAY, I'M HAPPY WE COULD MEET. SO THANKS!!!
SNIFF

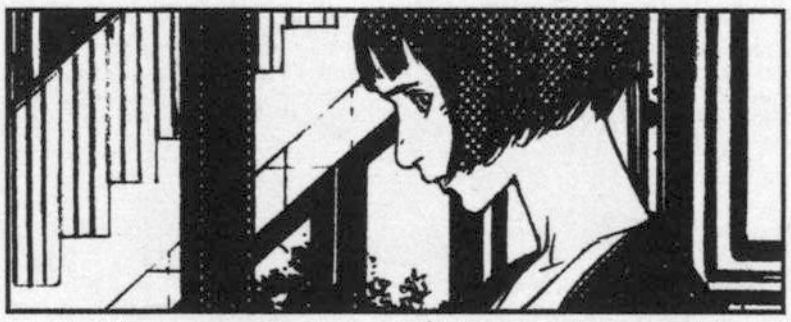

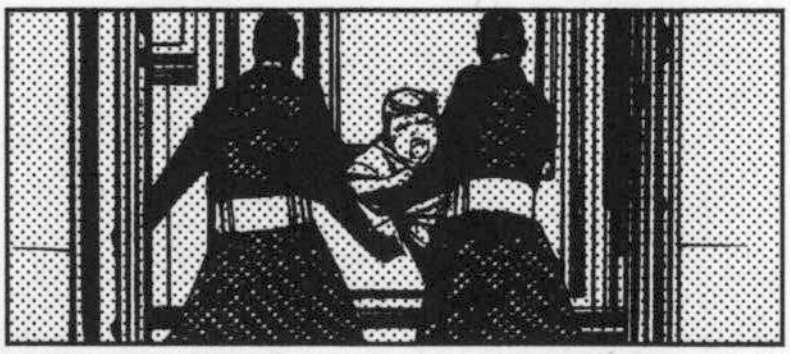

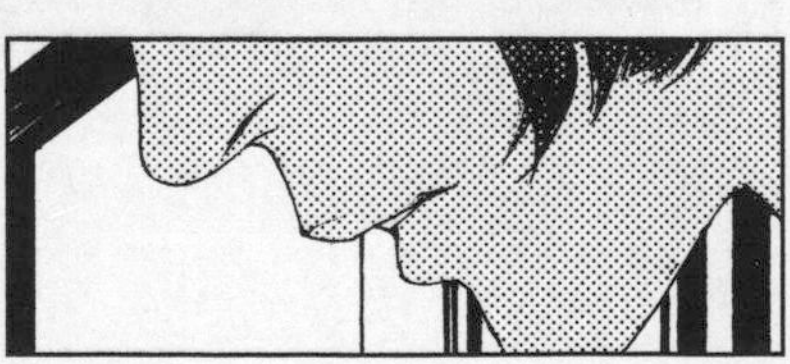

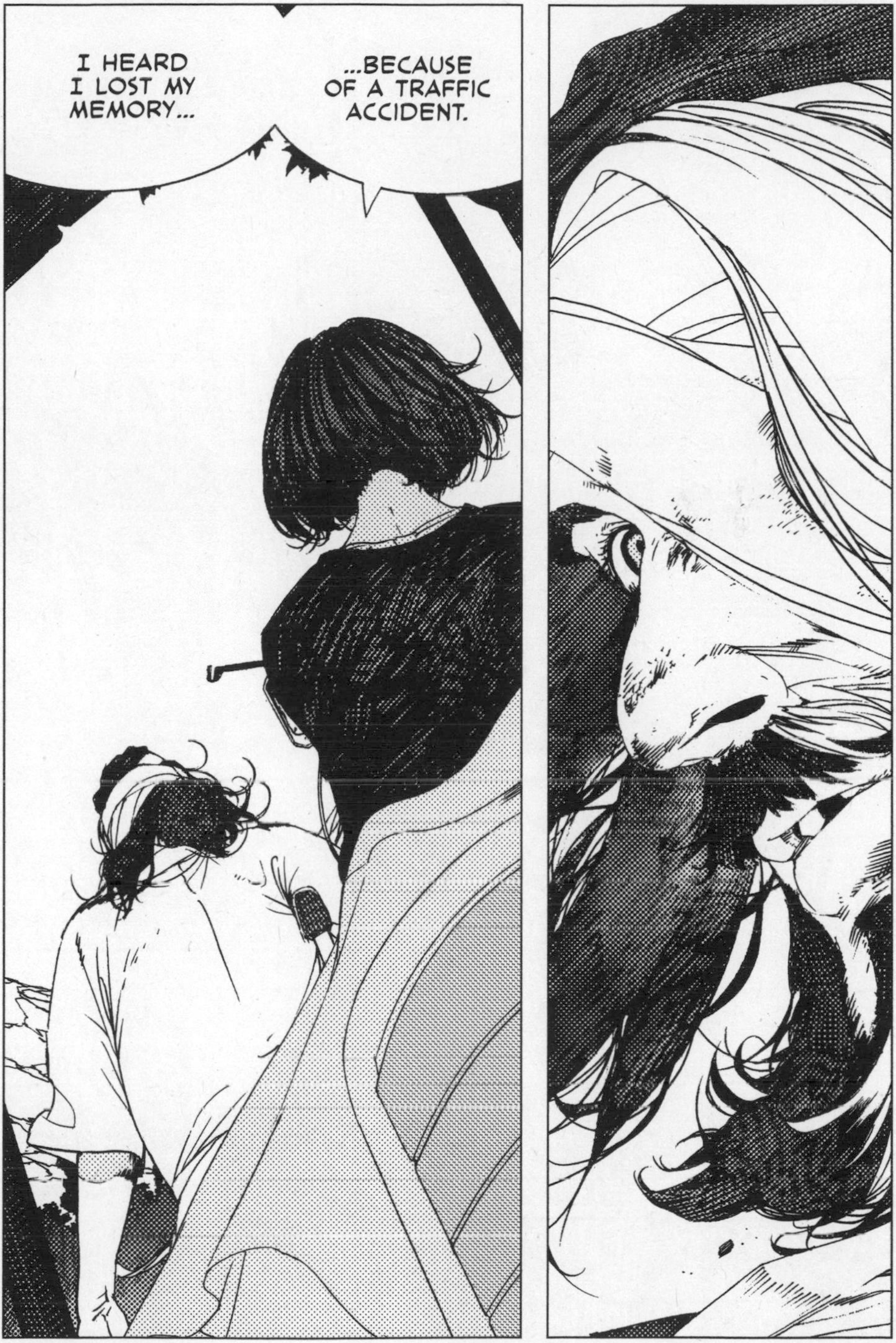
I HEARD I LOST MY MEMORY...
...BECAUSE OF A TRAFFIC ACCIDENT.

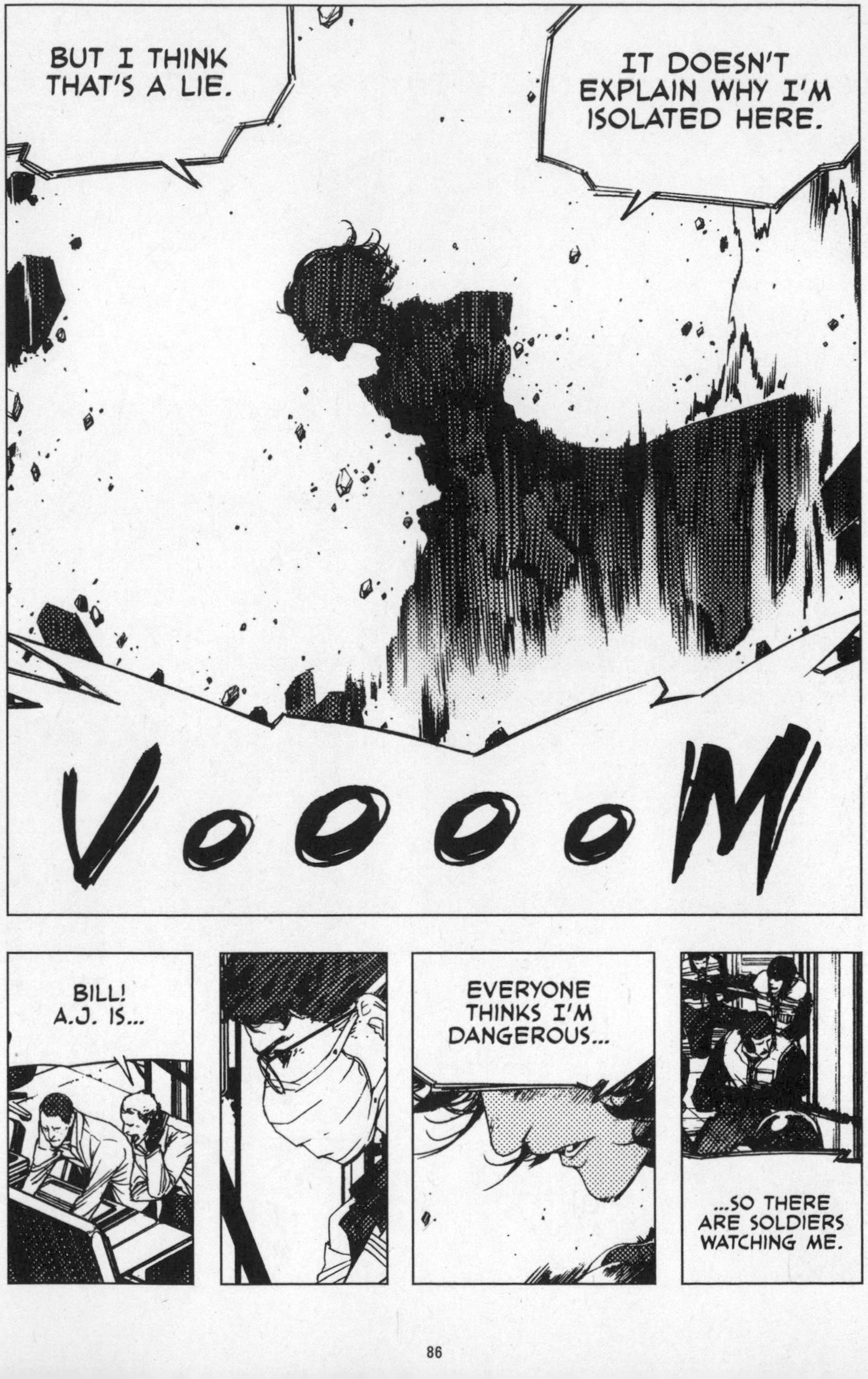
BUT I THINK THAT'S A LIE.
IT DOESN'T EXPLAIN WHY I'M ISOLATED HERE.
VOOOOM
BILL! A.J. IS...
EVERYONE THINKS I'M DANGEROUS...
...SO THERE ARE SOLDIERS WATCHING ME.

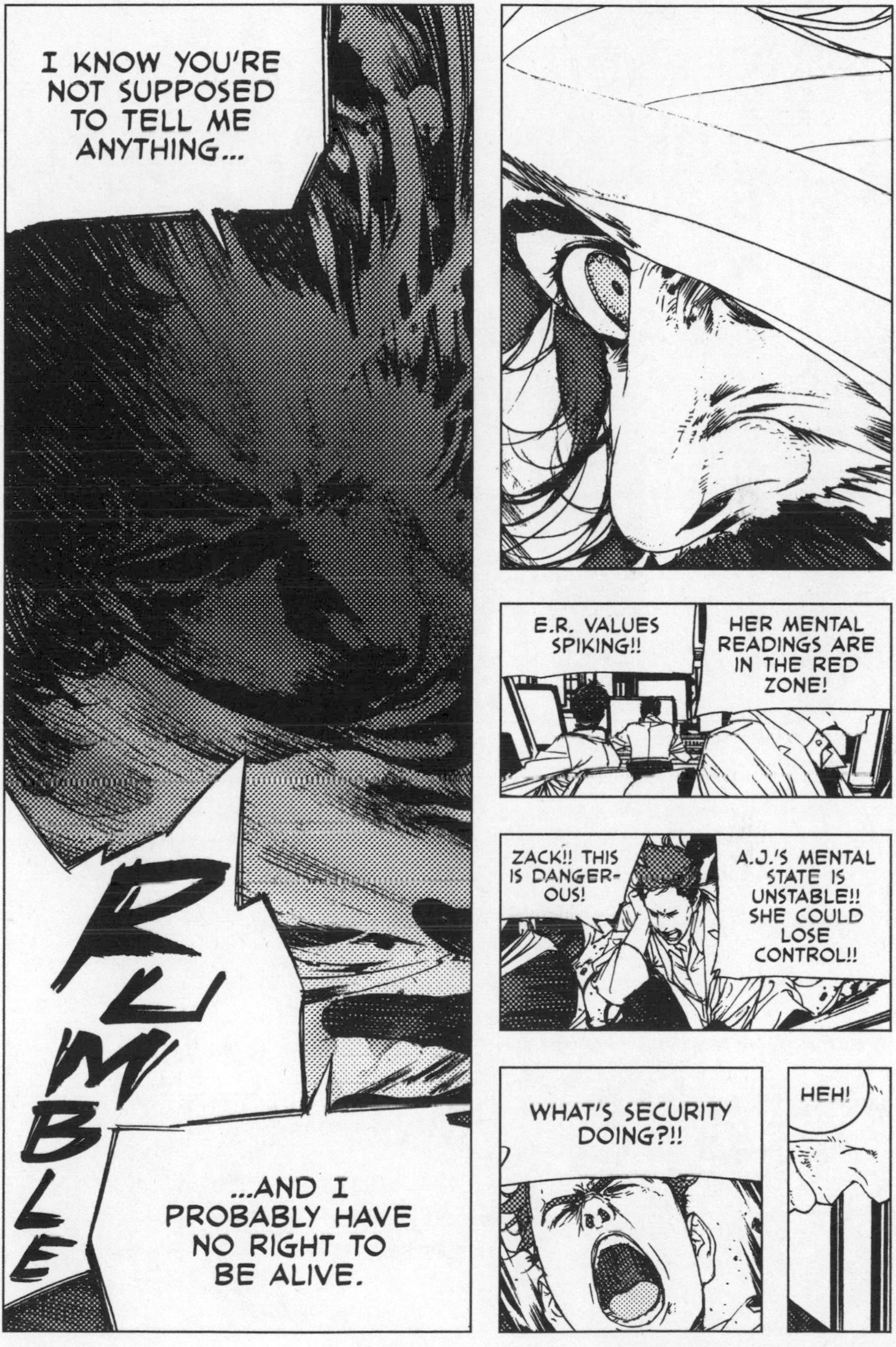
I KNOW YOU'RE NOT SUPPOSED TO TELL ME ANYTHING...
...AND I PROBABLY HAVE NO RIGHT TO BE ALIVE.
RUMBLE
E.R. VALUES SPIKING!!
HER MENTAL READINGS ARE IN THE RED ZONE!
ZACK!! THIS IS DANGER-OUS!
A.J.'S MENTAL STATE IS UNSTABLE!! SHE COULD LOSE CONTROL!!
WHAT'S SECURITY DOING?!!
HEH!

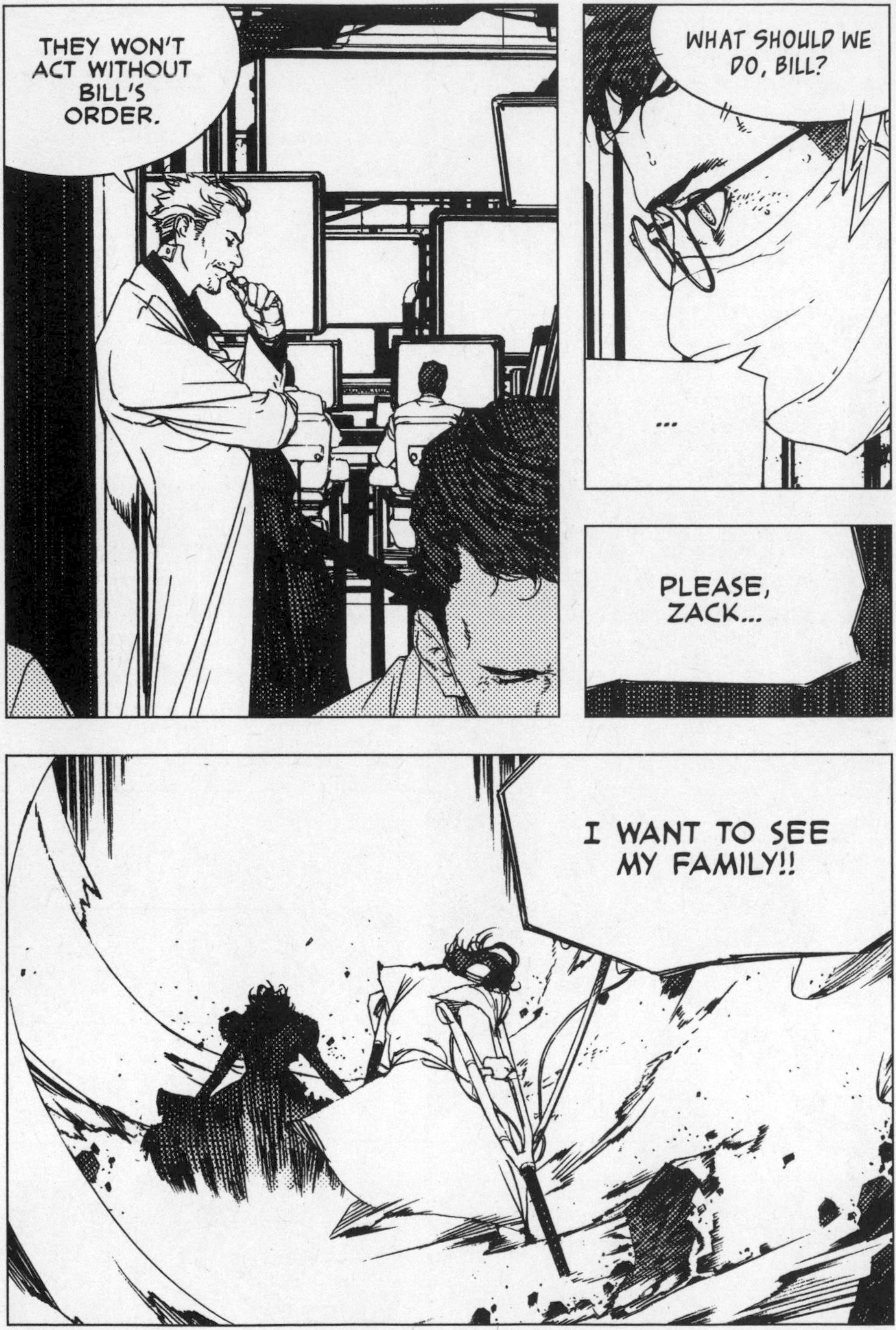
WHAT SHOULD WE DO, BILL?
...
PLEASE, ZACK...
THEY WON'T ACT WITHOUT BILL'S ORDER.
I WANT TO SEE MY FAMILY!!

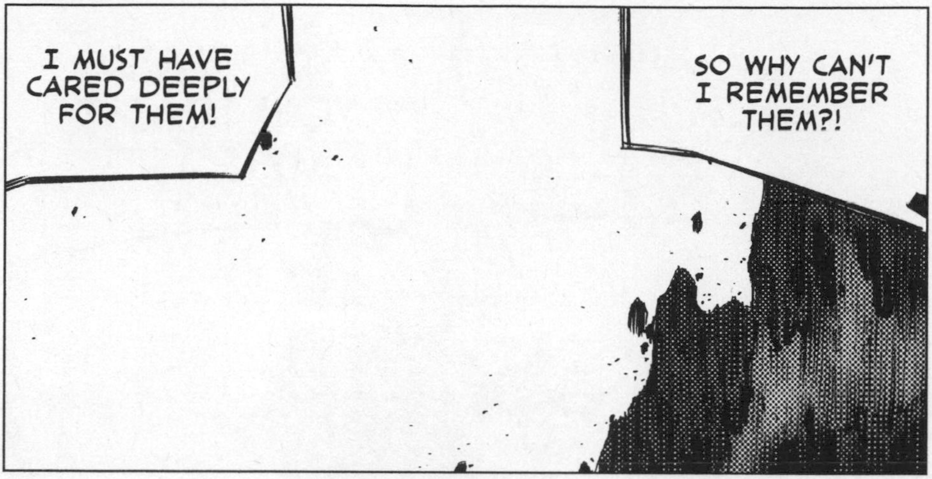
SO WHY CAN'T I REMEMBER THEM?!
I MUST HAVE CARED DEEPLY FOR THEM!
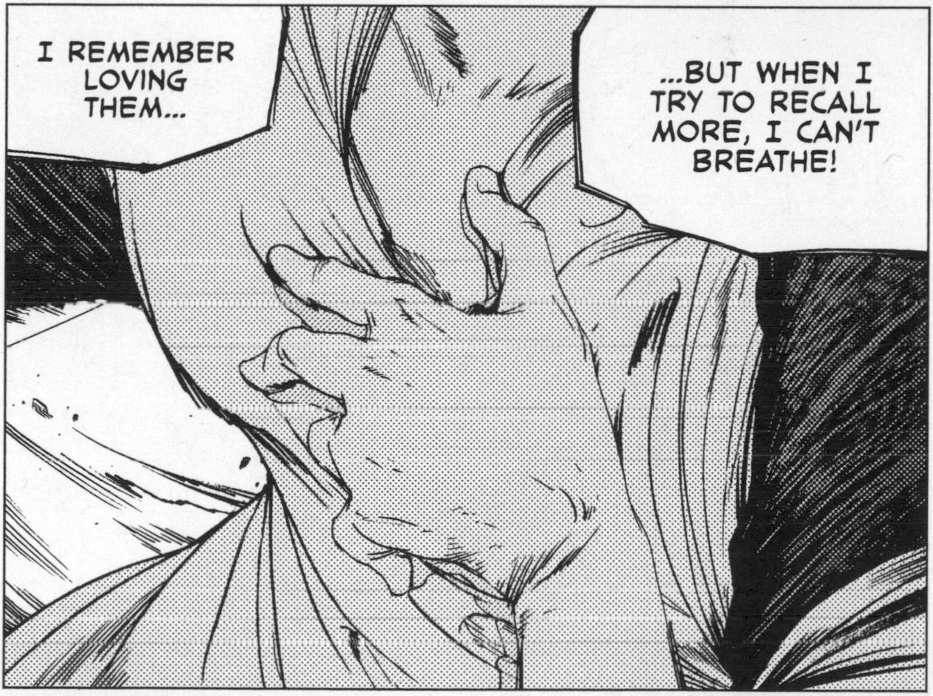
I REMEMBER LOVING THEM...
...BUT WHEN I TRY TO RECALL MORE, I CAN'T BREATHE!
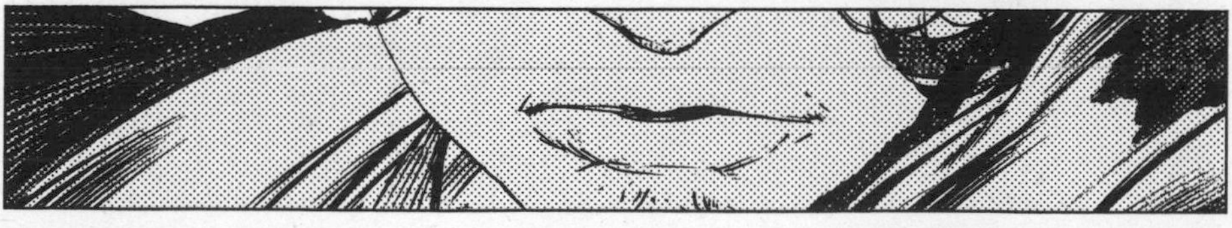

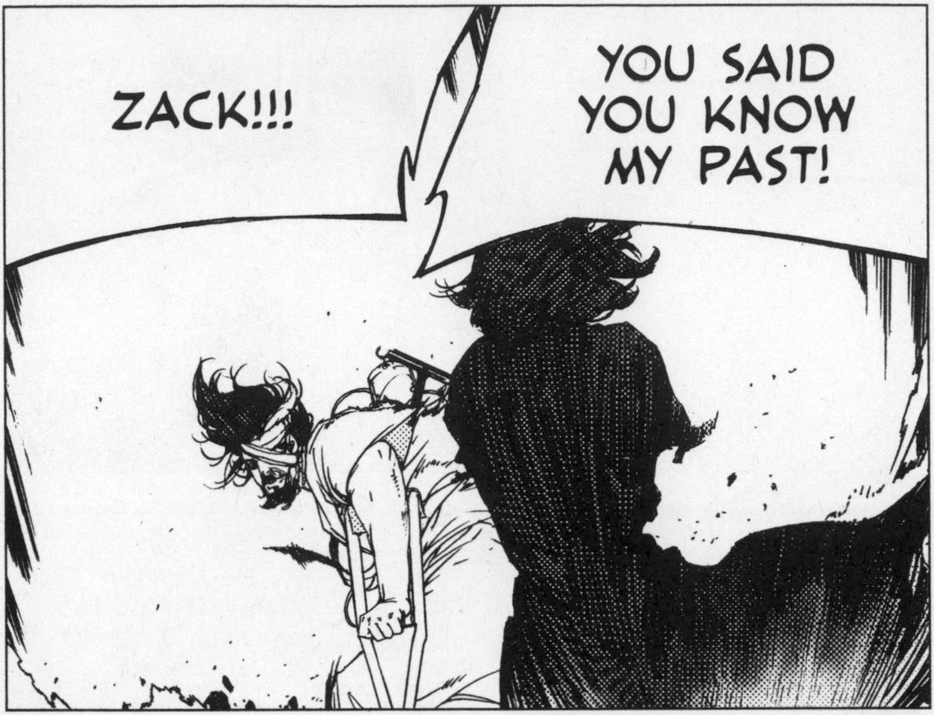
ZACK!!!
YOU SAID YOU KNOW MY PAST!

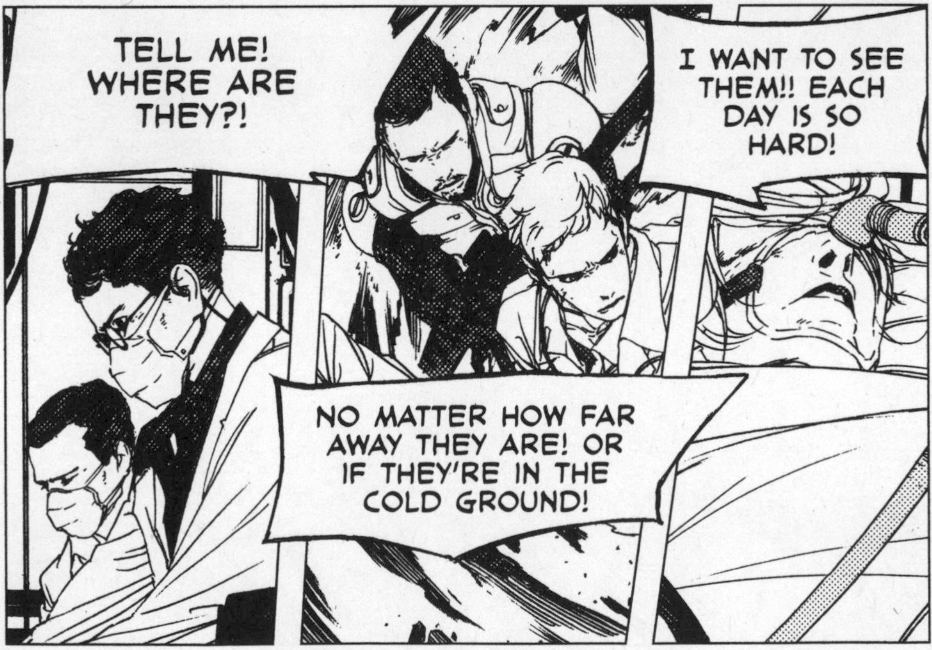
TELL ME! WHERE ARE THEY?!
I WANT TO SEE THEM!! EACH DAY IS SO HARD!
NO MATTER HOW FAR AWAY THEY ARE! OR IF THEY'RE IN THE COLD GROUND!

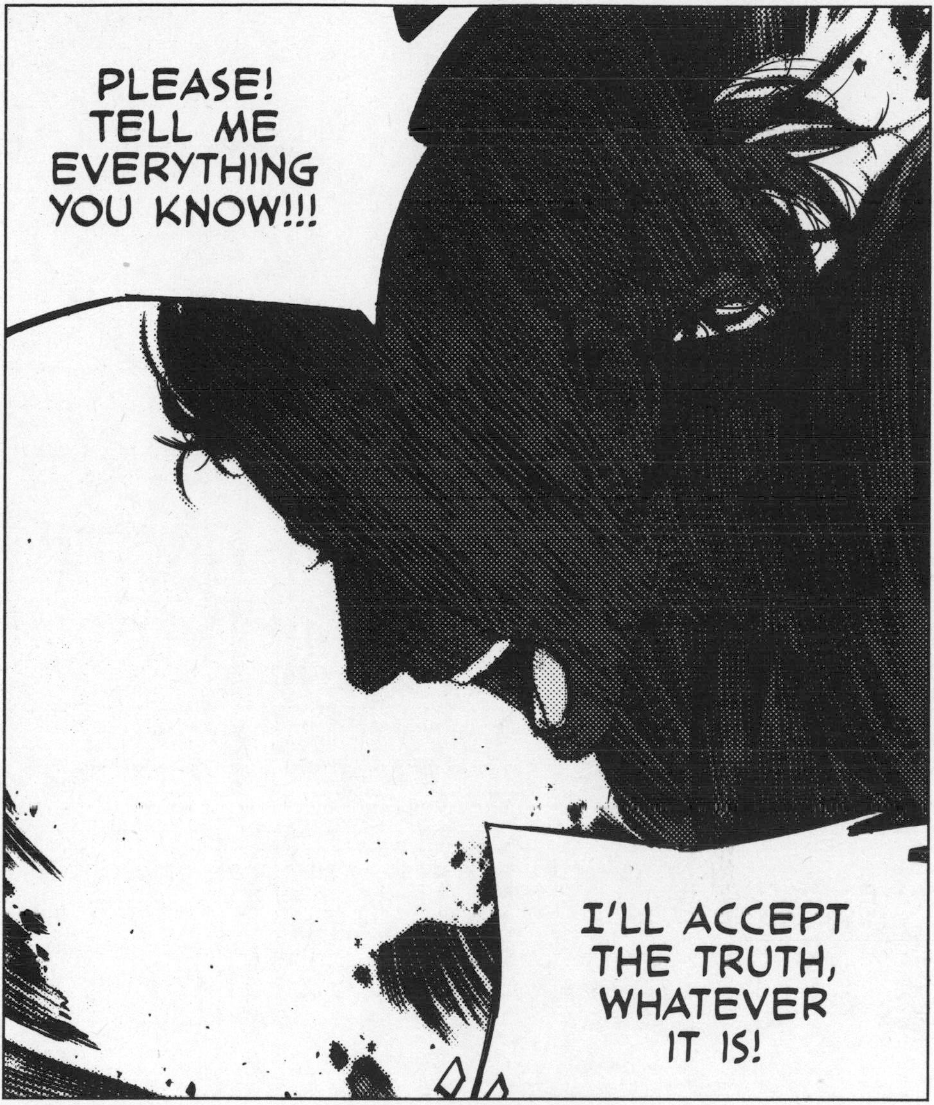
PLEASE! TELL ME EVERYTHING YOU KNOW!!!
I'LL ACCEPT THE TRUTH, WHATEVER IT IS!
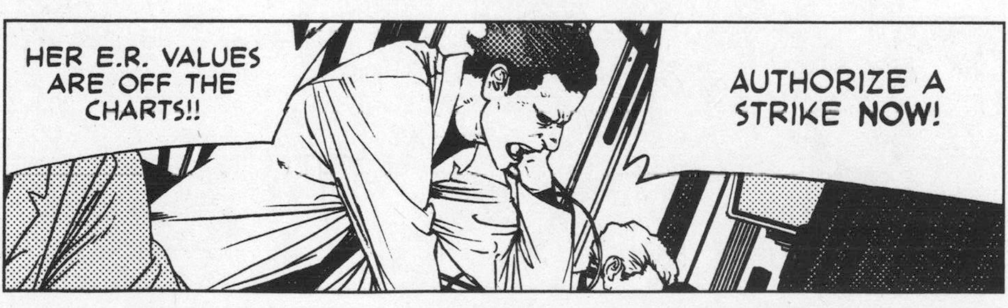
AUTHORIZE A STRIKE NOW!
HER E.R. VALUES ARE OFF THE CHARTS!!

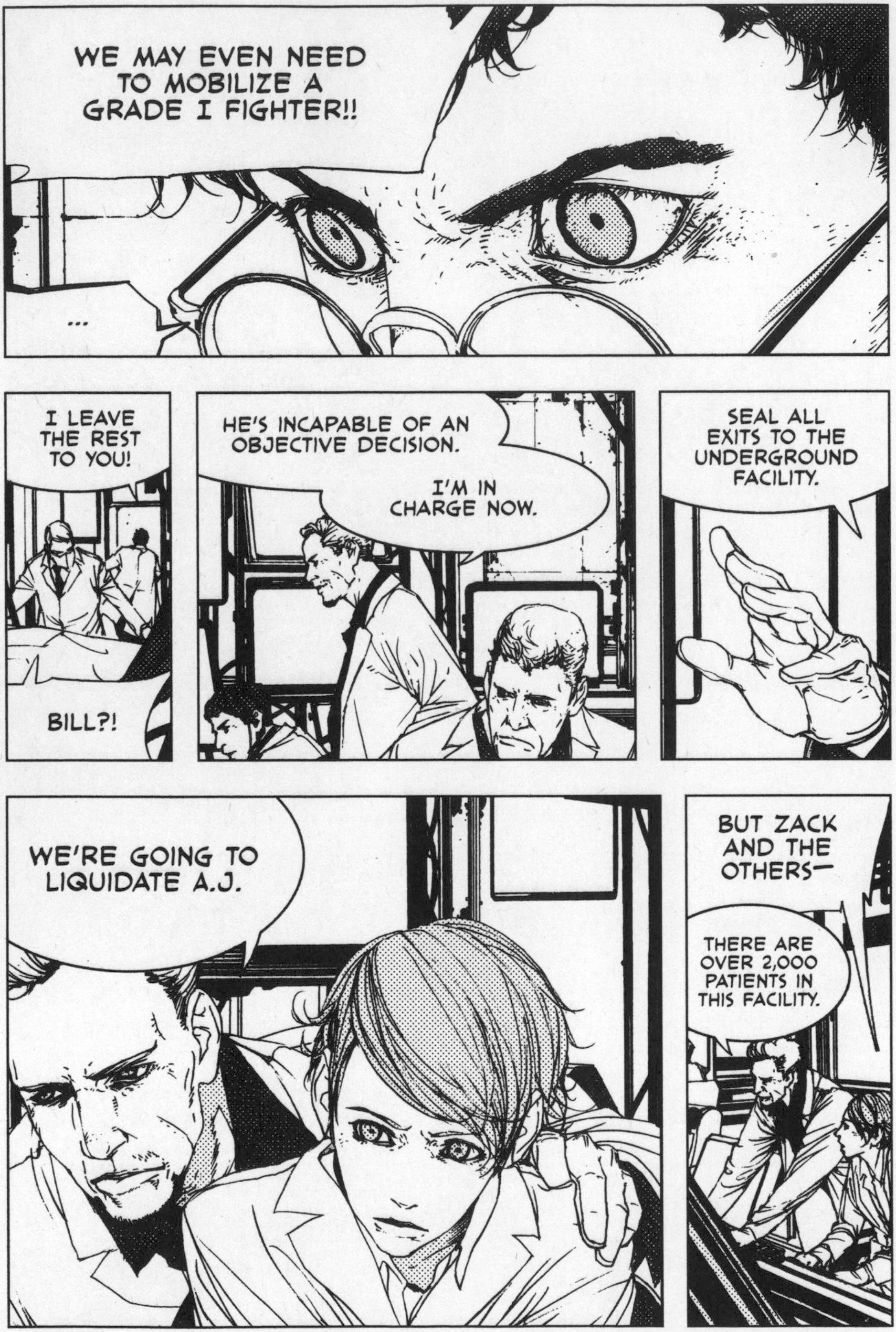
WE MAY EVEN NEED TO MOBILIZE A GRADE I FIGHTER!!
...
I LEAVE THE REST TO YOU!
BILL?!
HE'S INCAPABLE OF AN OBJECTIVE DECISION.
I'M IN CHARGE NOW.
SEAL ALL EXITS TO THE UNDERGROUND FACILITY.
WE'RE GOING TO LIQUIDATE A.J.
BUT ZACK AND THE OTHERS—
THERE ARE OVER 2,000 PATIENTS IN THIS FACILITY.

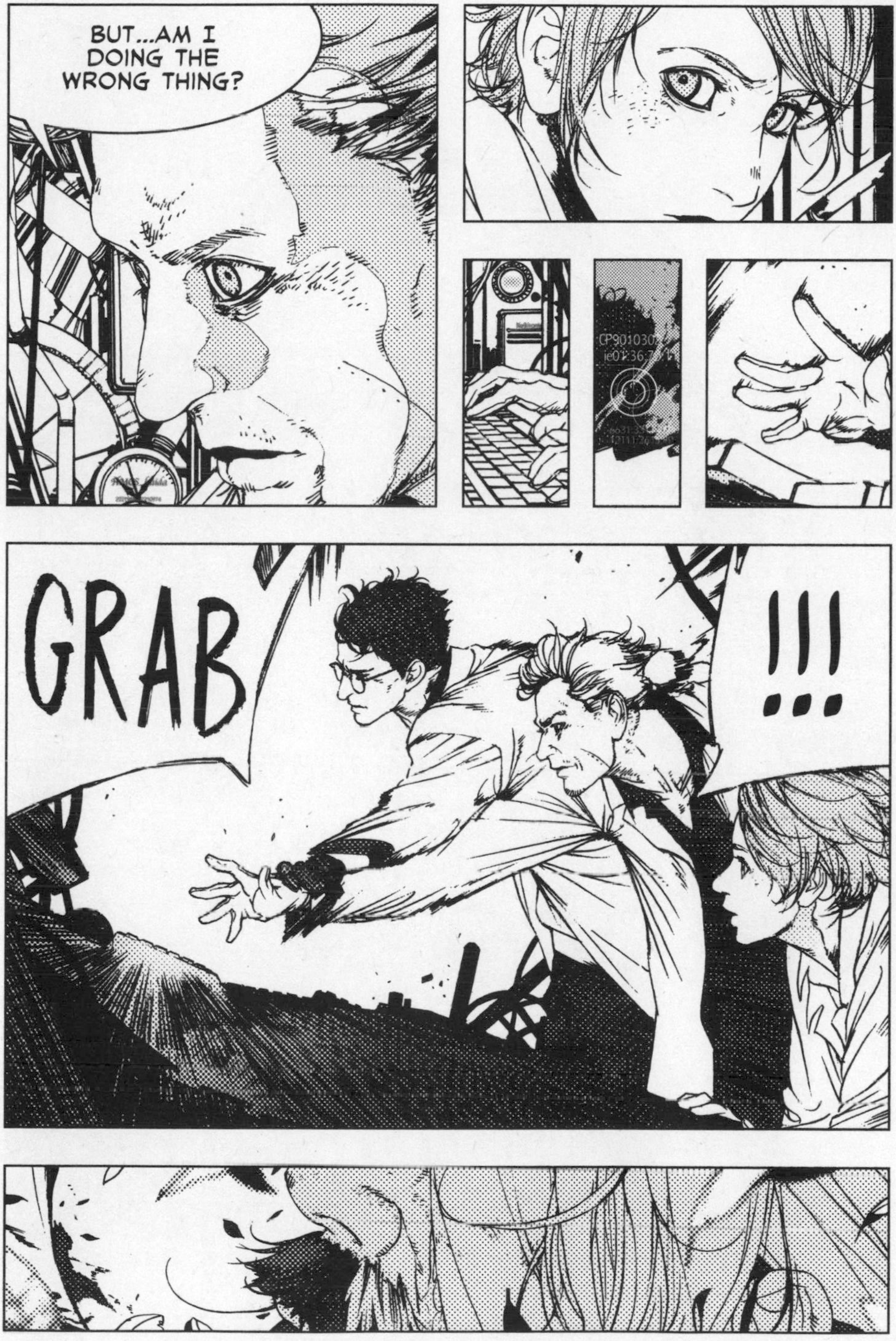
BUT...AM I DOING THE WRONG THING?
GRAB
!!!

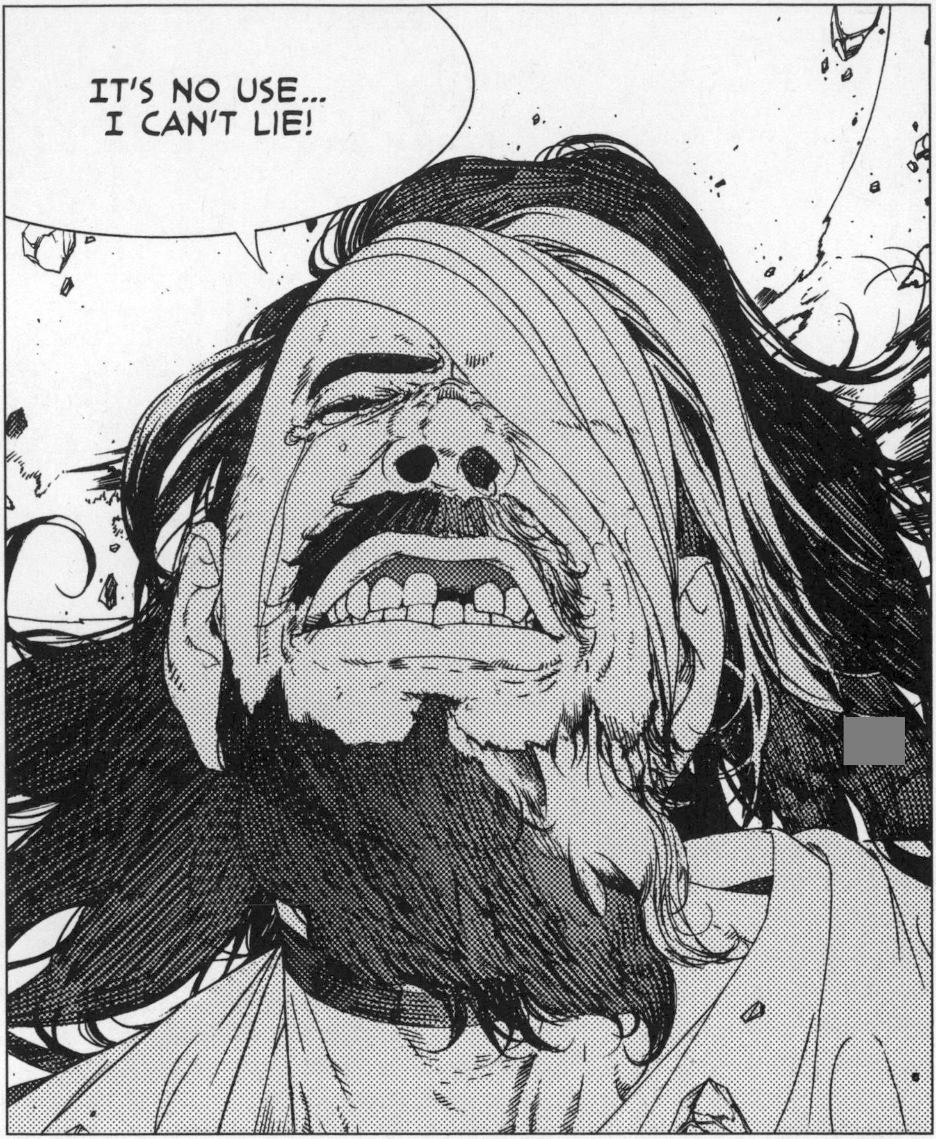
IT'S NO USE... I CAN'T LIE!

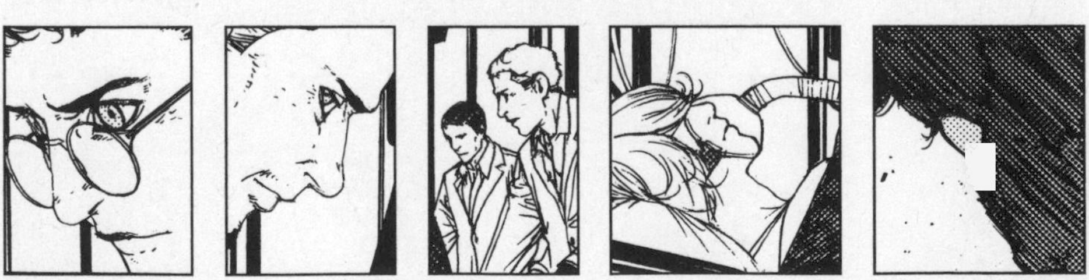

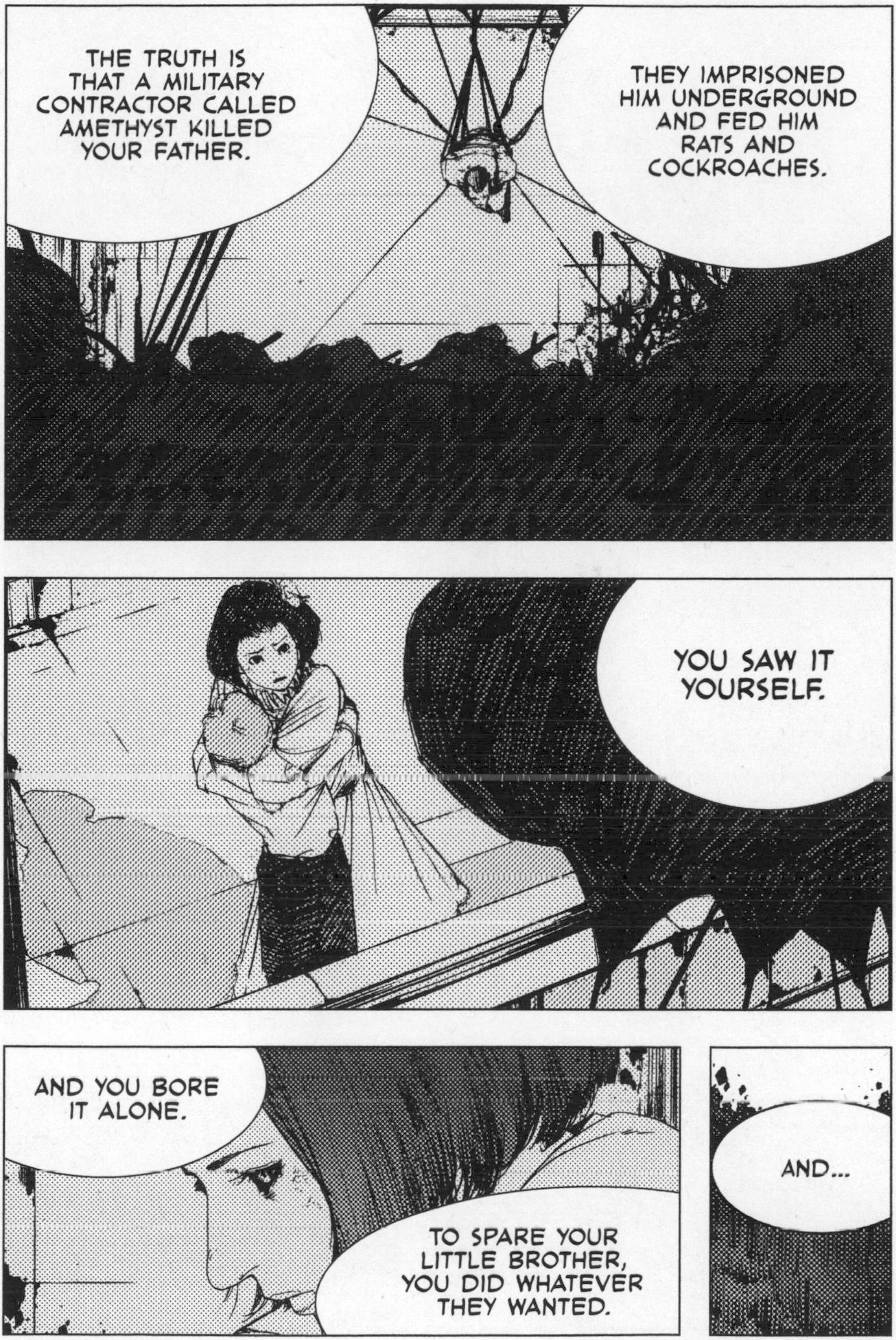
THE TRUTH IS THAT A MILITARY CONTRACTOR CALLED AMETHYST KILLED YOUR FATHER.
THEY IMPRISONED HIM UNDERGROUND AND FED HIM RATS AND COCKROACHES.
YOU SAW IT YOURSELF.
AND YOU BORE IT ALONE.
TO SPARE YOUR LITTLE BROTHER, YOU DID WHATEVER THEY WANTED.
AND...

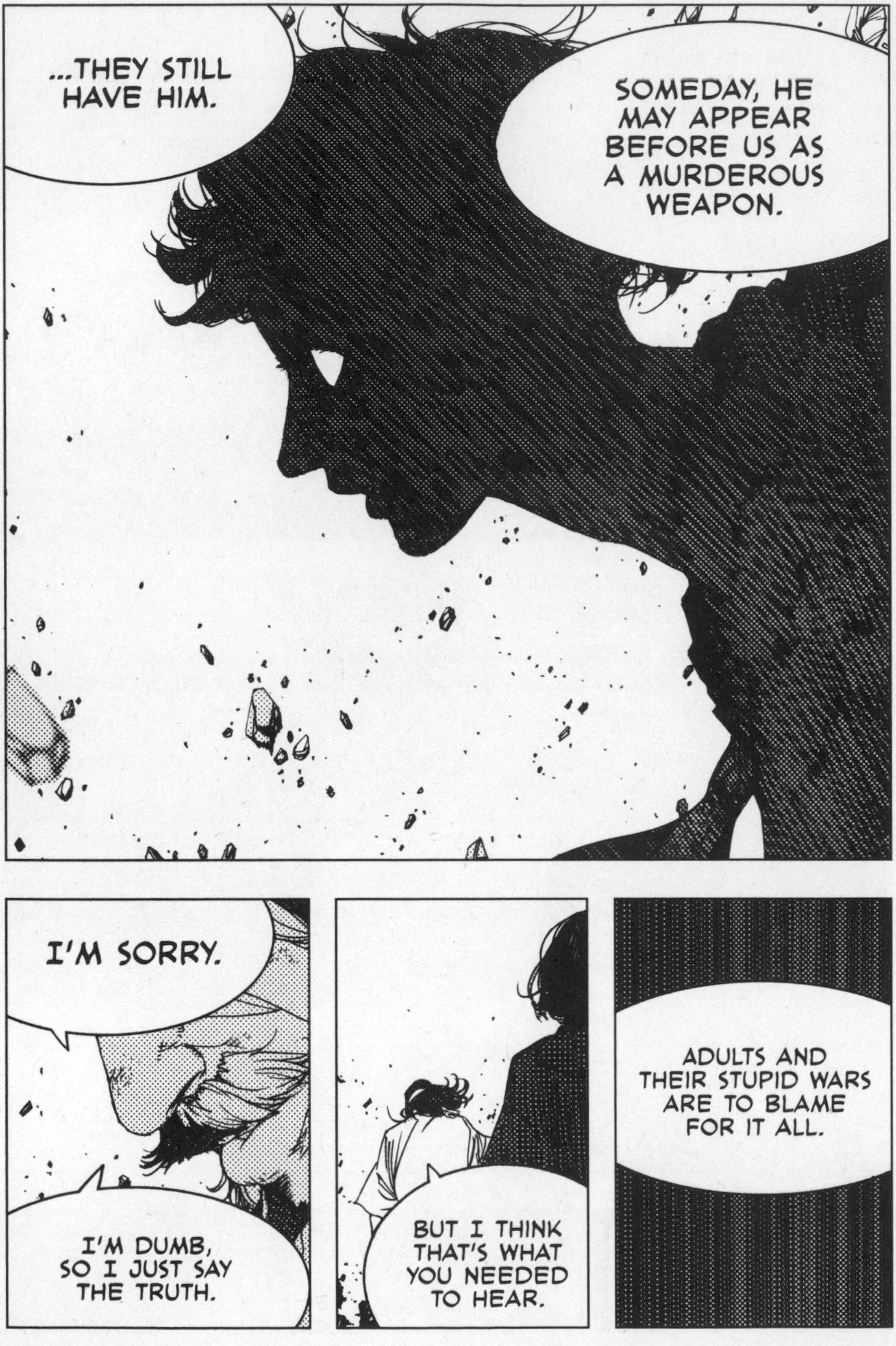
...THEY STILL HAVE HIM.
SOMEDAY, HE MAY APPEAR BEFORE US AS A MURDEROUS WEAPON.
ADULTS AND THEIR STUPID WARS ARE TO BLAME FOR IT ALL.
BUT I THINK THAT'S WHAT YOU NEEDED TO HEAR.
I'M SORRY.
I'M DUMB, SO I JUST SAY THE TRUTH.

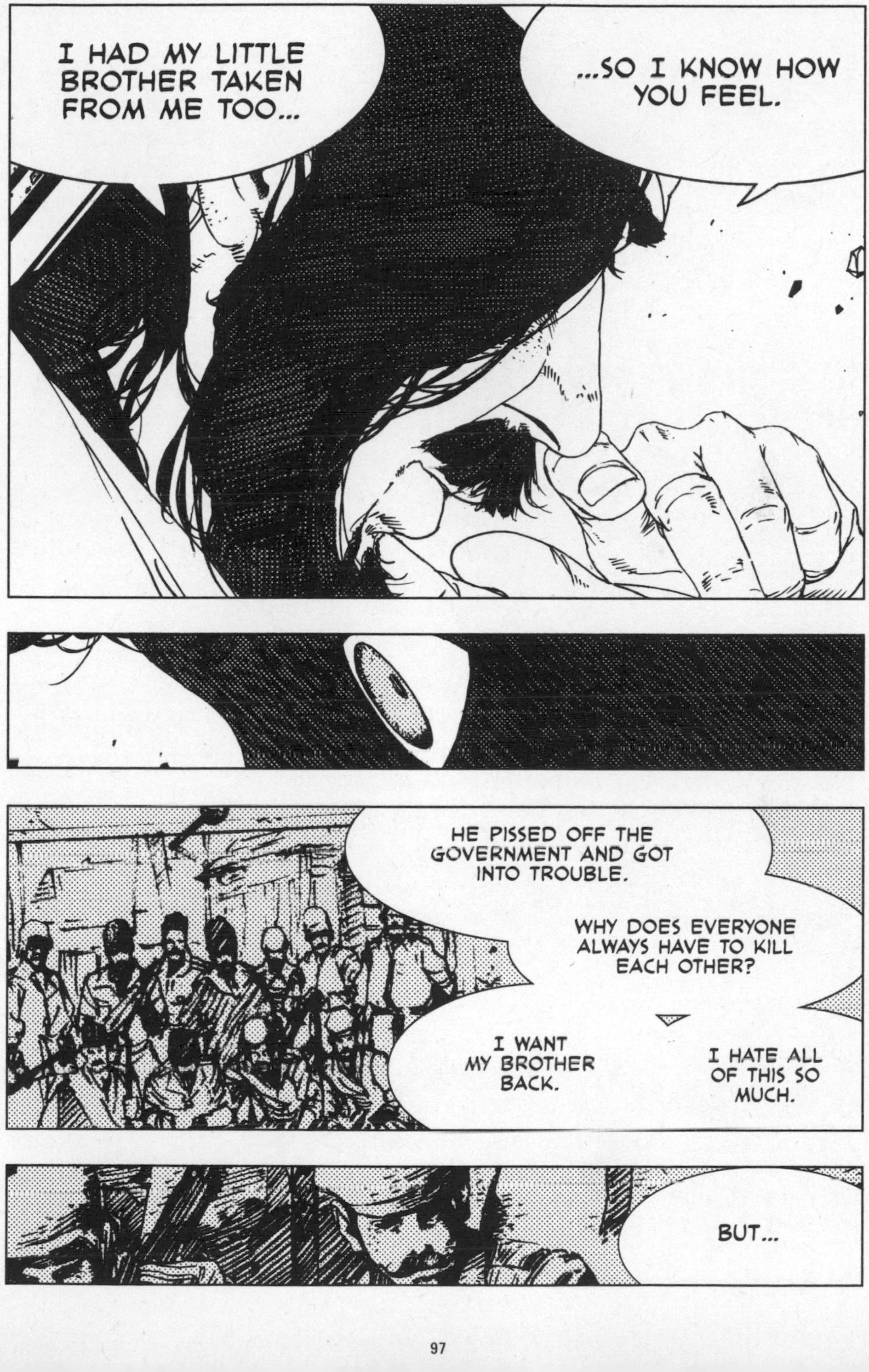
I HAD MY LITTLE BROTHER TAKEN FROM ME TOO...
...SO I KNOW HOW YOU FEEL.
HE PISSED OFF THE GOVERNMENT AND GOT INTO TROUBLE.
WHY DOES EVERYONE ALWAYS HAVE TO KILL EACH OTHER?
I WANT MY BROTHER BACK.
I HATE ALL OF THIS SO MUCH.
BUT...

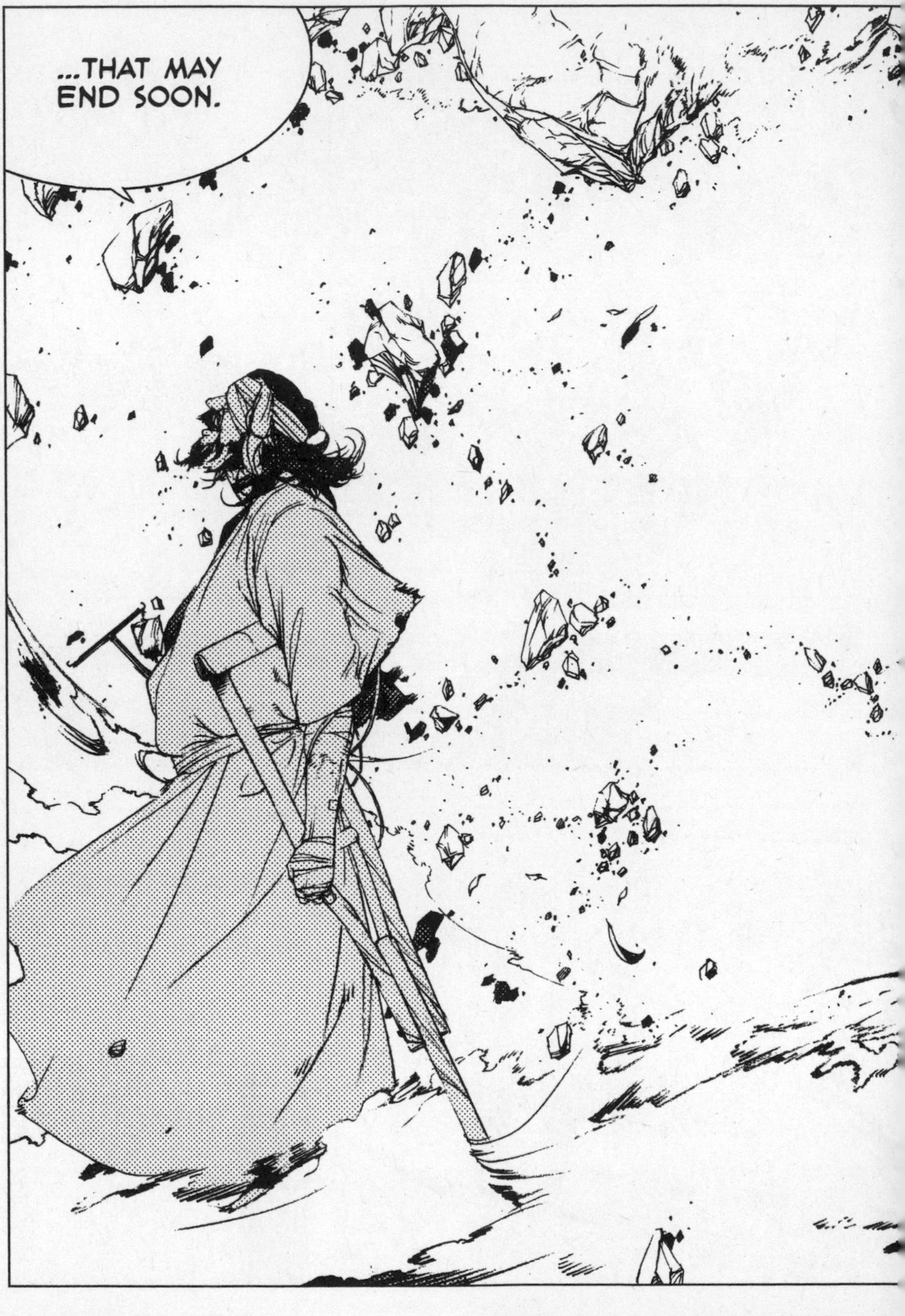
...THAT MAY END SOON.

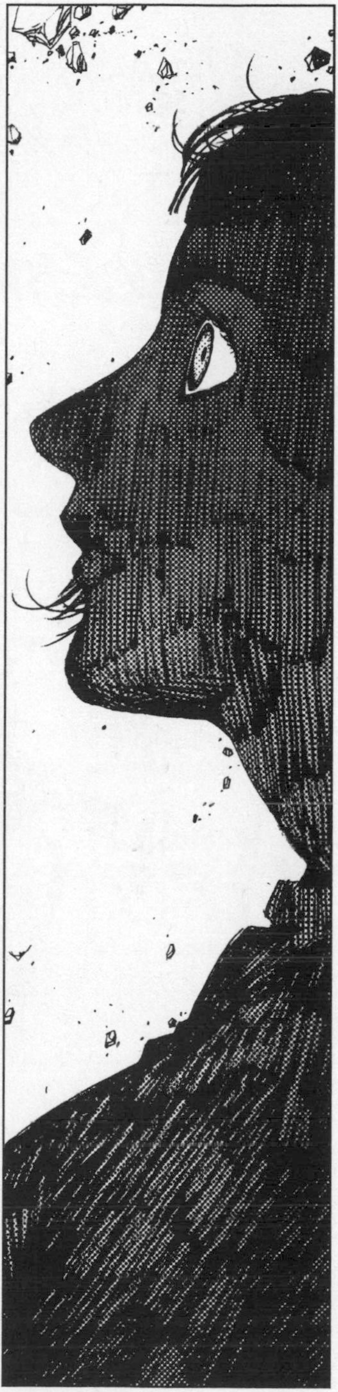
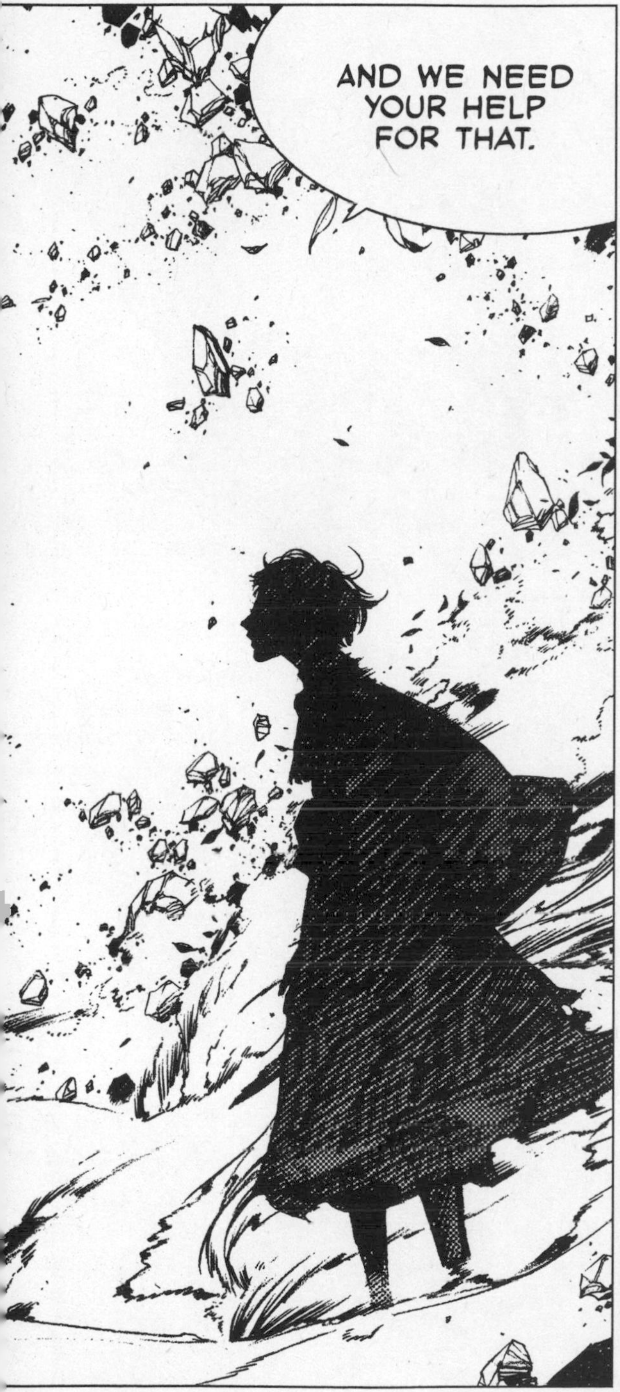
AND WE NEED YOUR HELP FOR THAT.

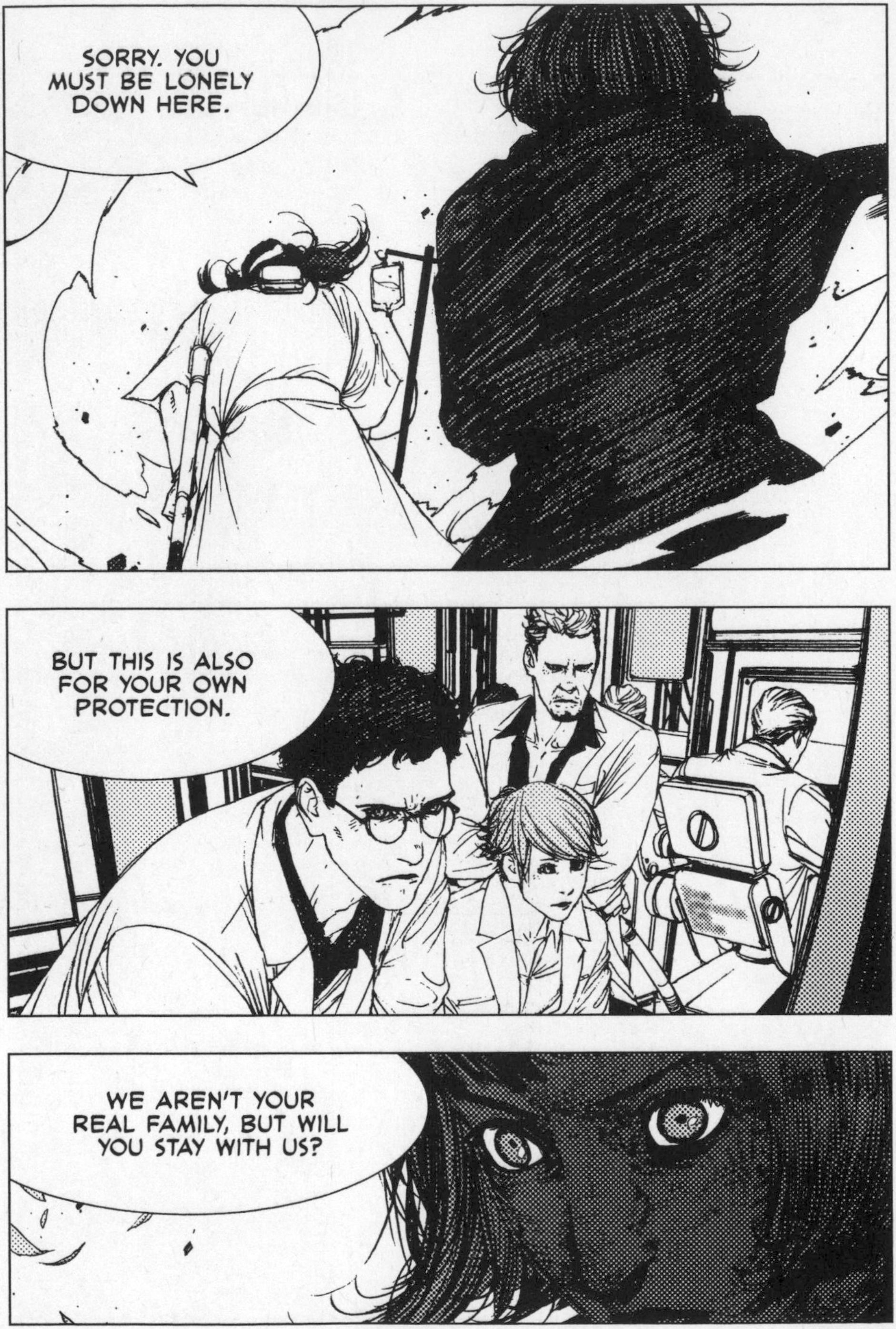
SORRY. YOU MUST BE LONELY DOWN HERE.
BUT THIS IS ALSO FOR YOUR OWN PROTECTION.
WE AREN'T YOUR REAL FAMILY, BUT WILL YOU STAY WITH US?

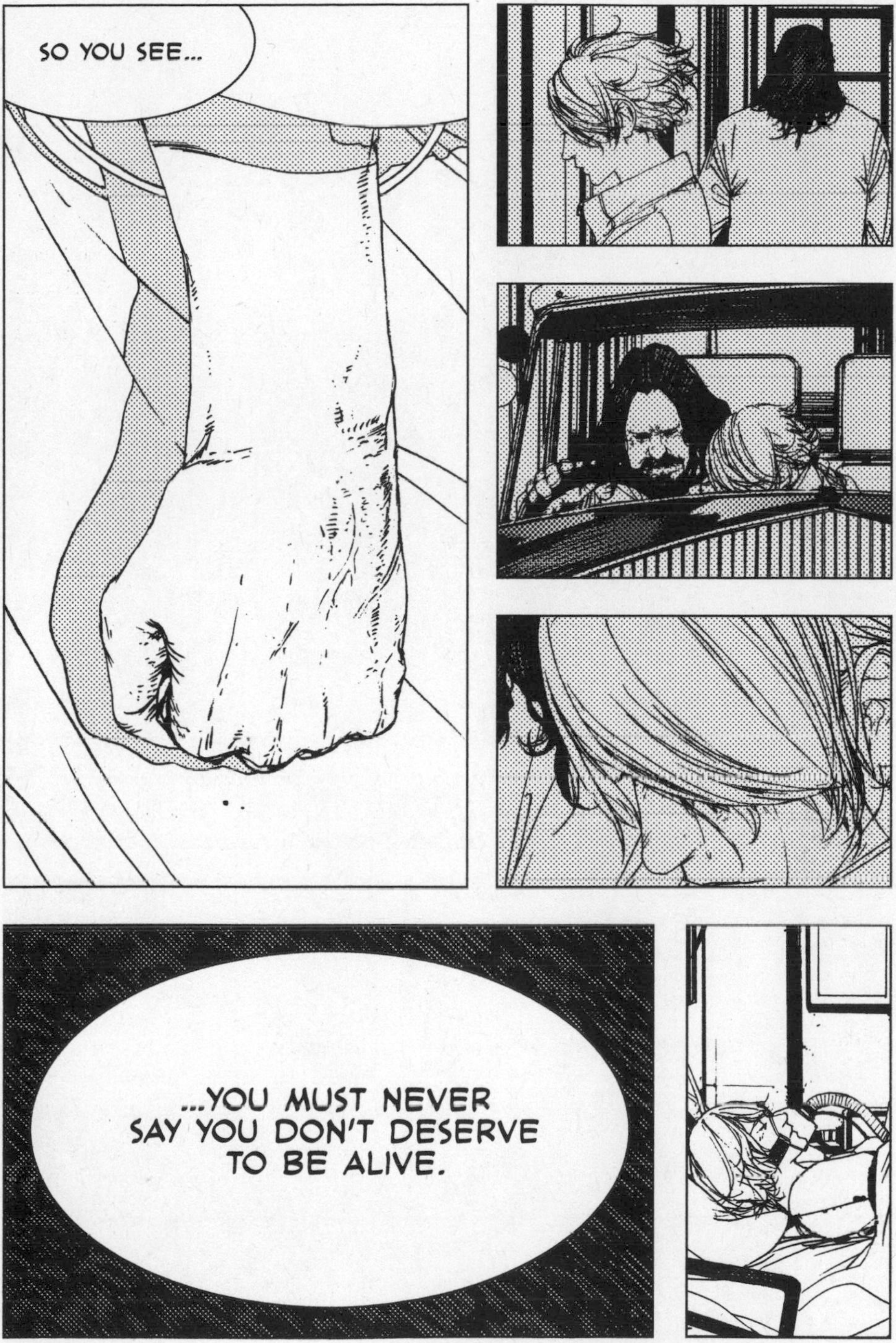
SO YOU SEE...
...YOU MUST NEVER SAY YOU DON'T DESERVE TO BE ALIVE.

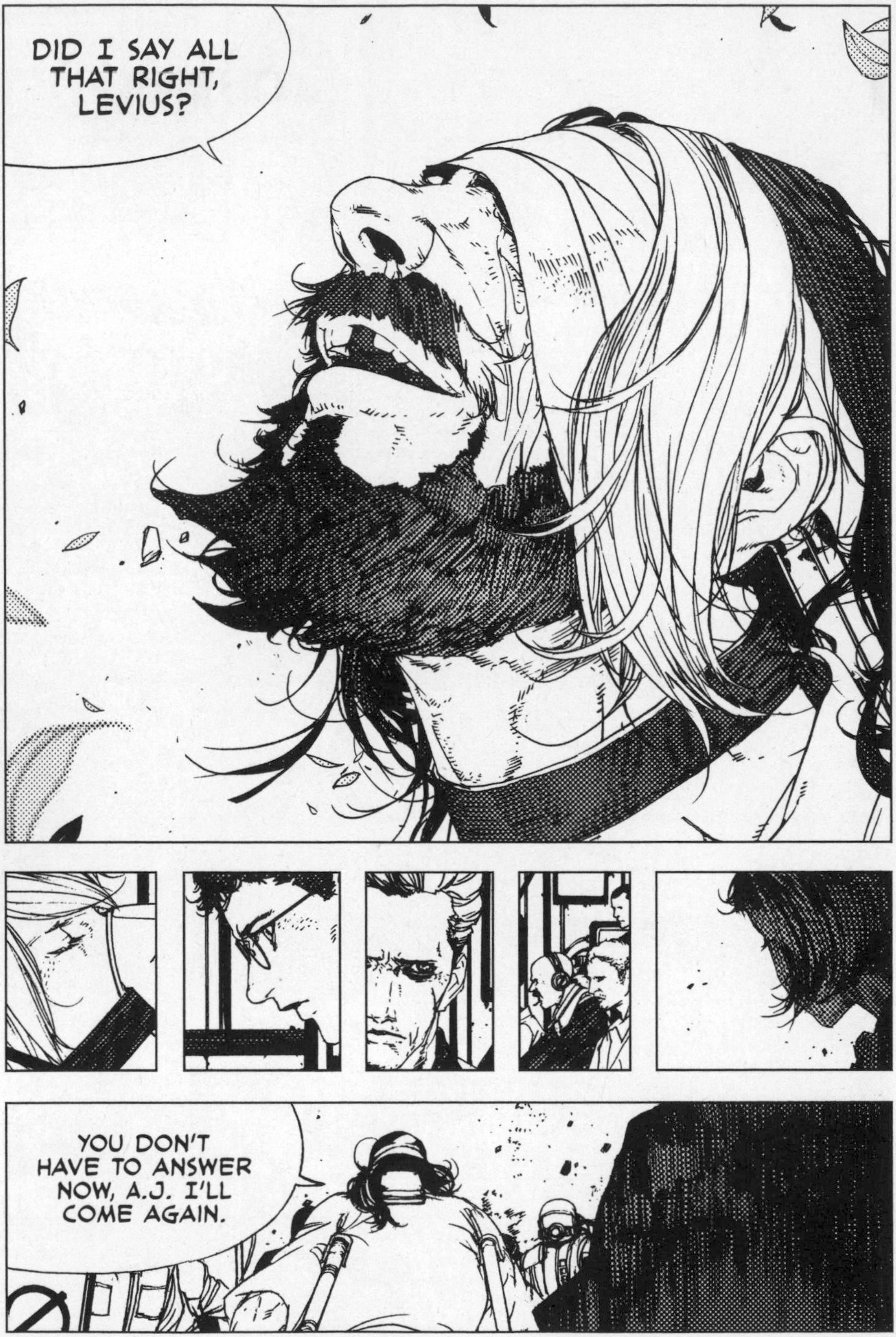
DID I SAY ALL THAT RIGHT, LEVIUS?
YOU DON'T HAVE TO ANSWER NOW, A.J. I'LL COME AGAIN.

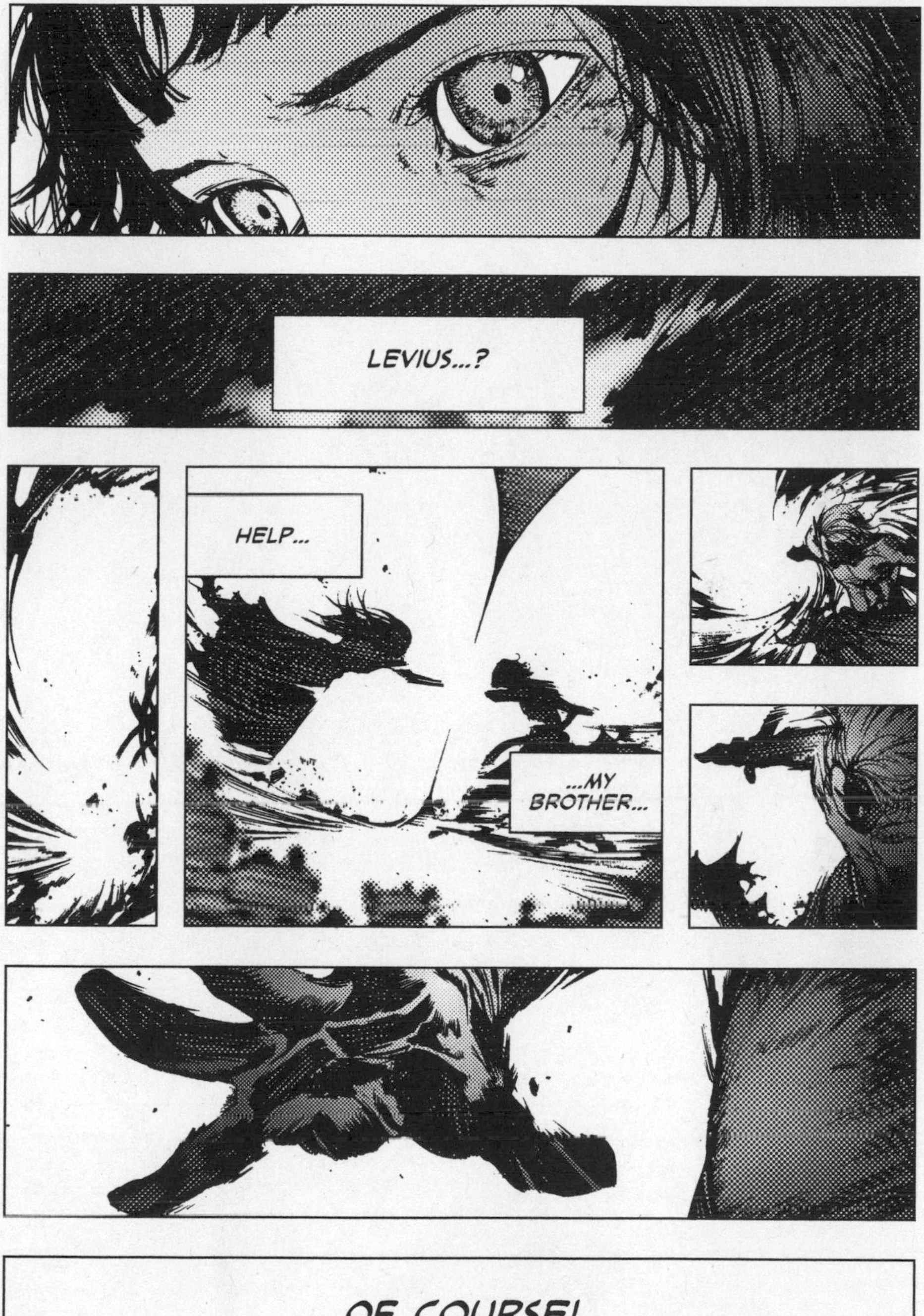
LEVIUS...?
HELP...
...MY BROTHER...
OF COURSE!

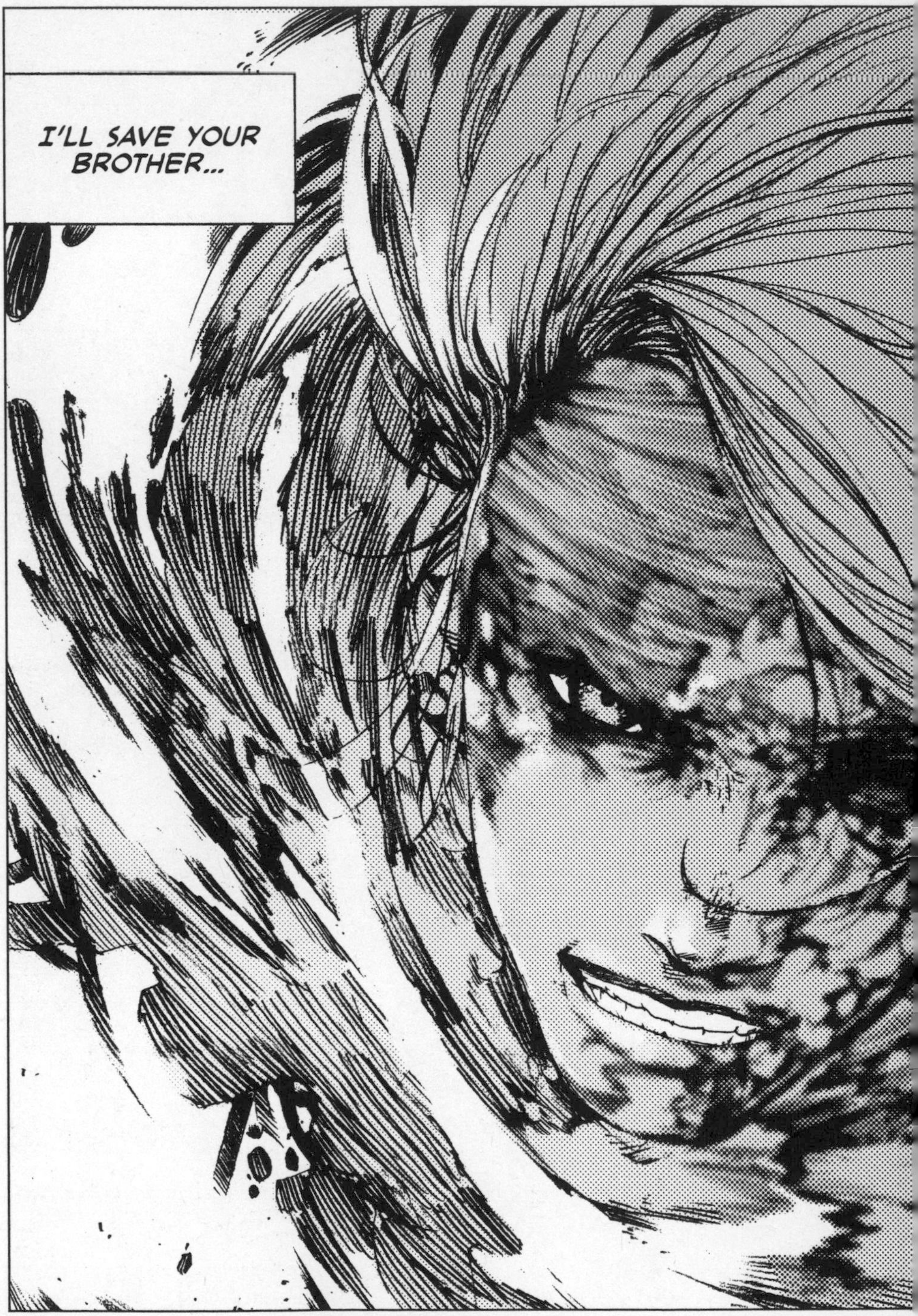
I'LL SAVE YOUR BROTHER...

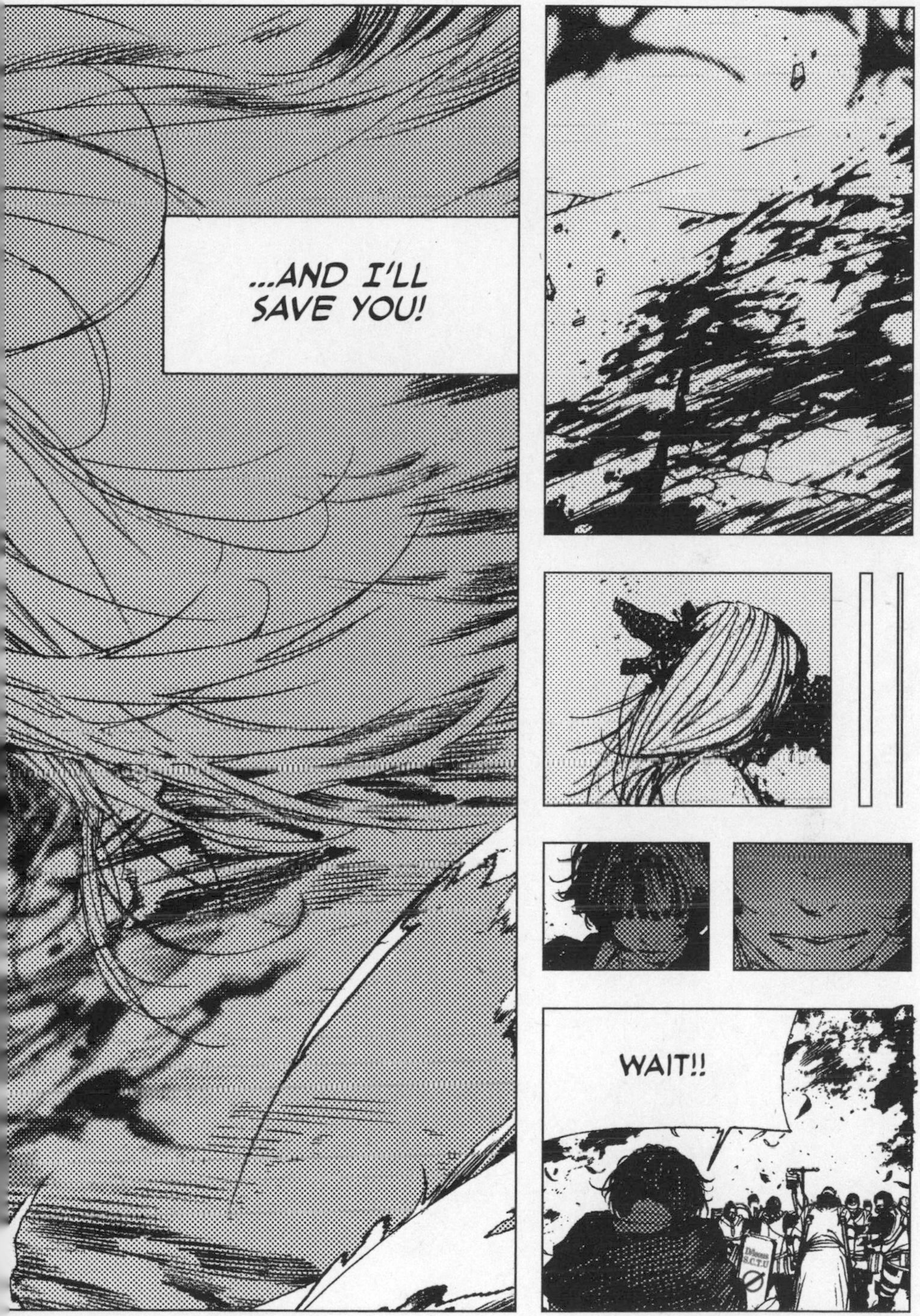
WAIT!!
...AND I'LL SAVE YOU!

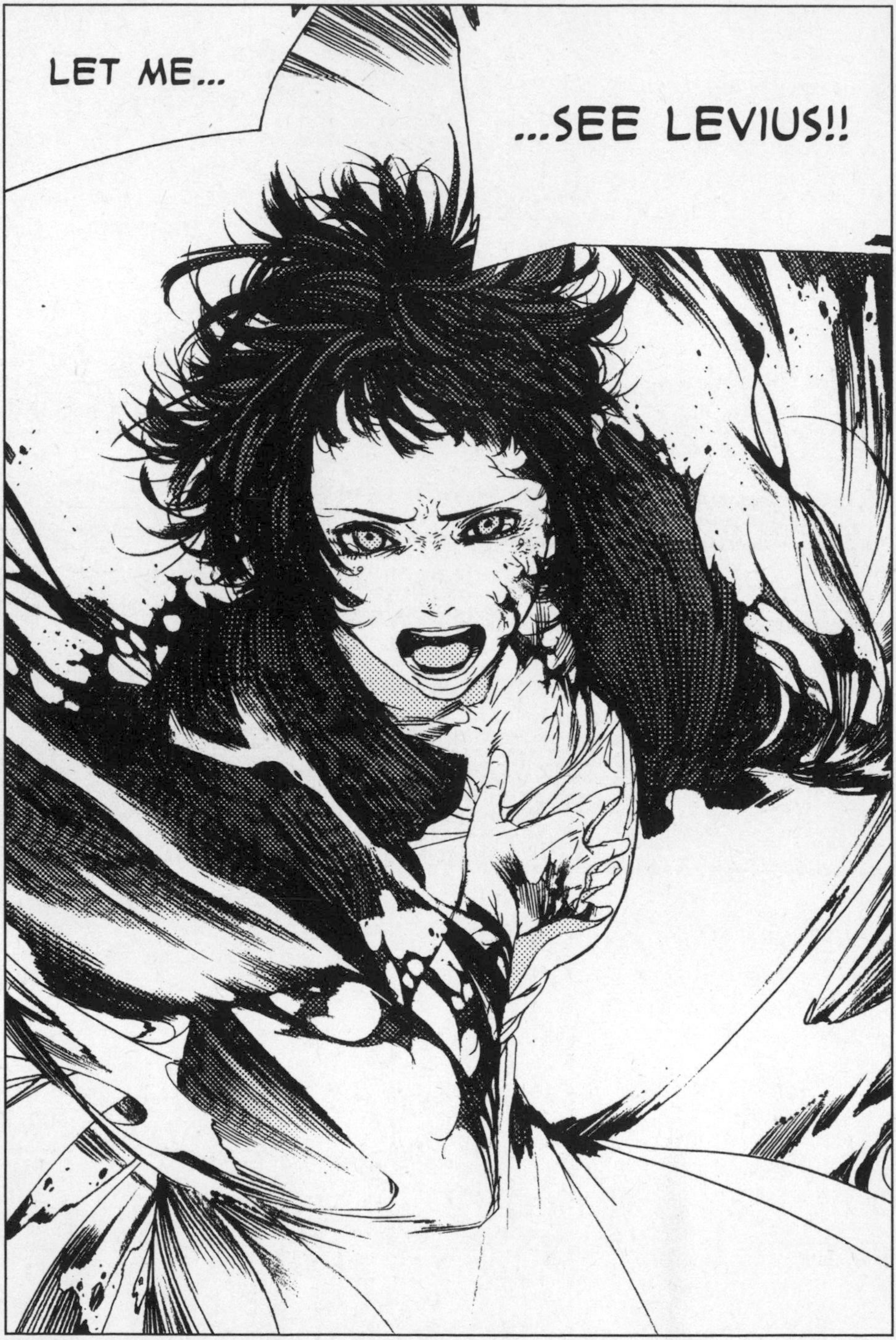
LET ME...
...SEE LEVIUS!!

Levius/est
VOL. 1

Chapter 03

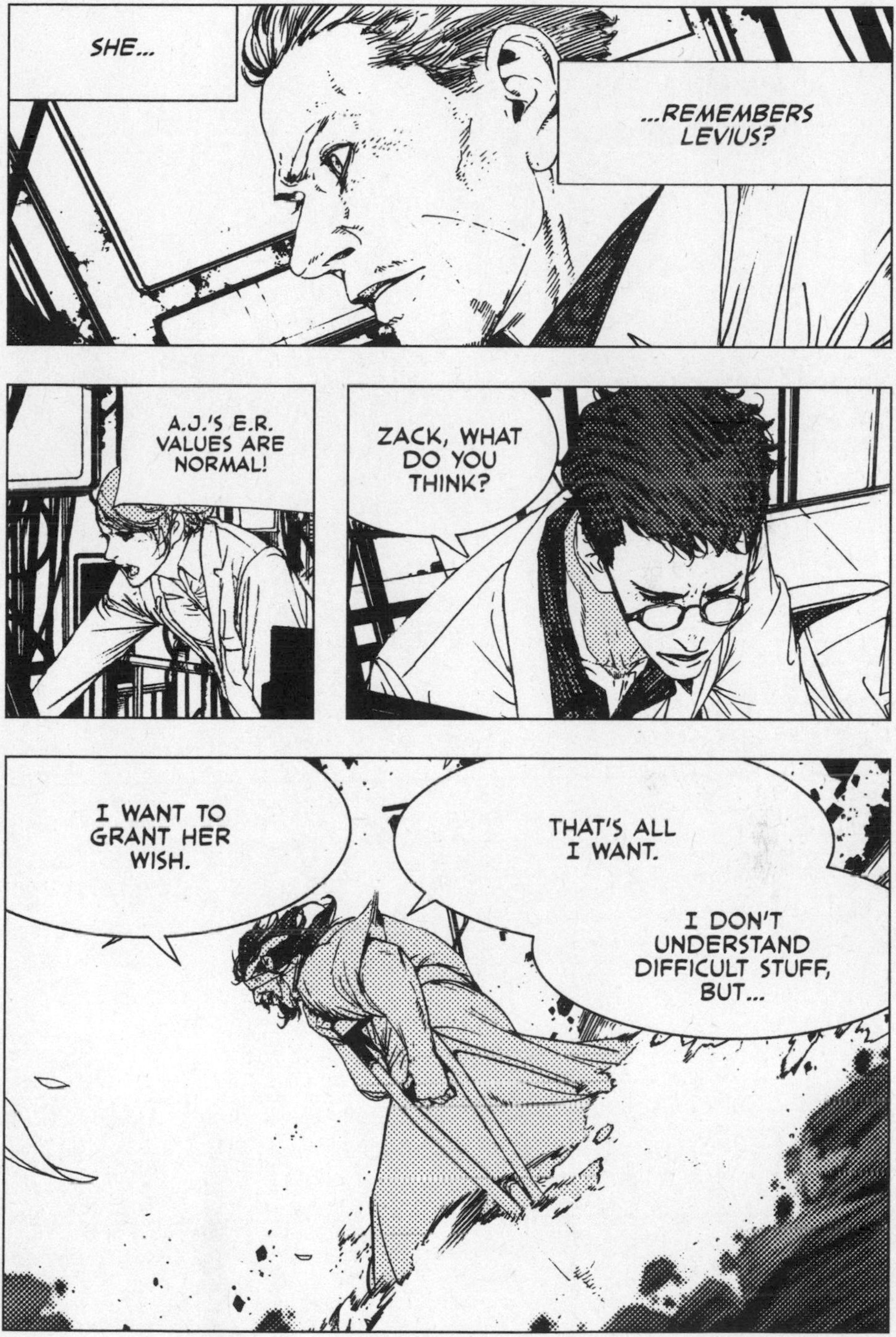
SHE...
...REMEMBERS LEVIUS?
A.J.'S E.R. VALUES ARE NORMAL!
ZACK, WHAT DO YOU THINK?
I WANT TO GRANT HER WISH.
THAT'S ALL I WANT.
I DON'T UNDERSTAND DIFFICULT STUFF, BUT...

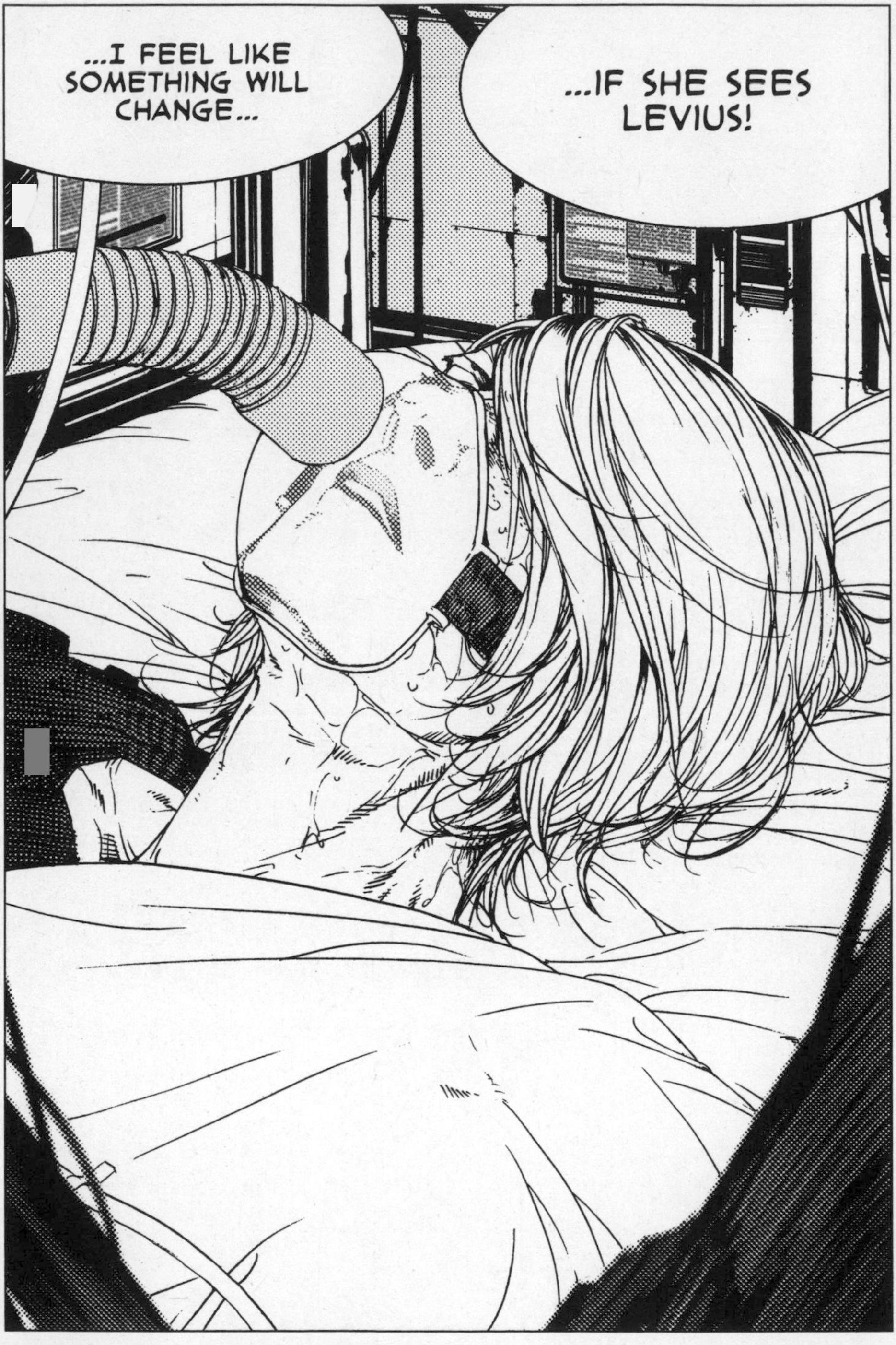
...IF SHE SEES LEVIUS!
...I FEEL LIKE SOMETHING WILL CHANGE...

ALTERING THE ELEVATOR ROUTE...

...TO HEAD FOR THE OPERATING ROOM ON FLOOR 22!

"AN ENGINEER WHO CAN'T TAKE LIVES CAN'T **SAVE** LIVES."

YOU WERE A FAMOUS ENGINEER IN THE EUROPEAN WAR WHEN YOU SAID THAT.

WHERE IS THAT MAN NOW, BILL WEINBERG?

PASSING FLOOR 10! ARRIVING SHORTLY!

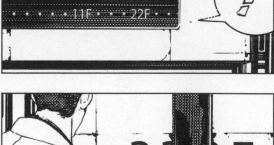

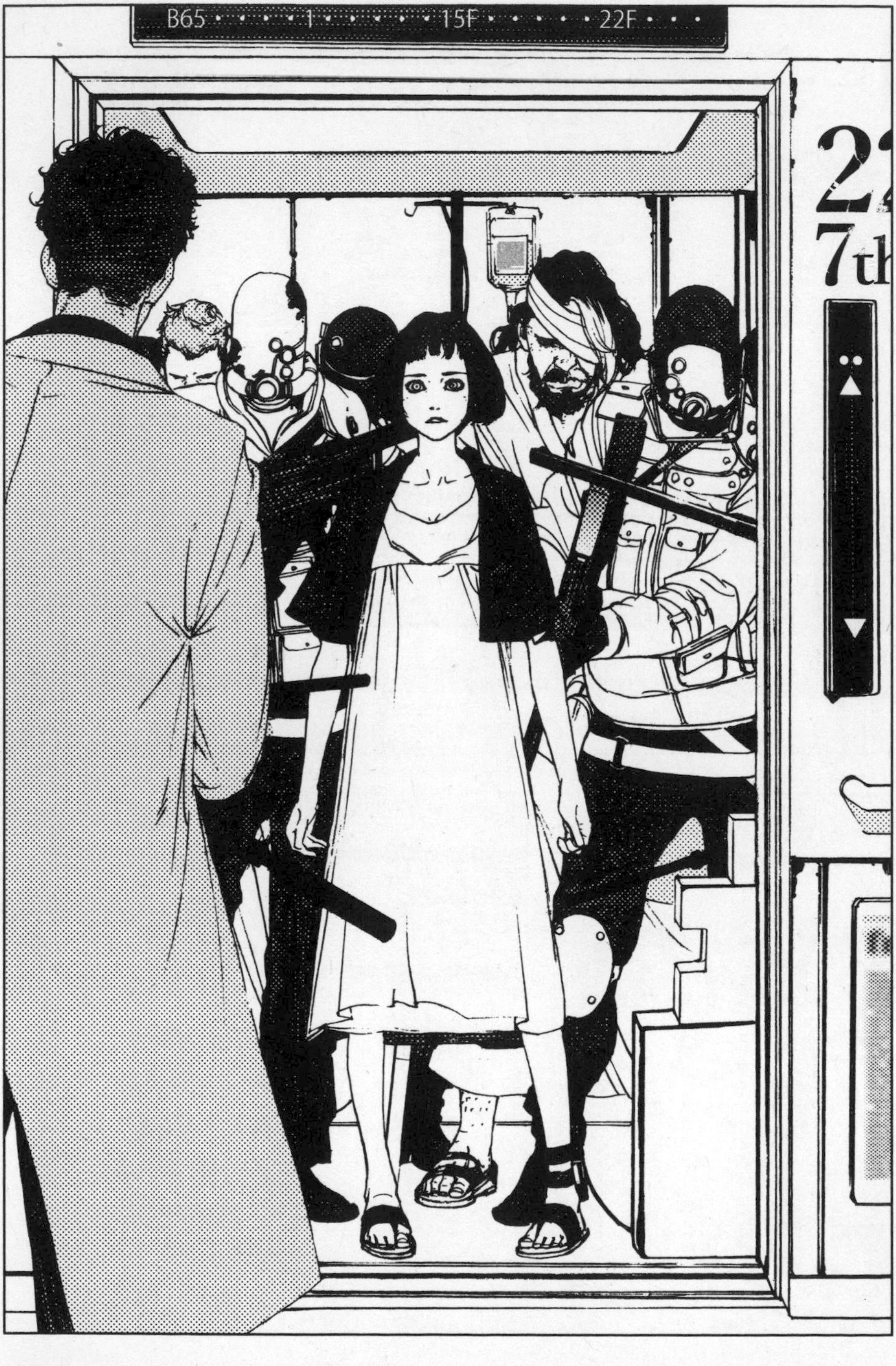
B65 • • • • • 1 • • • • • • 15F • • • • • • 22F • • •
22
7th

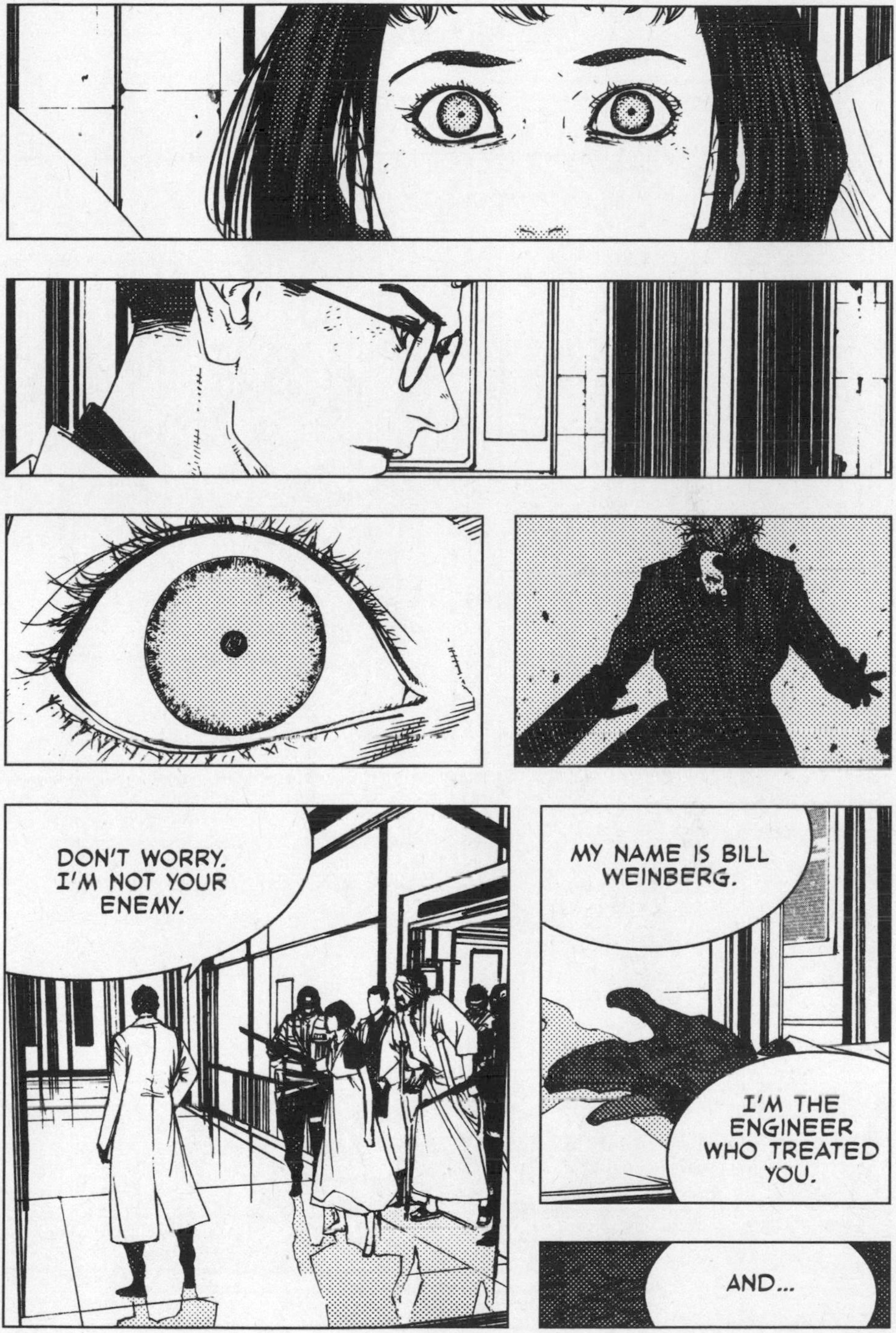
DON'T WORRY. I'M NOT YOUR ENEMY.
MY NAME IS BILL WEINBERG.
I'M THE ENGINEER WHO TREATED YOU.
AND...

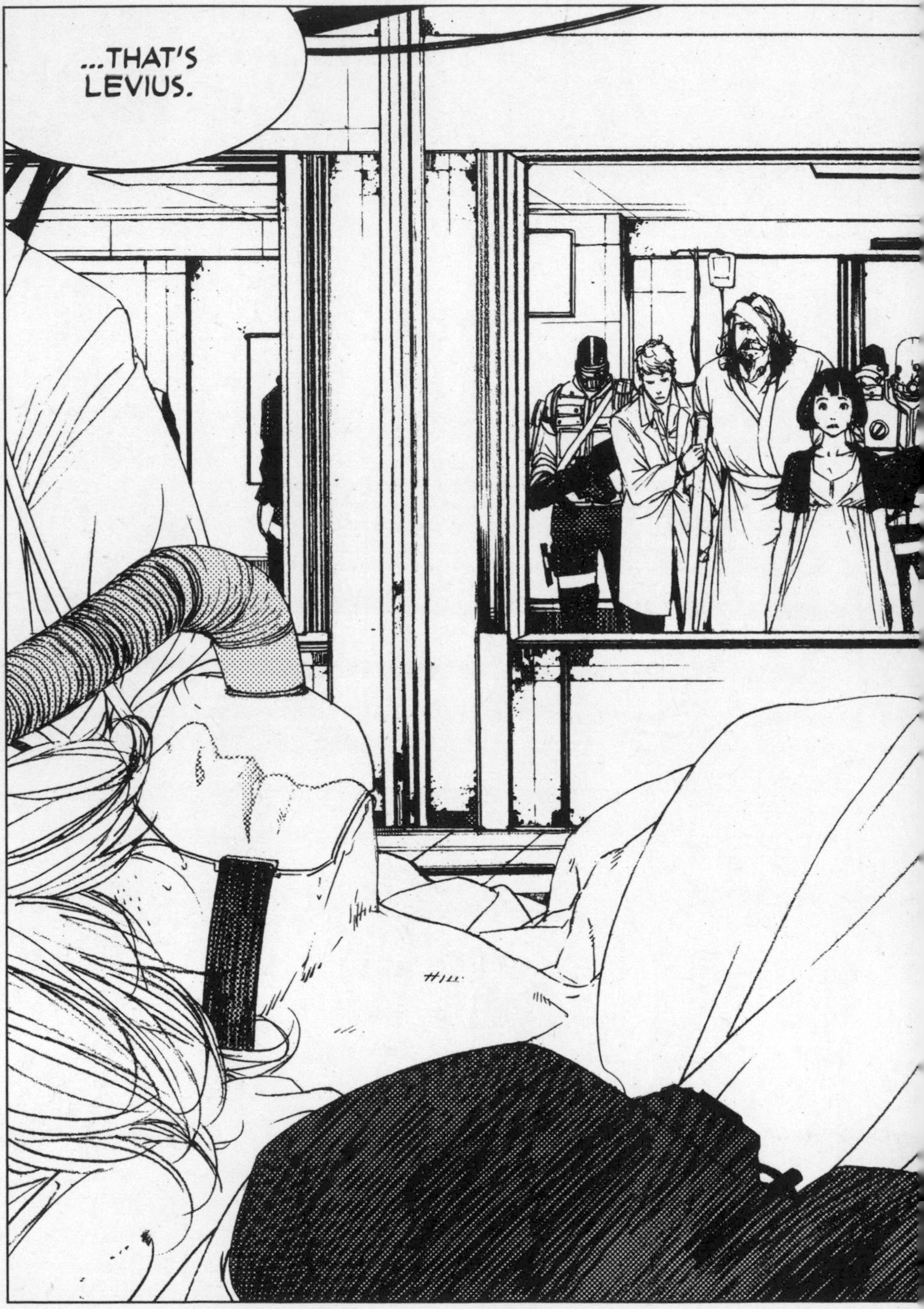
...THAT'S LEVIUS.

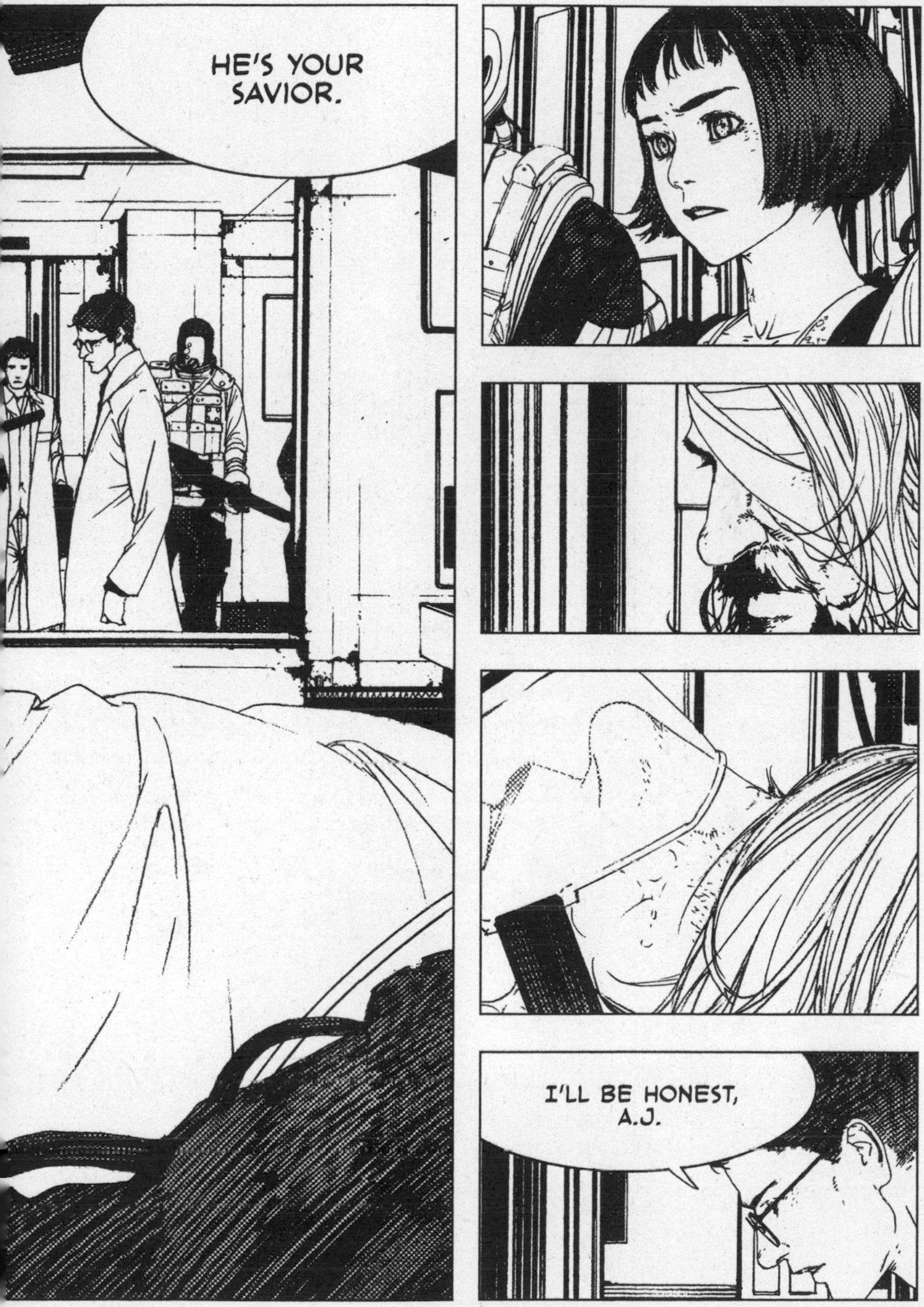
I'LL BE HONEST, A.J.
HE'S YOUR SAVIOR.

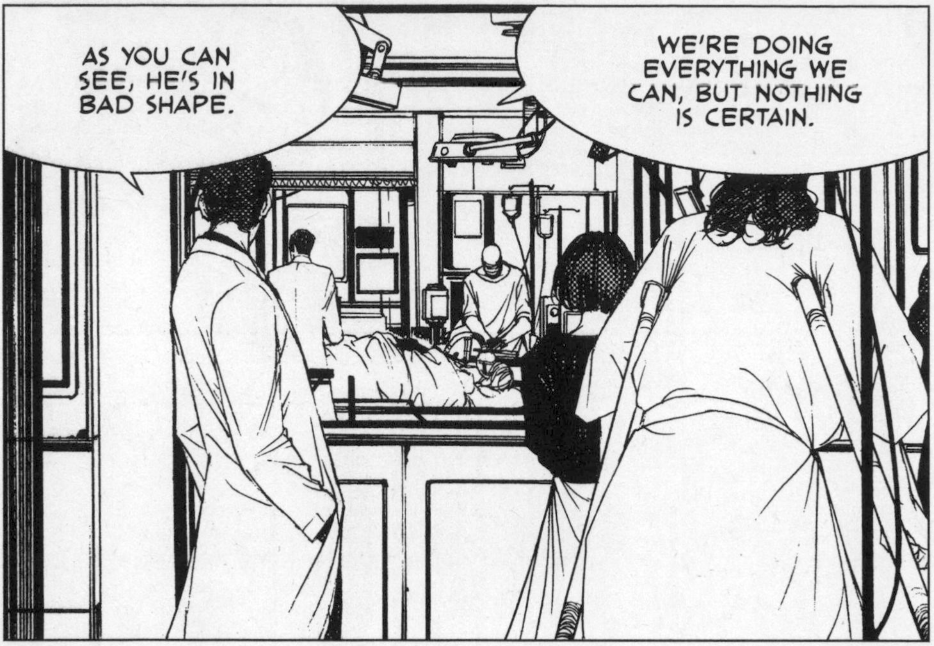
AS YOU CAN SEE, HE'S IN BAD SHAPE.
WE'RE DOING EVERYTHING WE CAN, BUT NOTHING IS CERTAIN.
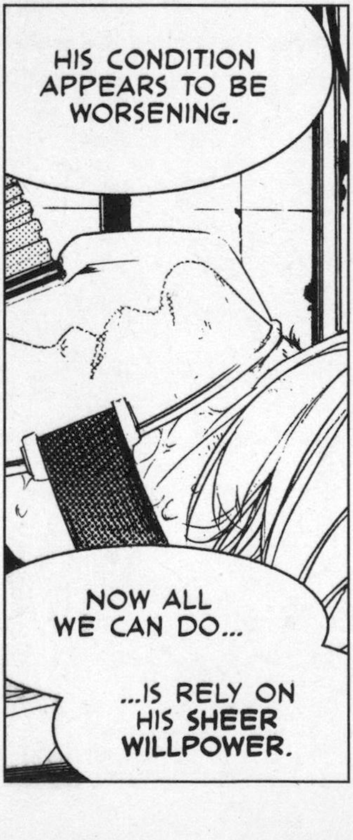
HIS CONDITION APPEARS TO BE WORSENING.
NOW ALL WE CAN DO...
...IS RELY ON HIS SHEER WILLPOWER.
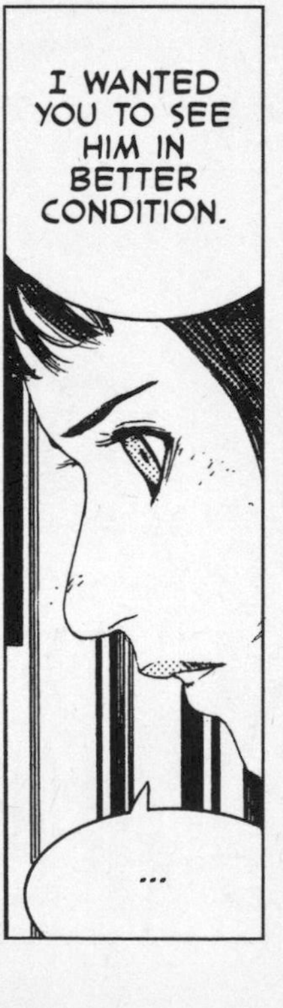
I WANTED YOU TO SEE HIM IN BETTER CONDITION.
...
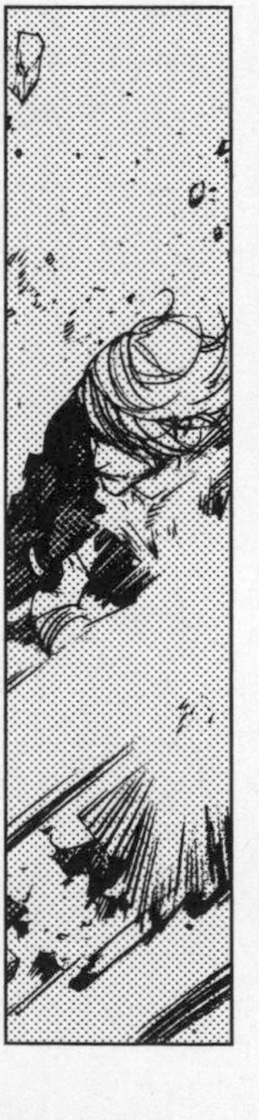
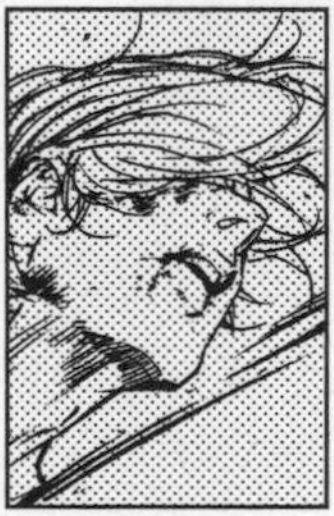
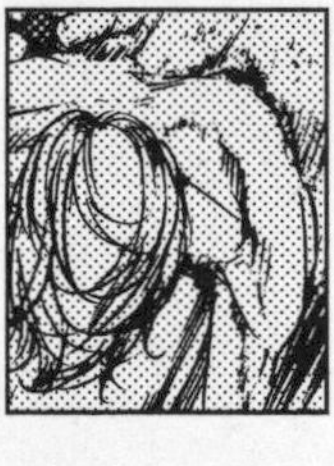
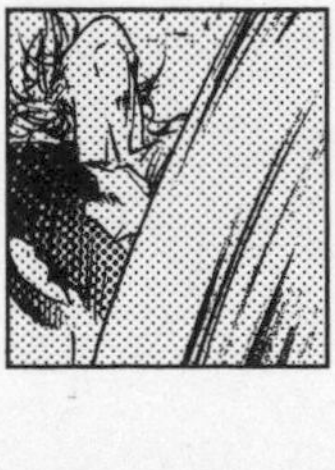

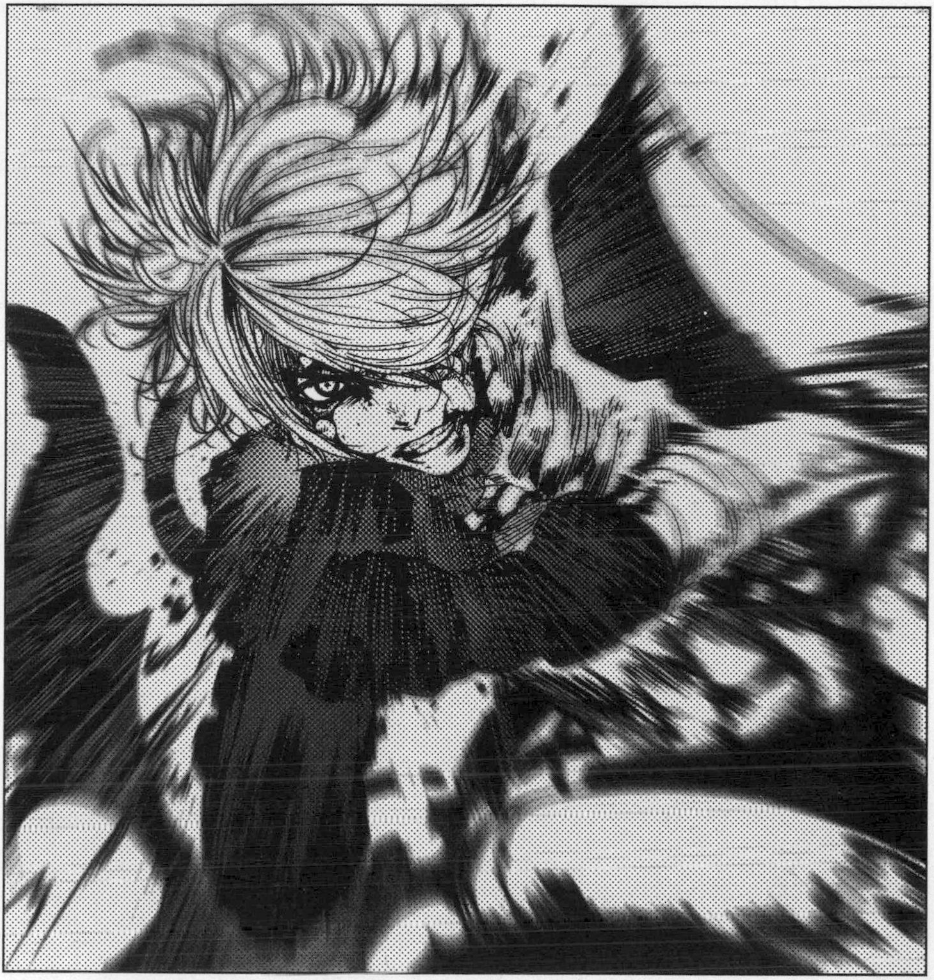
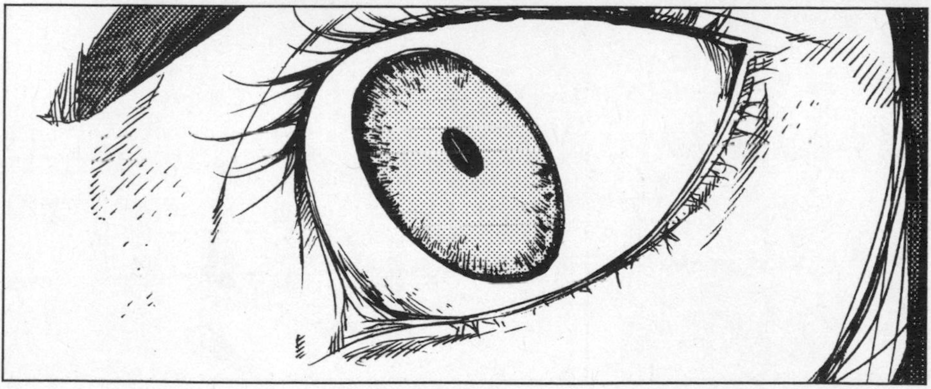

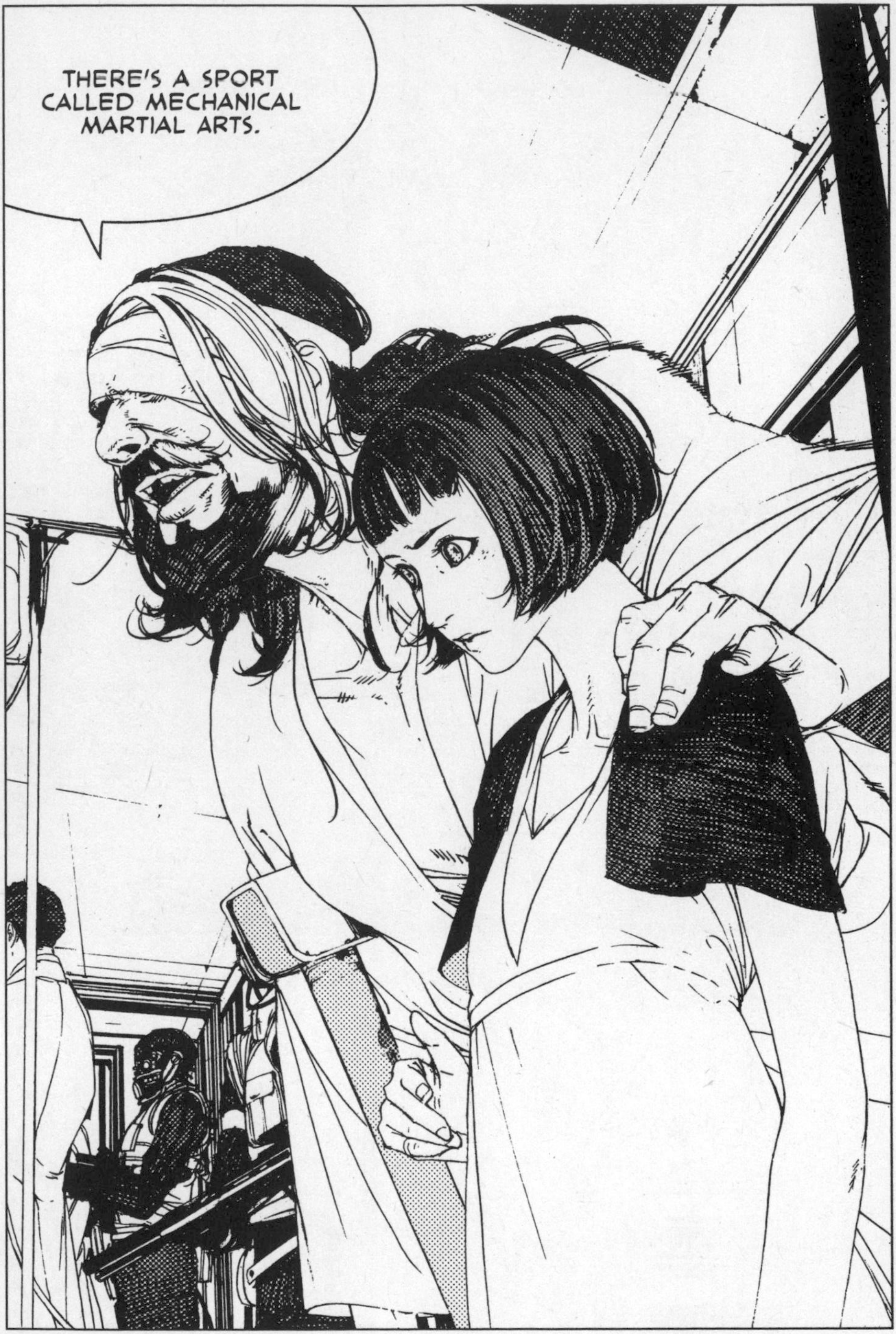
THERE'S A SPORT CALLED MECHANICAL MARTIAL ARTS.

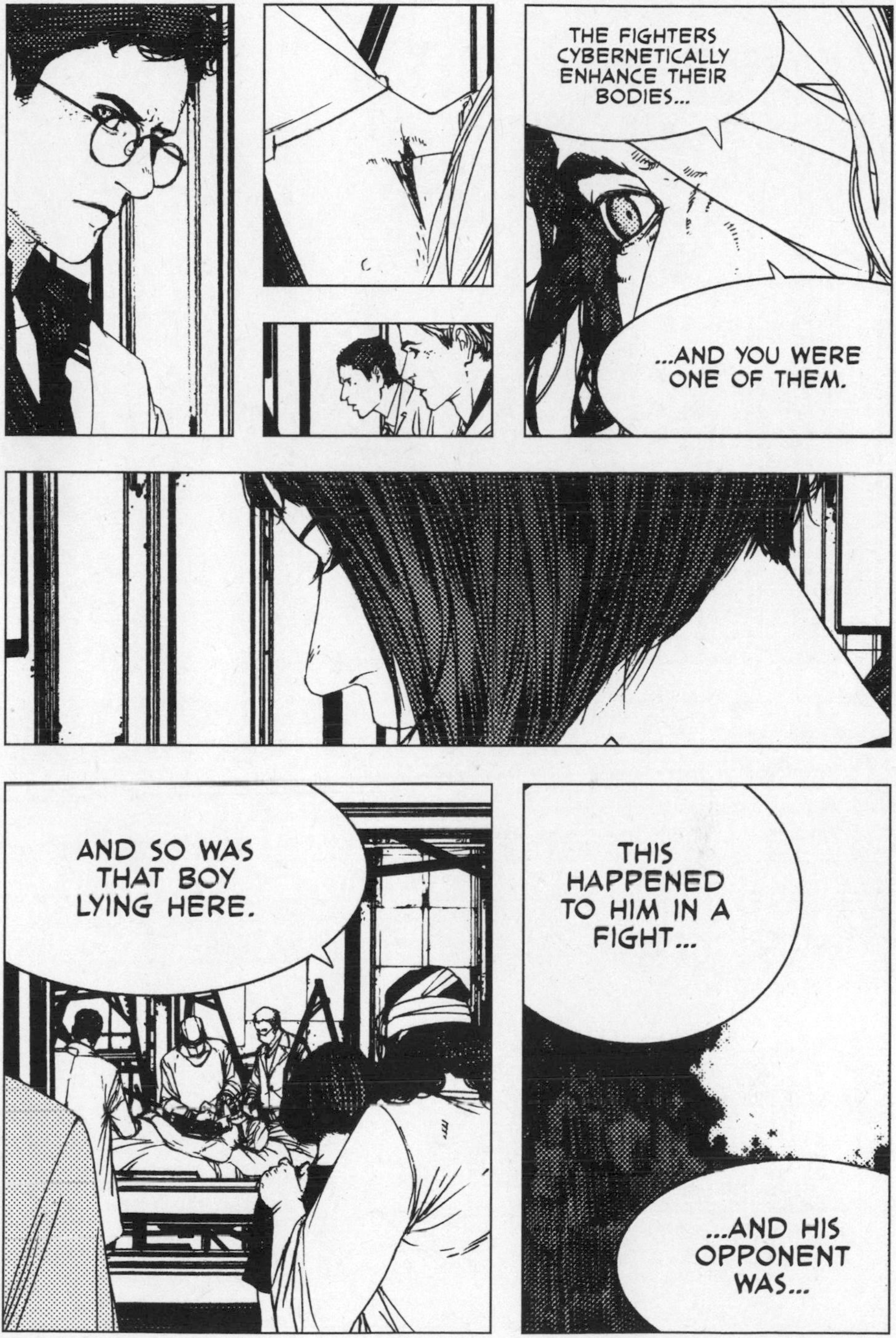
THE FIGHTERS CYBERNETICALLY ENHANCE THEIR BODIES...
...AND YOU WERE ONE OF THEM.
AND SO WAS THAT BOY LYING HERE.
THIS HAPPENED TO HIM IN A FIGHT...
...AND HIS OPPONENT WAS...

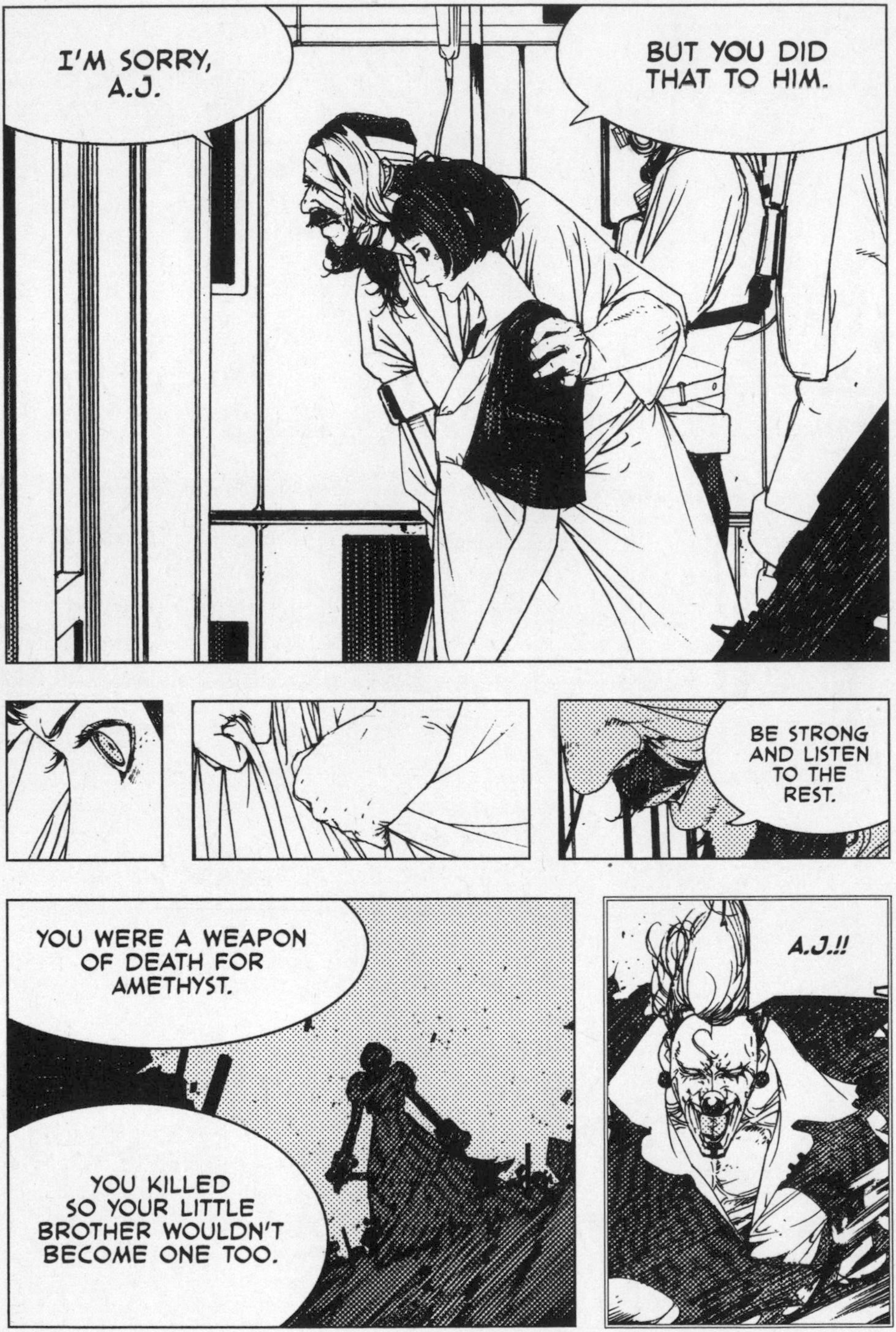
I'M SORRY, A.J.
BUT YOU DID THAT TO HIM.
BE STRONG AND LISTEN TO THE REST.
YOU WERE A WEAPON OF DEATH FOR AMETHYST.
YOU KILLED SO YOUR LITTLE BROTHER WOULDN'T BECOME ONE TOO.
A.J.!!

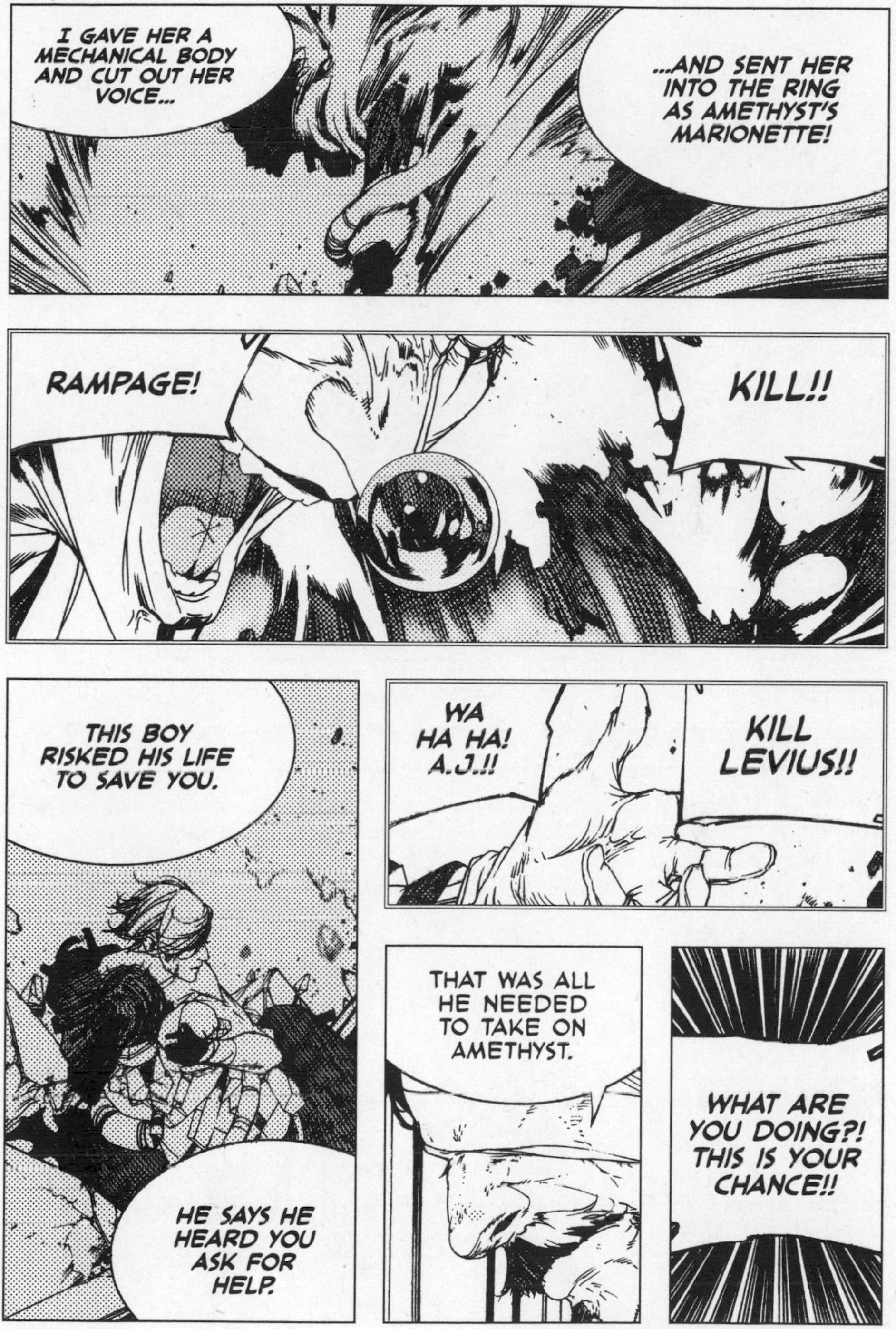
I GAVE HER A MECHANICAL BODY AND CUT OUT HER VOICE...
...AND SENT HER INTO THE RING AS AMETHYST'S MARIONETTE!
RAMPAGE!
KILL!!
THIS BOY RISKED HIS LIFE TO SAVE YOU.
HE SAYS HE HEARD YOU ASK FOR HELP.
WA HA HA! A.J.!!
KILL LEVIUS!!
THAT WAS ALL HE NEEDED TO TAKE ON AMETHYST.
WHAT ARE YOU DOING?! THIS IS YOUR CHANCE!!

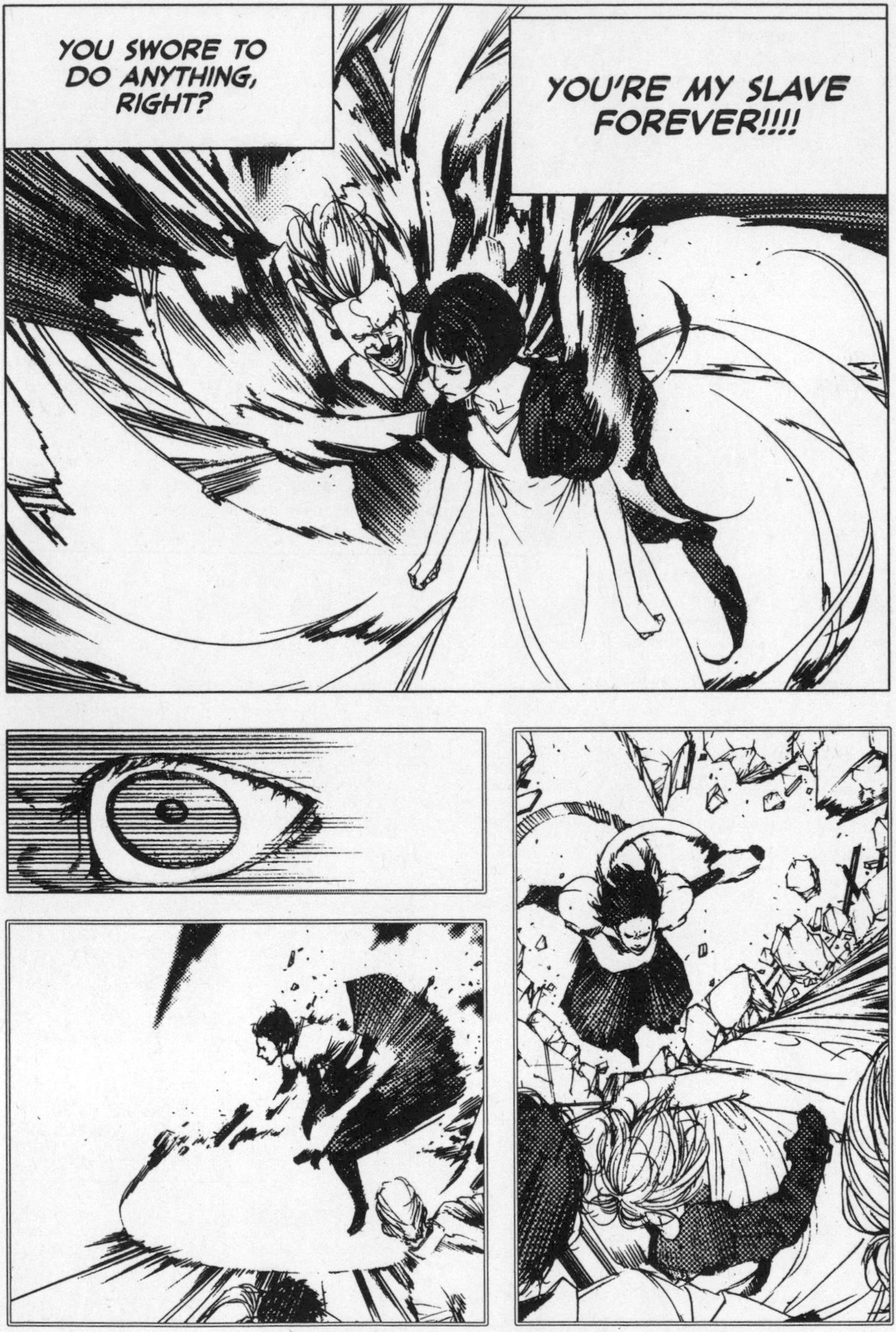
YOU'RE MY SLAVE FOREVER!!!!
YOU SWORE TO DO ANYTHING, RIGHT?

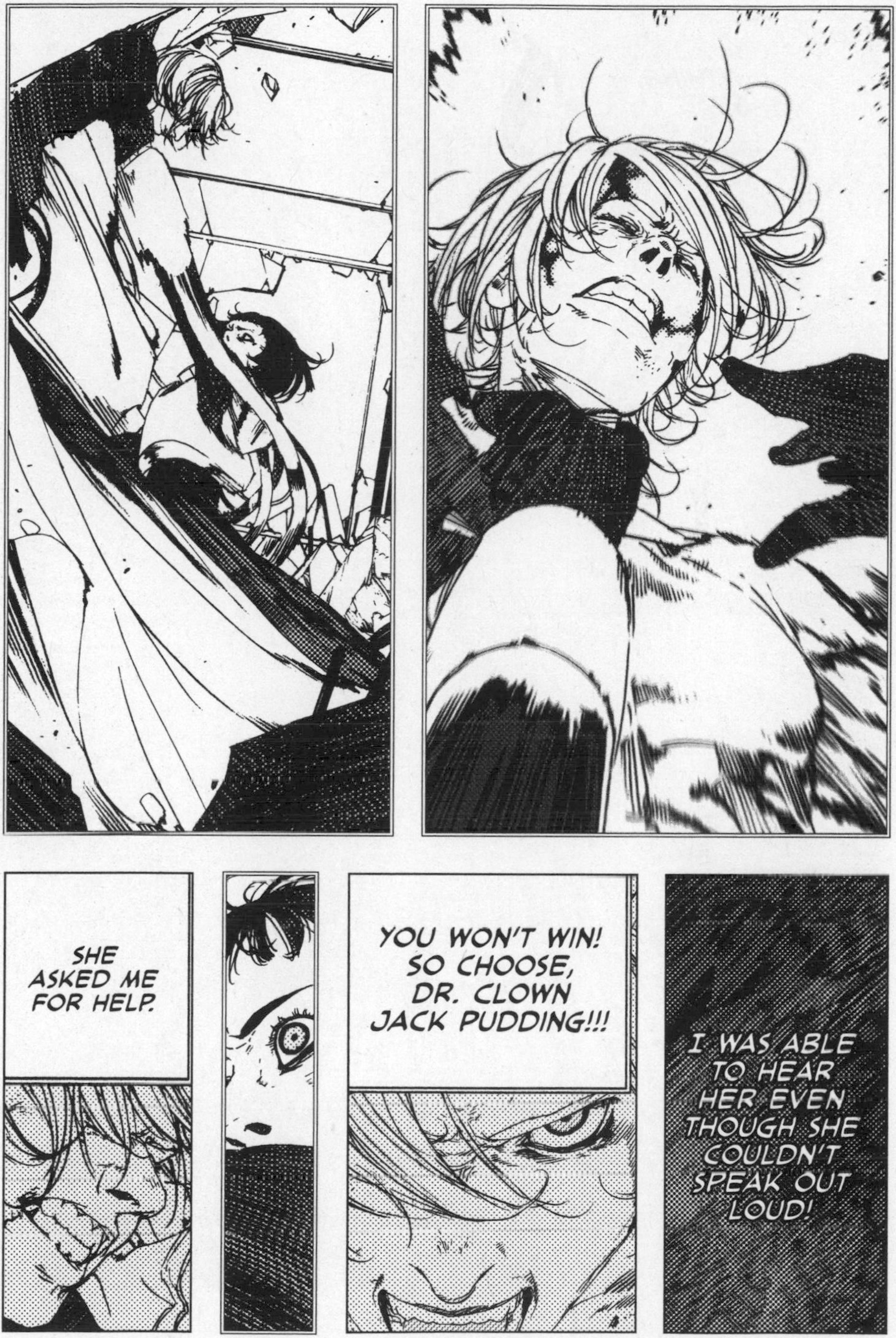
I WAS ABLE TO HEAR HER EVEN THOUGH SHE COULDN'T SPEAK OUT LOUD!
YOU WON'T WIN! SO CHOOSE, DR. CLOWN JACK PUDDING!!!
SHE ASKED ME FOR HELP.

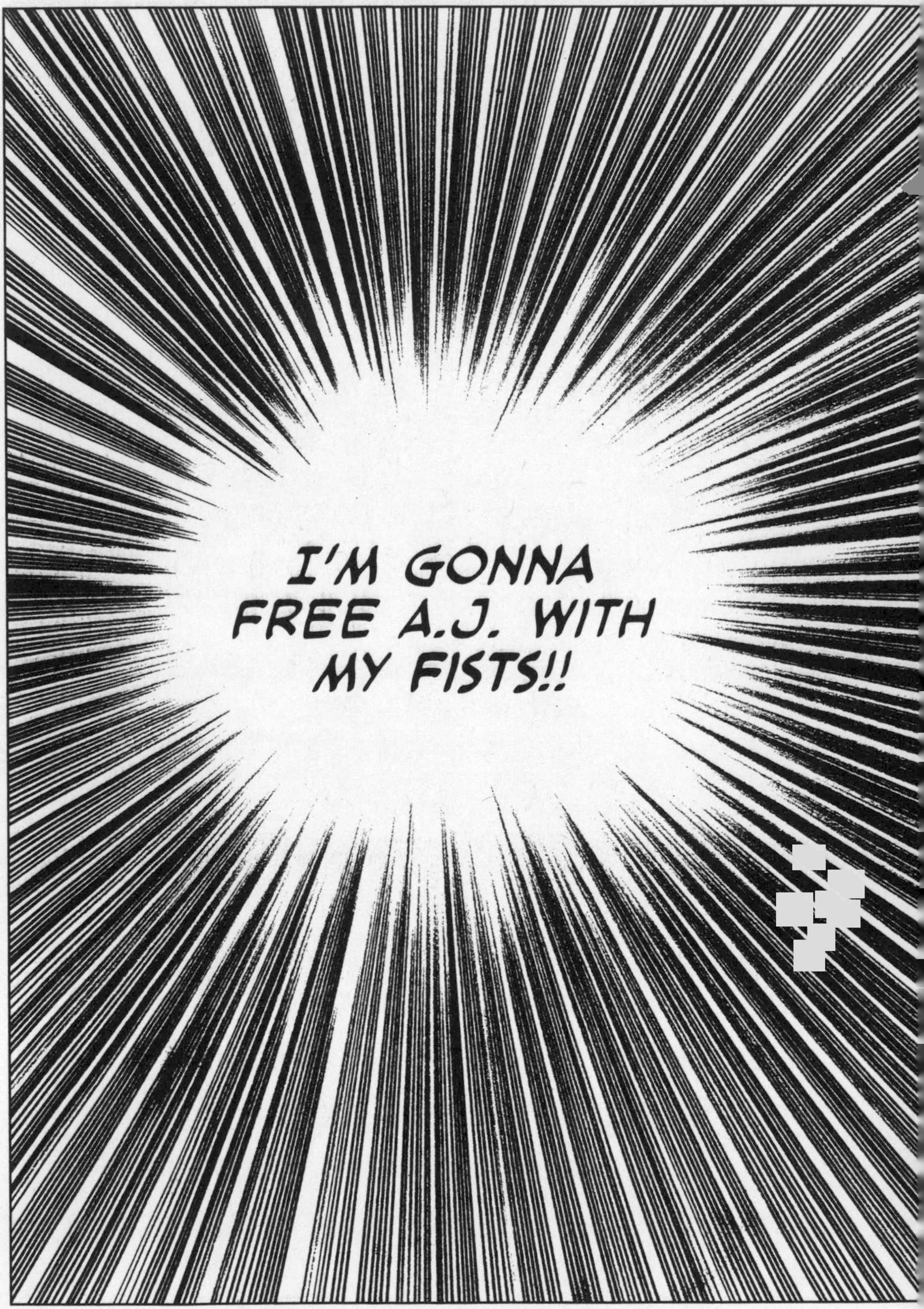
I'M GONNA FREE A.J. WITH MY FISTS!!

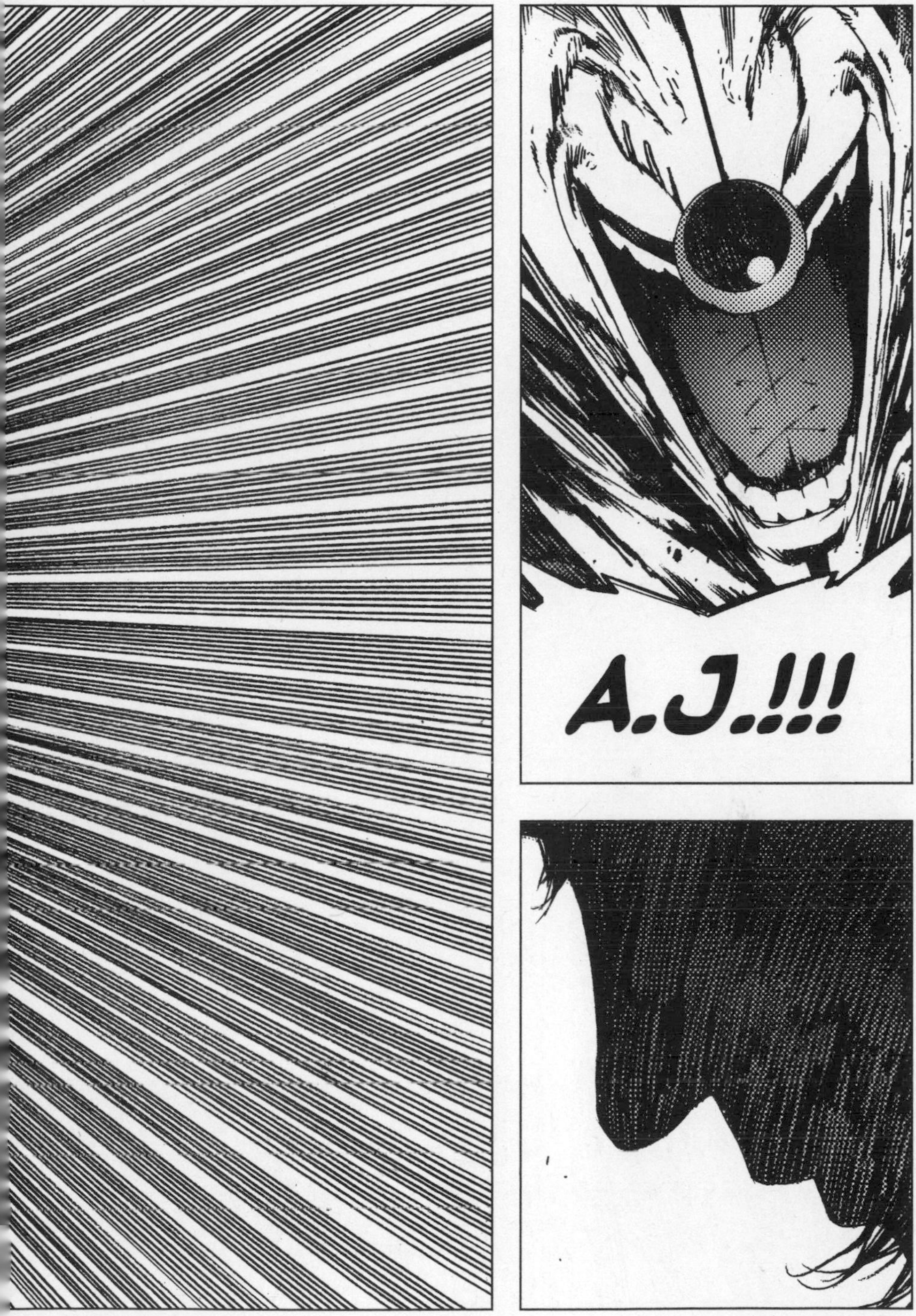
A.J..!!!

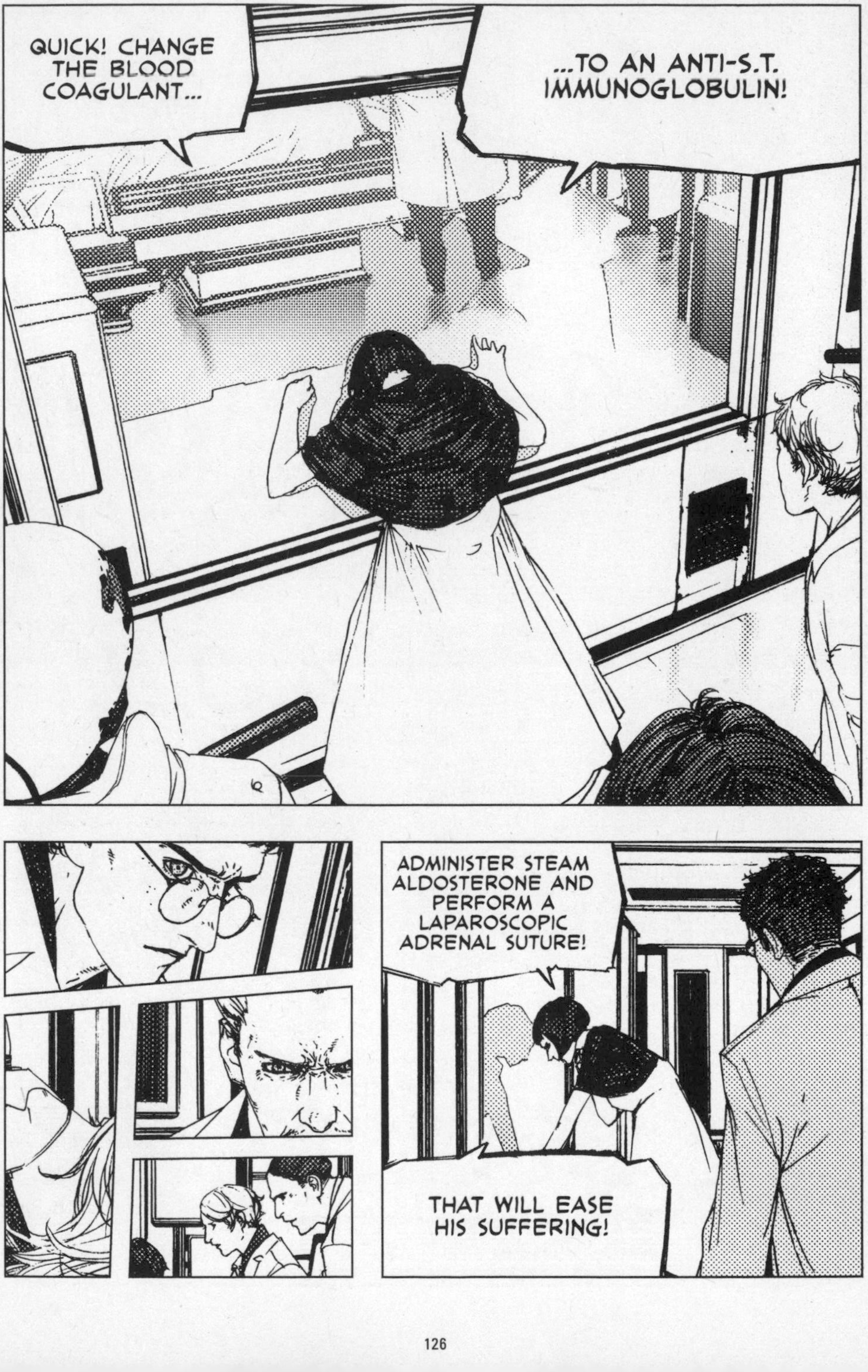
QUICK! CHANGE THE BLOOD COAGULANT...
...TO AN ANTI-S.T. IMMUNOGLOBULIN!
ADMINISTER STEAM ALDOSTERONE AND PERFORM A LAPAROSCOPIC ADRENAL SUTURE!
THAT WILL EASE HIS SUFFERING!

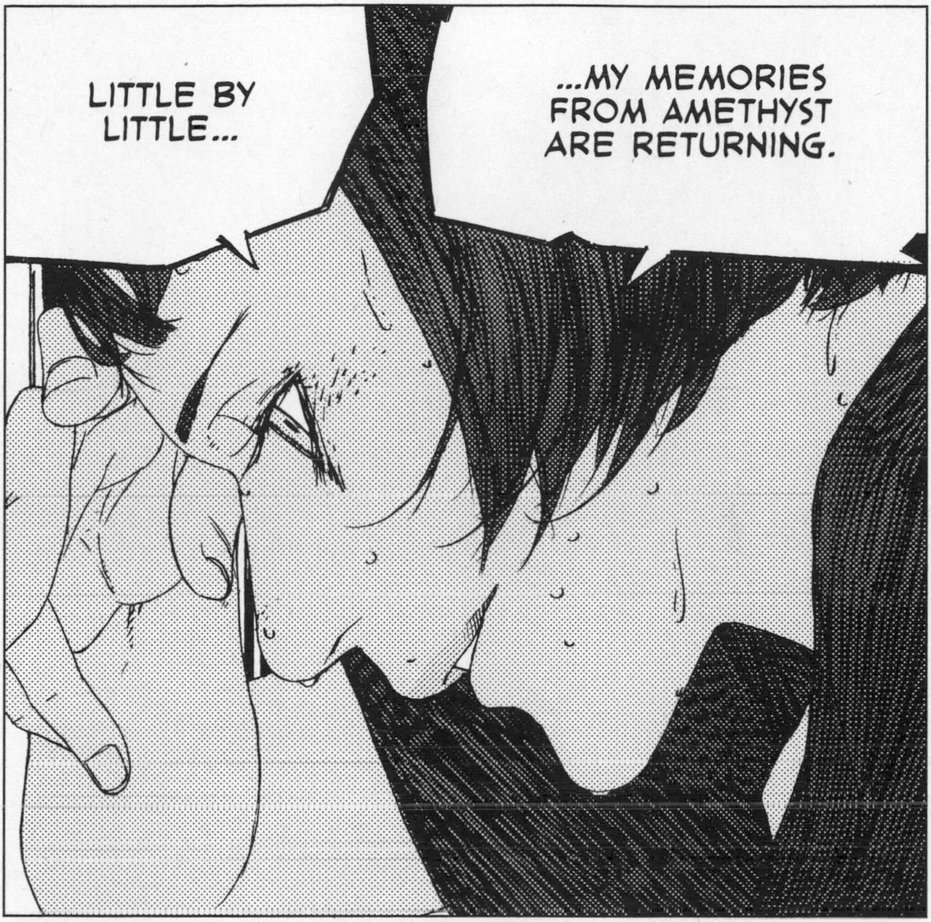
LITTLE BY LITTLE...
...MY MEMORIES FROM AMETHYST ARE RETURNING.
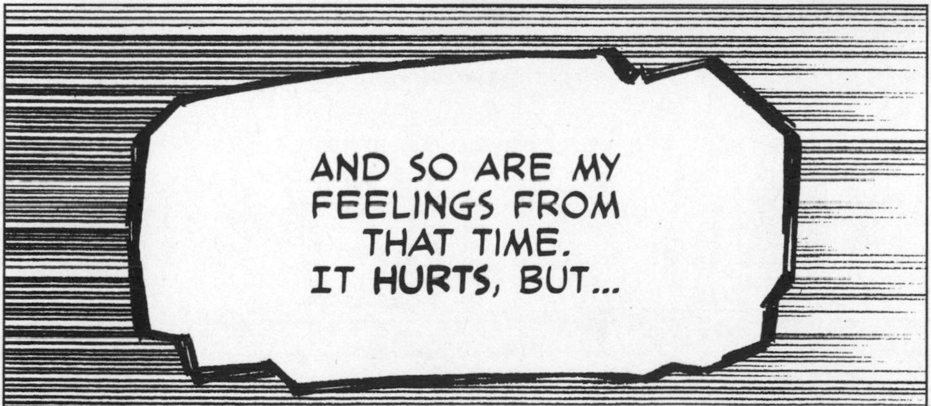
AND SO ARE MY FEELINGS FROM THAT TIME. IT HURTS, BUT...

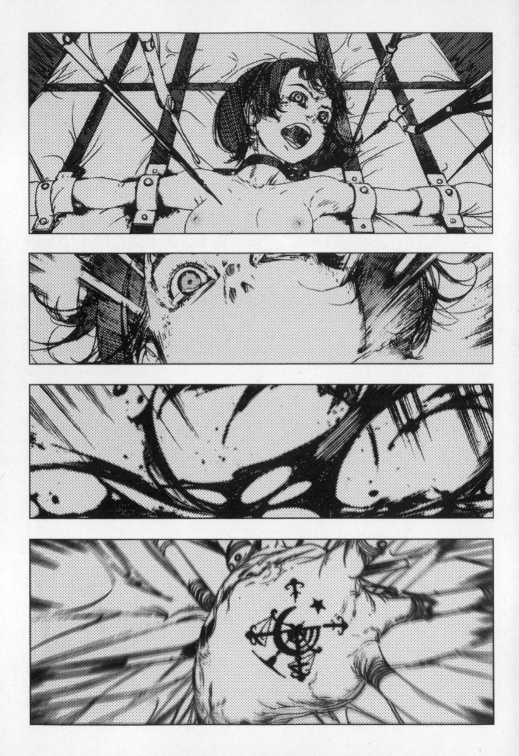

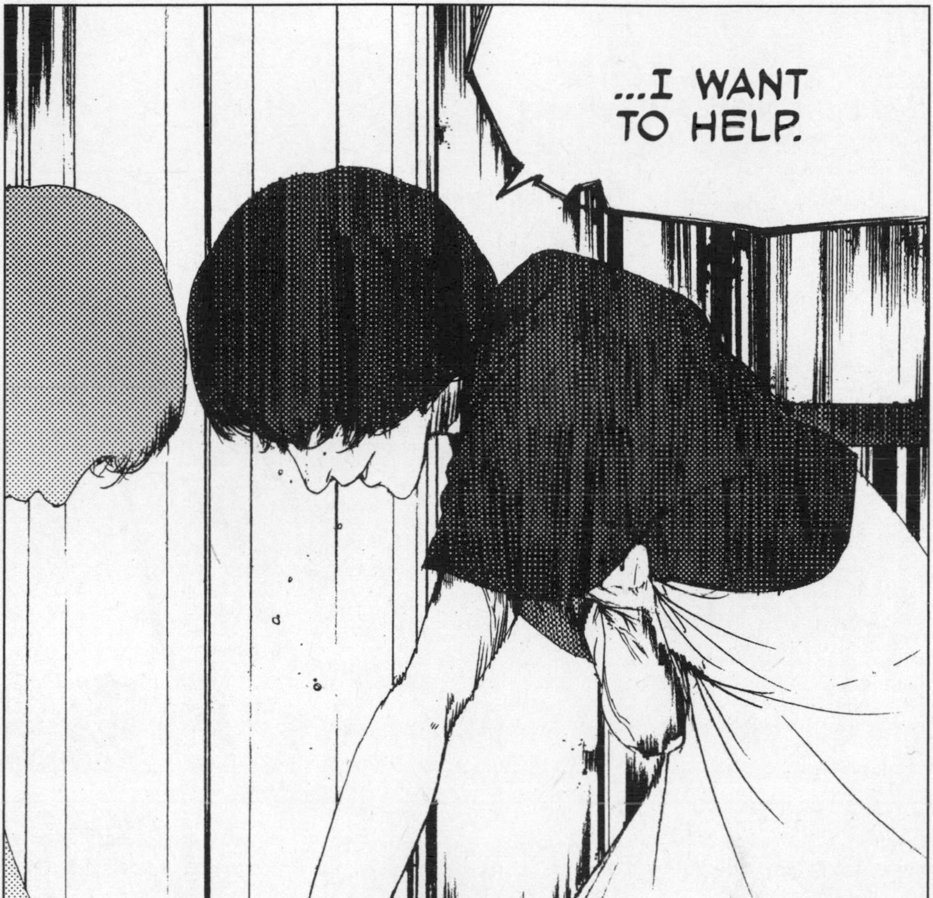
...I WANT TO HELP.
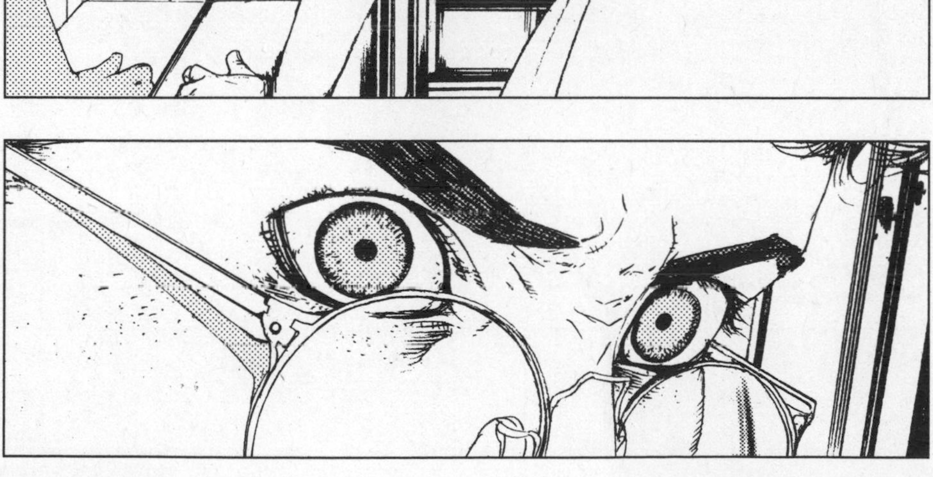

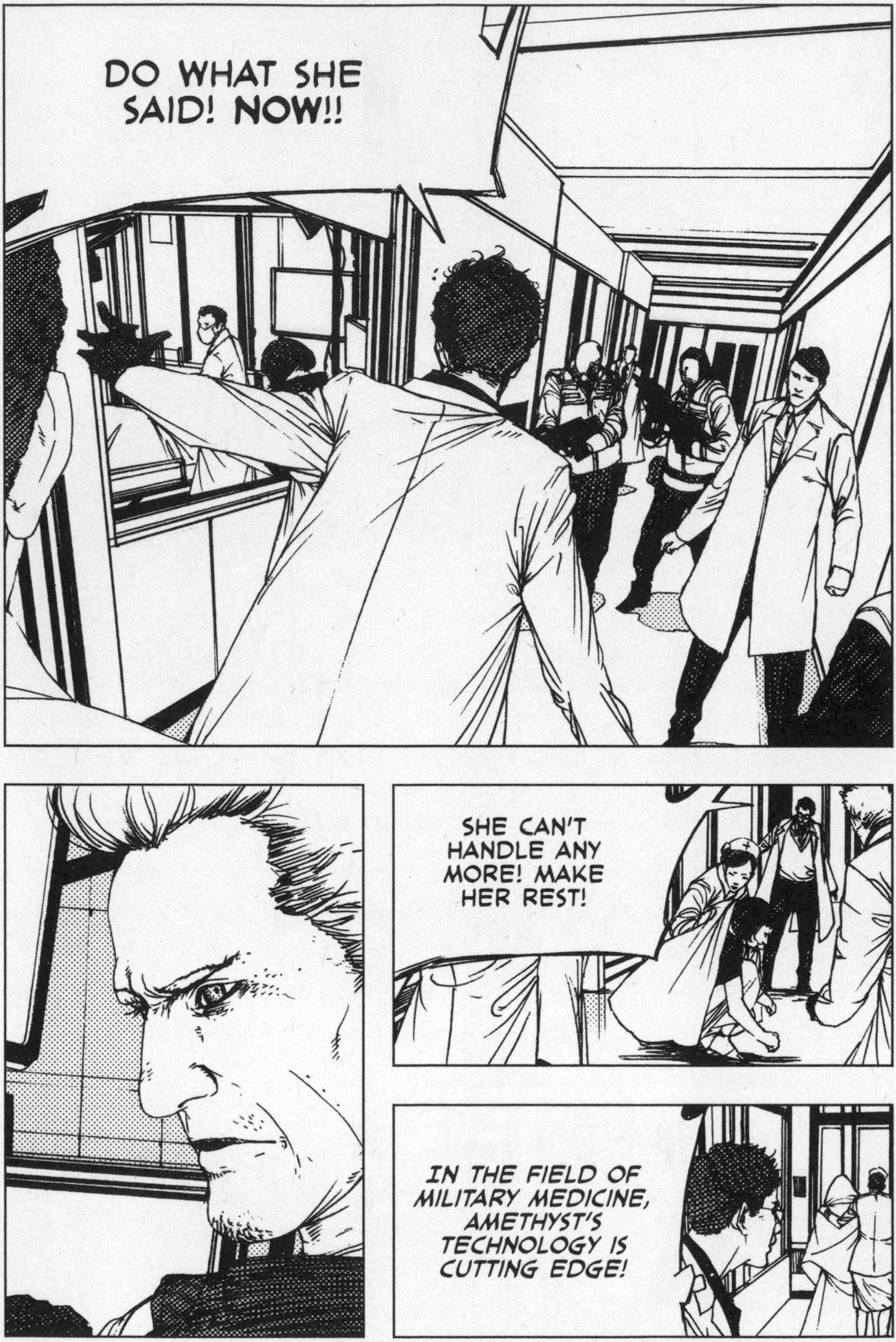
DO WHAT SHE SAID! NOW!!
SHE CAN'T HANDLE ANY MORE! MAKE HER REST!
IN THE FIELD OF MILITARY MEDICINE, AMETHYST'S TECHNOLOGY IS CUTTING EDGE!

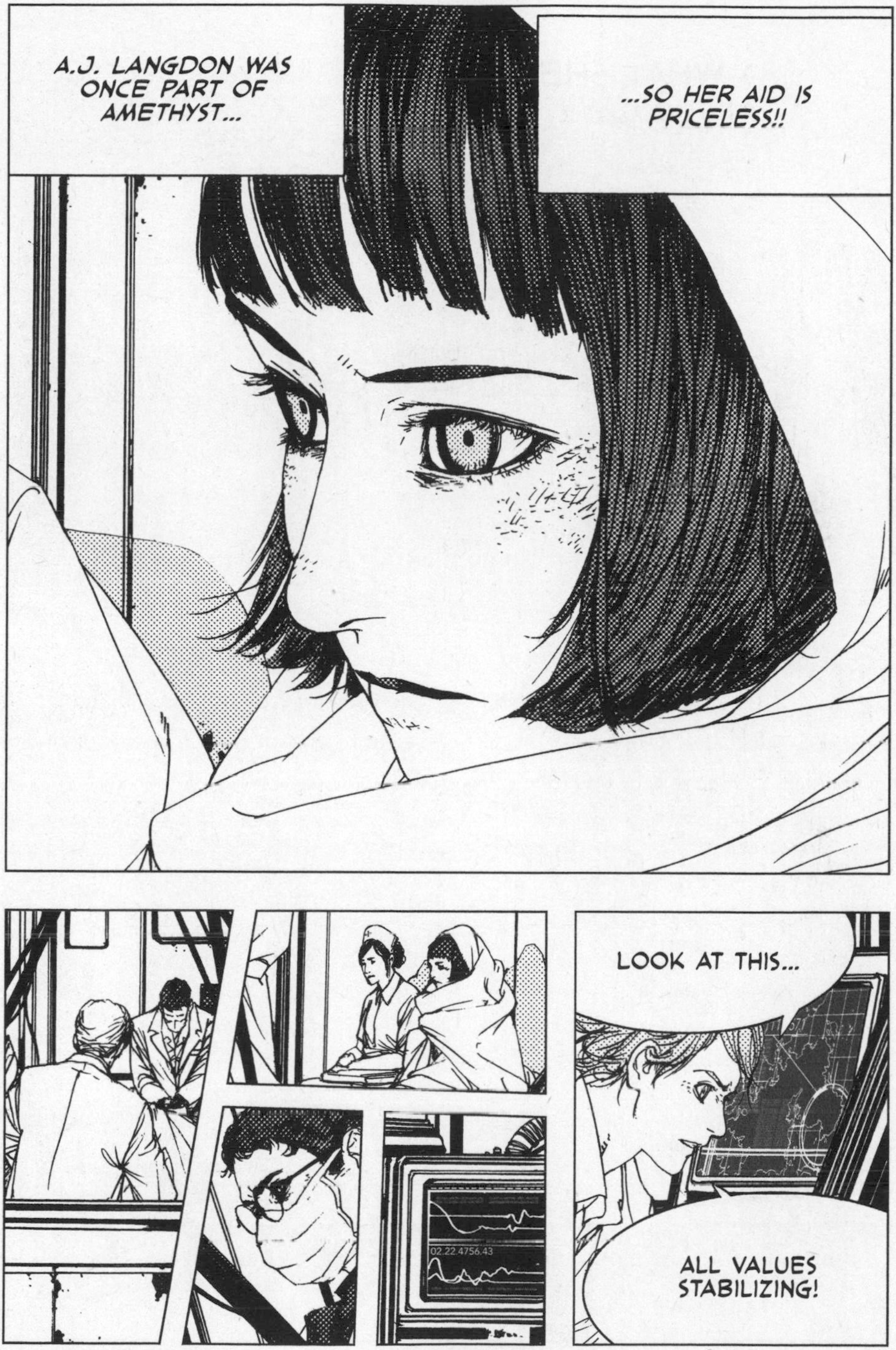
A.J. LANGDON WAS ONCE PART OF AMETHYST...
...SO HER AID IS PRICELESS!!
02.22.4756.43
LOOK AT THIS...
ALL VALUES STABILIZING!

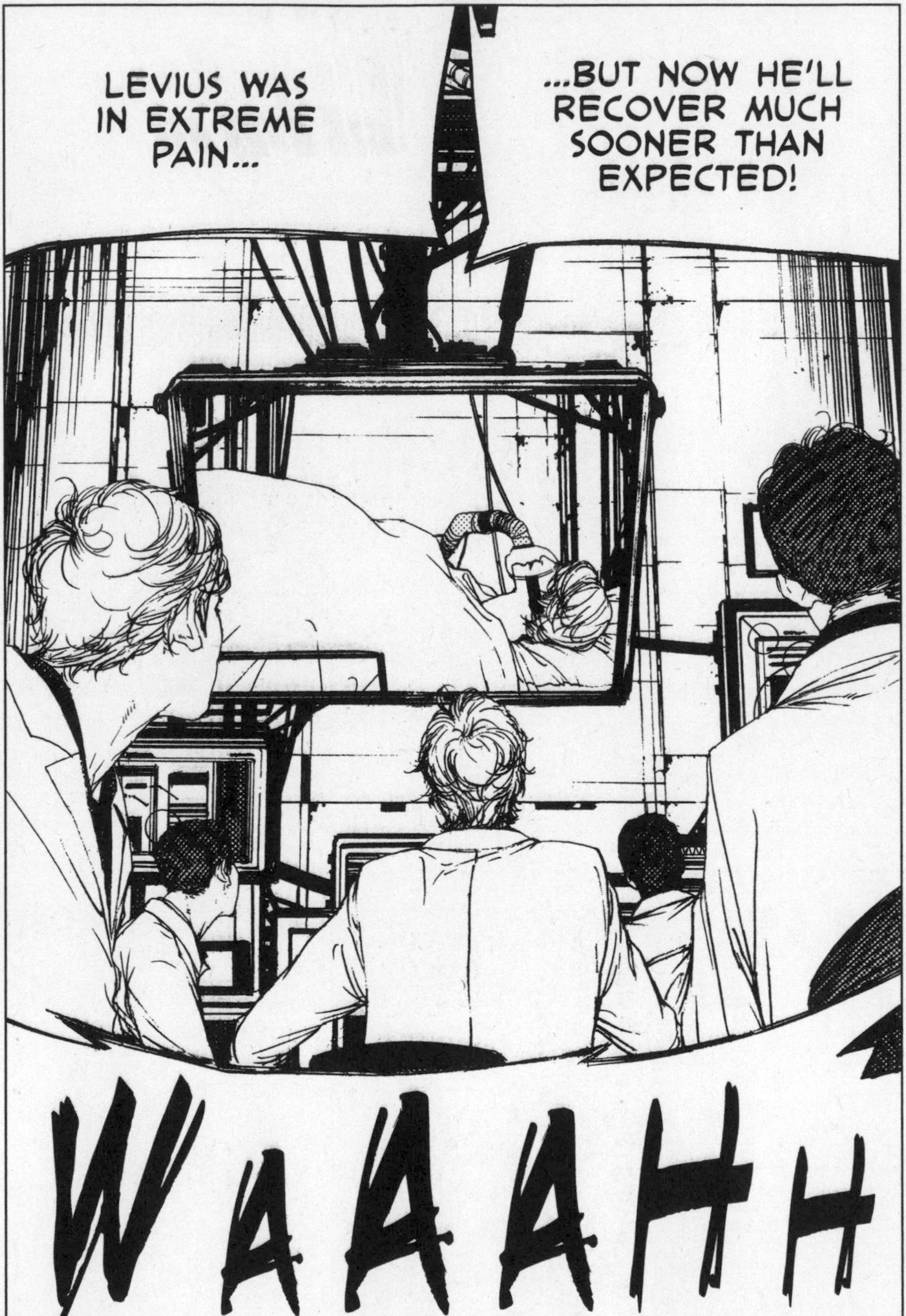
...BUT NOW HE'LL RECOVER MUCH SOONER THAN EXPECTED!
LEVIUS WAS IN EXTREME PAIN...
WAAAHH

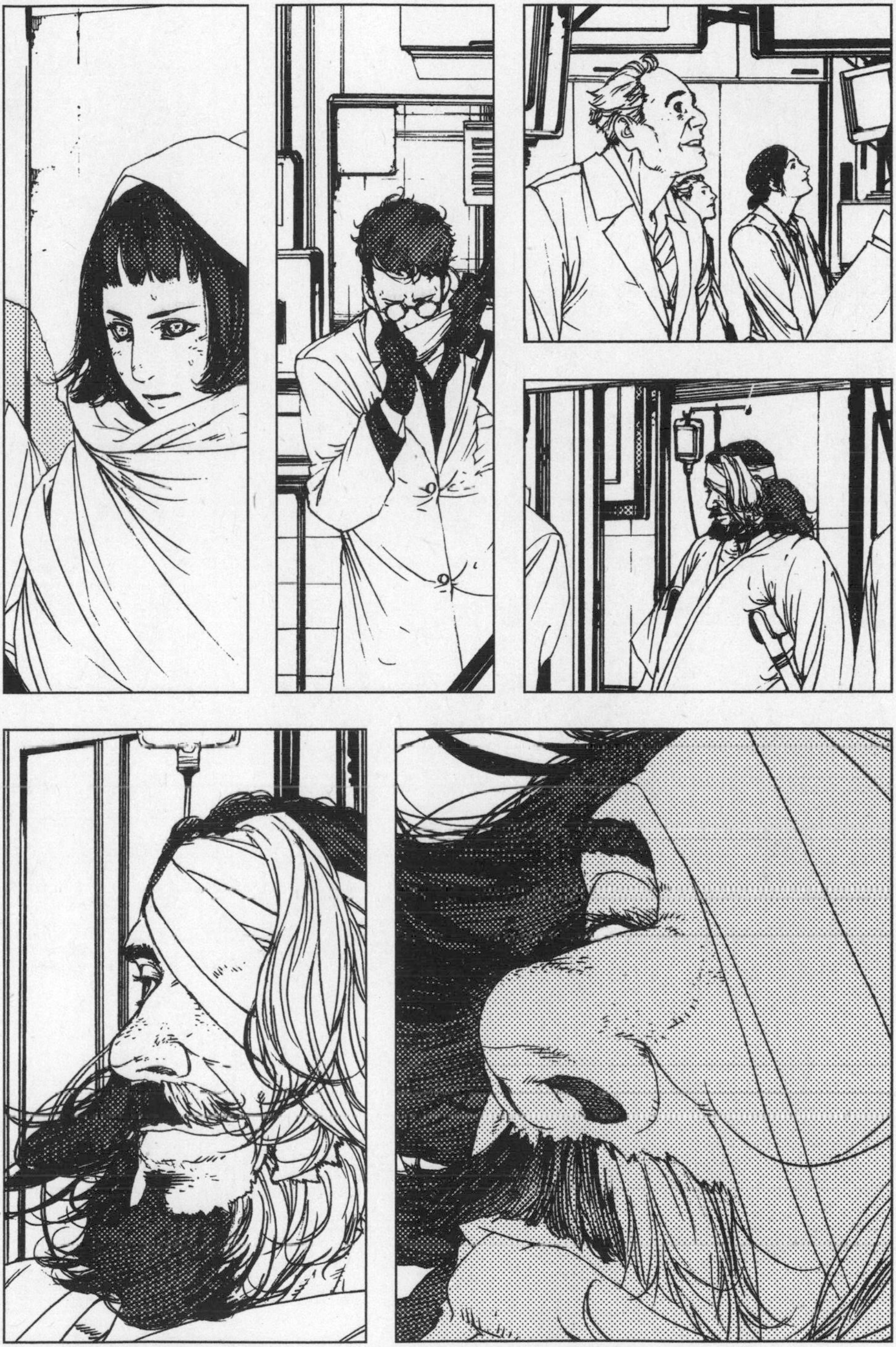

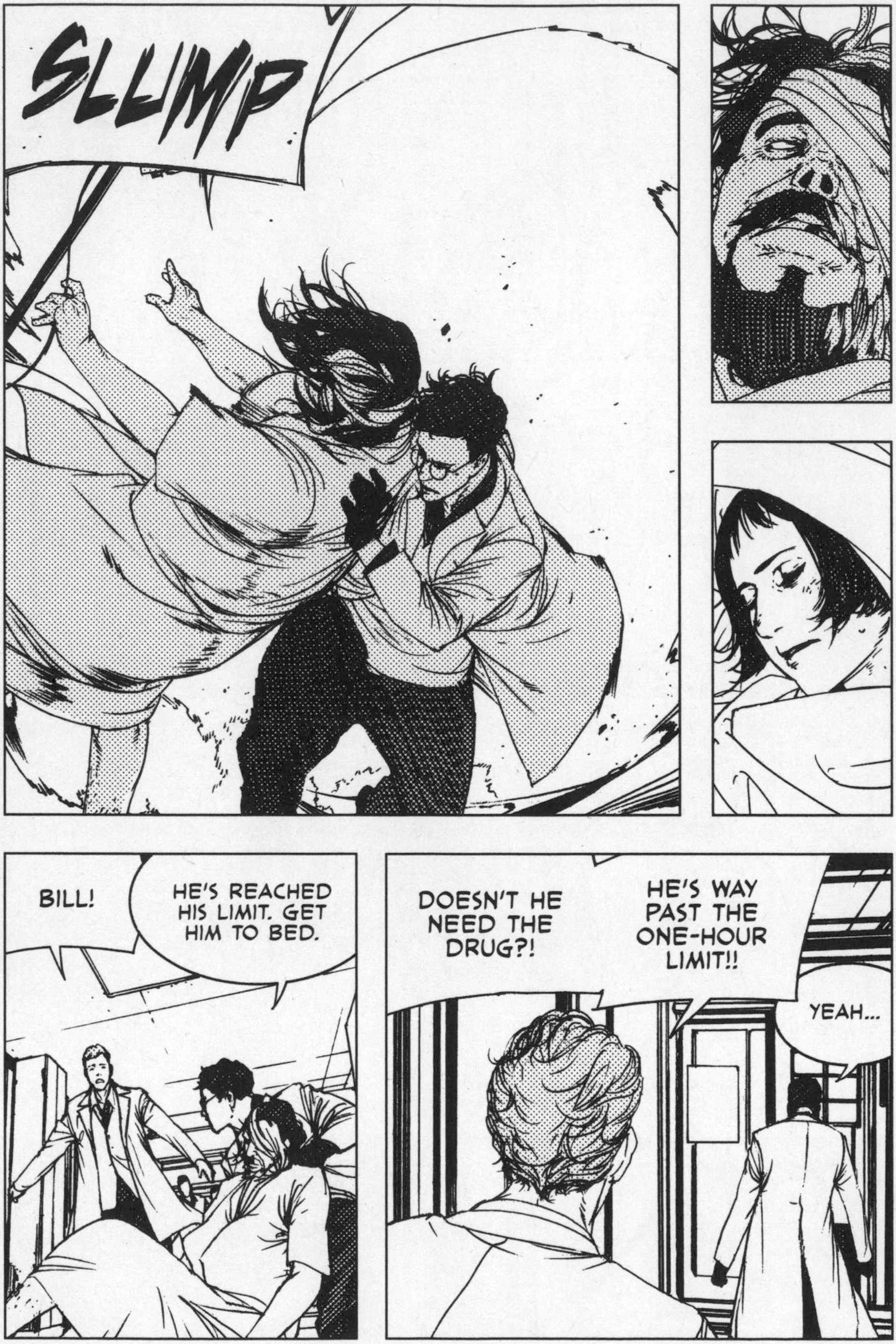
SLUMP
BILL!
HE'S REACHED HIS LIMIT. GET HIM TO BED.
DOESN'T HE NEED THE DRUG?!
HE'S WAY PAST THE ONE-HOUR LIMIT!!
YEAH...

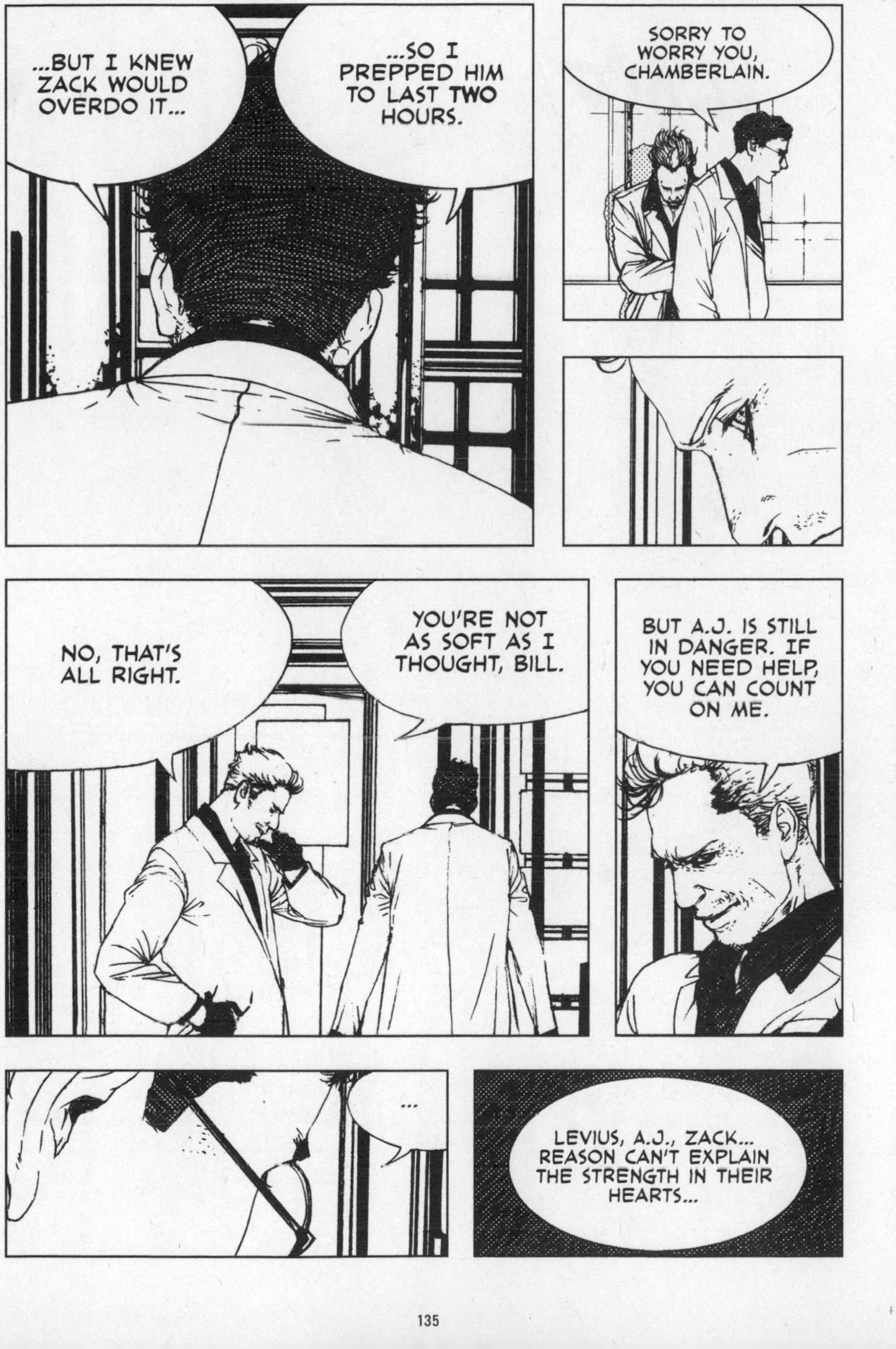
...BUT I KNEW ZACK WOULD OVERDO IT...
...SO I PREPPED HIM TO LAST TWO HOURS.
SORRY TO WORRY YOU, CHAMBERLAIN.
NO, THAT'S ALL RIGHT.
YOU'RE NOT AS SOFT AS I THOUGHT, BILL.
BUT A.J. IS STILL IN DANGER. IF YOU NEED HELP, YOU CAN COUNT ON ME.
...
LEVIUS, A.J., ZACK... REASON CAN'T EXPLAIN THE STRENGTH IN THEIR HEARTS...

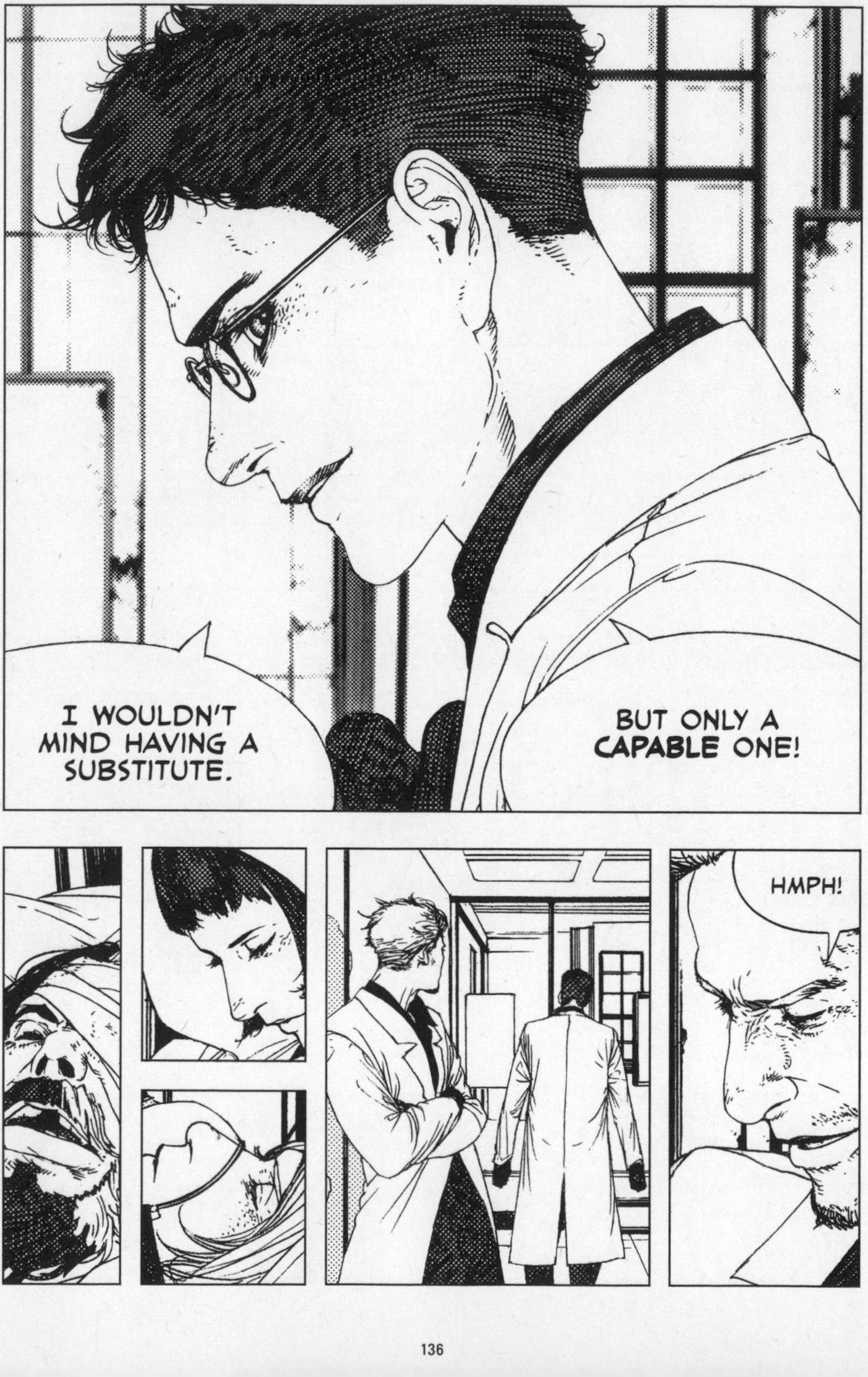
I WOULDN'T MIND HAVING A SUBSTITUTE.
BUT ONLY A CAPABLE ONE!
HMPH!

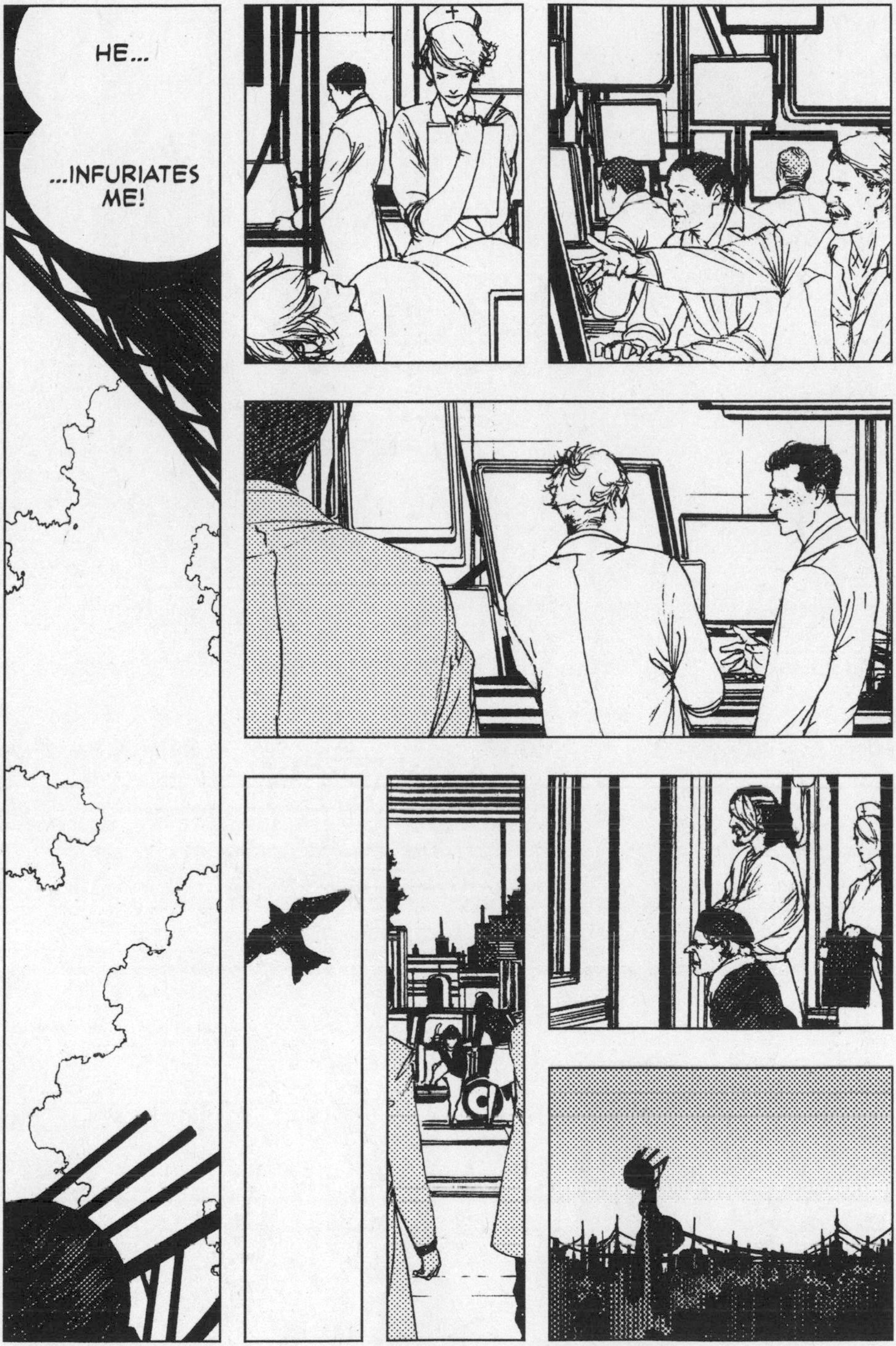
HE...
...INFURIATES ME!

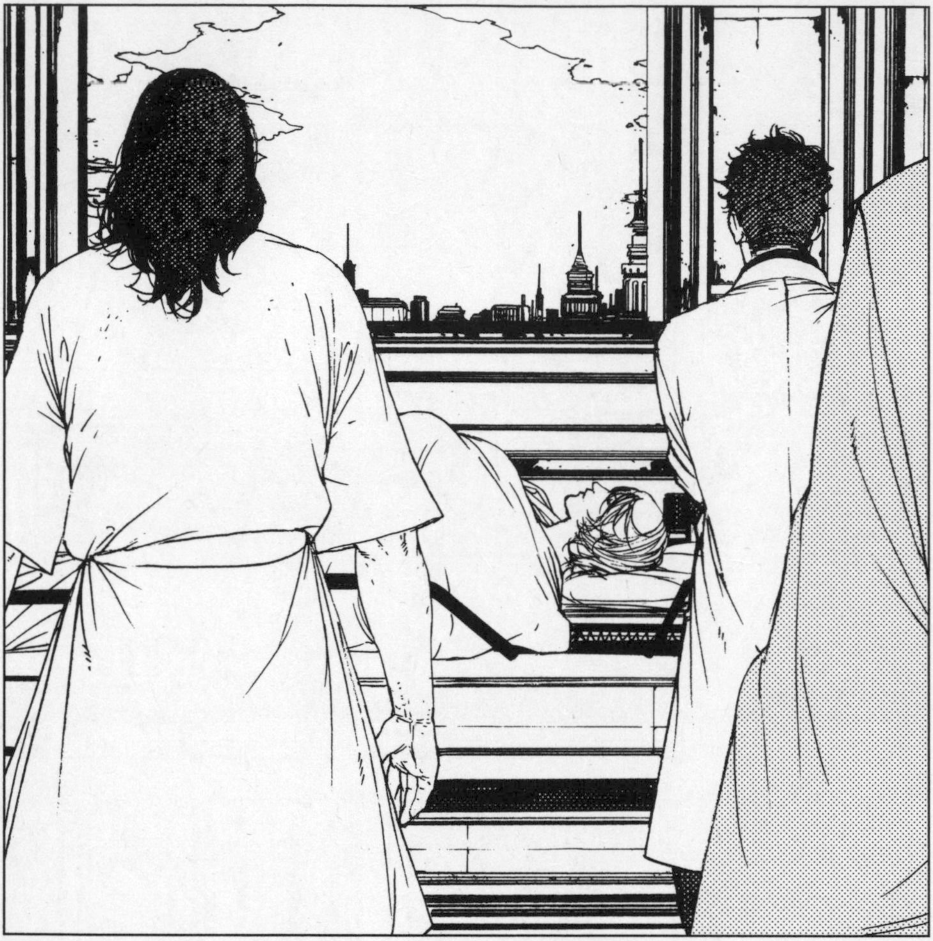
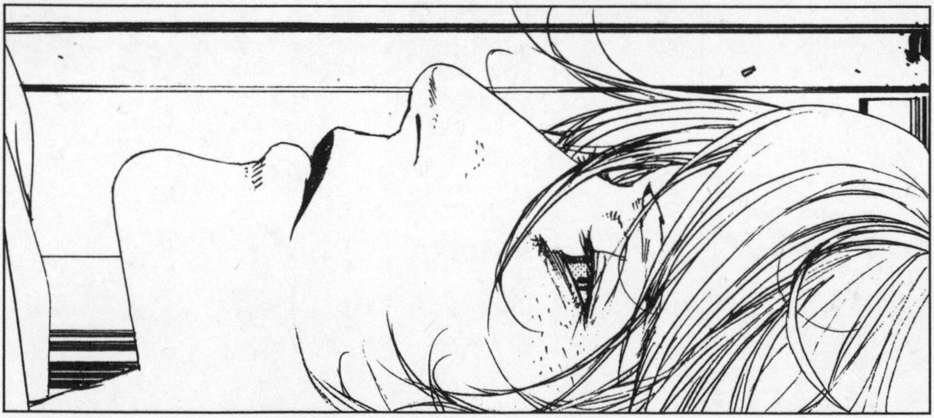

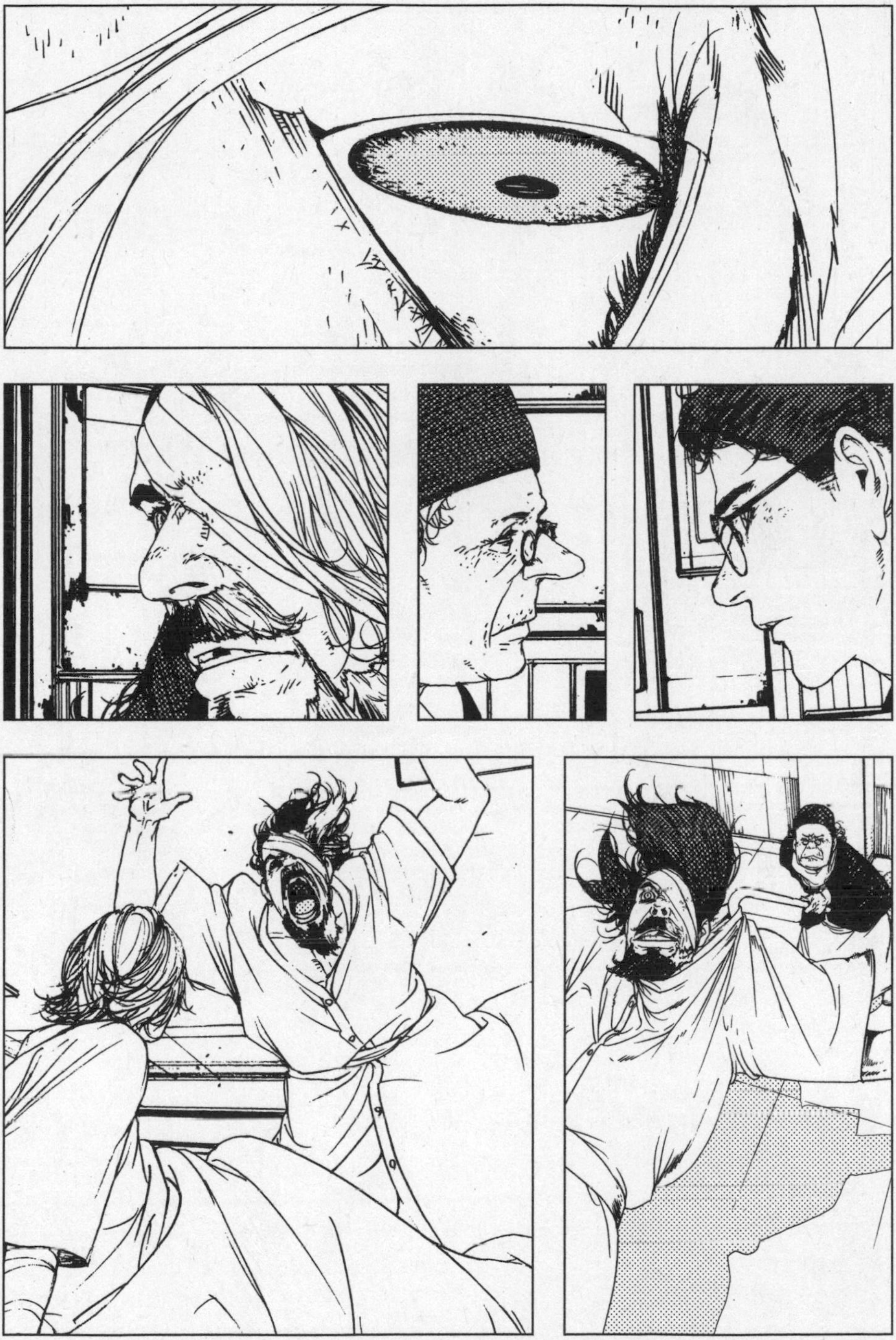

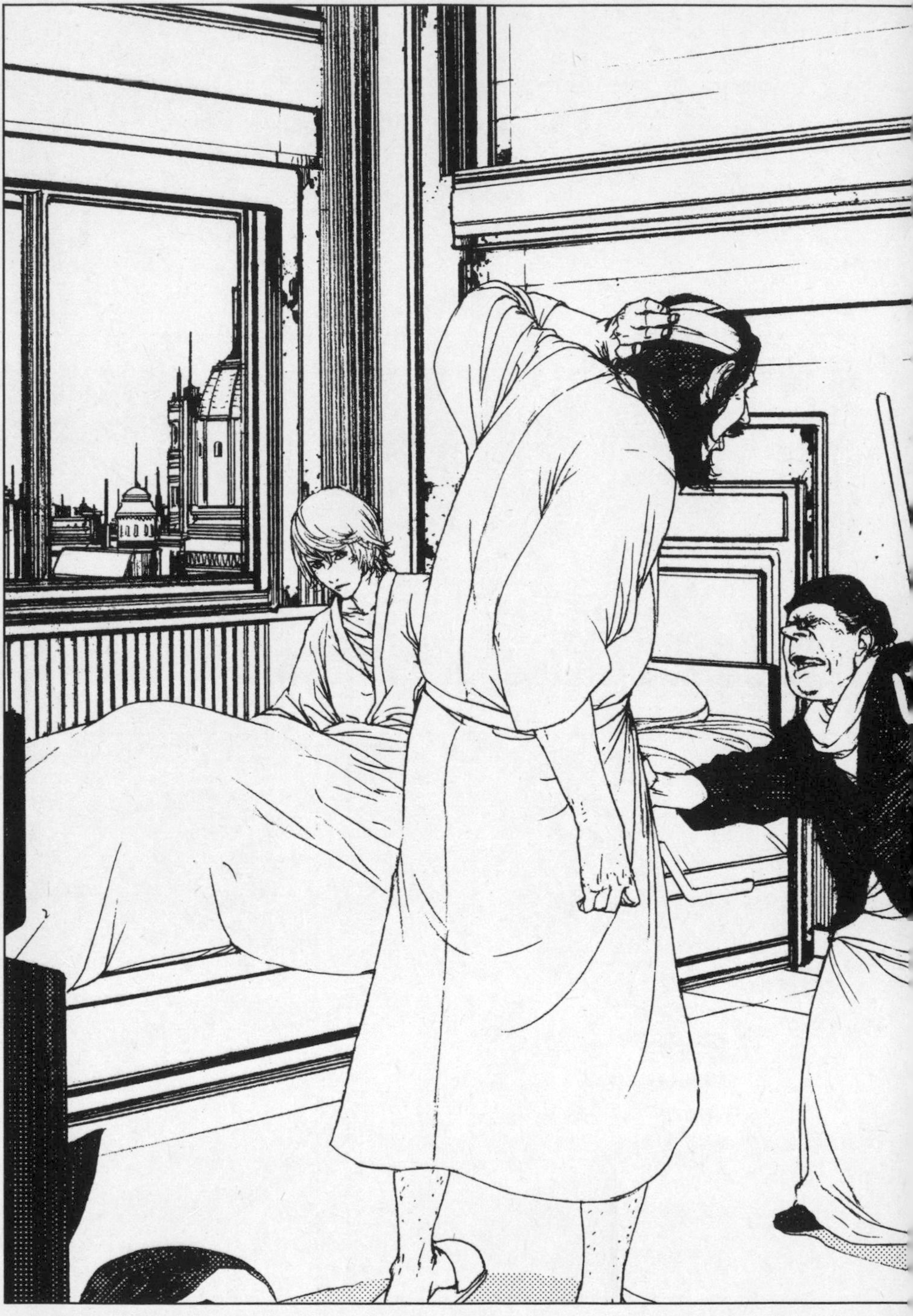

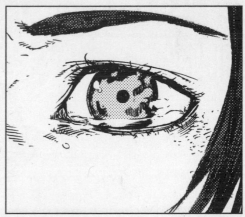

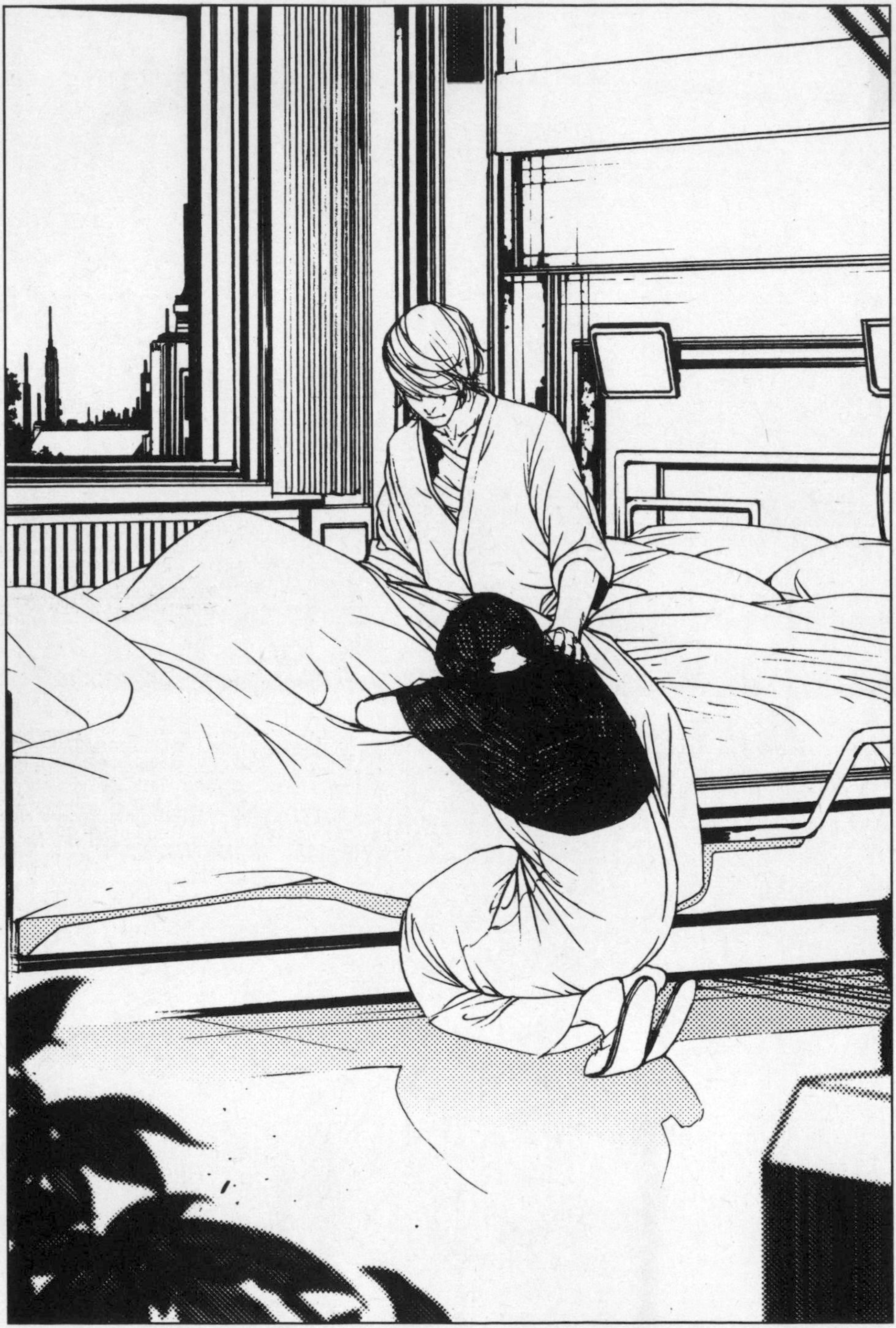

Levius/est
VOL. 1

Chapter 04

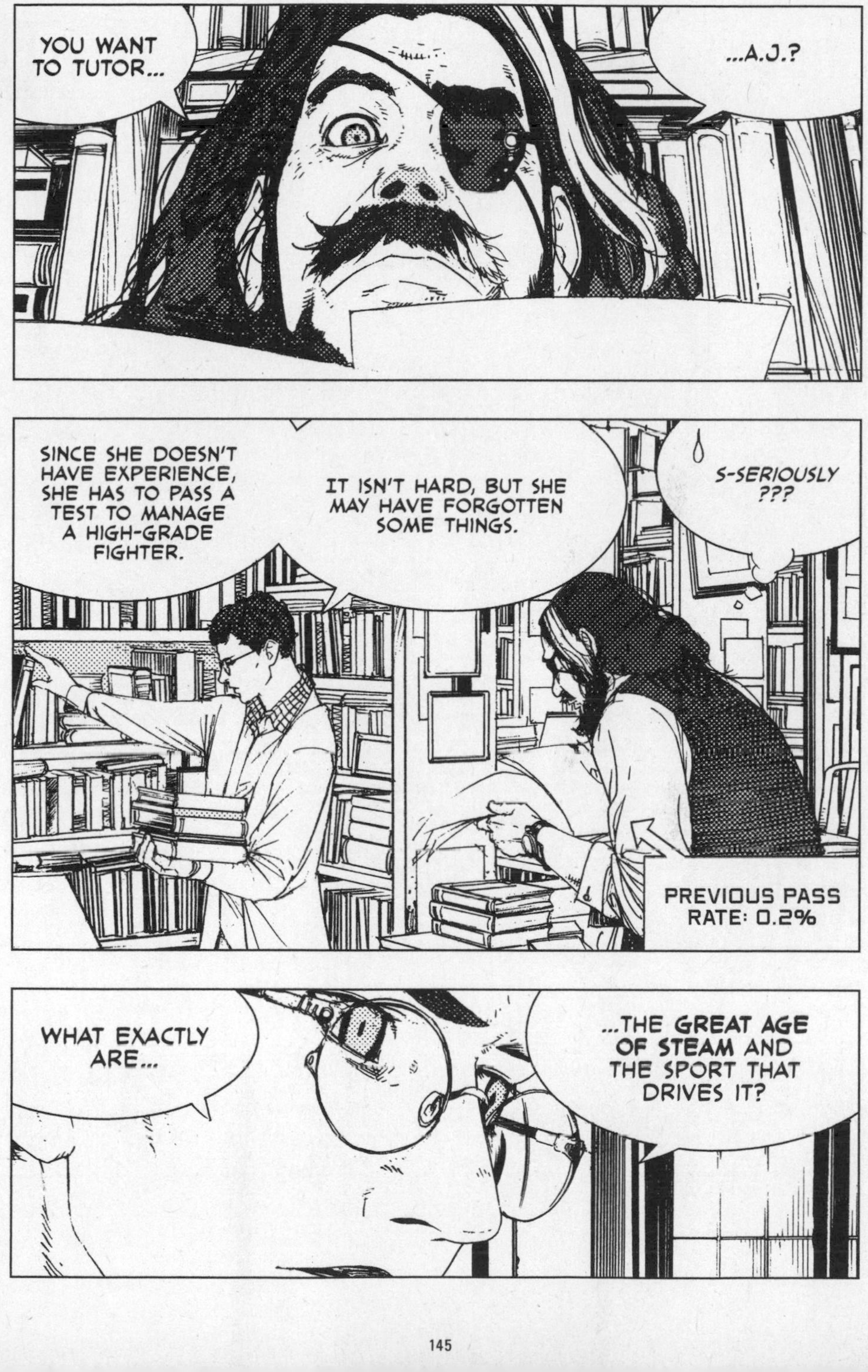
YOU WANT TO TUTOR...
...A.J.?
SINCE SHE DOESN'T HAVE EXPERIENCE, SHE HAS TO PASS A TEST TO MANAGE A HIGH-GRADE FIGHTER.
IT ISN'T HARD, BUT SHE MAY HAVE FORGOTTEN SOME THINGS.
S-SERIOUSLY ???
PREVIOUS PASS RATE: 0.2%
WHAT EXACTLY ARE...
...THE GREAT AGE OF STEAM AND THE SPORT THAT DRIVES IT?

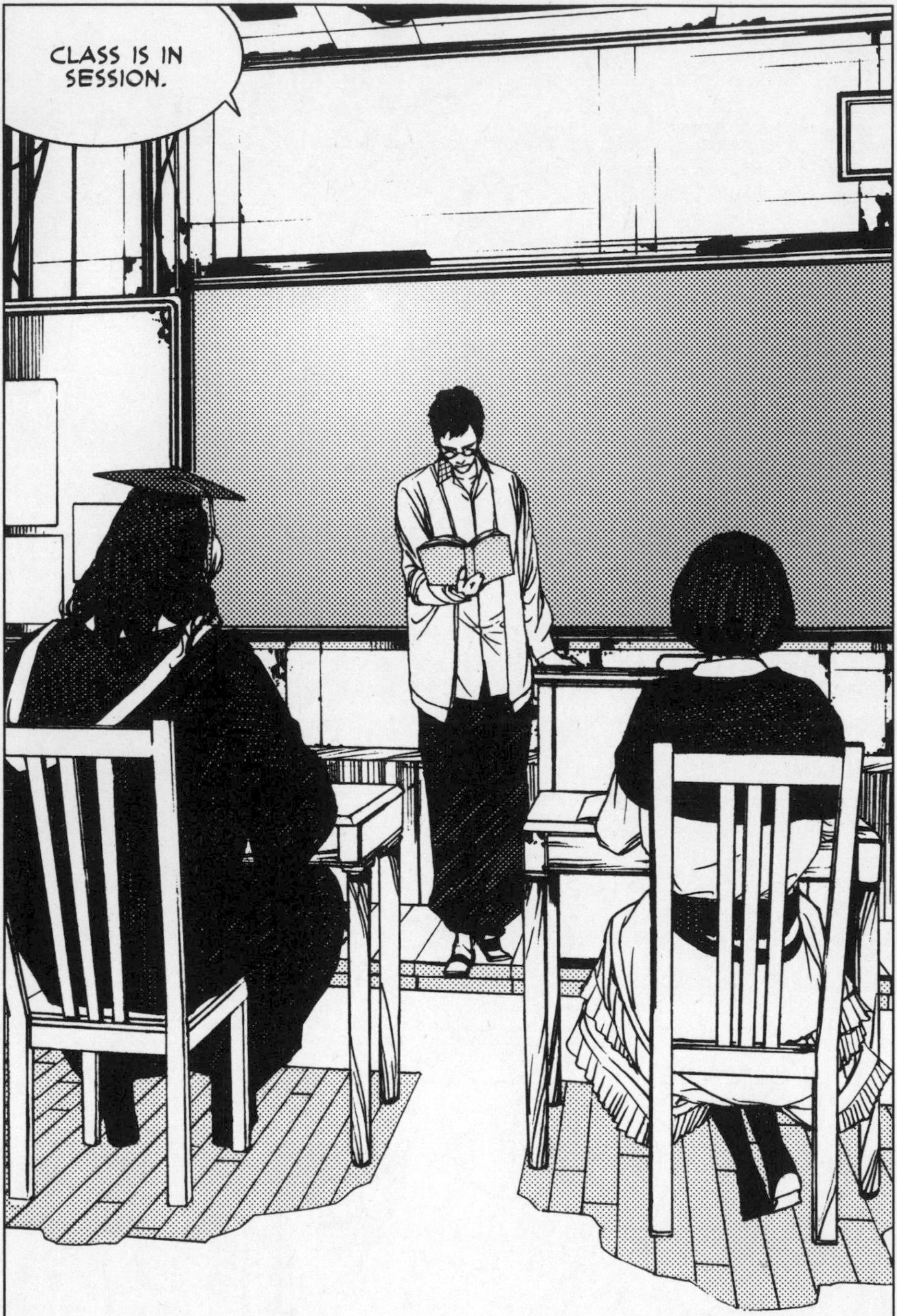
CLASS IS IN SESSION.

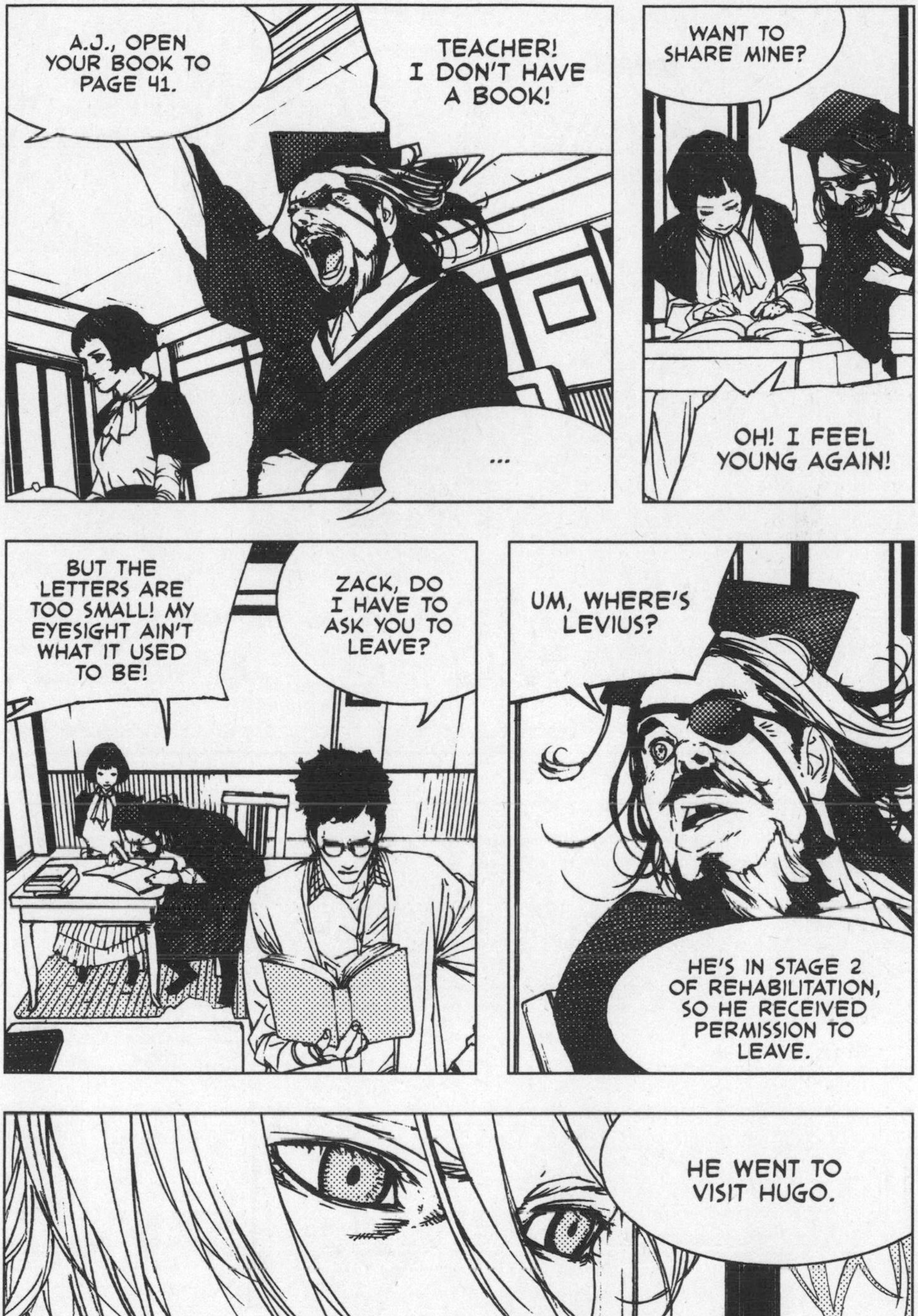
A.J., OPEN YOUR BOOK TO PAGE 41.
TEACHER! I DON'T HAVE A BOOK!
...
WANT TO SHARE MINE?
OH! I FEEL YOUNG AGAIN!
BUT THE LETTERS ARE TOO SMALL! MY EYESIGHT AIN'T WHAT IT USED TO BE!
ZACK, DO I HAVE TO ASK YOU TO LEAVE?
UM, WHERE'S LEVIUS?
HE'S IN STAGE 2 OF REHABILITATION, SO HE RECEIVED PERMISSION TO LEAVE.
HE WENT TO VISIT HUGO.

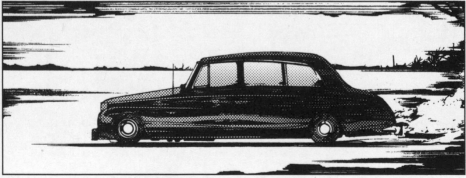

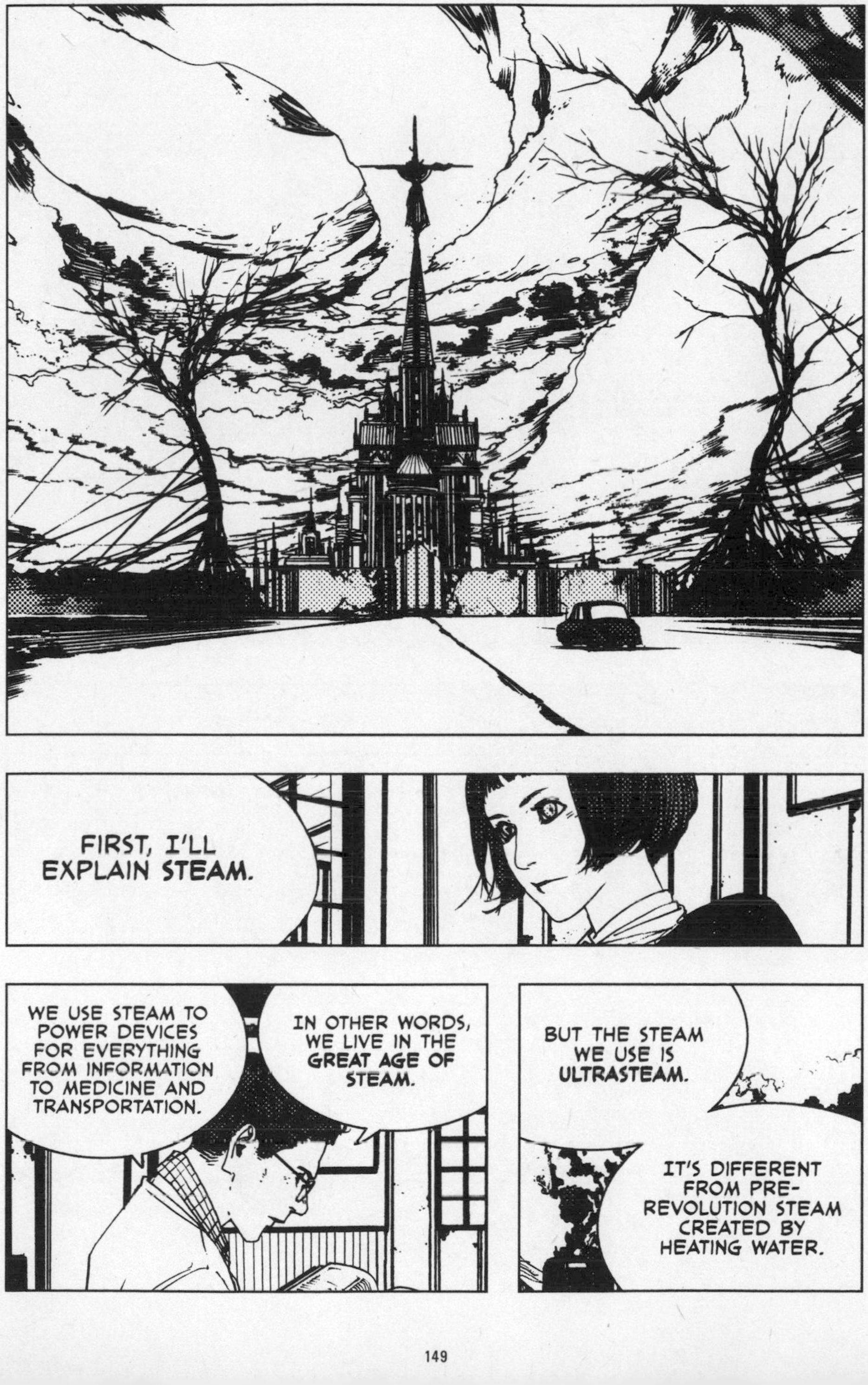
FIRST, I'LL EXPLAIN STEAM.
WE USE STEAM TO POWER DEVICES FOR EVERYTHING FROM INFORMATION TO MEDICINE AND TRANSPORTATION.
IN OTHER WORDS, WE LIVE IN THE GREAT AGE OF STEAM.
BUT THE STEAM WE USE IS ULTRASTEAM.
IT'S DIFFERENT FROM PRE-REVOLUTION STEAM CREATED BY HEATING WATER.

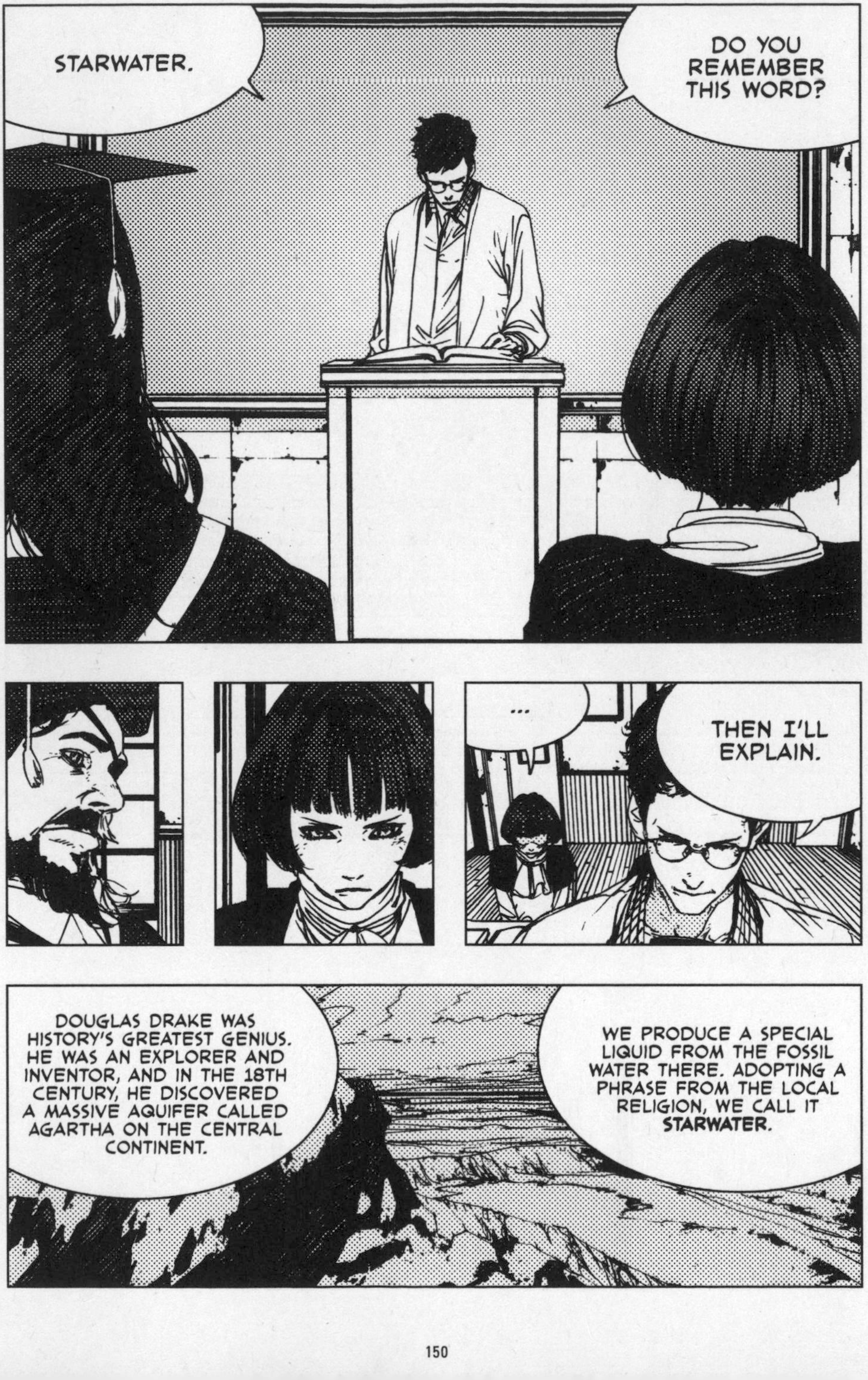
STARWATER.
DO YOU REMEMBER THIS WORD?
...
THEN I'LL EXPLAIN.
DOUGLAS DRAKE WAS HISTORY'S GREATEST GENIUS. HE WAS AN EXPLORER AND INVENTOR, AND IN THE 18TH CENTURY, HE DISCOVERED A MASSIVE AQUIFER CALLED AGARTHA ON THE CENTRAL CONTINENT.
WE PRODUCE A SPECIAL LIQUID FROM THE FOSSIL WATER THERE. ADOPTING A PHRASE FROM THE LOCAL RELIGION, WE CALL IT **STARWATER**.

THAT WATER HAS A SPECIAL CHARACTERISTIC NOT FOUND IN OTHER SUBSTANCES.
WATCH.
SRK

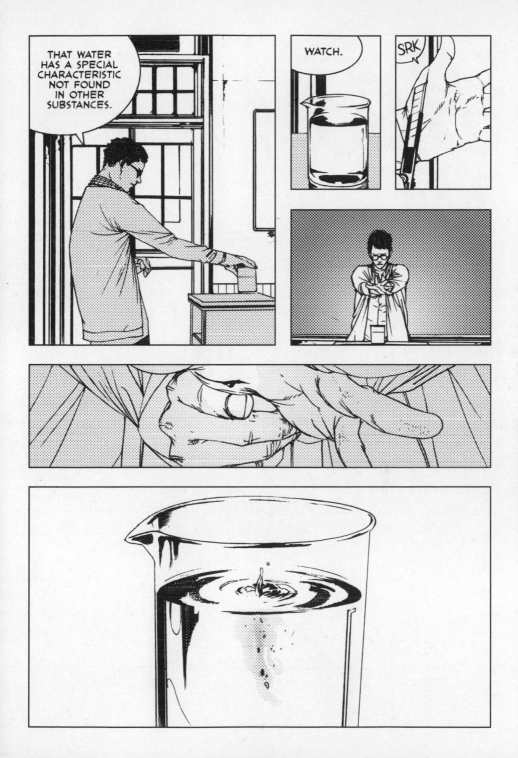

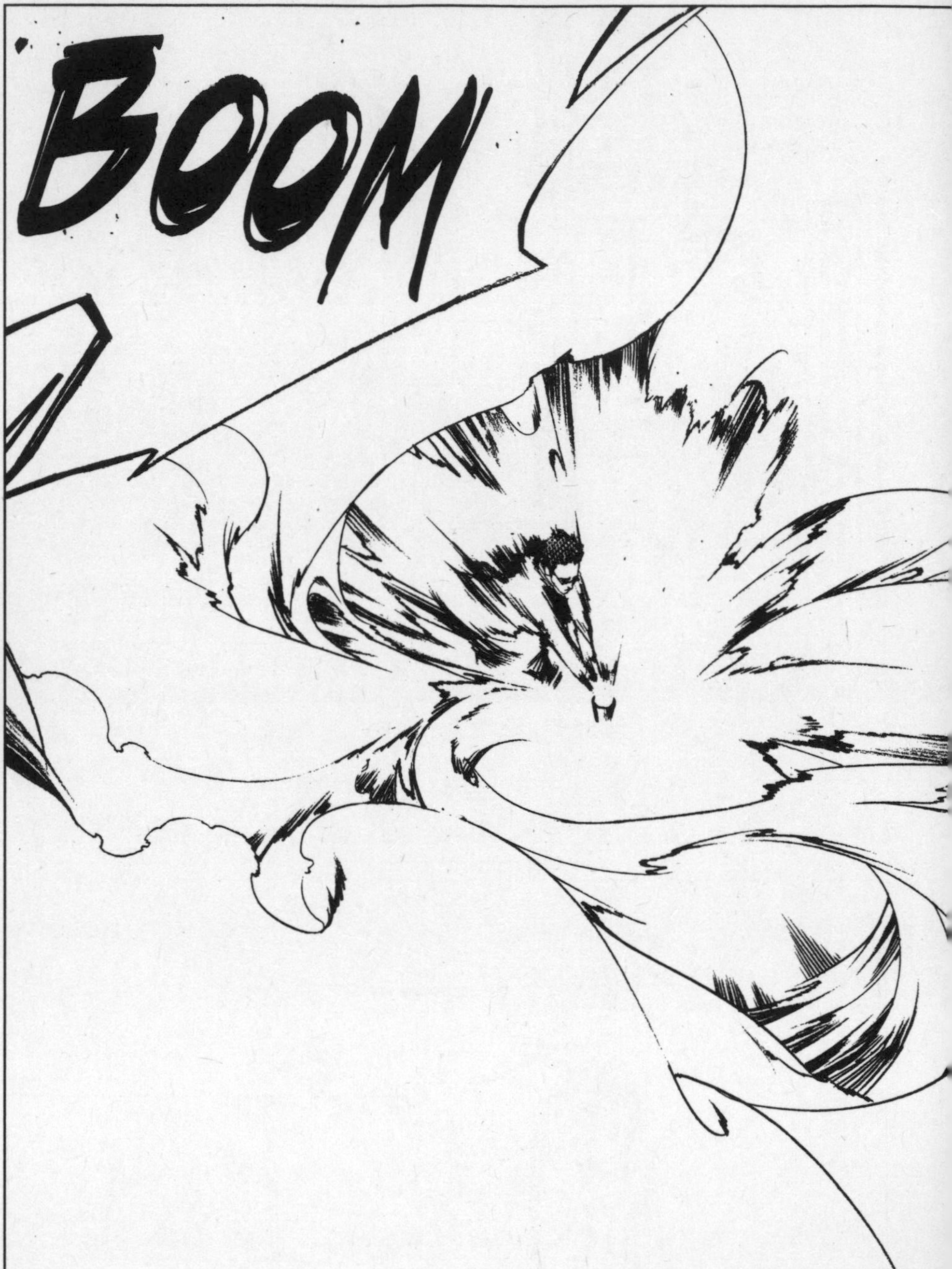
BOOM

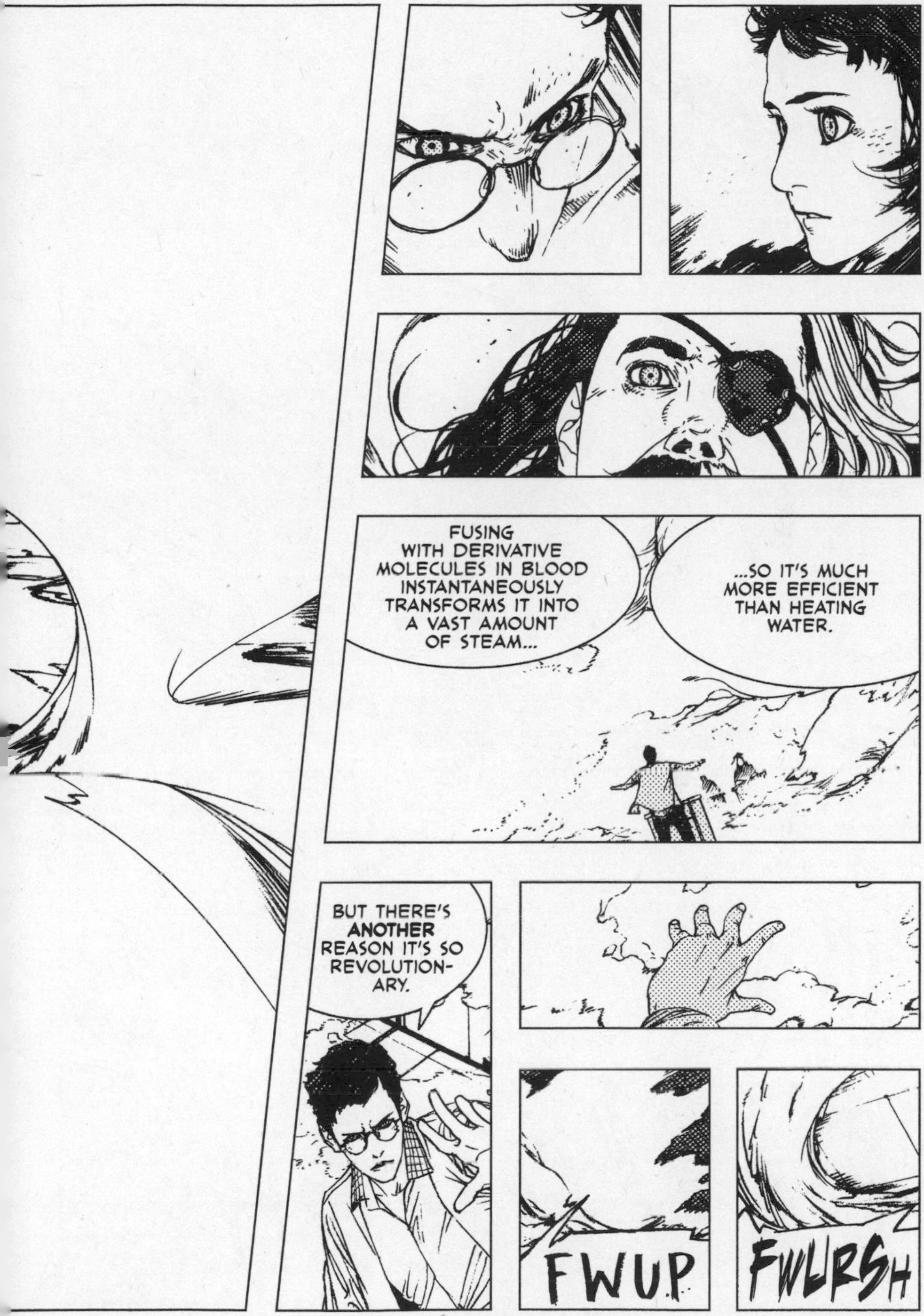
FUSING WITH DERIVATIVE MOLECULES IN BLOOD INSTANTANEOUSLY TRANSFORMS IT INTO A VAST AMOUNT OF STEAM...
...SO IT'S MUCH MORE EFFICIENT THAN HEATING WATER.
FWURSH
FWUP
BUT THERE'S **ANOTHER** REASON IT'S SO REVOLUTION-ARY.

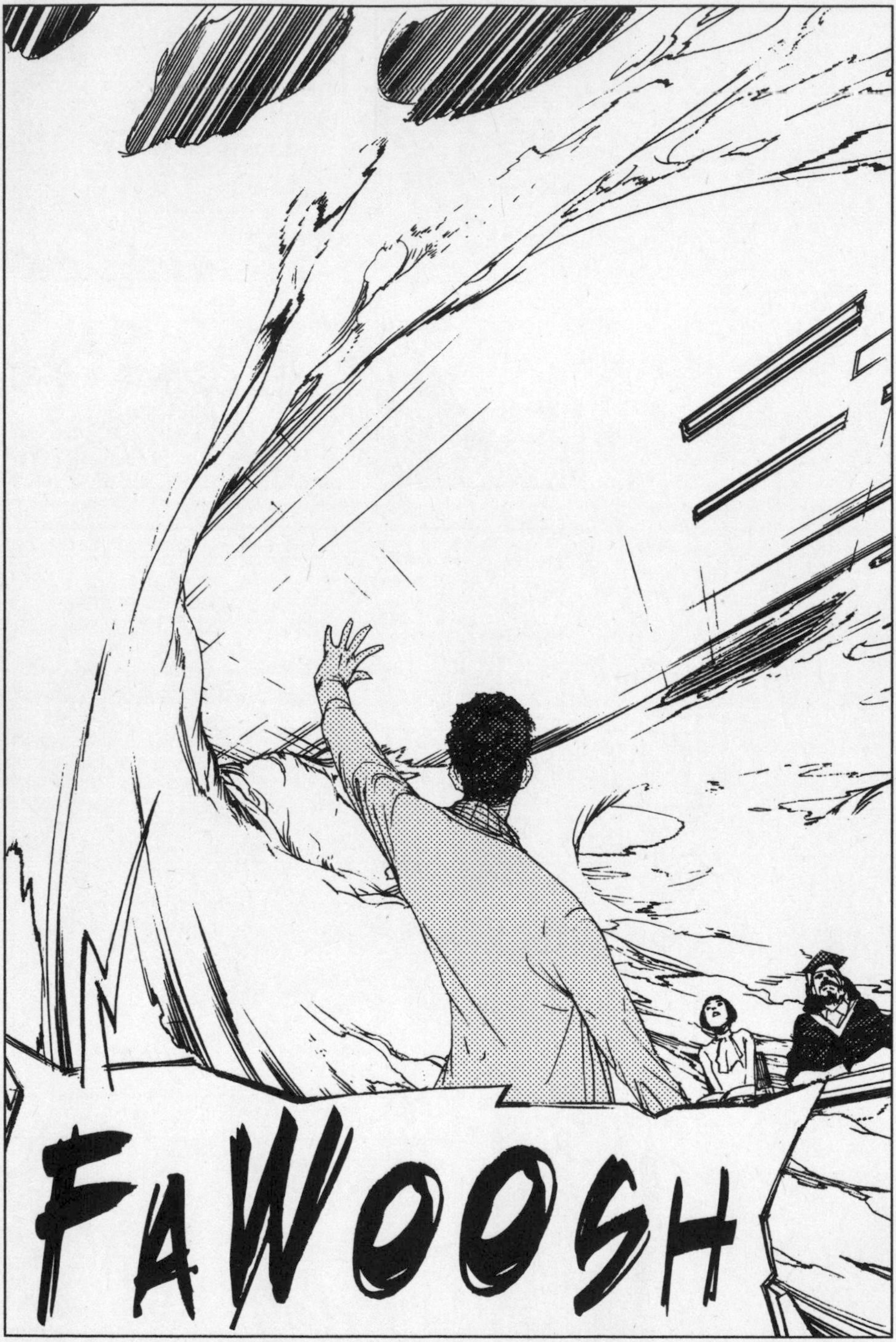
FAWOOSH

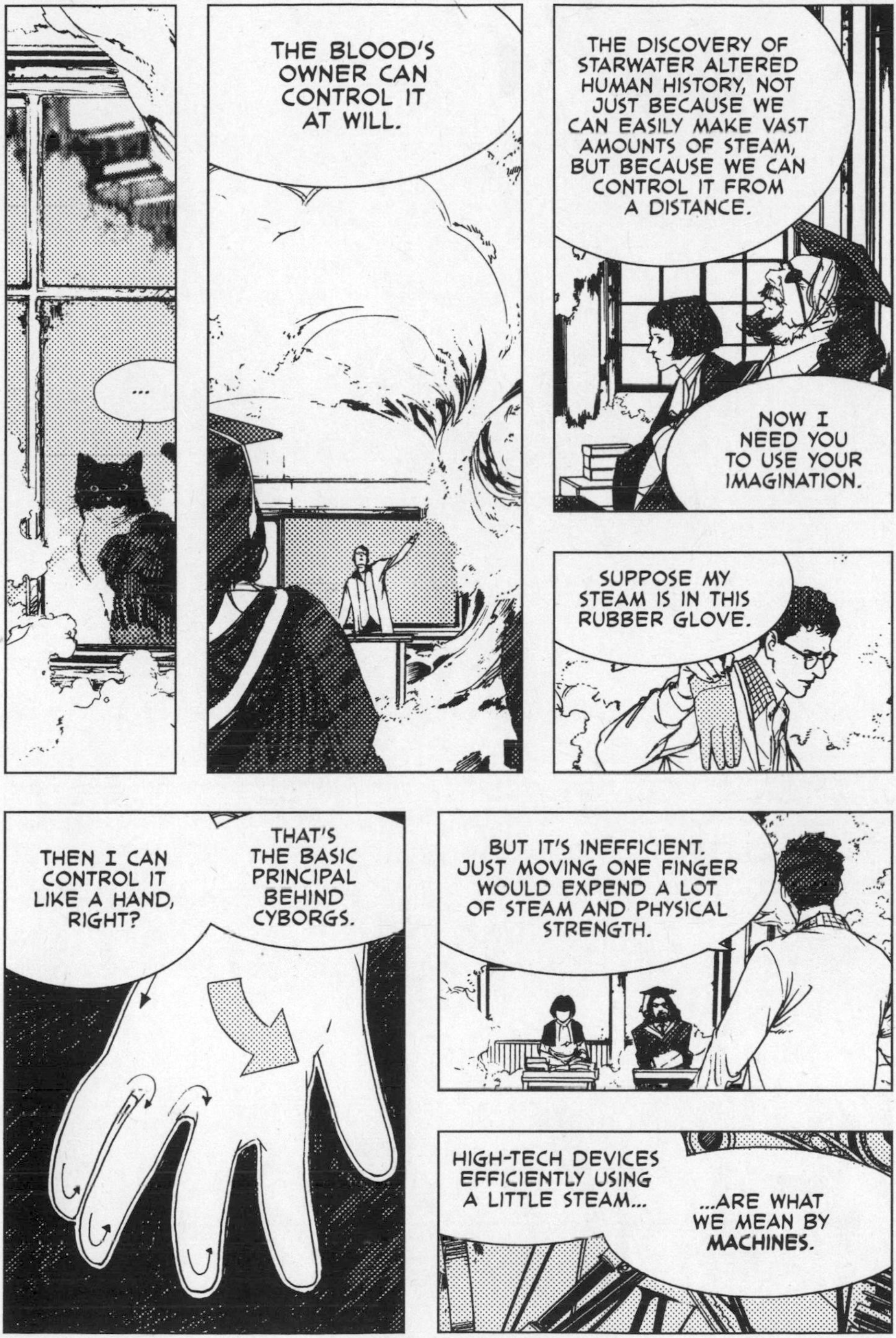
...
THE BLOOD'S OWNER CAN CONTROL IT AT WILL.
THE DISCOVERY OF STARWATER ALTERED HUMAN HISTORY, NOT JUST BECAUSE WE CAN EASILY MAKE VAST AMOUNTS OF STEAM, BUT BECAUSE WE CAN CONTROL IT FROM A DISTANCE.
NOW I NEED YOU TO USE YOUR IMAGINATION.
SUPPOSE MY STEAM IS IN THIS RUBBER GLOVE.
THEN I CAN CONTROL IT LIKE A HAND, RIGHT?
THAT'S THE BASIC PRINCIPAL BEHIND CYBORGS.
BUT IT'S INEFFICIENT. JUST MOVING ONE FINGER WOULD EXPEND A LOT OF STEAM AND PHYSICAL STRENGTH.
HIGH-TECH DEVICES EFFICIENTLY USING A LITTLE STEAM...
...ARE WHAT WE MEAN BY MACHINES.

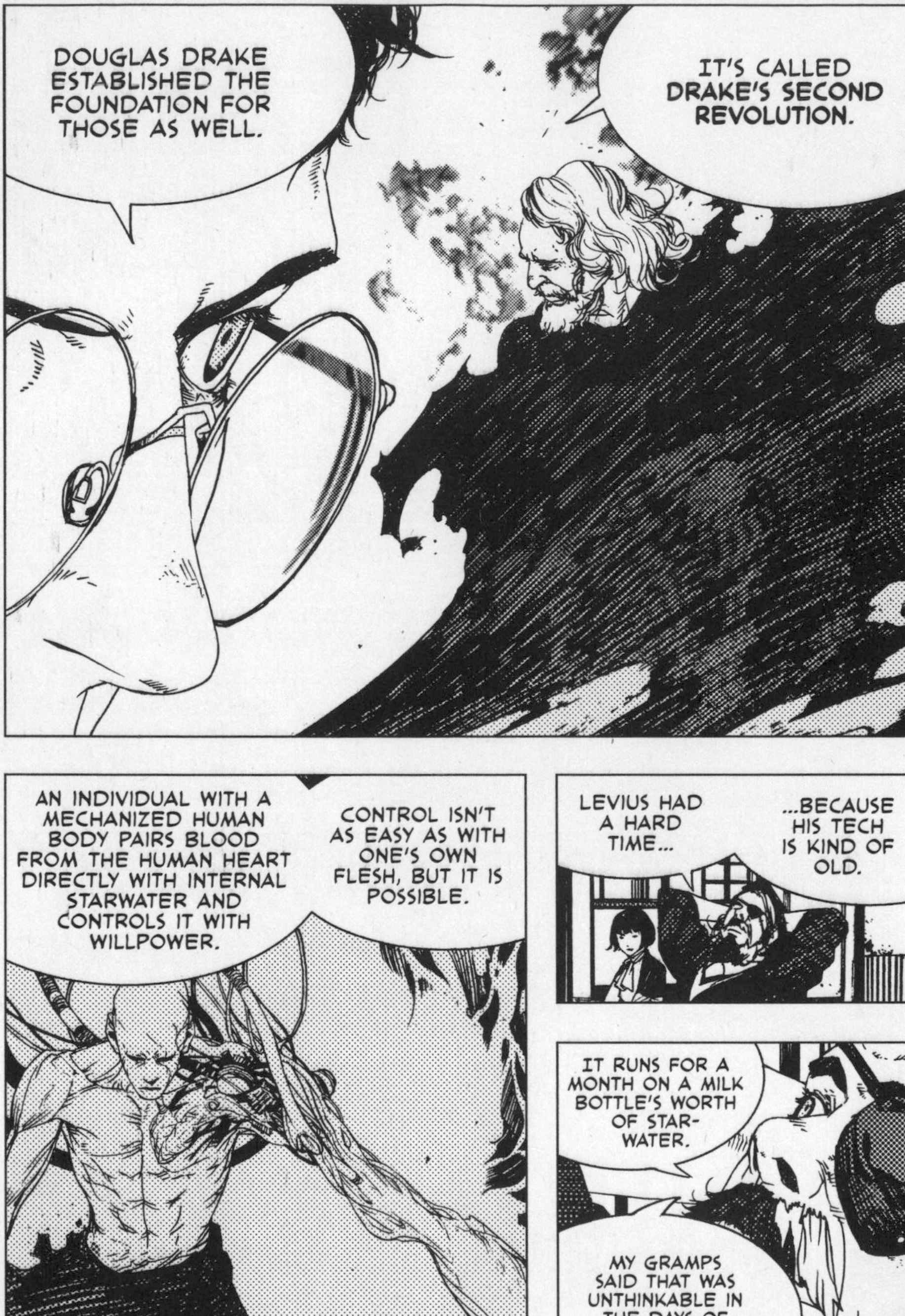
DOUGLAS DRAKE ESTABLISHED THE FOUNDATION FOR THOSE AS WELL.
IT'S CALLED DRAKE'S SECOND REVOLUTION.
AN INDIVIDUAL WITH A MECHANIZED HUMAN BODY PAIRS BLOOD FROM THE HUMAN HEART DIRECTLY WITH INTERNAL STARWATER AND CONTROLS IT WITH WILLPOWER.
CONTROL ISN'T AS EASY AS WITH ONE'S OWN FLESH, BUT IT IS POSSIBLE.
LEVIUS HAD A HARD TIME...
...BECAUSE HIS TECH IS KIND OF OLD.
IT RUNS FOR A MONTH ON A MILK BOTTLE'S WORTH OF STAR-WATER.
MY GRAMPS SAID THAT WAS UNTHINKABLE IN THE DAYS OF BOILING WATER.

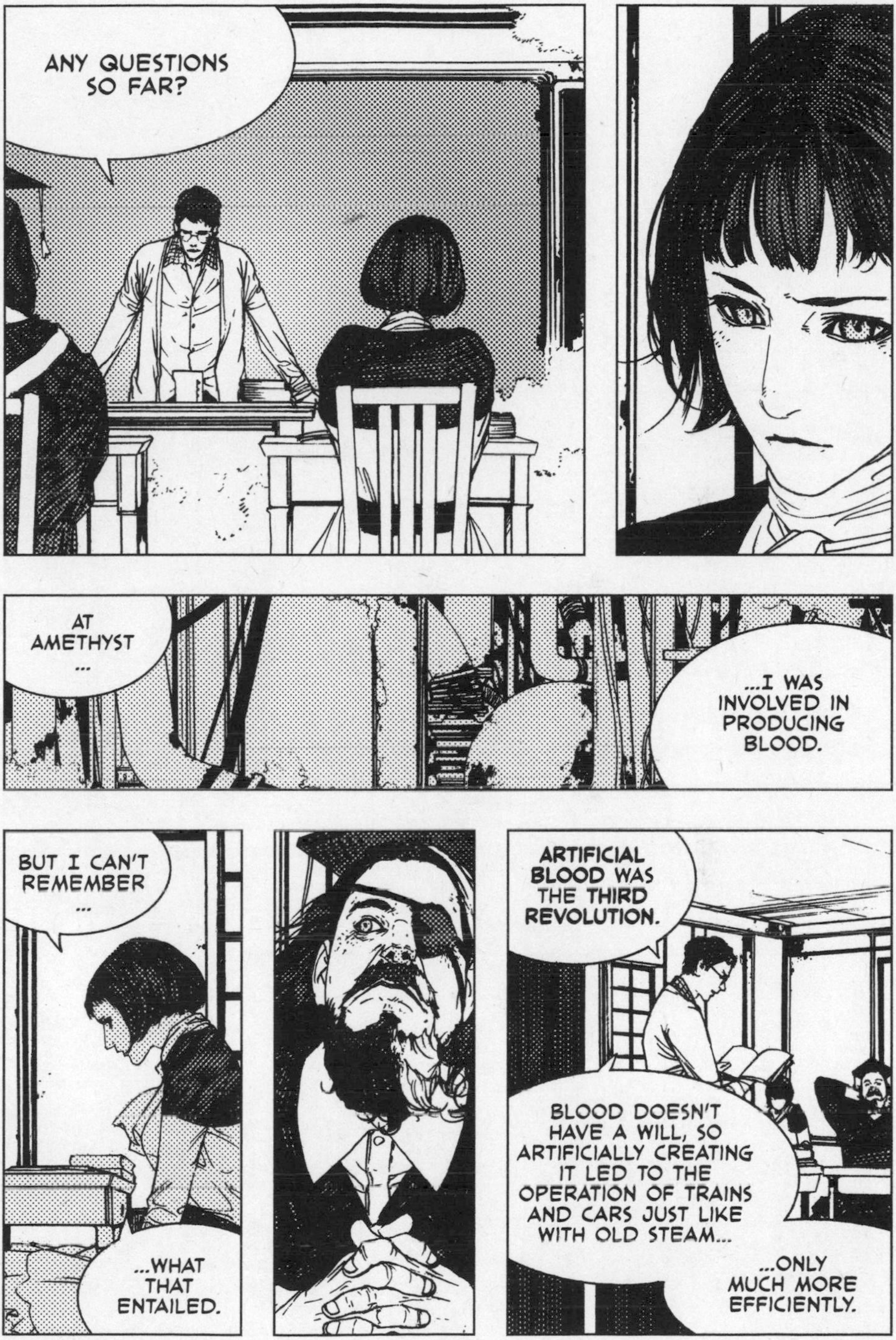
ANY QUESTIONS SO FAR?
AT AMETHYST ...
...I WAS INVOLVED IN PRODUCING BLOOD.
BUT I CAN'T REMEMBER ...
...WHAT THAT ENTAILED.
ARTIFICIAL BLOOD WAS THE THIRD REVOLUTION.
BLOOD DOESN'T HAVE A WILL, SO ARTIFICIALLY CREATING IT LED TO THE OPERATION OF TRAINS AND CARS JUST LIKE WITH OLD STEAM...
...ONLY MUCH MORE EFFICIENTLY.

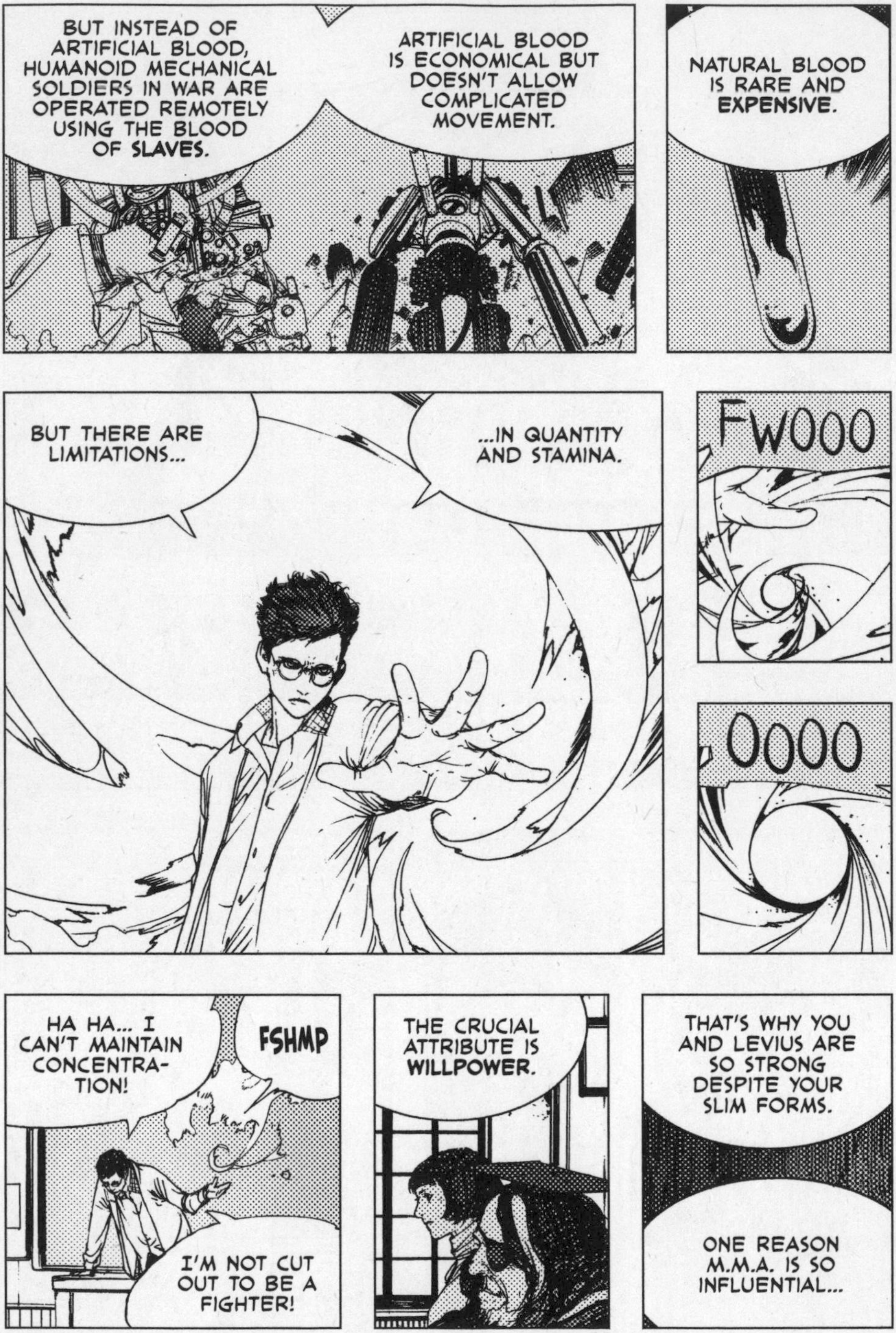
BUT INSTEAD OF ARTIFICIAL BLOOD, HUMANOID MECHANICAL SOLDIERS IN WAR ARE OPERATED REMOTELY USING THE BLOOD OF SLAVES.
ARTIFICIAL BLOOD IS ECONOMICAL BUT DOESN'T ALLOW COMPLICATED MOVEMENT.
NATURAL BLOOD IS RARE AND EXPENSIVE.
BUT THERE ARE LIMITATIONS...
...IN QUANTITY AND STAMINA.
FWOOO
OOOO
HA HA... I CAN'T MAINTAIN CONCENTRA-TION!
FSHMP
I'M NOT CUT OUT TO BE A FIGHTER!
THE CRUCIAL ATTRIBUTE IS WILLPOWER.
THAT'S WHY YOU AND LEVIUS ARE SO STRONG DESPITE YOUR SLIM FORMS.
ONE REASON M.M.A. IS SO INFLUENTIAL...

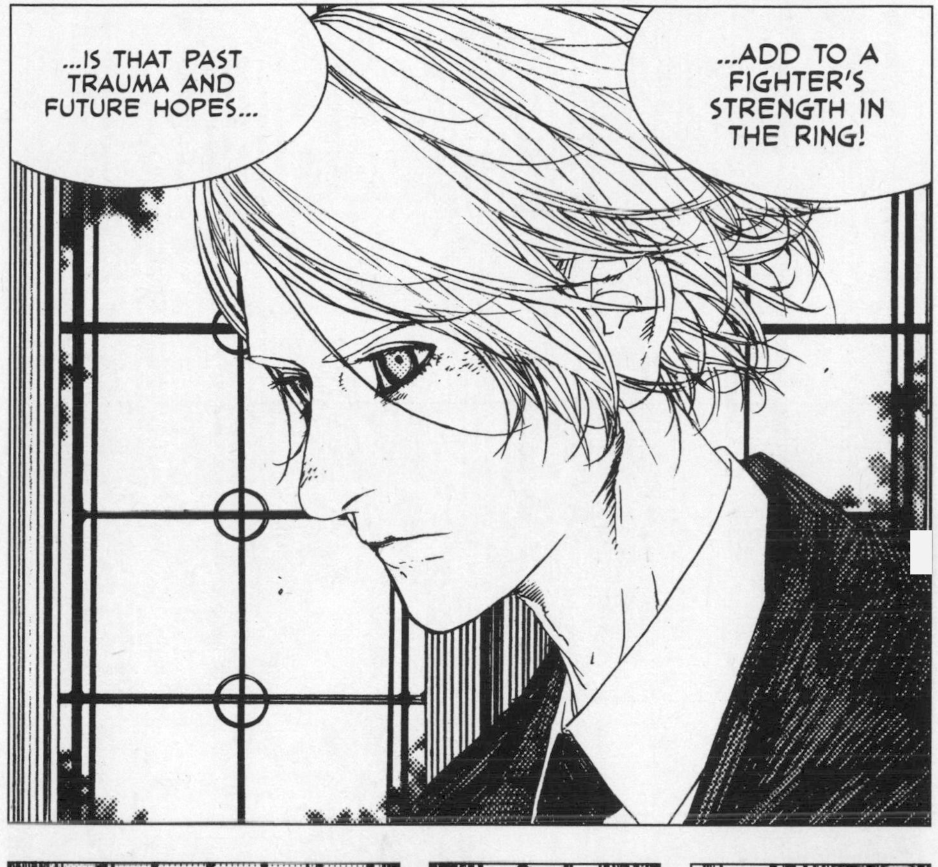
...IS THAT PAST TRAUMA AND FUTURE HOPES...
...ADD TO A FIGHTER'S STRENGTH IN THE RING!

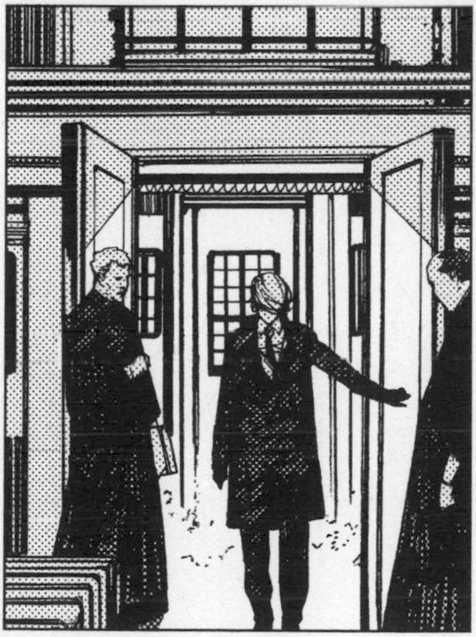

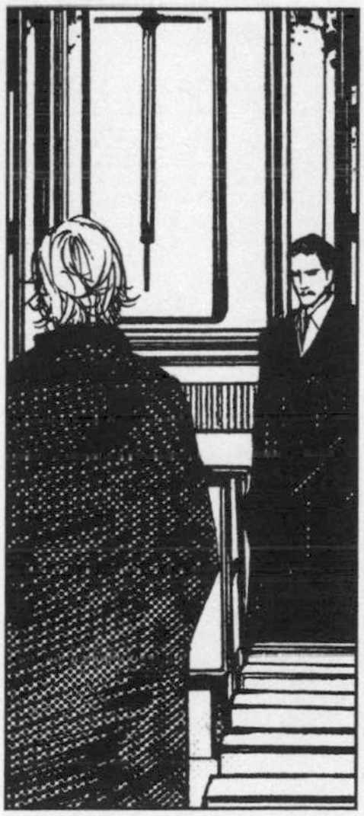

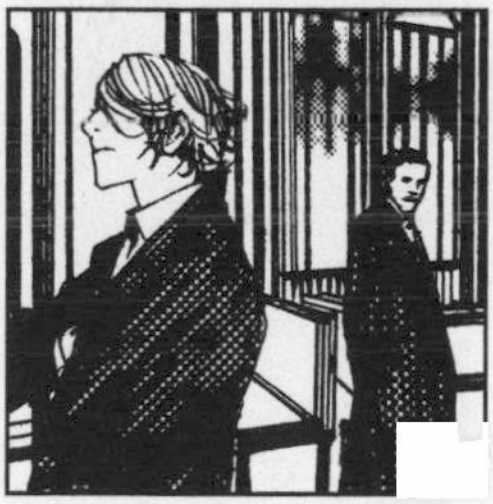

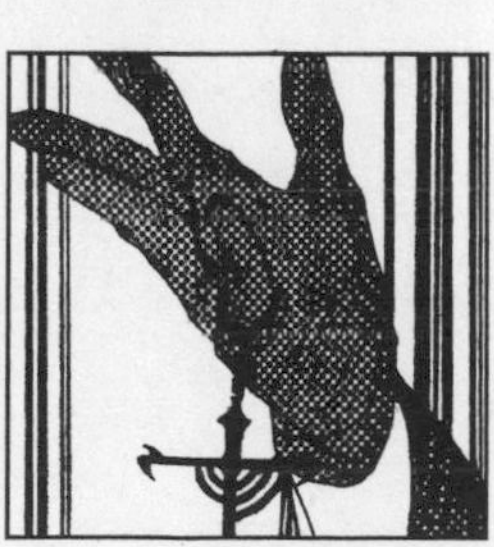

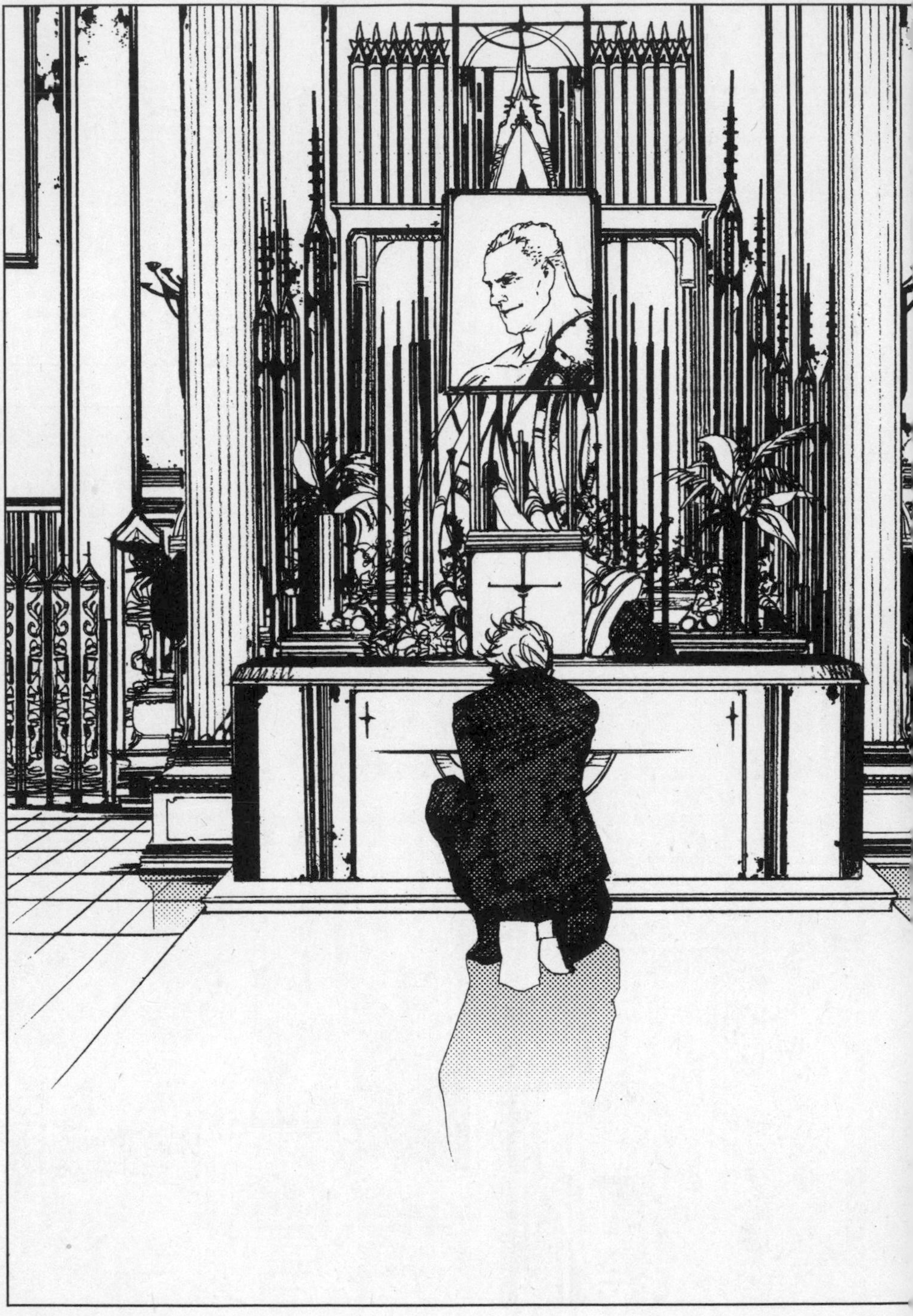

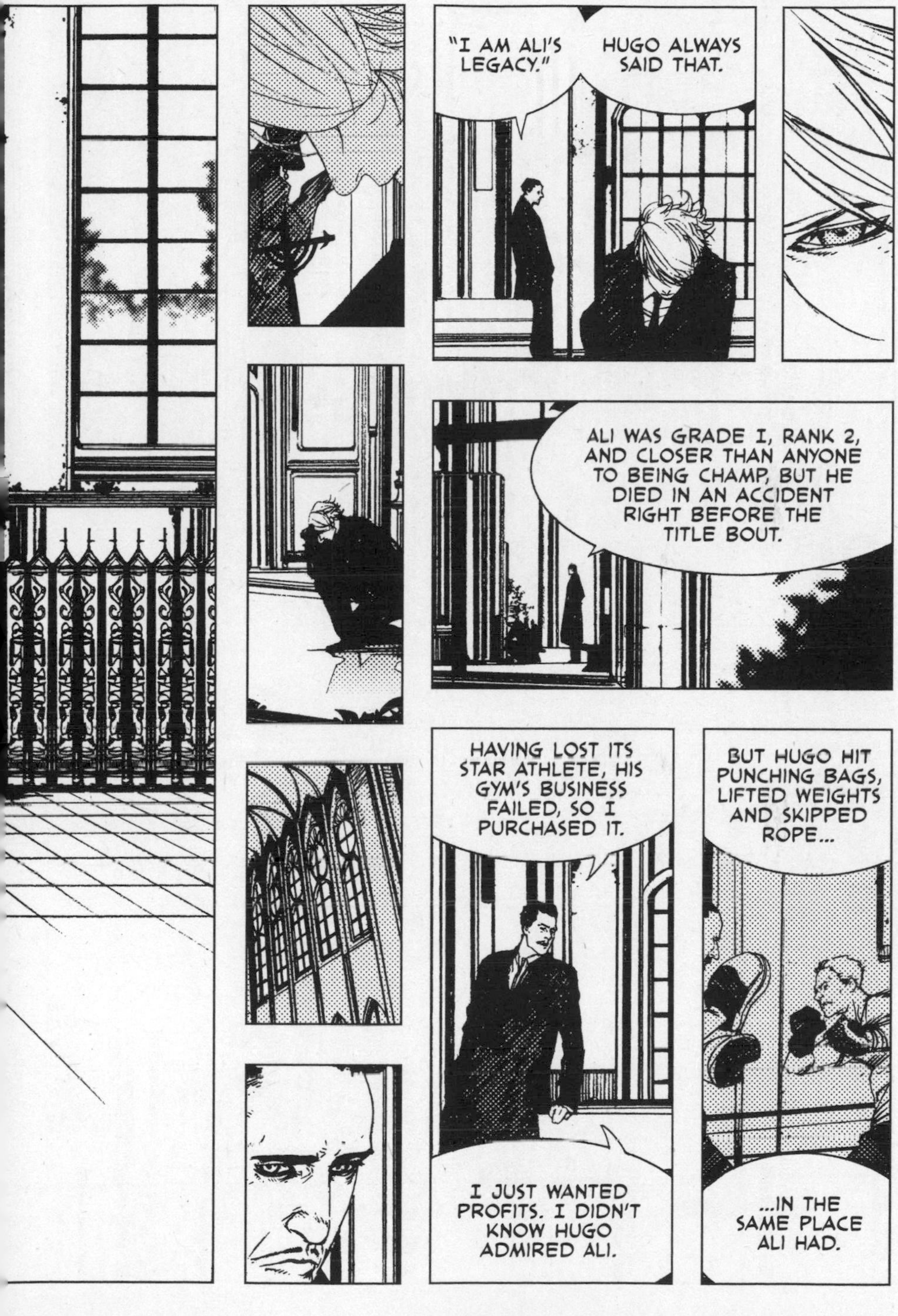
"I AM ALI'S LEGACY."
HUGO ALWAYS SAID THAT.
ALI WAS GRADE 1, RANK 2, AND CLOSER THAN ANYONE TO BEING CHAMP, BUT HE DIED IN AN ACCIDENT RIGHT BEFORE THE TITLE BOUT.
HAVING LOST ITS STAR ATHLETE, HIS GYM'S BUSINESS FAILED, SO I PURCHASED IT.
I JUST WANTED PROFITS. I DIDN'T KNOW HUGO ADMIRED ALI.
BUT HUGO HIT PUNCHING BAGS, LIFTED WEIGHTS AND SKIPPED ROPE...
...IN THE SAME PLACE ALI HAD.

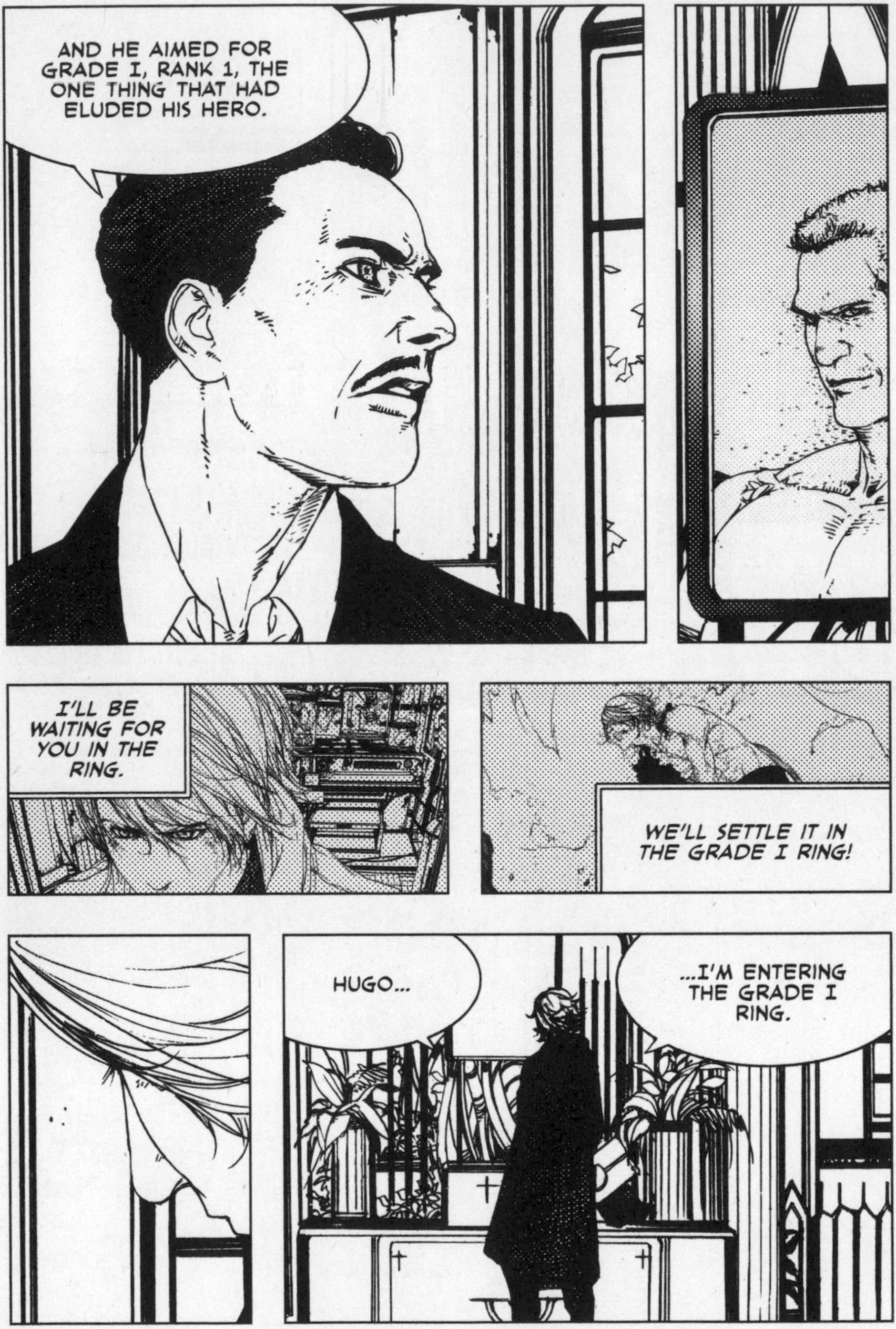
AND HE AIMED FOR GRADE I, RANK 1, THE ONE THING THAT HAD ELUDED HIS HERO.
I'LL BE WAITING FOR YOU IN THE RING.
WE'LL SETTLE IT IN THE GRADE I RING!
HUGO...
...I'M ENTERING THE GRADE I RING.

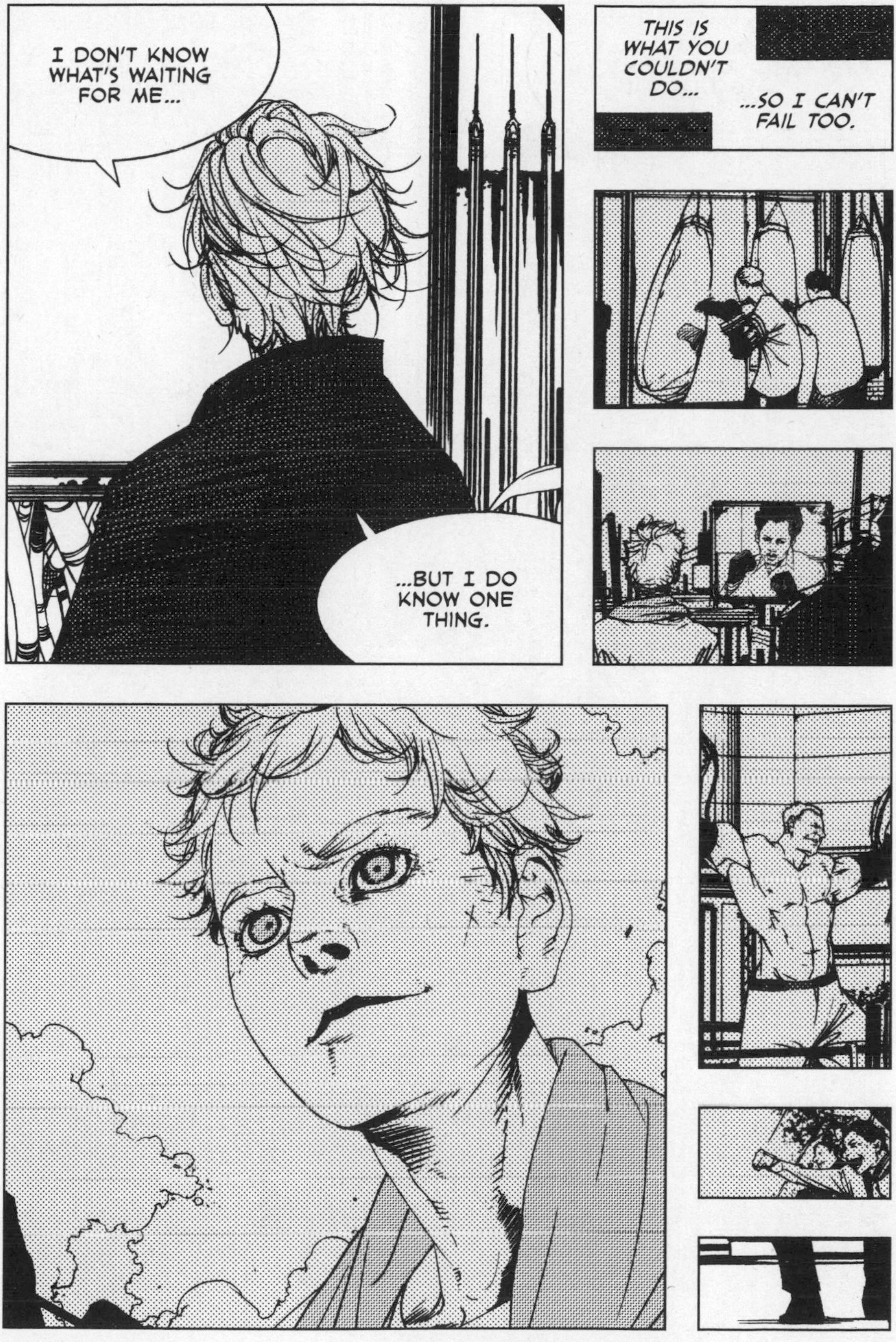
I DON'T KNOW WHAT'S WAITING FOR ME...
...BUT I DO KNOW ONE THING.
THIS IS WHAT YOU COULDN'T DO...
...SO I CAN'T FAIL TOO.

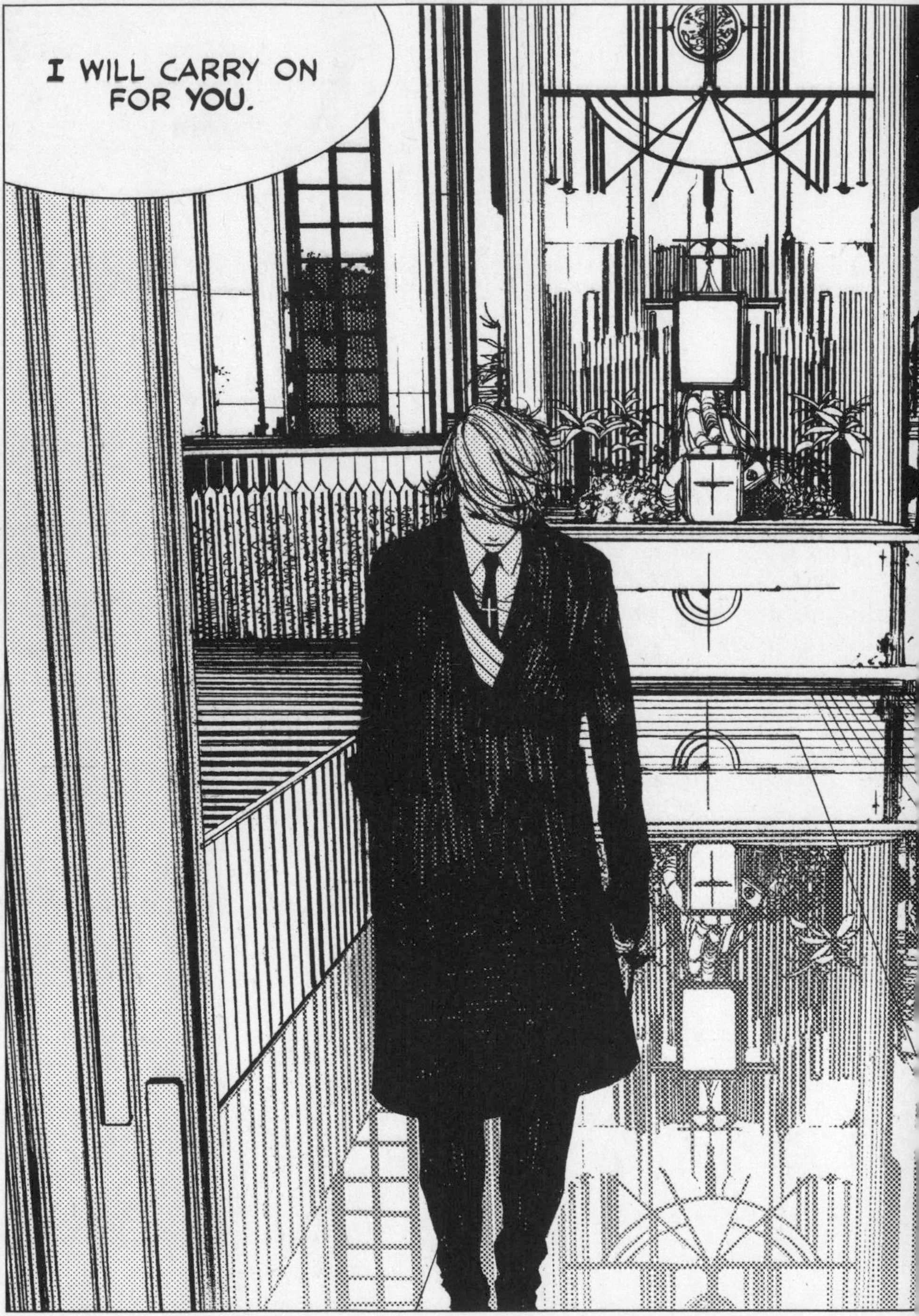
I WILL CARRY ON FOR YOU.

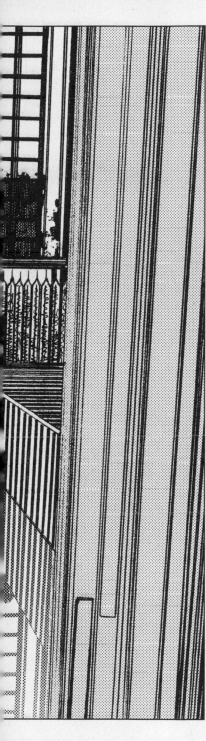

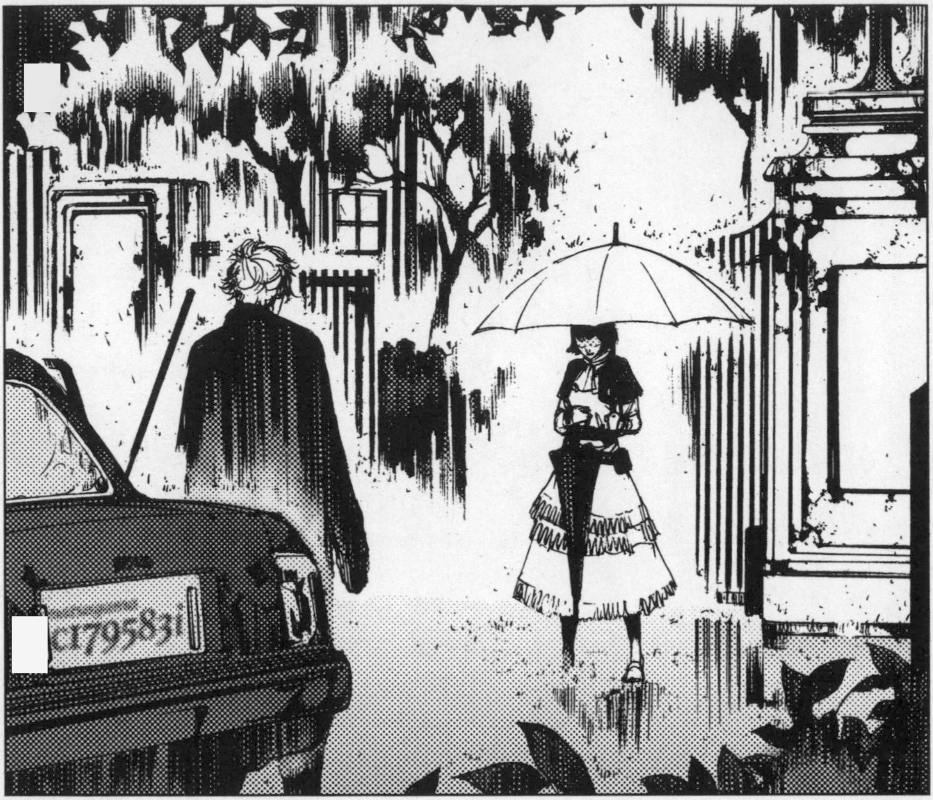
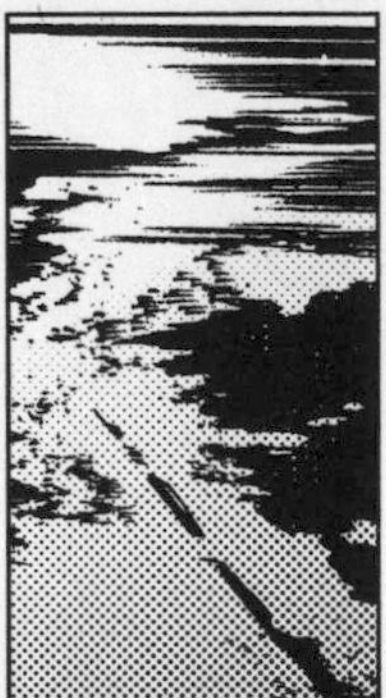
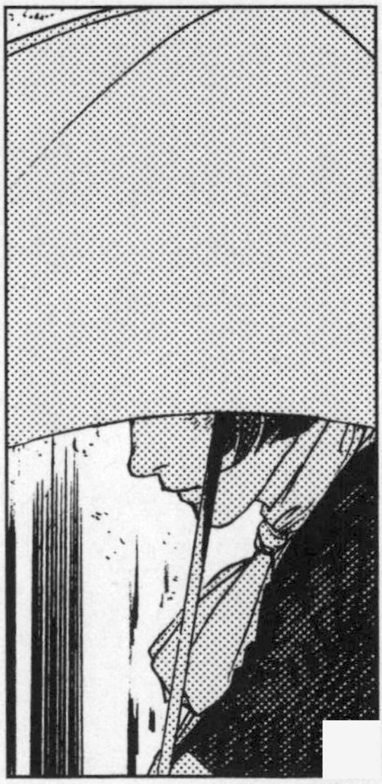
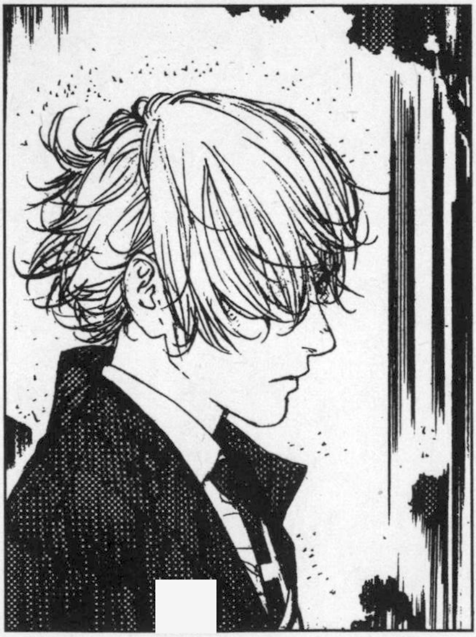

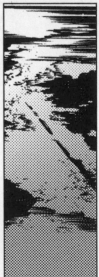

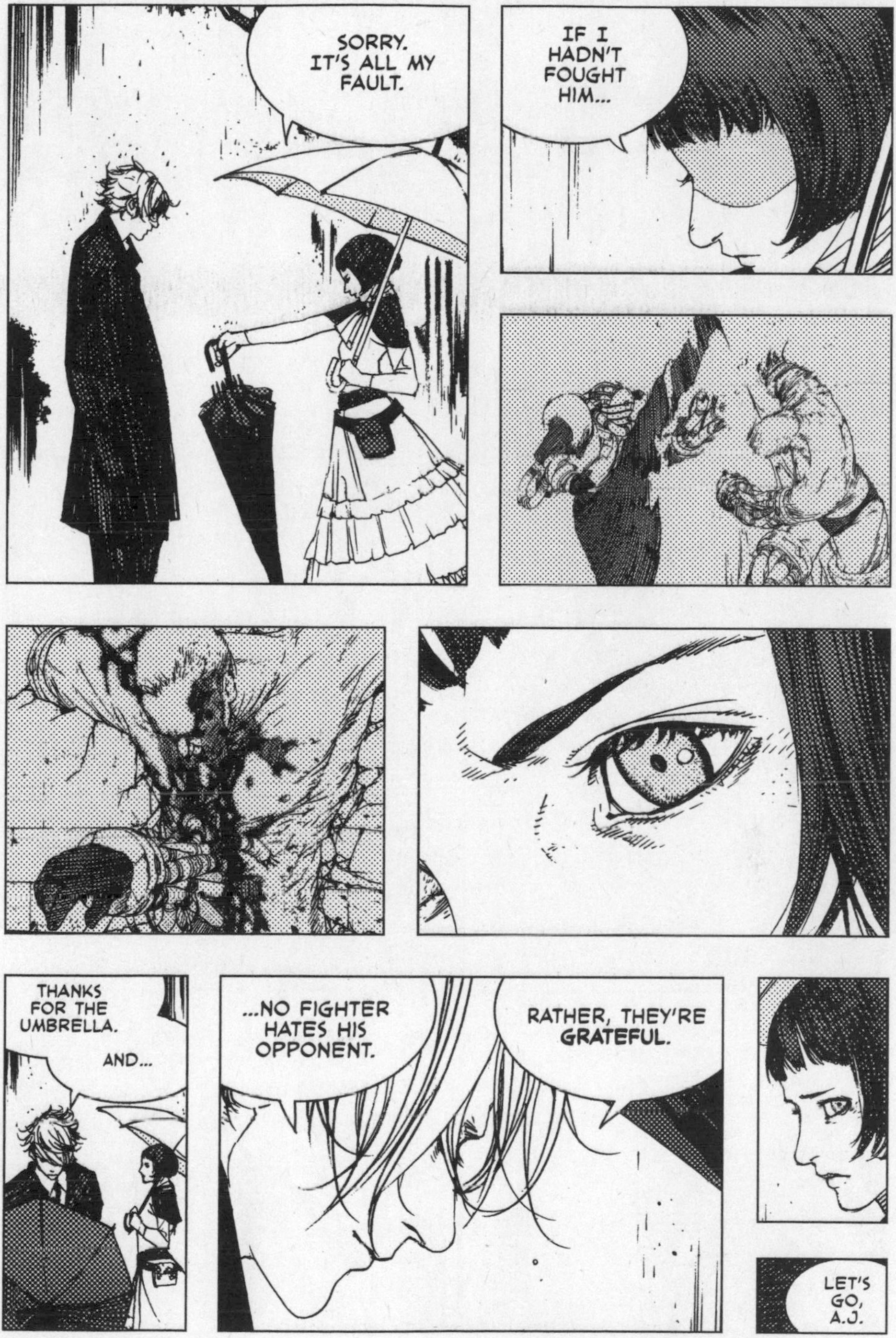
SORRY. IT'S ALL MY FAULT.
IF I HADN'T FOUGHT HIM...
THANKS FOR THE UMBRELLA.
AND...
...NO FIGHTER HATES HIS OPPONENT.
RATHER, THEY'RE GRATEFUL.
LET'S GO, A.J.

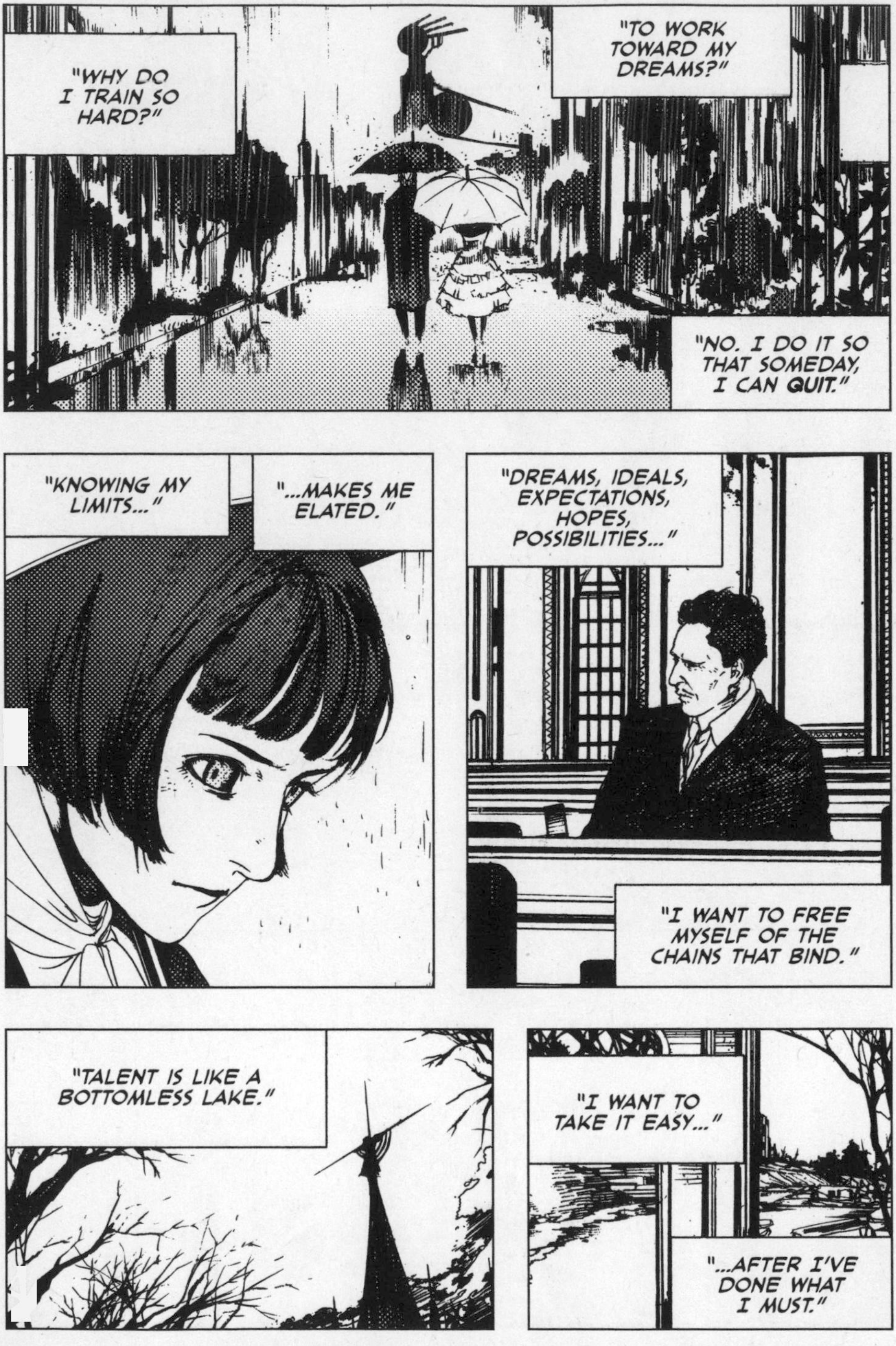
"WHY DO I TRAIN SO HARD?"
"TO WORK TOWARD MY DREAMS?"
"NO. I DO IT SO THAT SOMEDAY, I CAN QUIT."
"KNOWING MY LIMITS..."
"...MAKES ME ELATED."
"DREAMS, IDEALS, EXPECTATIONS, HOPES, POSSIBILITIES..."
"I WANT TO FREE MYSELF OF THE CHAINS THAT BIND."
"TALENT IS LIKE A BOTTOMLESS LAKE."
"I WANT TO TAKE IT EASY..."
"...AFTER I'VE DONE WHAT I MUST."

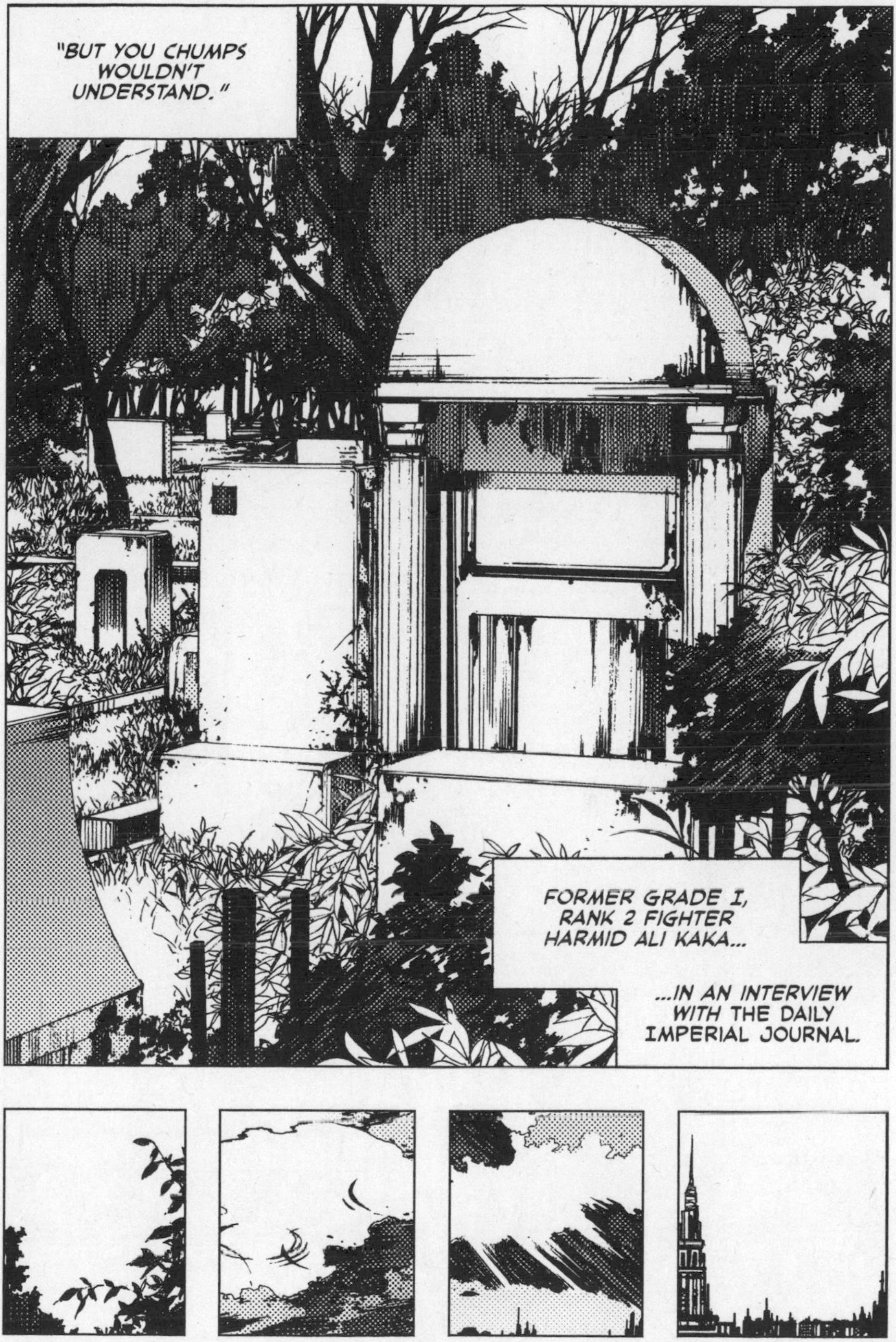
"BUT YOU CHUMPS WOULDN'T UNDERSTAND."
FORMER GRADE I, RANK 2 FIGHTER HARMID ALI KAKA...
...IN AN INTERVIEW WITH THE DAILY IMPERIAL JOURNAL.

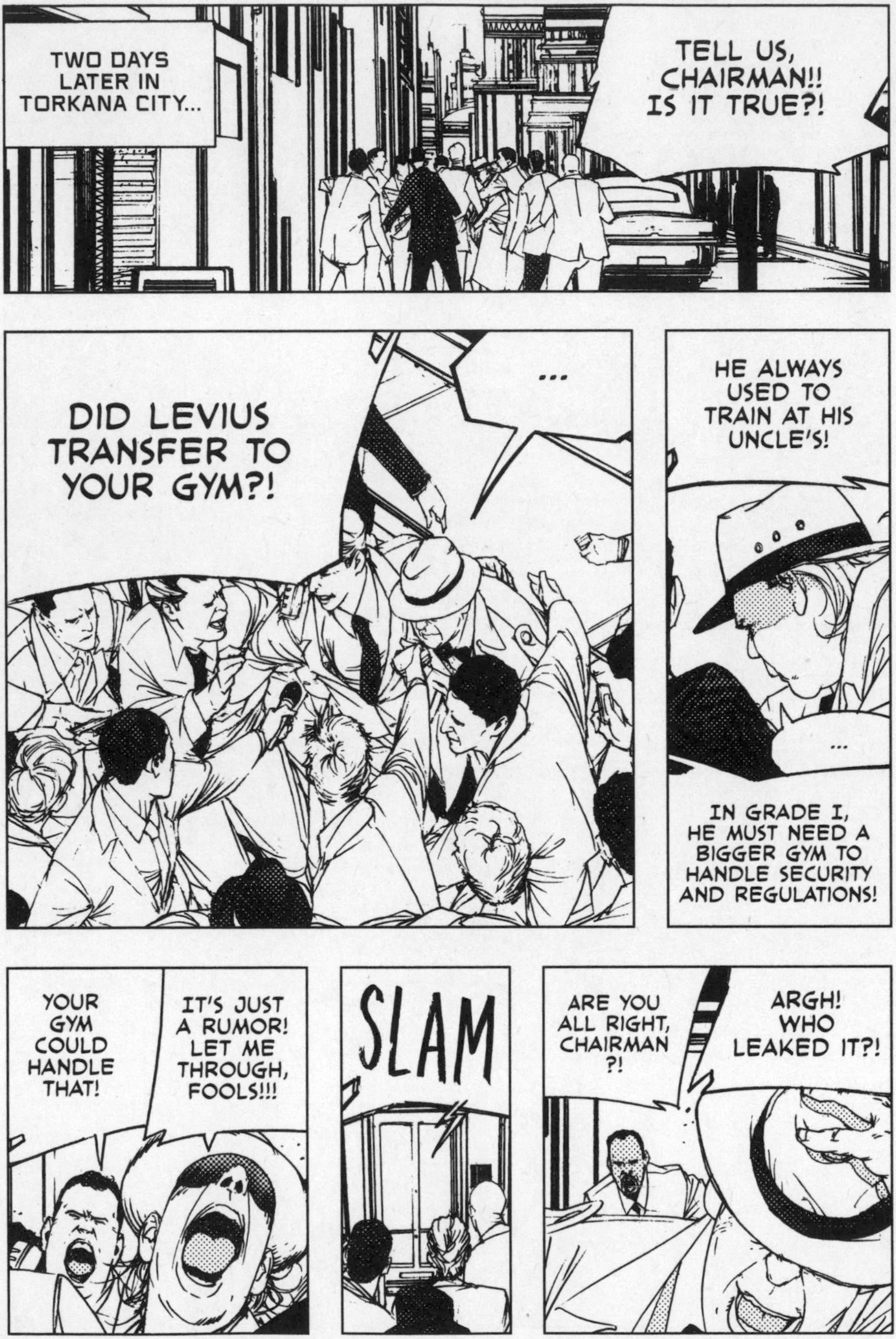
TWO DAYS LATER IN TORKANA CITY...
TELL US, CHAIRMAN!! IS IT TRUE?!
DID LEVIUS TRANSFER TO YOUR GYM?!
...
HE ALWAYS USED TO TRAIN AT HIS UNCLE'S!
...
IN GRADE I, HE MUST NEED A BIGGER GYM TO HANDLE SECURITY AND REGULATIONS!
YOUR GYM COULD HANDLE THAT!
IT'S JUST A RUMOR! LET ME THROUGH, FOOLS!!!
SLAM
ARE YOU ALL RIGHT, CHAIRMAN ?!
ARGH! WHO LEAKED IT?!

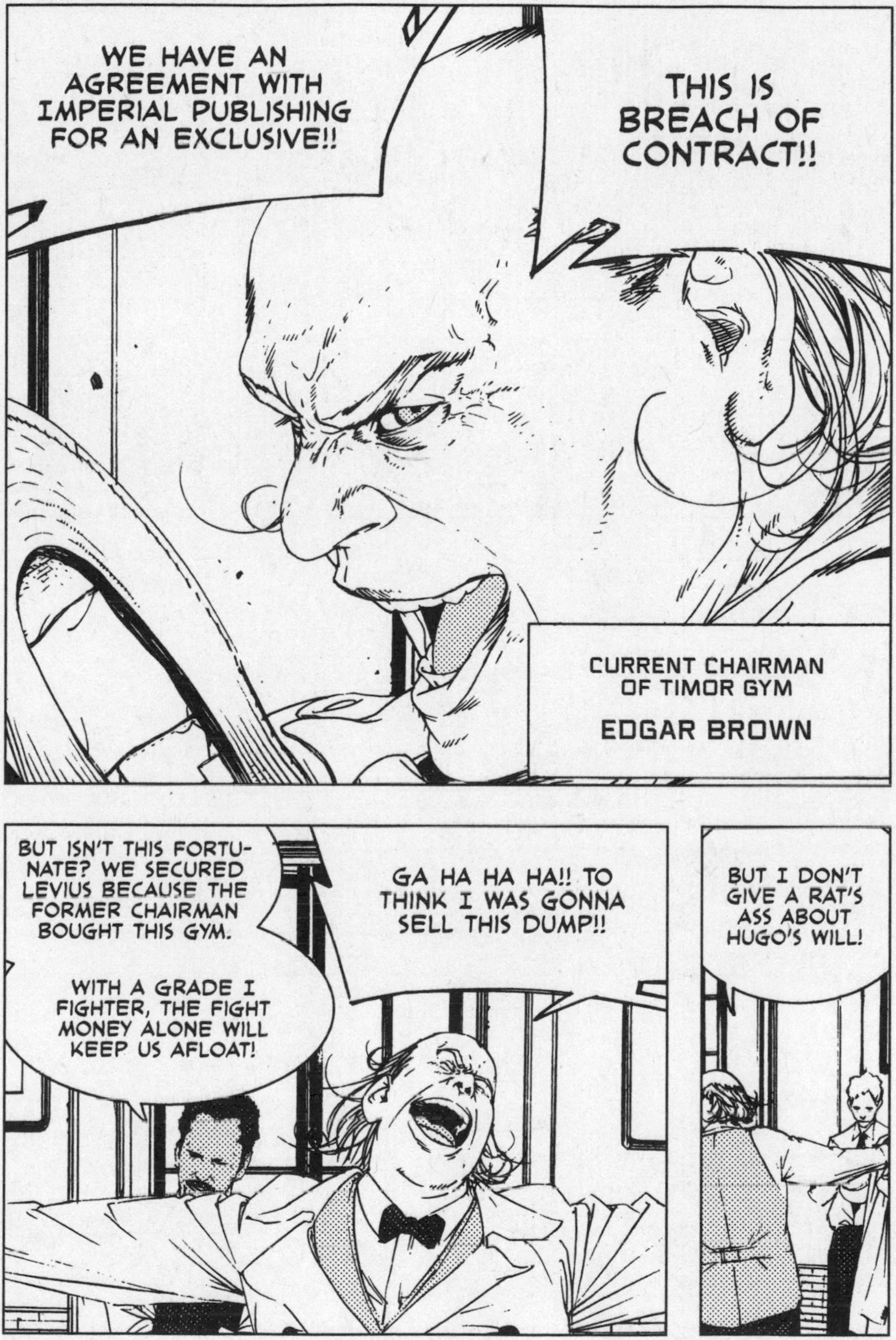
WE HAVE AN AGREEMENT WITH IMPERIAL PUBLISHING FOR AN EXCLUSIVE!!
THIS IS BREACH OF CONTRACT!!
CURRENT CHAIRMAN OF TIMOR GYM
EDGAR BROWN
BUT ISN'T THIS FORTUNATE? WE SECURED LEVIUS BECAUSE THE FORMER CHAIRMAN BOUGHT THIS GYM.
WITH A GRADE I FIGHTER, THE FIGHT MONEY ALONE WILL KEEP US AFLOAT!
GA HA HA HA!! TO THINK I WAS GONNA SELL THIS DUMP!!
BUT I DON'T GIVE A RAT'S ASS ABOUT HUGO'S WILL!

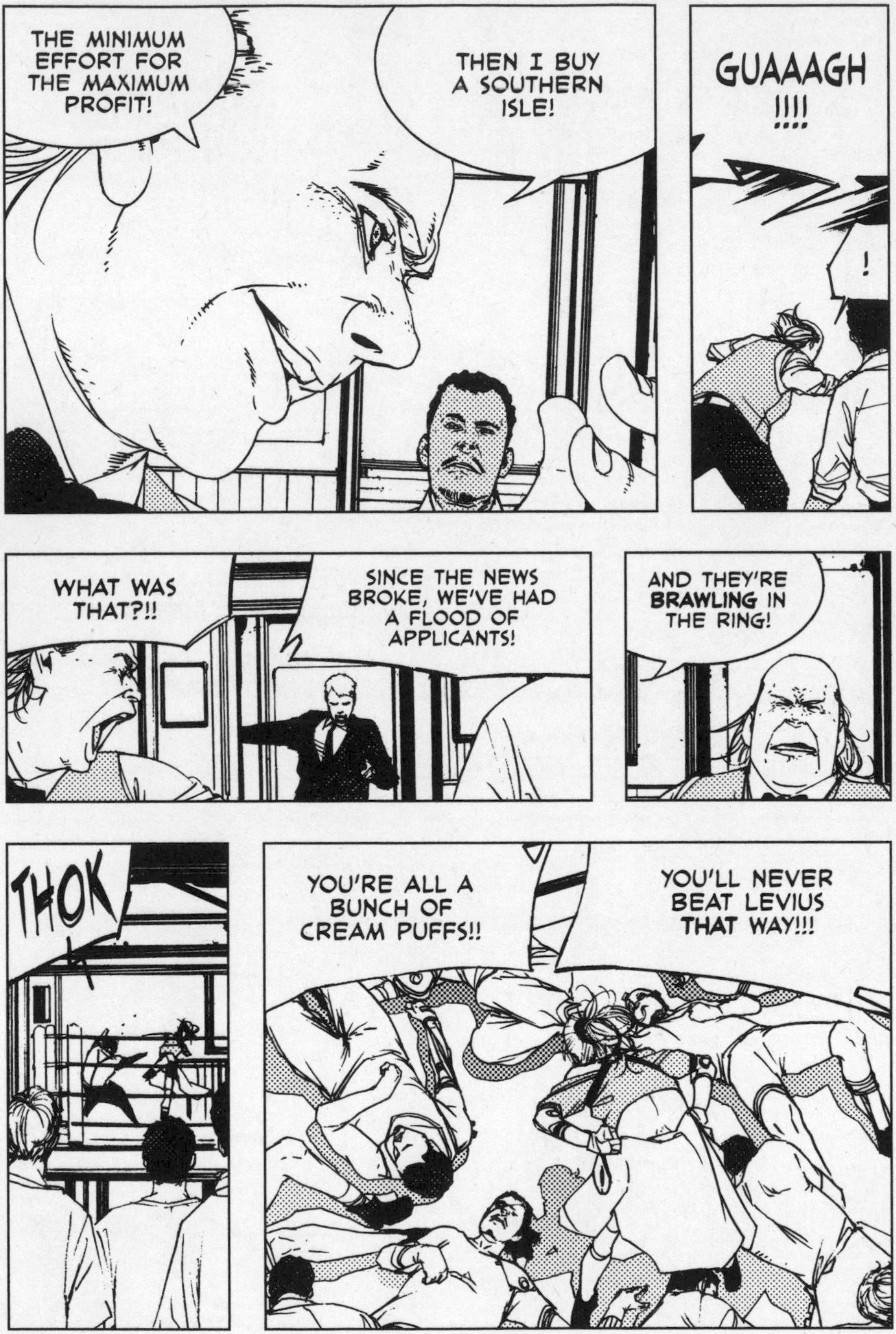
THE MINIMUM EFFORT FOR THE MAXIMUM PROFIT!
THEN I BUY A SOUTHERN ISLE!
GUAAAGH !!!!
!
WHAT WAS THAT?!!
SINCE THE NEWS BROKE, WE'VE HAD A FLOOD OF APPLICANTS!
AND THEY'RE **BRAWLING** IN THE RING!
THOK
YOU'RE ALL A BUNCH OF CREAM PUFFS!!
YOU'LL NEVER BEAT LEVIUS **THAT WAY!!!**

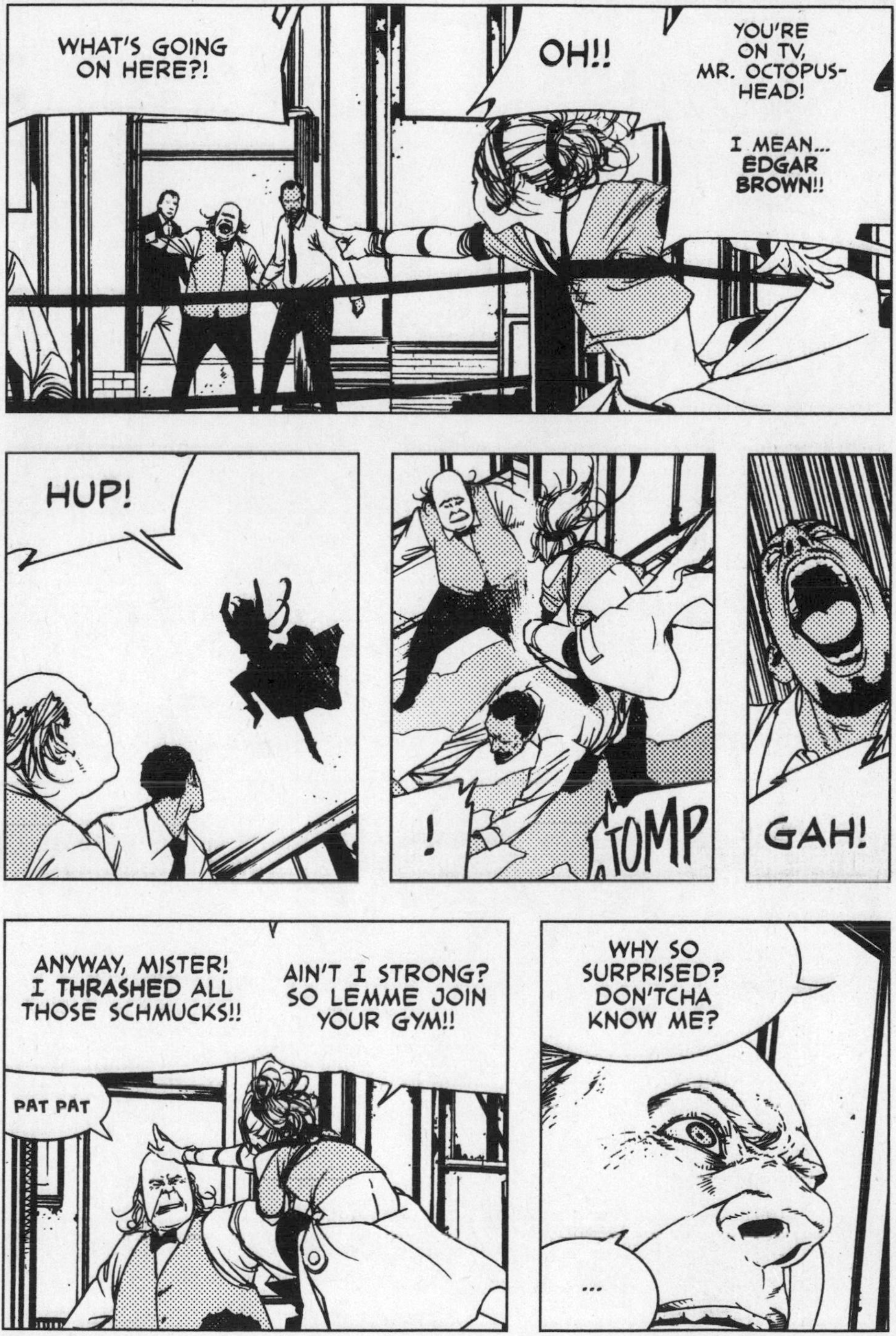
WHAT'S GOING ON HERE?!
OH!!
YOU'RE ON TV, MR. OCTOPUS-HEAD!
I MEAN... EDGAR BROWN!!
HUP!
!
TOMP
GAH!
ANYWAY, MISTER! I THRASHED ALL THOSE SCHMUCKS!!
AIN'T I STRONG? SO LEMME JOIN YOUR GYM!!
PAT PAT
WHY SO SURPRISED? DON'TCHA KNOW ME?
...

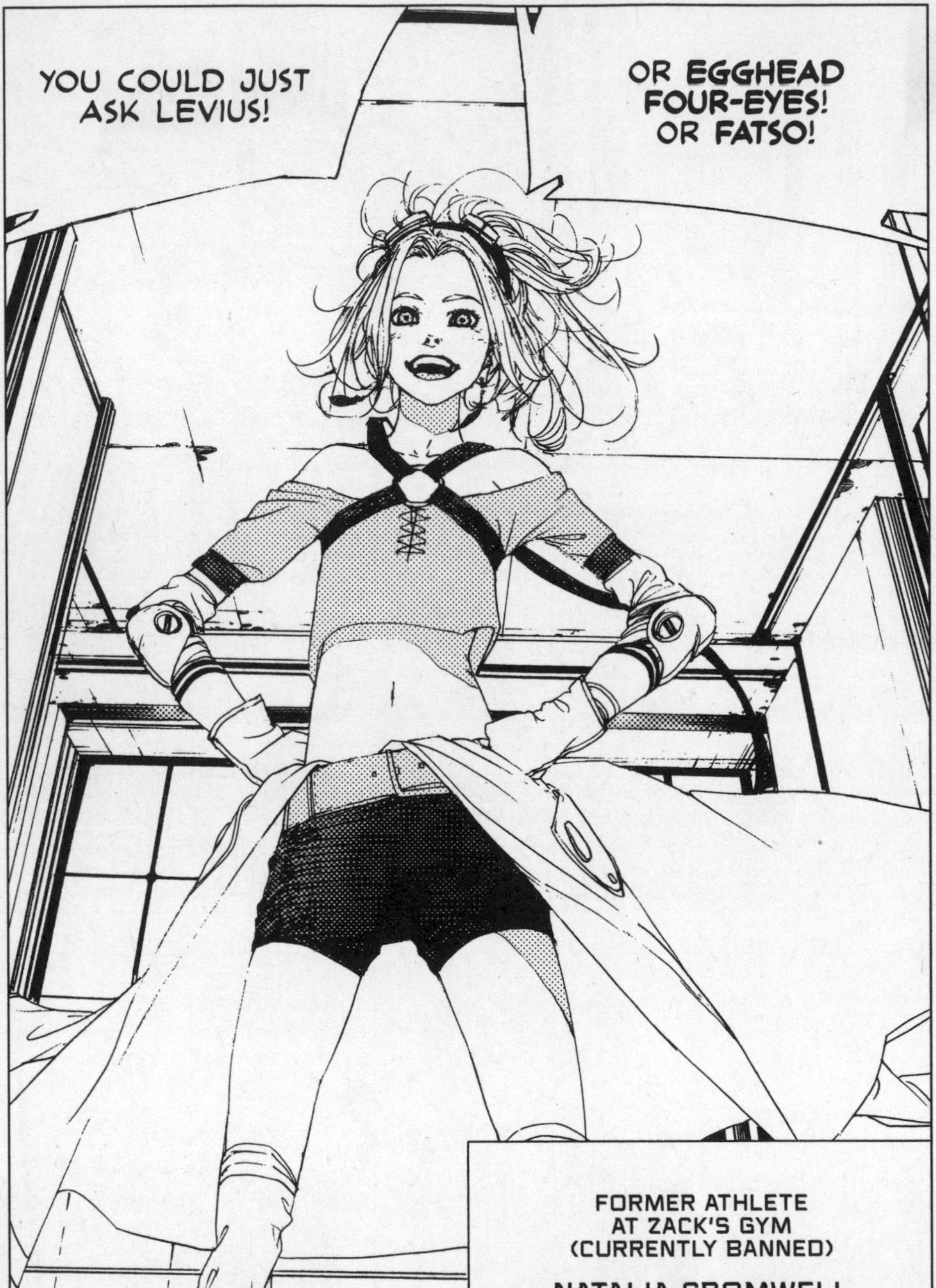
YOU COULD JUST ASK LEVIUS!
OR EGGHEAD FOUR-EYES! OR FATSO!
FORMER ATHLETE AT ZACK'S GYM (CURRENTLY BANNED)
NATALIA CROMWELL

Levius/est
VOL. 1

Chapter 05

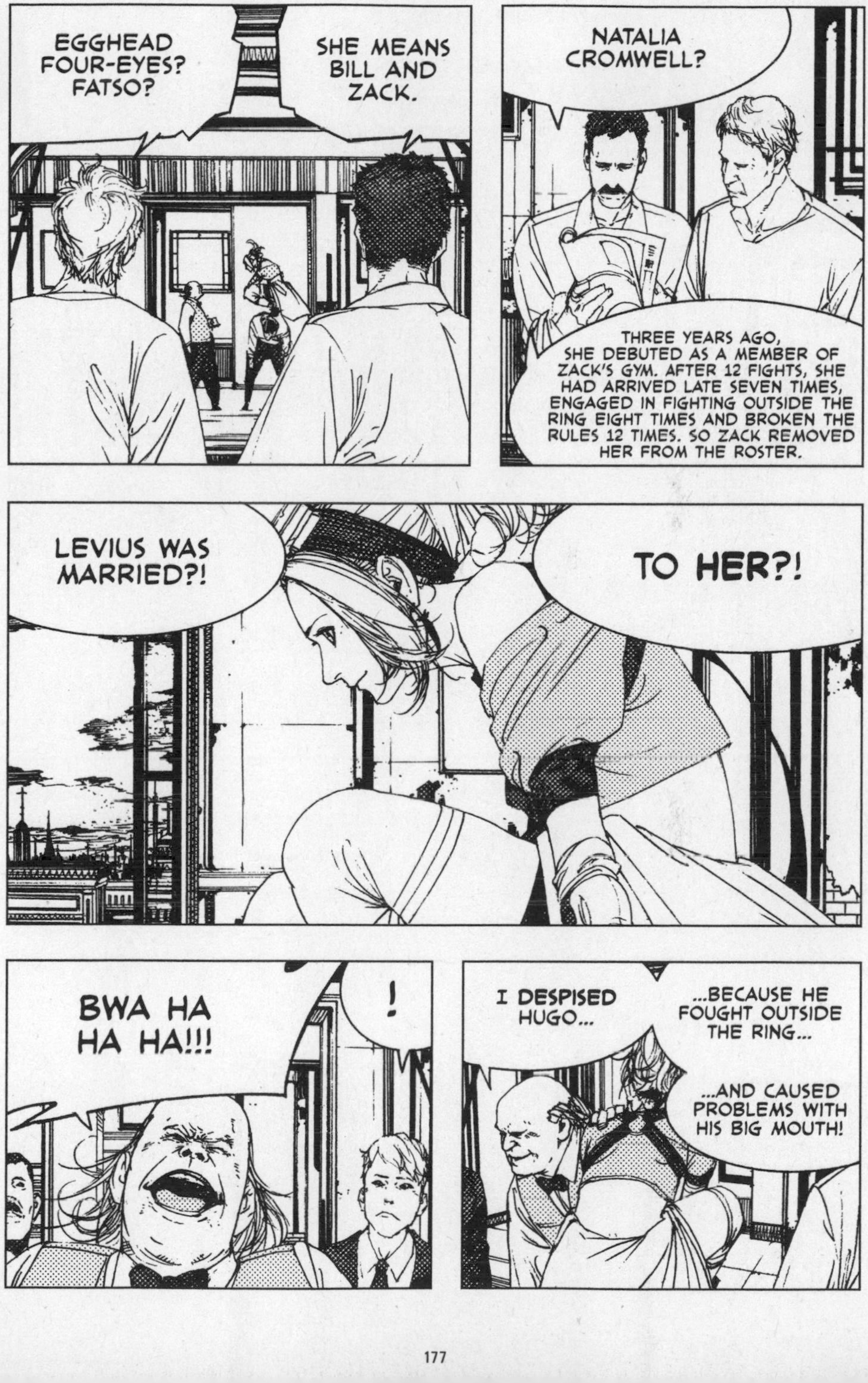
EGGHEAD FOUR-EYES? FATSO?
SHE MEANS BILL AND ZACK.
NATALIA CROMWELL?
THREE YEARS AGO, SHE DEBUTED AS A MEMBER OF ZACK'S GYM. AFTER 12 FIGHTS, SHE HAD ARRIVED LATE SEVEN TIMES, ENGAGED IN FIGHTING OUTSIDE THE RING EIGHT TIMES AND BROKEN THE RULES 12 TIMES. SO ZACK REMOVED HER FROM THE ROSTER.
LEVIUS WAS MARRIED?!
TO **HER**?!
BWA HA HA HA!!!
!
I DESPISED HUGO...
...BECAUSE HE FOUGHT OUTSIDE THE RING...
...AND CAUSED PROBLEMS WITH HIS BIG MOUTH!

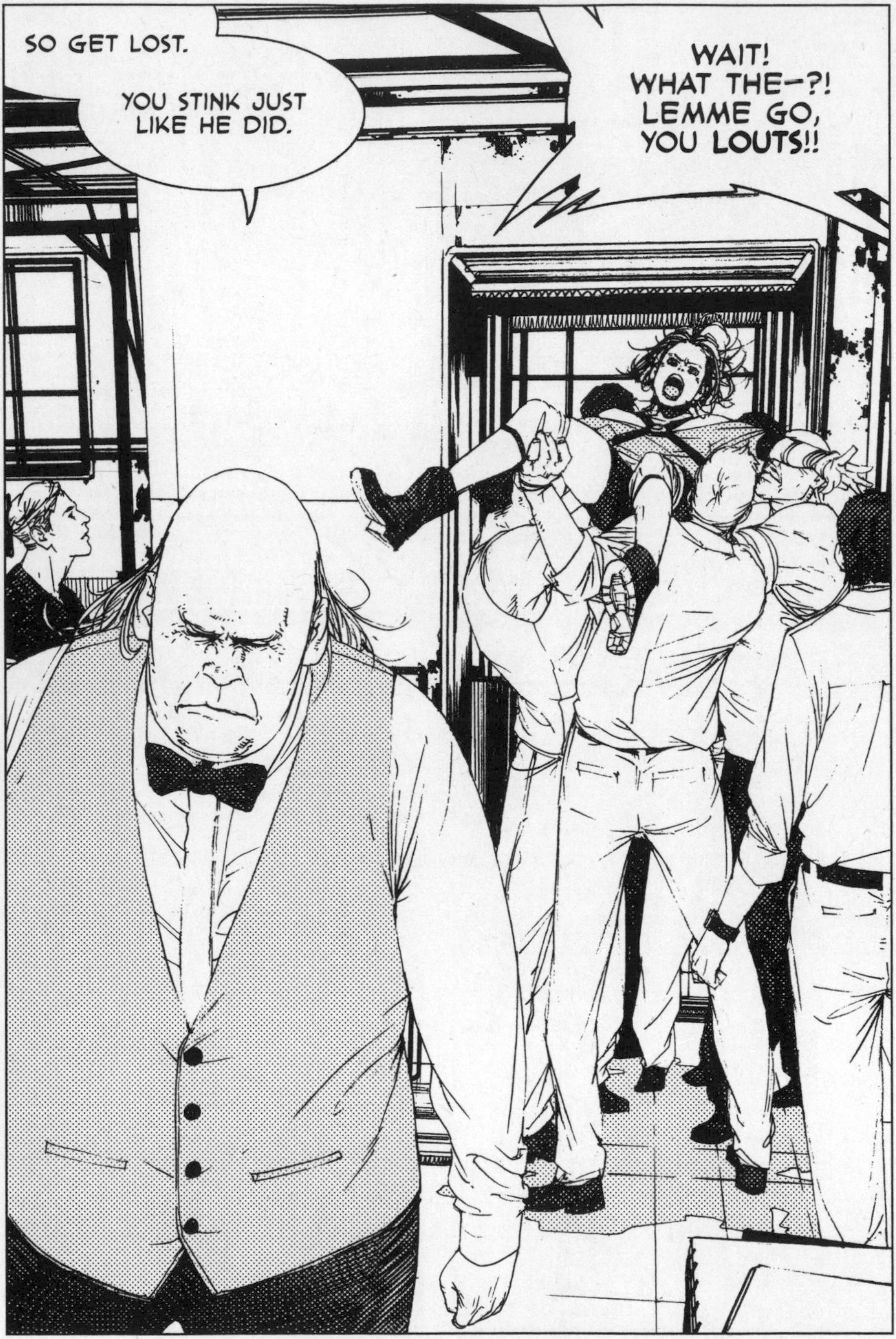
WAIT! WHAT THE–?! LEMME GO, YOU LOUTS!!
SO GET LOST.
YOU STINK JUST LIKE HE DID.

YOU DON'T KNOW ANYTHING ABOUT ME, OCTOPUS-HEAD!!

I'M A GRADE III PHENOM IN ROSALIA! THEY SAY I'M A COMBINATION OF BEAUTY AND BRAWN THAT ONLY APPEARS ONCE A MILLENNIUM!!

I SELL OUT TICKETS OVERNIGHT!! I DOMINATE FAN RANKINGS! I FILL THE STANDS WITH CROWDS!!

DON'T LUMP ME IN WITH THAT MEATHEAD!!

SH-SHE'S RIGHT. ROSALIA LEADS THE REGIONS IN ATTENDANCE.

SHE HAS A SMALL ARMY OF LOYAL AND RABID FANS.

BUT THE CASUAL FANS, THE MAJORITY OF THE AUDIENCE, THEY DON'T REALLY KNOW WHO SHE IS.

SHE'S GOT SOMETHING THOUGH. IF SHE WERE TO RISE IN THE RANKS, IF MORE PEOPLE SAW HER, SHE MIGHT JUST WIN OVER THE WHOLE WORLD!

...

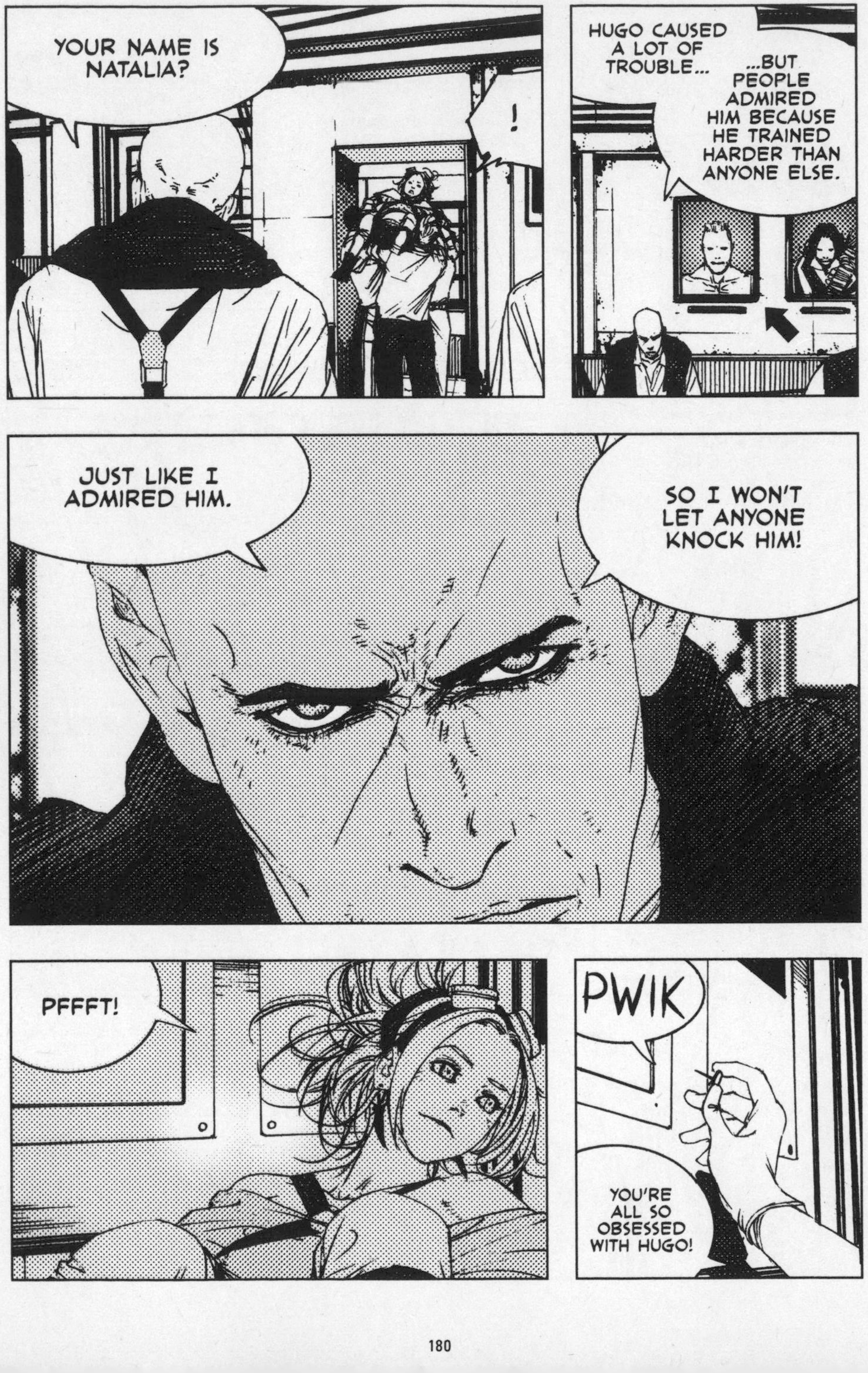
YOUR NAME IS NATALIA?
!
HUGO CAUSED A LOT OF TROUBLE...
...BUT PEOPLE ADMIRED HIM BECAUSE HE TRAINED HARDER THAN ANYONE ELSE.
JUST LIKE I ADMIRED HIM.
SO I WON'T LET ANYONE KNOCK HIM!
PFFFT!
PWIK
YOU'RE ALL SO OBSESSED WITH HUGO!

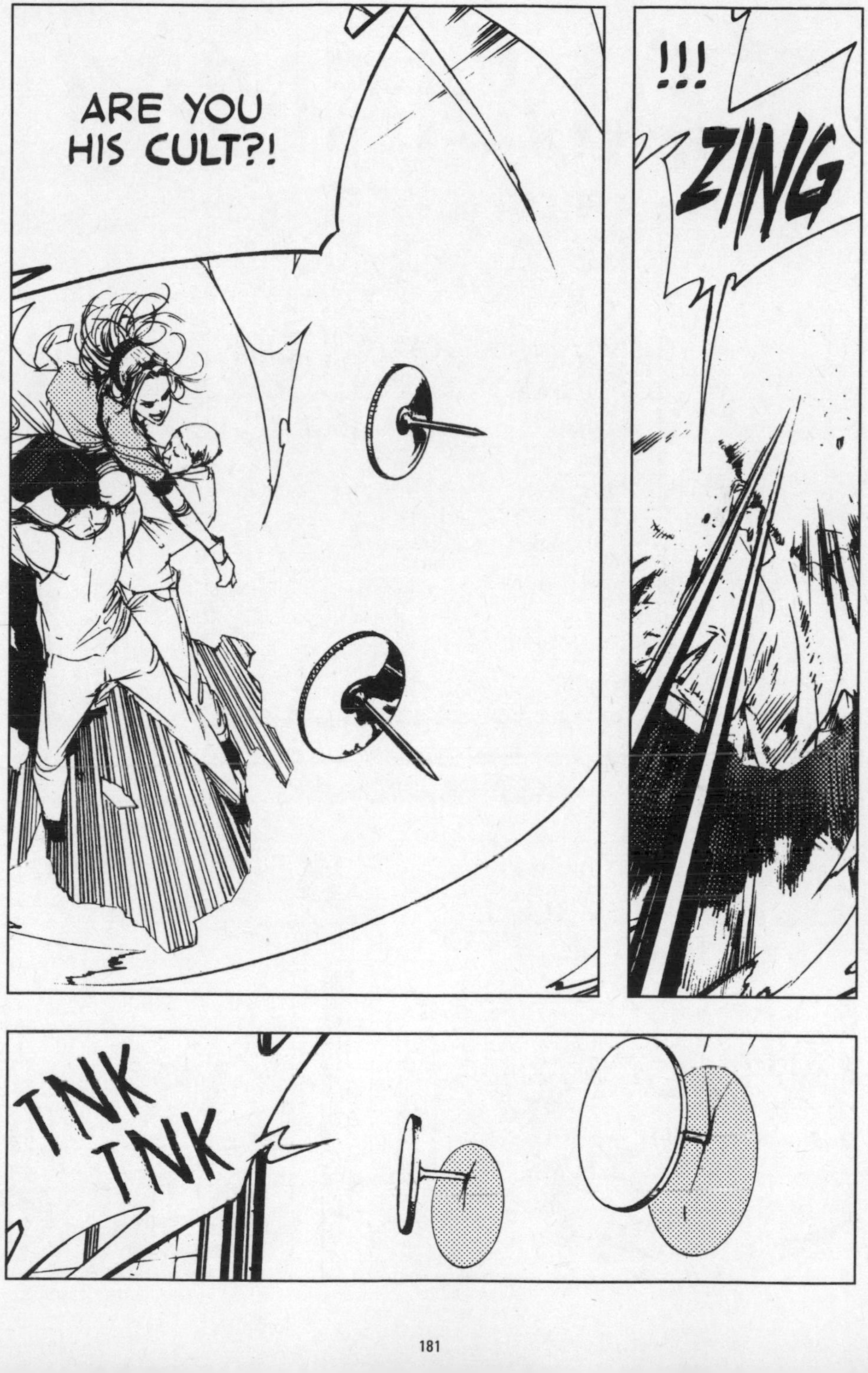
!!!
ZING
ARE YOU HIS CULT?!
TNK TNK

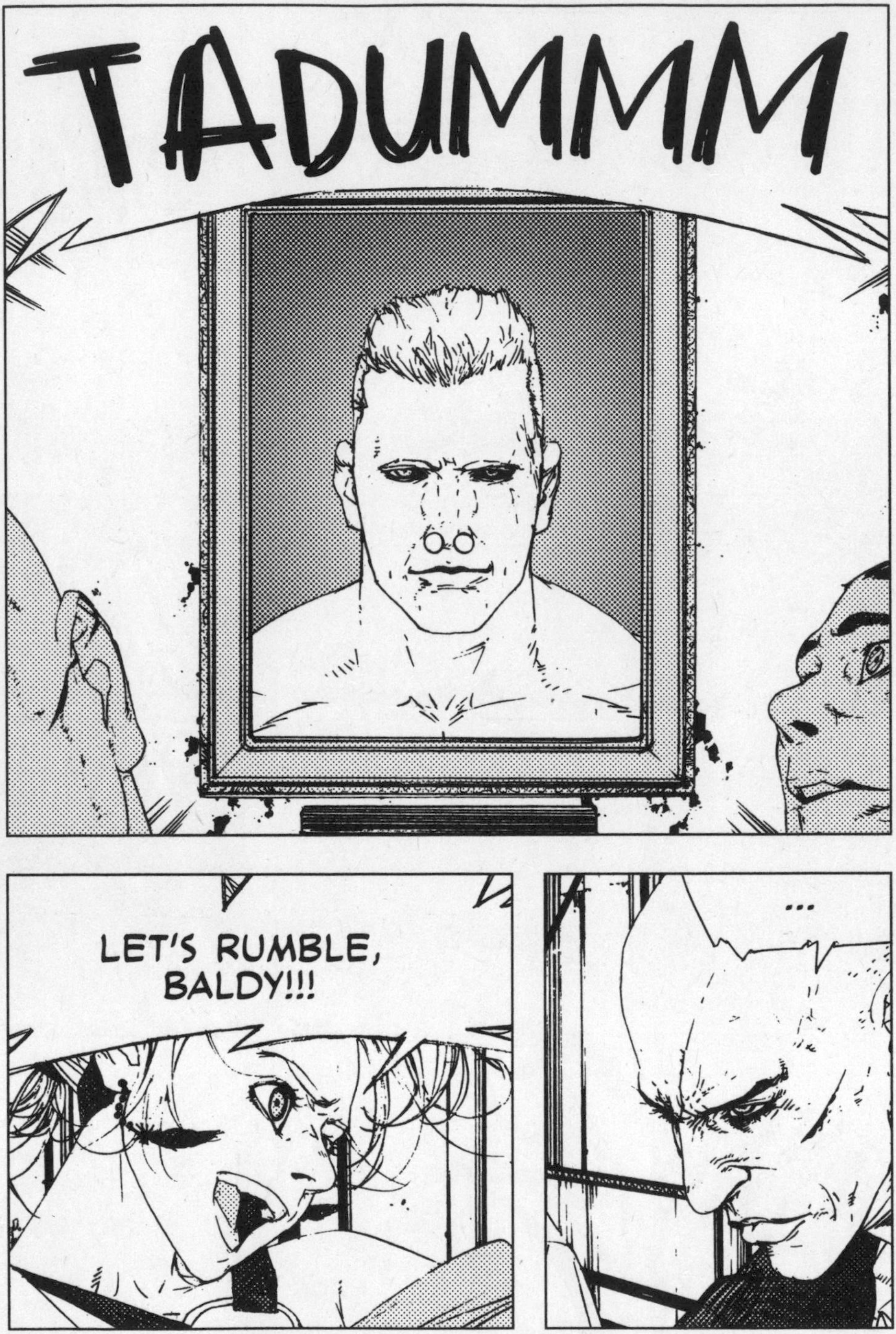
TADUMMM
...
LET'S RUMBLE, BALDY!!!

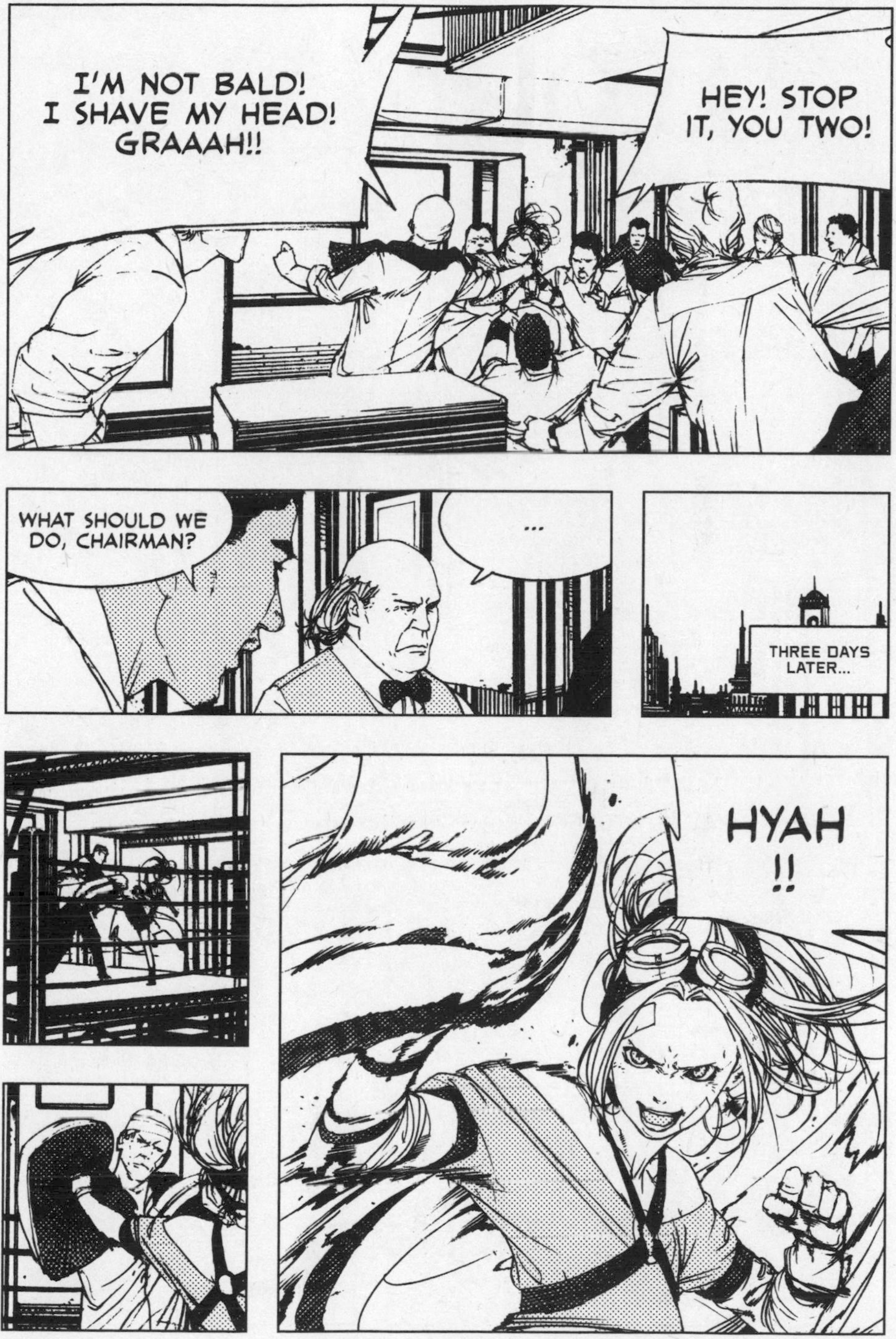
I'M NOT BALD! I SHAVE MY HEAD! GRAAAH!!
HEY! STOP IT, YOU TWO!
WHAT SHOULD WE DO, CHAIRMAN?
...
THREE DAYS LATER...
HYAH !!

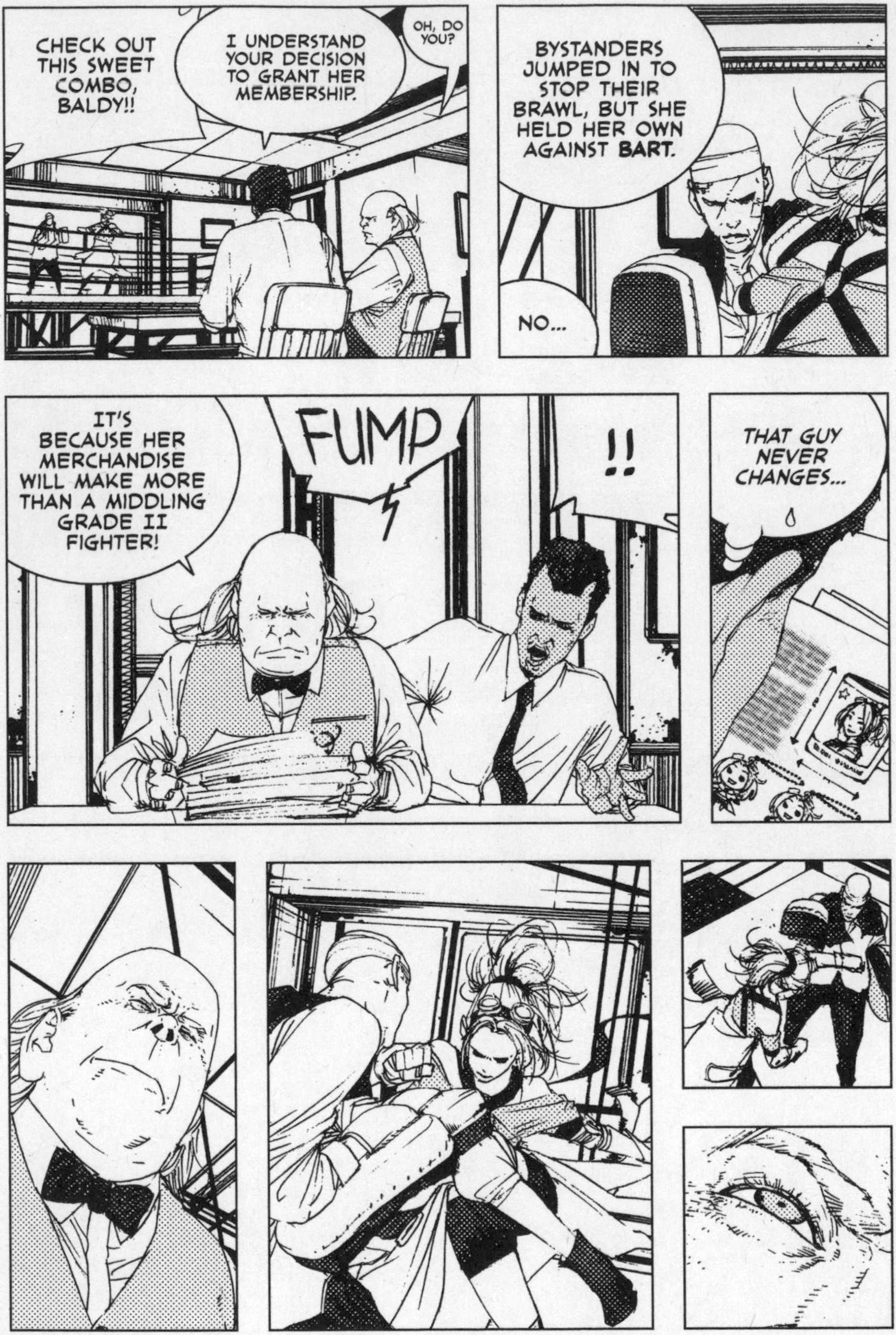
CHECK OUT THIS SWEET COMBO, BALDY!!
I UNDERSTAND YOUR DECISION TO GRANT HER MEMBERSHIP.
OH, DO YOU?
BYSTANDERS JUMPED IN TO STOP THEIR BRAWL, BUT SHE HELD HER OWN AGAINST BART.
NO...
IT'S BECAUSE HER MERCHANDISE WILL MAKE MORE THAN A MIDDLING GRADE II FIGHTER!
FUMP
!!
THAT GUY NEVER CHANGES...

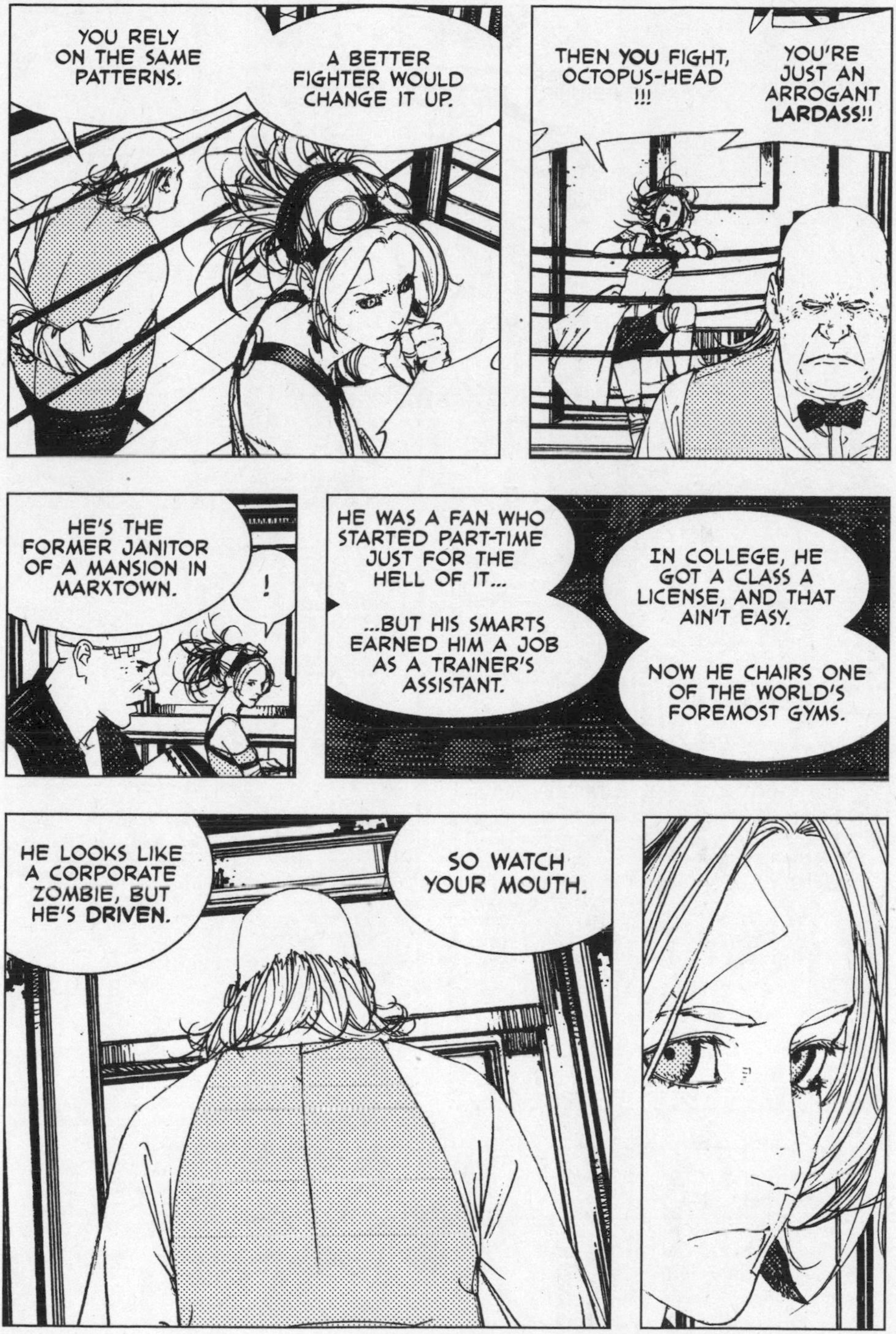
YOU RELY ON THE SAME PATTERNS.
A BETTER FIGHTER WOULD CHANGE IT UP.
THEN YOU FIGHT, OCTOPUS-HEAD !!!
YOU'RE JUST AN ARROGANT LARDASS!!
HE'S THE FORMER JANITOR OF A MANSION IN MARXTOWN.
!
HE WAS A FAN WHO STARTED PART-TIME JUST FOR THE HELL OF IT...
...BUT HIS SMARTS EARNED HIM A JOB AS A TRAINER'S ASSISTANT.
IN COLLEGE, HE GOT A CLASS A LICENSE, AND THAT AIN'T EASY.
NOW HE CHAIRS ONE OF THE WORLD'S FOREMOST GYMS.
HE LOOKS LIKE A CORPORATE ZOMBIE, BUT HE'S DRIVEN.
SO WATCH YOUR MOUTH.

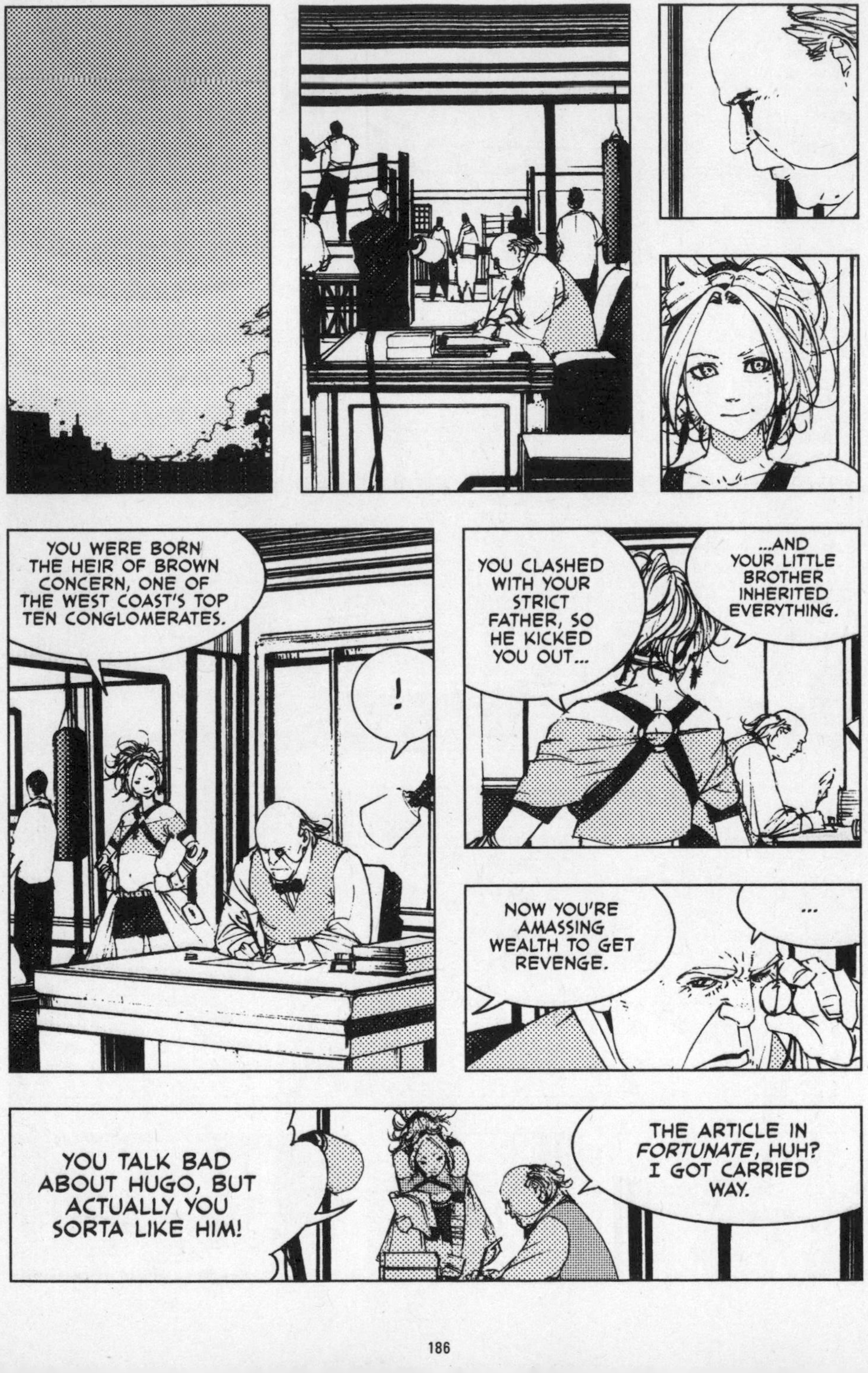
YOU WERE BORN THE HEIR OF BROWN CONCERN, ONE OF THE WEST COAST'S TOP TEN CONGLOMERATES.
!
YOU CLASHED WITH YOUR STRICT FATHER, SO HE KICKED YOU OUT...
...AND YOUR LITTLE BROTHER INHERITED EVERYTHING.
NOW YOU'RE AMASSING WEALTH TO GET REVENGE.
...
YOU TALK BAD ABOUT HUGO, BUT ACTUALLY YOU SORTA LIKE HIM!
THE ARTICLE IN *FORTUNATE*, HUH? I GOT CARRIED WAY.

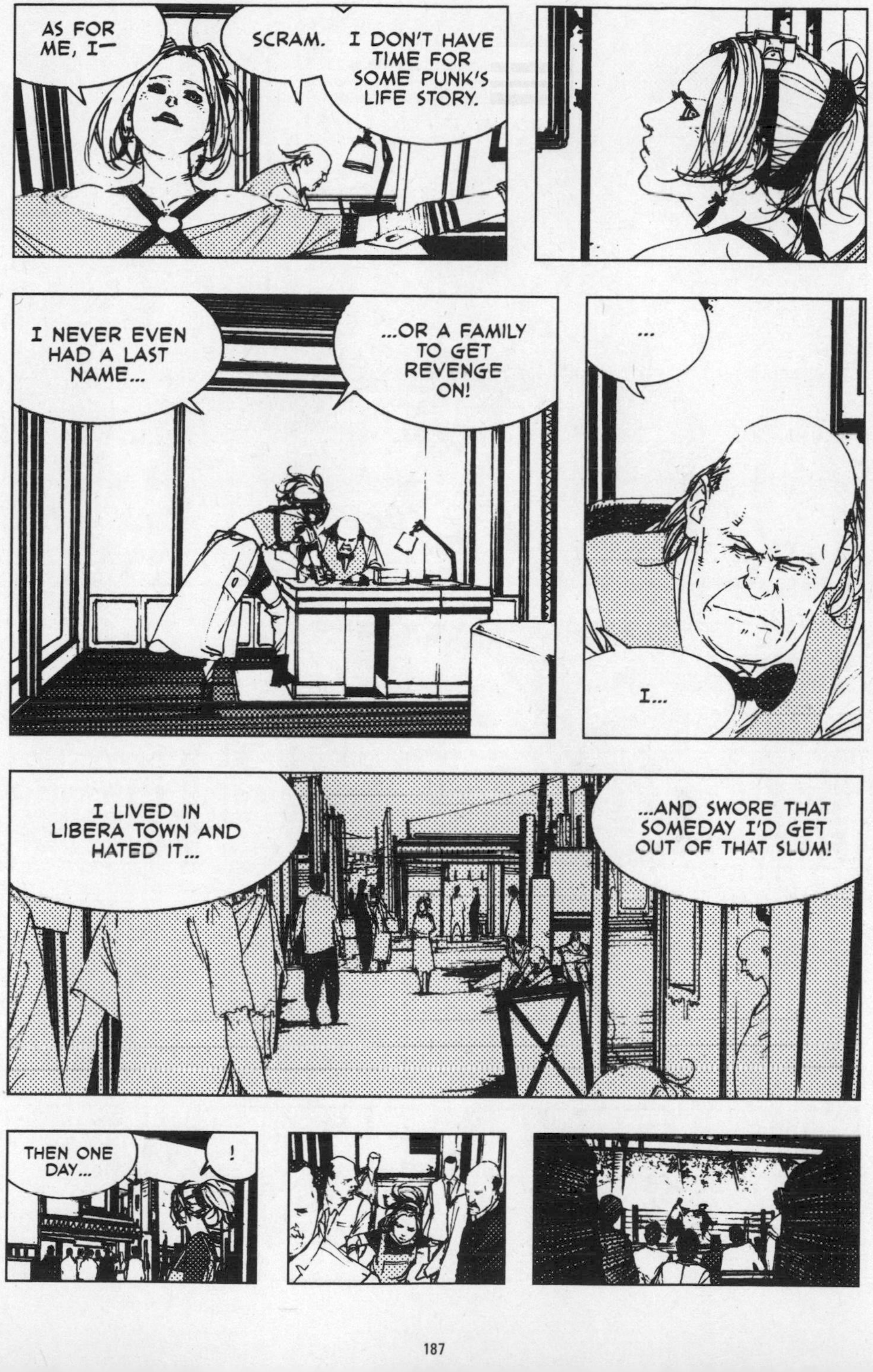
AS FOR ME, I—
SCRAM. I DON'T HAVE TIME FOR SOME PUNK'S LIFE STORY.
I NEVER EVEN HAD A LAST NAME...
...OR A FAMILY TO GET REVENGE ON!
...
I...
I LIVED IN LIBERA TOWN AND HATED IT...
...AND SWORE THAT SOMEDAY I'D GET OUT OF THAT SLUM!
THEN ONE DAY...
!

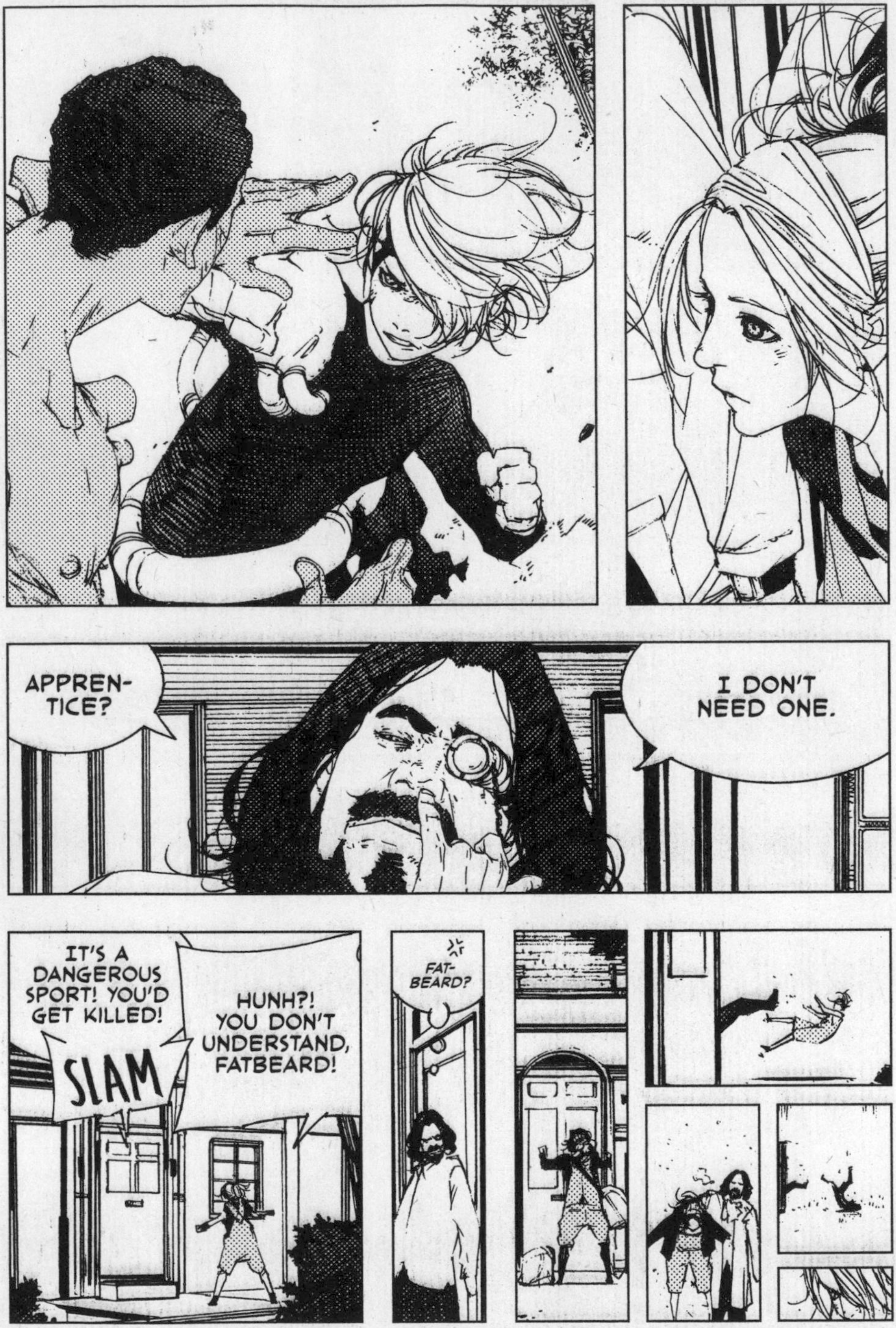
APPREN-
TICE?
I DON'T
NEED ONE.
IT'S A
DANGEROUS
SPORT! YOU'D
GET KILLED!
SLAM
HUNH?!
YOU DON'T
UNDERSTAND,
FATBEARD!
FAT-
BEARD?

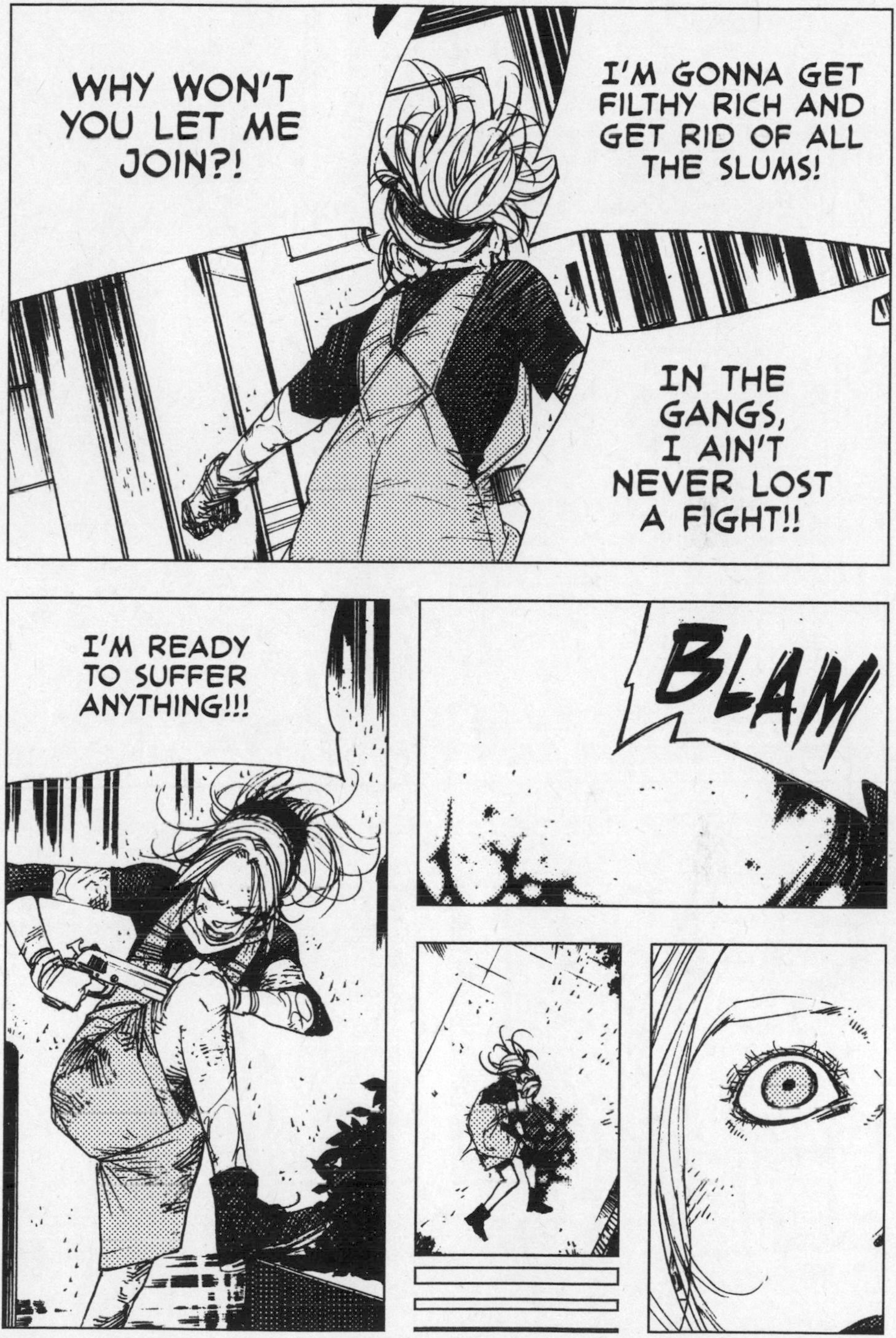
WHY WON'T YOU LET ME JOIN?!
I'M GONNA GET FILTHY RICH AND GET RID OF ALL THE SLUMS!
IN THE GANGS, I AIN'T NEVER LOST A FIGHT!!
I'M READY TO SUFFER ANYTHING!!!
BLAM

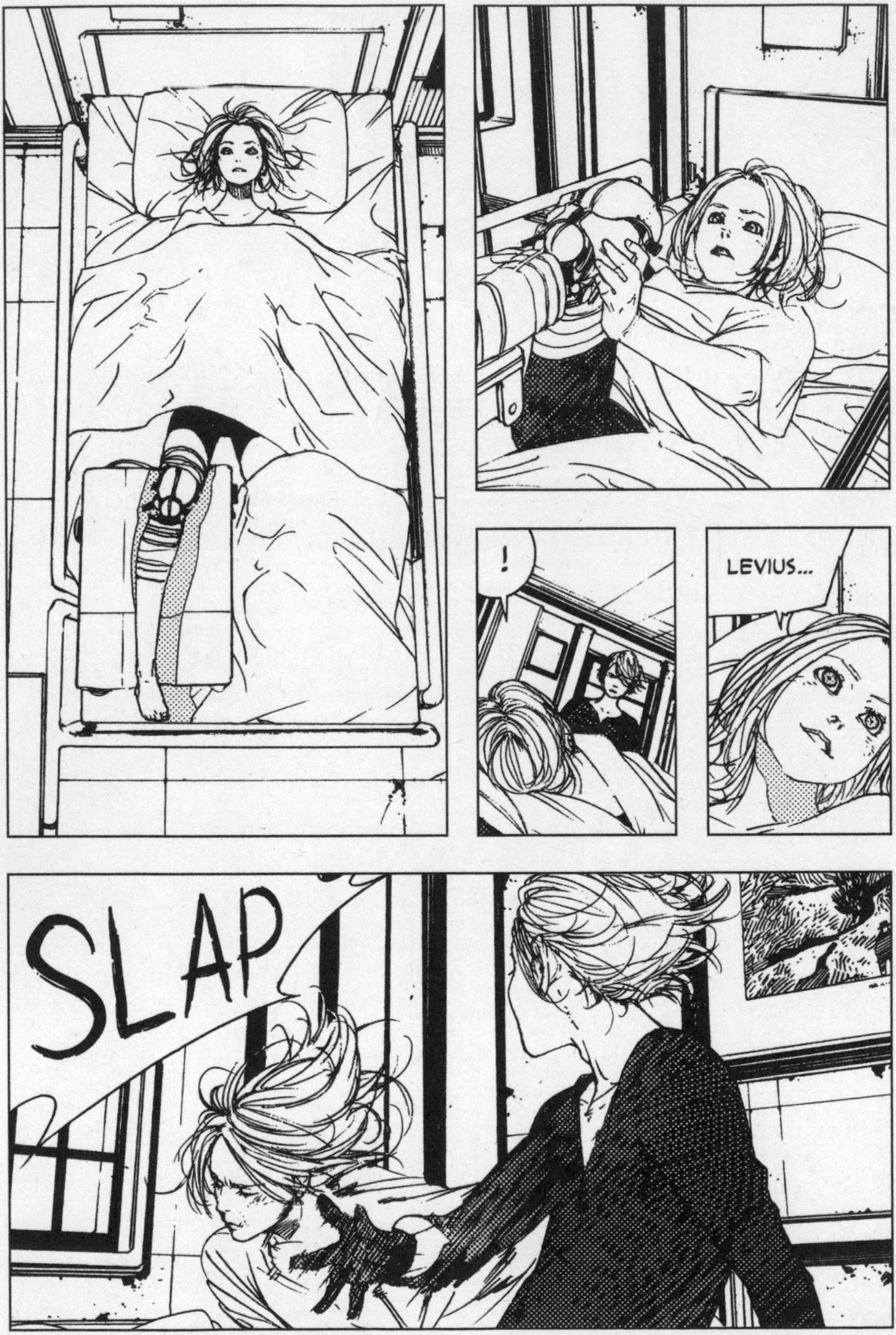

LEVIUS...
!
SLAP

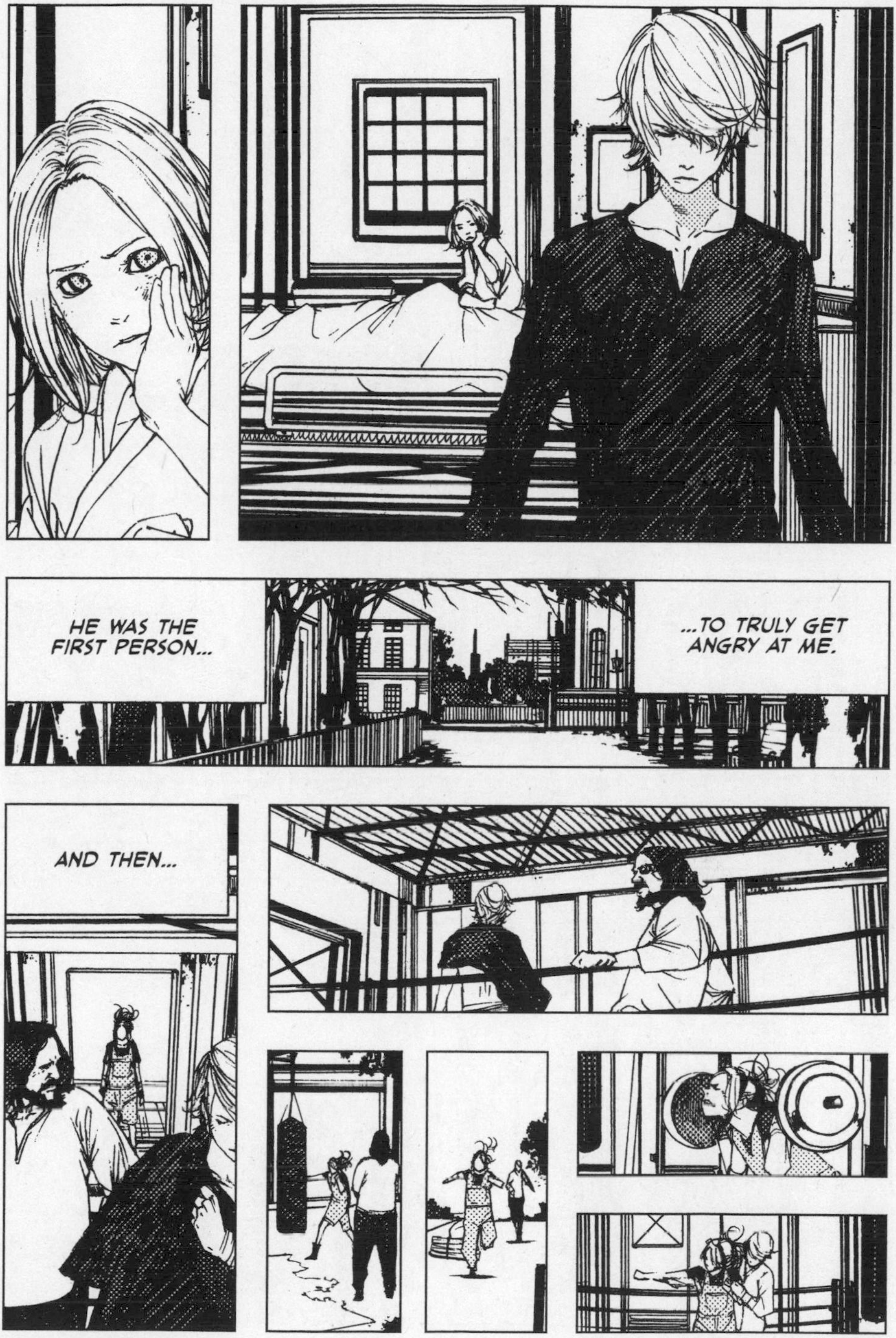
HE WAS THE FIRST PERSON...
...TO TRULY GET ANGRY AT ME.
AND THEN...

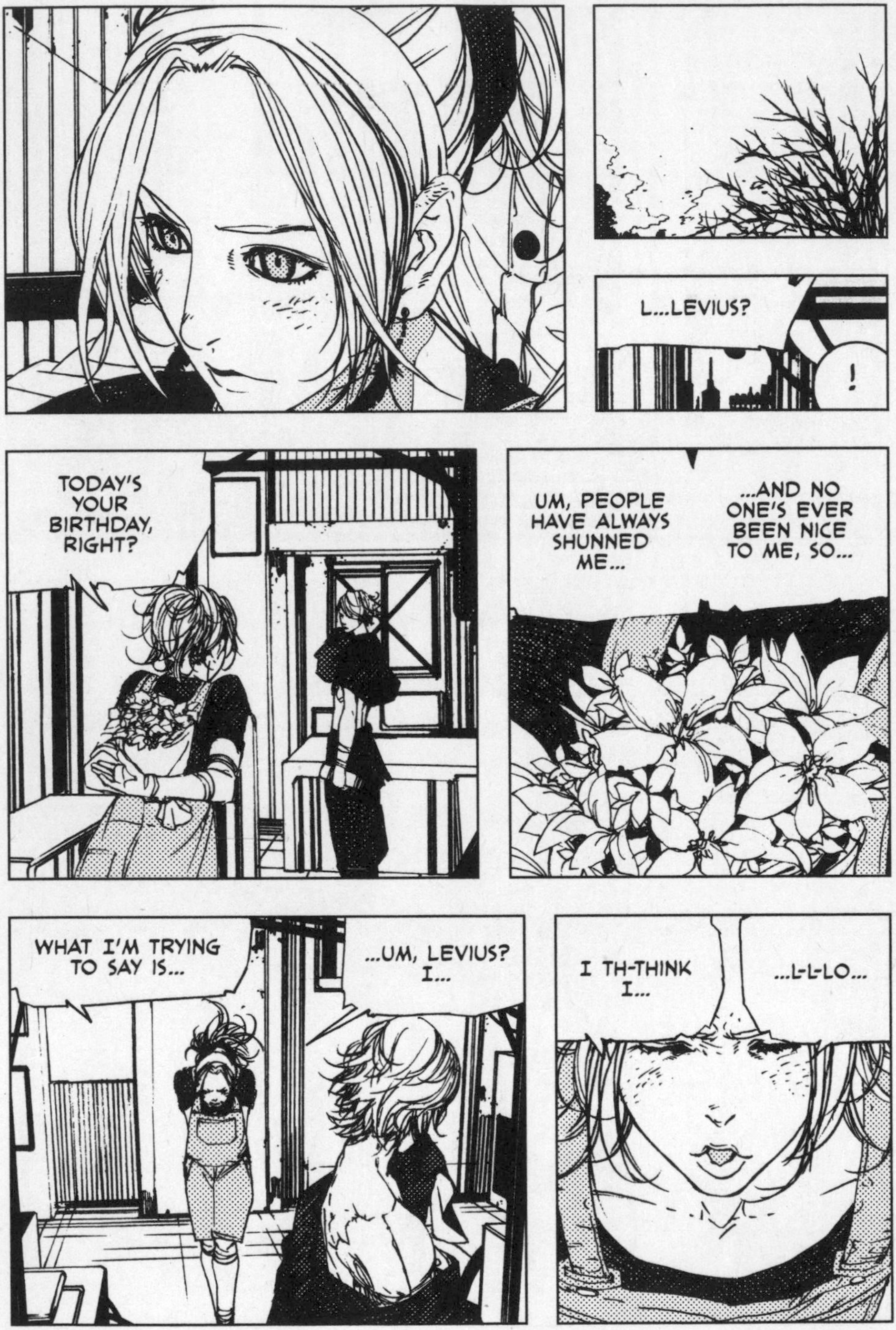
L...LEVIUS?
!
TODAY'S YOUR BIRTHDAY, RIGHT?
UM, PEOPLE HAVE ALWAYS SHUNNED ME...
...AND NO ONE'S EVER BEEN NICE TO ME, SO...
WHAT I'M TRYING TO SAY IS...
...UM, LEVIUS? I...
I TH-THINK I...
...L-L-LO...

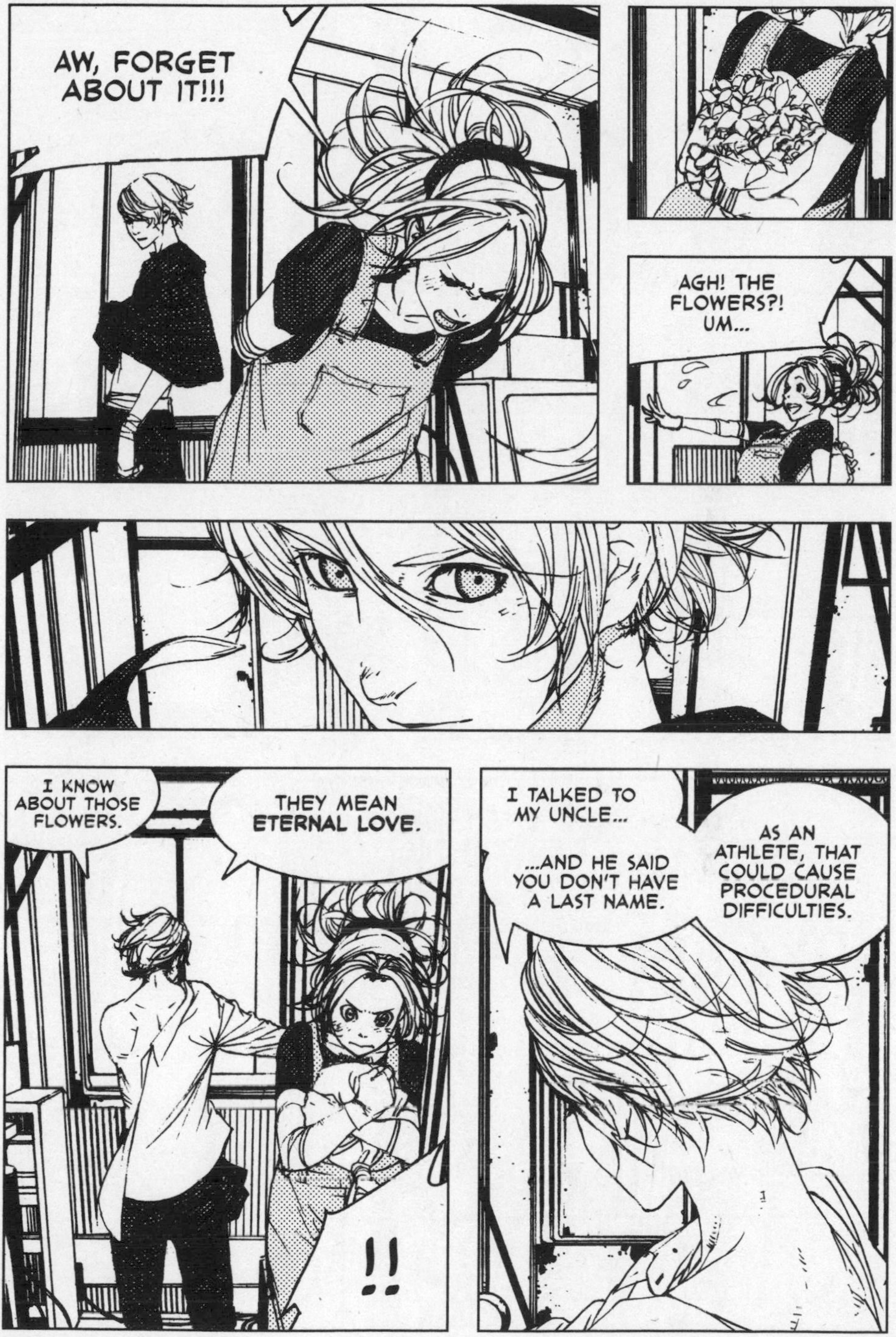
AW, FORGET ABOUT IT!!!
AGH! THE FLOWERS?! UM...
I KNOW ABOUT THOSE FLOWERS.
THEY MEAN ETERNAL LOVE.
!!
I TALKED TO MY UNCLE...
...AND HE SAID YOU DON'T HAVE A LAST NAME.
AS AN ATHLETE, THAT COULD CAUSE PROCEDURAL DIFFICULTIES.

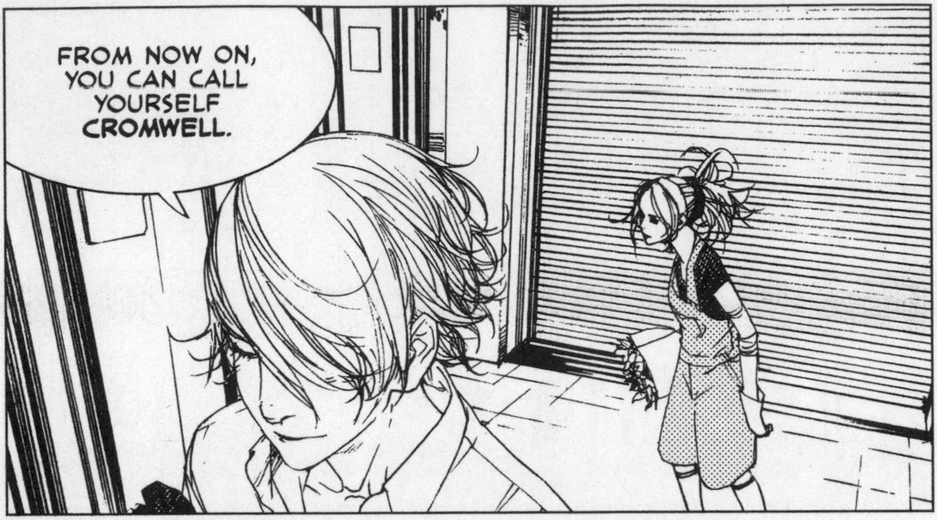
FROM NOW ON, YOU CAN CALL YOURSELF CROMWELL.

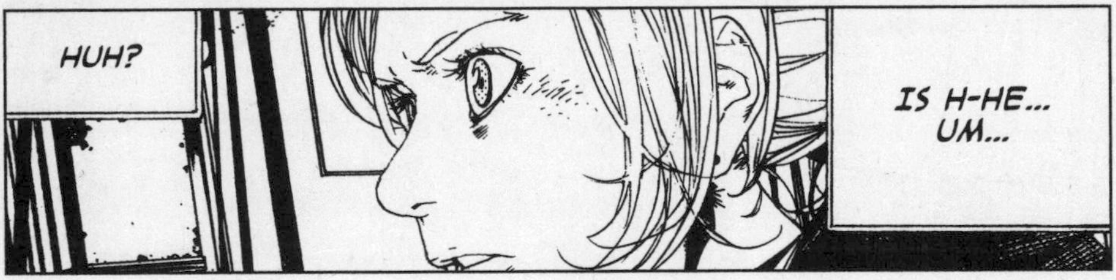
HUH?
IS H-HE... UM...

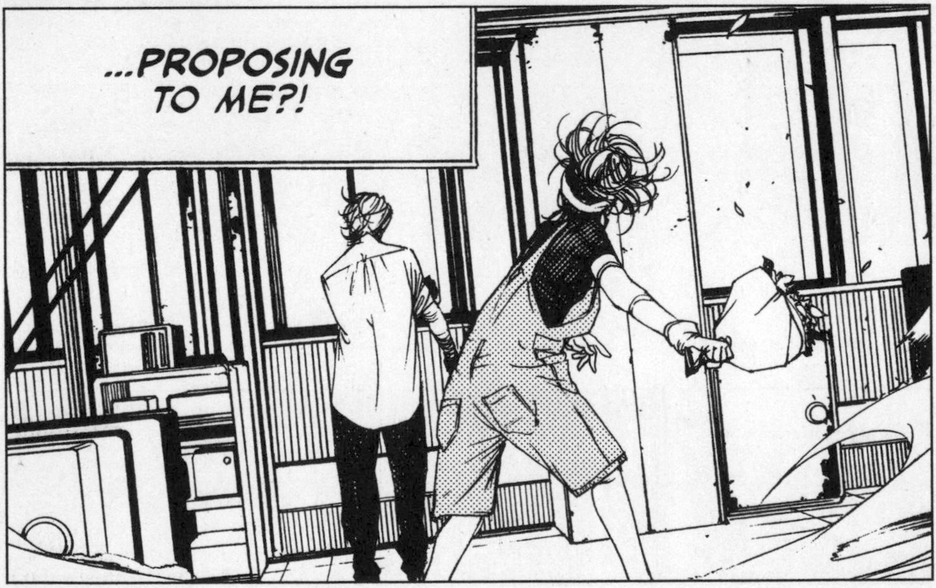
...PROPOSING TO ME?!

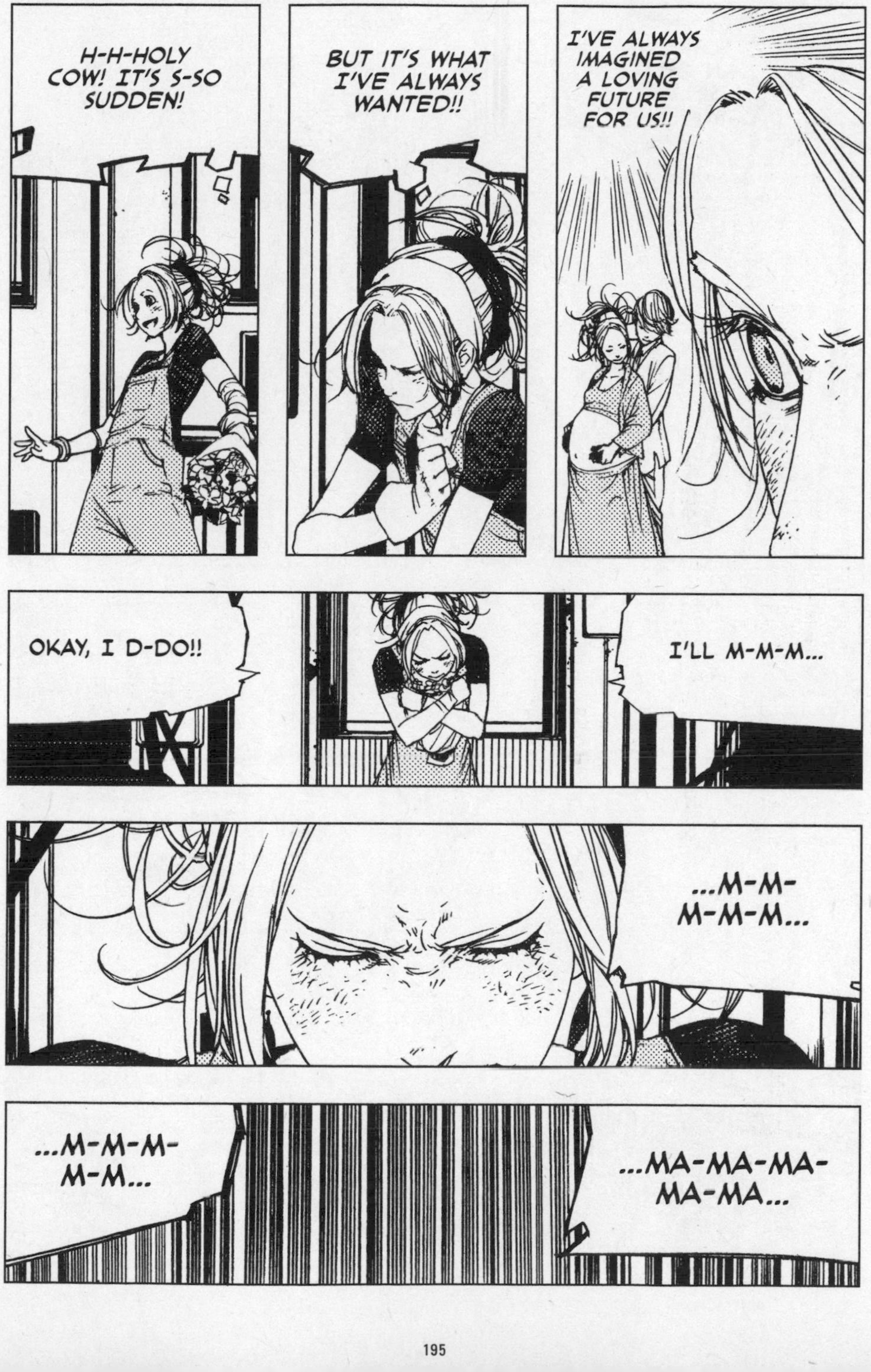
H-H-HOLY COW! IT'S S-SO SUDDEN!
BUT IT'S WHAT I'VE ALWAYS WANTED!!
I'VE ALWAYS IMAGINED A LOVING FUTURE FOR US!!
OKAY, I D-DO!!
I'LL M-M-M...
...M-M-M-M-M...
...M-M-M-M-M...
...MA-MA-MA-MA-MA...

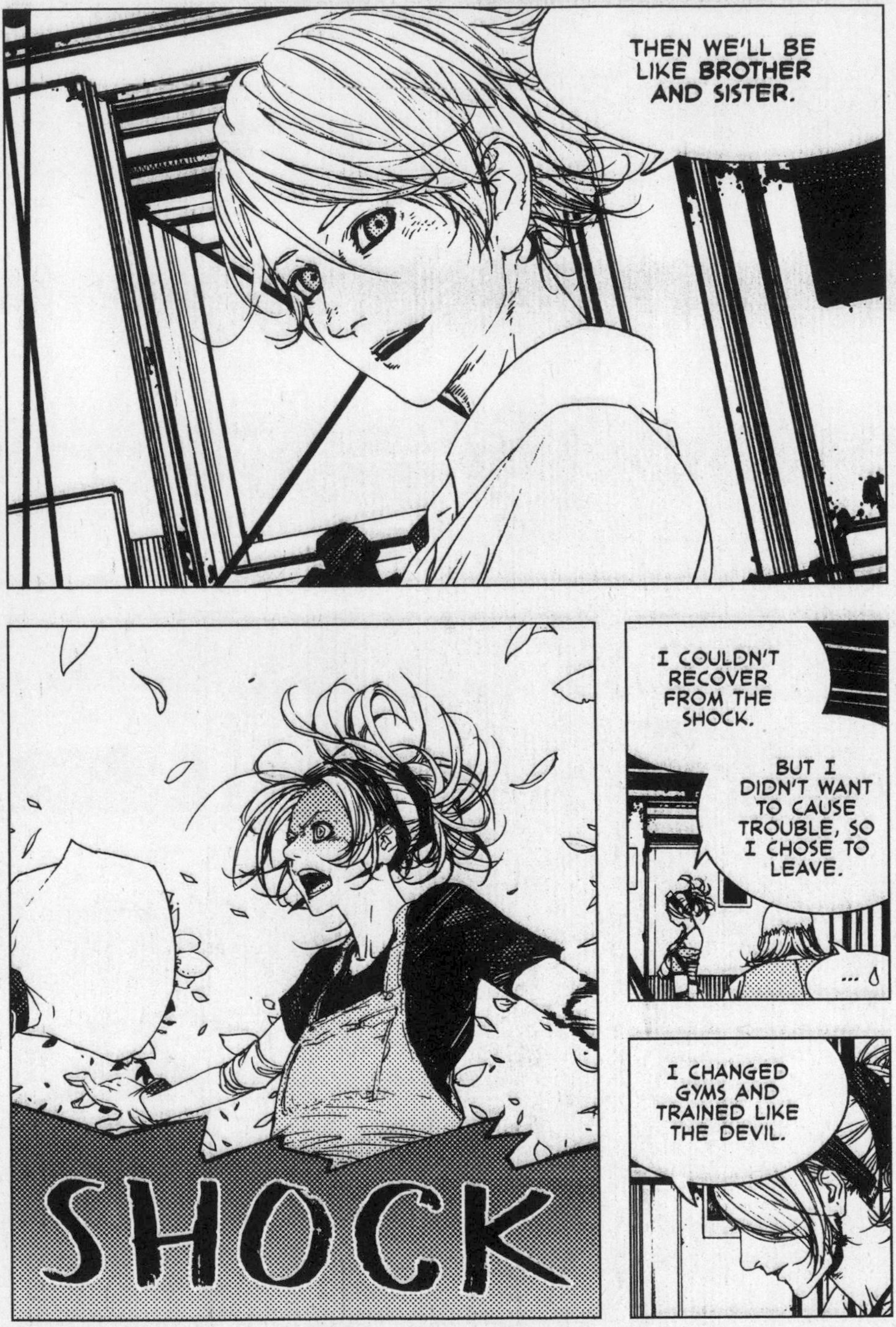
THEN WE'LL BE LIKE BROTHER AND SISTER.
I COULDN'T RECOVER FROM THE SHOCK.
BUT I DIDN'T WANT TO CAUSE TROUBLE, SO I CHOSE TO LEAVE.
...
I CHANGED GYMS AND TRAINED LIKE THE DEVIL.
SHOCK

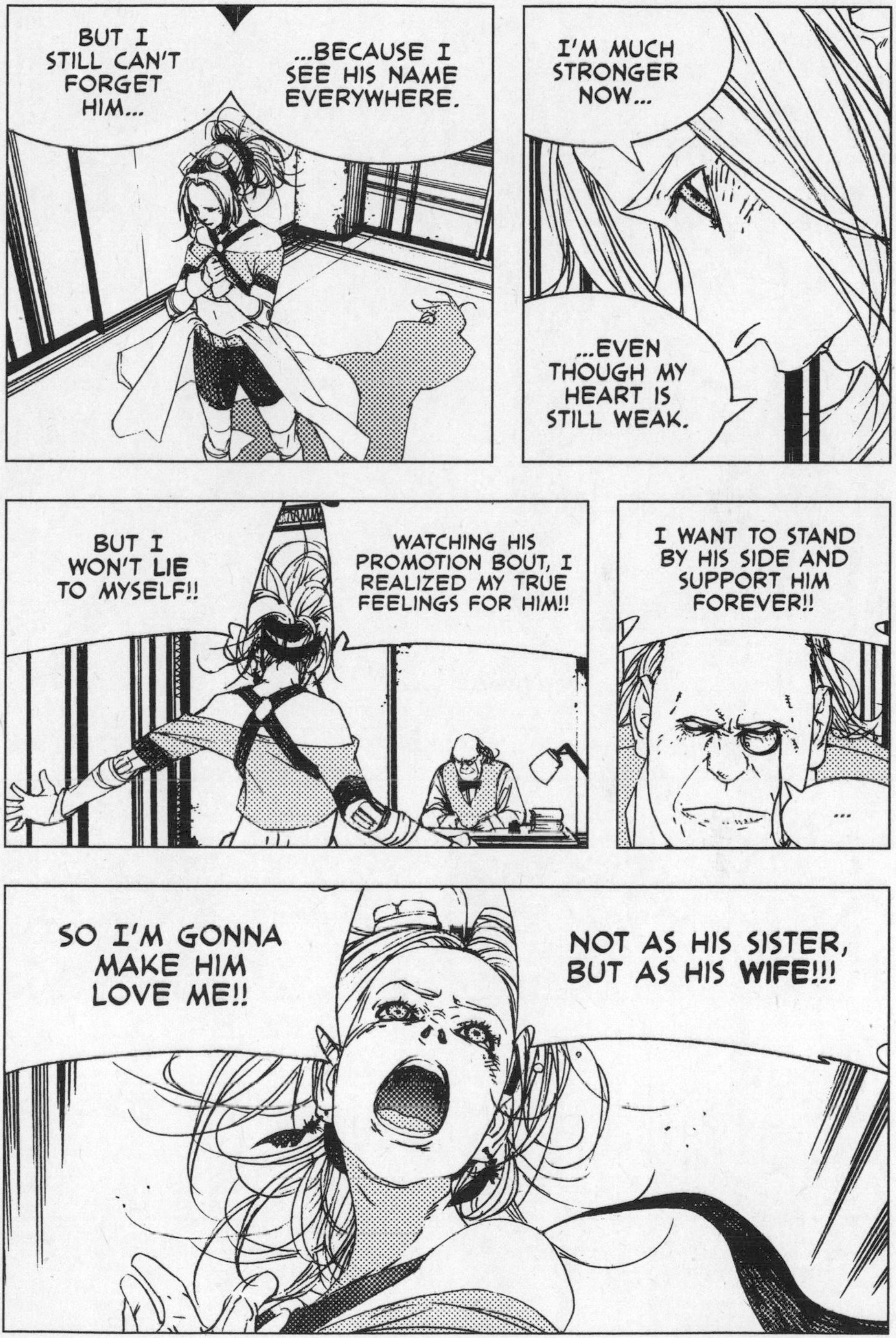
BUT I STILL CAN'T FORGET HIM...
...BECAUSE I SEE HIS NAME EVERYWHERE.
I'M MUCH STRONGER NOW...
...EVEN THOUGH MY HEART IS STILL WEAK.
BUT I WON'T LIE TO MYSELF!!
WATCHING HIS PROMOTION BOUT, I REALIZED MY TRUE FEELINGS FOR HIM!!
I WANT TO STAND BY HIS SIDE AND SUPPORT HIM FOREVER!!
...
SO I'M GONNA MAKE HIM LOVE ME!!
NOT AS HIS SISTER, BUT AS HIS WIFE!!!

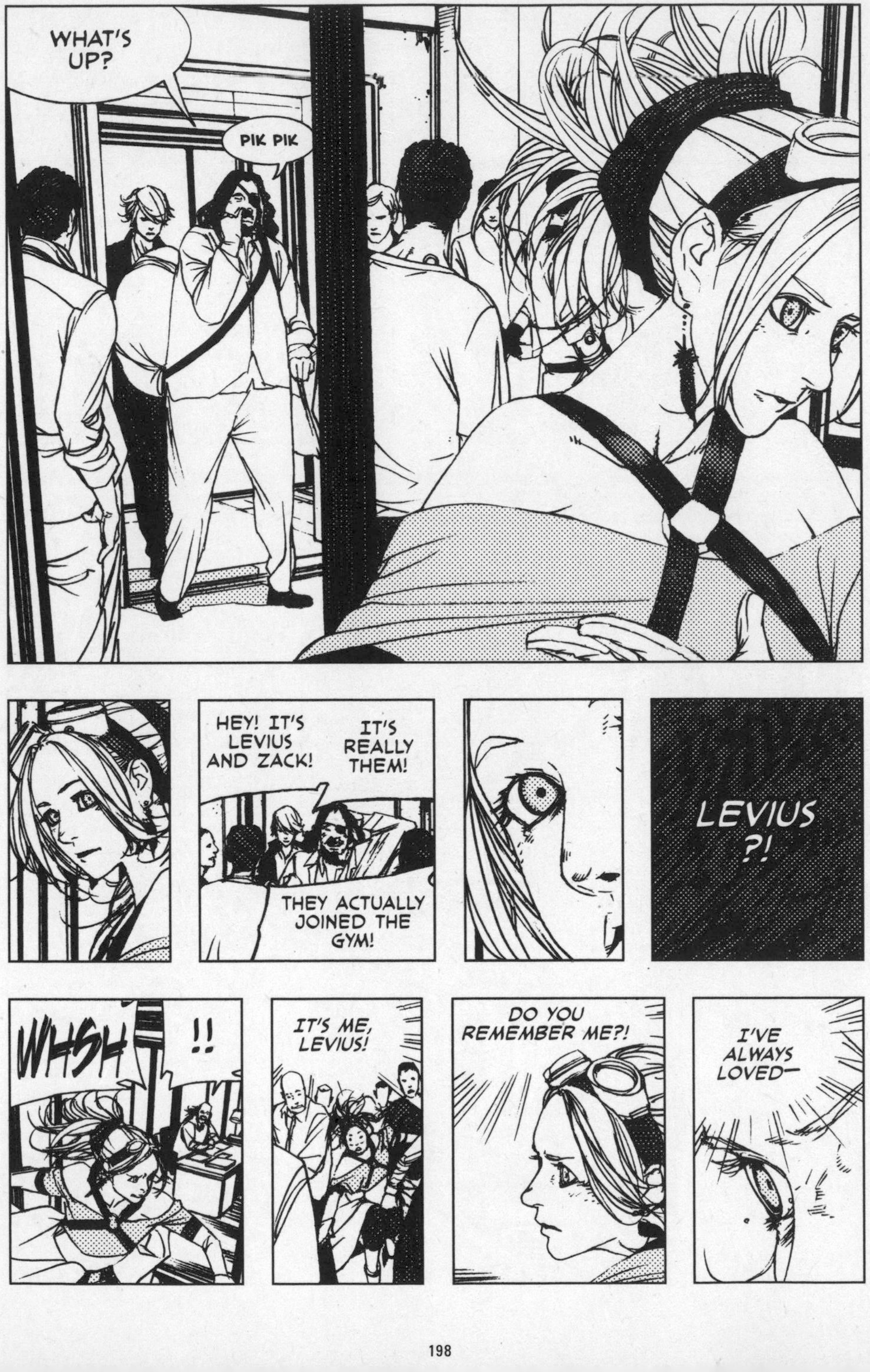
WHAT'S UP?
PIK PIK
HEY! IT'S LEVIUS AND ZACK!
IT'S REALLY THEM!
THEY ACTUALLY JOINED THE GYM!
LEVIUS ?!
WHSH
!!
IT'S ME, LEVIUS!
DO YOU REMEMBER ME?!
I'VE ALWAYS LOVED—

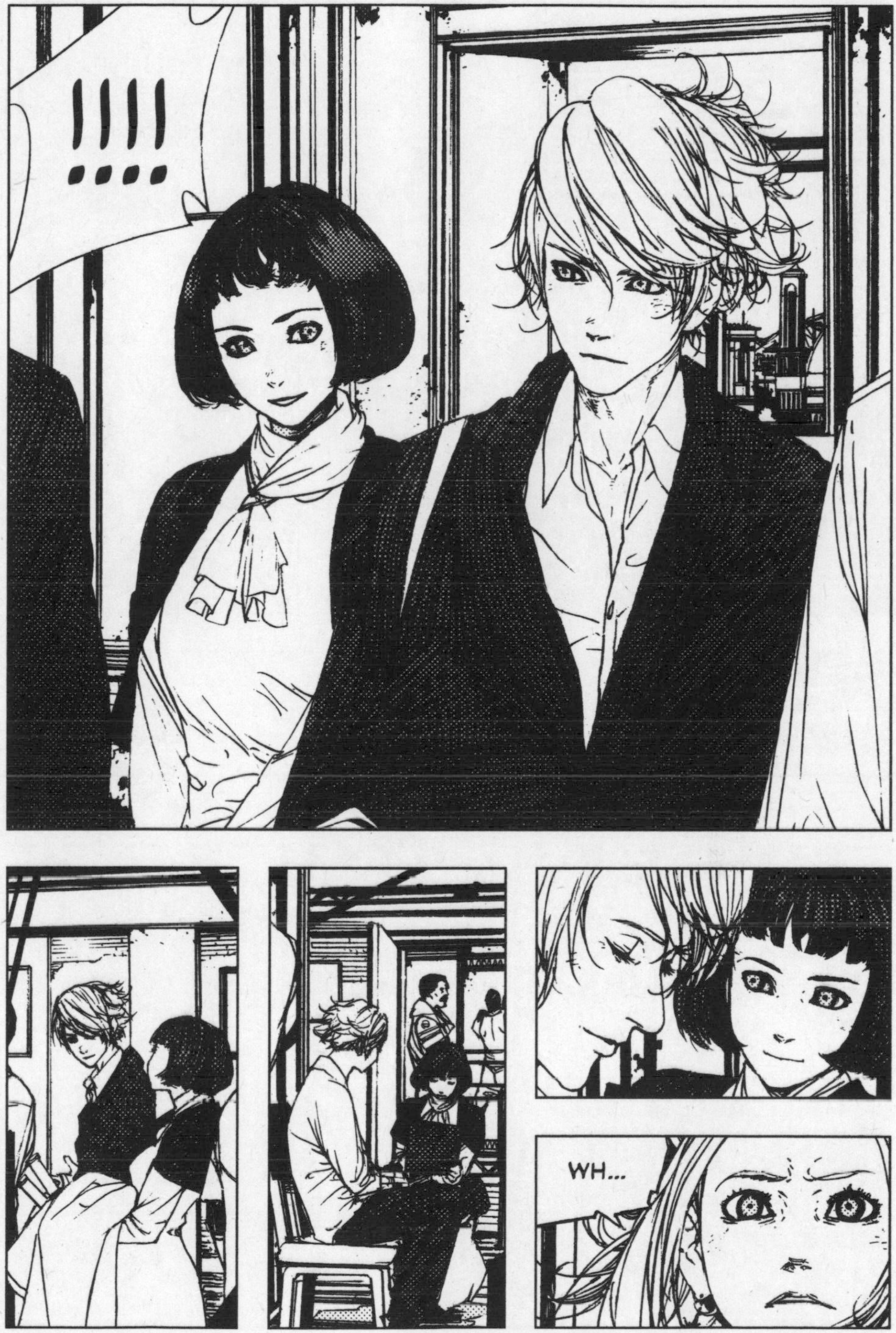
!!!!
WH...

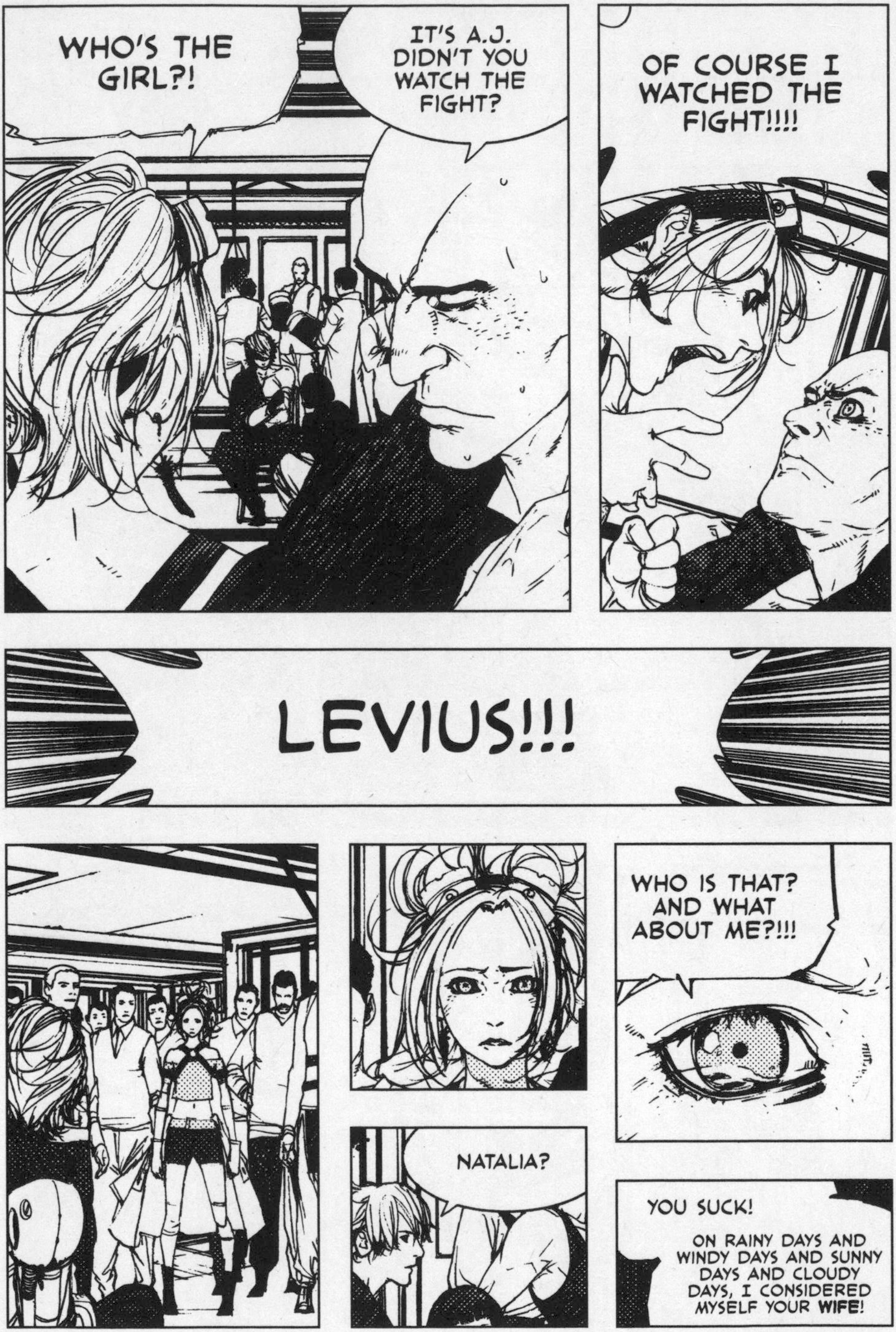
WHO'S THE GIRL?!
IT'S A.J. DIDN'T YOU WATCH THE FIGHT?
OF COURSE I WATCHED THE FIGHT!!!!
LEVIUS!!!
NATALIA?
WHO IS THAT? AND WHAT ABOUT ME?!!!
YOU SUCK!
ON RAINY DAYS AND WINDY DAYS AND SUNNY DAYS AND CLOUDY DAYS, I CONSIDERED MYSELF YOUR **WIFE**!

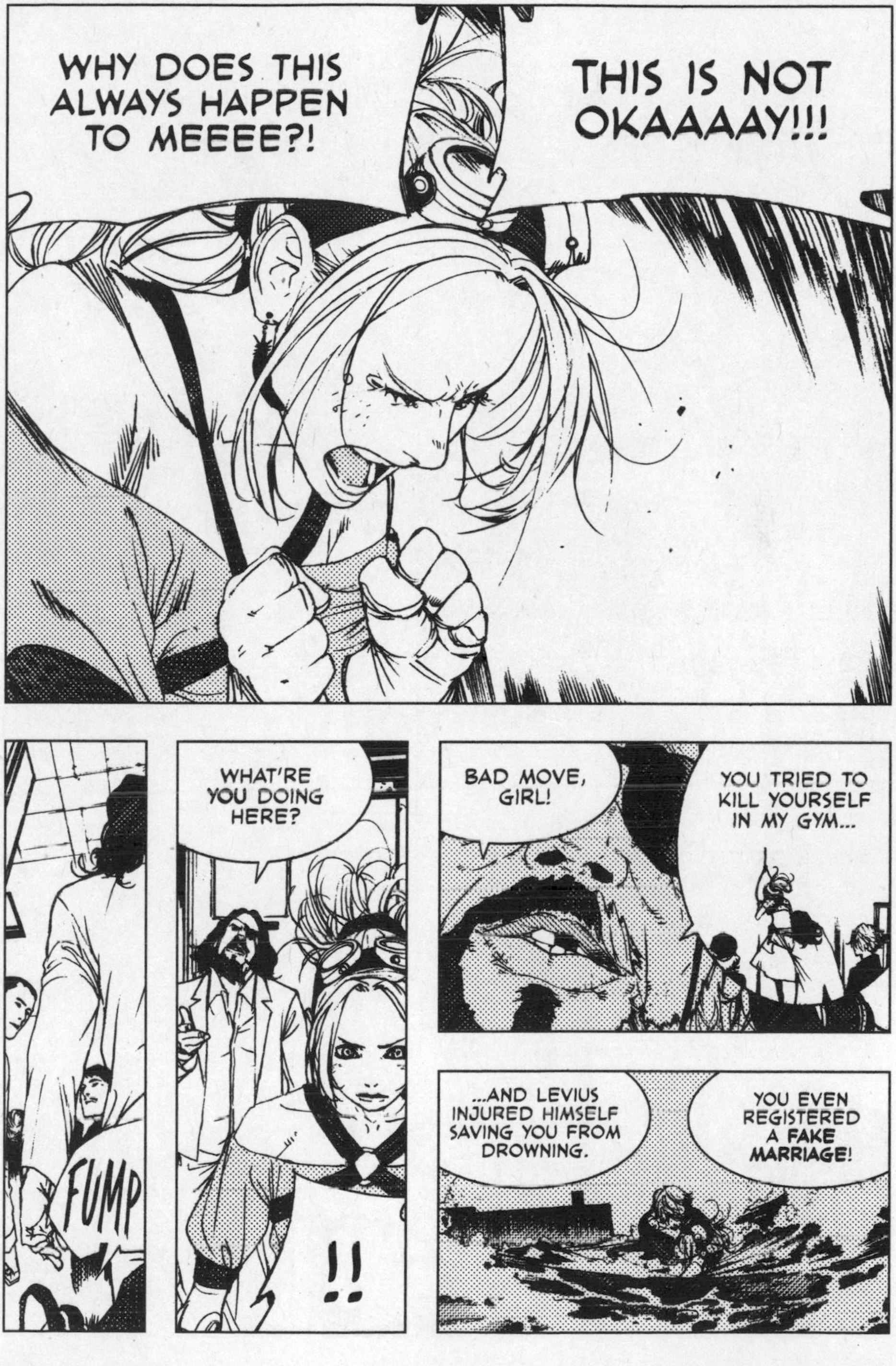
WHY DOES THIS ALWAYS HAPPEN TO MEEEE?!
THIS IS NOT OKAAAAY!!!
FUMP
WHAT'RE YOU DOING HERE?
!!
BAD MOVE, GIRL!
YOU TRIED TO KILL YOURSELF IN MY GYM...
...AND LEVIUS INJURED HIMSELF SAVING YOU FROM DROWNING.
YOU EVEN REGISTERED A FAKE MARRIAGE!

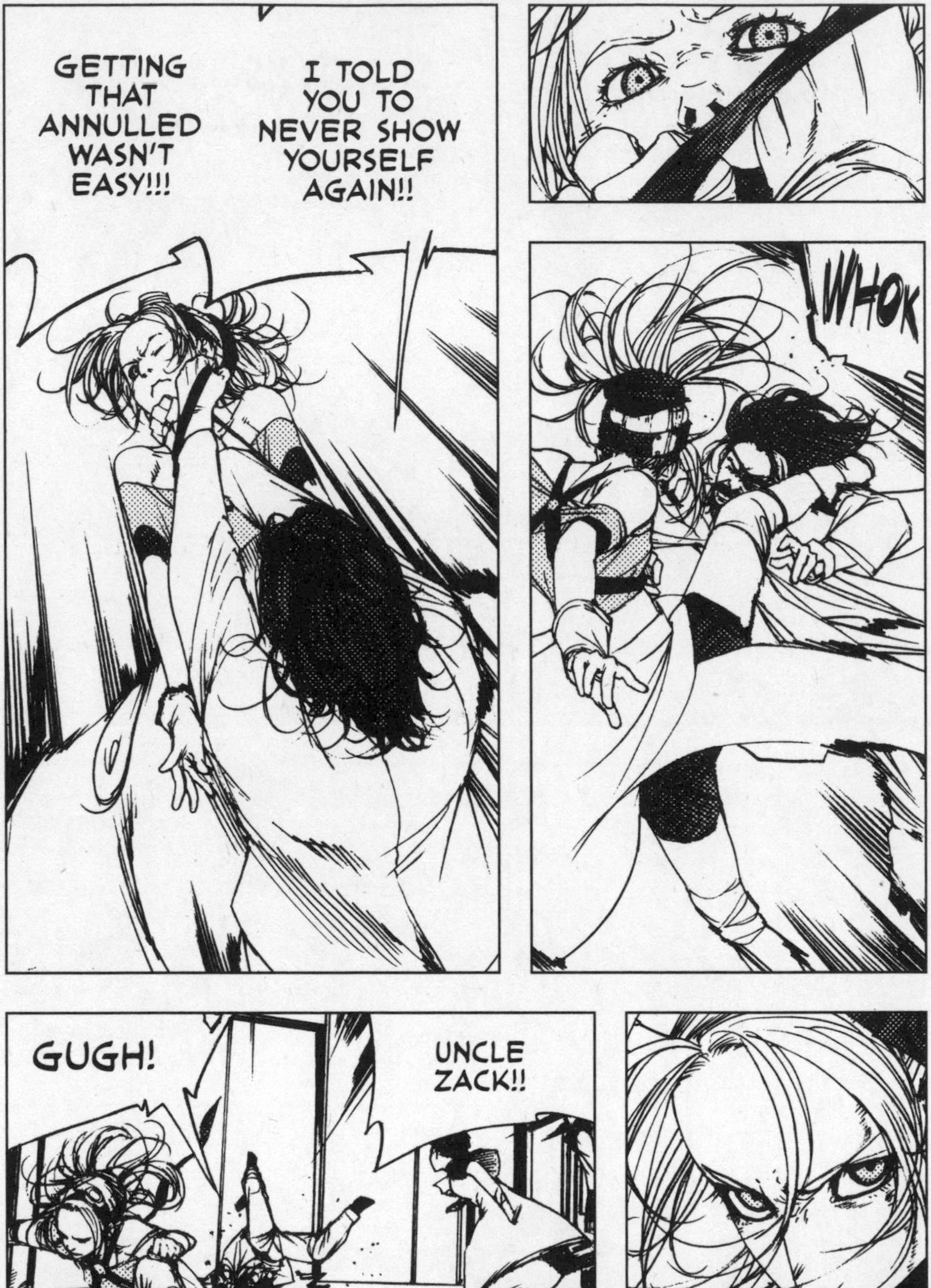
WHOK
I TOLD YOU TO NEVER SHOW YOURSELF AGAIN!!
GETTING THAT ANNULLED WASN'T EASY!!!
UNCLE ZACK!!
GUGH!

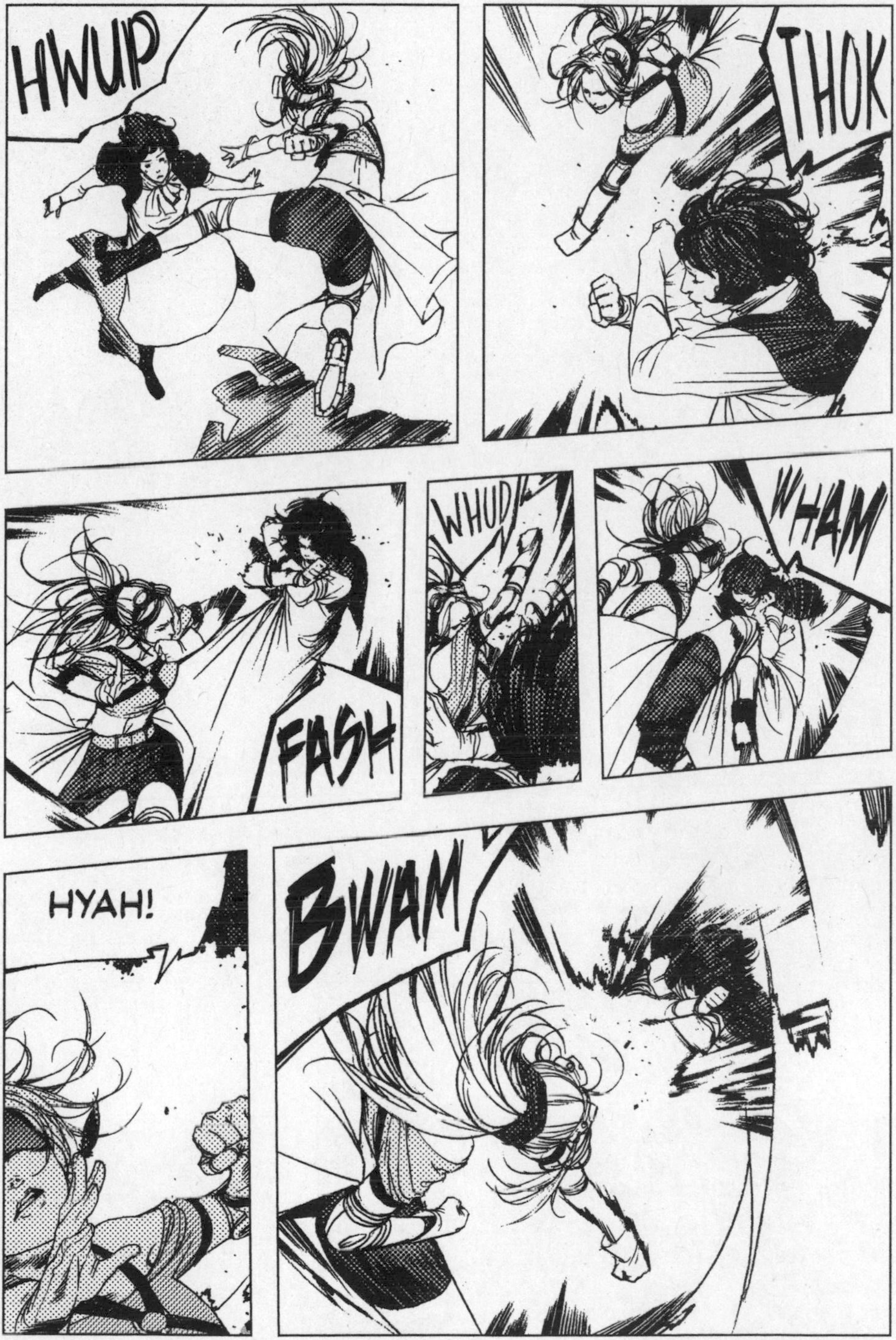
THOK
HWUP
WHAM
WHUD
FASH
BWAM
HYAH!

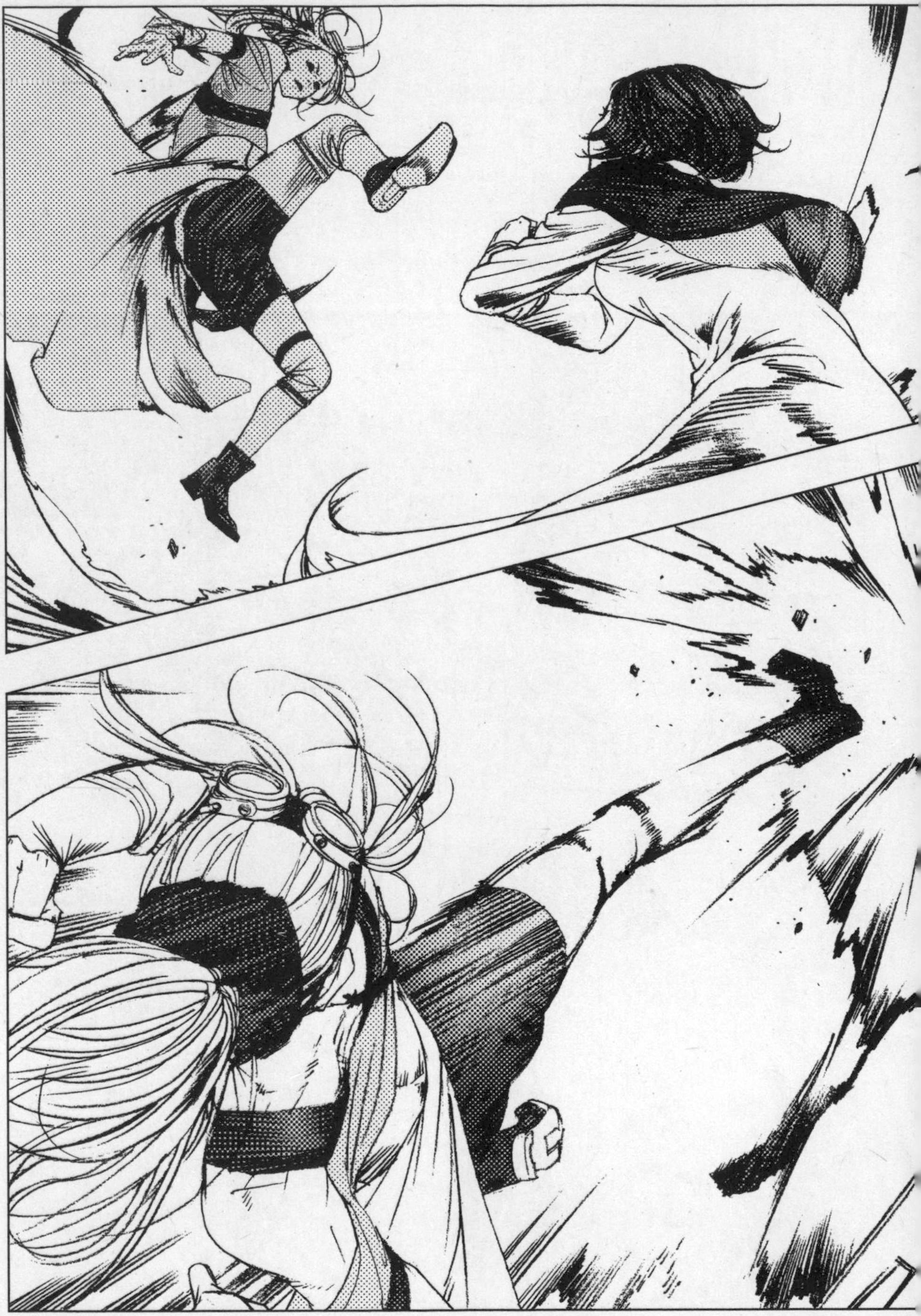

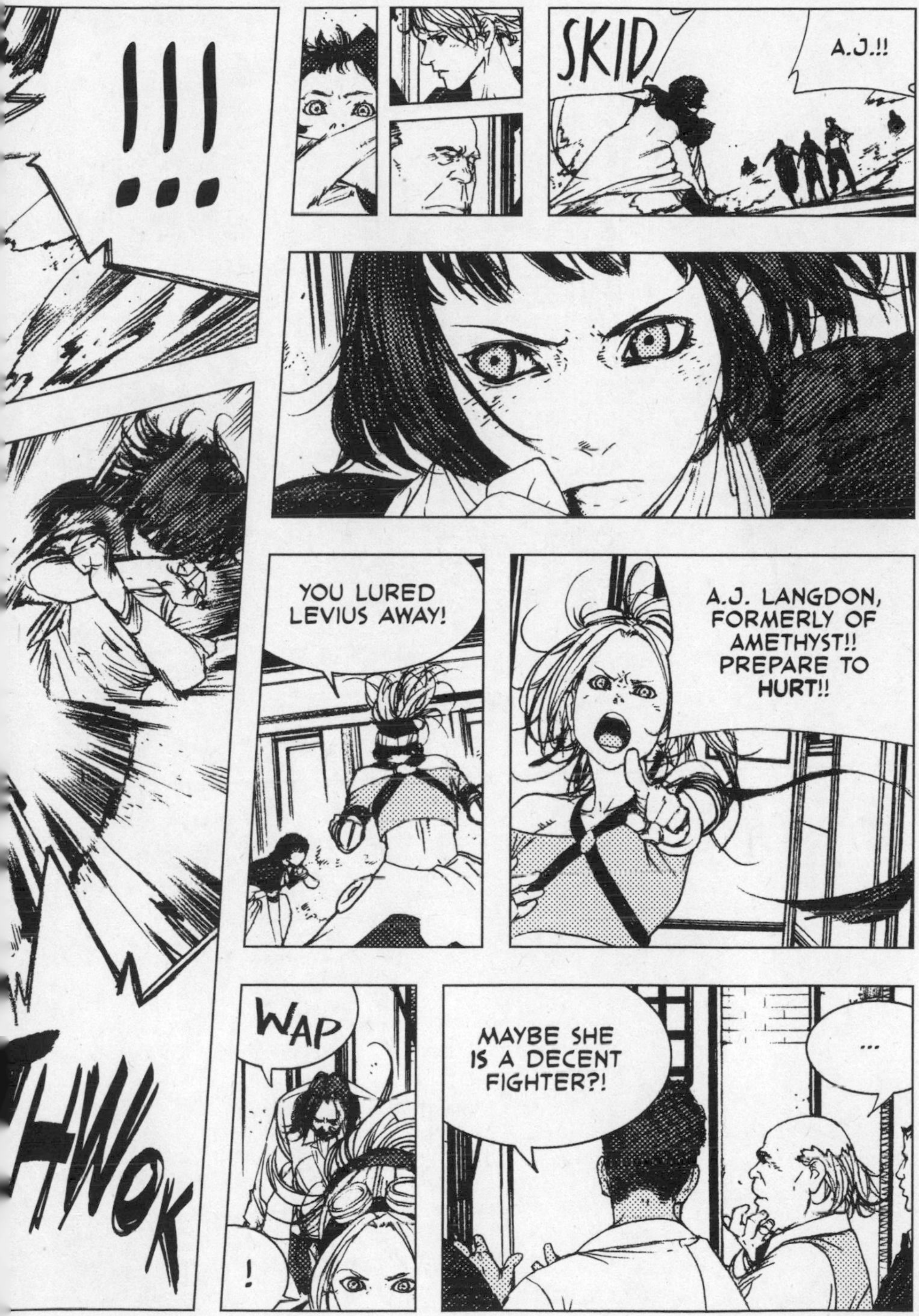
SKID
A.J.!!
A.J. LANGDON, FORMERLY OF AMETHYST!! PREPARE TO HURT!!
YOU LURED LEVIUS AWAY!
...
MAYBE SHE IS A DECENT FIGHTER?!
WAP
!
!!!...
THWOK

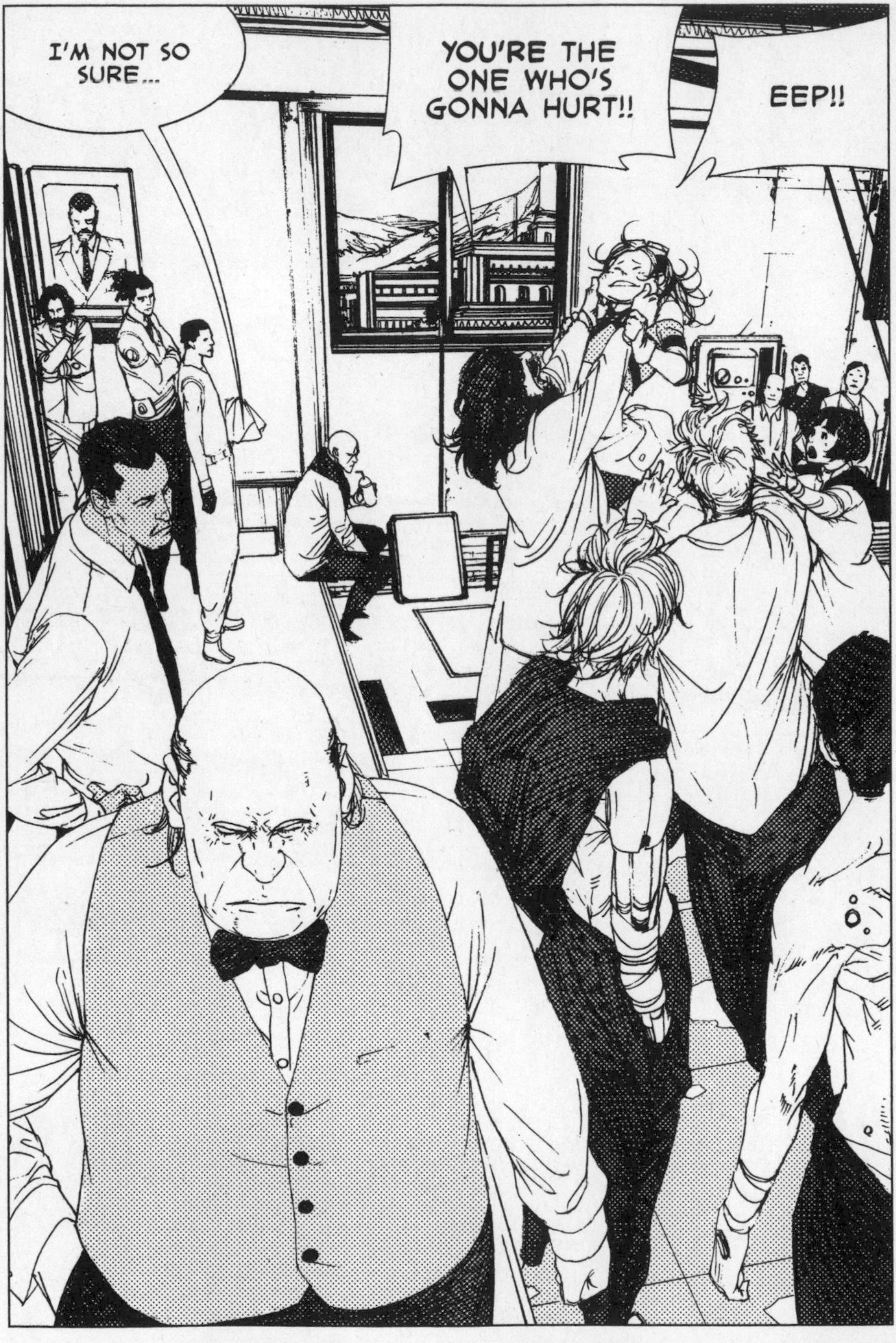
EEP!!
YOU'RE THE ONE WHO'S GONNA HURT!!
I'M NOT SO SURE...

To Be Continued...

Hana-Kimi

For You in Full Blossom

21

story and art by
HISAYA NAKAJO

HANA-KIMI
For You in Full Blossom
VOLUME 21

STORY & ART BY HISAYA NAKAJO

Translation & English Adaptation/David Ury
Touch-Up Art & Lettering/Primary Graphix
Design/Izumi Evers
Editor/Jason Thompson

Editor in Chief, Books/Alvin Lu
Editor in Chief, Magazines/Marc Weidenbaum
VP of Publishing Licensing/Rika Inouye
VP of Sales/Gonzalo Ferreyra
Sr. VP of Marketing/Liza Coppola
Publisher/Hyoe Narita

Hanazakari no Kimitachi he by Hisaya Nakajo © Hisaya Nakajo 2003
All rights reserved. First published in Japan in 2003 by HAKUSENSHA, Inc., Tokyo.
English language translation rights in America and Canada arranged with
HAKUSENSHA, Inc., Tokyo. New and adapted artwork and text © 2007 VIZ Media, LLC.
The HANA-KIMI logo is a trademark of VIZ Media, LLC. The stories, characters and
incidents mentioned in this publication are entirely fictional. Some artwork has been
modified for the English edition.

Printed in the U.S.A.

Published by VIZ Media, LLC, P.O. Box 77010, San Francisco, CA 94107

Shôjo Edition
10 9 8 7 6 5 4 3 2 1

First printing, December 2007

www.viz.com
store.viz.com

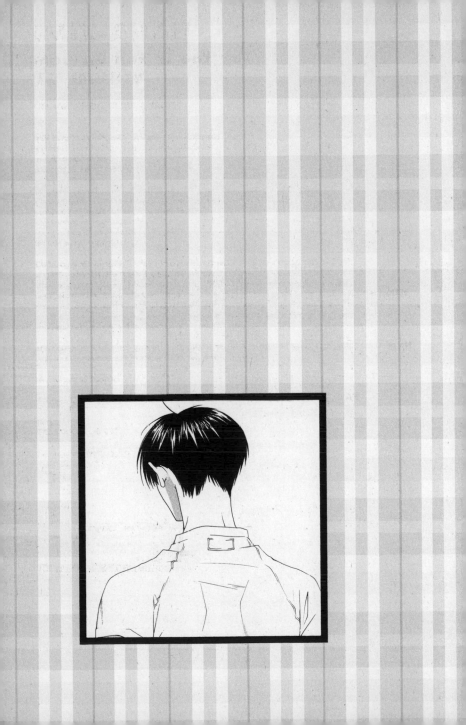

CONTENTS

Hana-Kimi Chapter 120 5

Hana-Kimi Chapter 121 23

Hana-Kimi Chapter 122 48

Hana-Kimi Chapter 123 75

Hana-Kimi Chapter 124 99

Hana-Kimi Chapter 125 119

Hana-Kimi Chapter 126 139

Hana-Kimi Chapter 127 163

Previews 184

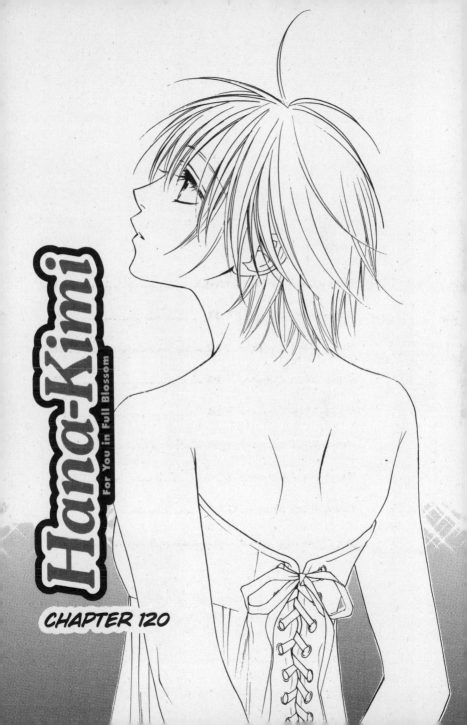

Hana-Kimi

For You in Full Blossom

CHAPTER 120

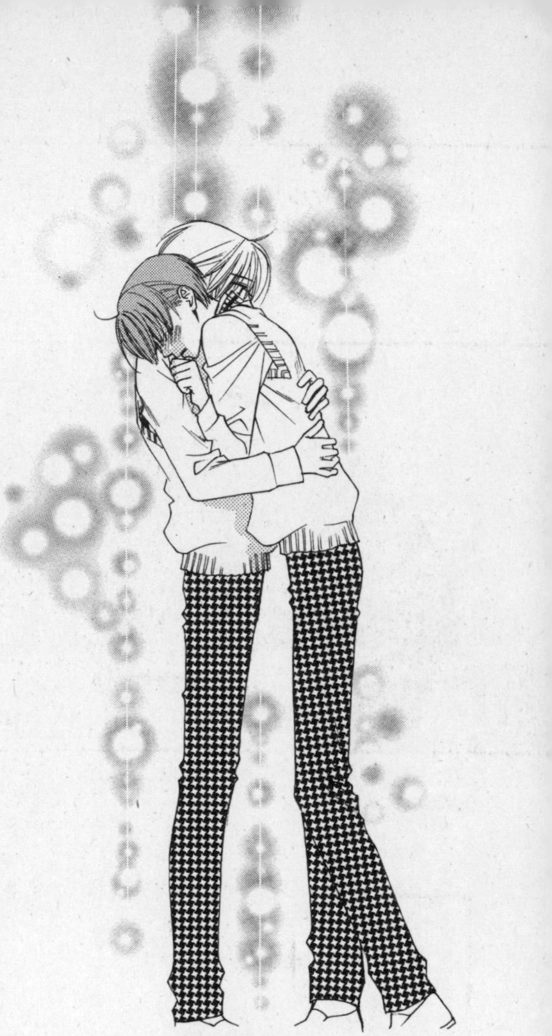

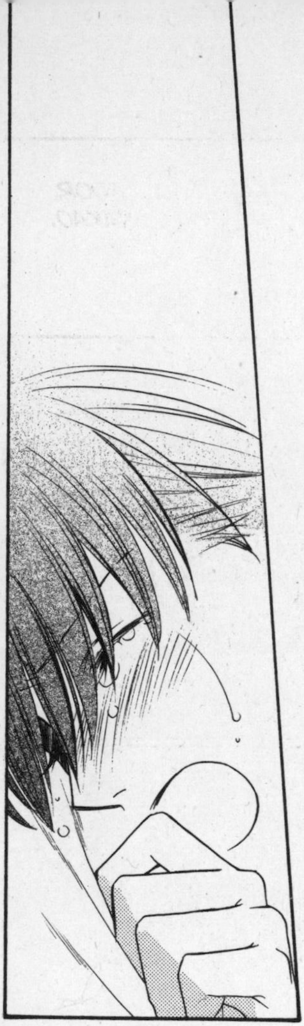

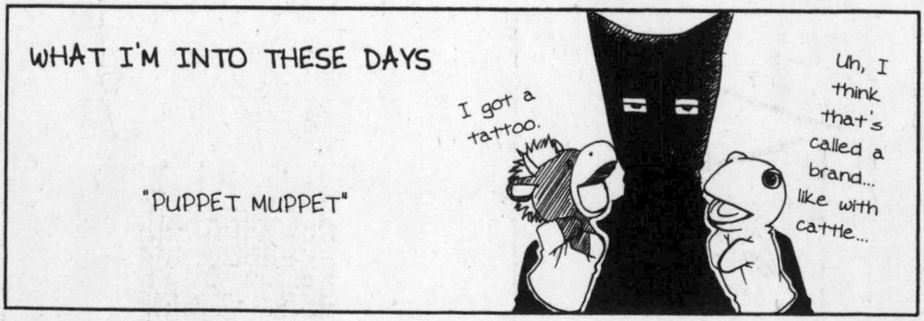

WHAT I'M INTO THESE DAYS
"PUPPET MUPPET"
I got a tattoo.
Uh, I think that's called a brand... like with cattle...

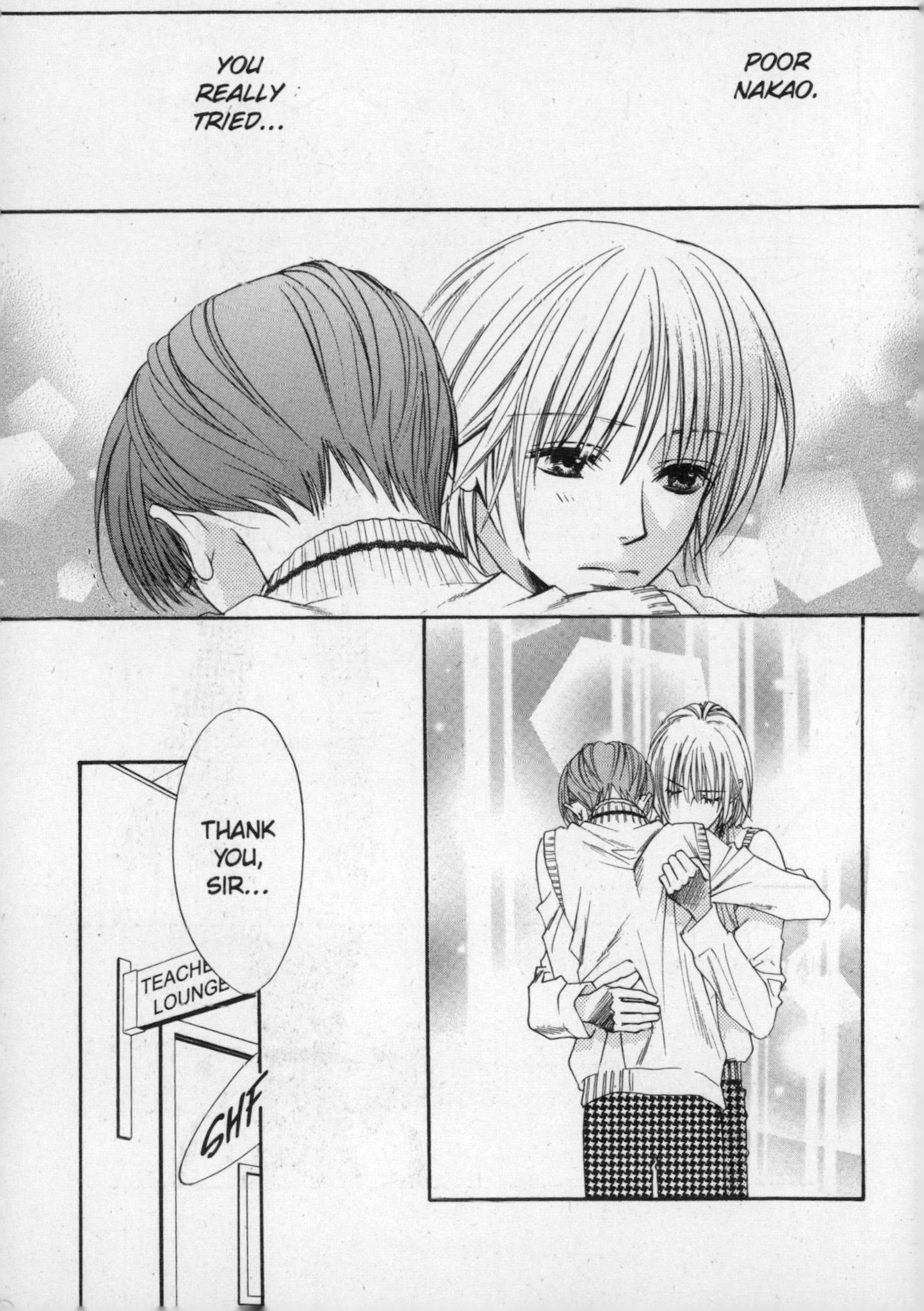
POOR NAKAO.
YOU REALLY TRIED...
THANK YOU, SIR...
TEACHE
LOUNGE
SHF

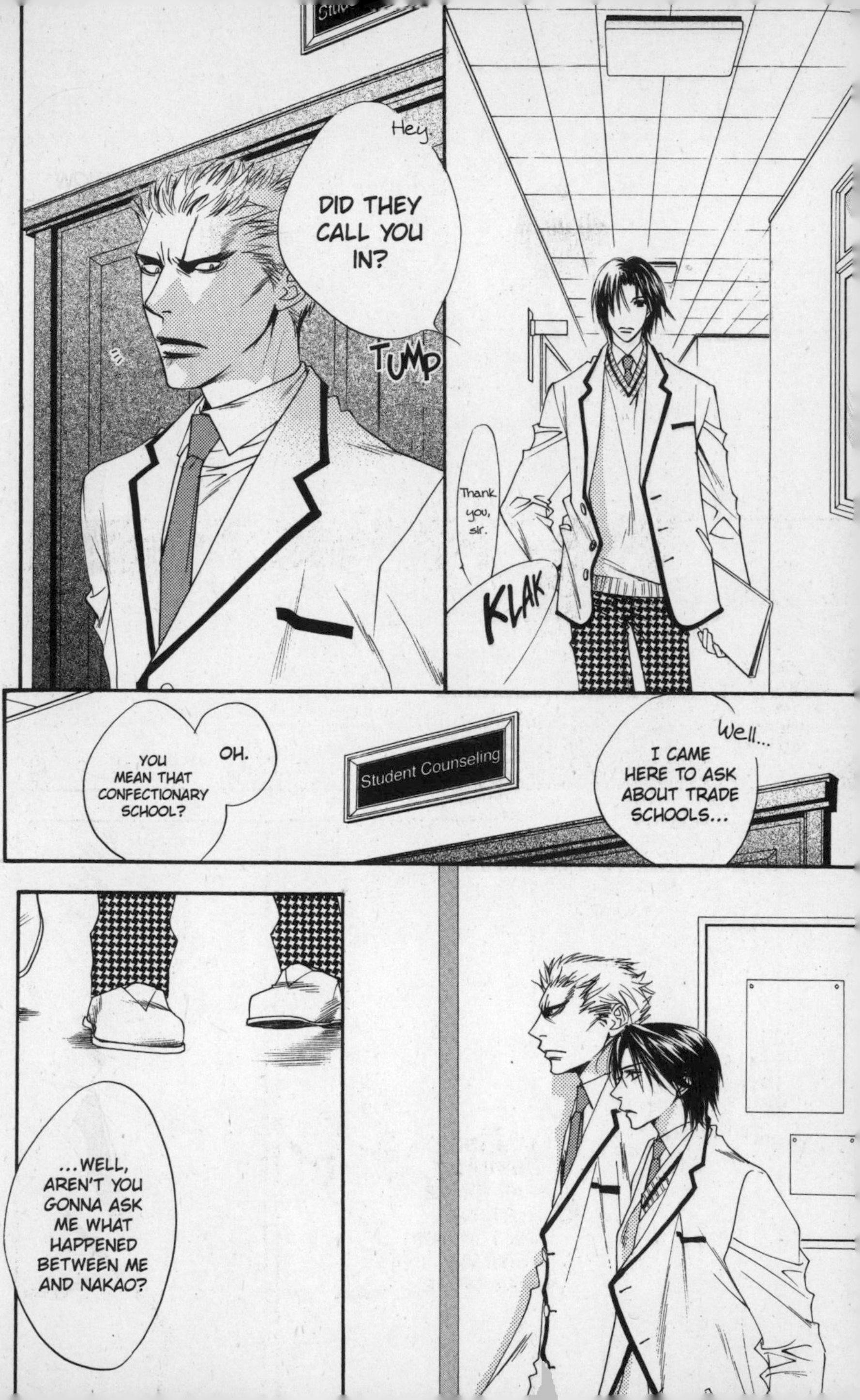
Thank you, sir.
KLAK
Hey.
DID THEY CALL YOU IN?
TUMP
Well...
I CAME HERE TO ASK ABOUT TRADE SCHOOLS...
Student Counseling
OH.
YOU MEAN THAT CONFECTIONARY SCHOOL?
...WELL, AREN'T YOU GONNA ASK ME WHAT HAPPENED BETWEEN ME AND NAKAO?

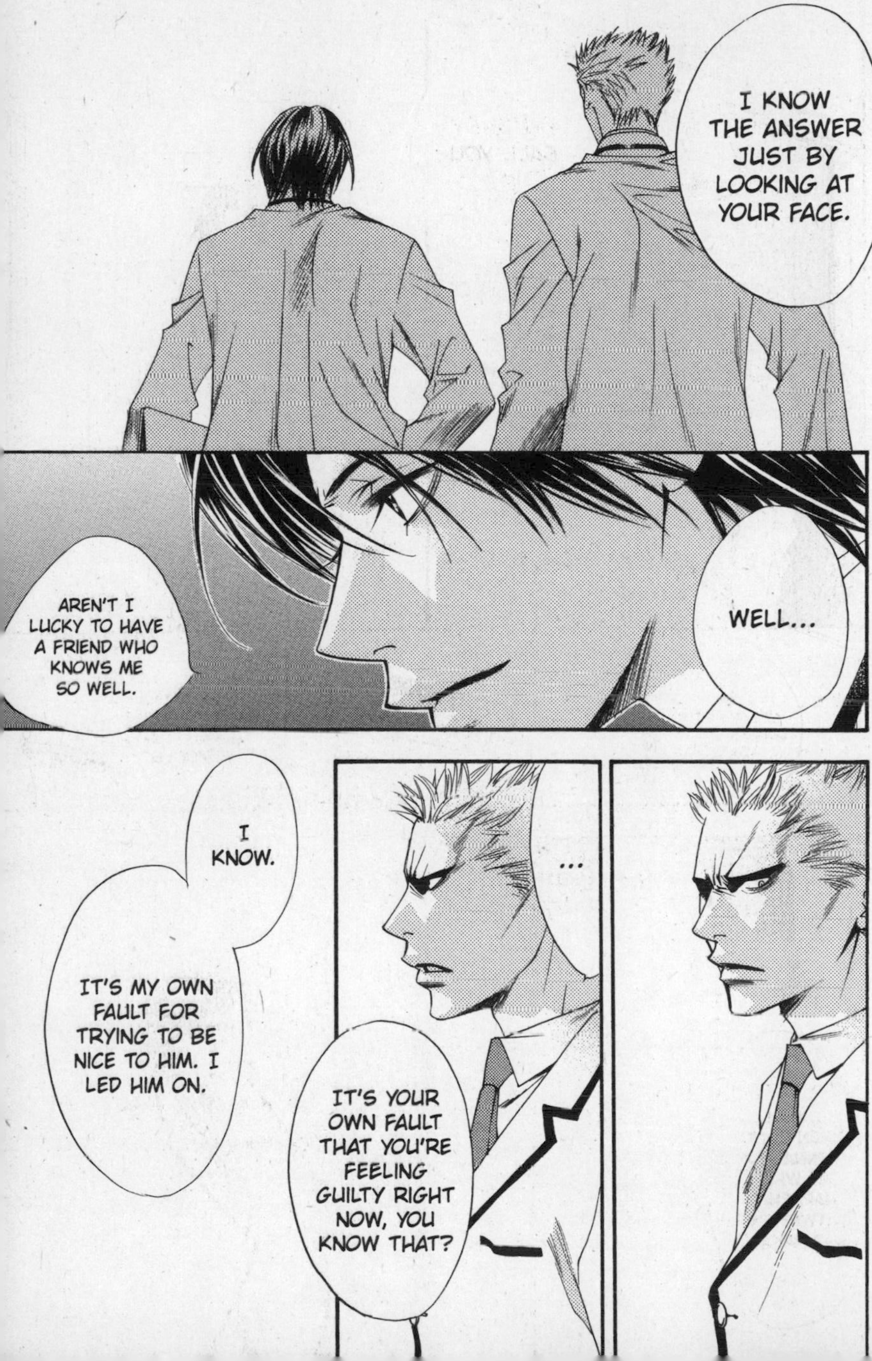
I KNOW THE ANSWER JUST BY LOOKING AT YOUR FACE.
WELL...
AREN'T I LUCKY TO HAVE A FRIEND WHO KNOWS ME SO WELL.
...
IT'S YOUR OWN FAULT THAT YOU'RE FEELING GUILTY RIGHT NOW, YOU KNOW THAT?
I KNOW.
IT'S MY OWN FAULT FOR TRYING TO BE NICE TO HIM. I LED HIM ON.

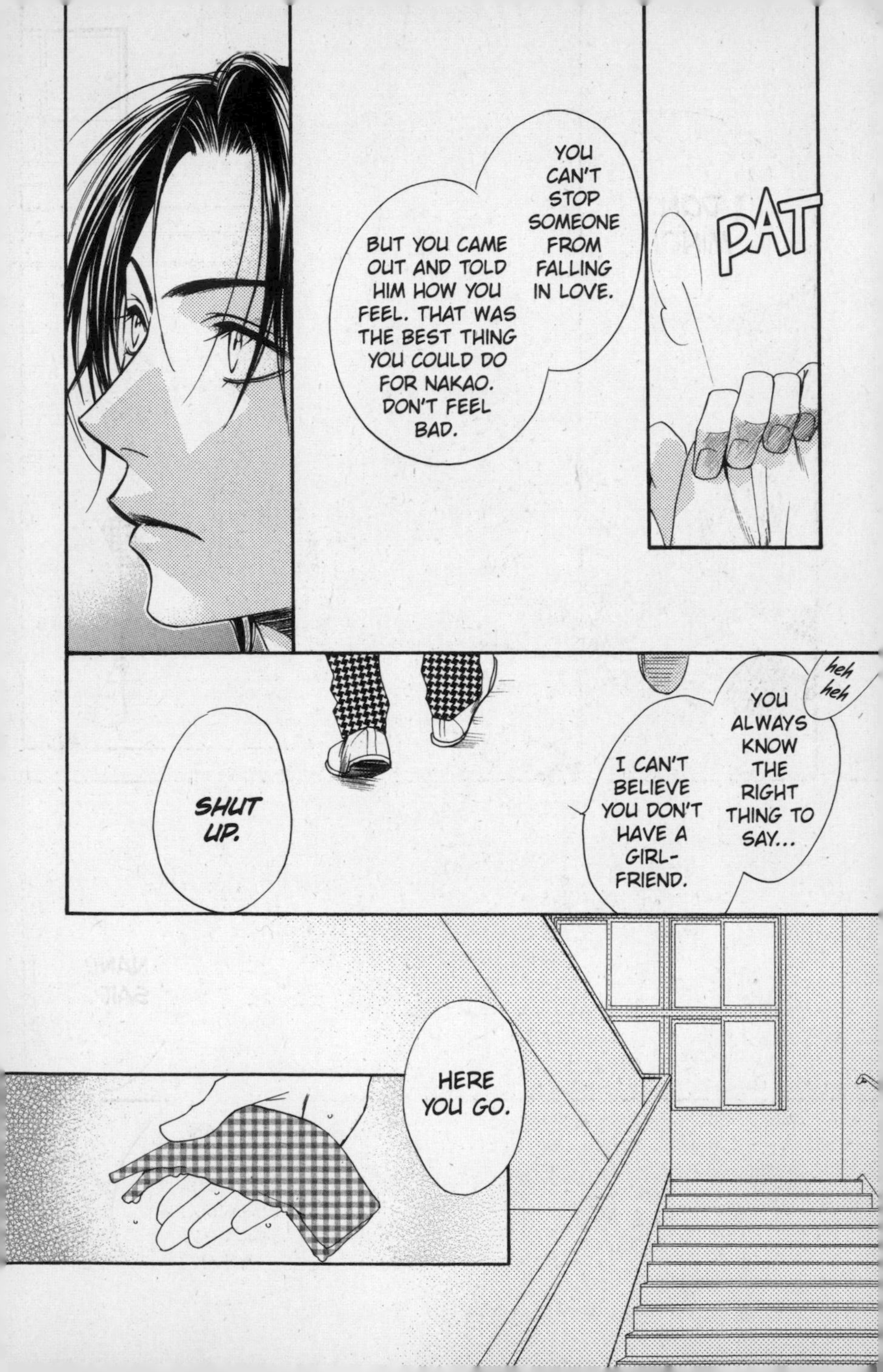
PAT
YOU CAN'T STOP SOMEONE FROM FALLING IN LOVE.
BUT YOU CAME OUT AND TOLD HIM HOW YOU FEEL. THAT WAS THE BEST THING YOU COULD DO FOR NAKAO. DON'T FEEL BAD.
heh heh
YOU ALWAYS KNOW THE RIGHT THING TO SAY...
I CAN'T BELIEVE YOU DON'T HAVE A GIRL-FRIEND.
SHUT UP.
HERE YOU GO.

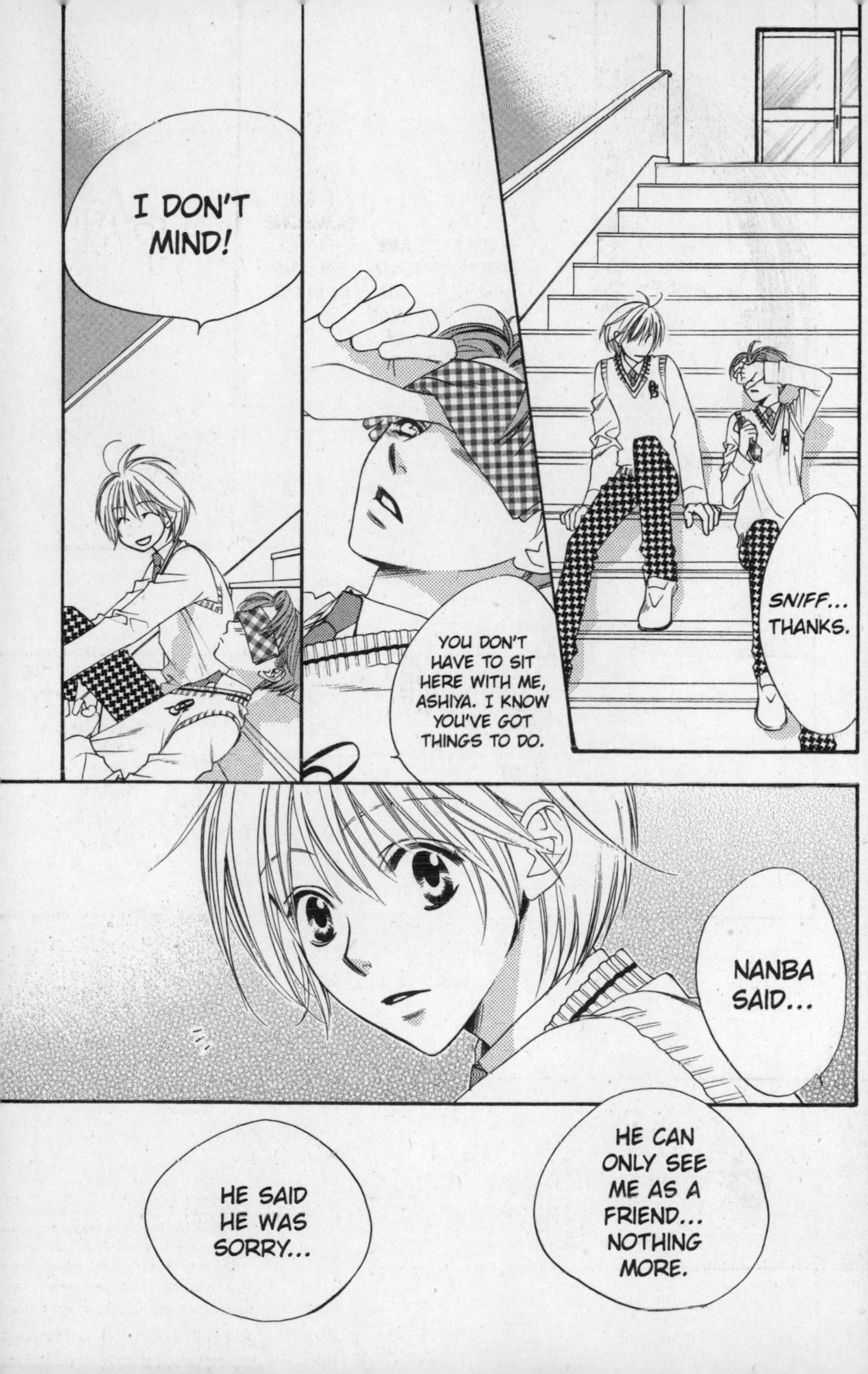
SNIFF... THANKS.
YOU DON'T HAVE TO SIT HERE WITH ME, ASHIYA. I KNOW YOU'VE GOT THINGS TO DO.
I DON'T MIND!
NANBA SAID...
HE CAN ONLY SEE ME AS A FRIEND... NOTHING MORE.
HE SAID HE WAS SORRY...

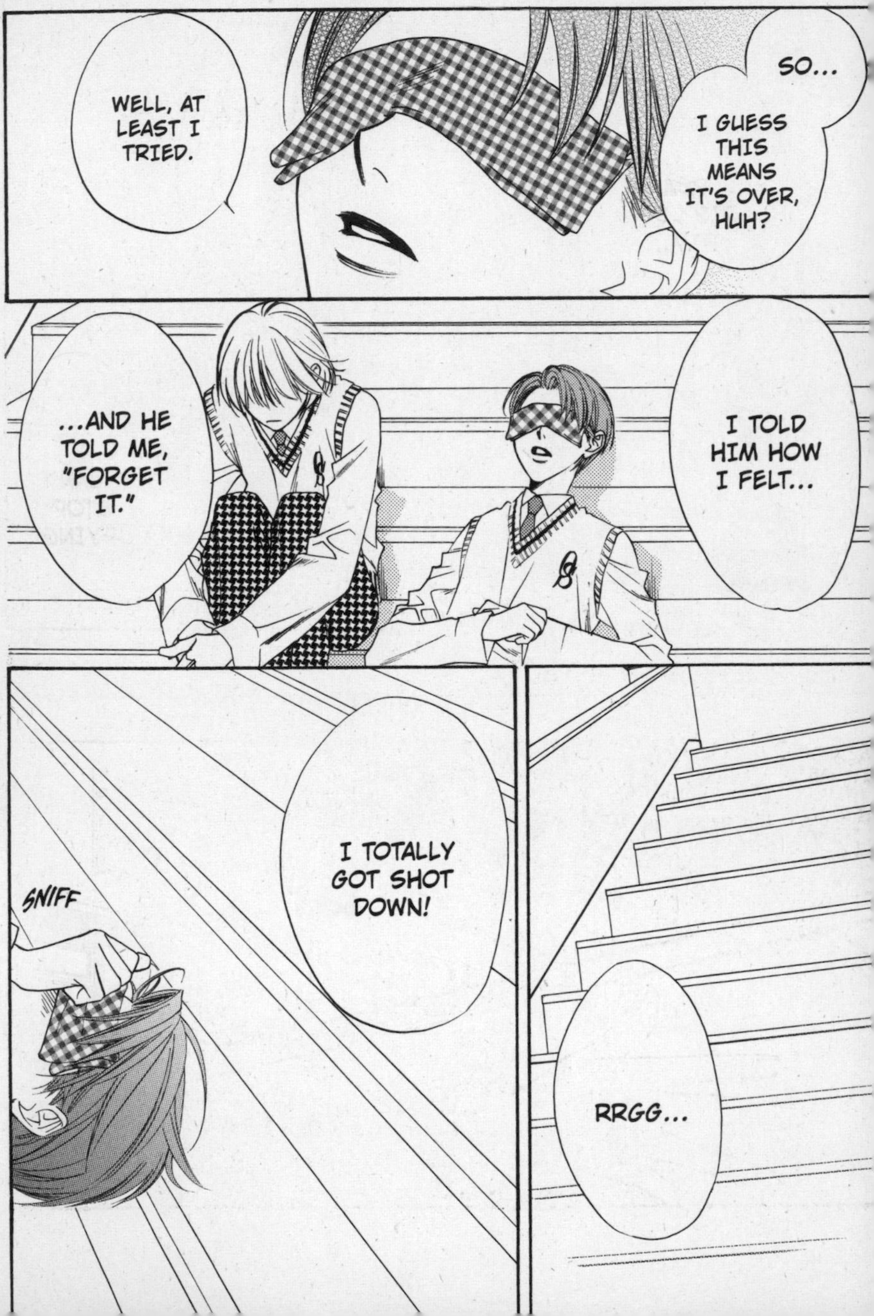
SO...
I GUESS THIS MEANS IT'S OVER, HUH?
WELL, AT LEAST I TRIED.
I TOLD HIM HOW I FELT...
...AND HE TOLD ME, "FORGET IT."
RRGG...
I TOTALLY GOT SHOT DOWN!
SNIFF

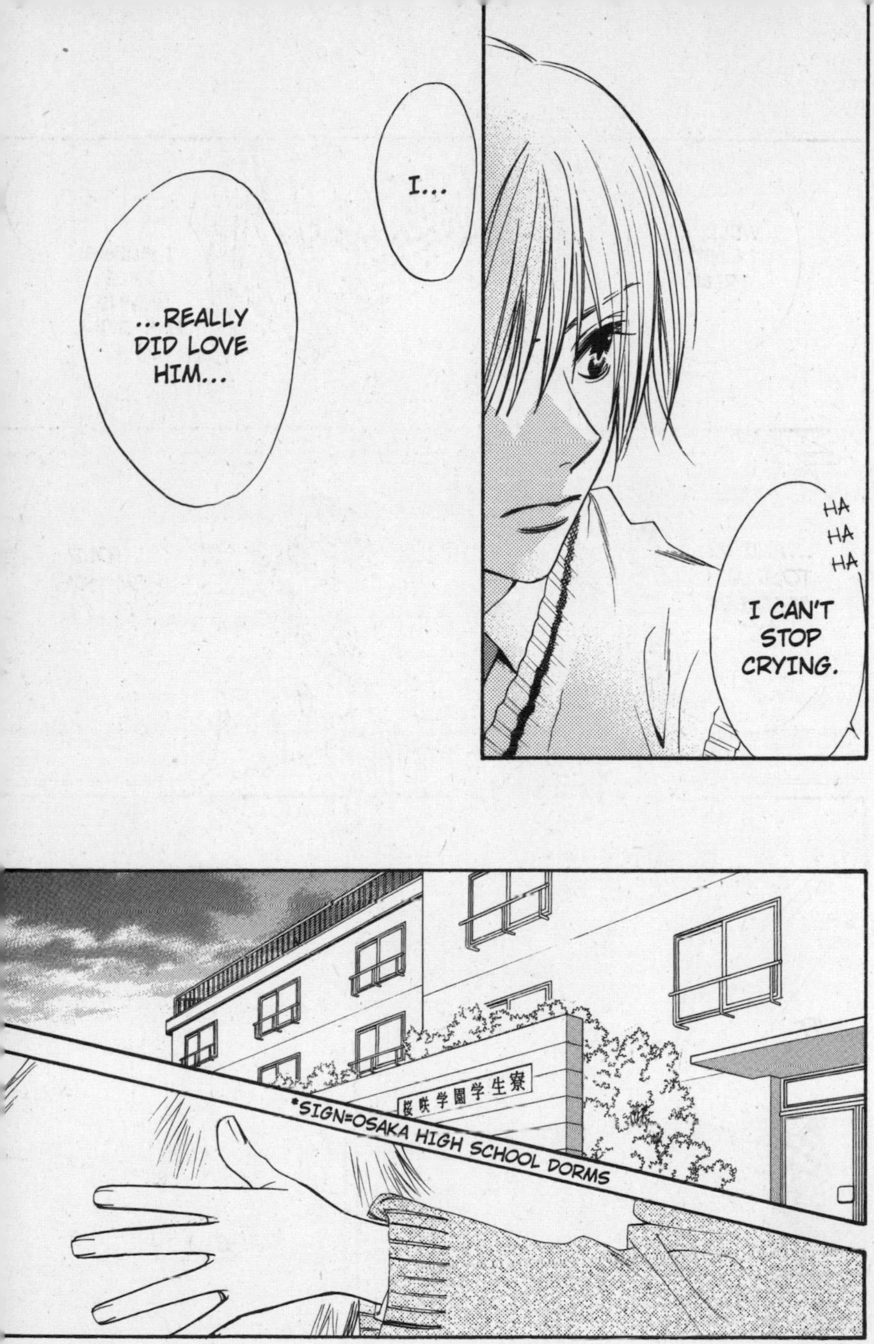
I...
...REALLY DID LOVE HIM...
HA HA HA
I CAN'T STOP CRYING.
桜咲学園学生寮
*SIGN=OSAKA HIGH SCHOOL DORMS

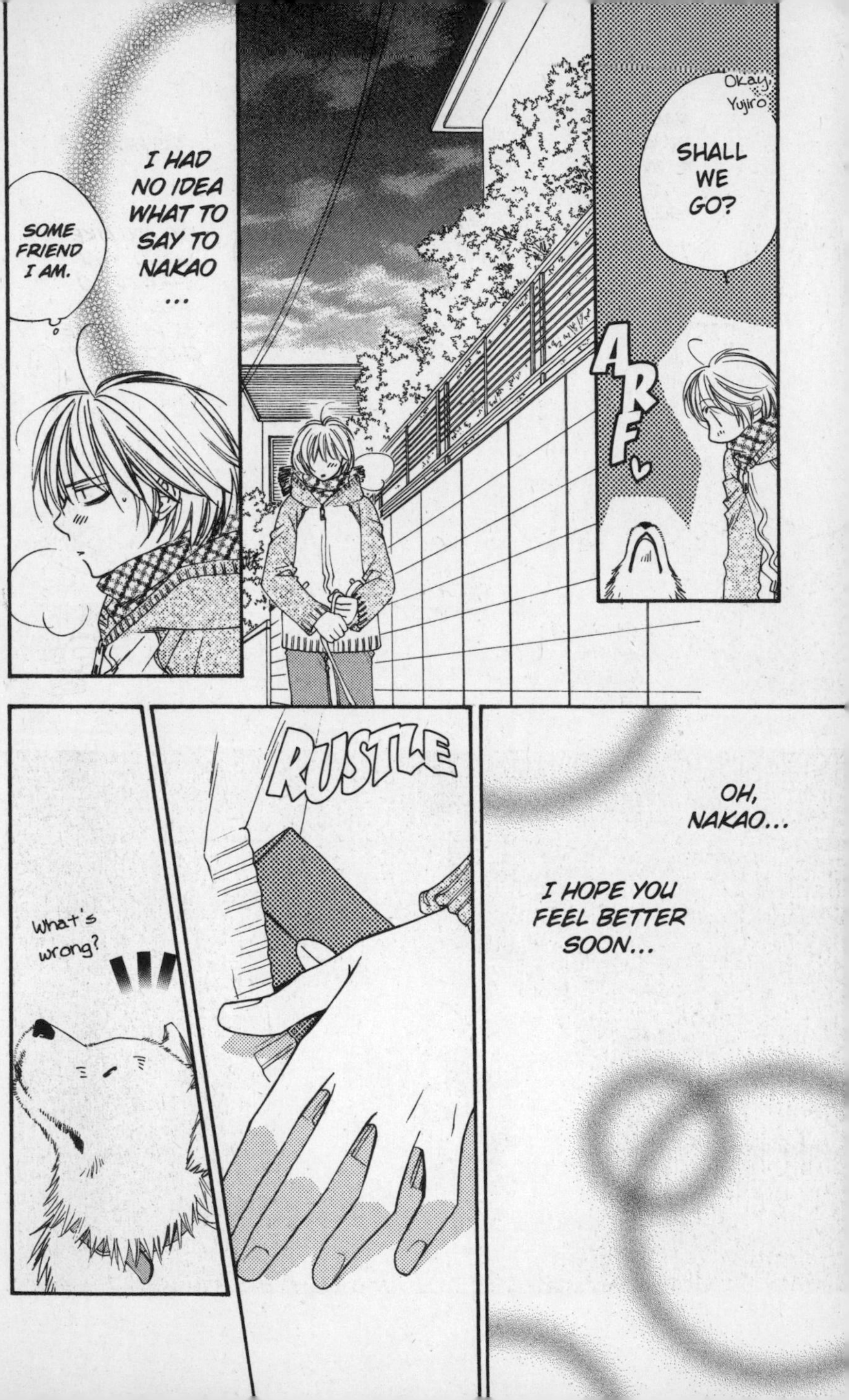
Okay, Yujiro
SHALL WE GO?
ARF
I HAD NO IDEA WHAT TO SAY TO NAKAO...
SOME FRIEND I AM.
OH, NAKAO...
I HOPE YOU FEEL BETTER SOON...
RUSTLE
What's wrong?

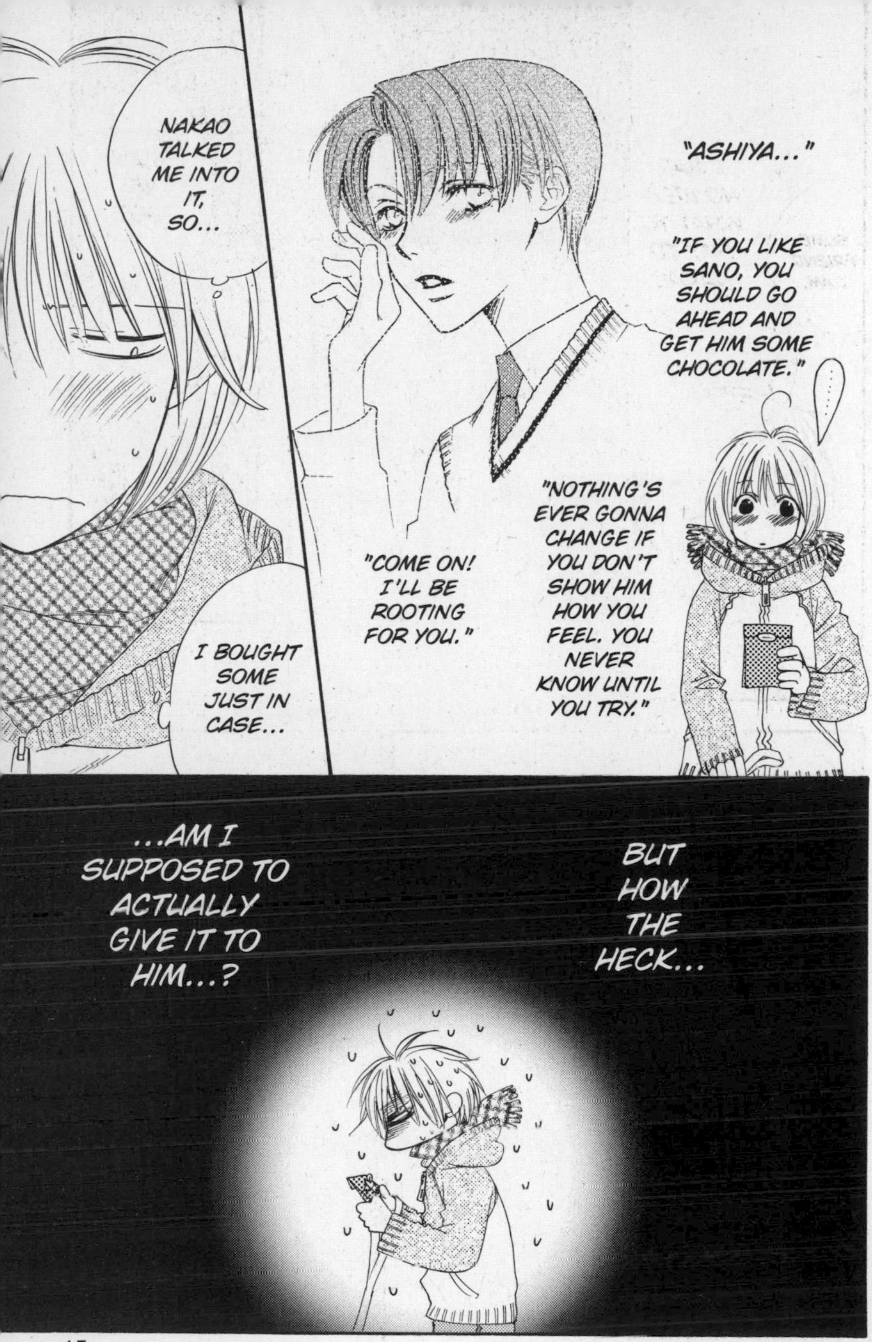
"ASHIYA..."
"IF YOU LIKE SANO, YOU SHOULD GO AHEAD AND GET HIM SOME CHOCOLATE."
"NOTHING'S EVER GONNA CHANGE IF YOU DON'T SHOW HIM HOW YOU FEEL. YOU NEVER KNOW UNTIL YOU TRY."
"COME ON! I'LL BE ROOTING FOR YOU."
NAKAO TALKED ME INTO IT, SO...
I BOUGHT SOME JUST IN CASE...
BUT HOW THE HECK...
...AM I SUPPOSED TO ACTUALLY GIVE IT TO HIM...?

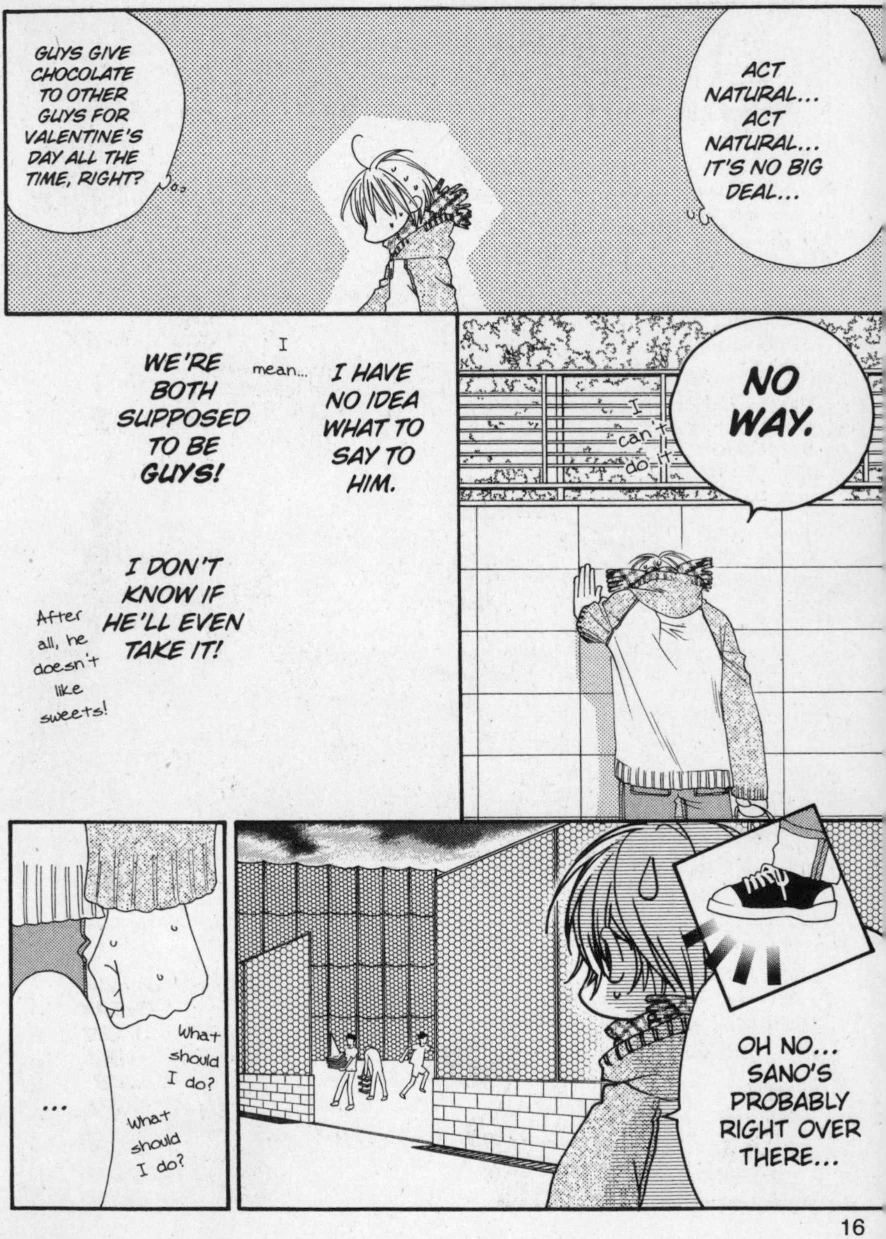
ACT NATURAL... ACT NATURAL... IT'S NO BIG DEAL...
GUYS GIVE CHOCOLATE TO OTHER GUYS FOR VALENTINE'S DAY ALL THE TIME, RIGHT?
NO WAY.
I can't do it
I HAVE NO IDEA WHAT TO SAY TO HIM.
I mean...
WE'RE BOTH SUPPOSED TO BE GUYS!
I DON'T KNOW IF HE'LL EVEN TAKE IT!
After all, he doesn't like sweets!
OH NO... SANO'S PROBABLY RIGHT OVER THERE...
What should I do?
What should I do?
...

21

Autinokku!

Apparently, if you hear this word backwards, it sounds like "Konnichiwa" (hello). Well, that was a long introduction... Hana-Kimi has finally reached volume 20! And this is volume 21! Ahh, I'm so glad I was able to publish volume 20 in the 20th century. (Ha ha!) Volume 21 includes 30% more romance than the average volume of Hana-Kimi. I mean, just look at the cover illustration. They're so obviously in love that it makes me blush...heh heh...and it's gonna get even more lovey dovey in book 22...Ah wah wah...!

I heard it on TV.

Only 30%...

21

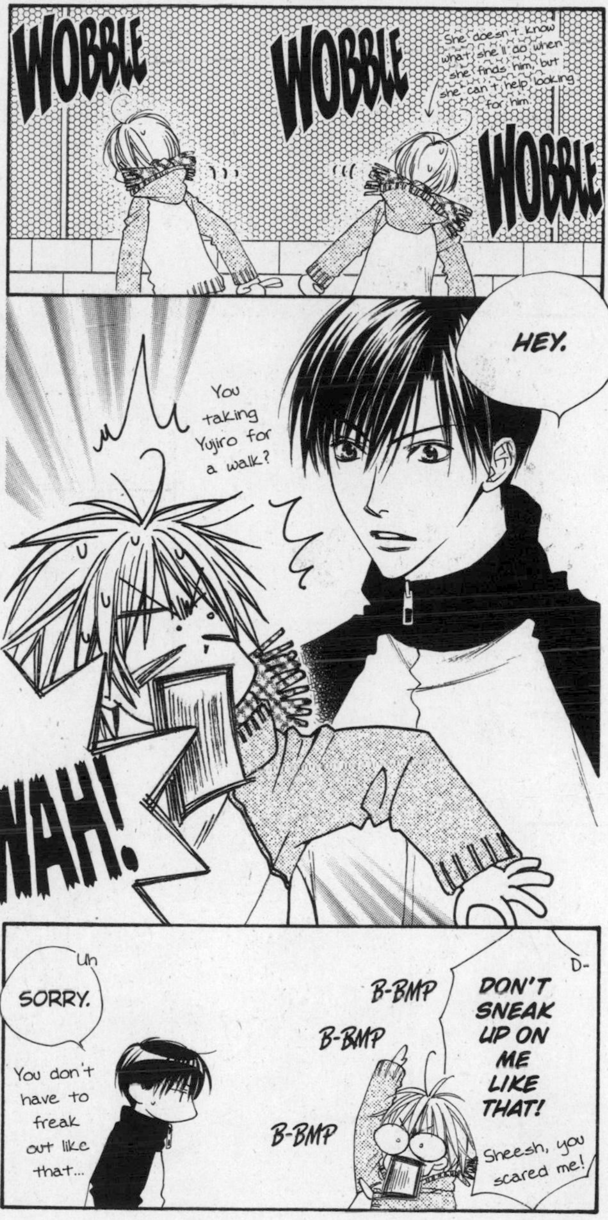
WOBBLE
WOBBLE
She doesn't know what she'll do when she finds him, but she can't help looking for him.
WOBBLE
HEY.
You taking Yujiro for a walk?
WAH!
D-
DON'T SNEAK UP ON ME LIKE THAT!
B-BMP
B-BMP
B-BMP
Sheesh, you scared me!
Uh
SORRY.
You don't have to freak out like that...

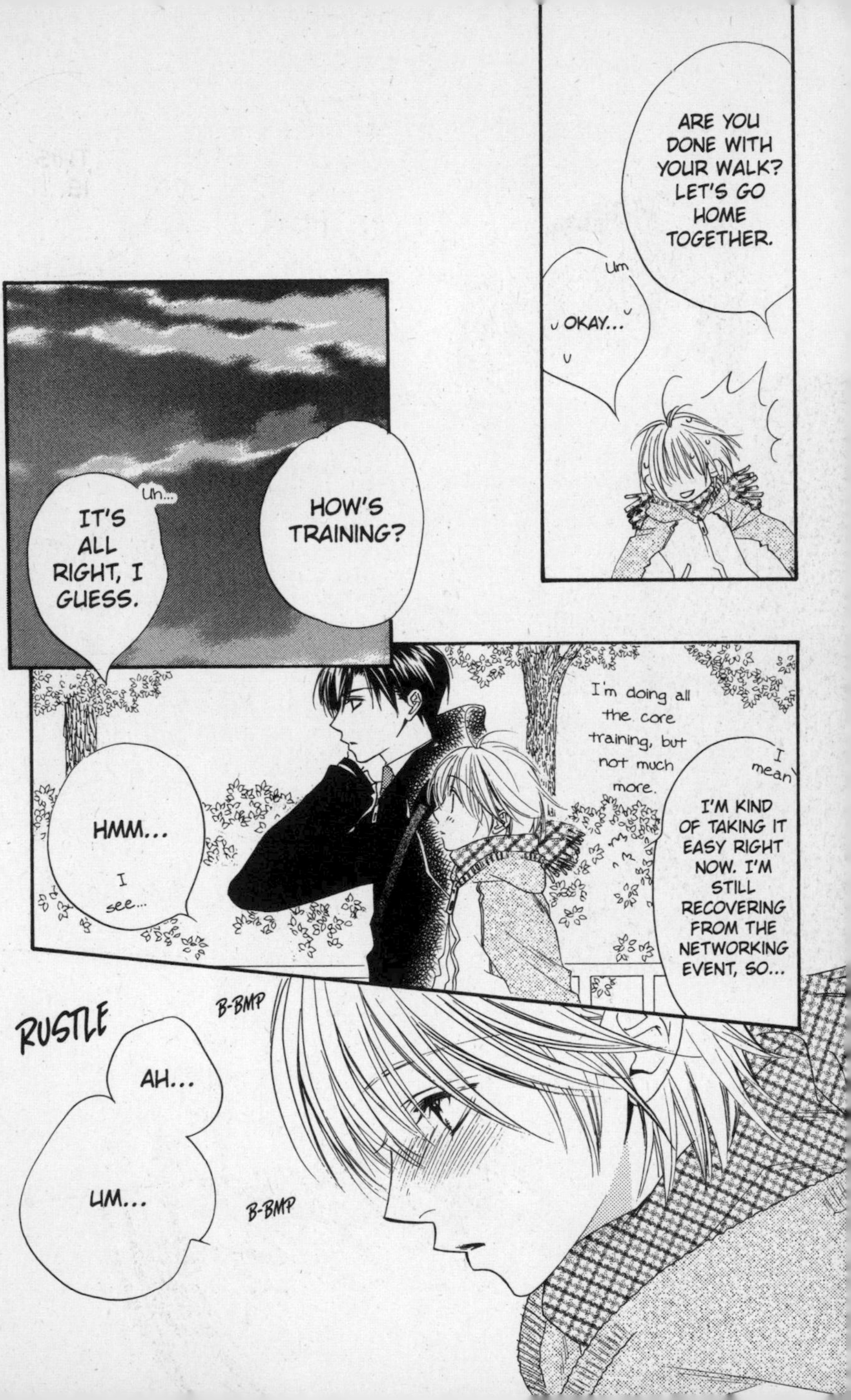
ARE YOU DONE WITH YOUR WALK? LET'S GO HOME TOGETHER.
Um
OKAY...
HOW'S TRAINING?
Uh...
IT'S ALL RIGHT, I GUESS.
I'm doing all the core training, but not much more.
I mean
I'M KIND OF TAKING IT EASY RIGHT NOW. I'M STILL RECOVERING FROM THE NETWORKING EVENT, SO...
HMM...
I see...
B-BMP
RUSTLE
AH...
B-BMP
UM...

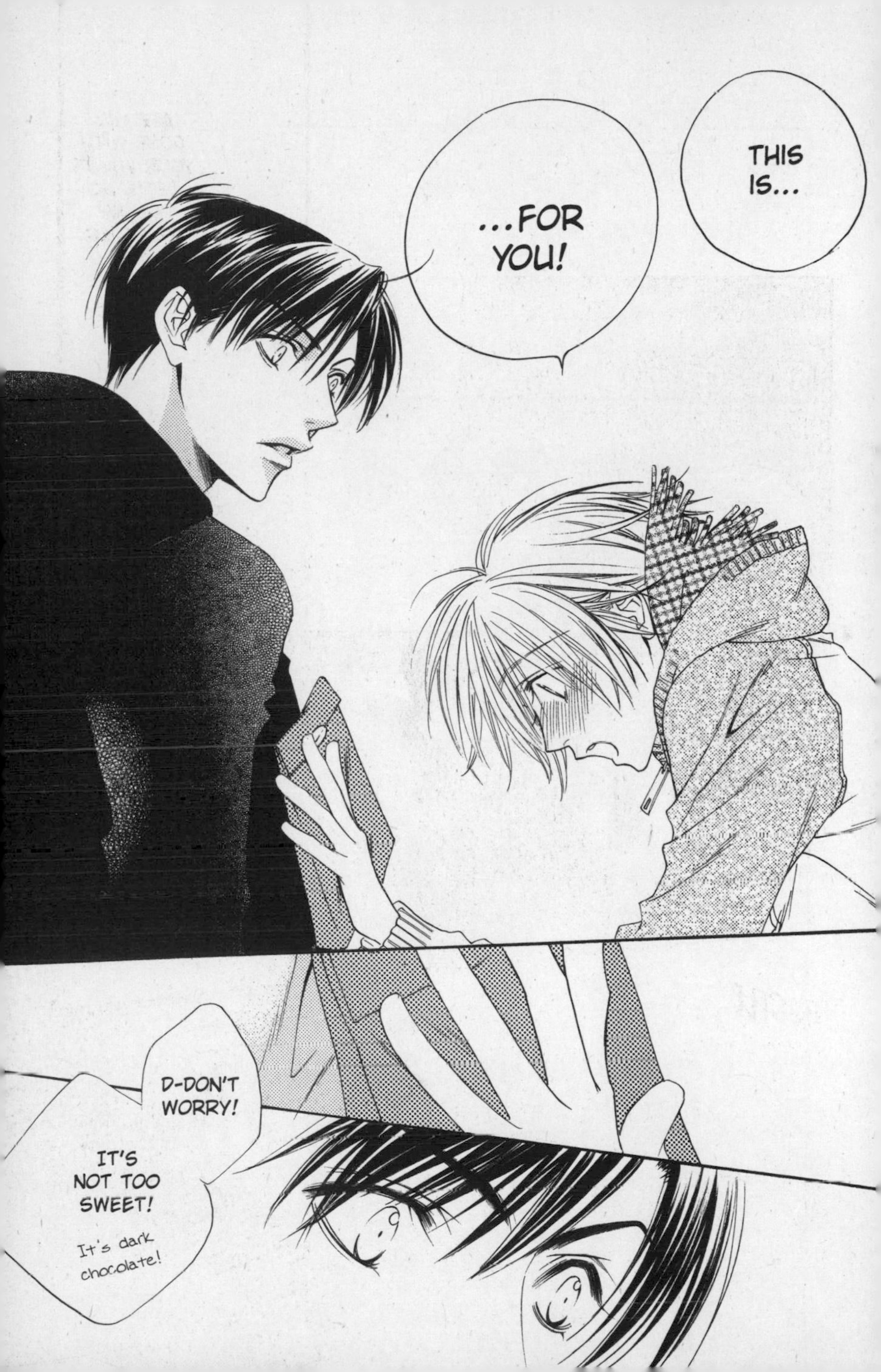
THIS IS...
...FOR YOU!
D-DON'T WORRY!
IT'S NOT TOO SWEET!
It's dark chocolate!

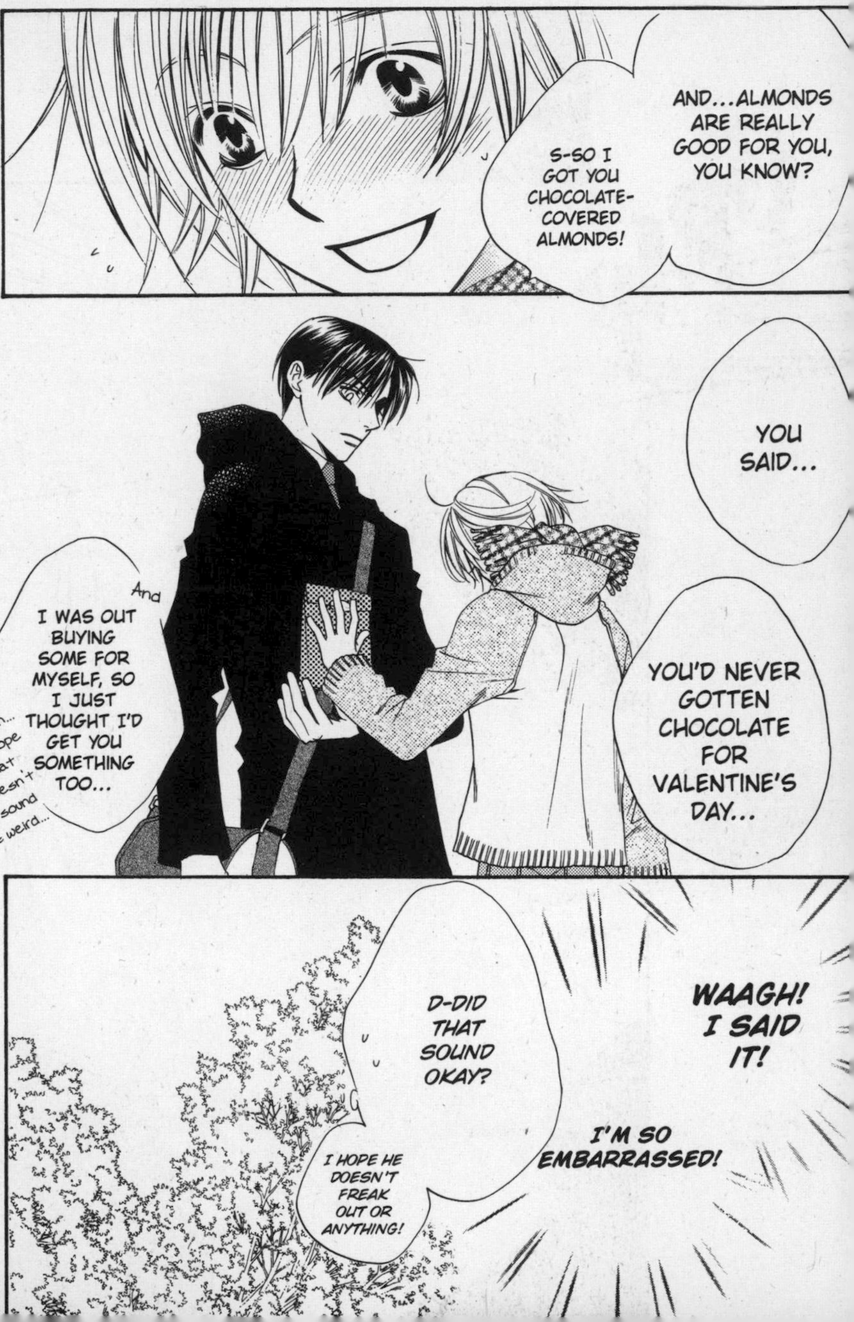
AND...ALMONDS ARE REALLY GOOD FOR YOU, YOU KNOW?
S-SO I GOT YOU CHOCOLATE-COVERED ALMONDS!
YOU SAID...
YOU'D NEVER GOTTEN CHOCOLATE FOR VALENTINE'S DAY...
And
I WAS OUT BUYING SOME FOR MYSELF, SO I JUST THOUGHT I'D GET YOU SOMETHING TOO...
I mean... I h-hope that doesn't sound weird...
WAAGH! I SAID IT!
I'M SO EMBARRASSED!
D-DID THAT SOUND OKAY?
I HOPE HE DOESN'T FREAK OUT OR ANYTHING!

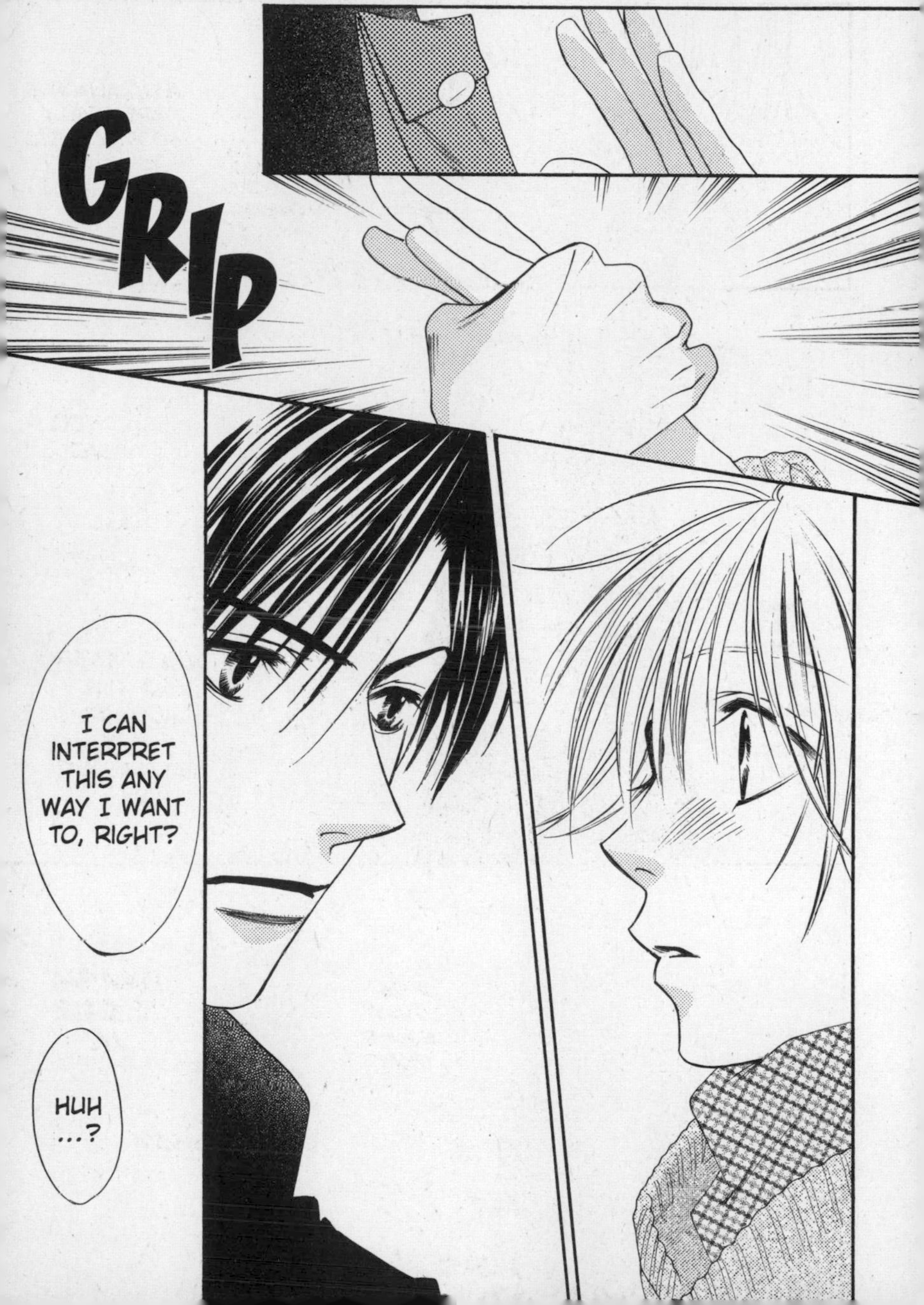
GRIP
I CAN INTERPRET THIS ANY WAY I WANT TO, RIGHT?
HUH ...?

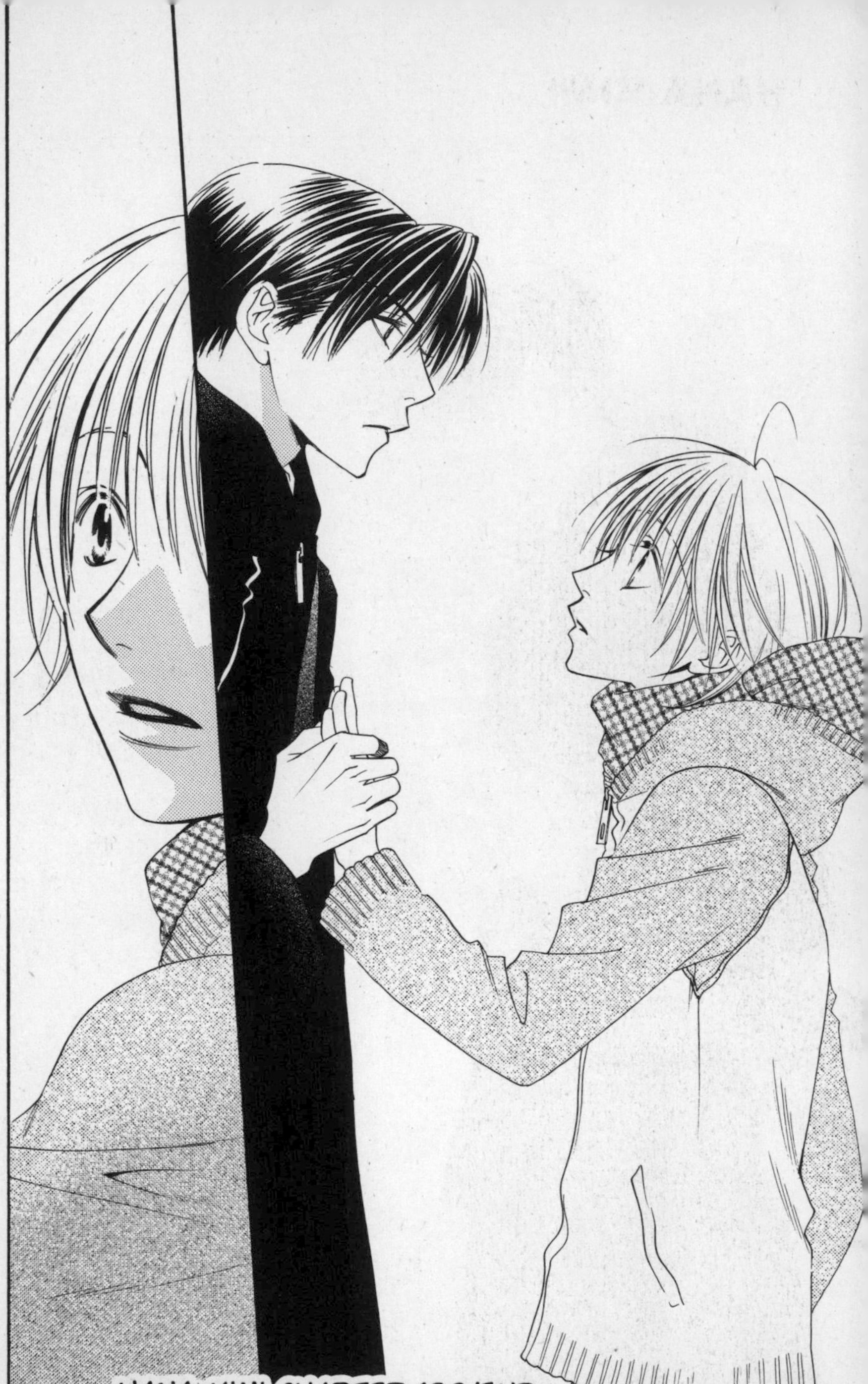

HANA-KIMI CHAPTER 120/END

HANA-KIMI

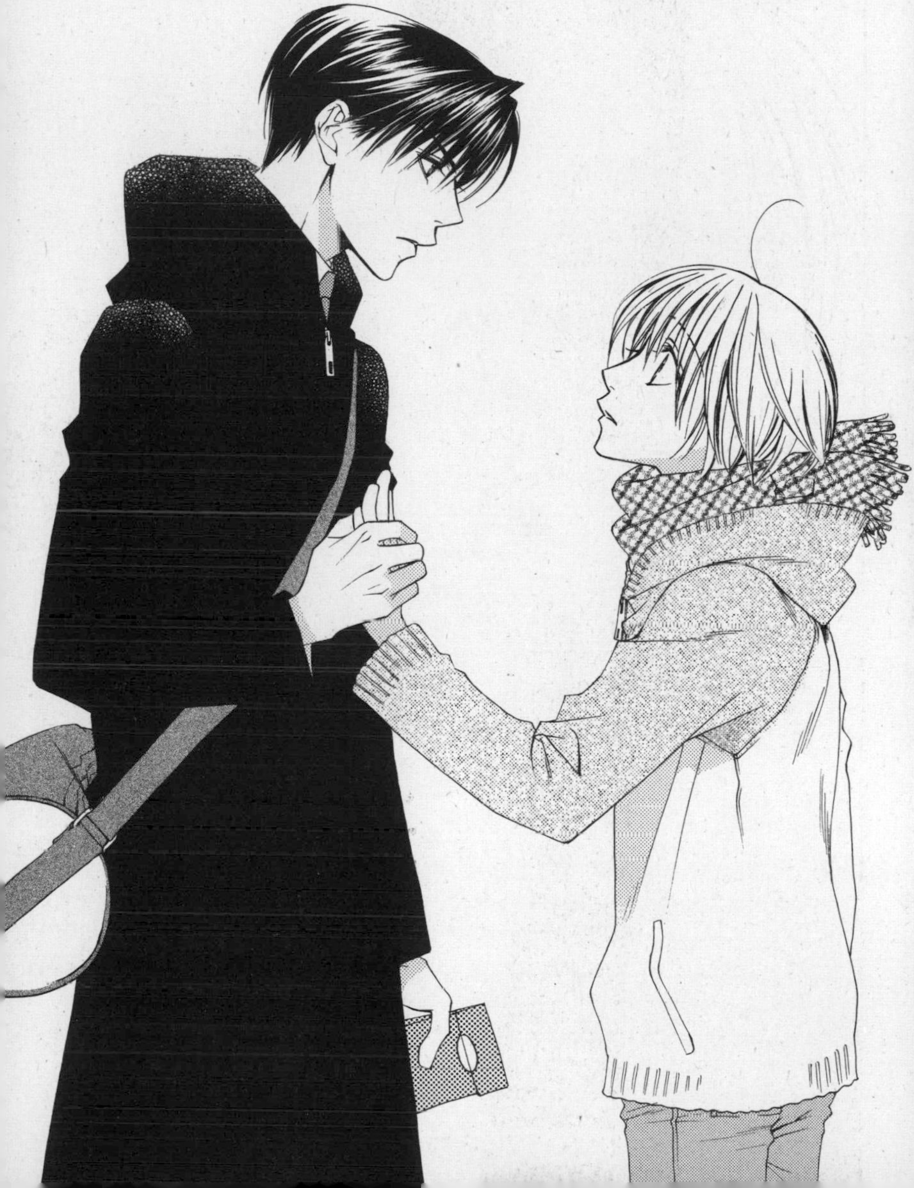

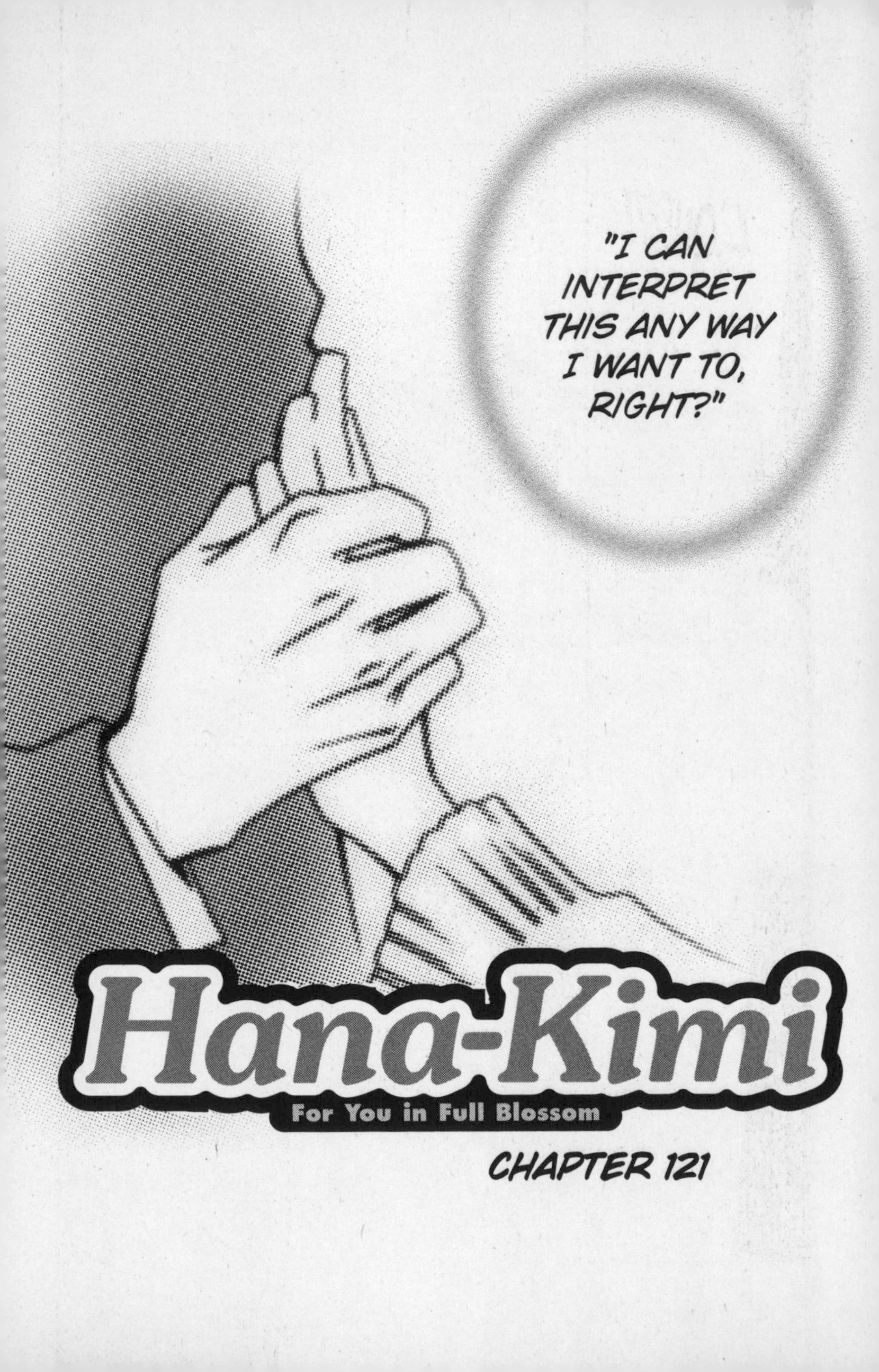
"I CAN INTERPRET THIS ANY WAY I WANT TO, RIGHT?"
Hana-Kimi
For You in Full Blossom
CHAPTER 121

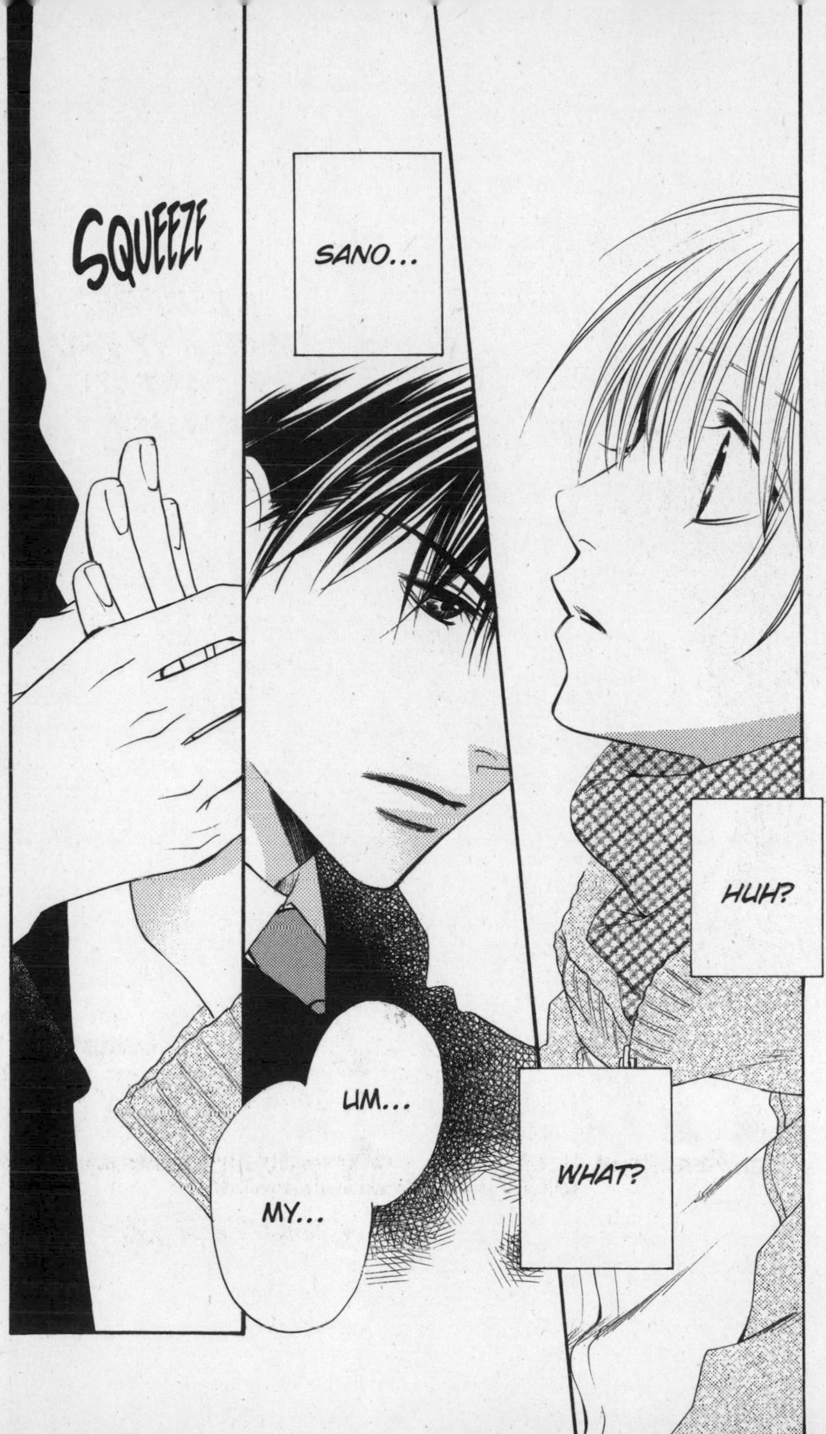
HUH?
WHAT?
SANO...
UM...
MY...
SQUEEZE

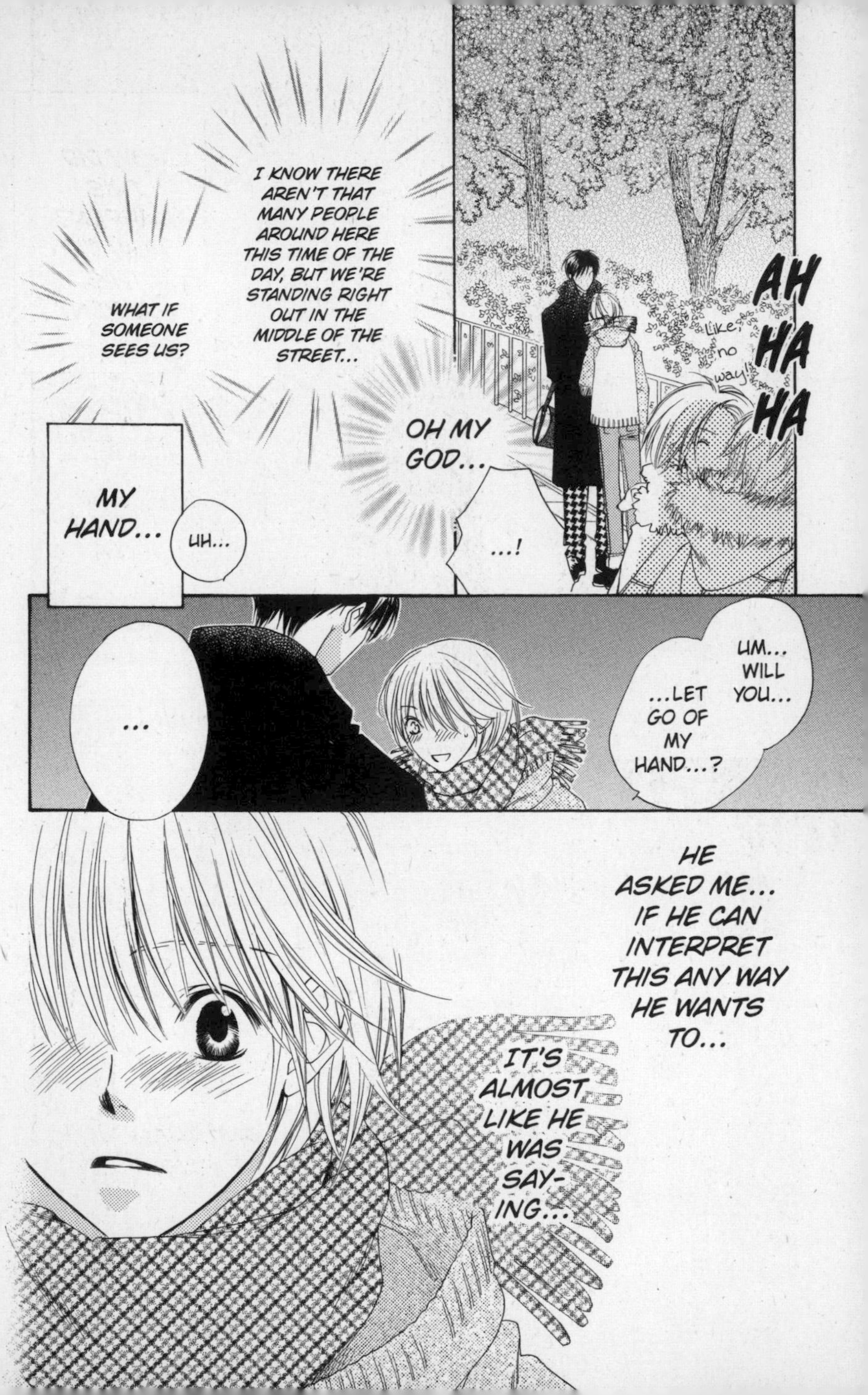
AH HA HA HA
Like, no way!
OH MY GOD...
...!
I KNOW THERE AREN'T THAT MANY PEOPLE AROUND HERE THIS TIME OF THE DAY, BUT WE'RE STANDING RIGHT OUT IN THE MIDDLE OF THE STREET...
WHAT IF SOMEONE SEES US?
MY HAND...
UH...
UM... WILL YOU...
...LET GO OF MY HAND...?
...
HE ASKED ME... IF HE CAN INTERPRET THIS ANY WAY HE WANTS TO...
IT'S ALMOST LIKE HE WAS SAY-ING...

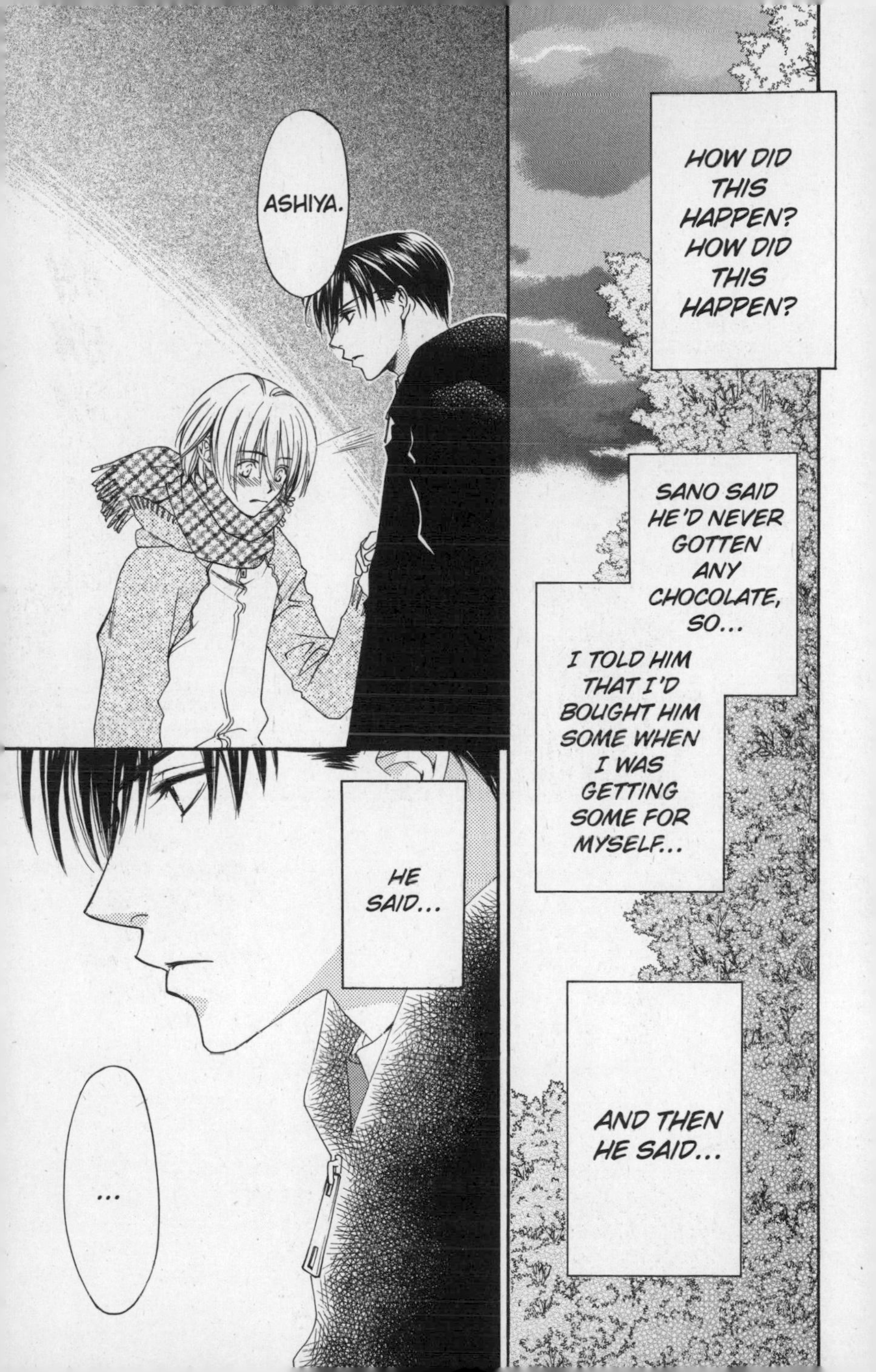
HOW DID THIS HAPPEN? HOW DID THIS HAPPEN?
SANO SAID HE'D NEVER GOTTEN ANY CHOCOLATE, SO...
I TOLD HIM THAT I'D BOUGHT HIM SOME WHEN I WAS GETTING SOME FOR MYSELF...
AND THEN HE SAID...
ASHIYA.
HE SAID...
...

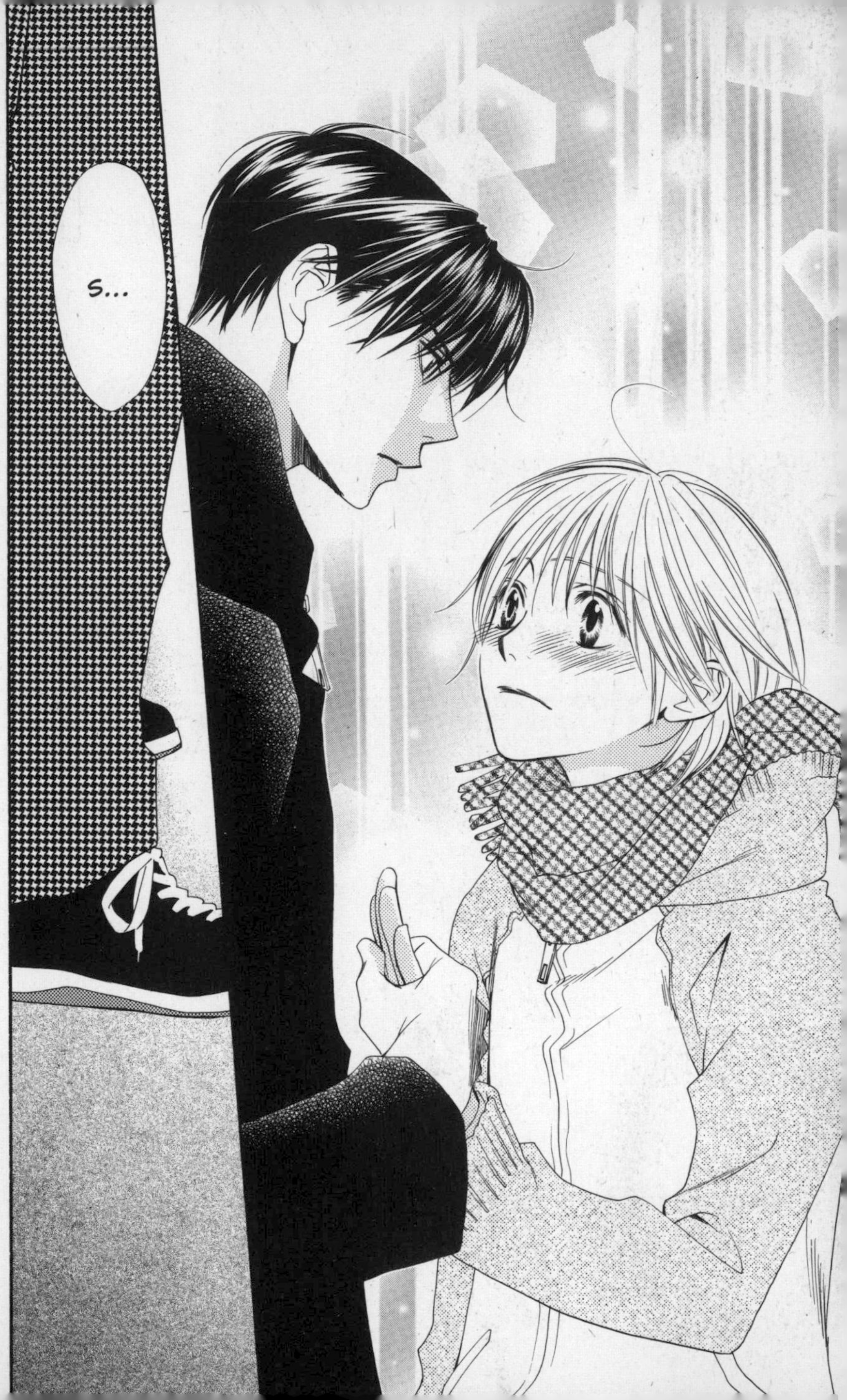
S...

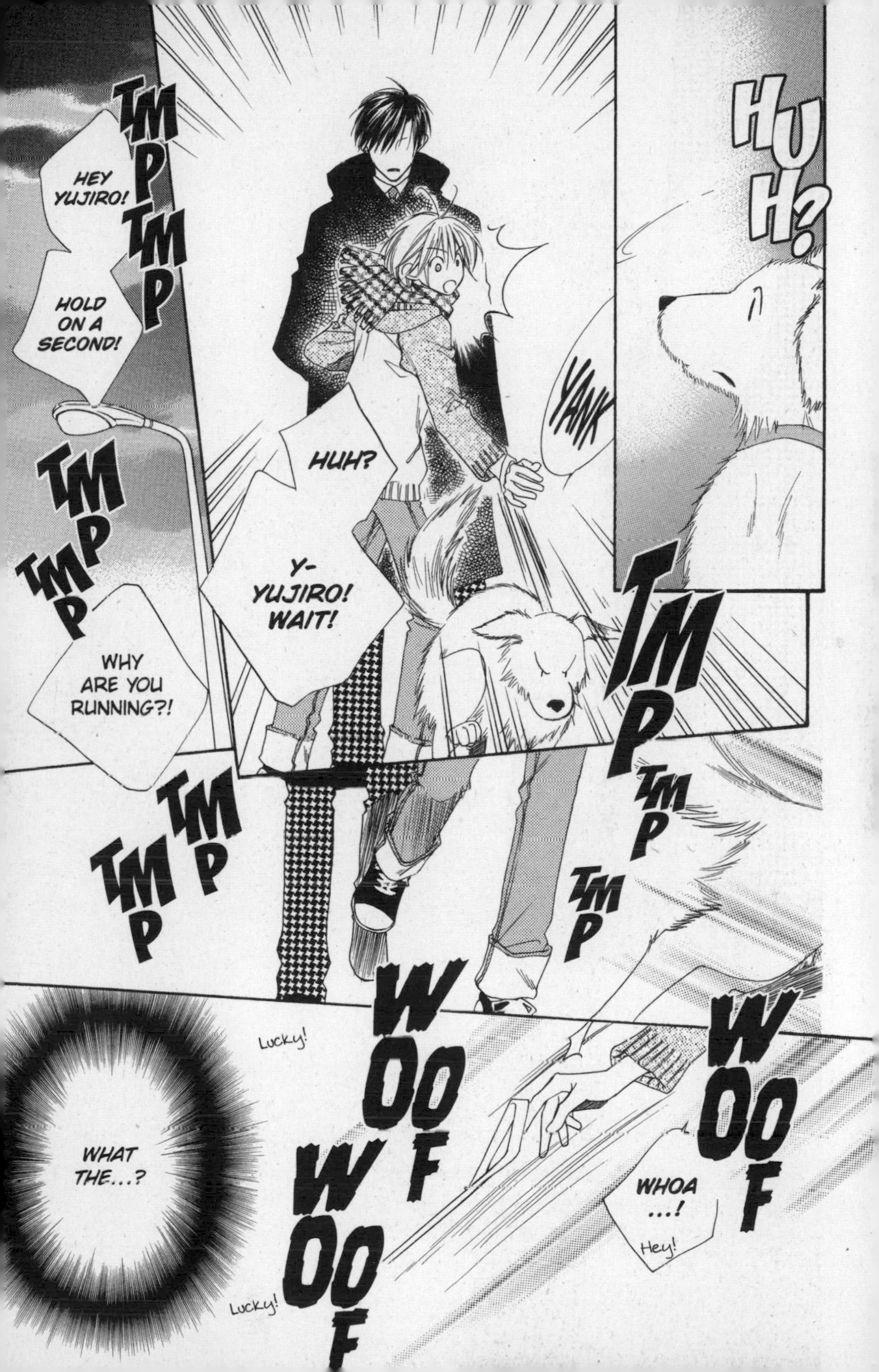
HUH?
YANK
TMP
TMP TMP
HEY YUJIRO!
HOLD ON A SECOND!
TMP TMP
HUH?
Y-YUJIRO! WAIT!
TMP TMP
WHY ARE YOU RUNNING?!
TMP
TMP
TMP
WOOF
WHOA ...!
Hey!
WOOF
Lucky!
WOOF
Lucky!
WHAT THE...?

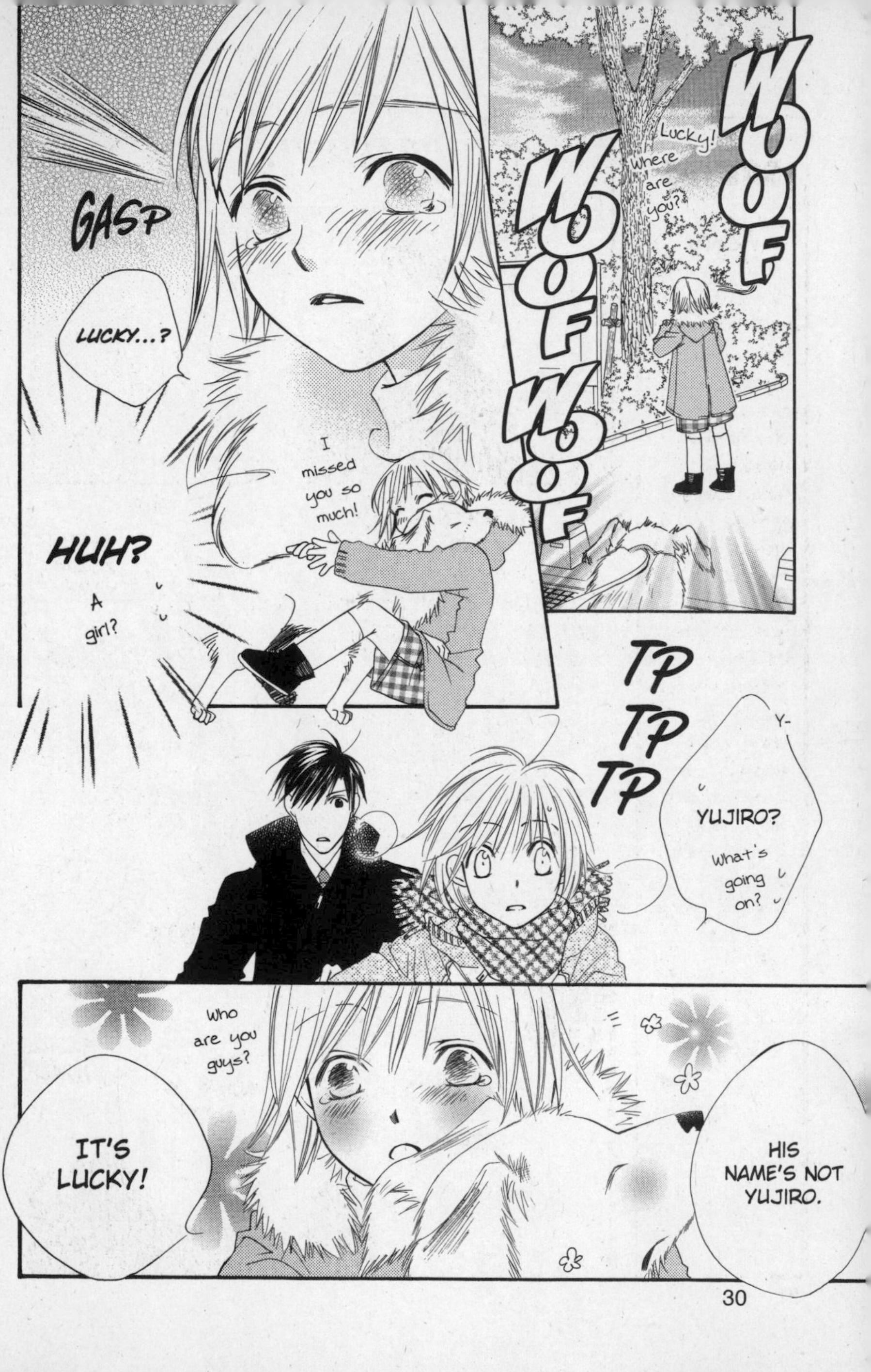

WOOF WOOF WOOF WOOF
Lucky! Where are you?
GASP
LUCKY...?
I missed you so much!
HUH?
A girl?
TP TP TP
Y-YUJIRO? What's going on?
HIS NAME'S NOT YUJIRO.
Who are you guys?
IT'S LUCKY!

DRINKS

"Aojiru"

Lately I've been really into aojiru ("green juice," a sort of health drink made of kale, barley grass, and other ingredients). ✿ My editor got me into it. It's pretty harsh to drink aojiru straight, so I mix it with apple juice. I feel much healthier now...

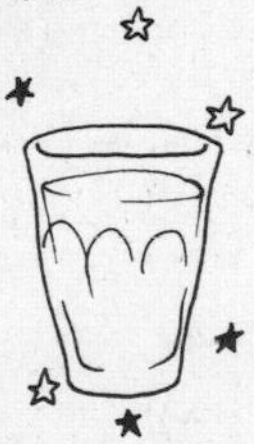

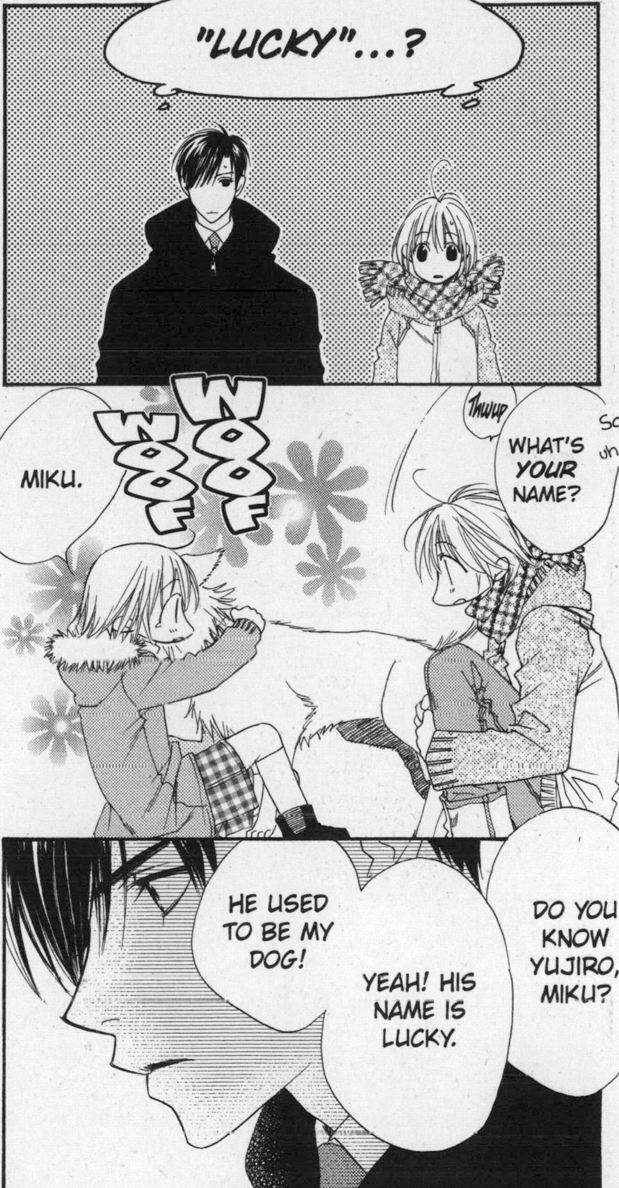
"LUCKY"...?
Thwup
So, uh...
WHAT'S YOUR NAME?
MIKU.
WOOF WOOF
DO YOU KNOW YUJIRO, MIKU?
YEAH! HIS NAME IS LUCKY.
HE USED TO BE MY DOG!

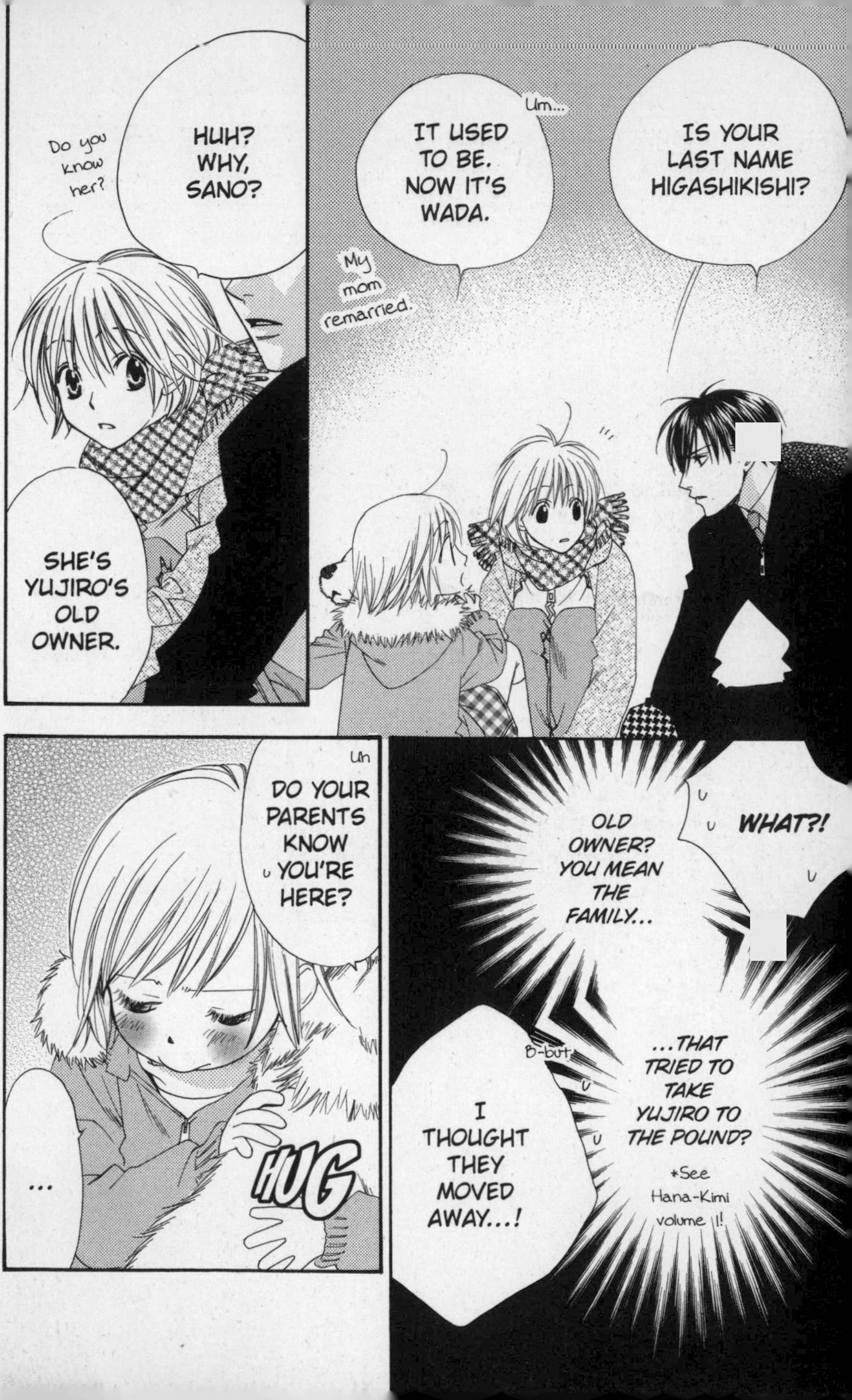
IS YOUR LAST NAME HIGASHIKISHI?
Um...
IT USED TO BE. NOW IT'S WADA.
My mom remarried.
HUH? WHY, SANO?
Do you know her?
SHE'S YUJIRO'S OLD OWNER.
WHAT?!
OLD OWNER? YOU MEAN THE FAMILY...
...THAT TRIED TO TAKE YUJIRO TO THE POUND?
*See Hana-Kimi volume 1!
B-but
I THOUGHT THEY MOVED AWAY...!
Un
DO YOUR PARENTS KNOW YOU'RE HERE?
HUG
...

I DON'T CARE IF THEY KNOW!
I HATE MY MOM!
SHE RAN AWAY FROM HOME...
She ran away from home once, too.
He's sort of running away right now.
YOU KNOW, MIKU...
YOUR PARENTS ARE PROBABLY WORRIED ABOUT YOU.
BUT...
BUT...MY MOM LIED TO ME.
ONE DAY I CAME HOME FROM KINDERGARTEN AND LUCKY WAS GONE.
MOM SAID LUCKY RAN AWAY WHILE SHE WAS OUT WALKING HIM...
BUT IT WAS ALL A LIE.

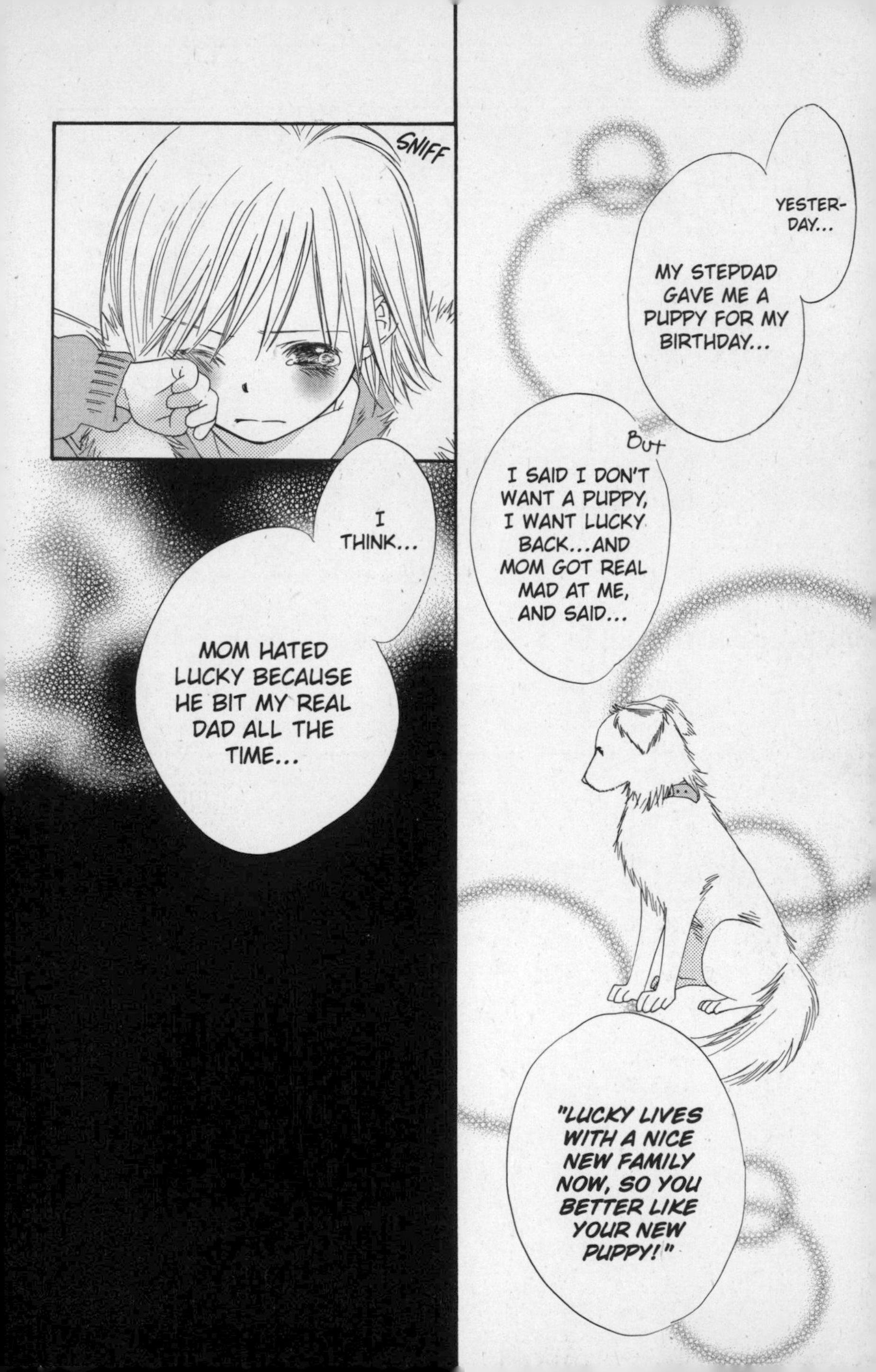
YESTER-DAY...
MY STEPDAD GAVE ME A PUPPY FOR MY BIRTHDAY...
But
I SAID I DON'T WANT A PUPPY, I WANT LUCKY BACK...AND MOM GOT REAL MAD AT ME, AND SAID...
"LUCKY LIVES WITH A NICE NEW FAMILY NOW, SO YOU BETTER LIKE YOUR NEW PUPPY!"
SNIFF
I THINK...
MOM HATED LUCKY BECAUSE HE BIT MY REAL DAD ALL THE TIME...

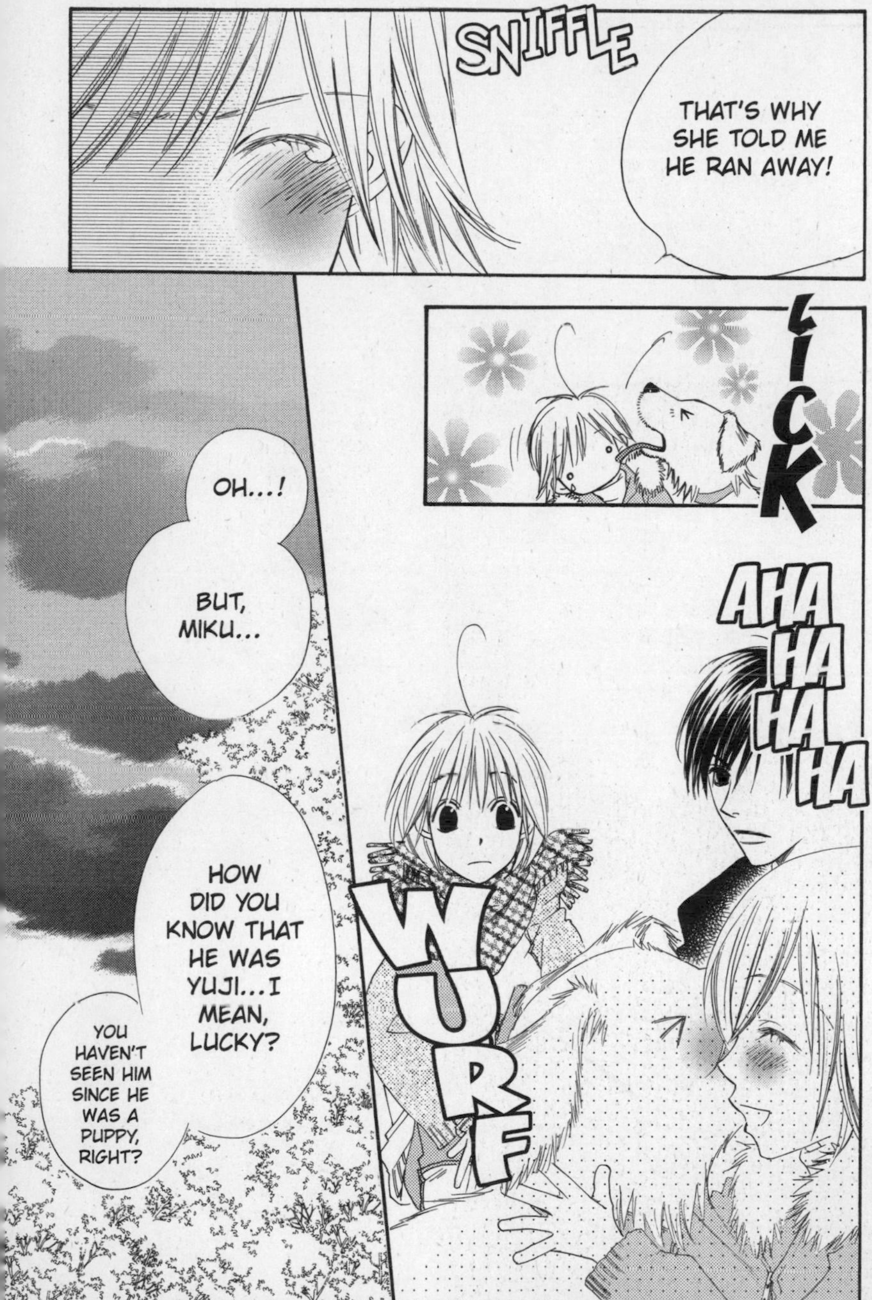
SNIFFLE
THAT'S WHY SHE TOLD ME HE RAN AWAY!
LICK
AHAHAHAHAHA
WURF
OH...!
BUT, MIKU...
HOW DID YOU KNOW THAT HE WAS YUJI...I MEAN, LUCKY?
YOU HAVEN'T SEEN HIM SINCE HE WAS A PUPPY, RIGHT?

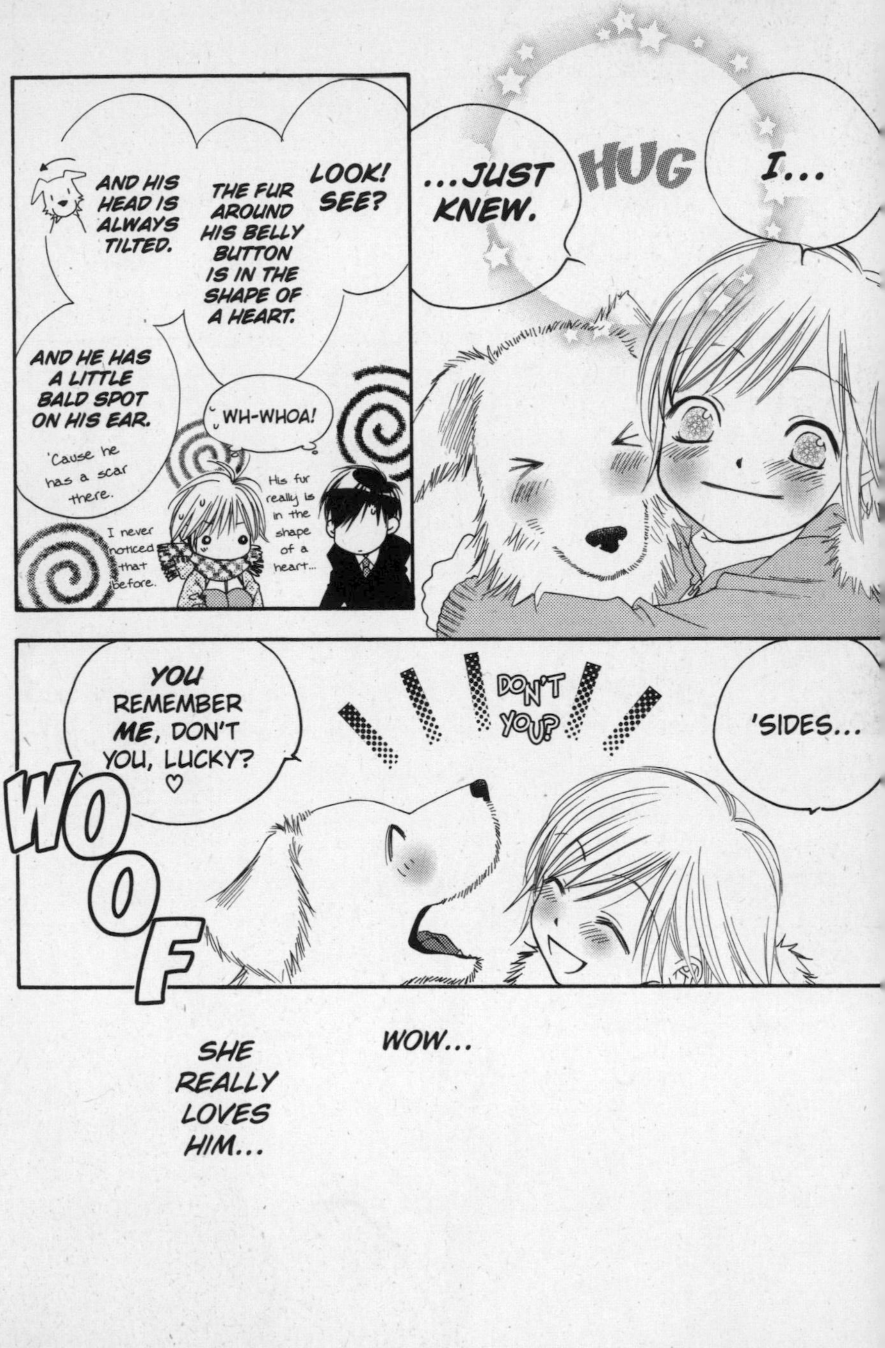
I...
HUG
...JUST KNEW.
LOOK! SEE?
THE FUR AROUND HIS BELLY BUTTON IS IN THE SHAPE OF A HEART.
AND HIS HEAD IS ALWAYS TILTED.
AND HE HAS A LITTLE BALD SPOT ON HIS EAR.
'Cause he has a scar there.
WH-WHOA!
His fur really is in the shape of a heart...
I never noticed that before.
'SIDES...
DON'T YOU?
YOU REMEMBER ME, DON'T YOU, LUCKY? ♡
WOOF
WOW...
SHE REALLY LOVES HIM...

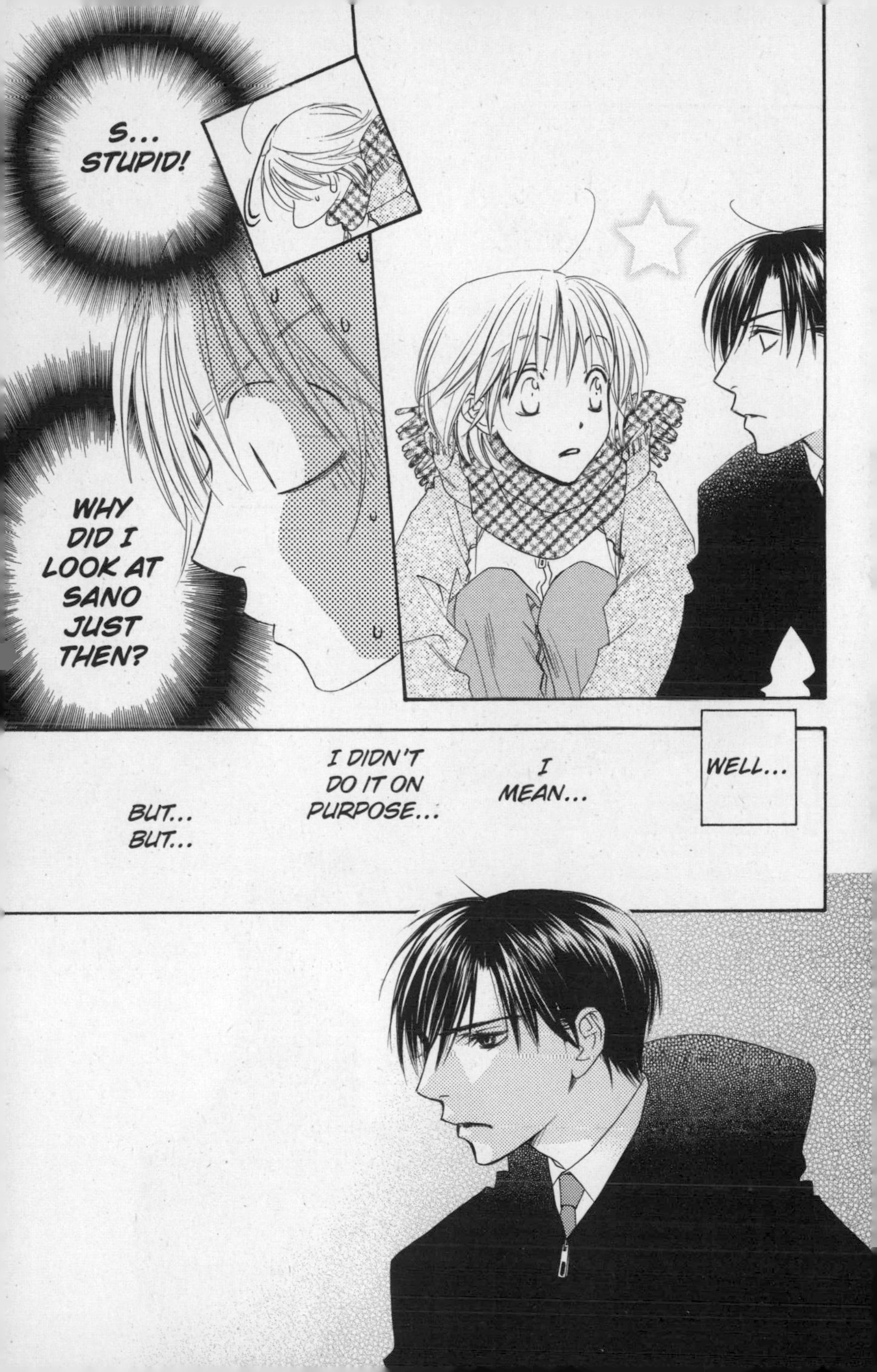
S... STUPID!
WHY DID I LOOK AT SANO JUST THEN?
WELL...
I MEAN...
I DIDN'T DO IT ON PURPOSE...
BUT... BUT...

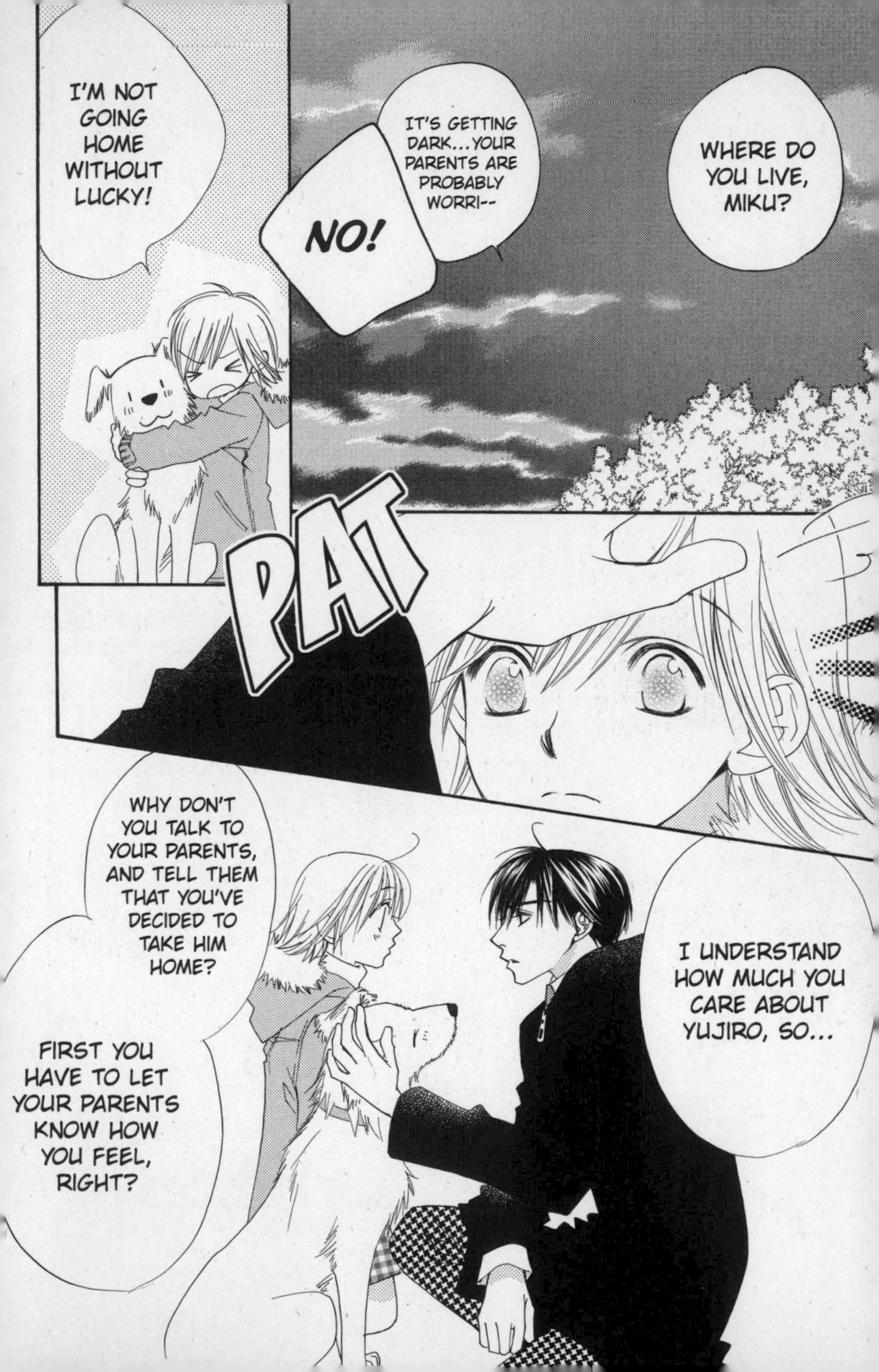
WHERE DO YOU LIVE, MIKU?
IT'S GETTING DARK...YOUR PARENTS ARE PROBABLY WORRI--
NO!
I'M NOT GOING HOME WITHOUT LUCKY!
PAT
I UNDERSTAND HOW MUCH YOU CARE ABOUT YUJIRO, SO...
WHY DON'T YOU TALK TO YOUR PARENTS, AND TELL THEM THAT YOU'VE DECIDED TO TAKE HIM HOME?
FIRST YOU HAVE TO LET YOUR PARENTS KNOW HOW YOU FEEL, RIGHT?

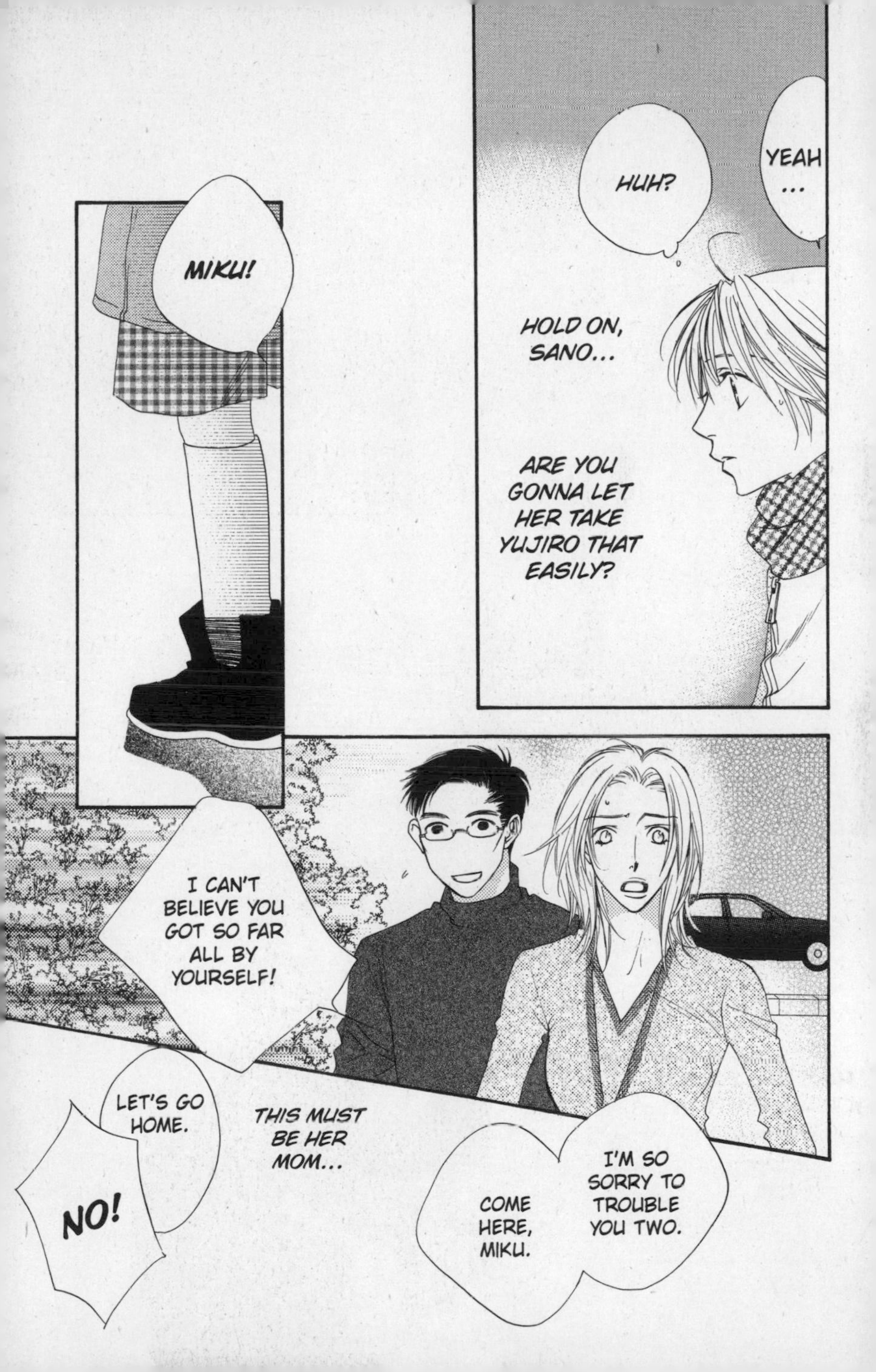
YEAH...
HUH?
HOLD ON, SANO...
ARE YOU GONNA LET HER TAKE YUJIRO THAT EASILY?
MIKU!
I CAN'T BELIEVE YOU GOT SO FAR ALL BY YOURSELF!
I'M SO SORRY TO TROUBLE YOU TWO.
COME HERE, MIKU.
THIS MUST BE HER MOM...
LET'S GO HOME.
NO!

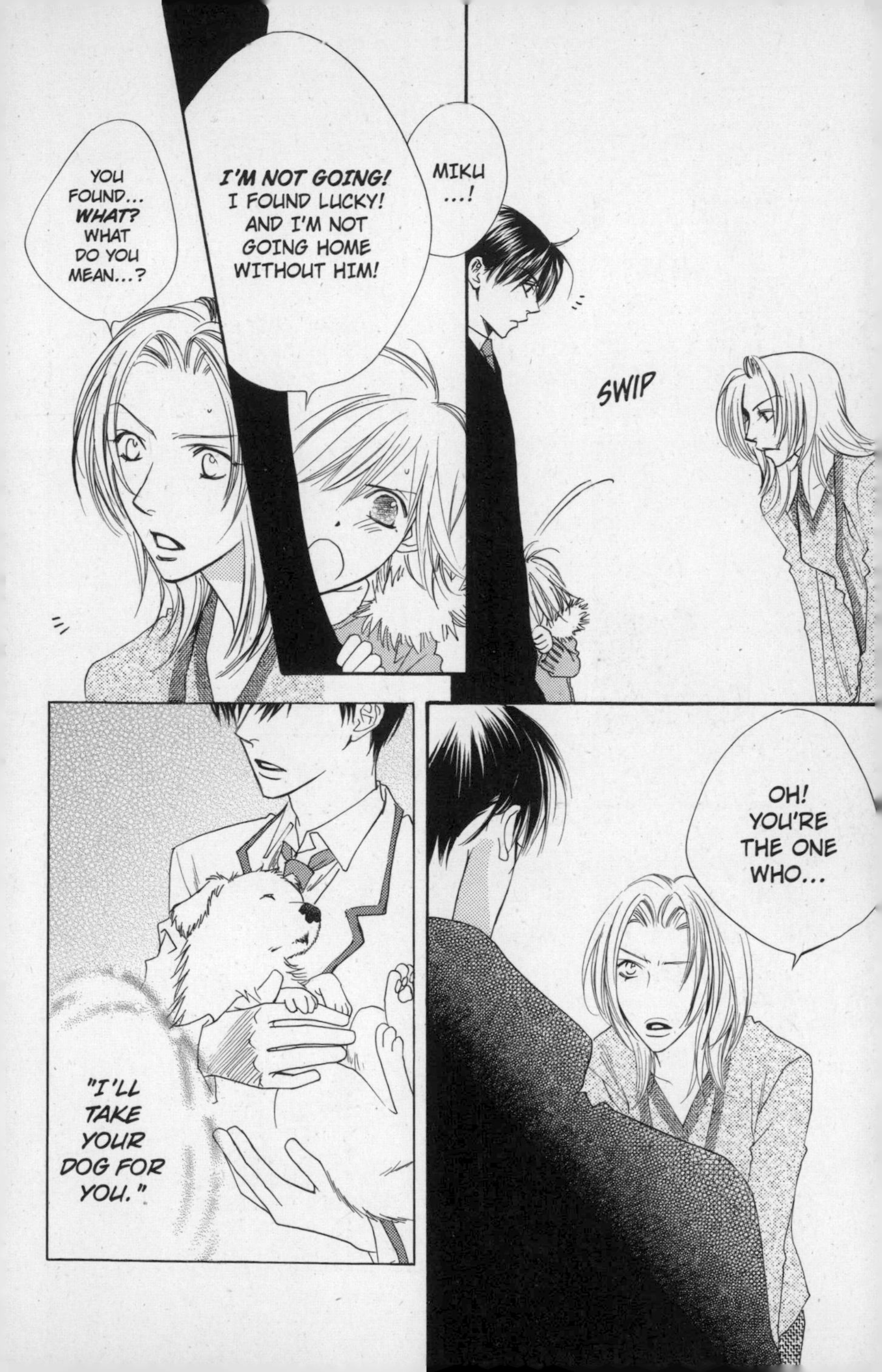
MIKU ...!
SWIP
I'M NOT GOING! I FOUND LUCKY! AND I'M NOT GOING HOME WITHOUT HIM!
YOU FOUND... *WHAT?* WHAT DO YOU MEAN...?
OH! YOU'RE THE ONE WHO...
"I'LL TAKE YOUR DOG FOR YOU."

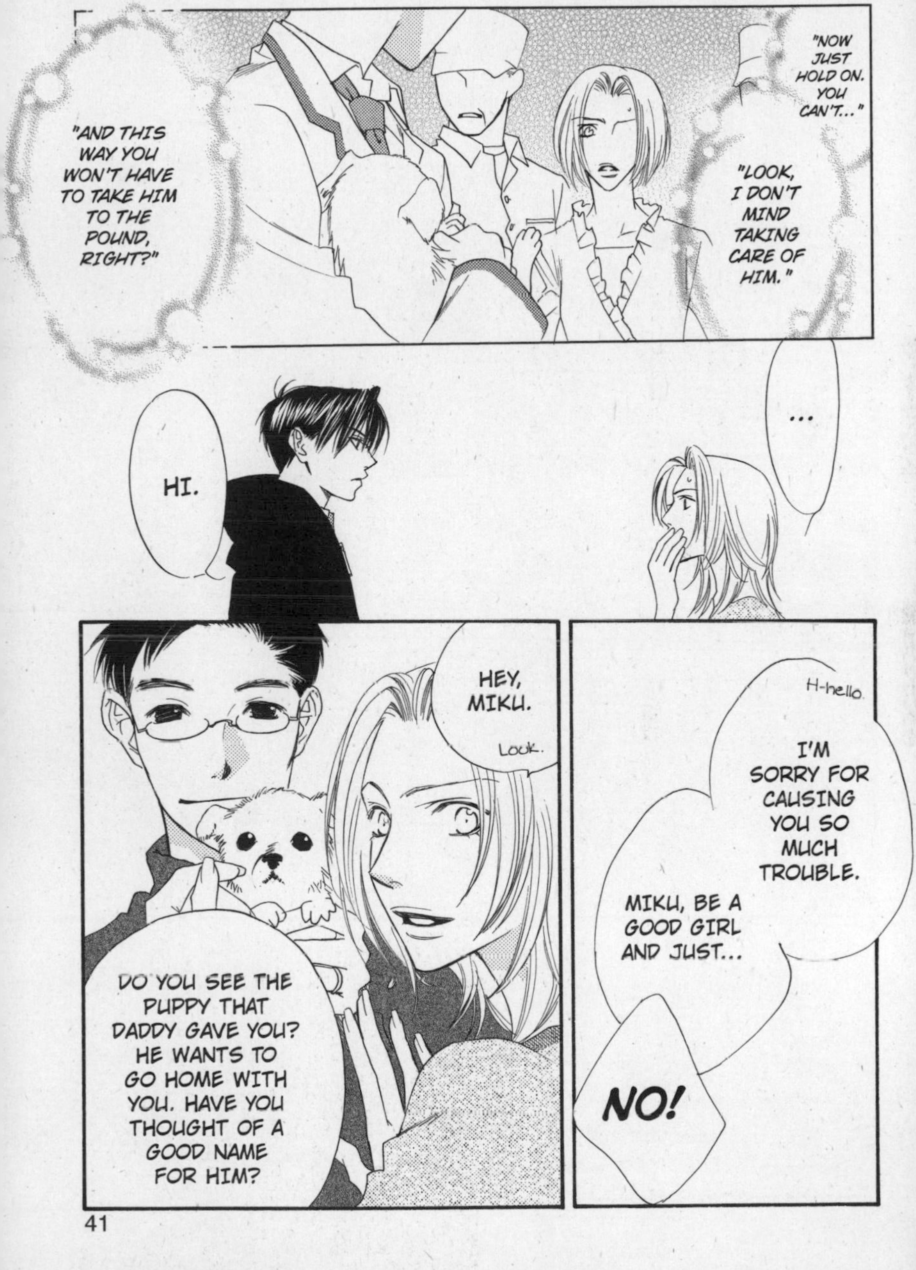
"NOW JUST HOLD ON. YOU CAN'T..."
"LOOK, I DON'T MIND TAKING CARE OF HIM."
"AND THIS WAY YOU WON'T HAVE TO TAKE HIM TO THE POUND, RIGHT?"
...
HI.
H-hello.
I'M SORRY FOR CAUSING YOU SO MUCH TROUBLE.
MIKU, BE A GOOD GIRL AND JUST...
NO!
HEY, MIKU.
Look.
DO YOU SEE THE PUPPY THAT DADDY GAVE YOU? HE WANTS TO GO HOME WITH YOU. HAVE YOU THOUGHT OF A GOOD NAME FOR HIM?

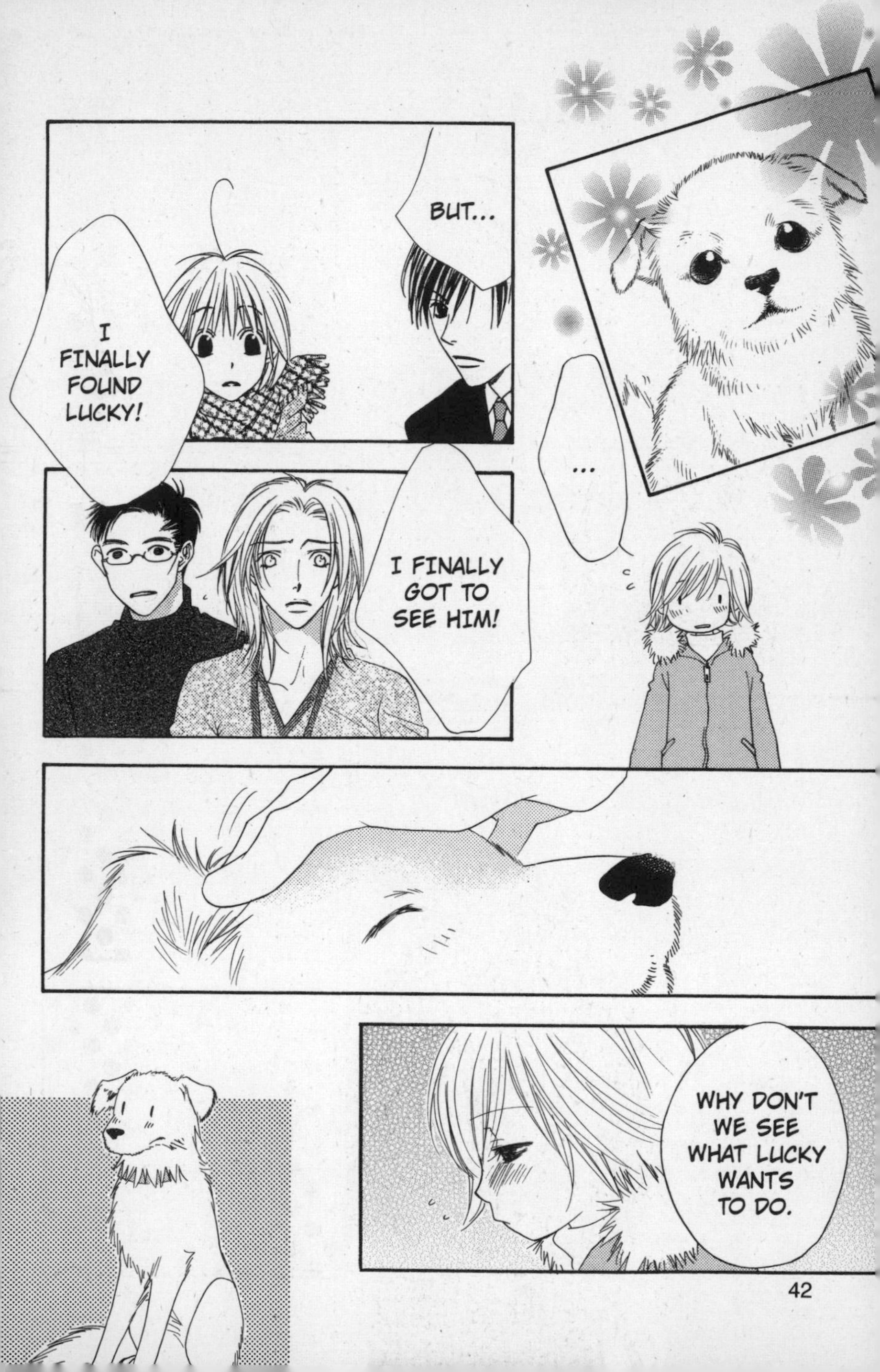
...
BUT...
I FINALLY FOUND LUCKY!
I FINALLY GOT TO SEE HIM!
WHY DON'T WE SEE WHAT LUCKY WANTS TO DO.

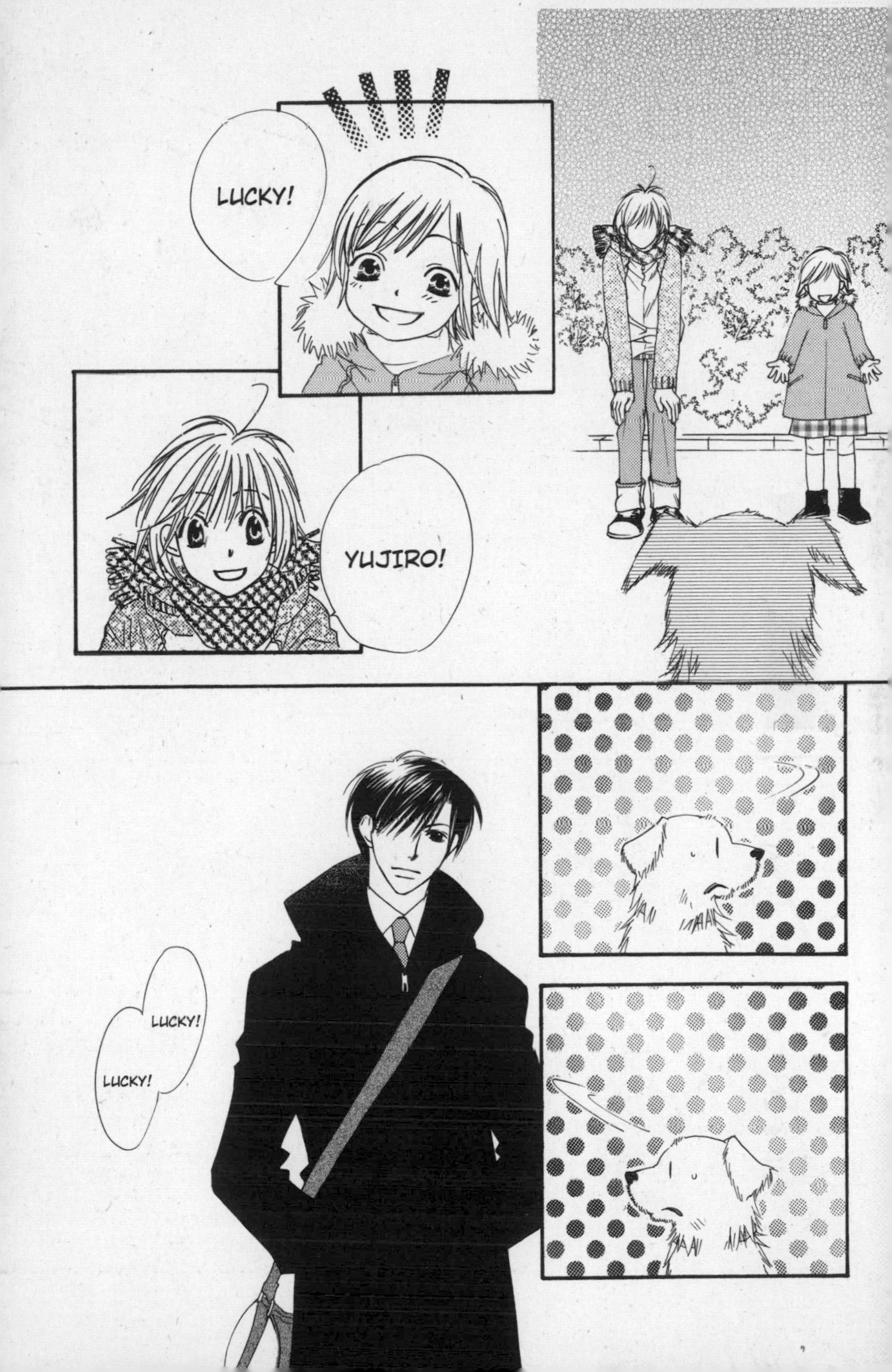
LUCKY!
YUJIRO!
LUCKY!
LUCKY!

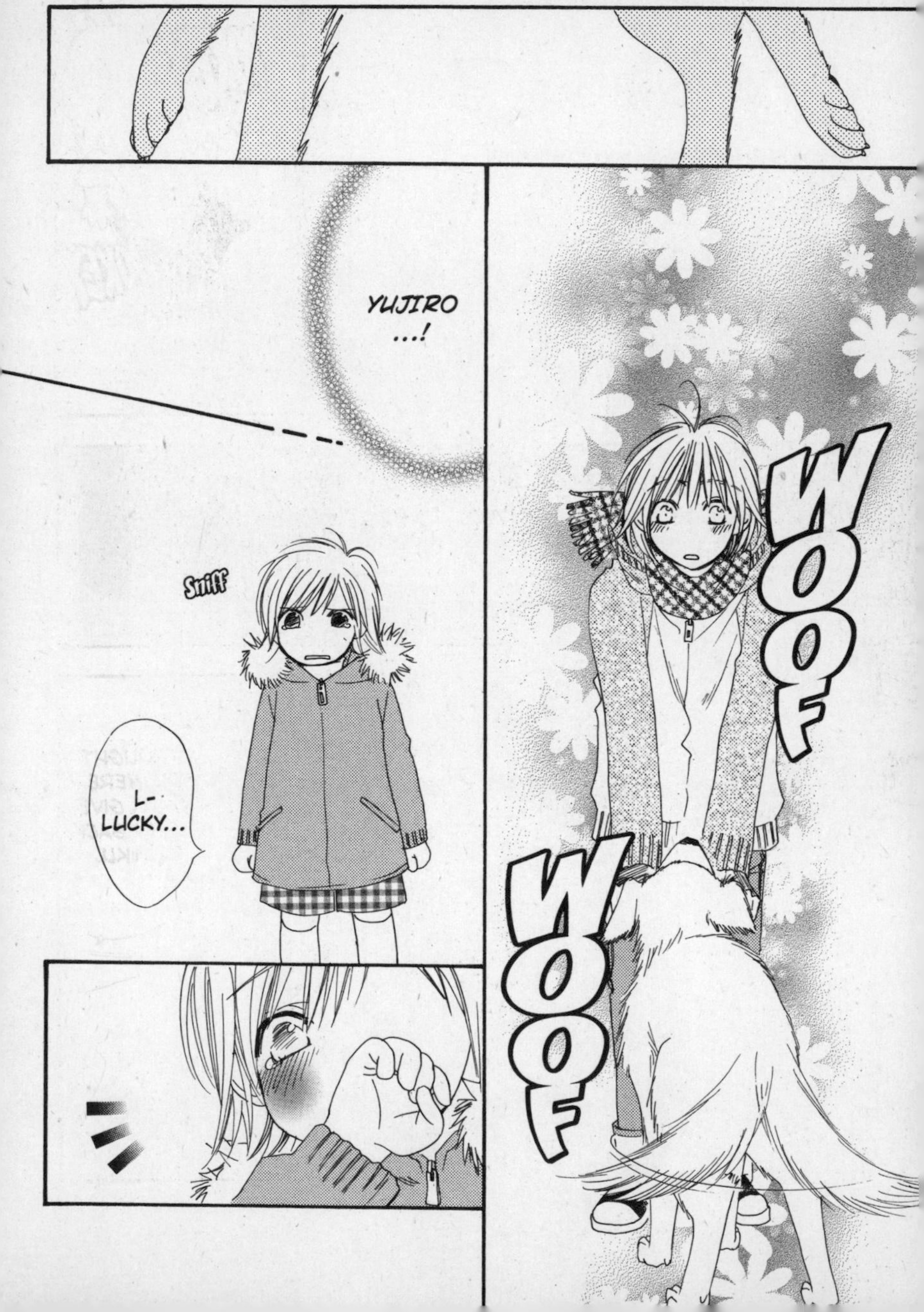
WOOF
WOOF
YUJIRO ...!
Sniff
L- LUCKY...

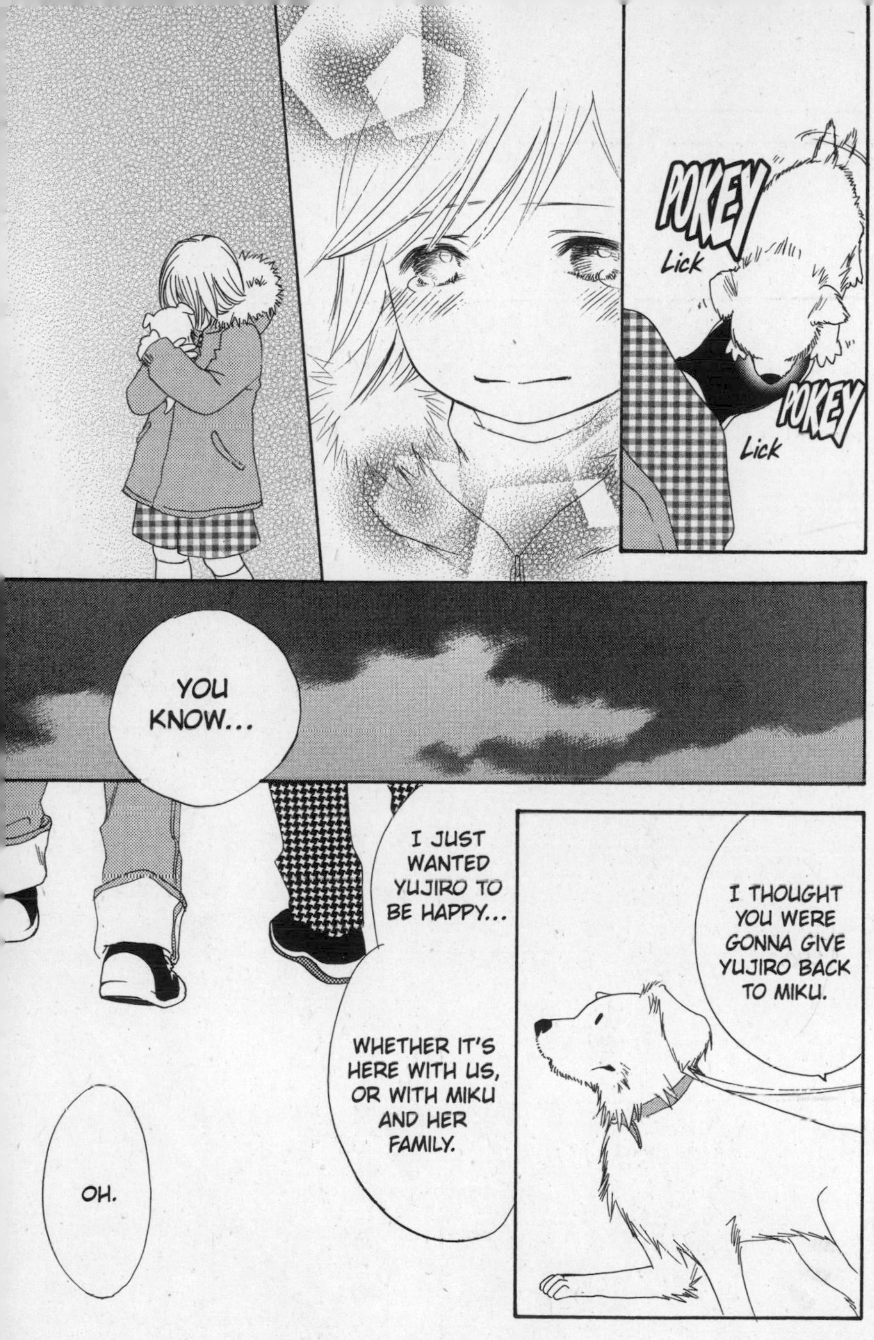
POKEY
Lick
POKEY
Lick
YOU KNOW...
I THOUGHT YOU WERE GONNA GIVE YUJIRO BACK TO MIKU.
I JUST WANTED YUJIRO TO BE HAPPY...
WHETHER IT'S HERE WITH US, OR WITH MIKU AND HER FAMILY.
OH.

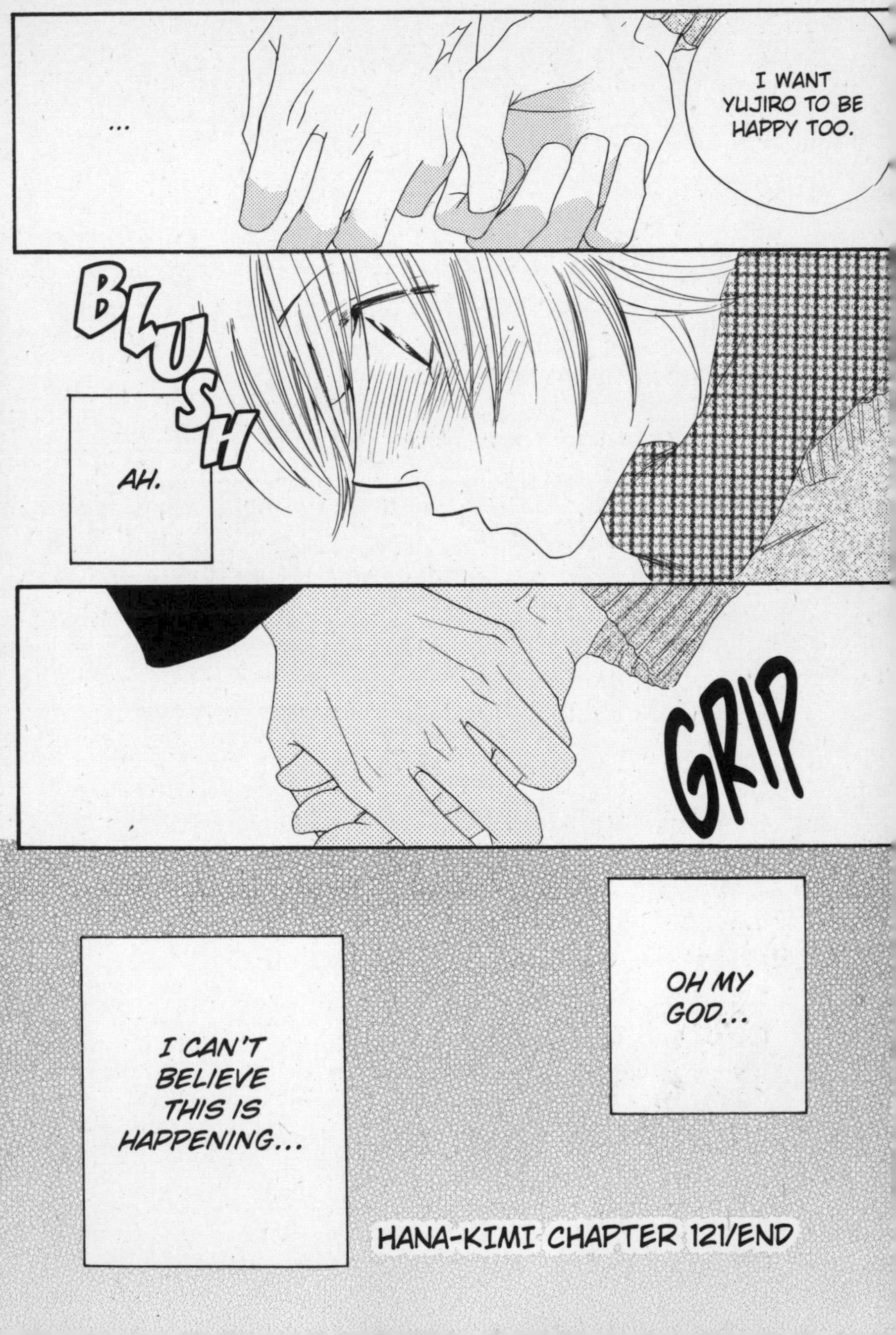
I WANT YUJIRO TO BE HAPPY TOO.
...
BLUSH
AH.
GRIP
OH MY GOD...
I CAN'T BELIEVE THIS IS HAPPENING...
HANA-KIMI CHAPTER 121/END

HYAA!
IT'S SO HEAVY!

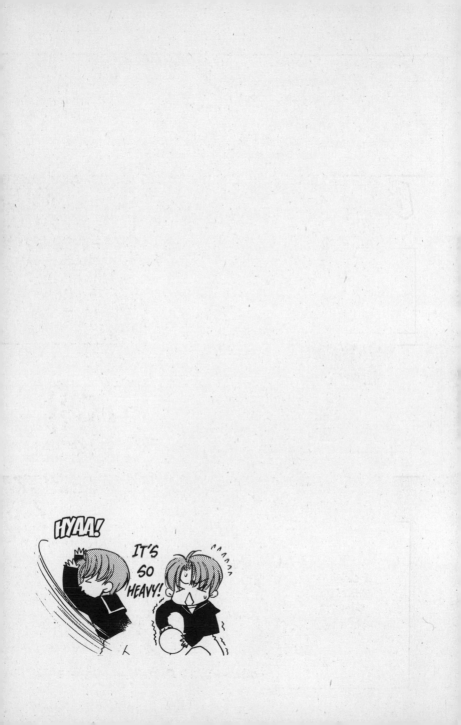

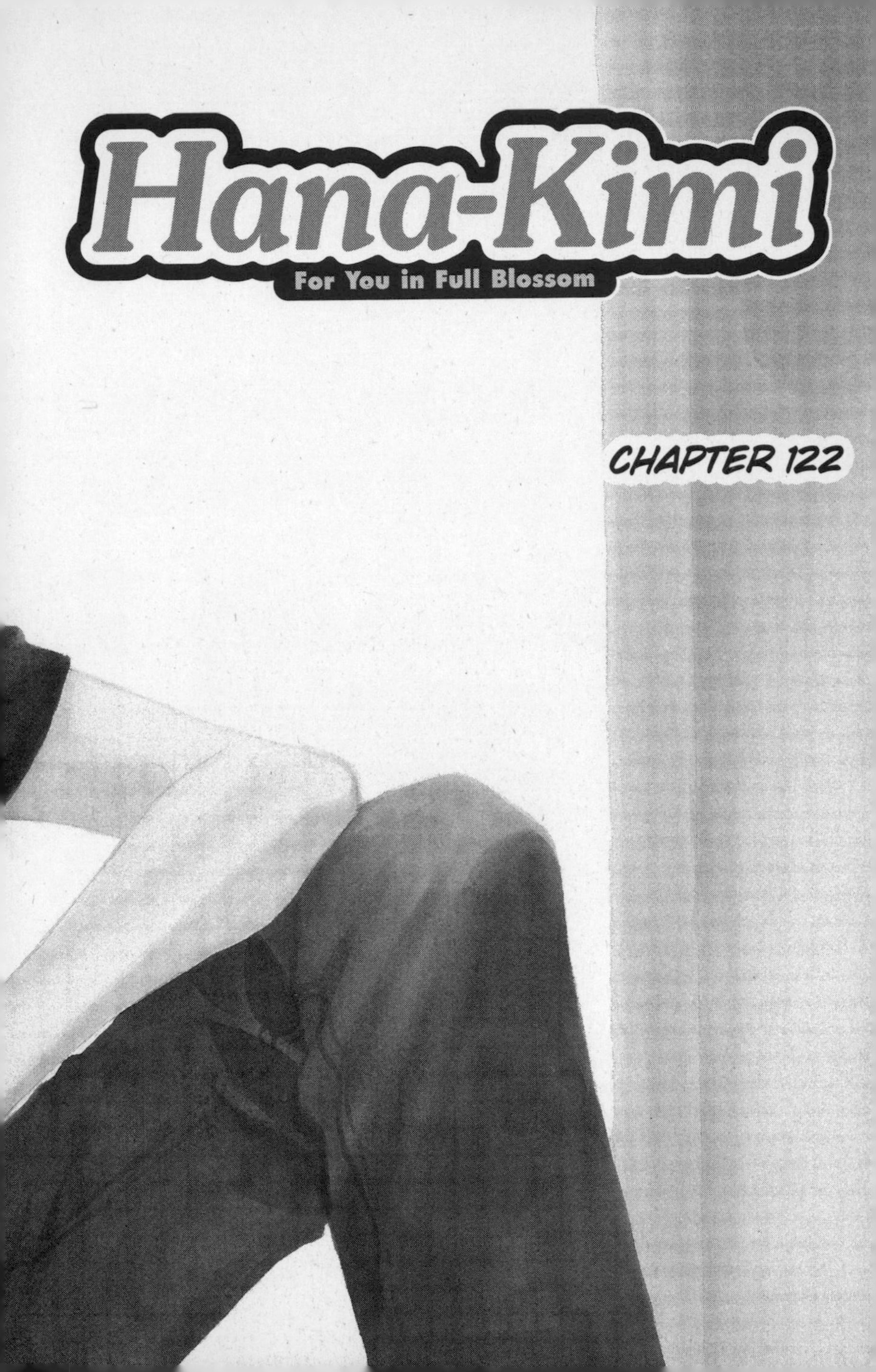
Hana-Kimi
For You in Full Blossom
CHAPTER 122

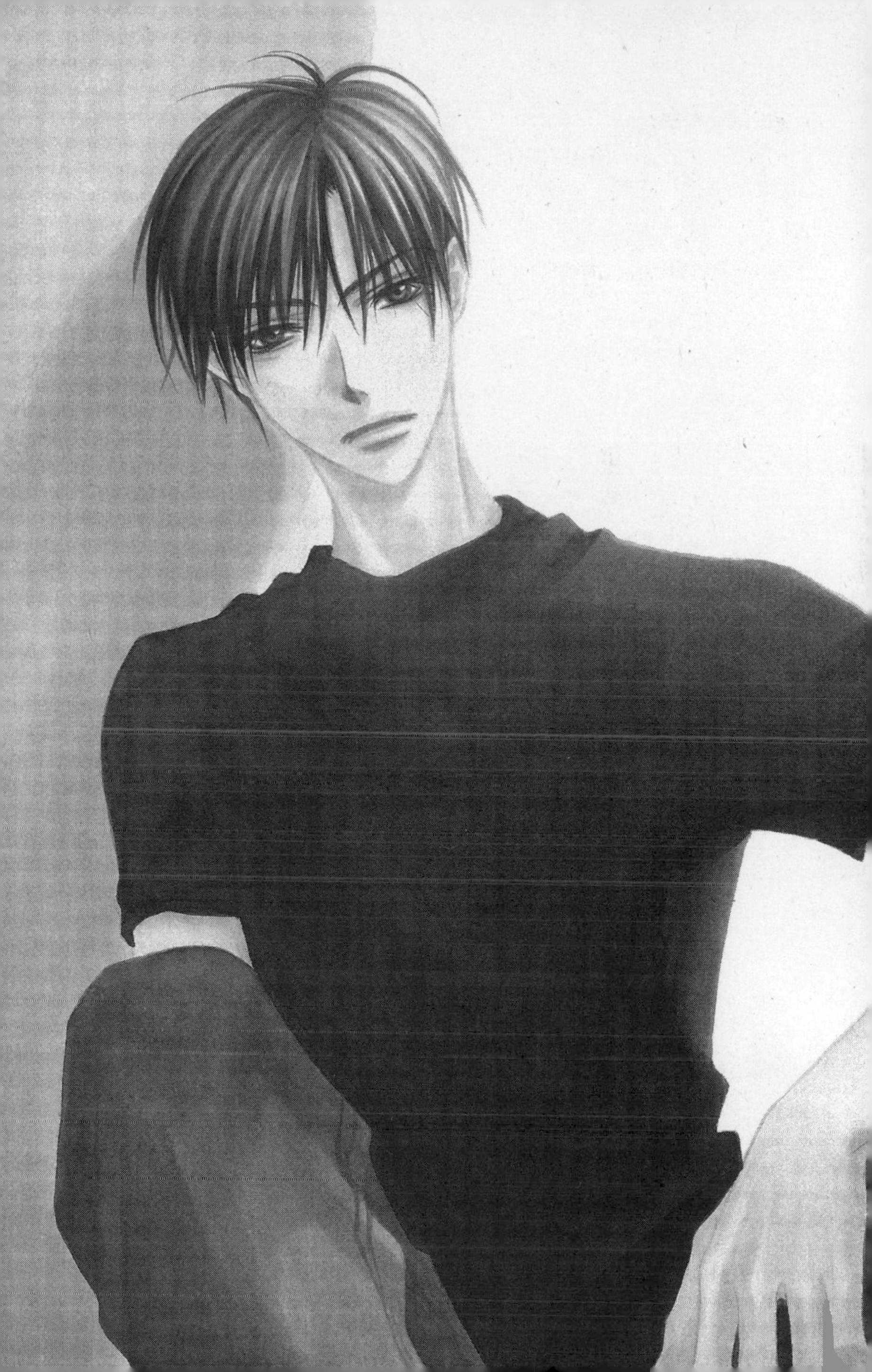

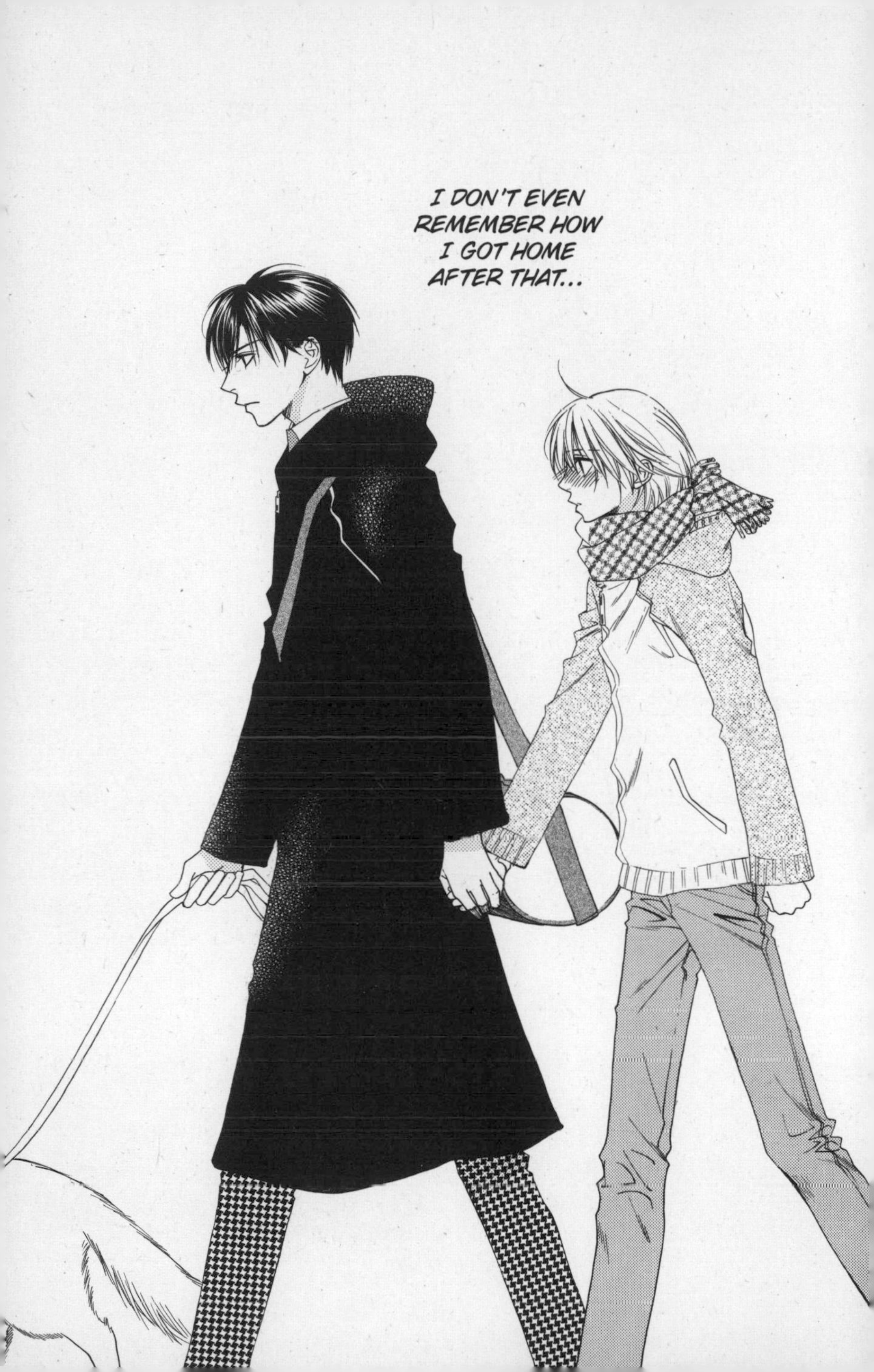
I DON'T EVEN REMEMBER HOW I GOT HOME AFTER THAT...

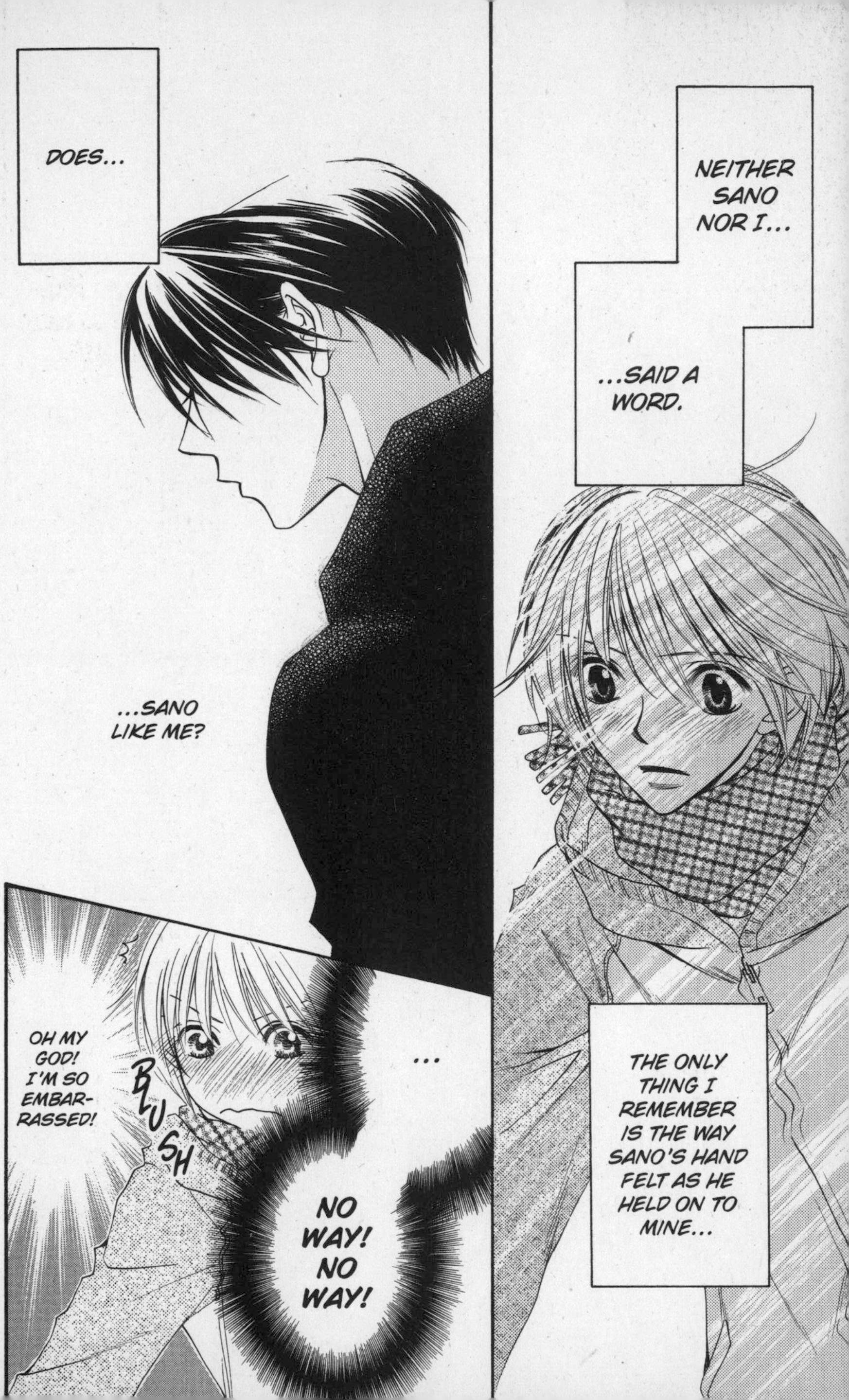
NEITHER SANO NOR I...
...SAID A WORD.
THE ONLY THING I REMEMBER IS THE WAY SANO'S HAND FELT AS HE HELD ON TO MINE...
DOES...
...SANO LIKE ME?
...
NO WAY! NO WAY!
BLUSH
OH MY GOD! I'M SO EMBARRASSED!

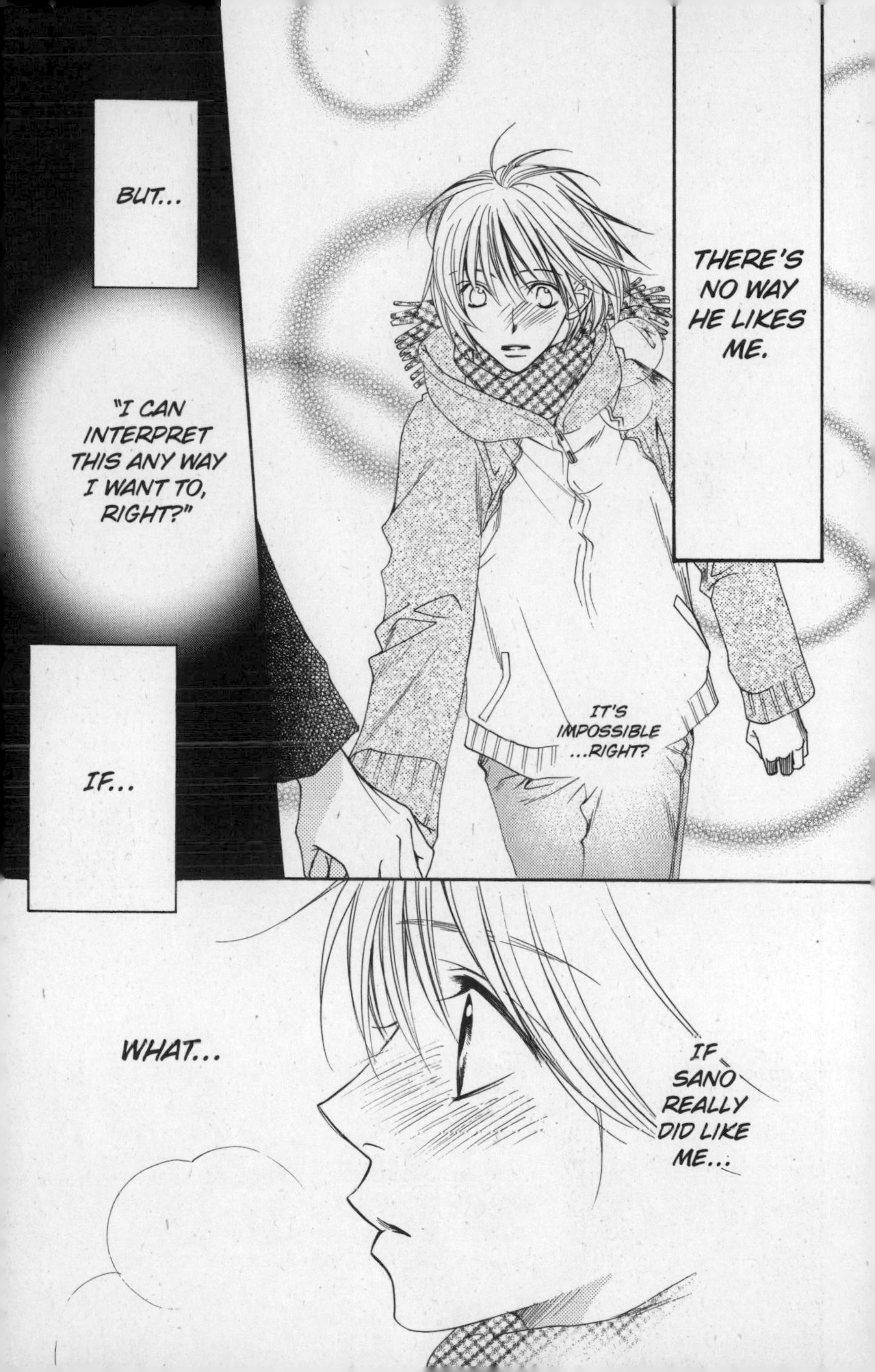
THERE'S NO WAY HE LIKES ME.
BUT...
"I CAN INTERPRET THIS ANY WAY I WANT TO, RIGHT?"
IT'S IMPOSSIBLE ...RIGHT?
IF...
IF SANO REALLY DID LIKE ME...
WHAT...

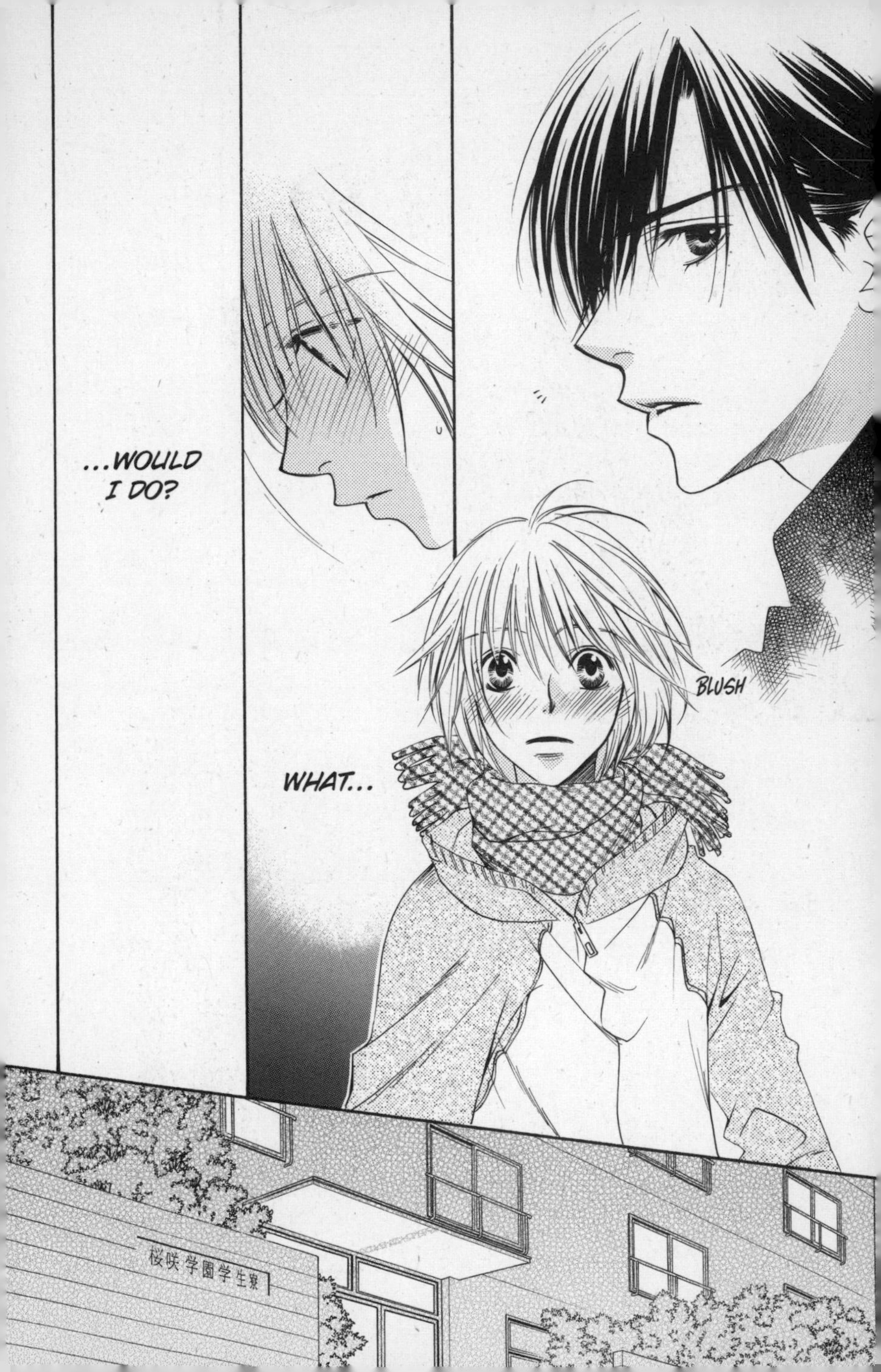
BLUSH
WHAT...
...WOULD I DO?
桜咲学園学生寮

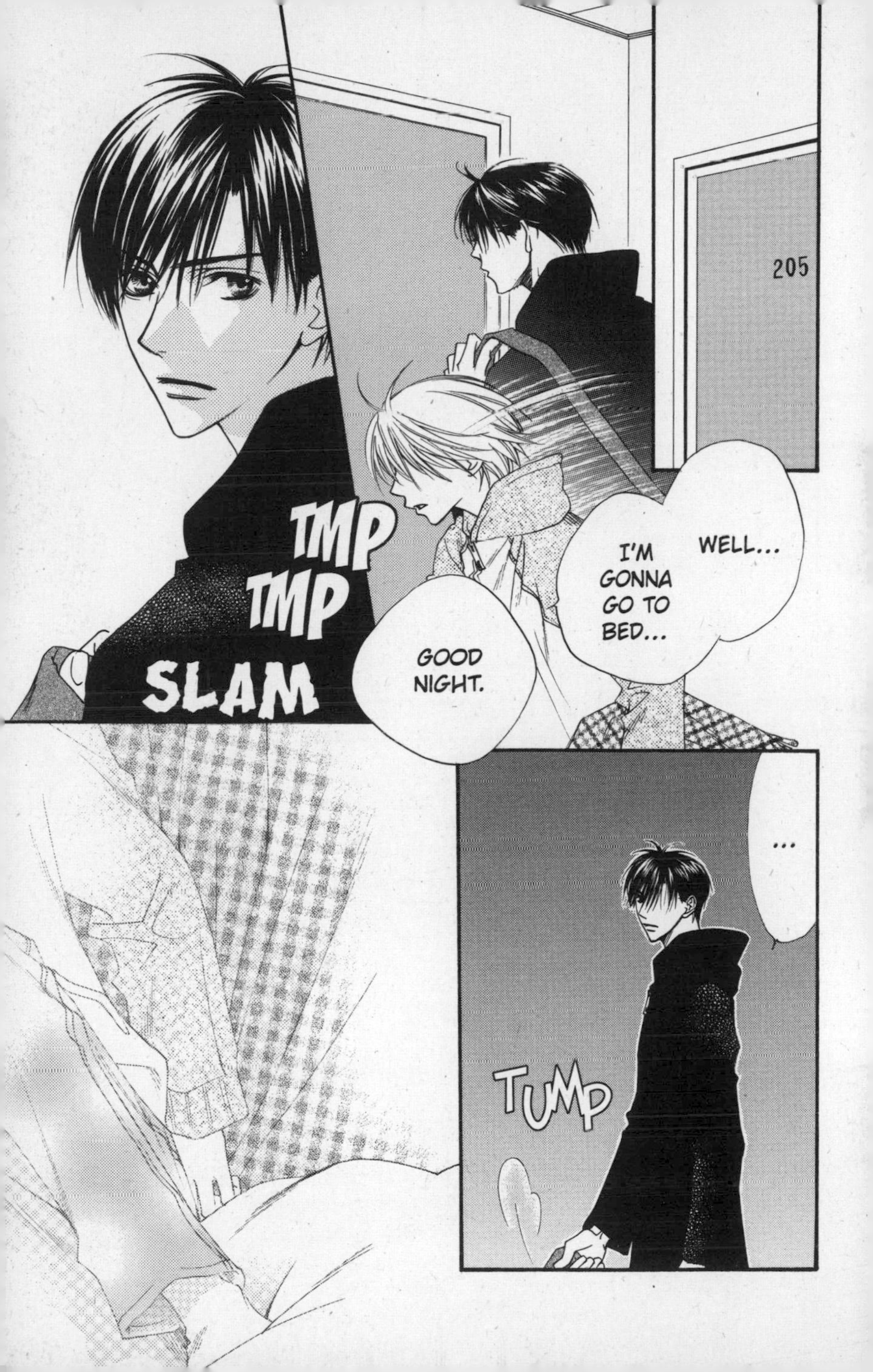
205
WELL...
I'M GONNA GO TO BED...
GOOD NIGHT.
TMP
TMP
SLAM
...
TUMP

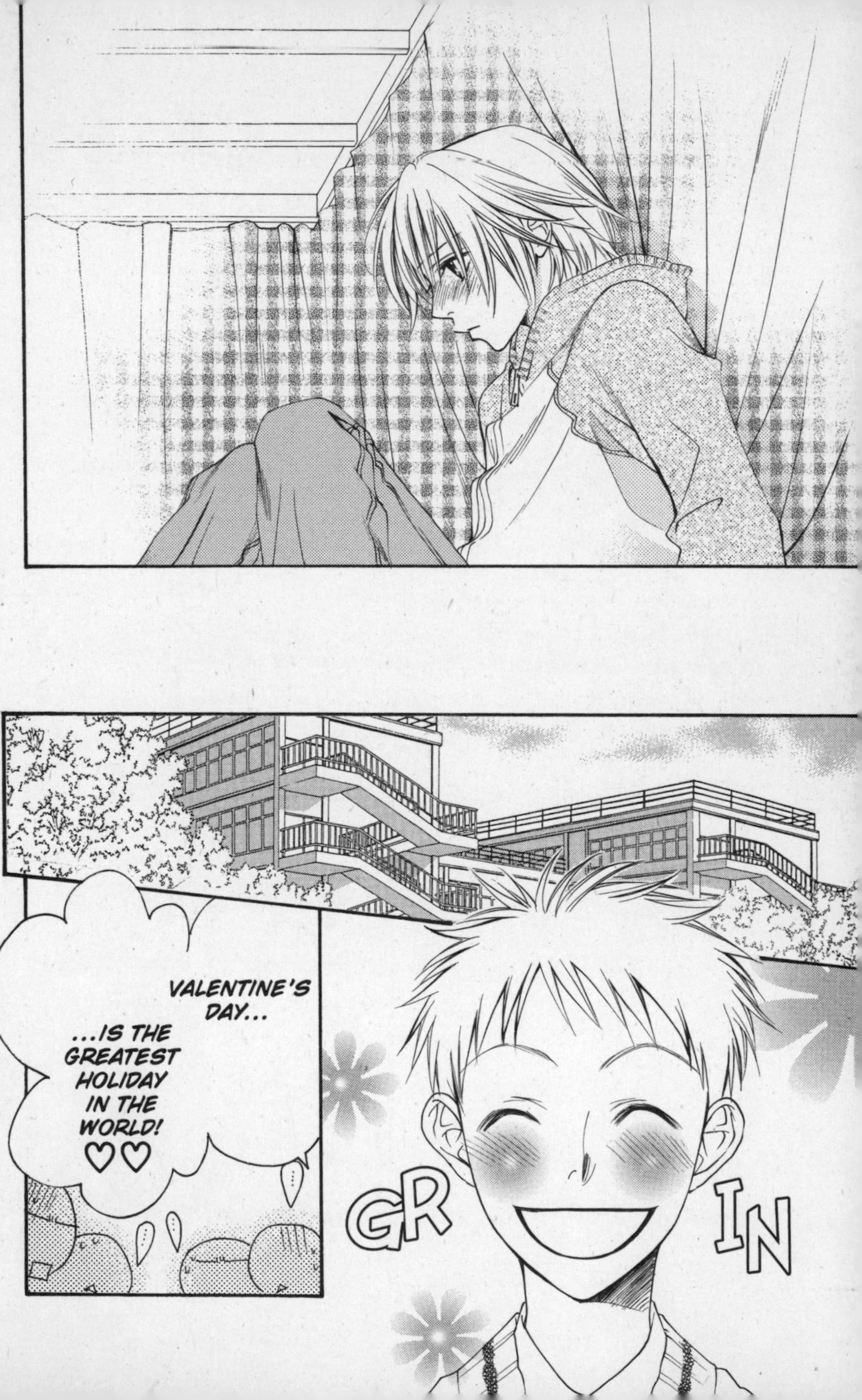
VALENTINE'S DAY...
...IS THE GREATEST HOLIDAY IN THE WORLD! ♡♡
GRIN

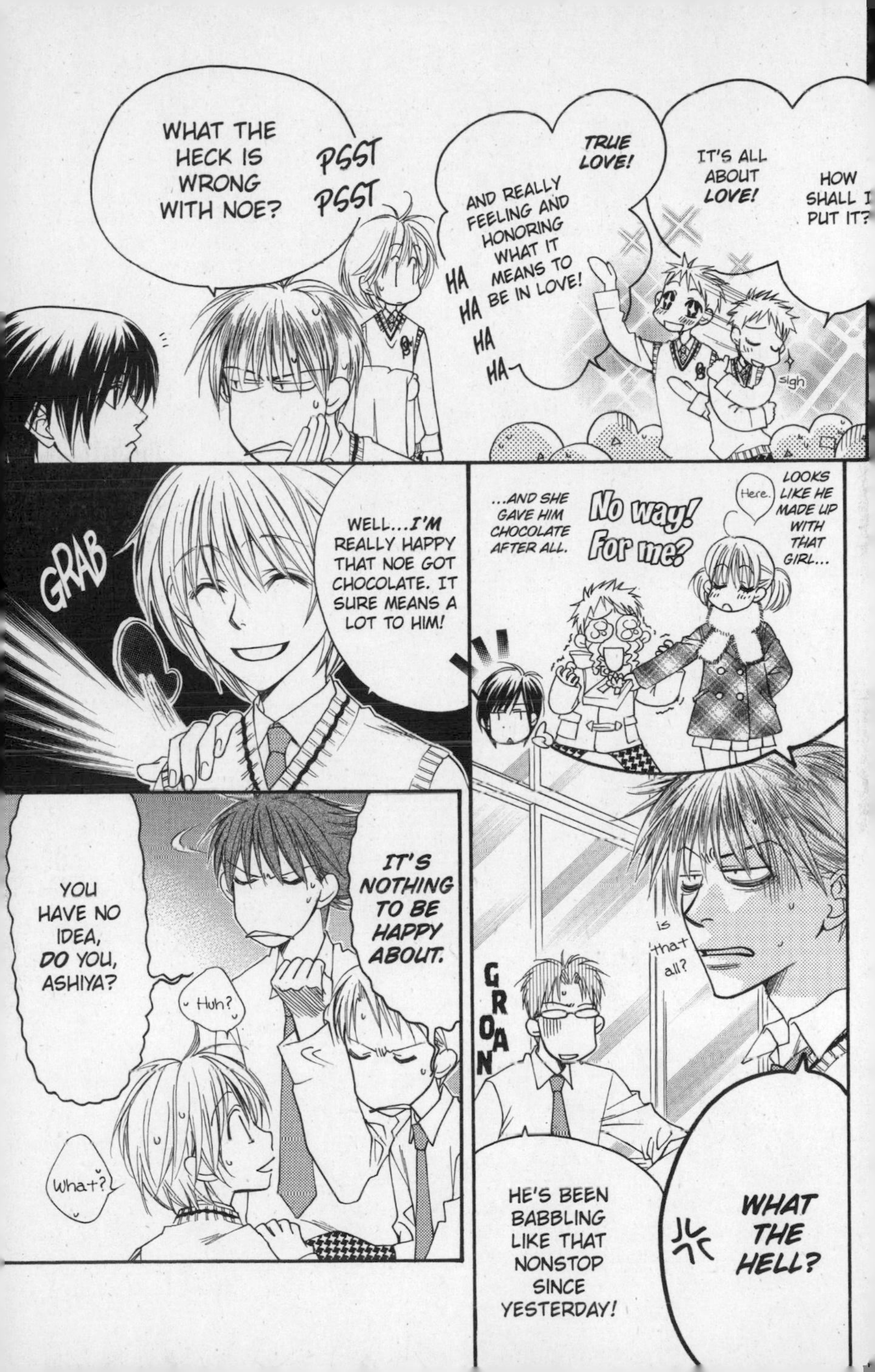
HOW SHALL I PUT IT?
IT'S ALL ABOUT LOVE!
TRUE LOVE!
AND REALLY FEELING AND HONORING WHAT IT MEANS TO BE IN LOVE!
HA HA HA HA
sigh
PSST PSST
WHAT THE HECK IS WRONG WITH NOE?
LOOKS LIKE HE MADE UP WITH THAT GIRL...
Here.
No way! For me?
...AND SHE GAVE HIM CHOCOLATE AFTER ALL.
is that all?
GROAN
WHAT THE HELL?
HE'S BEEN BABBLING LIKE THAT NONSTOP SINCE YESTERDAY!
WELL...I'M REALLY HAPPY THAT NOE GOT CHOCOLATE. IT SURE MEANS A LOT TO HIM!
GRAB
IT'S NOTHING TO BE HAPPY ABOUT.
YOU HAVE NO IDEA, DO YOU, ASHIYA?
Huh?
What?

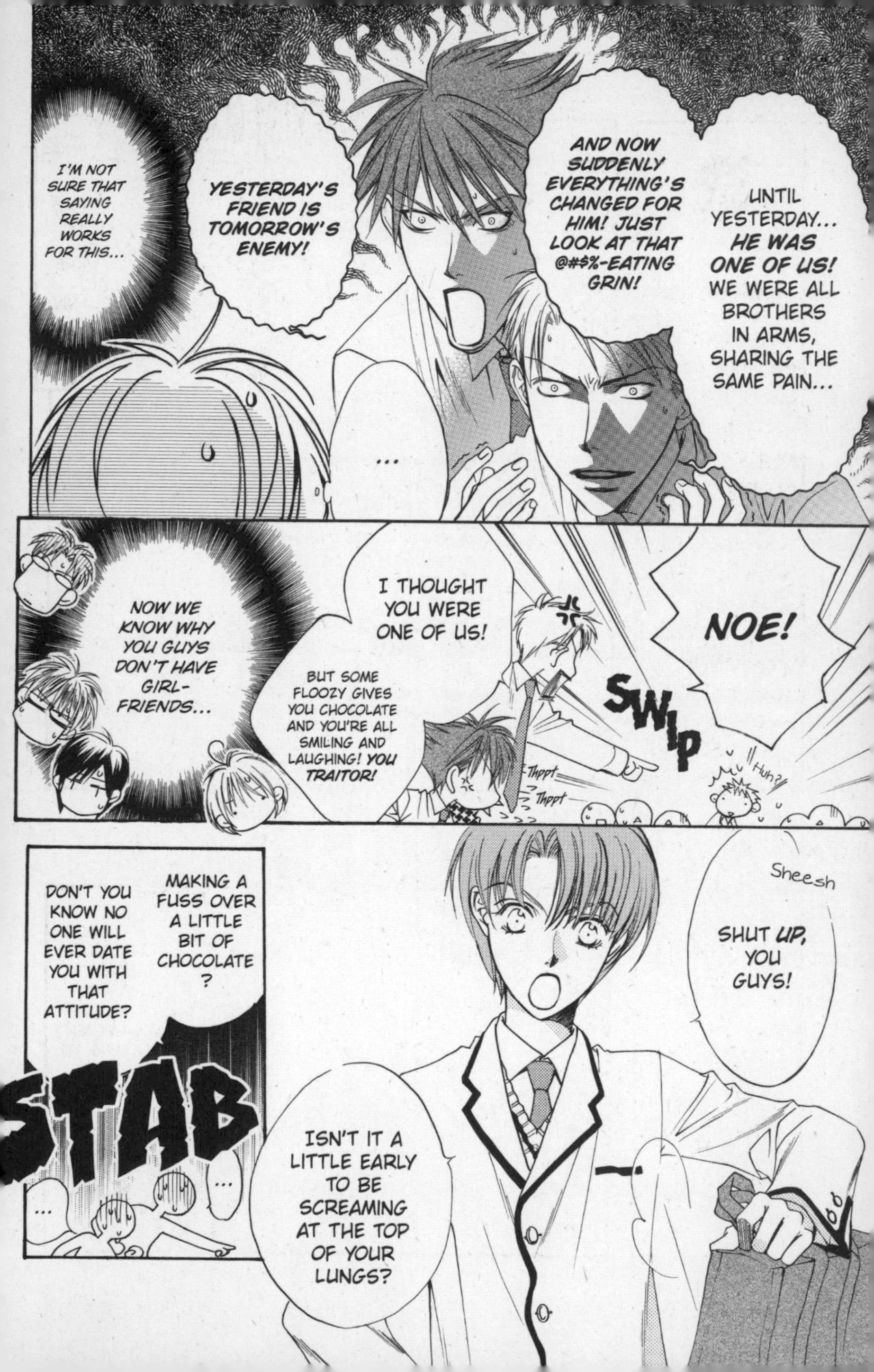
UNTIL YESTERDAY... HE WAS ONE OF US! WE WERE ALL BROTHERS IN ARMS, SHARING THE SAME PAIN...
AND NOW SUDDENLY EVERYTHING'S CHANGED FOR HIM! JUST LOOK AT THAT @#$%-EATING GRIN!
YESTERDAY'S FRIEND IS TOMORROW'S ENEMY!
...
I'M NOT SURE THAT SAYING REALLY WORKS FOR THIS...
NOE!
SWIP
Huh?
Thppt
Thppt
I THOUGHT YOU WERE ONE OF US!
BUT SOME FLOOZY GIVES YOU CHOCOLATE AND YOU'RE ALL SMILING AND LAUGHING! YOU TRAITOR!
NOW WE KNOW WHY YOU GUYS DON'T HAVE GIRL-FRIENDS...
Sheesh
SHUT UP, YOU GUYS!
ISN'T IT A LITTLE EARLY TO BE SCREAMING AT THE TOP OF YOUR LUNGS?
MAKING A FUSS OVER A LITTLE BIT OF CHOCOLATE?
DON'T YOU KNOW NO ONE WILL EVER DATE YOU WITH THAT ATTITUDE?
STAB
...
...

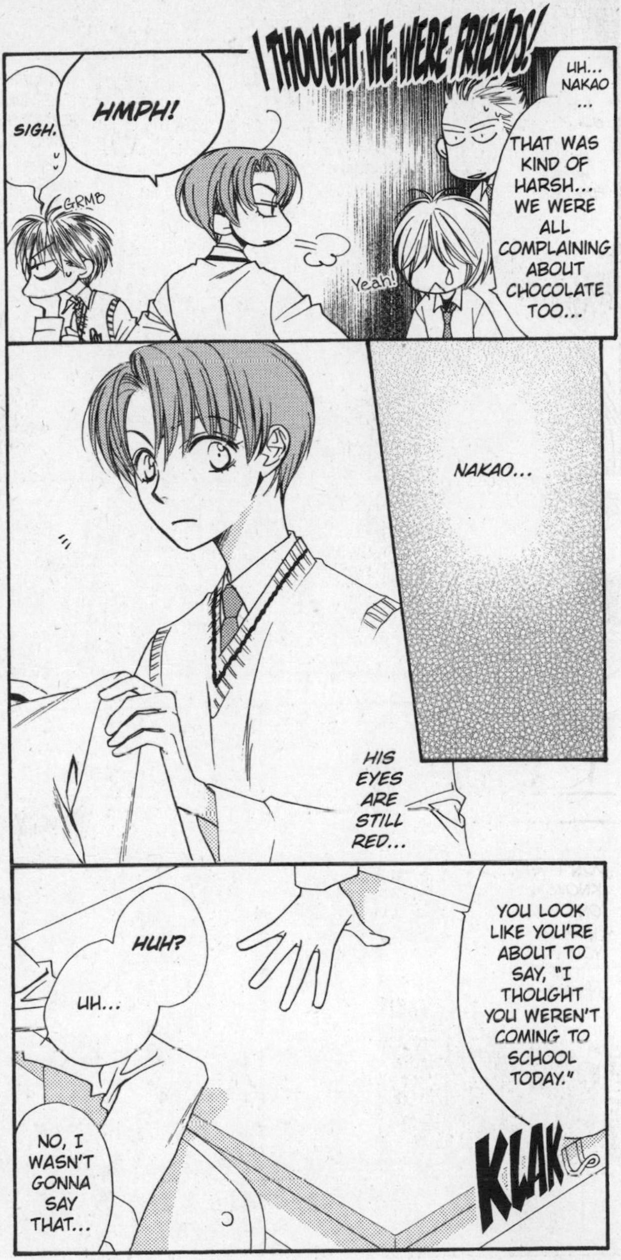
I THOUGHT WE WERE FRIENDS!
UH... NAKAO...
THAT WAS KIND OF HARSH... WE WERE ALL COMPLAINING ABOUT CHOCOLATE TOO...
Yeah!
HMPH!
SIGH.
GRMB
NAKAO...
HIS EYES ARE STILL RED...
YOU LOOK LIKE YOU'RE ABOUT TO SAY, "I THOUGHT YOU WEREN'T COMING TO SCHOOL TODAY."
KLAK
HUH?
UH...
NO, I WASN'T GONNA SAY THAT...

洗

washing

BODY BRUSH

My friend gave me this body brush I'd wanted for a long time (for my back). It was my birthday present! I'm so happy. It really feels great...I've been having the best baths ever. ✿

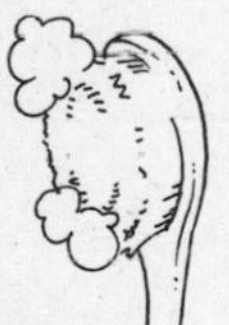

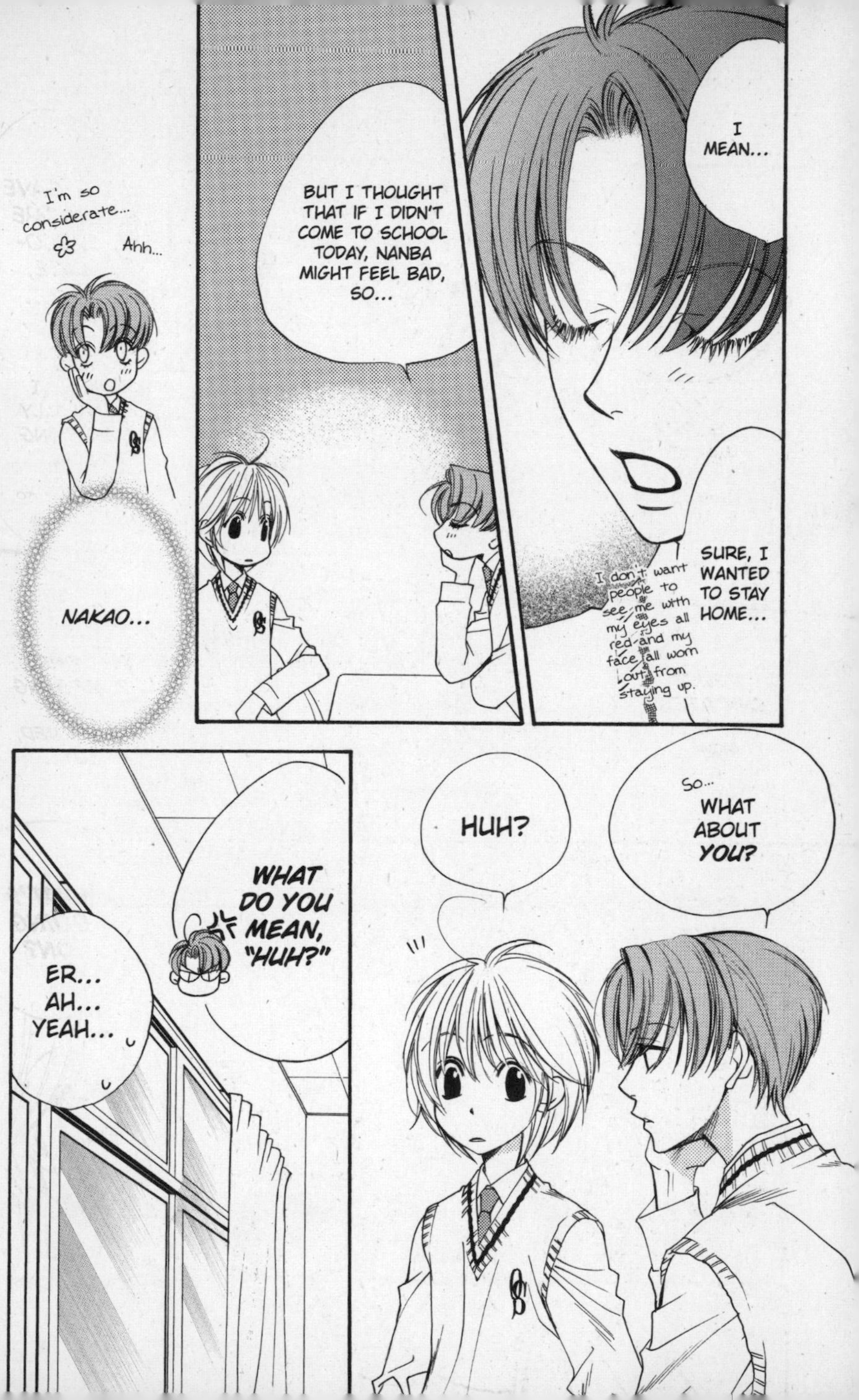
I MEAN...
SURE, I WANTED TO STAY HOME...
I don't want people to see me with my eyes all red and my face all worn out from staying up.
BUT I THOUGHT THAT IF I DIDN'T COME TO SCHOOL TODAY, NANBA MIGHT FEEL BAD, SO...
I'm so considerate...
Ahh...
NAKAO...
So... WHAT ABOUT YOU?
HUH?
WHAT DO YOU MEAN, "HUH?"
ER... AH... YEAH...

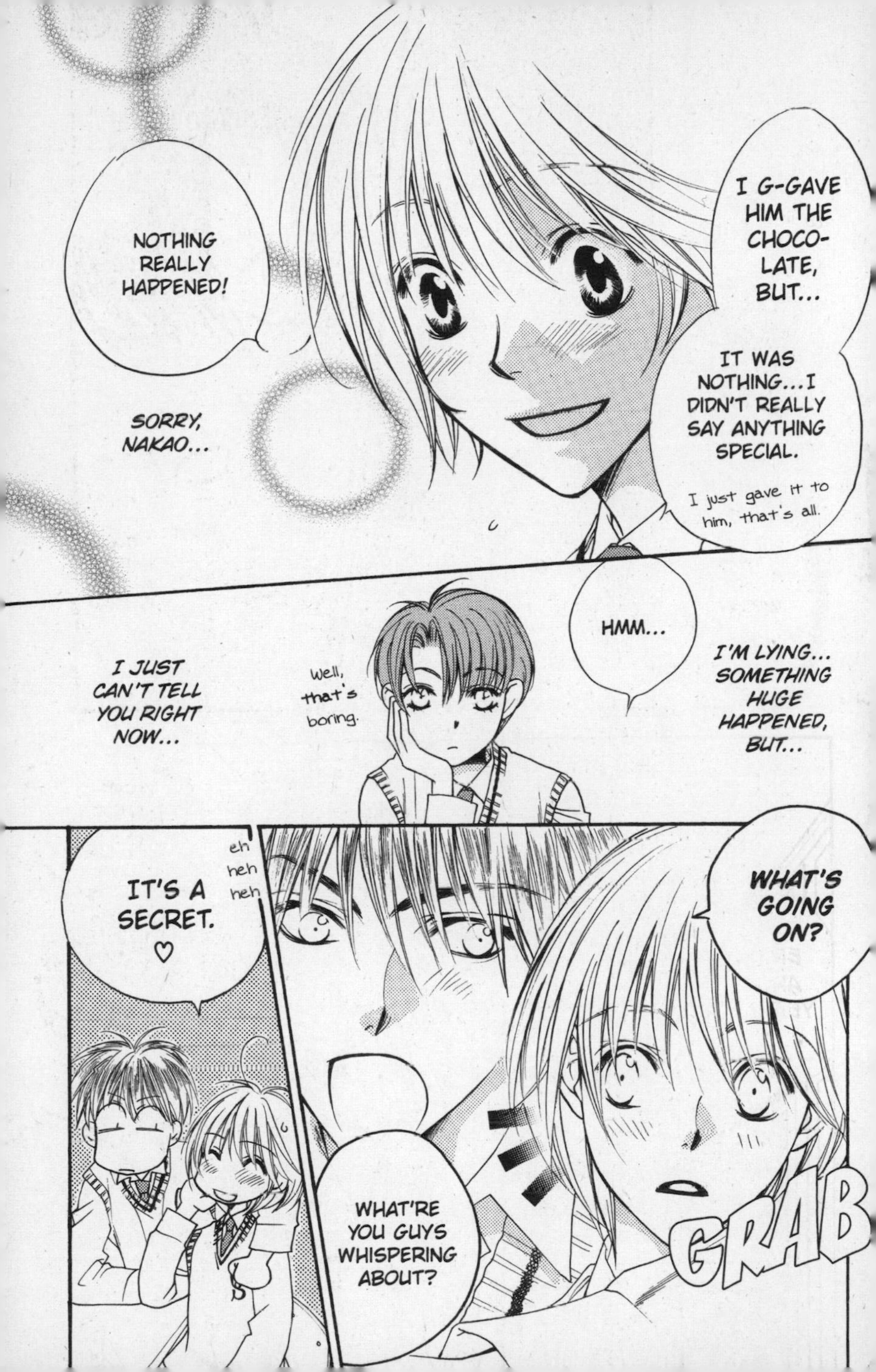
I G-GAVE HIM THE CHOCO-LATE, BUT...
IT WAS NOTHING...I DIDN'T REALLY SAY ANYTHING SPECIAL.
I just gave it to him, that's all.
NOTHING REALLY HAPPENED!
SORRY, NAKAO...
HMM...
I'M LYING... SOMETHING HUGE HAPPENED, BUT...
Well, that's boring.
I JUST CAN'T TELL YOU RIGHT NOW...
WHAT'S GOING ON?
GRAB
WHAT'RE YOU GUYS WHISPERING ABOUT?
eh heh heh
IT'S A SECRET. ♡

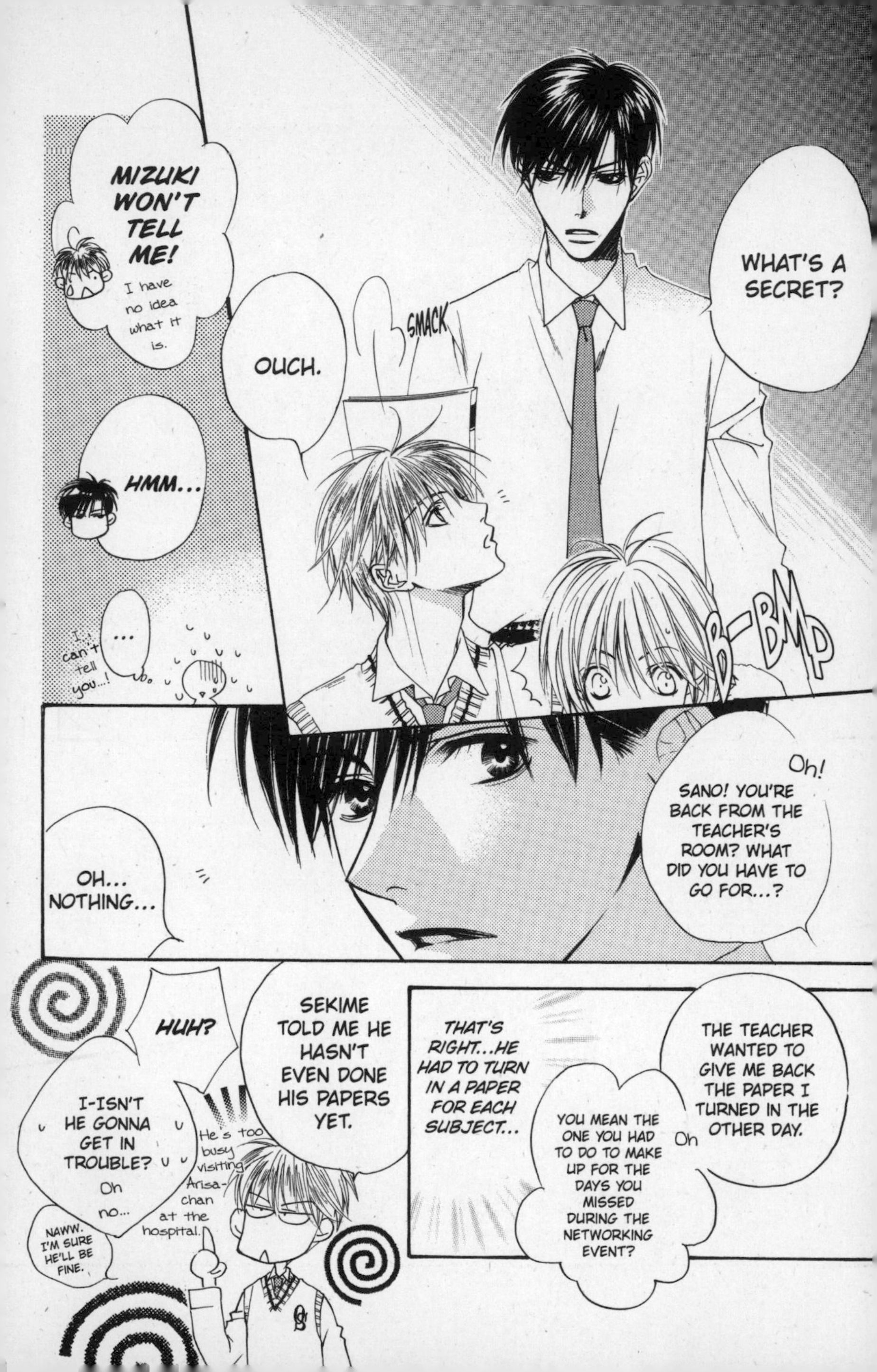
WHAT'S A SECRET?
SMACK
OUCH.
B-BMP
MIZUKI WON'T TELL ME! I have no idea what it is.
HMM...
...
I... can't tell you...!
Oh!
SANO! YOU'RE BACK FROM THE TEACHER'S ROOM? WHAT DID YOU HAVE TO GO FOR...?
OH... NOTHING...
THE TEACHER WANTED TO GIVE ME BACK THE PAPER I TURNED IN THE OTHER DAY.
Oh
YOU MEAN THE ONE YOU HAD TO DO TO MAKE UP FOR THE DAYS YOU MISSED DURING THE NETWORKING EVENT?
THAT'S RIGHT...HE HAD TO TURN IN A PAPER FOR EACH SUBJECT...
SEKIME TOLD ME HE HASN'T EVEN DONE HIS PAPERS YET.
HUH?
I-ISN'T HE GONNA GET IN TROUBLE?
Oh no...
He's too busy visiting Arisa-chan at the hospital.
NAWW. I'M SURE HE'LL BE FINE.

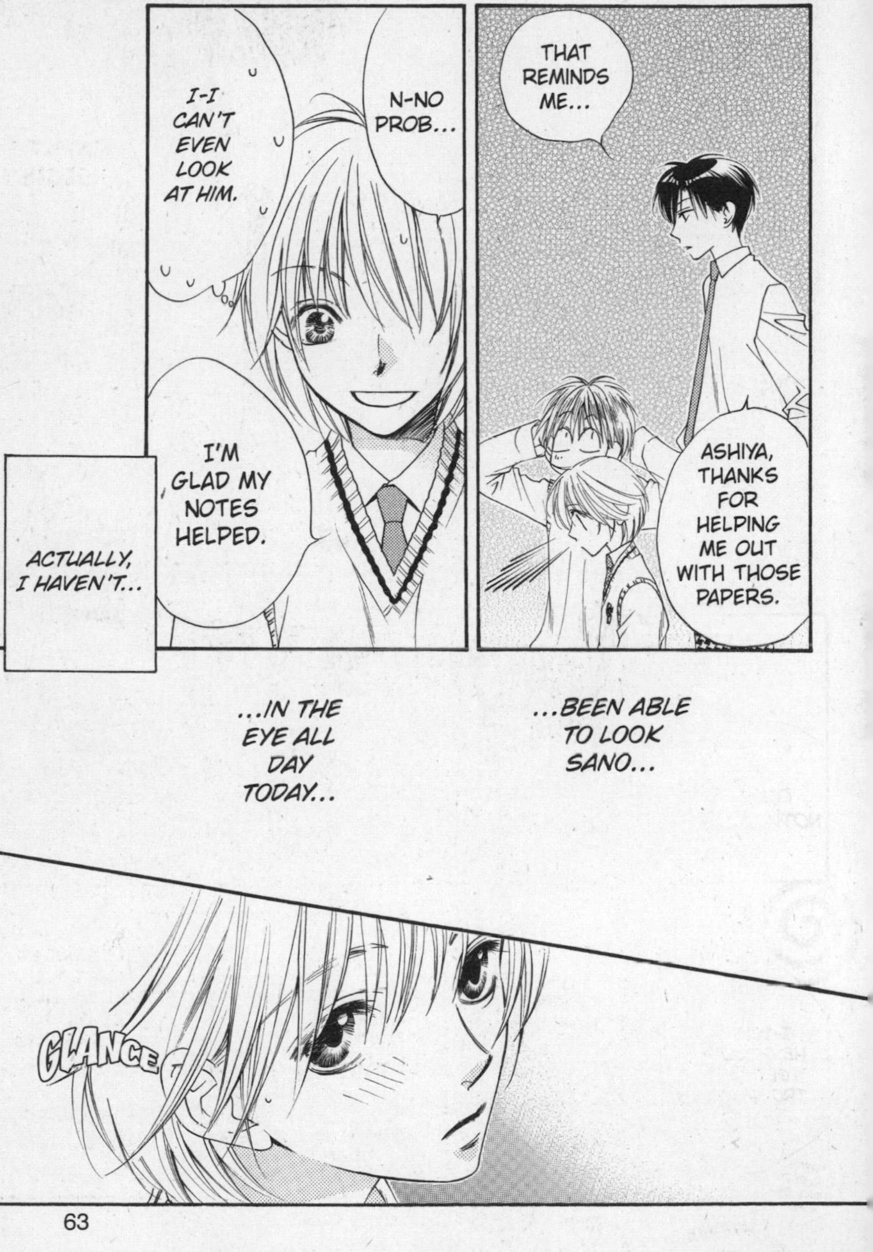
THAT REMINDS ME...
ASHIYA, THANKS FOR HELPING ME OUT WITH THOSE PAPERS.
N-NO PROB...
I-I CAN'T EVEN LOOK AT HIM.
I'M GLAD MY NOTES HELPED.
ACTUALLY, I HAVEN'T...
...BEEN ABLE TO LOOK SANO...
...IN THE EYE ALL DAY TODAY...
GLANCE

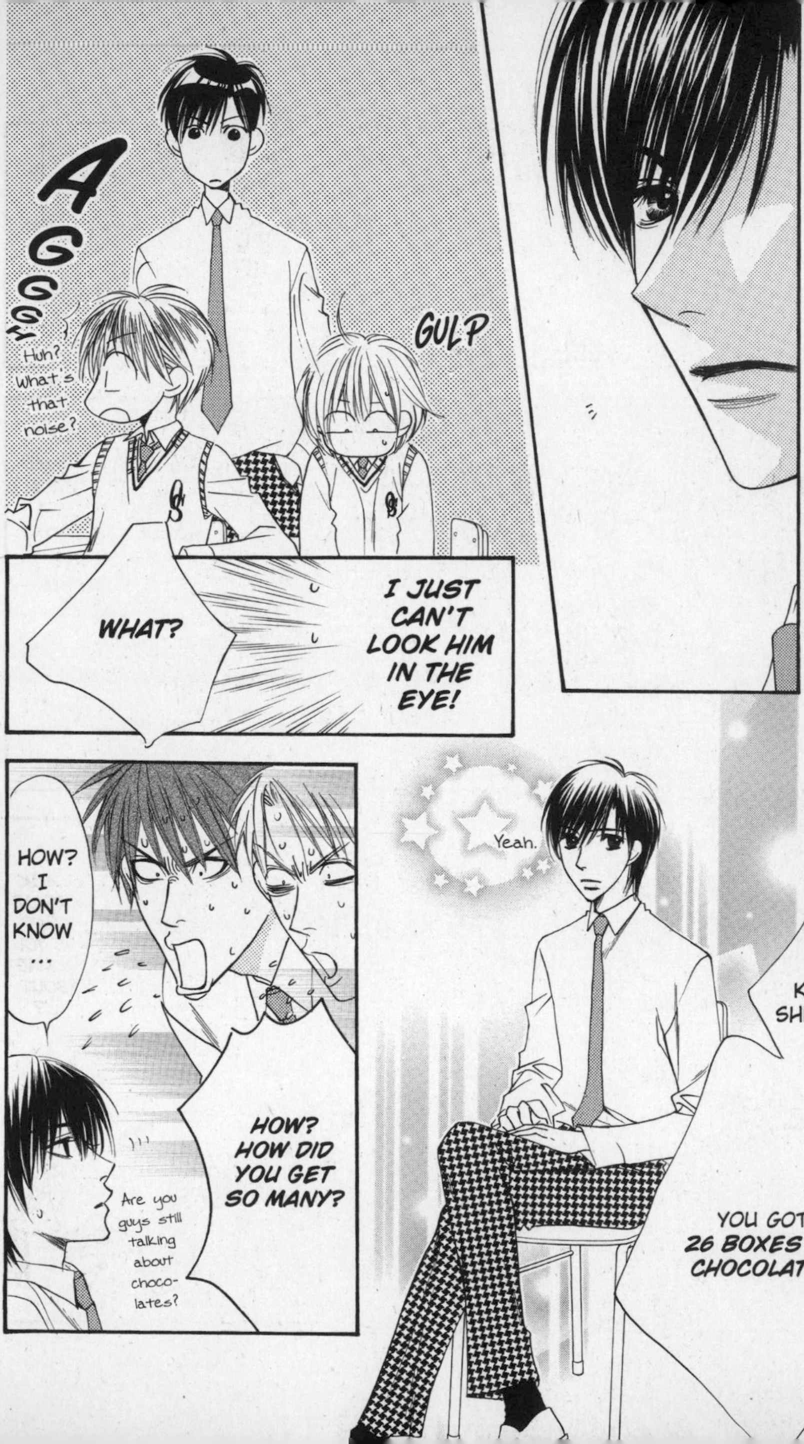
AGGGr
GULP
Huh? What's that noise?
I JUST CAN'T LOOK HIM IN THE EYE!
WHAT?
KAYA-SHIMA...
YOU GOT 26 BOXES OF CHOCOLATE?
Yeah.
HOW? HOW DID YOU GET SO MANY?
HOW? I DON'T KNOW...
Are you guys still talking about chocolates?

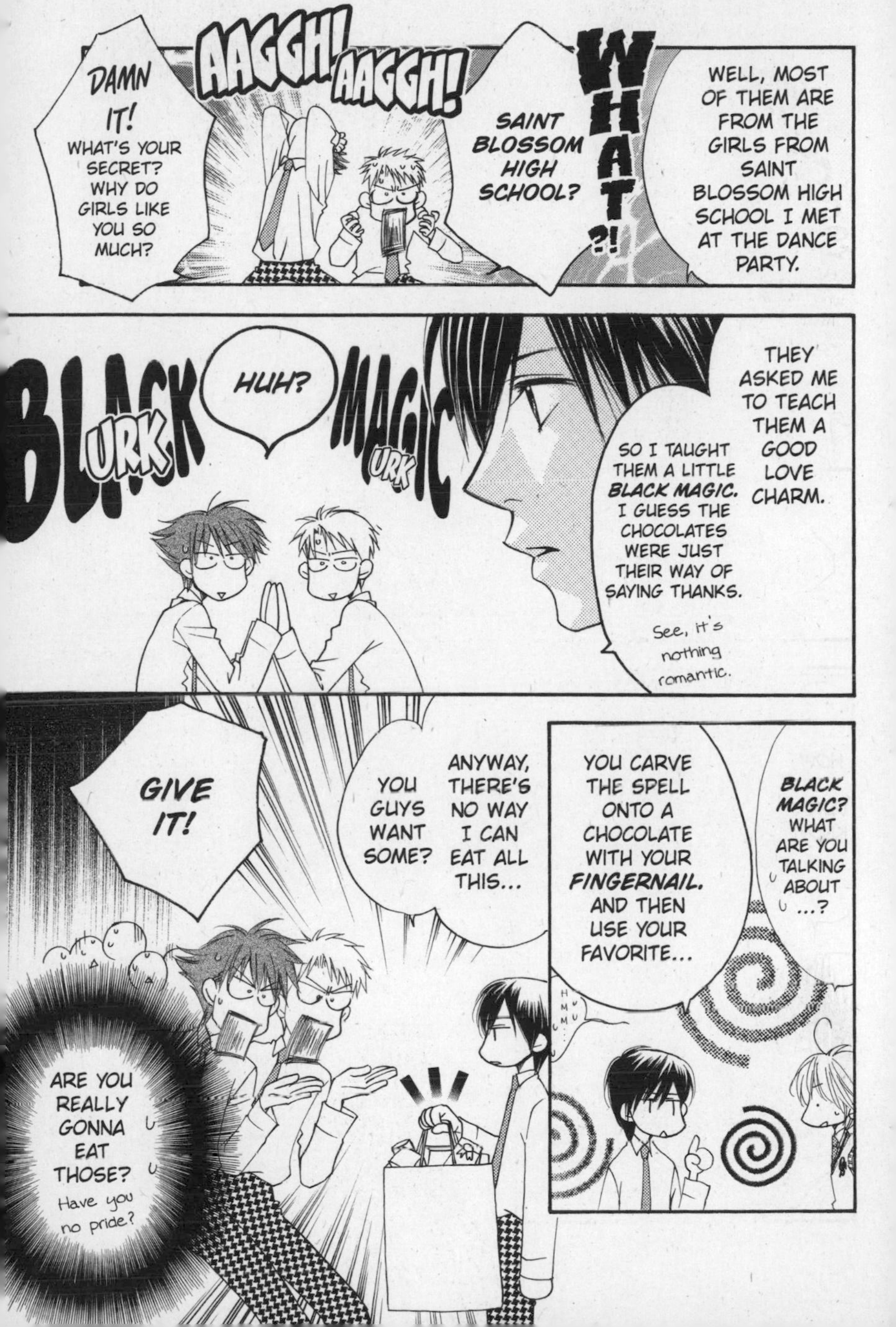
WELL, MOST OF THEM ARE FROM THE GIRLS FROM SAINT BLOSSOM HIGH SCHOOL I MET AT THE DANCE PARTY.
WHAT?!
SAINT BLOSSOM HIGH SCHOOL?
AAGGH! AAGGH!
DAMN IT! WHAT'S YOUR SECRET? WHY DO GIRLS LIKE YOU SO MUCH?
THEY ASKED ME TO TEACH THEM A GOOD LOVE CHARM.
SO I TAUGHT THEM A LITTLE BLACK MAGIC. I GUESS THE CHOCOLATES WERE JUST THEIR WAY OF SAYING THANKS.
See, it's nothing romantic.
MAGIC
URK
HUH?
BLACK
URK
BLACK MAGIC? WHAT ARE YOU TALKING ABOUT...?
YOU CARVE THE SPELL ONTO A CHOCOLATE WITH YOUR FINGERNAIL. AND THEN USE YOUR FAVORITE...
HMM...
ANYWAY, THERE'S NO WAY I CAN EAT ALL THIS...
YOU GUYS WANT SOME?
GIVE IT!
ARE YOU REALLY GONNA EAT THOSE?
Have you no pride?

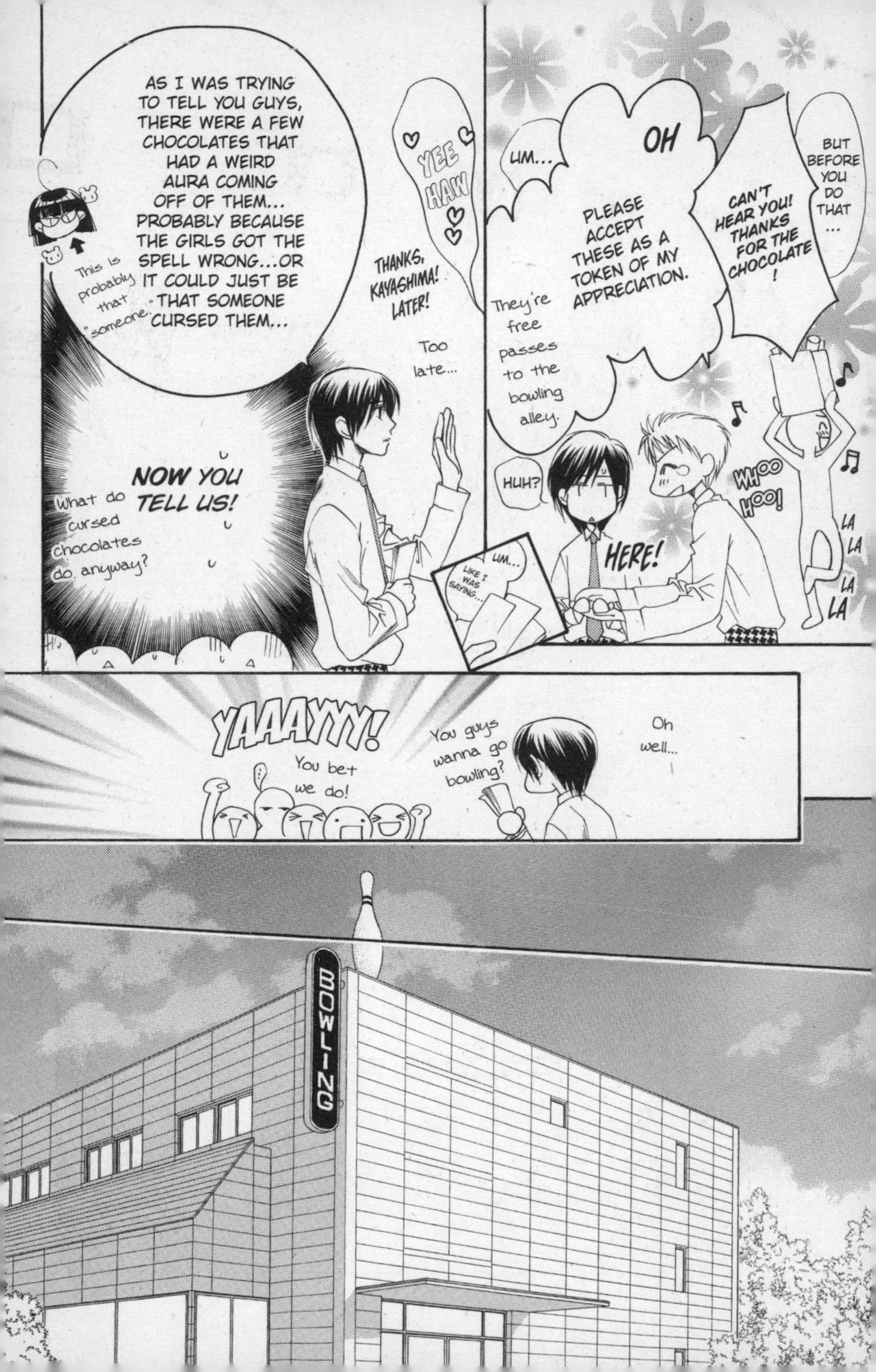
BUT BEFORE YOU DO THAT...
CAN'T HEAR YOU! THANKS FOR THE CHOCOLATE!
OH
UM...
PLEASE ACCEPT THESE AS A TOKEN OF MY APPRECIATION.
They're free passes to the bowling alley.
WHOO HOO!
LA LA LA LA
HERE!
HUH?
UM...
LIKE I WAS SAYING...
YEE HAW
THANKS, KAYASHIMA! LATER!
Too late...
AS I WAS TRYING TO TELL YOU GUYS, THERE WERE A FEW CHOCOLATES THAT HAD A WEIRD AURA COMING OFF OF THEM... PROBABLY BECAUSE THE GIRLS GOT THE SPELL WRONG...OR IT COULD JUST BE THAT SOMEONE CURSED THEM...
This is probably that "someone."
NOW YOU TELL US!
What do cursed chocolates do anyway?
Oh well...
You guys wanna go bowling?
YAAAYYY!
You bet we do!
BOWLING

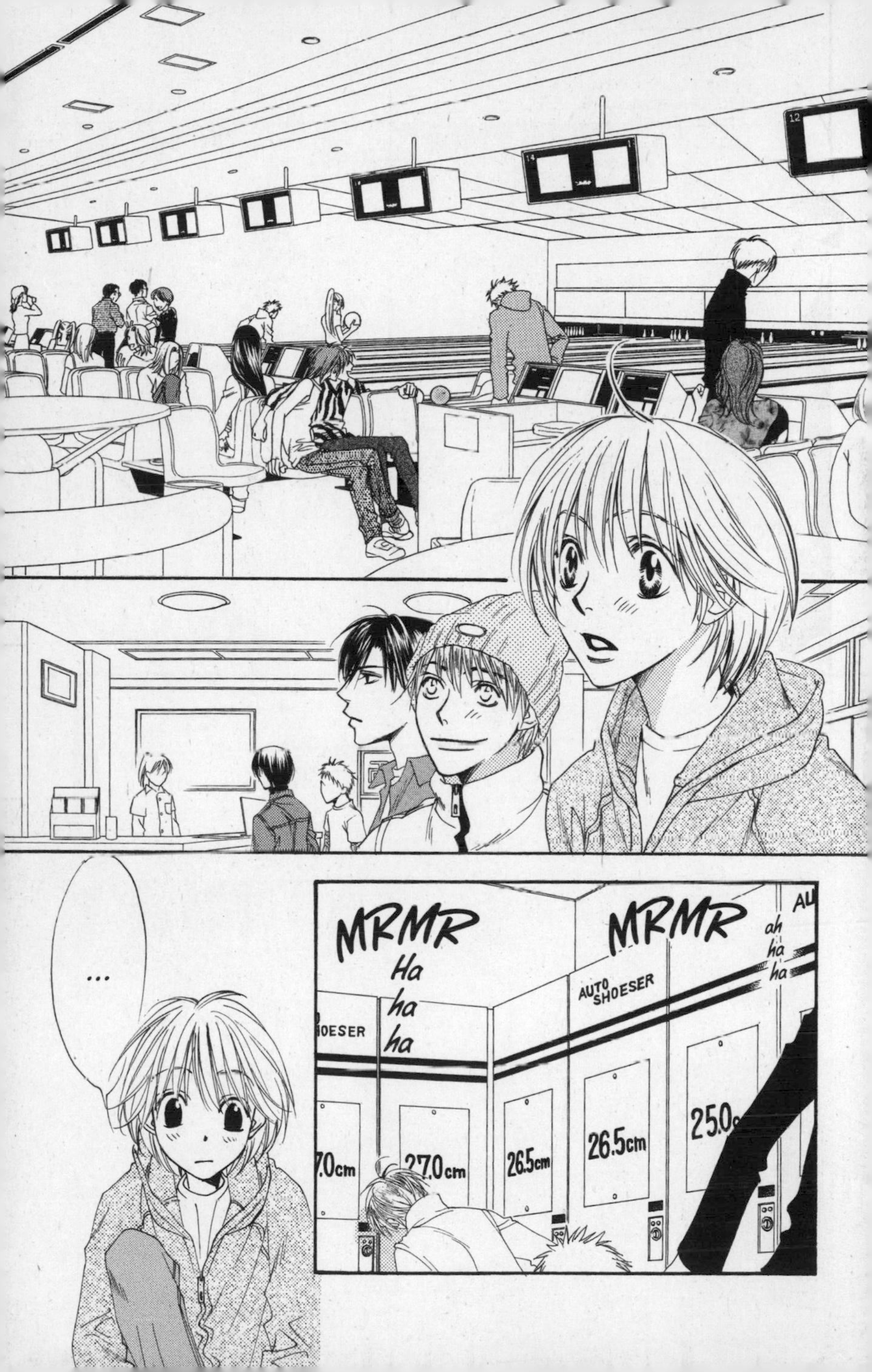
MRMR
ah ha ha
MRMR
Ha ha ha
AUTO SHOESER
27.0cm
26.5cm
26.5cm
...

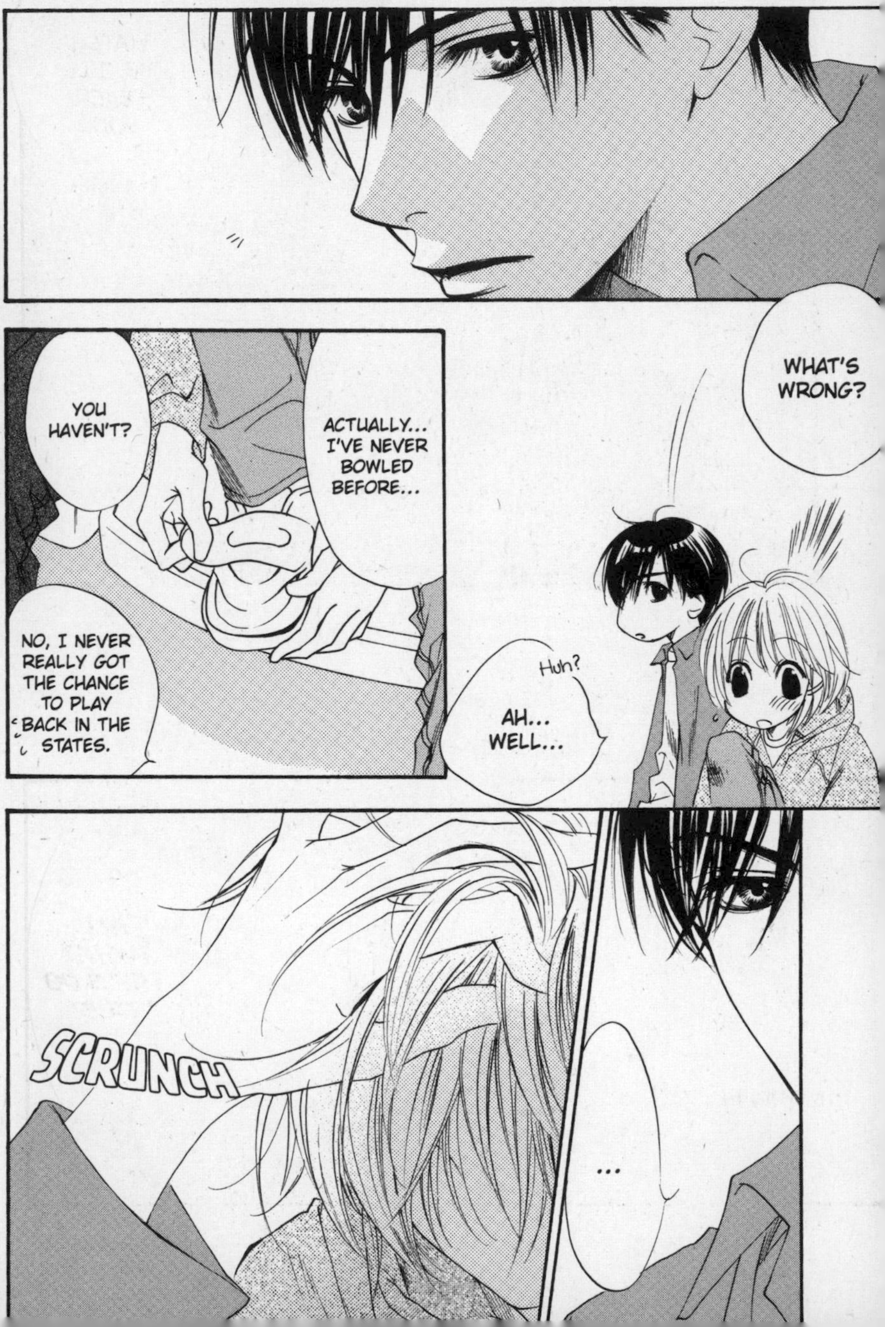
WHAT'S WRONG?
Huh?
AH... WELL...
ACTUALLY... I'VE NEVER BOWLED BEFORE...
YOU HAVEN'T?
NO, I NEVER REALLY GOT THE CHANCE TO PLAY BACK IN THE STATES.
SCRUNCH
...

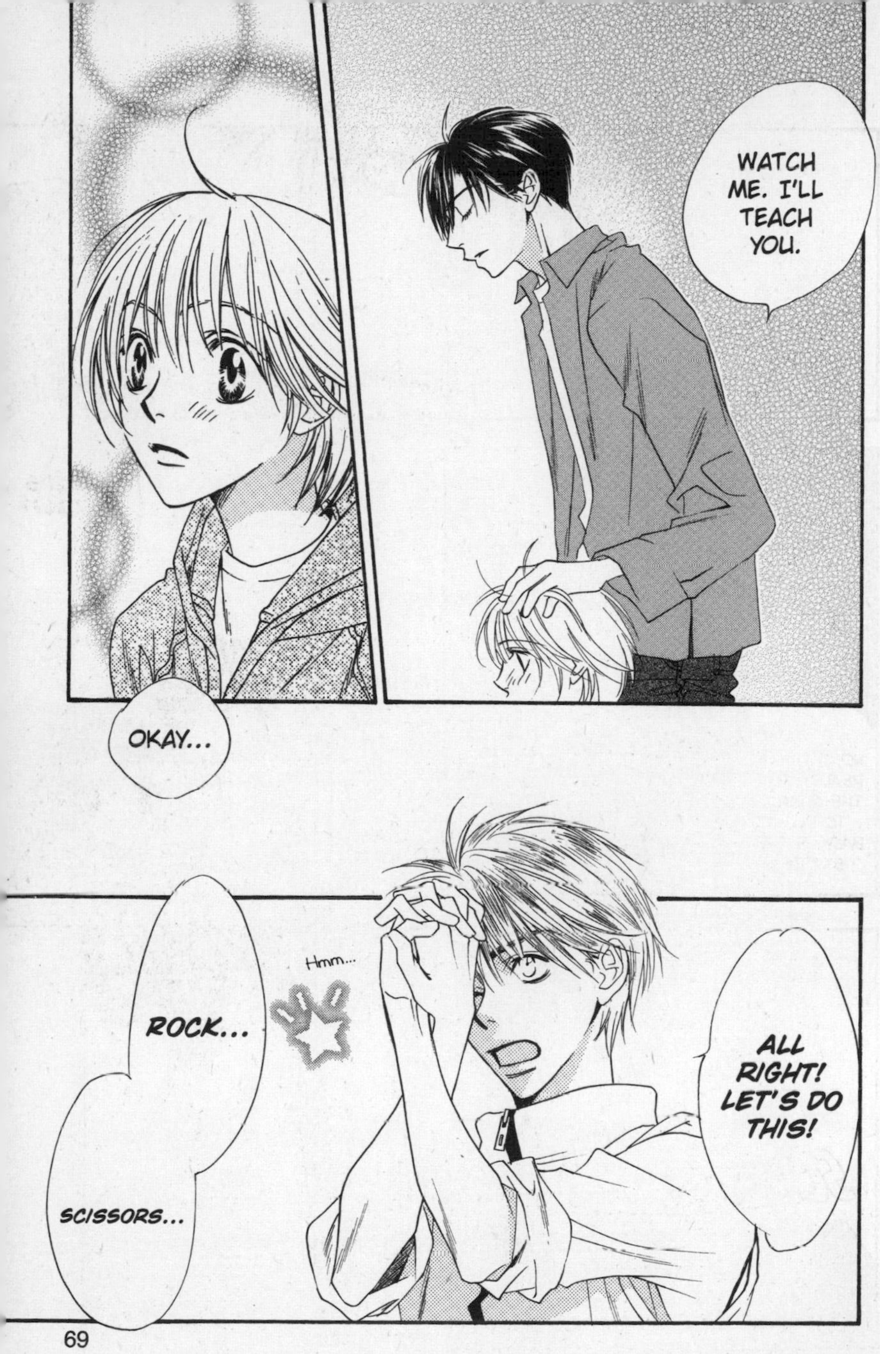
WATCH ME. I'LL TEACH YOU.
OKAY...
ALL RIGHT! LET'S DO THIS!
Hmm...
ROCK...
SCISSORS...

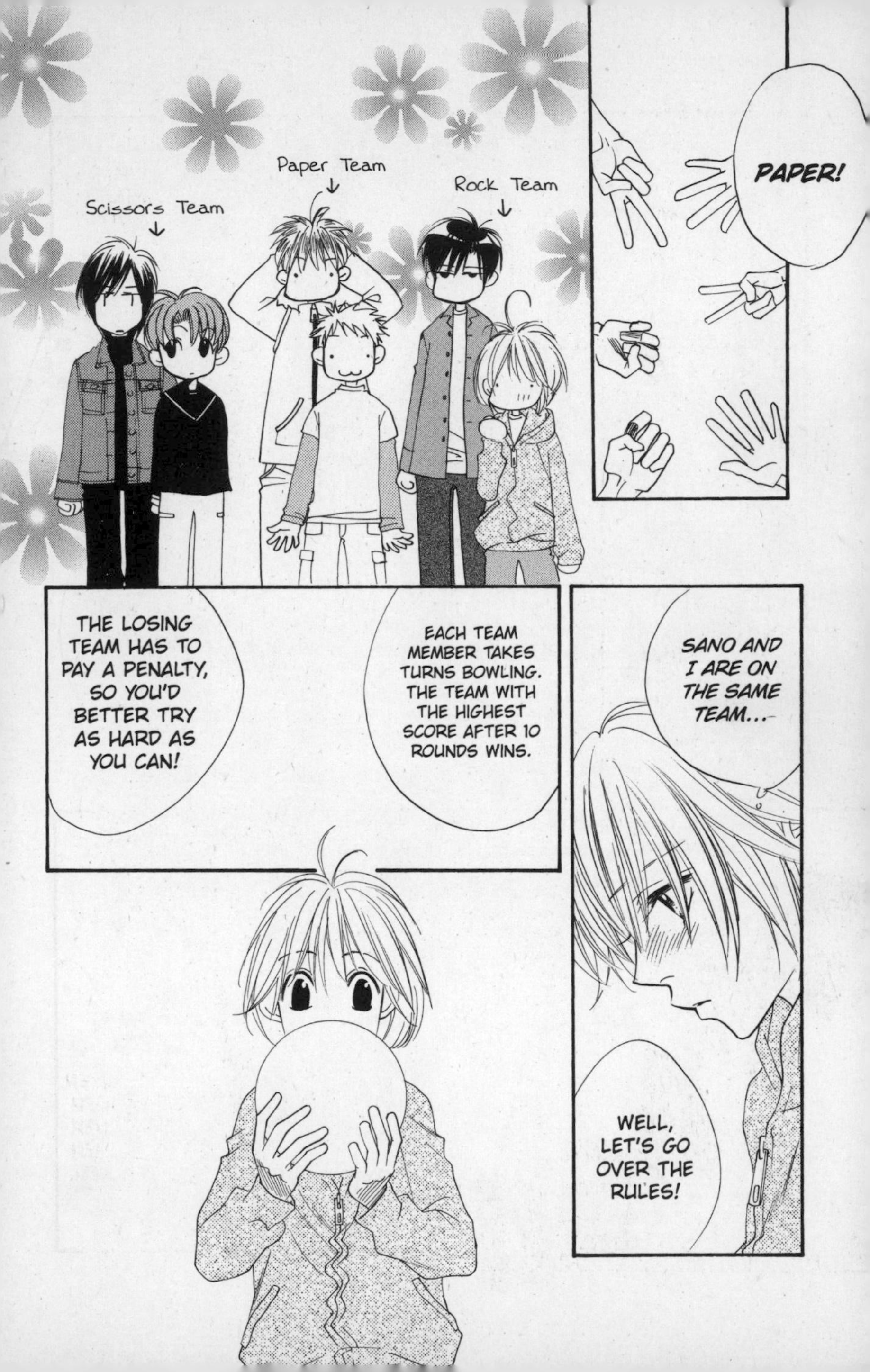
PAPER!
Rock Team
Paper Team
Scissors Team
SANO AND I ARE ON THE SAME TEAM...
WELL, LET'S GO OVER THE RULES!
EACH TEAM MEMBER TAKES TURNS BOWLING. THE TEAM WITH THE HIGHEST SCORE AFTER 10 ROUNDS WINS.
THE LOSING TEAM HAS TO PAY A PENALTY, SO YOU'D BETTER TRY AS HARD AS YOU CAN!

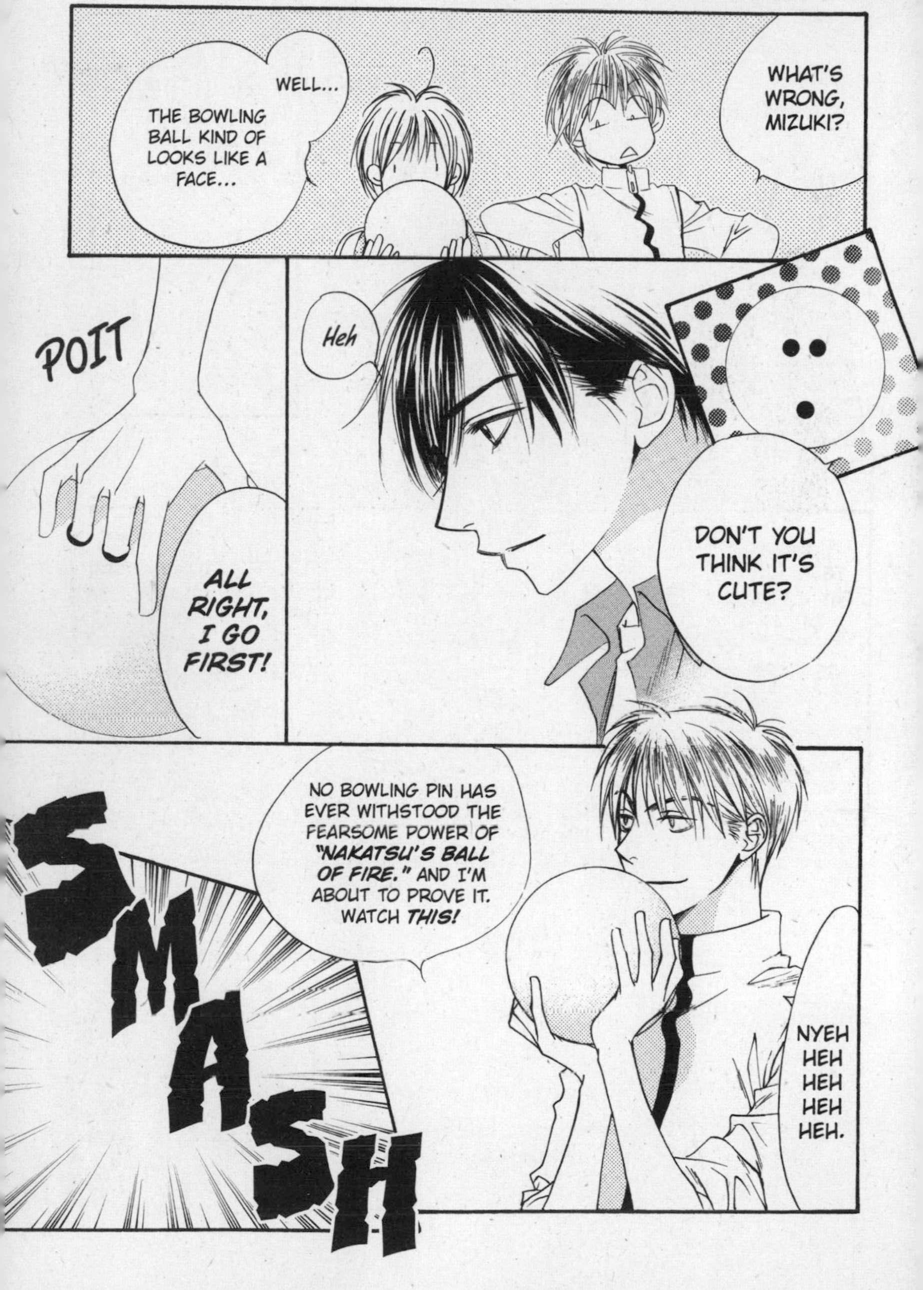
WHAT'S WRONG, MIZUKI?
WELL...
THE BOWLING BALL KIND OF LOOKS LIKE A FACE...
DON'T YOU THINK IT'S CUTE?
Heh
POIT
ALL RIGHT, I GO FIRST!
NO BOWLING PIN HAS EVER WITHSTOOD THE FEARSOME POWER OF "NAKATSU'S BALL OF FIRE." AND I'M ABOUT TO PROVE IT. WATCH THIS!
NYEH HEH HEH HEH HEH.
SMASH

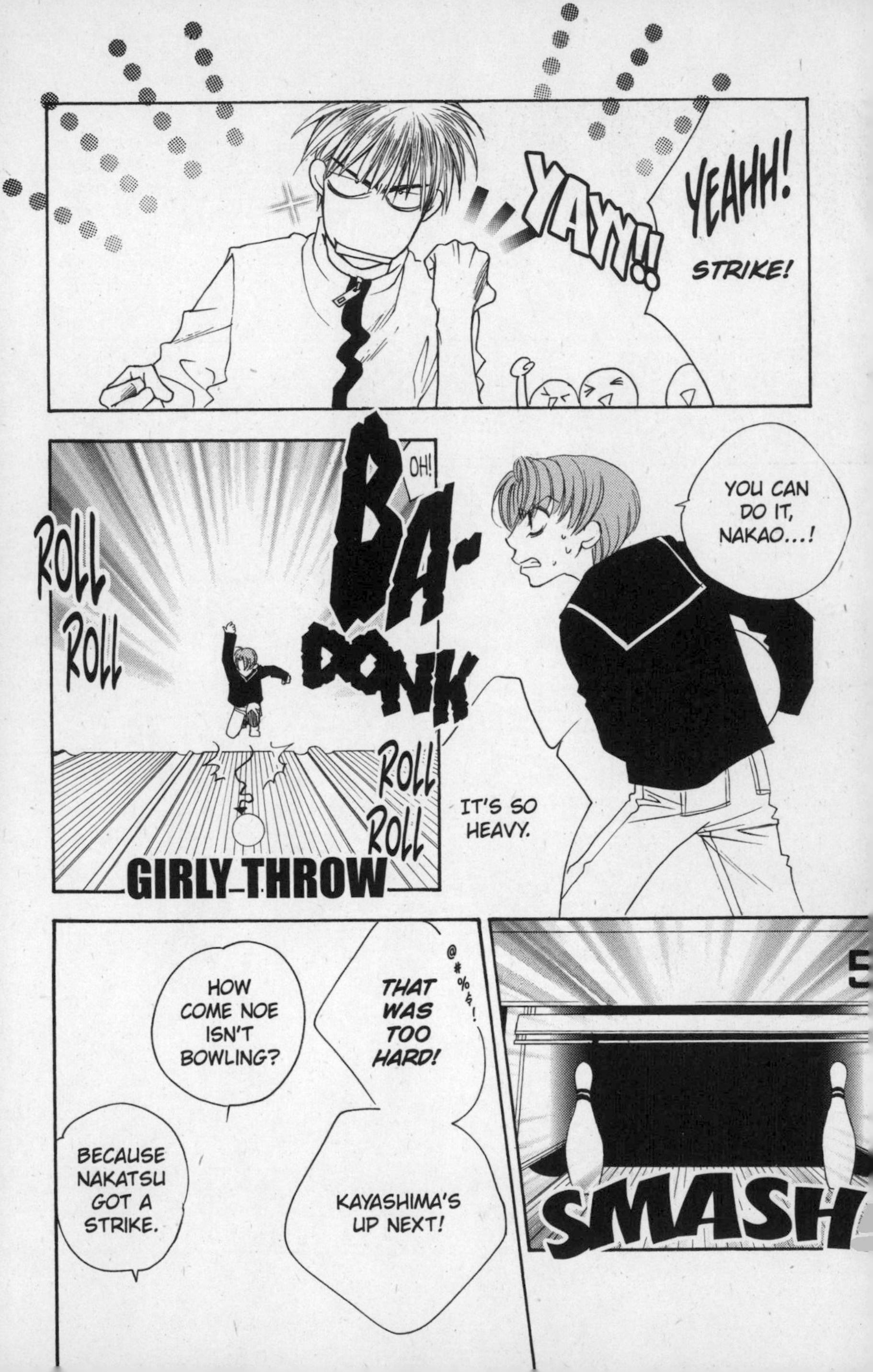
YEAHH!
STRIKE!
YAYY!!
YOU CAN DO IT, NAKAO...!
IT'S SO HEAVY.
OH!
BA-DONK
ROLL ROLL
ROLL ROLL
GIRLY THROW
SMASH
THAT WAS TOO HARD!
HOW COME NOE ISN'T BOWLING?
KAYASHIMA'S UP NEXT!
BECAUSE NAKATSU GOT A STRIKE.

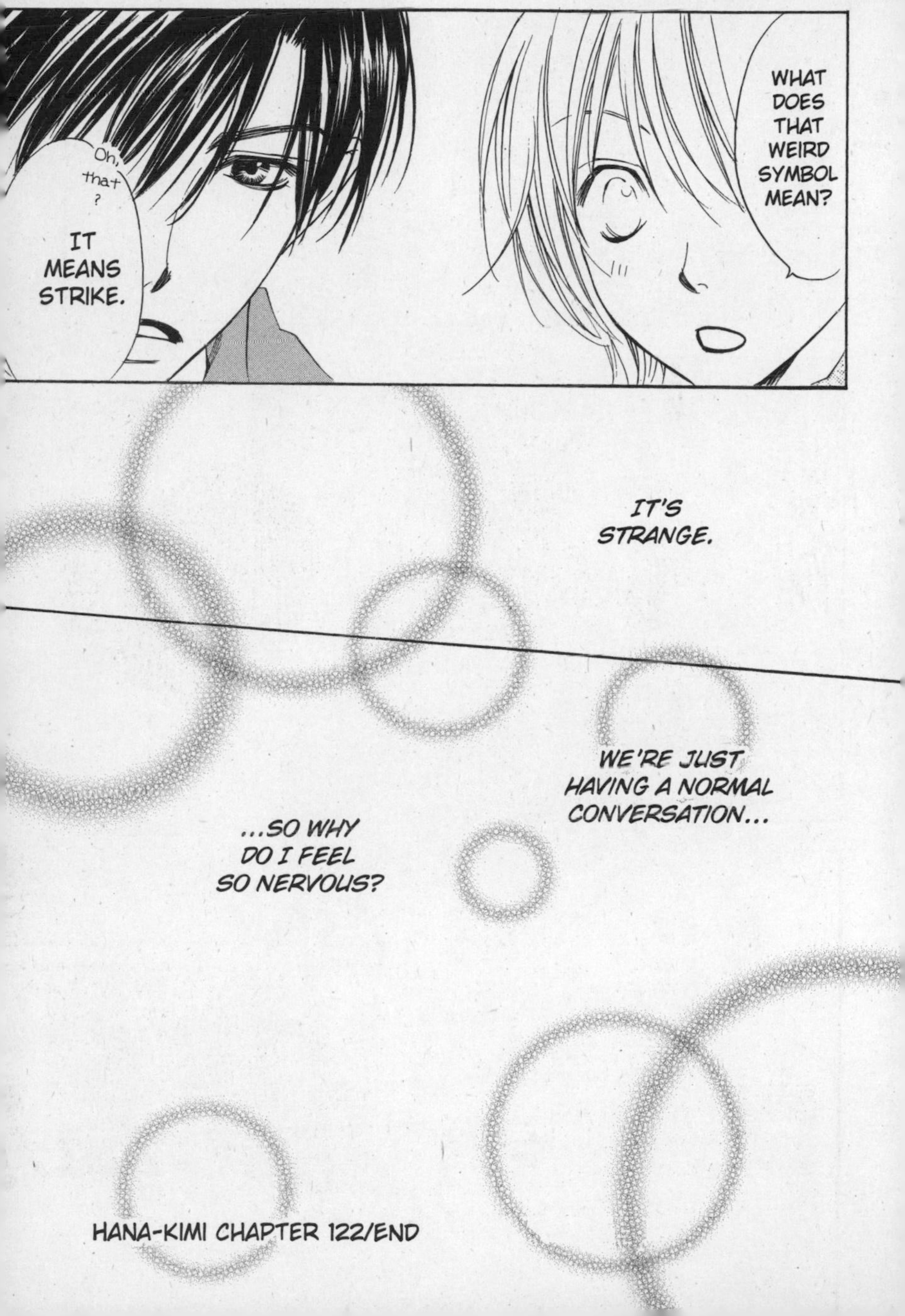
WHAT DOES THAT WEIRD SYMBOL MEAN?
Oh, that?
IT MEANS STRIKE.
IT'S STRANGE.
WE'RE JUST HAVING A NORMAL CONVERSATION...
...SO WHY DO I FEEL SO NERVOUS?
HANA-KIMI CHAPTER 122/END

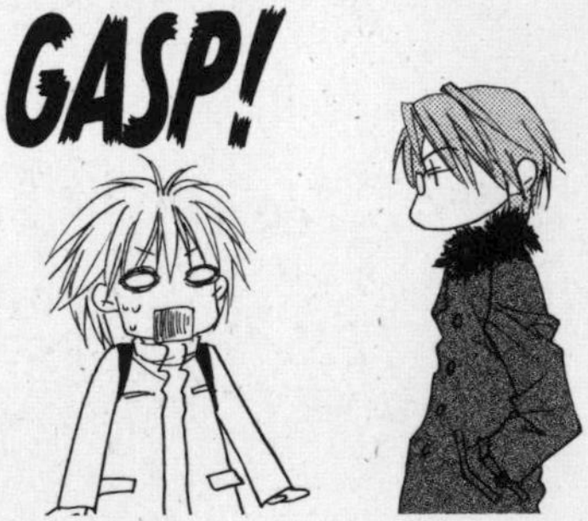
GASP!

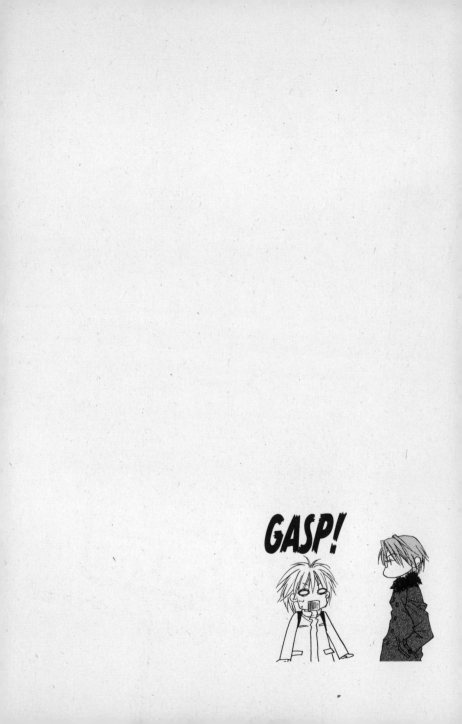

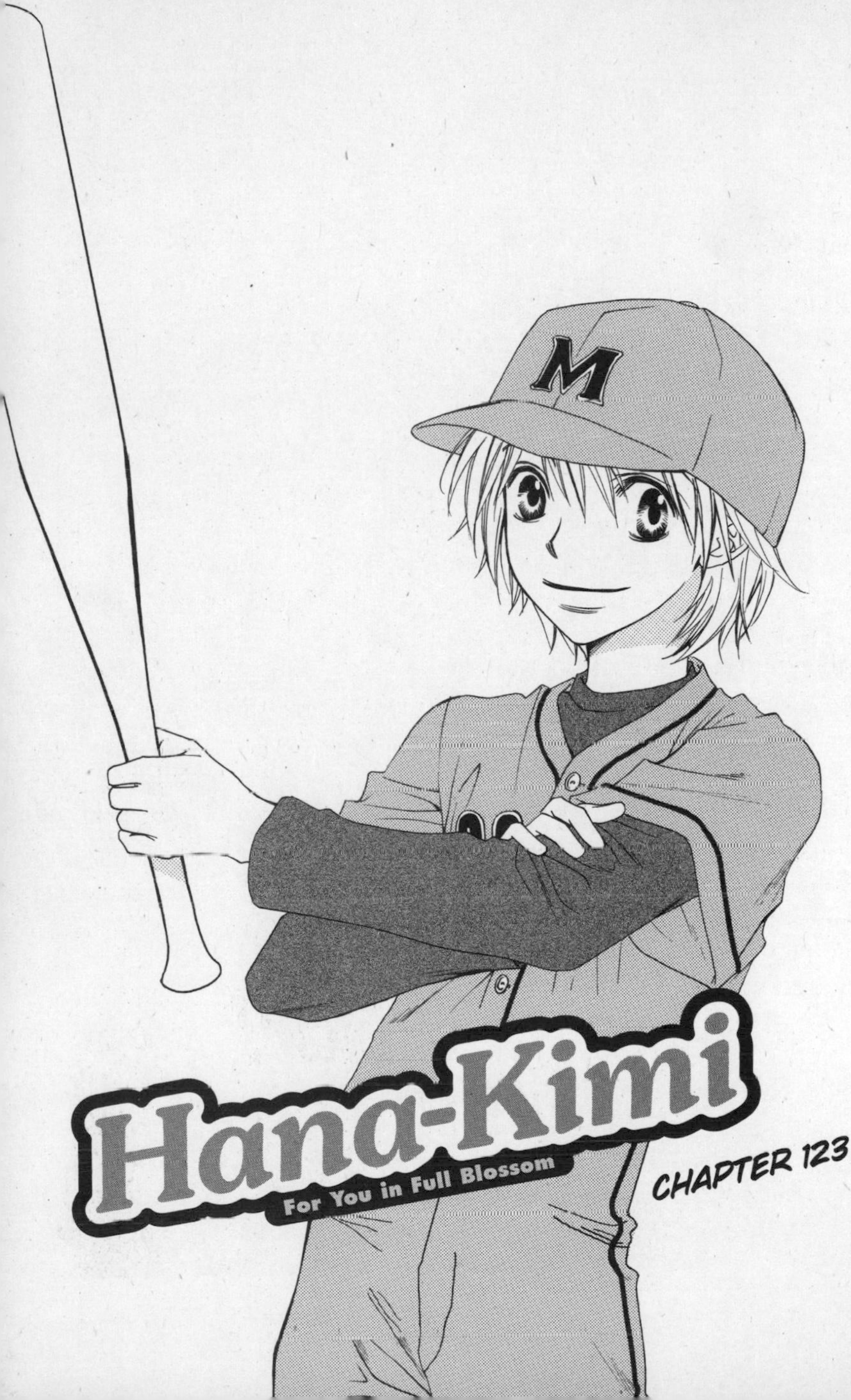
Hana-Kimi
For You in Full Blossom
CHAPTER 123

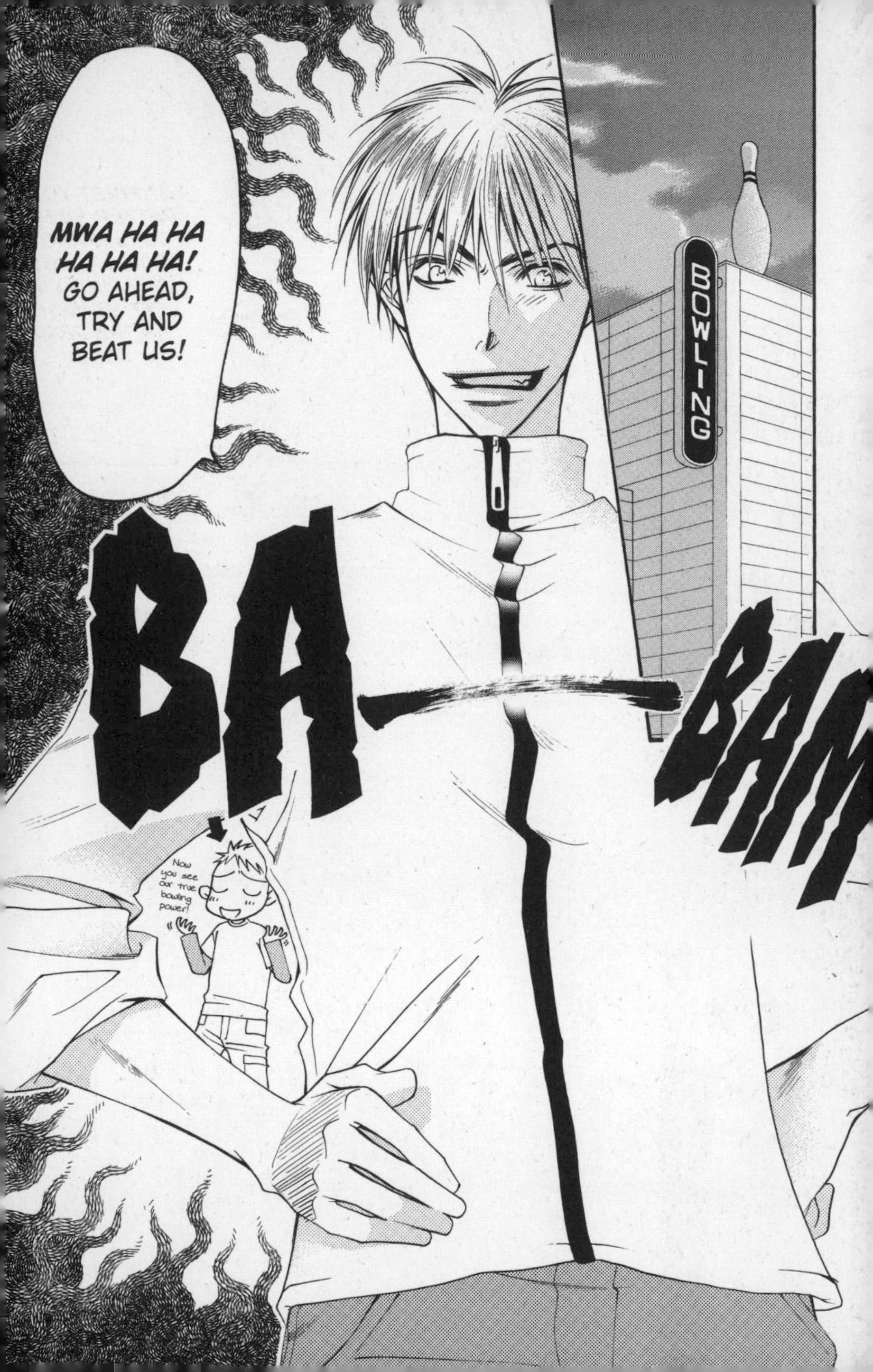
MWA HA HA HA HA HA! GO AHEAD, TRY AND BEAT US!
BOWLING
BA-BAM
Now you see our true bowling power!

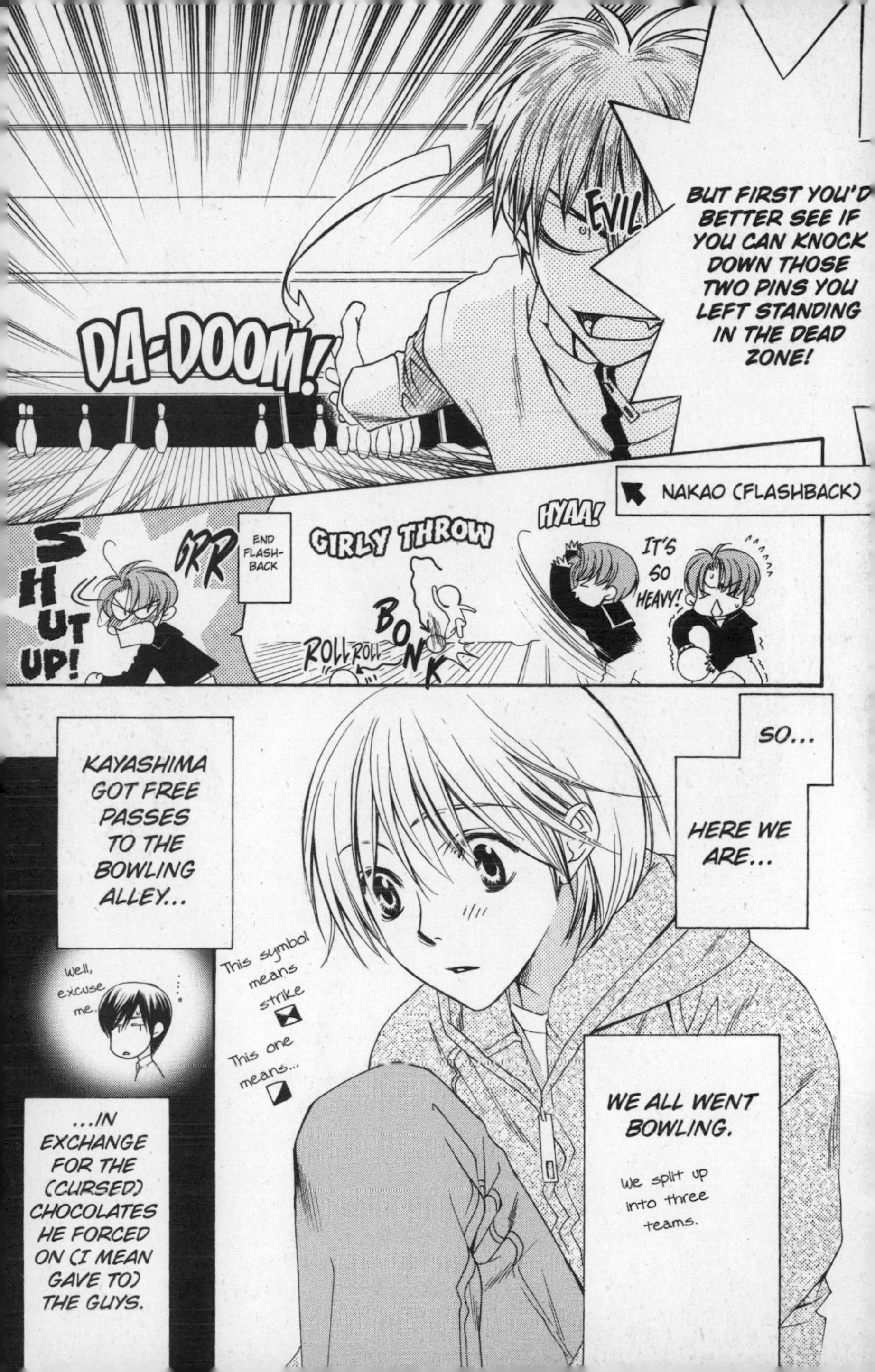
BUT FIRST YOU'D BETTER SEE IF YOU CAN KNOCK DOWN THOSE TWO PINS YOU LEFT STANDING IN THE DEAD ZONE!
EVIL
DA-DOOM!
NAKAO (FLASHBACK)
IT'S SO HEAVY!
HYAA!
GIRLY THROW
BONK
ROLL ROLL
END FLASH-BACK
GRR
SHUT UP!
SO...
HERE WE ARE...
KAYASHIMA GOT FREE PASSES TO THE BOWLING ALLEY...
WE ALL WENT BOWLING.
We split up into three teams.
This symbol means strike
This one means...
Well, excuse me...
...IN EXCHANGE FOR THE (CURSED) CHOCOLATES HE FORCED ON (I MEAN GAVE TO) THE GUYS.

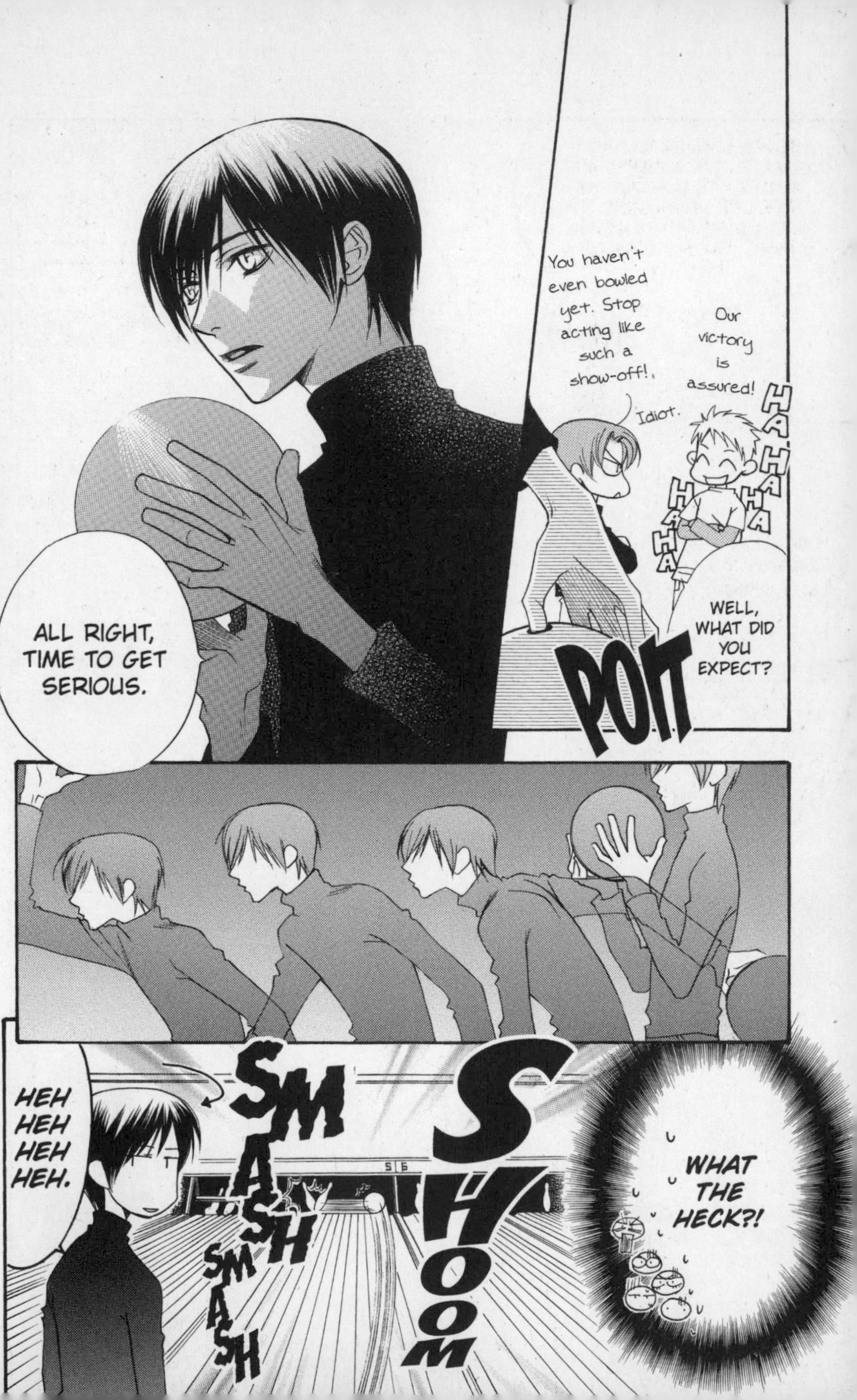
Our victory is assured!
HAHAHA
HAHAHA
You haven't even bowled yet. Stop acting like such a show-off!
Idiot.
WELL, WHAT DID YOU EXPECT?
POIT
ALL RIGHT, TIME TO GET SERIOUS.
WHAT THE HECK?!
SHOOOM
SMASH
SMASH
HEH HEH HEH HEH.

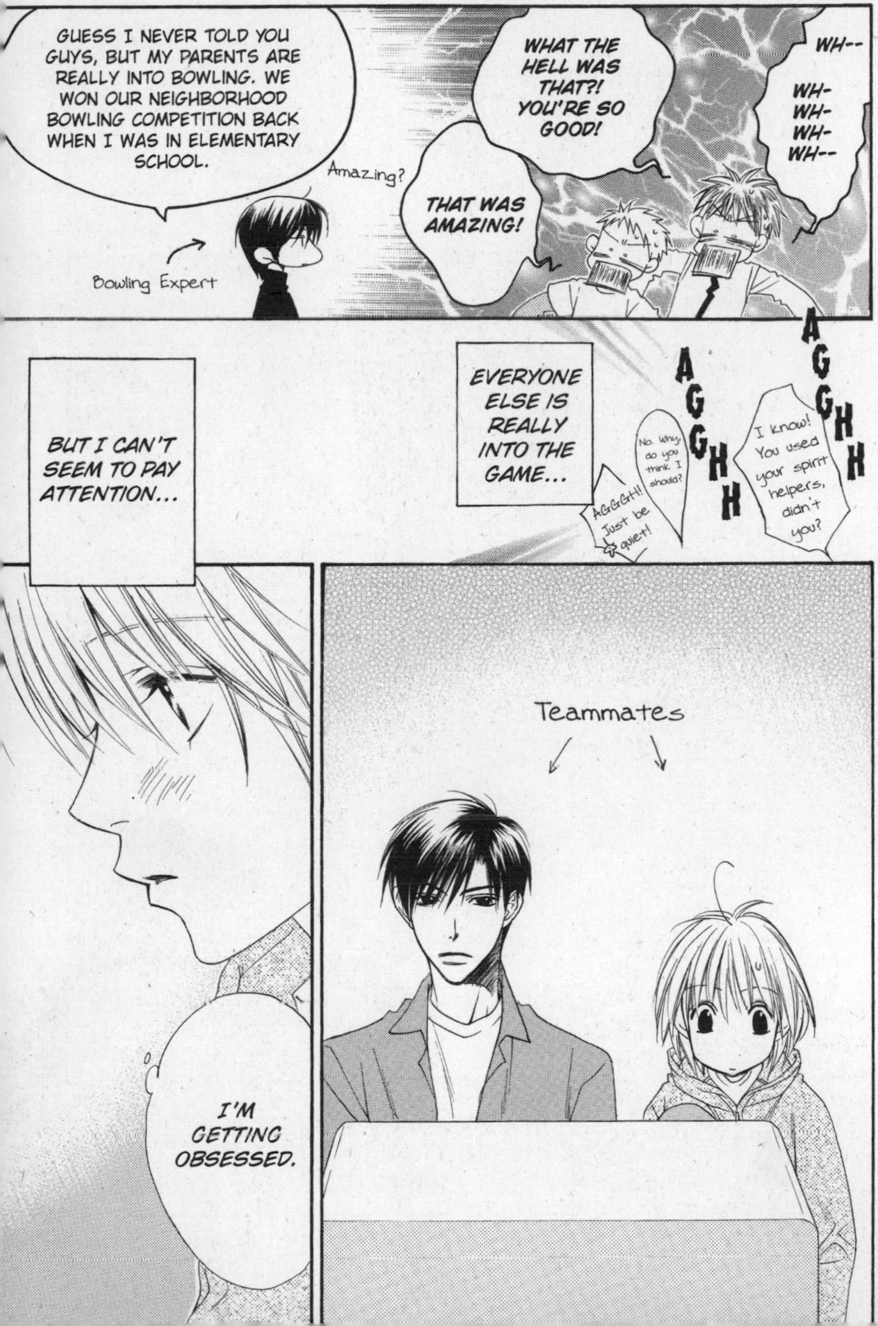
WH--
WH- WH- WH- WH--
WHAT THE HELL WAS THAT?! YOU'RE SO GOOD!
THAT WAS AMAZING!
Amazing?
GUESS I NEVER TOLD YOU GUYS, BUT MY PARENTS ARE REALLY INTO BOWLING. WE WON OUR NEIGHBORHOOD BOWLING COMPETITION BACK WHEN I WAS IN ELEMENTARY SCHOOL.
Bowling Expert
AGGHH
AGGHH
I know! You used your spirit helpers, didn't you?
No. Why do you think I should?
AGGGH! Just be quiet!
EVERYONE ELSE IS REALLY INTO THE GAME...
BUT I CAN'T SEEM TO PAY ATTENTION...
Teammates
I'M GETTING OBSESSED.

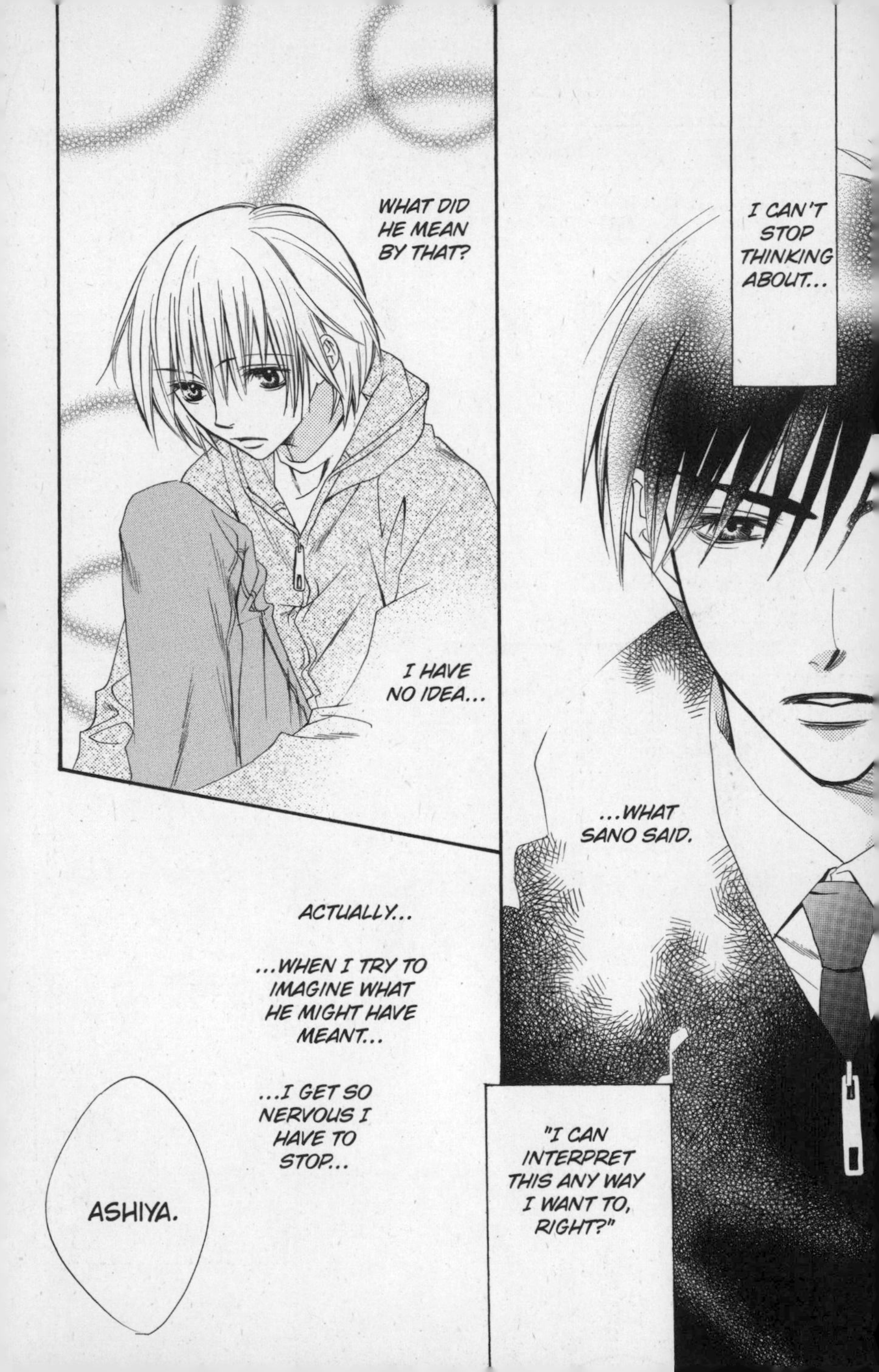
I CAN'T STOP THINKING ABOUT...
...WHAT SANO SAID.
"I CAN INTERPRET THIS ANY WAY I WANT TO, RIGHT?"
WHAT DID HE MEAN BY THAT?
I HAVE NO IDEA...
ACTUALLY...
...WHEN I TRY TO IMAGINE WHAT HE MIGHT HAVE MEANT...
...I GET SO NERVOUS I HAVE TO STOP...
ASHIYA.

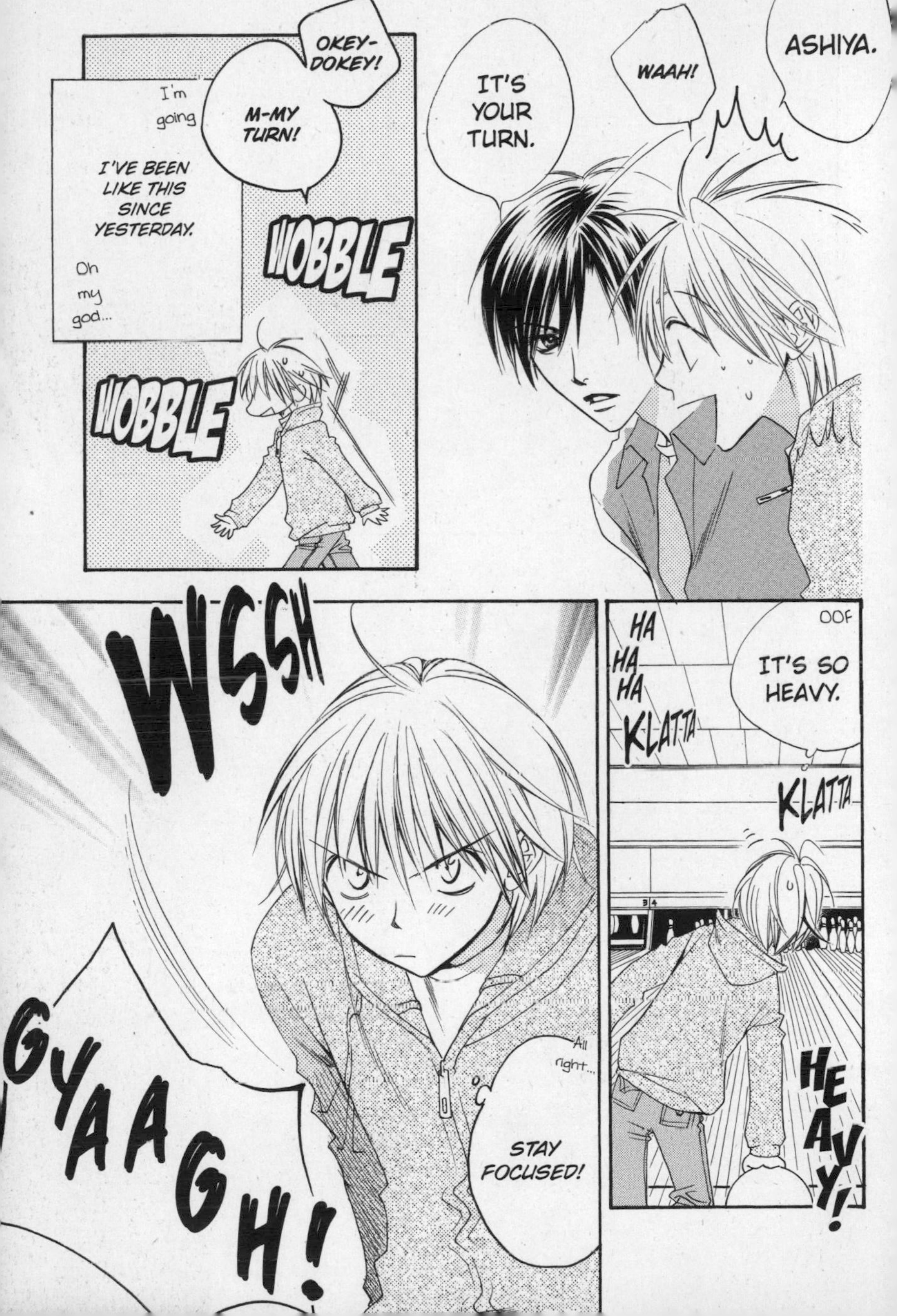
ASHIYA.
WAAH!
IT'S YOUR TURN.
OKEY-DOKEY!
M-MY TURN!
WOBBLE
WOBBLE
I'm going
I'VE BEEN LIKE THIS SINCE YESTERDAY.
Oh my god...
OOF
IT'S SO HEAVY.
HA HA HA
KLATTA
KLATTA
HEAVY!
WSSH
All right...
STAY FOCUSED!
GYAAGH!

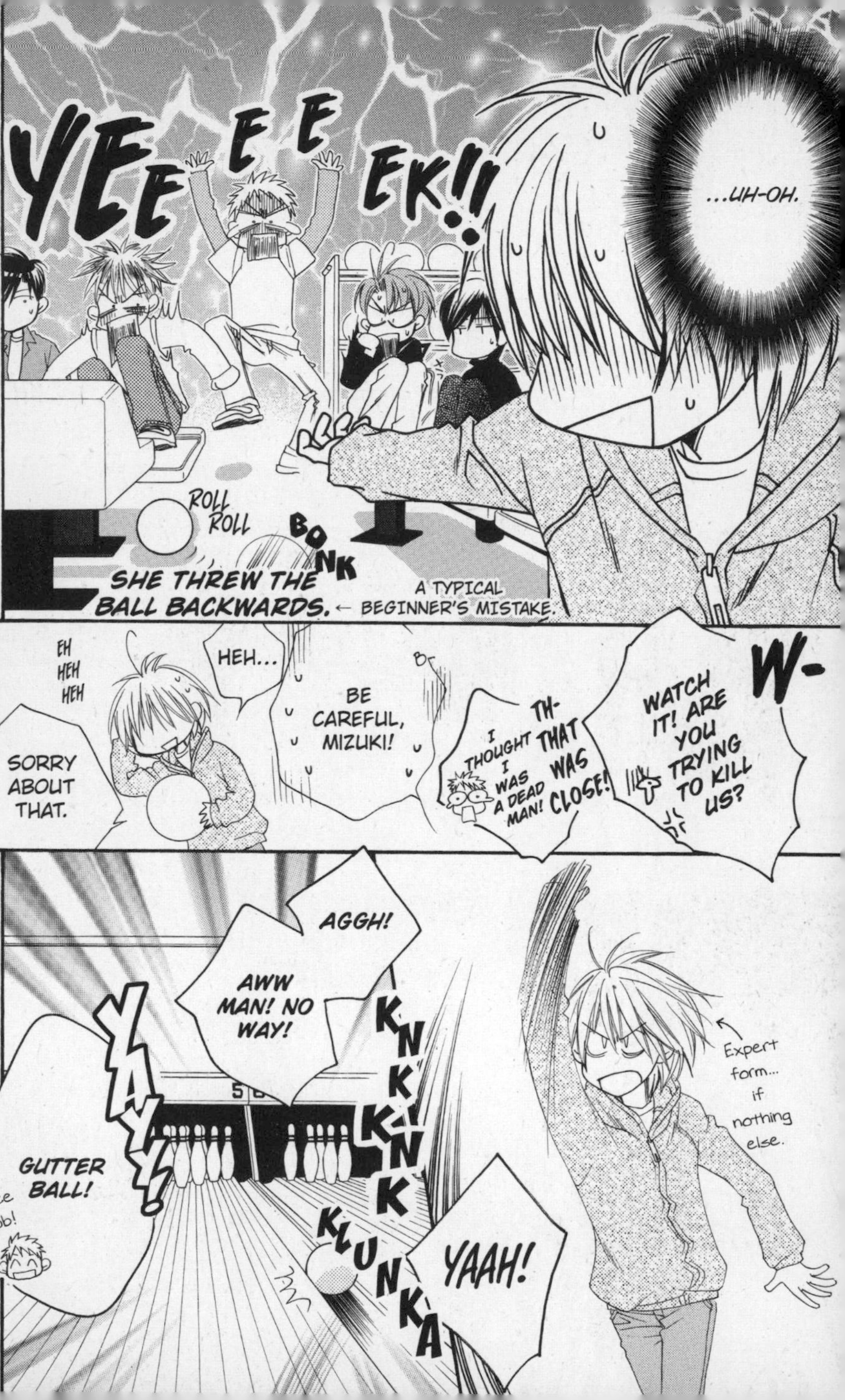
...UH-OH.
YEEEEEEK!!!
ROLL ROLL
BONK
SHE THREW THE BALL BACKWARDS. ← A TYPICAL BEGINNER'S MISTAKE.
W-WATCH IT! ARE YOU TRYING TO KILL US?
TH-THAT WAS CLOSE!
I THOUGHT I WAS A DEAD MAN!
BE CAREFUL, MIZUKI!
HEH...
EH HEH HEH
SORRY ABOUT THAT.
Expert form... if nothing else.
YAAH!
KNK KNK KNK KLUNKA
AGGH!
AWW MAN! NO WAY!
YAAAY!
GUTTER BALL!
Nice job!

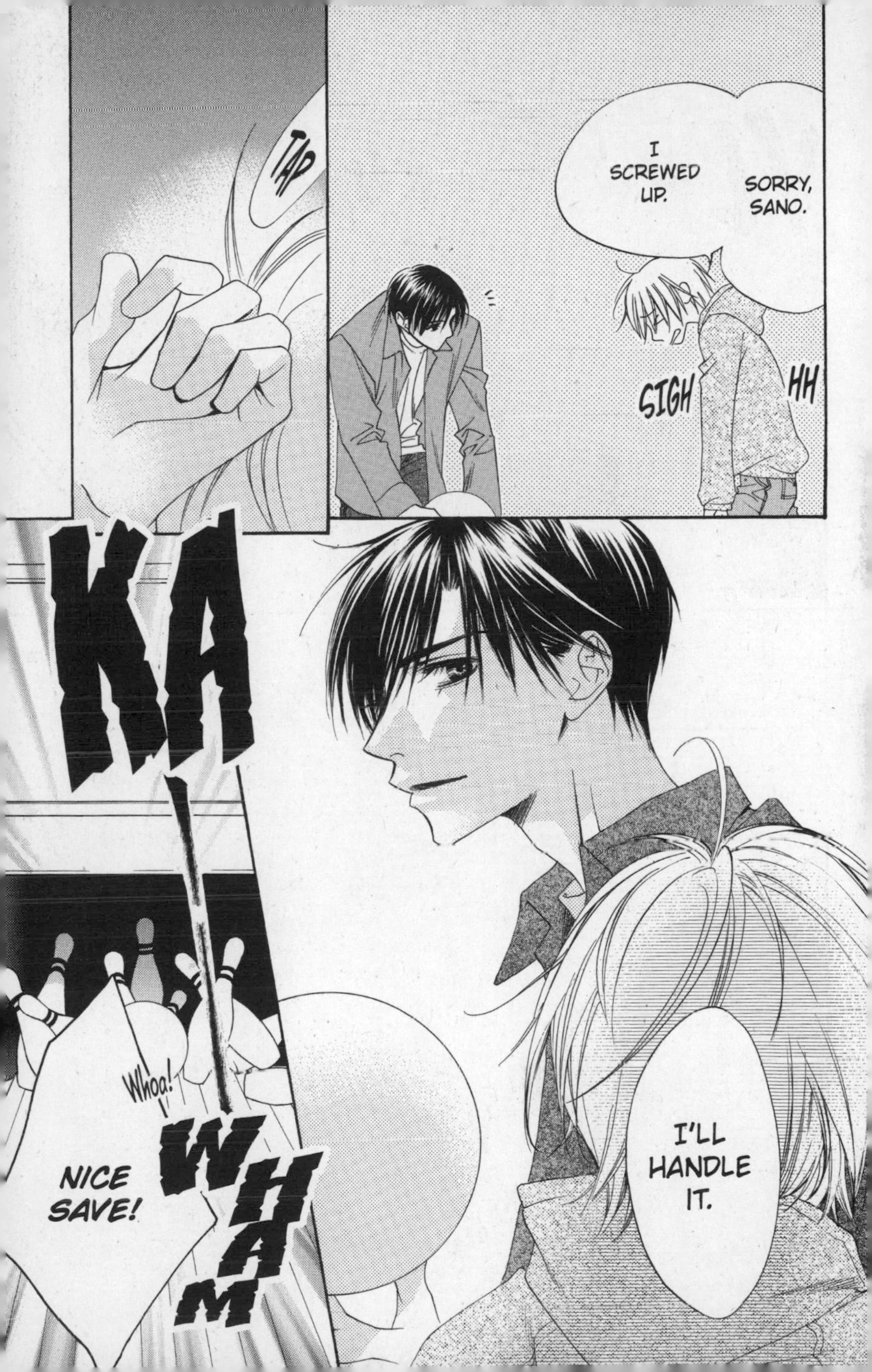

SORRY, SANO.
I SCREWED UP.
SIGH
HH
TAP
I'LL HANDLE IT.
KA
WHAM
Whoa!
NICE SAVE!

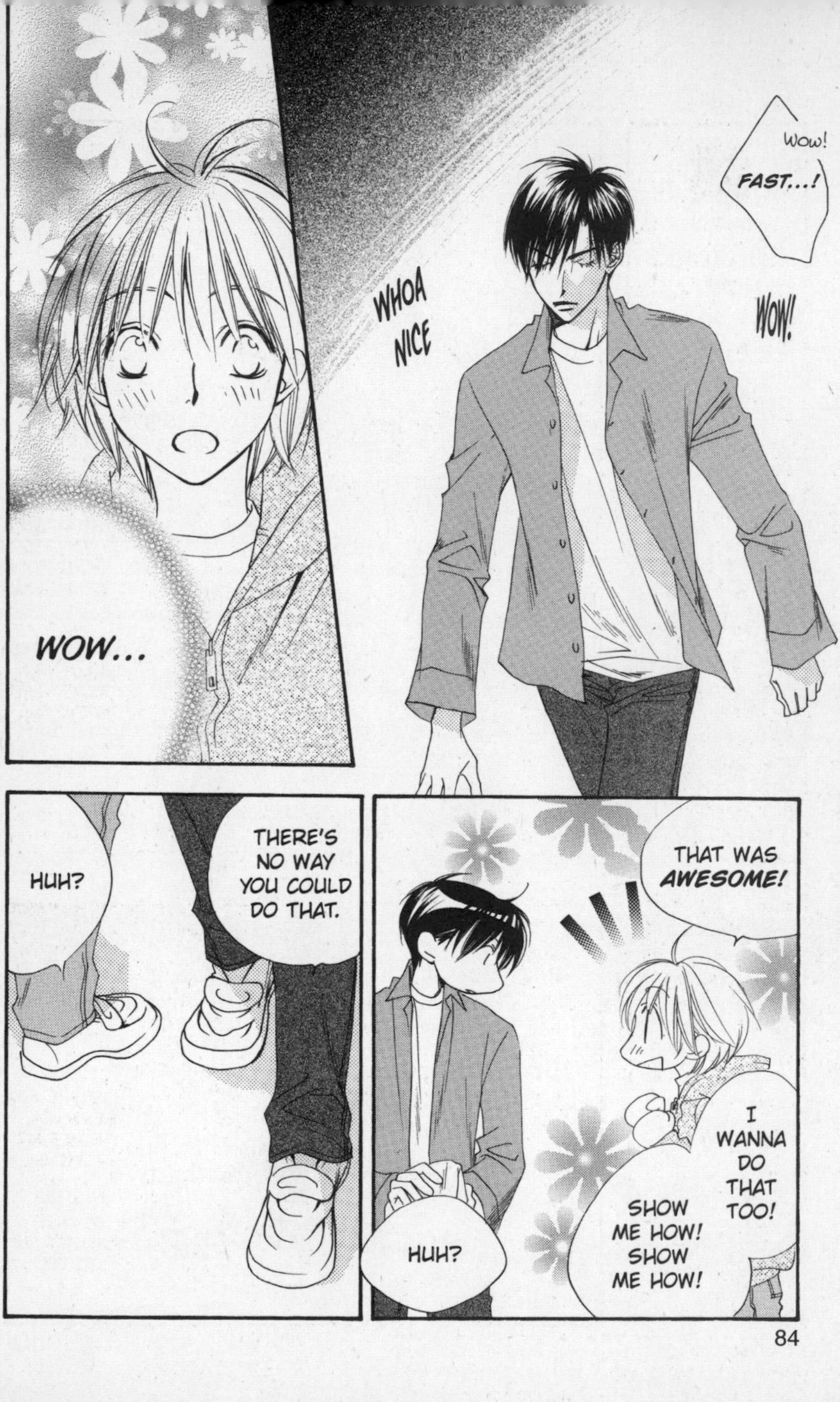

Wow! FAST...!
WOW!
WHOA NICE
WOW...
THAT WAS AWESOME!
I WANNA DO THAT TOO!
SHOW ME HOW! SHOW ME HOW!
HUH?
THERE'S NO WAY YOU COULD DO THAT.
HUH?

演

THEATER

THE MIRACLE WORKER

I went to see "The Miracle Worker" starring An Suzuki as Helen, and Shinobu Ootake as Miss Sullivan. The play was filled with big name actors! I saw An live for the first time, and I was totally carried away. But I was soon distracted by Ootake's amazing acting. Wow, it was such a great play! An's version of Helen was so cute that it made me wanna protect her. Helen and Miss Sullivan were both really powerful and emotional characters. I cried so hard watching the last scene, where Helen learns the word "water"! The audience was sniffling and clapping at the same time! It was really moving.

She was as cute as when she was paying the role of Maya in "Glass no Kamen" (Mask of Glass).

WHY NOT?
Heh
TO KNOCK ALL THE PINS DOWN AT ONCE YOU'VE GOT TO GET SERIOUS SPEED.
AND YOU NEED A LOT OF STRENGTH TO THROW THE BALL THAT FAST.
HMPH...
THUMP
THUMP
YOU'RE A BEGINNER. THERE'S NO POINT IN TRYING TO BOWL STRIKES RIGHT FROM THE GET GO.
WHY DON'T YOU START OUT BY JUST TRYING TO KEEP THE BALL OUT OF THE GUTTER? JUST TAKE IT ONE PIN AT A TIME.
Oh, okay.

I was planning on going to see the play a second time, but I couldn't make it. Later, I heard that Okada from V6 was there the day I was supposed to go and I really regretted that I didn't make it.

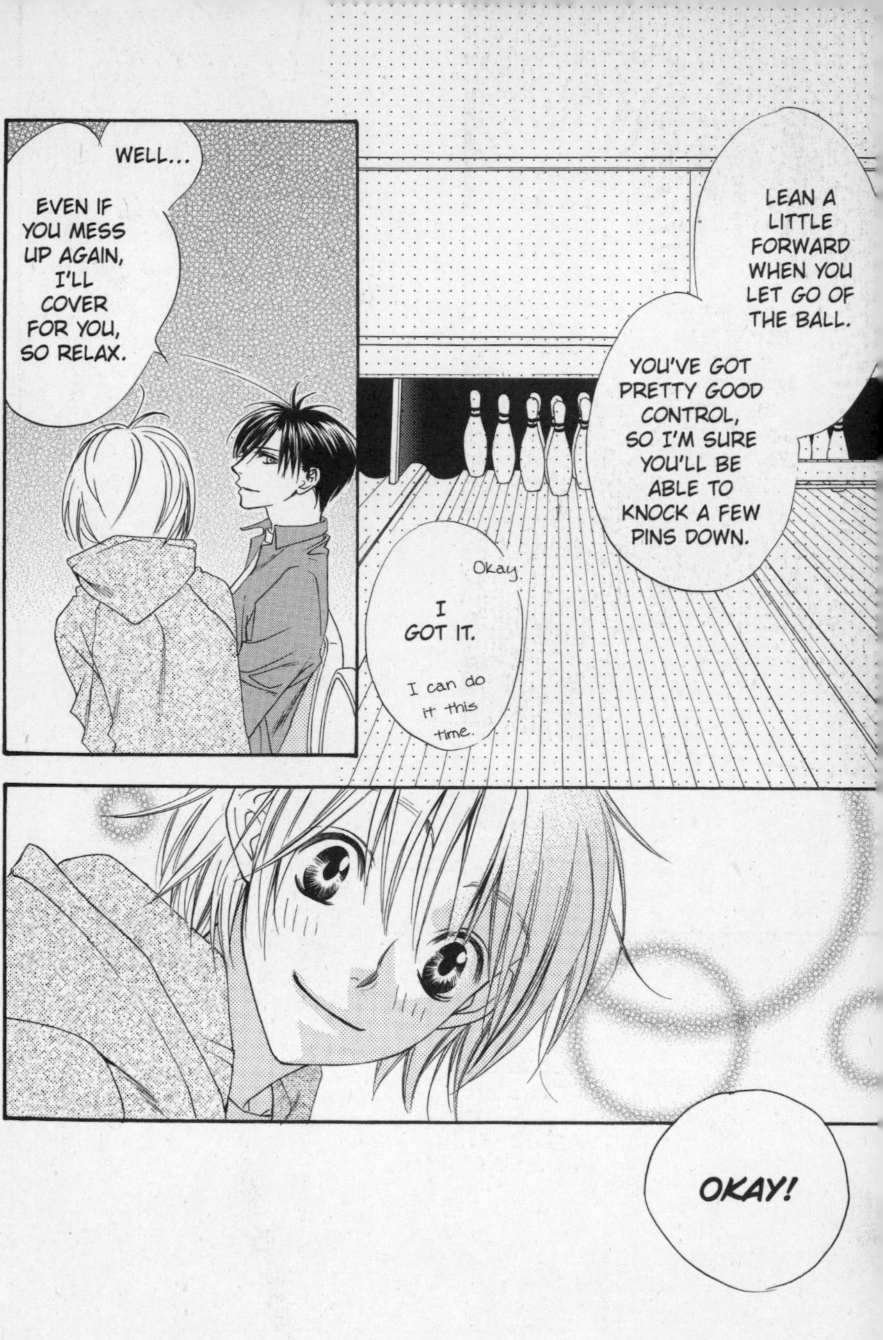
LEAN A LITTLE FORWARD WHEN YOU LET GO OF THE BALL.
YOU'VE GOT PRETTY GOOD CONTROL, SO I'M SURE YOU'LL BE ABLE TO KNOCK A FEW PINS DOWN.
Okay.
I GOT IT.
I can do it this time.
WELL...
EVEN IF YOU MESS UP AGAIN, I'LL COVER FOR YOU, SO RELAX.
OKAY!

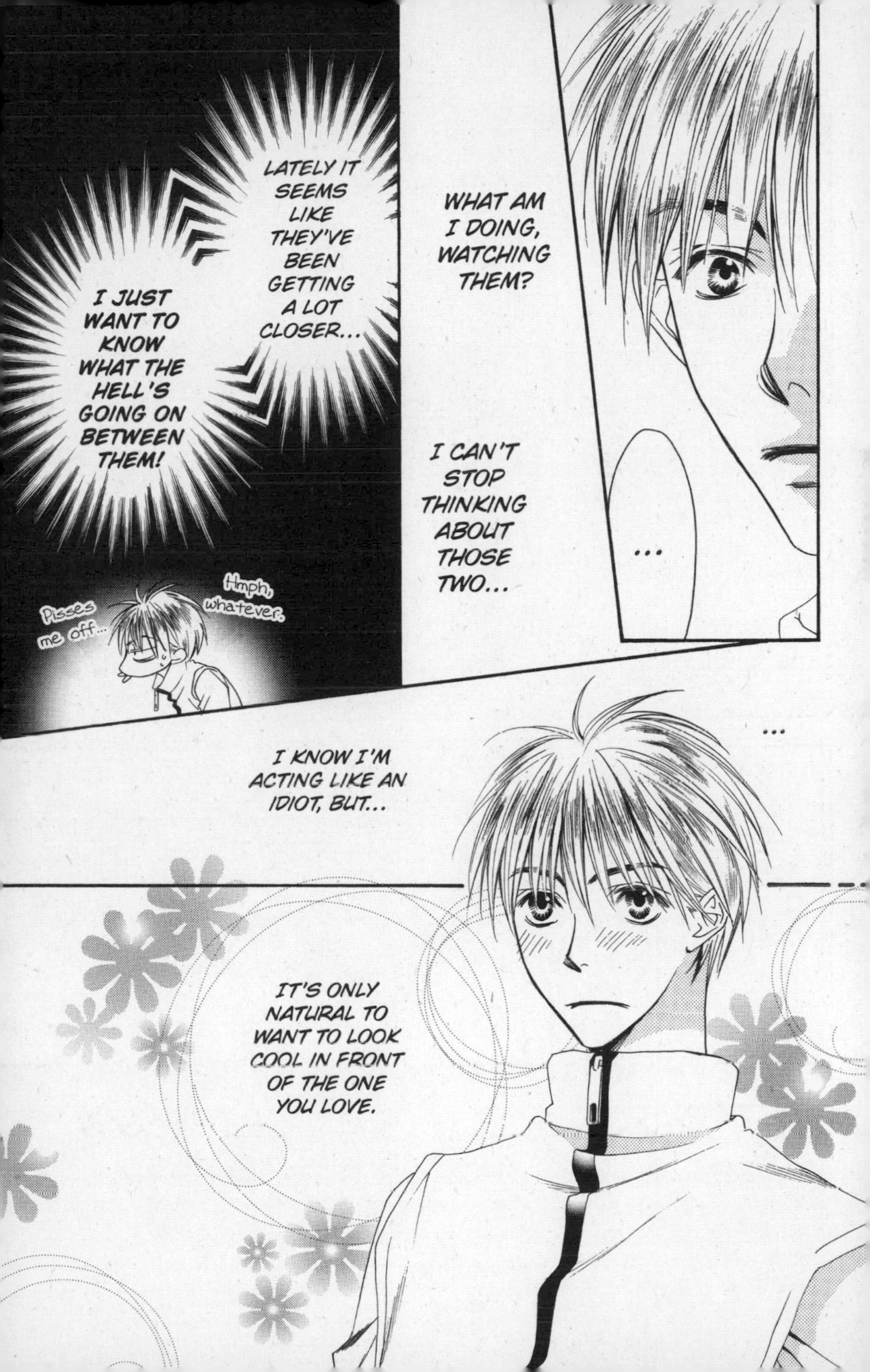
WHAT AM I DOING, WATCHING THEM?
I CAN'T STOP THINKING ABOUT THOSE TWO...
...
LATELY IT SEEMS LIKE THEY'VE BEEN GETTING A LOT CLOSER...
I JUST WANT TO KNOW WHAT THE HELL'S GOING ON BETWEEN THEM!
Hmph, whatever.
Pisses me off...
...
I KNOW I'M ACTING LIKE AN IDIOT, BUT...
IT'S ONLY NATURAL TO WANT TO LOOK COOL IN FRONT OF THE ONE YOU LOVE.

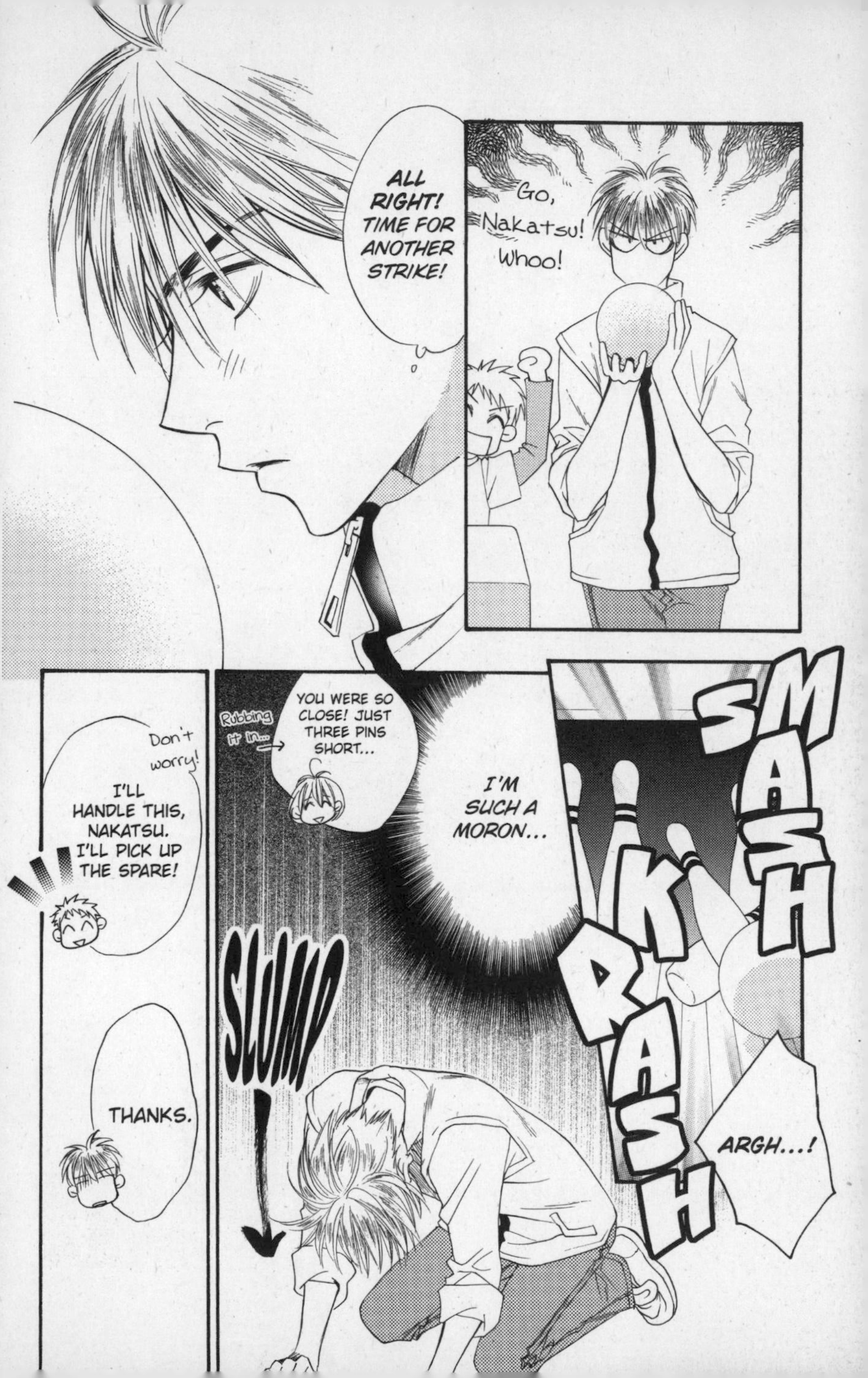
Go, Nakatsu! Whoo!
ALL RIGHT! TIME FOR ANOTHER STRIKE!
SMASH
KRASH
ARGH...!
I'M SUCH A MORON...
YOU WERE SO CLOSE! JUST THREE PINS SHORT...
Rubbing it in...
SLUMP
Don't worry!
I'LL HANDLE THIS, NAKATSU. I'LL PICK UP THE SPARE!
THANKS.

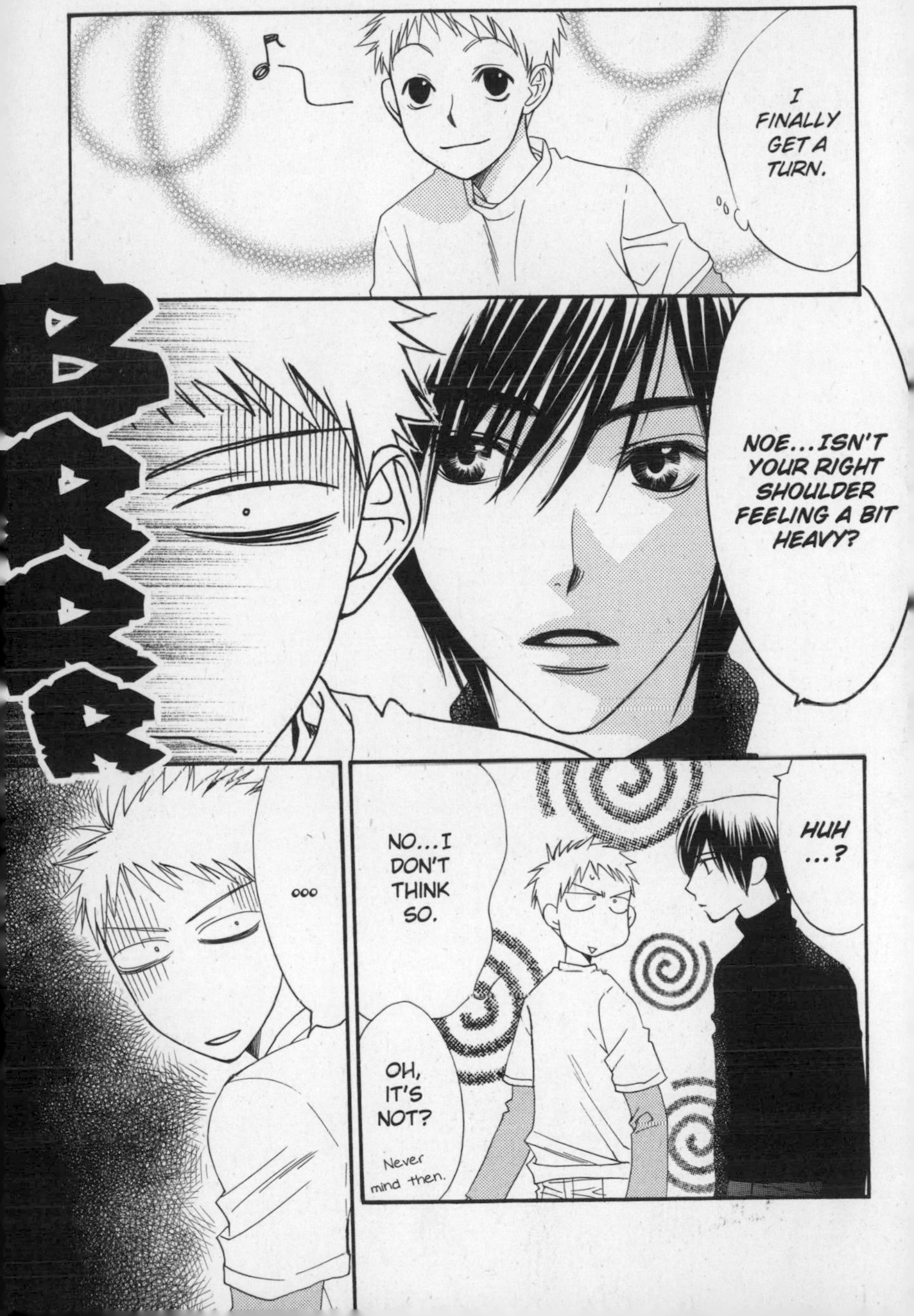
I FINALLY GET A TURN.
NOE...ISN'T YOUR RIGHT SHOULDER FEELING A BIT HEAVY?
HUH ...?
NO...I DON'T THINK SO.
OH, IT'S NOT?
Never mind then.
...

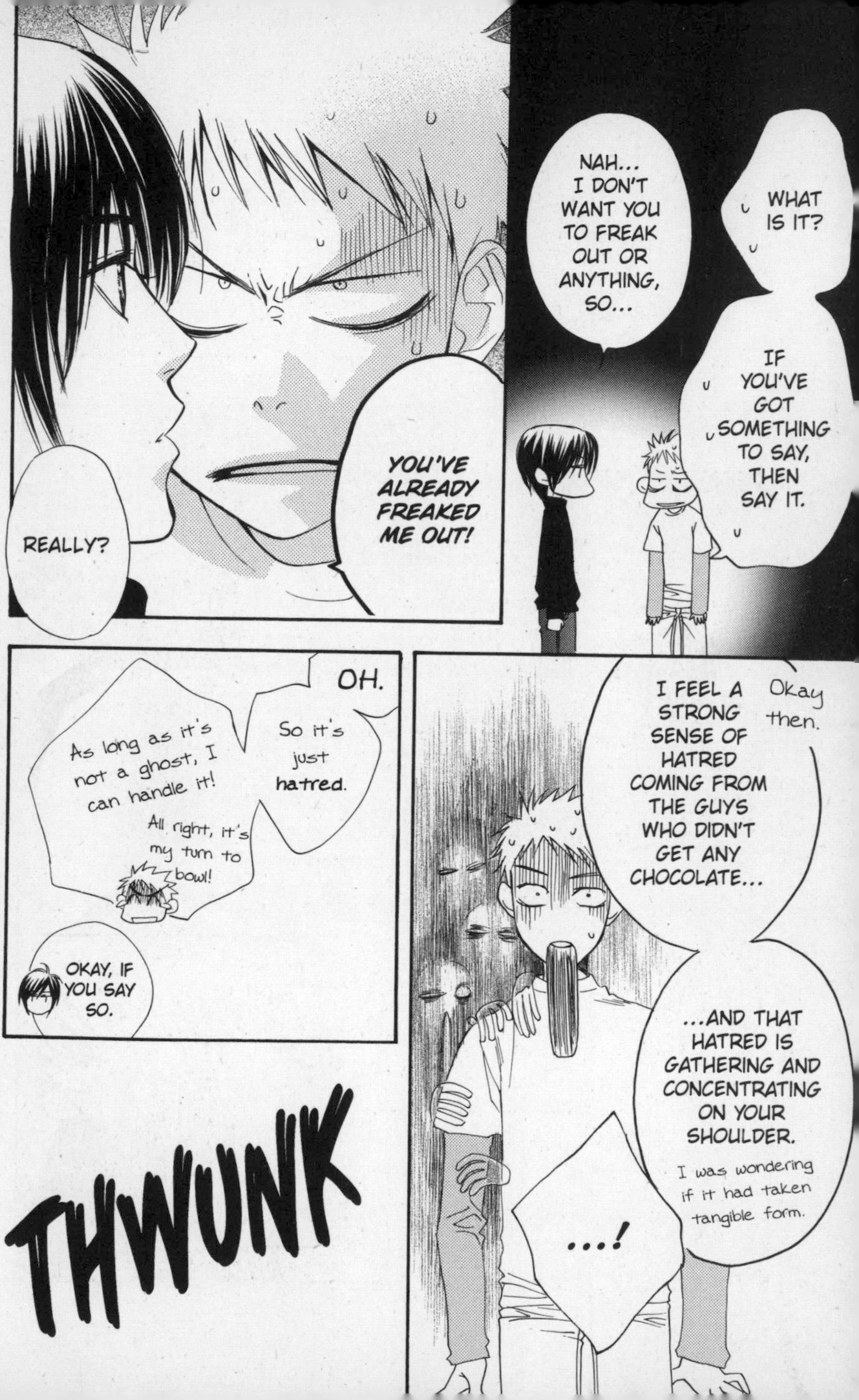

WHAT IS IT?
NAH... I DON'T WANT YOU TO FREAK OUT OR ANYTHING, SO...
IF YOU'VE GOT SOMETHING TO SAY, THEN SAY IT.
YOU'VE ALREADY FREAKED ME OUT!
REALLY?
Okay then.
I FEEL A STRONG SENSE OF HATRED COMING FROM THE GUYS WHO DIDN'T GET ANY CHOCOLATE...
...AND THAT HATRED IS GATHERING AND CONCENTRATING ON YOUR SHOULDER.
I was wondering if it had taken tangible form.
...!
OH.
So it's just hatred.
As long as it's not a ghost, I can handle it!
All right, it's my turn to bowl!
OKAY, IF YOU SAY SO.
THWUNK

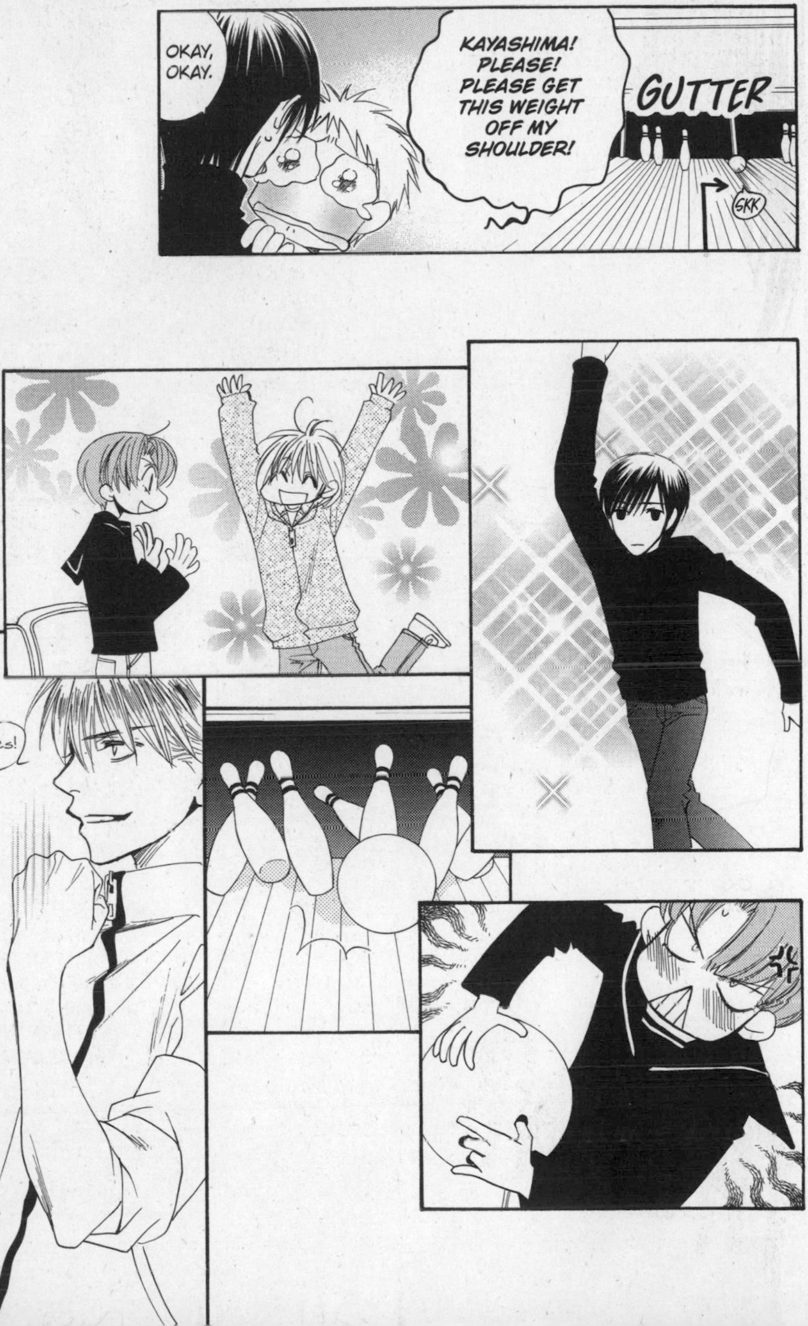
GUTTER
SKK
KAYASHIMA! PLEASE! PLEASE GET THIS WEIGHT OFF MY SHOULDER!
OKAY, OKAY.
Yes!

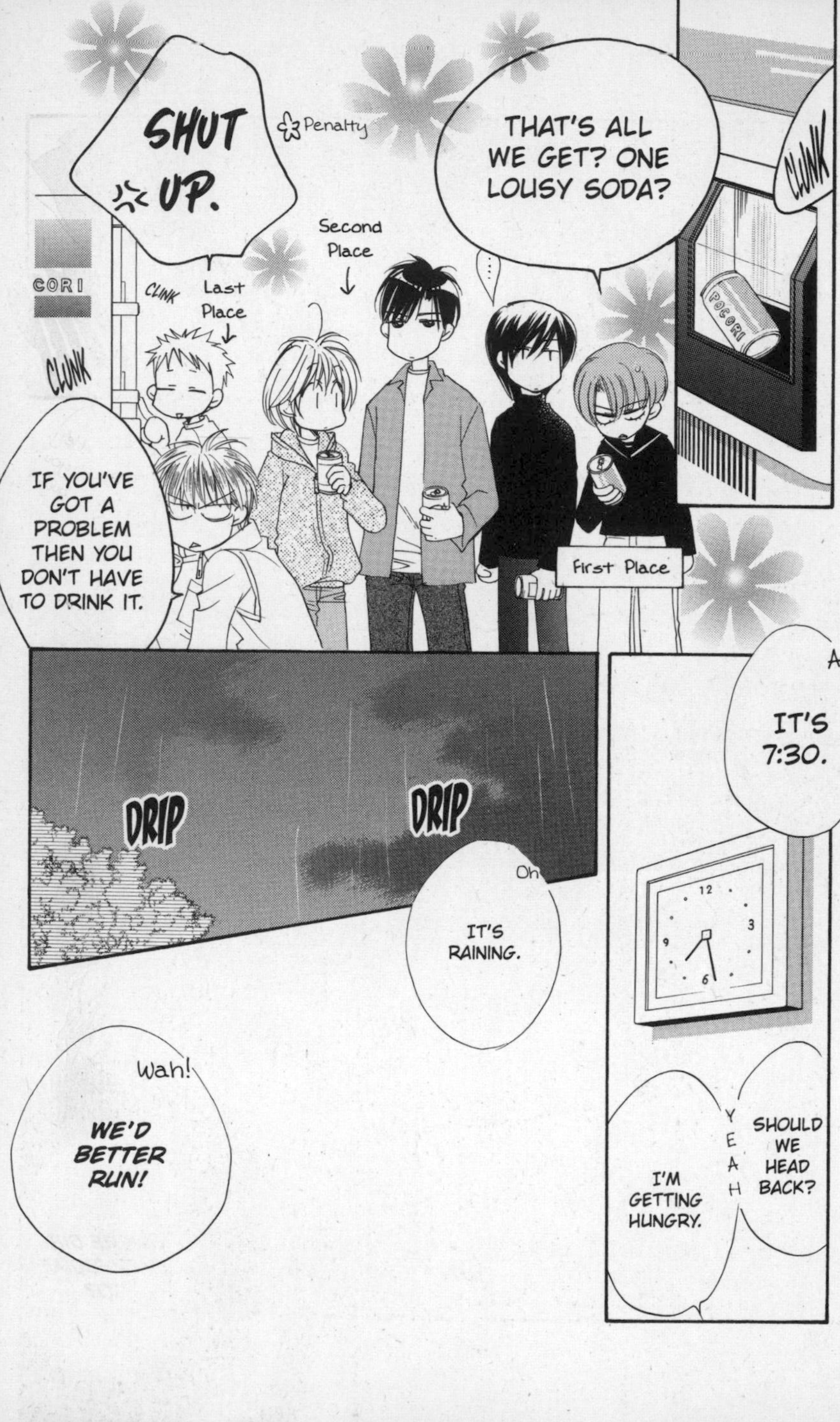

CLUNK
POCORI
THAT'S ALL WE GET? ONE LOUSY SODA?
...
SHUT UP.
Penalty
Second Place
Last Place
CLINK
CLUNK
CORI
First Place
IF YOU'VE GOT A PROBLEM THEN YOU DON'T HAVE TO DRINK IT.
An
IT'S 7:30.
DRIP
DRIP
Oh
IT'S RAINING.
SHOULD WE HEAD BACK?
YEAH
I'M GETTING HUNGRY.
Wah!
WE'D BETTER RUN!

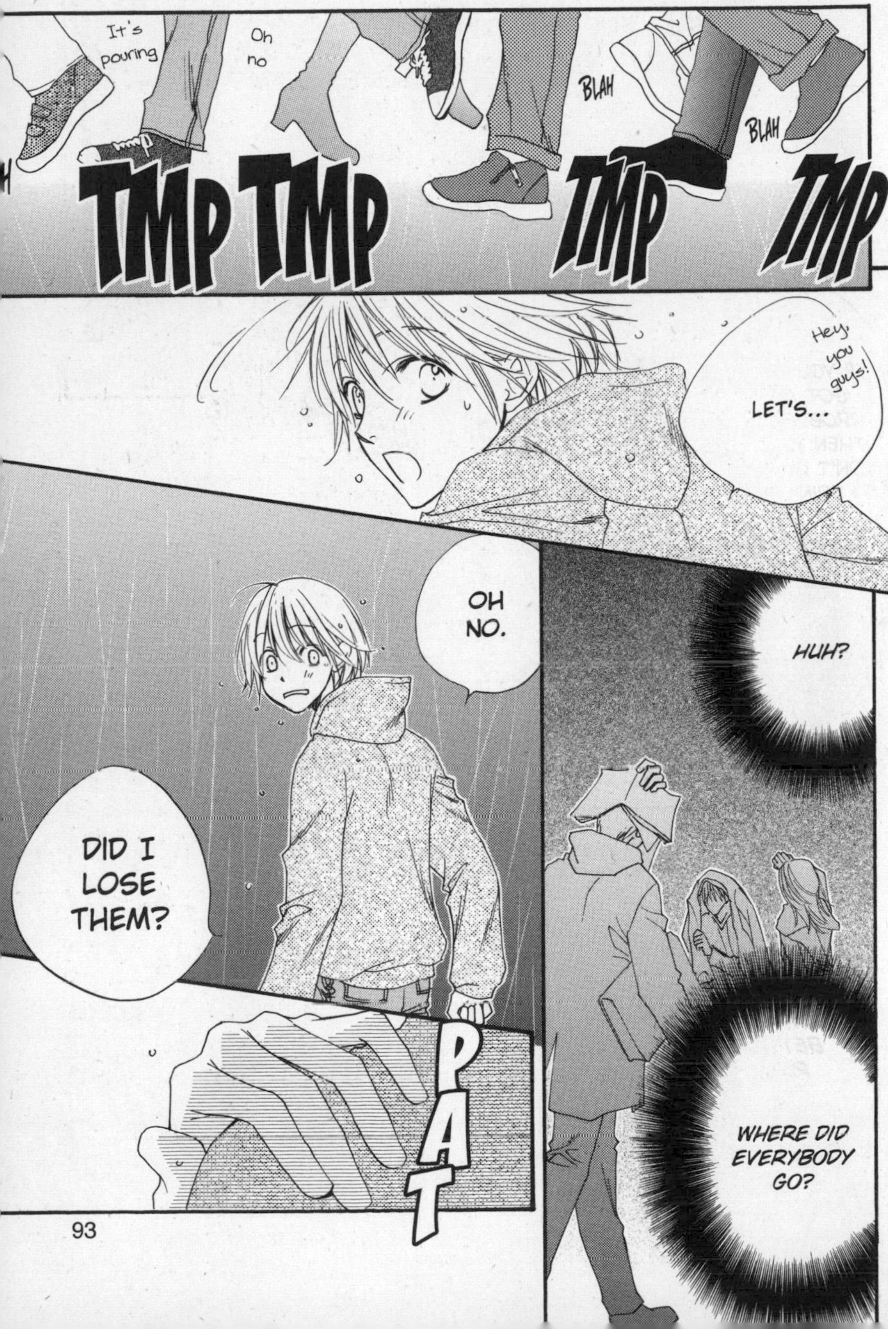
BLAH
BLAH
TMP
TMP
TMP TMP
Oh no
It's pouring
Hey, you guys!
LET'S...
HUH?
WHERE DID EVERYBODY GO?
OH NO.
DID I LOSE THEM?
PAT

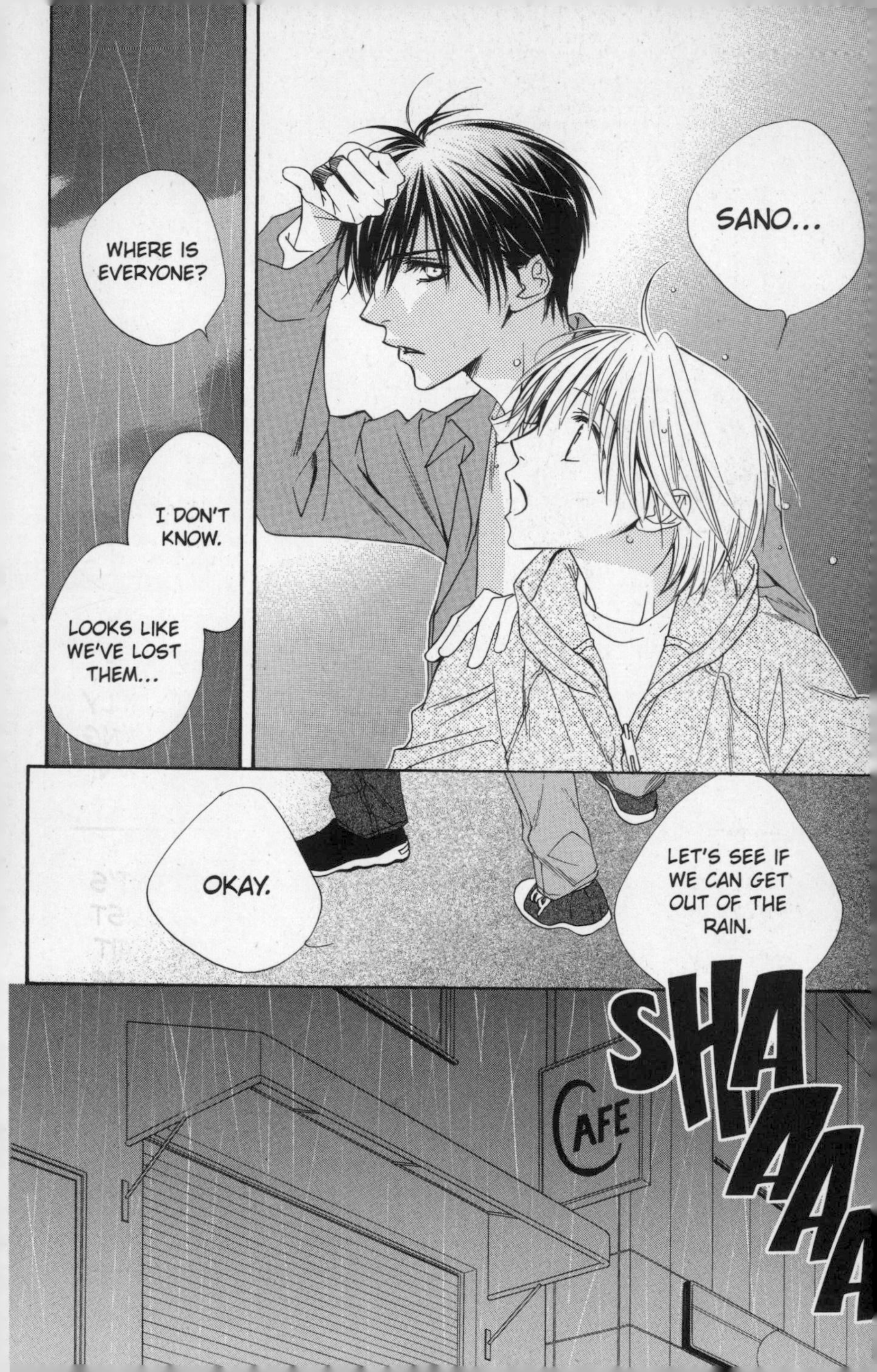
SANO...
WHERE IS EVERYONE?
I DON'T KNOW.
LOOKS LIKE WE'VE LOST THEM...
LET'S SEE IF WE CAN GET OUT OF THE RAIN.
OKAY.
SHAAAA
CAFE

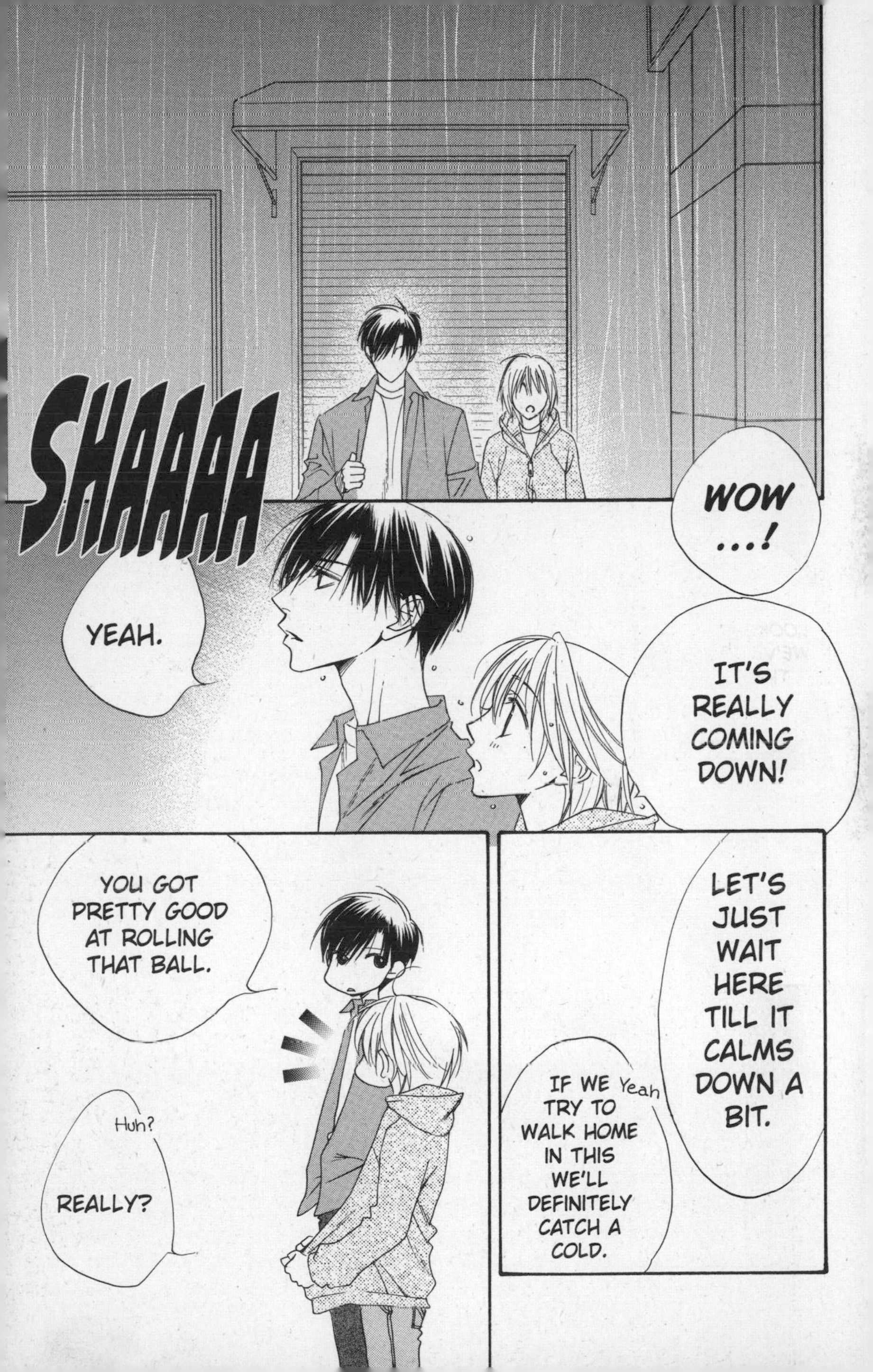
SHAAAA
WOW ...!
IT'S REALLY COMING DOWN!
YEAH.
LET'S JUST WAIT HERE TILL IT CALMS DOWN A BIT.
IF WE TRY TO WALK HOME IN THIS WE'LL DEFINITELY CATCH A COLD.
Yeah
YOU GOT PRETTY GOOD AT ROLLING THAT BALL.
Huh?
REALLY?

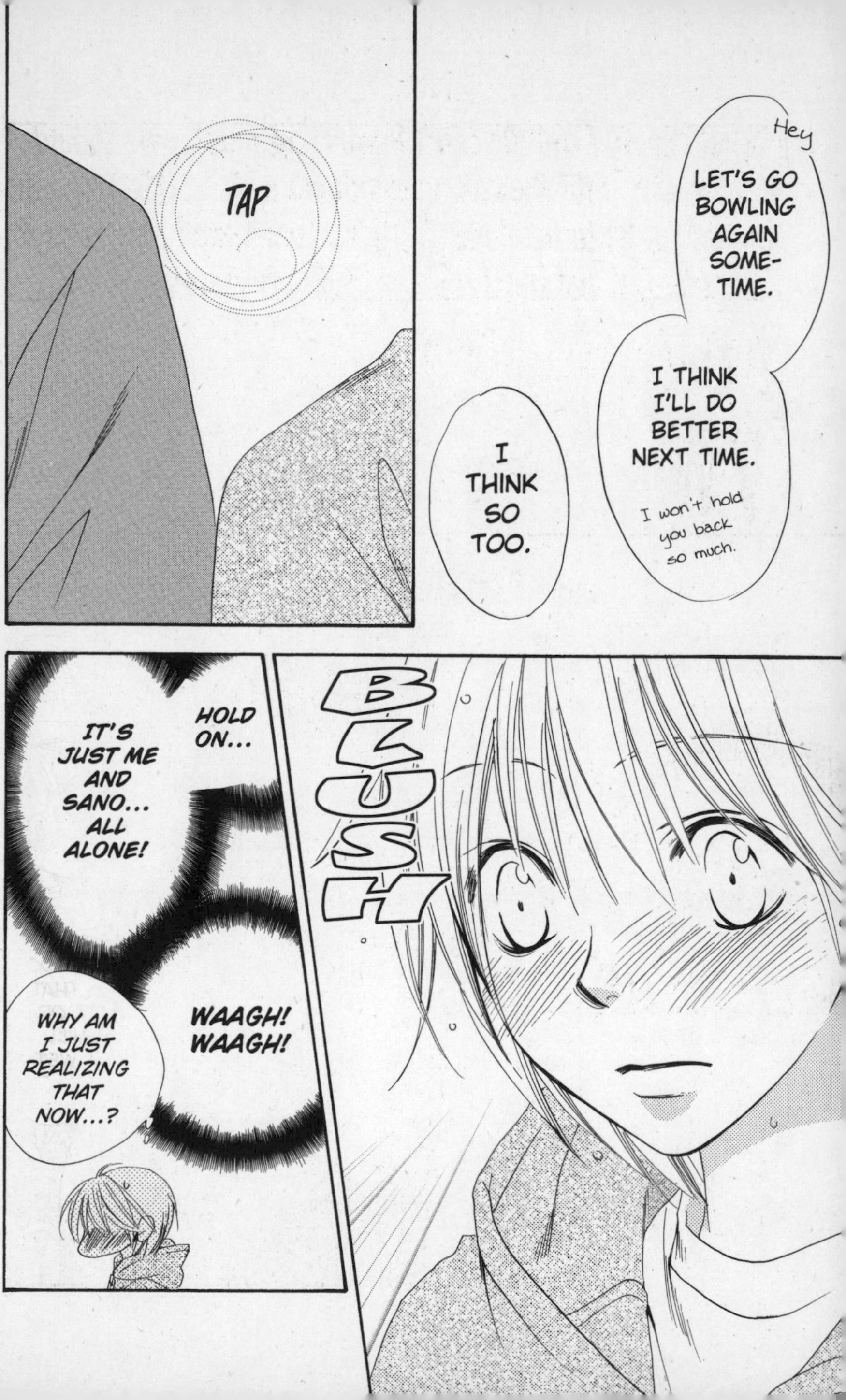
Hey
LET'S GO BOWLING AGAIN SOME-TIME.
I THINK I'LL DO BETTER NEXT TIME.
I won't hold you back so much.
I THINK SO TOO.
TAP
BLUSH
HOLD ON...
IT'S JUST ME AND SANO... ALL ALONE!
WAAGH! WAAGH!
WHY AM I JUST REALIZING THAT NOW...?

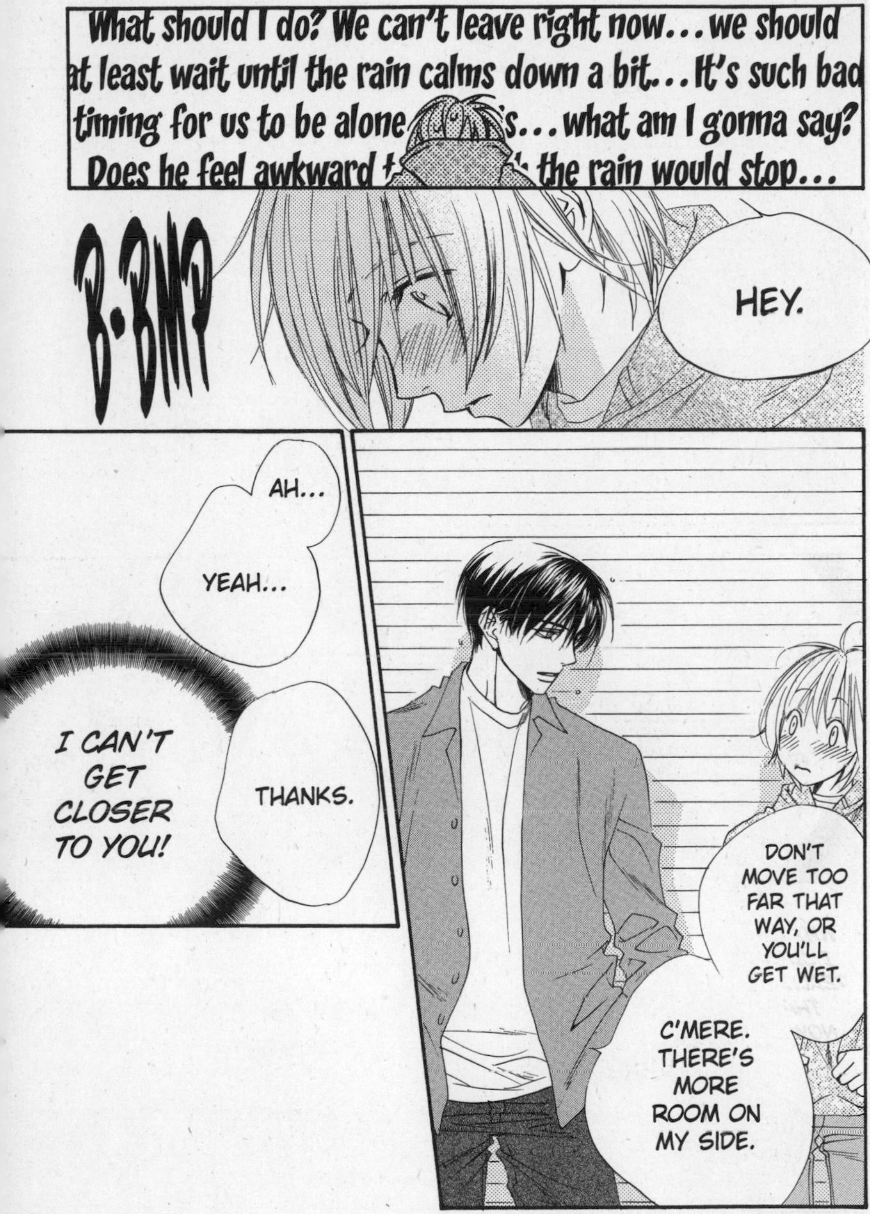
What should I do? We can't leave right now...we should at least wait until the rain calms down a bit...It's such bad timing for us to be alone
s...what am I gonna say? Does he feel awkward t
the rain would stop...
B-BMP
HEY.
DON'T MOVE TOO FAR THAT WAY, OR YOU'LL GET WET.
C'MERE. THERE'S MORE ROOM ON MY SIDE.
AH...
YEAH...
THANKS.
I CAN'T GET CLOSER TO YOU!

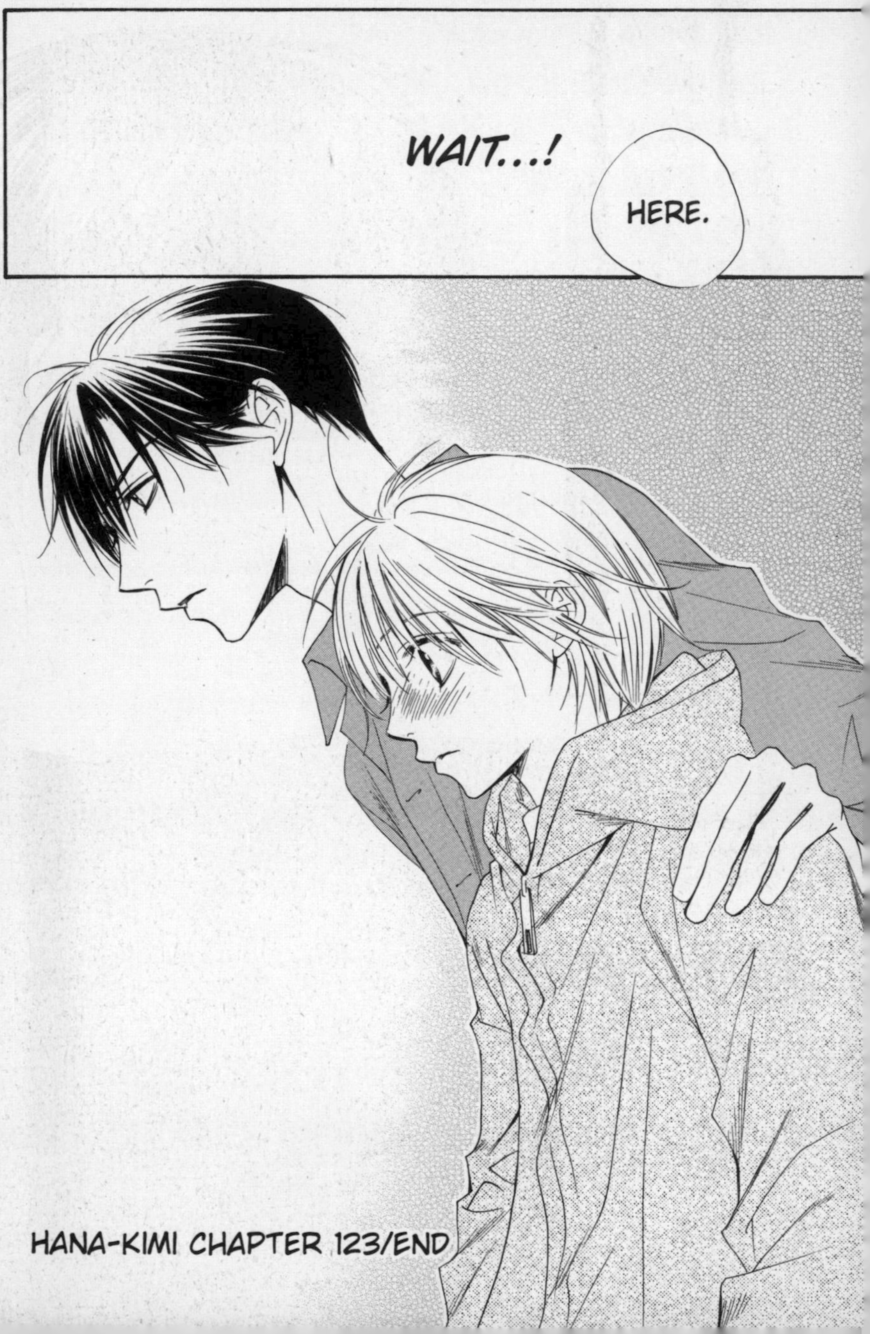
HERE.
WAIT...!
HANA-KIMI CHAPTER 123/END

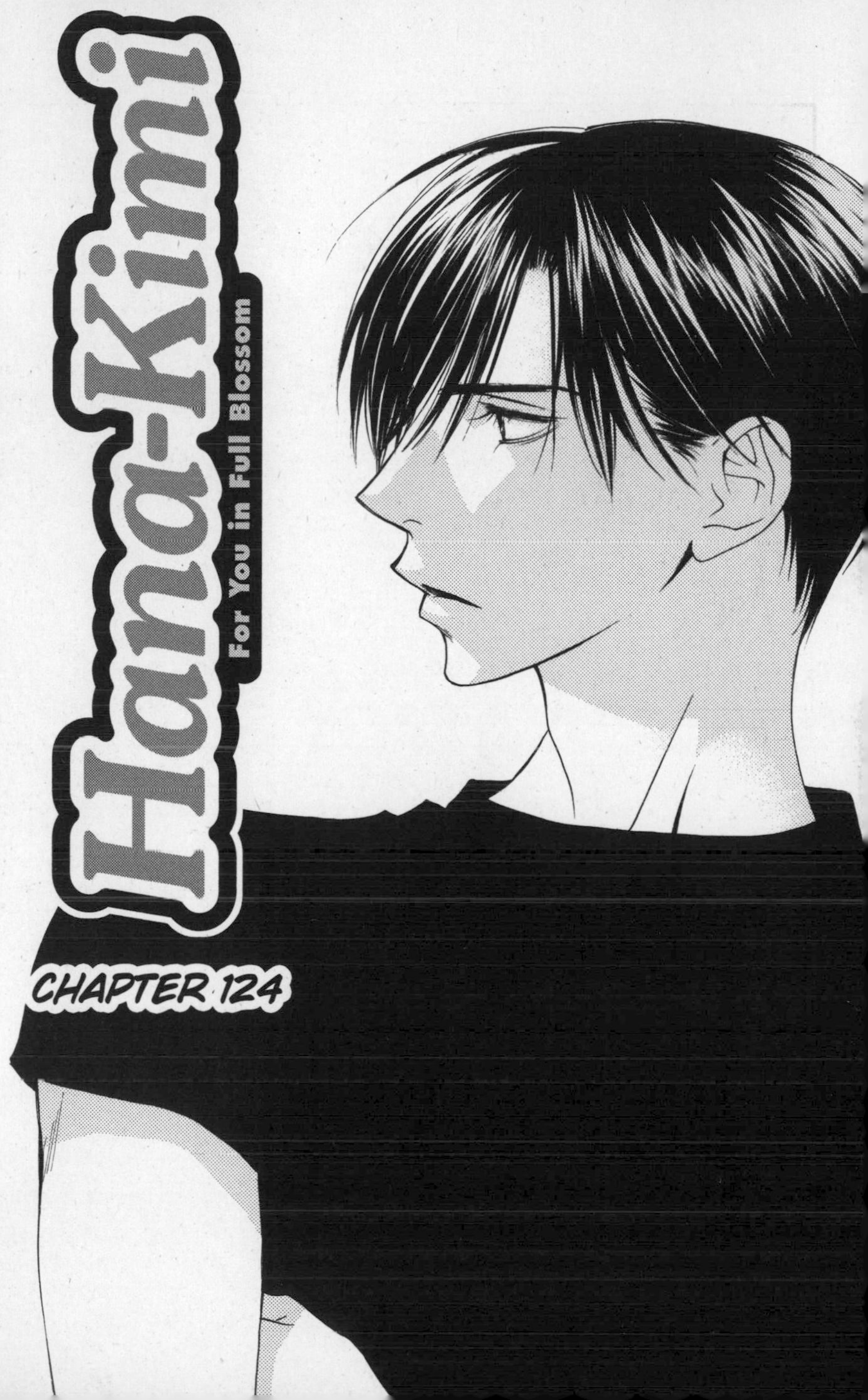
Hana-Kimi
For You in Full Blossom
CHAPTER 124

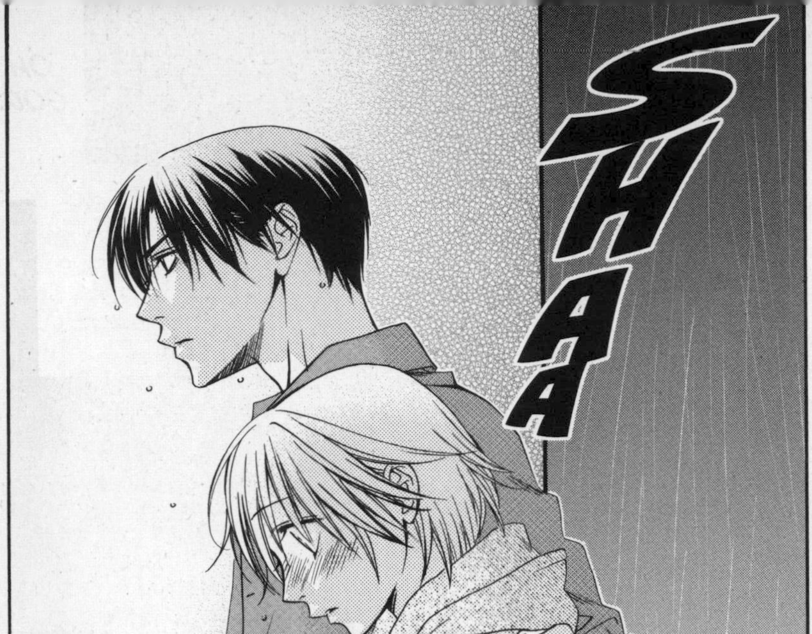
SHAAA

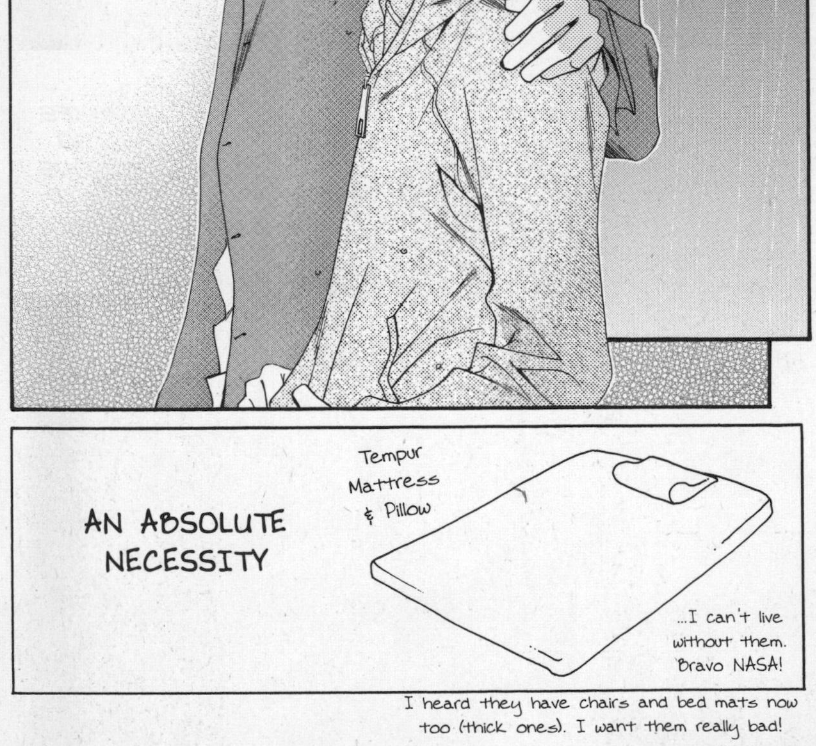
AN ABSOLUTE NECESSITY
Tempur Mattress & Pillow
...I can't live without them. Bravo NASA!

I heard they have chairs and bed mats now too (thick ones). I want them really bad!

OH GOD.
JUST BEING ALONE WITH SANO...
...MAKES ME SO NERVOUS I COULD DIE...
"DON'T MOVE TOO FAR THAT WAY, OR YOU'LL GET WET."
"C'MERE. THERE'S MORE ROOM ON MY SIDE."
WHAT'S WRONG WITH THIS SITUATION ...?

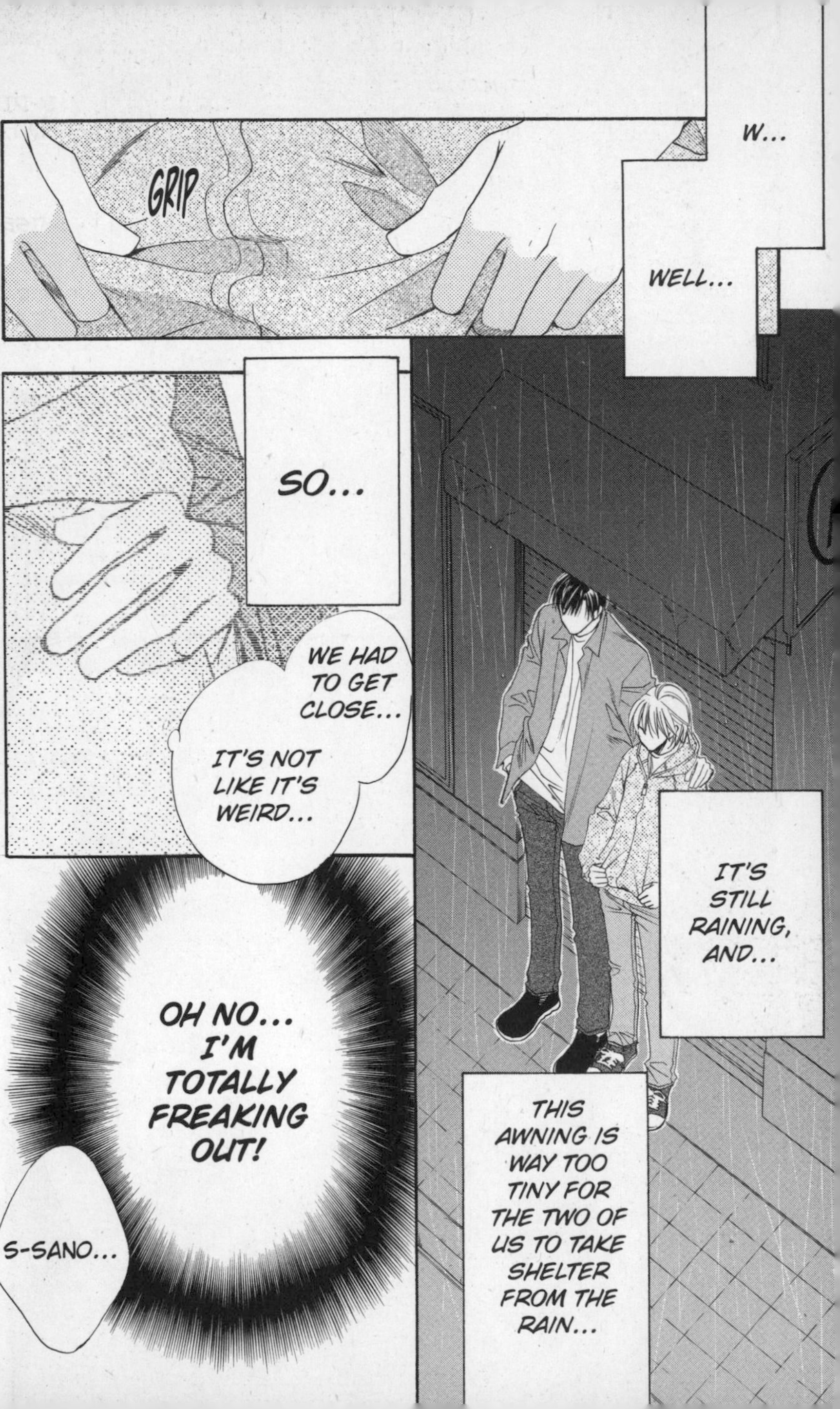
W...
WELL...
GRIP
IT'S STILL RAINING, AND...
THIS AWNING IS WAY TOO TINY FOR THE TWO OF US TO TAKE SHELTER FROM THE RAIN...
SO...
WE HAD TO GET CLOSE...
IT'S NOT LIKE IT'S WEIRD...
OH NO... I'M TOTALLY FREAKING OUT!
S-SANO...

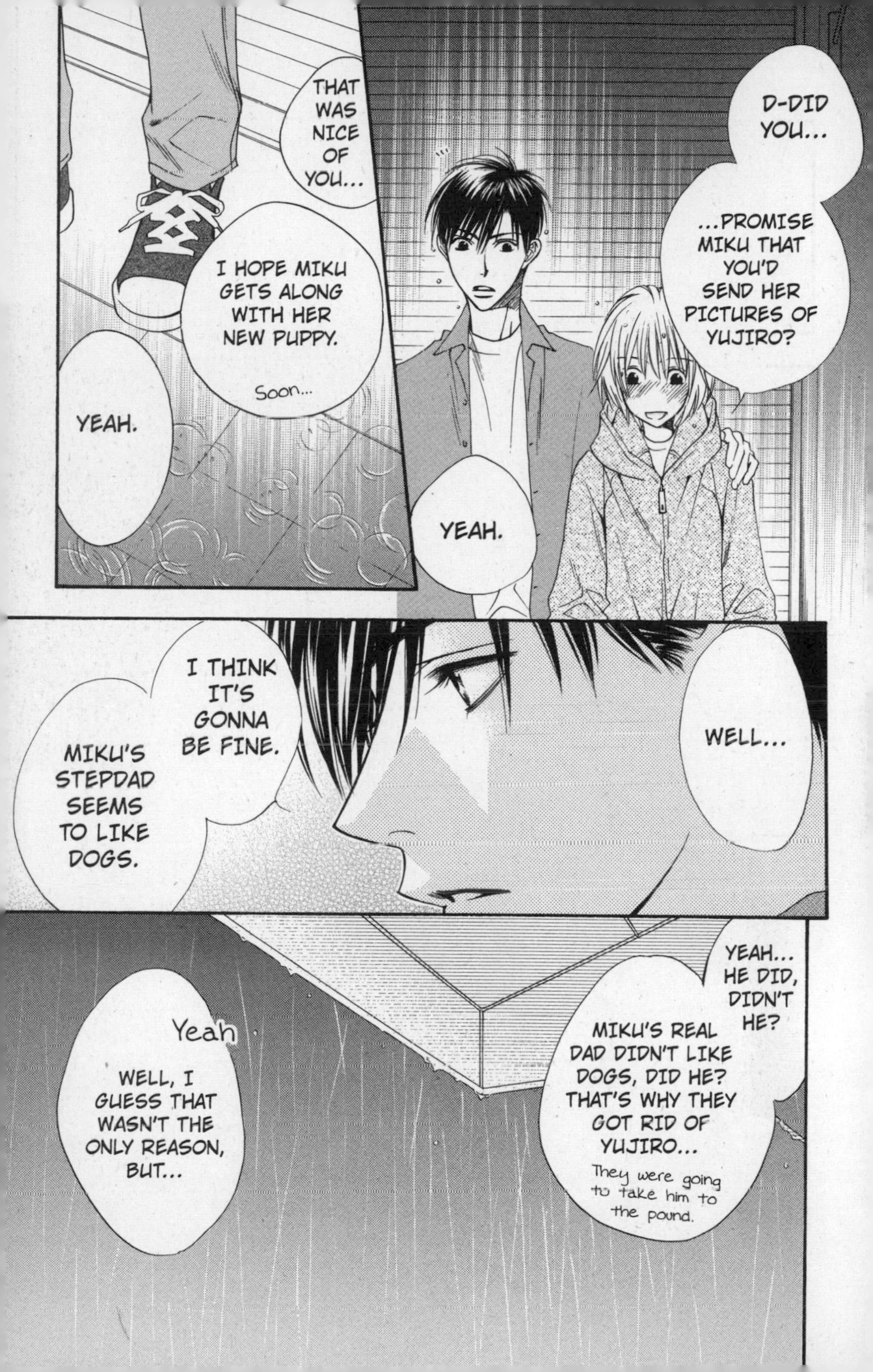
D-DID YOU...
...PROMISE MIKU THAT YOU'D SEND HER PICTURES OF YUJIRO?
YEAH.
THAT WAS NICE OF YOU...
I HOPE MIKU GETS ALONG WITH HER NEW PUPPY.
Soon...
YEAH.
WELL...
I THINK IT'S GONNA BE FINE.
MIKU'S STEPDAD SEEMS TO LIKE DOGS.
MIKU'S REAL DAD DIDN'T LIKE DOGS, DID HE? THAT'S WHY THEY GOT RID OF YUJIRO...
They were going to take him to the pound.
YEAH... HE DID, DIDN'T HE?
Yeah
WELL, I GUESS THAT WASN'T THE ONLY REASON, BUT...

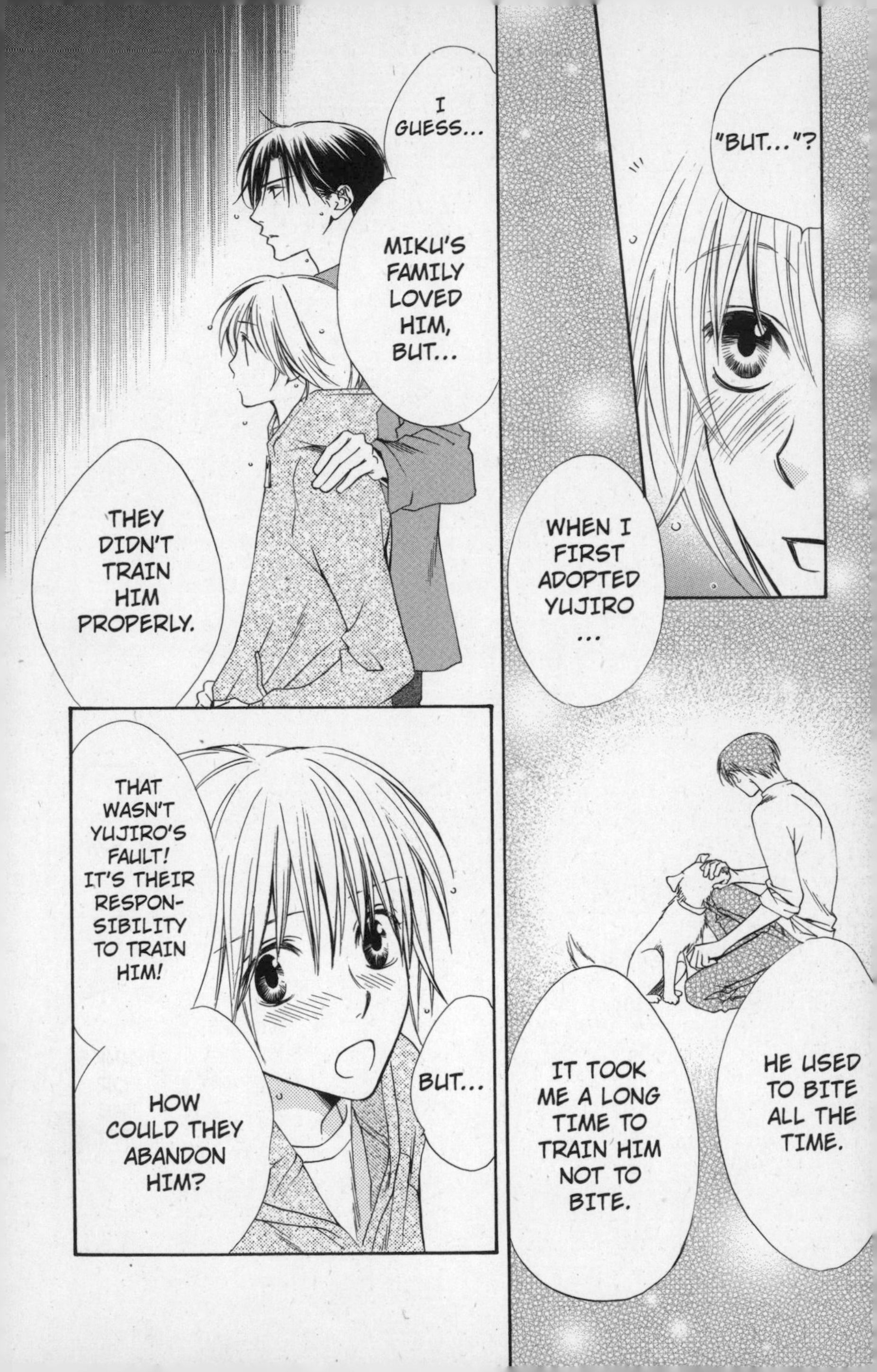
I GUESS...
MIKU'S FAMILY LOVED HIM, BUT...
THEY DIDN'T TRAIN HIM PROPERLY.
THAT WASN'T YUJIRO'S FAULT! IT'S THEIR RESPON-SIBILITY TO TRAIN HIM!
BUT...
HOW COULD THEY ABANDON HIM?
"BUT..."?
WHEN I FIRST ADOPTED YUJIRO ...
HE USED TO BITE ALL THE TIME.
IT TOOK ME A LONG TIME TO TRAIN HIM NOT TO BITE.

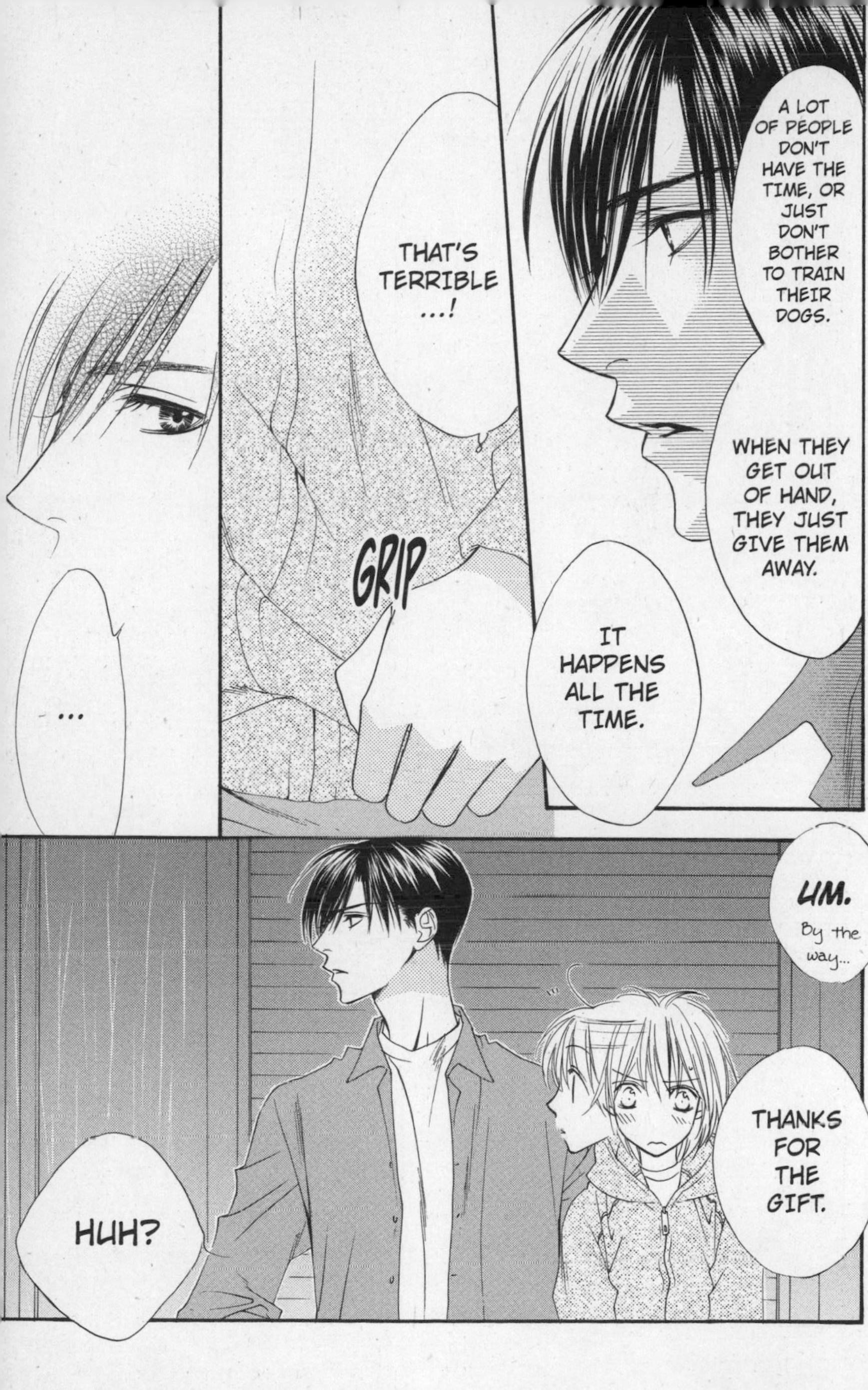
A LOT OF PEOPLE DON'T HAVE THE TIME, OR JUST DON'T BOTHER TO TRAIN THEIR DOGS.
WHEN THEY GET OUT OF HAND, THEY JUST GIVE THEM AWAY.
IT HAPPENS ALL THE TIME.
THAT'S TERRIBLE ...!
GRIP
...
UM.
By the way...
THANKS FOR THE GIFT.
HUH?

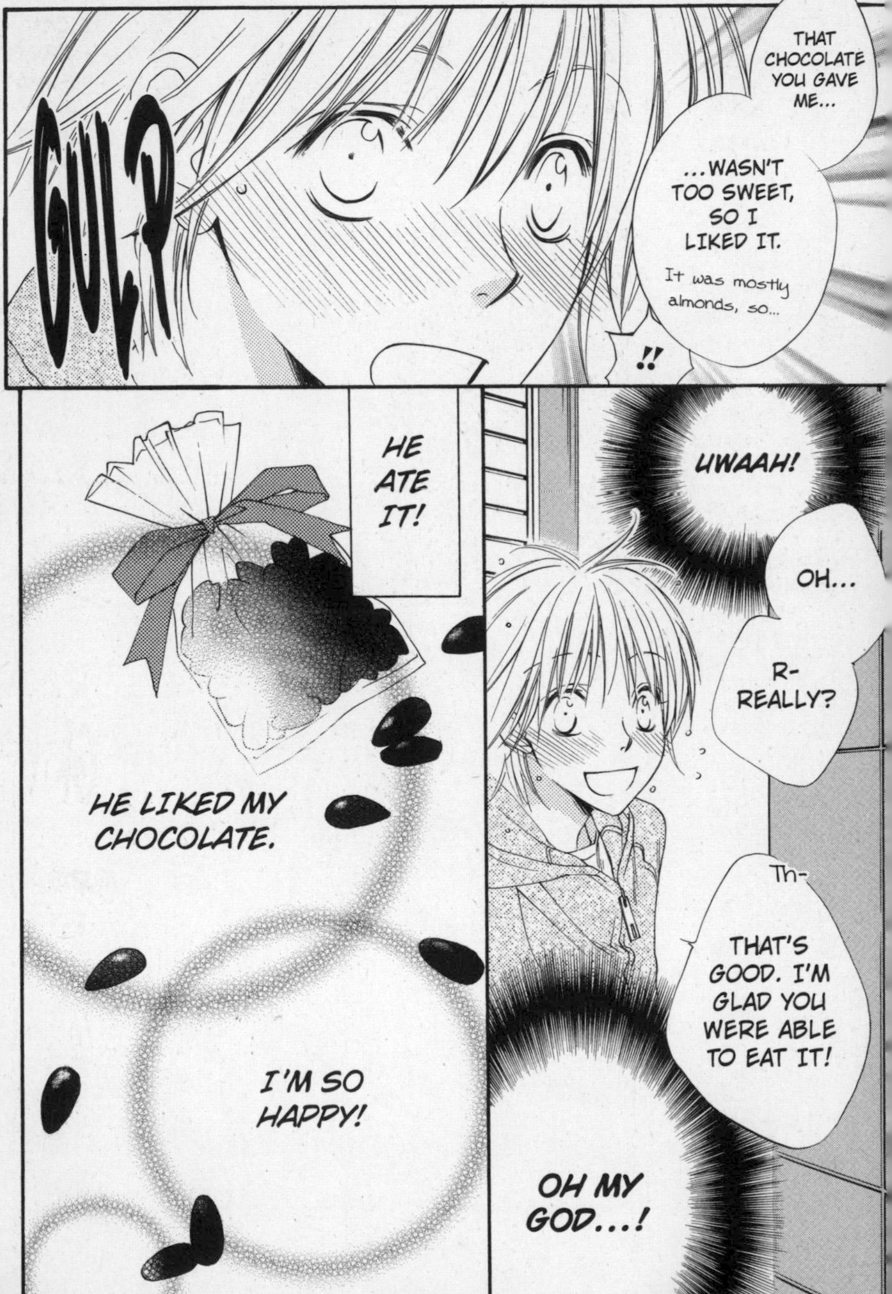
THAT CHOCOLATE YOU GAVE ME...
...WASN'T TOO SWEET, SO I LIKED IT.
It was mostly almonds, so...
!!
GULP
UWAAH!
OH...
R-REALLY?
Th-
THAT'S GOOD. I'M GLAD YOU WERE ABLE TO EAT IT!
OH MY GOD...!
HE ATE IT!
HE LIKED MY CHOCOLATE.
I'M SO HAPPY!

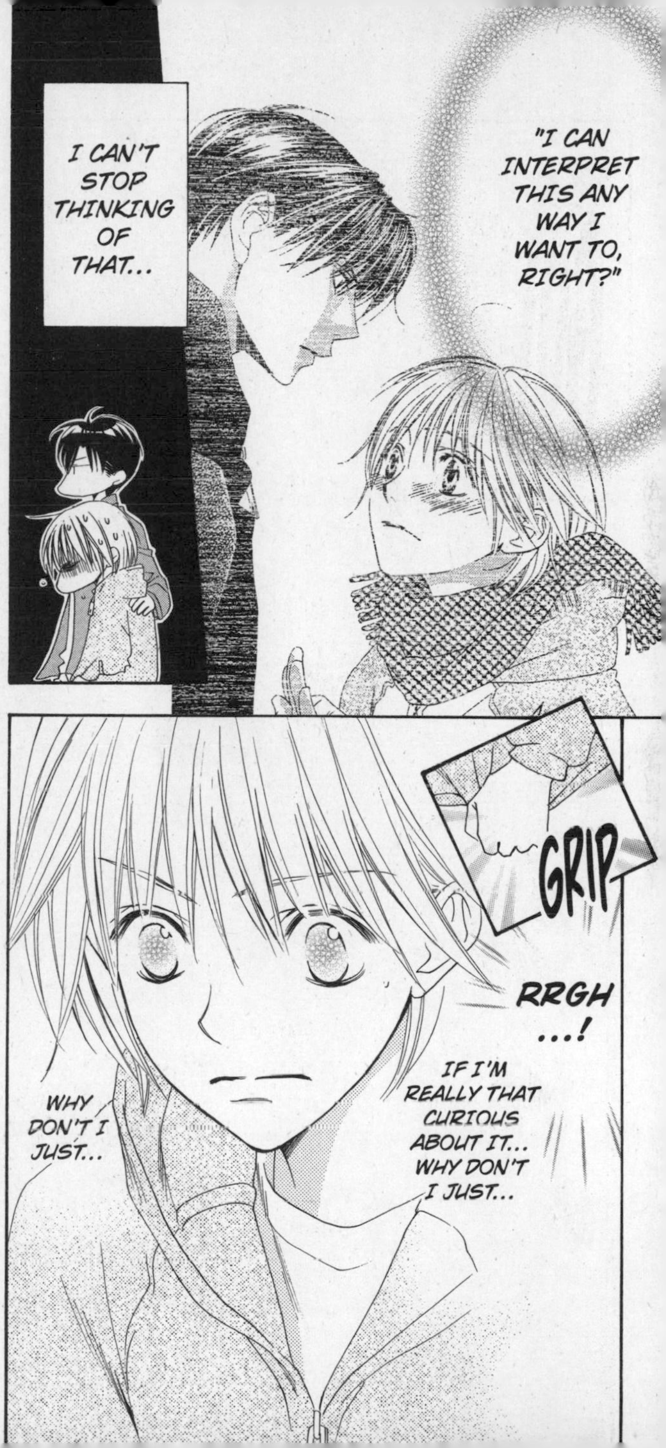
"I CAN INTERPRET THIS ANY WAY I WANT TO, RIGHT?"
I CAN'T STOP THINKING OF THAT...
GRIP
RRGH ...!
IF I'M REALLY THAT CURIOUS ABOUT IT... WHY DON'T I JUST...
WHY DON'T I JUST...

演

THEATER

"Elektra"

I went to see this Greek tragedy directed by Yukio Ninagawa. Shinobu Ootake played Elektra, and Junichi Okada from V6 played Elektra's brother Orestes! It was a tragedy, so the story was pretty heavy, but it was also very emotional! I cried so hard when the siblings reunited. The acting was amazing, but I was also moved by the wonderful directing! I'm not an expert, so I don't know anything about the details, but the set design and the wardrobe were fabulous! Especially at the end. After the lights faded out, the chorus group looked so beautiful onstage...it gave me goosebumps.

I had awesome seats, right in the second row! Orestes came onto the stage from the audience, so I was within about three feet of Okada! He looked so gorgeous live...

Sayaka Yamaguchi did a great job as Chrysothemis! I was really moved!

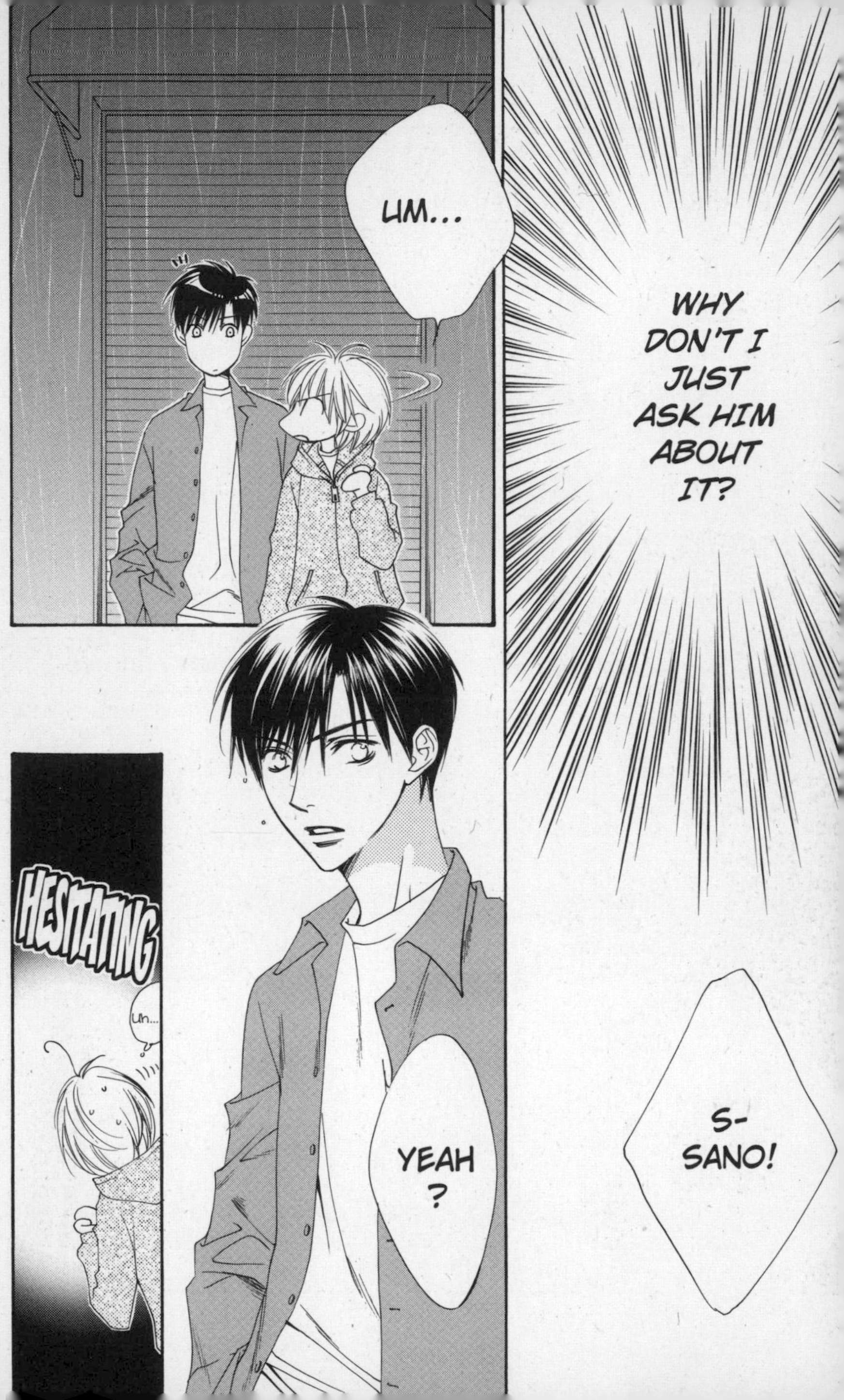
WHY DON'T I JUST ASK HIM ABOUT IT?
S-SANO!
UM...
YEAH?
HESITATING
Un...

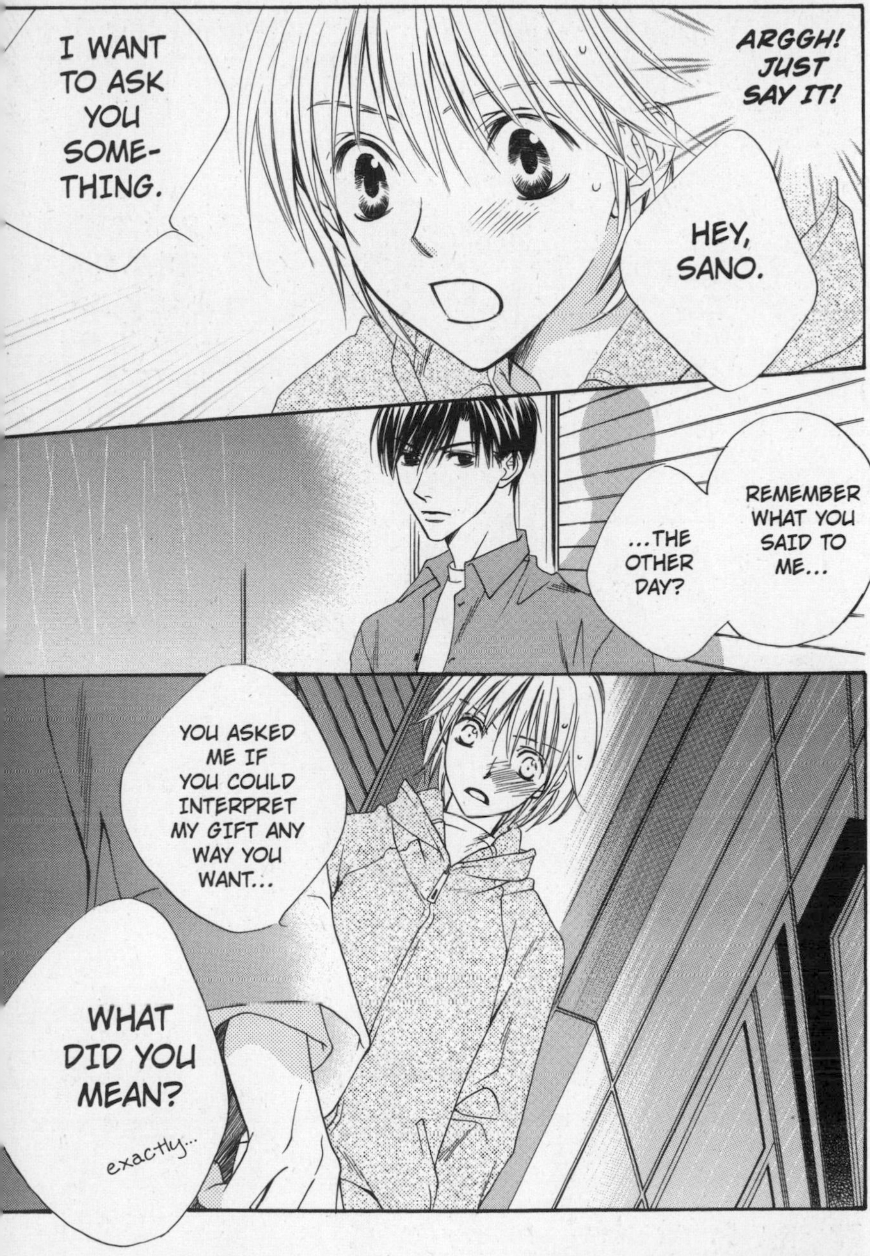
ARGGH! JUST SAY IT!
HEY, SANO.
I WANT TO ASK YOU SOME-THING.
REMEMBER WHAT YOU SAID TO ME...
...THE OTHER DAY?
YOU ASKED ME IF YOU COULD INTERPRET MY GIFT ANY WAY YOU WANT...
WHAT DID YOU MEAN?
exactly...

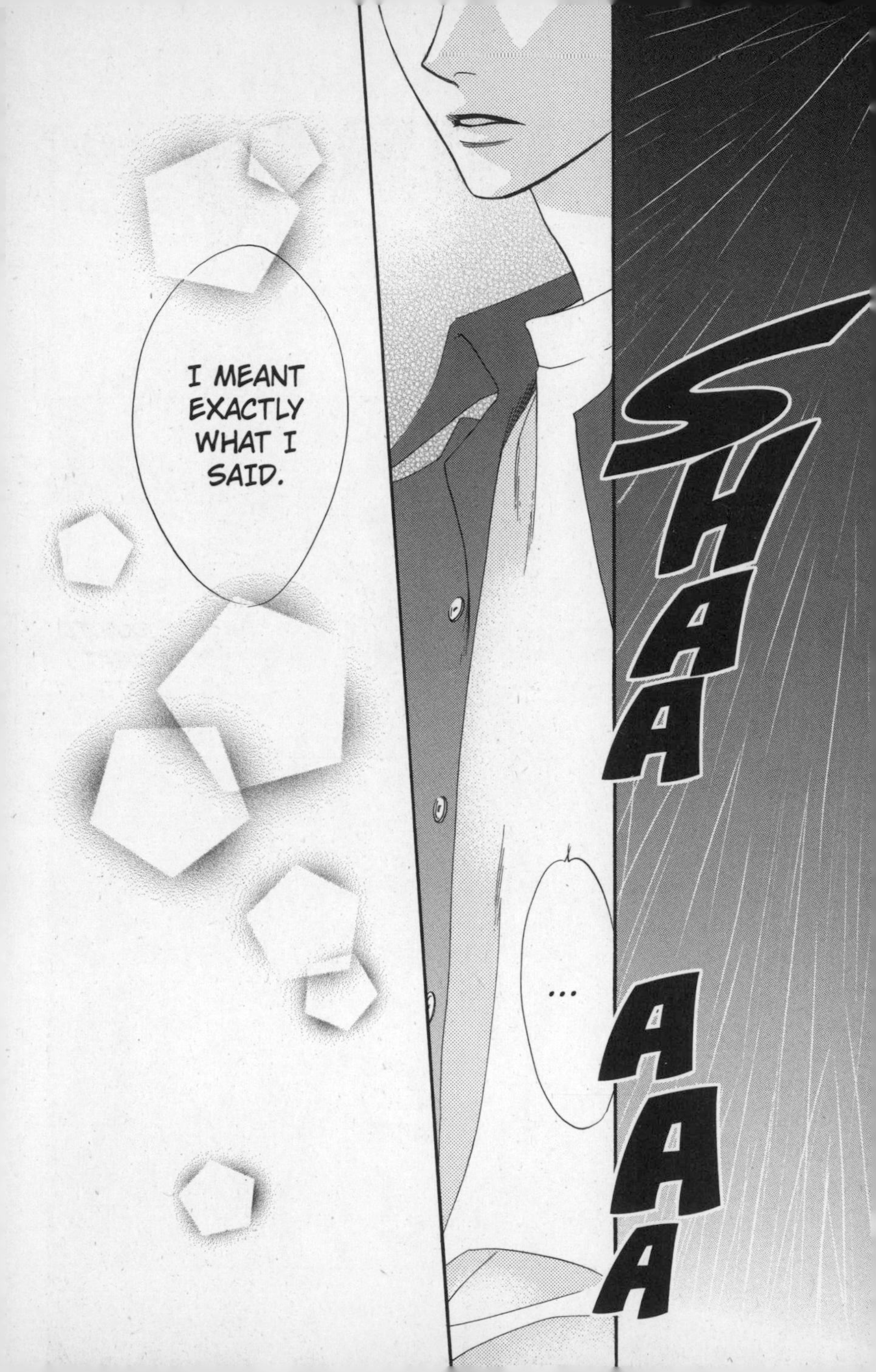
SHAAAA
AAAA
...
I MEANT EXACTLY WHAT I SAID.

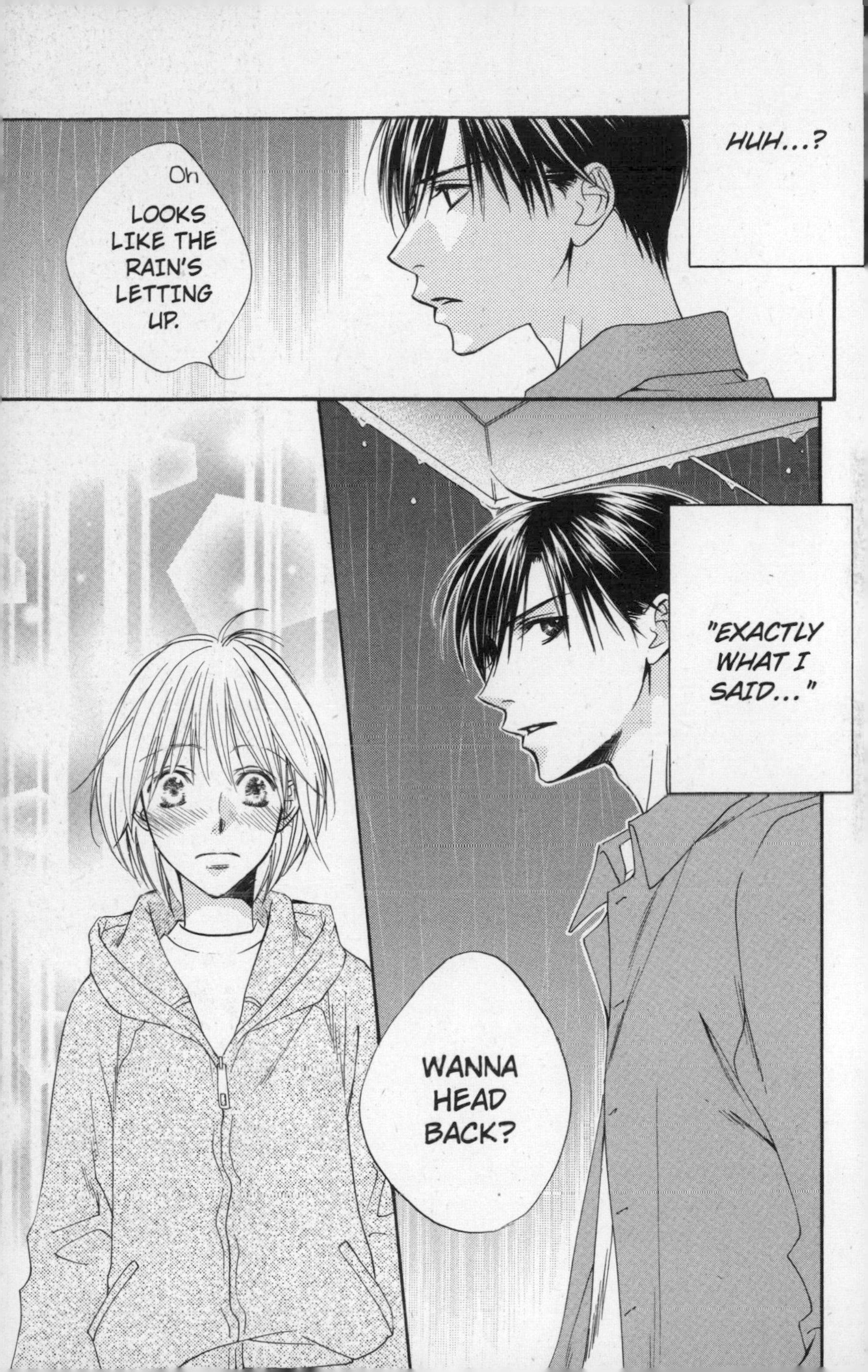
HUH...?
Oh LOOKS LIKE THE RAIN'S LETTING UP.
"EXACTLY WHAT I SAID..."
WANNA HEAD BACK?

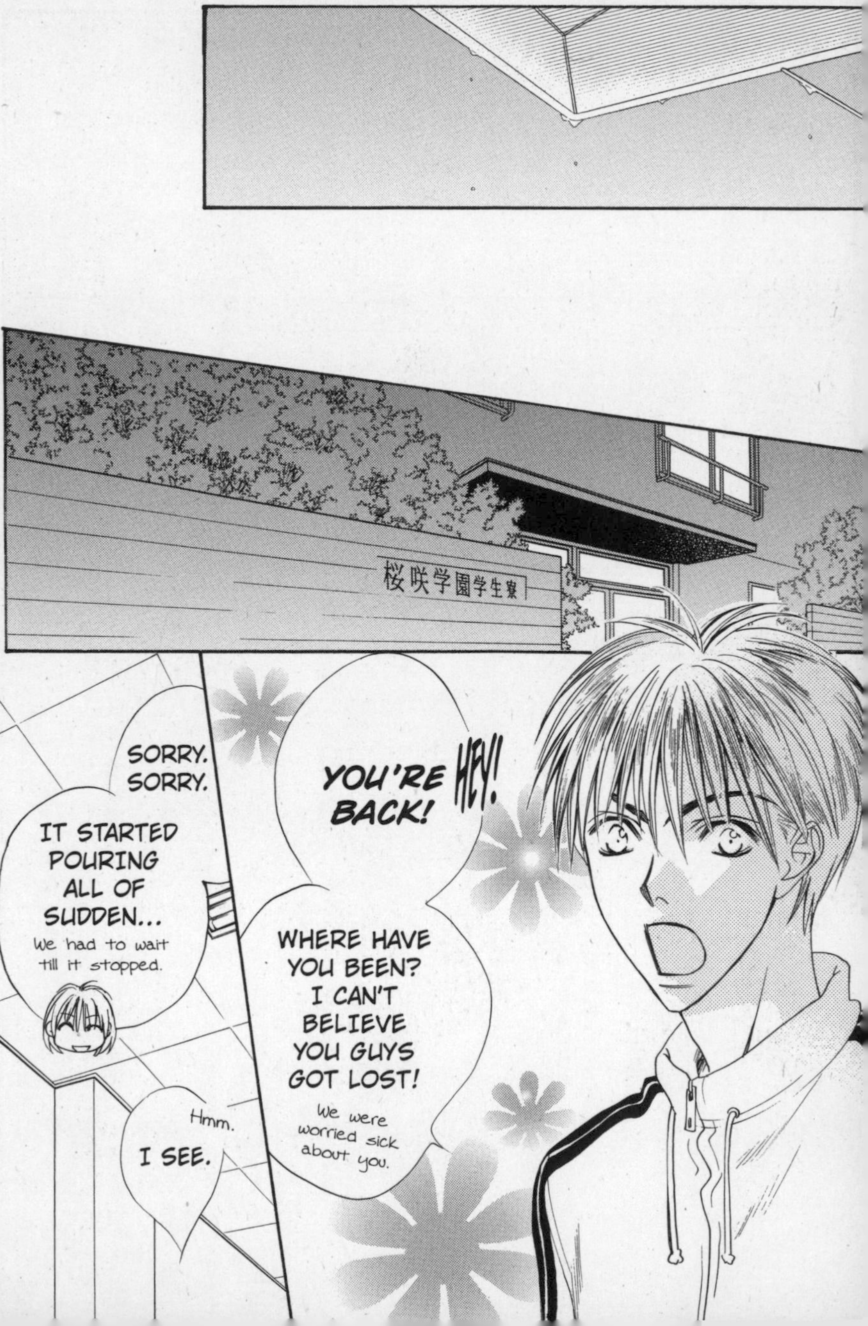
桜咲学園学生寮
HEY!
YOU'RE BACK!
WHERE HAVE YOU BEEN? I CAN'T BELIEVE YOU GUYS GOT LOST!
We were worried sick about you.
SORRY. SORRY.
IT STARTED POURING ALL OF SUDDEN...
We had to wait till it stopped.
Hmm.
I SEE.

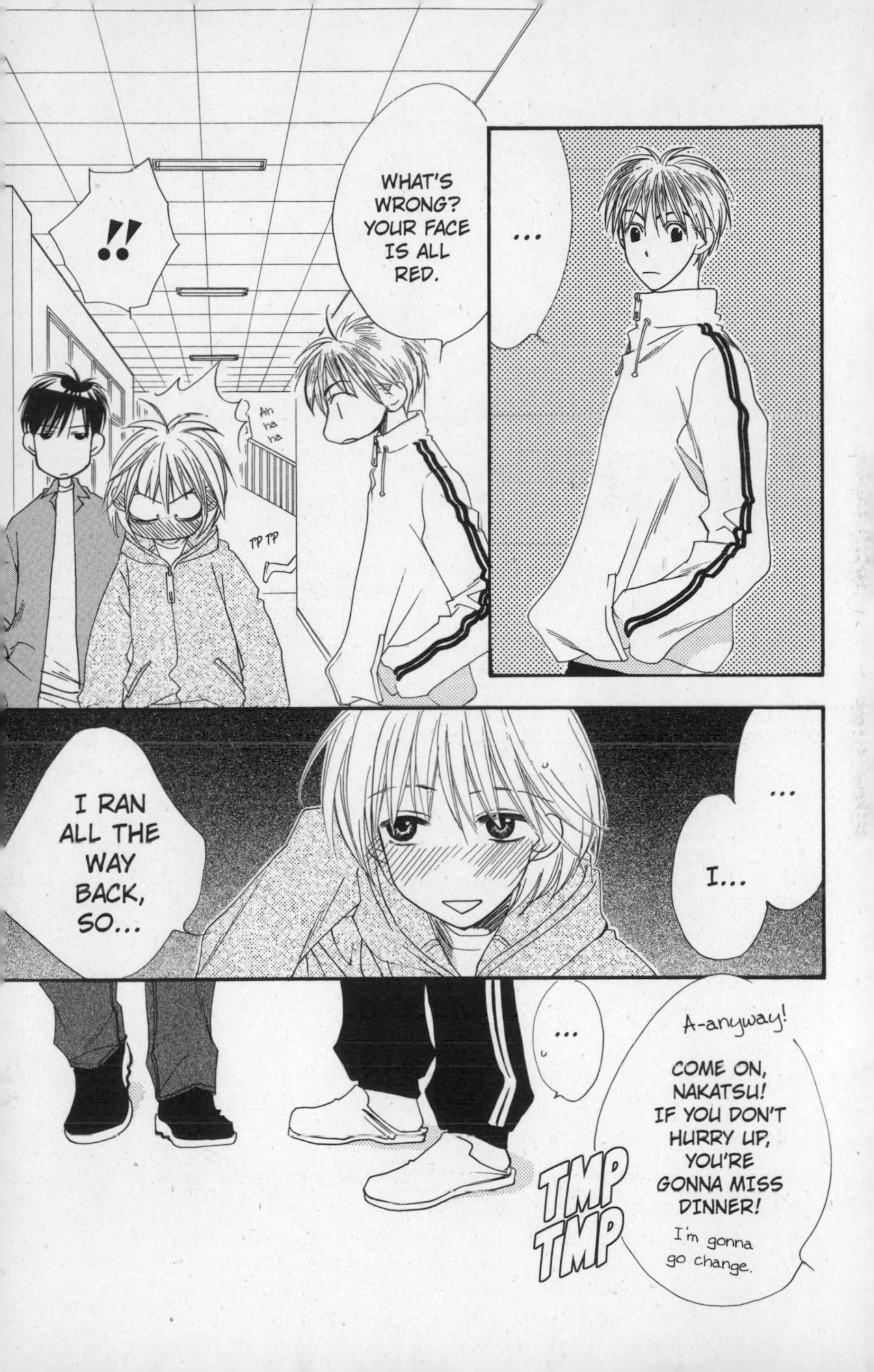
...
WHAT'S WRONG? YOUR FACE IS ALL RED.
!!
Ah ha ha
TP TP
...
I...
I RAN ALL THE WAY BACK, SO...
A-anyway!
COME ON, NAKATSU! IF YOU DON'T HURRY UP, YOU'RE GONNA MISS DINNER!
I'm gonna go change.
TMP TMP
...

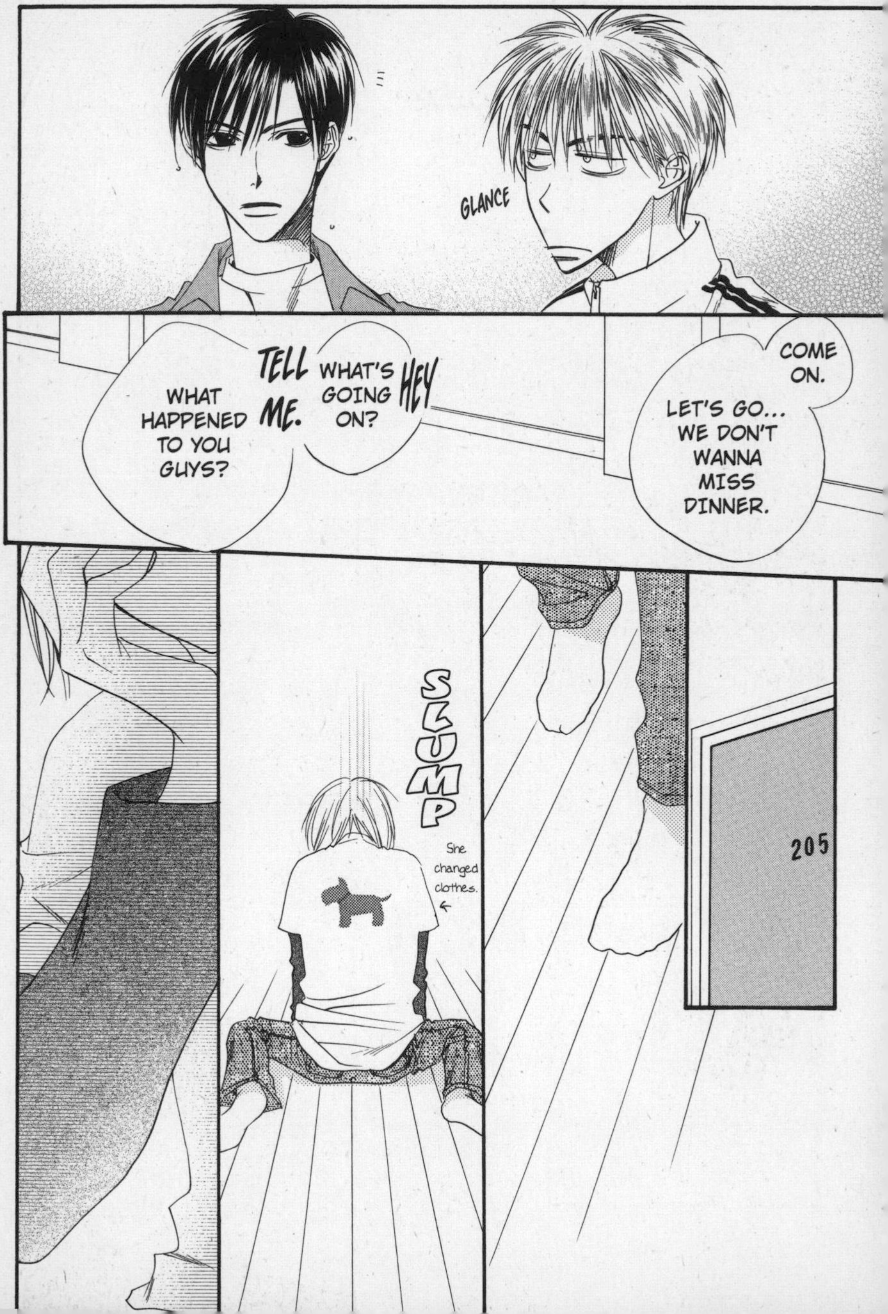
GLANCE
COME ON. LET'S GO... WE DON'T WANNA MISS DINNER.
HEY
WHAT'S GOING ON?
TELL ME.
WHAT HAPPENED TO YOU GUYS?
205
SLUMP
She changed clothes.

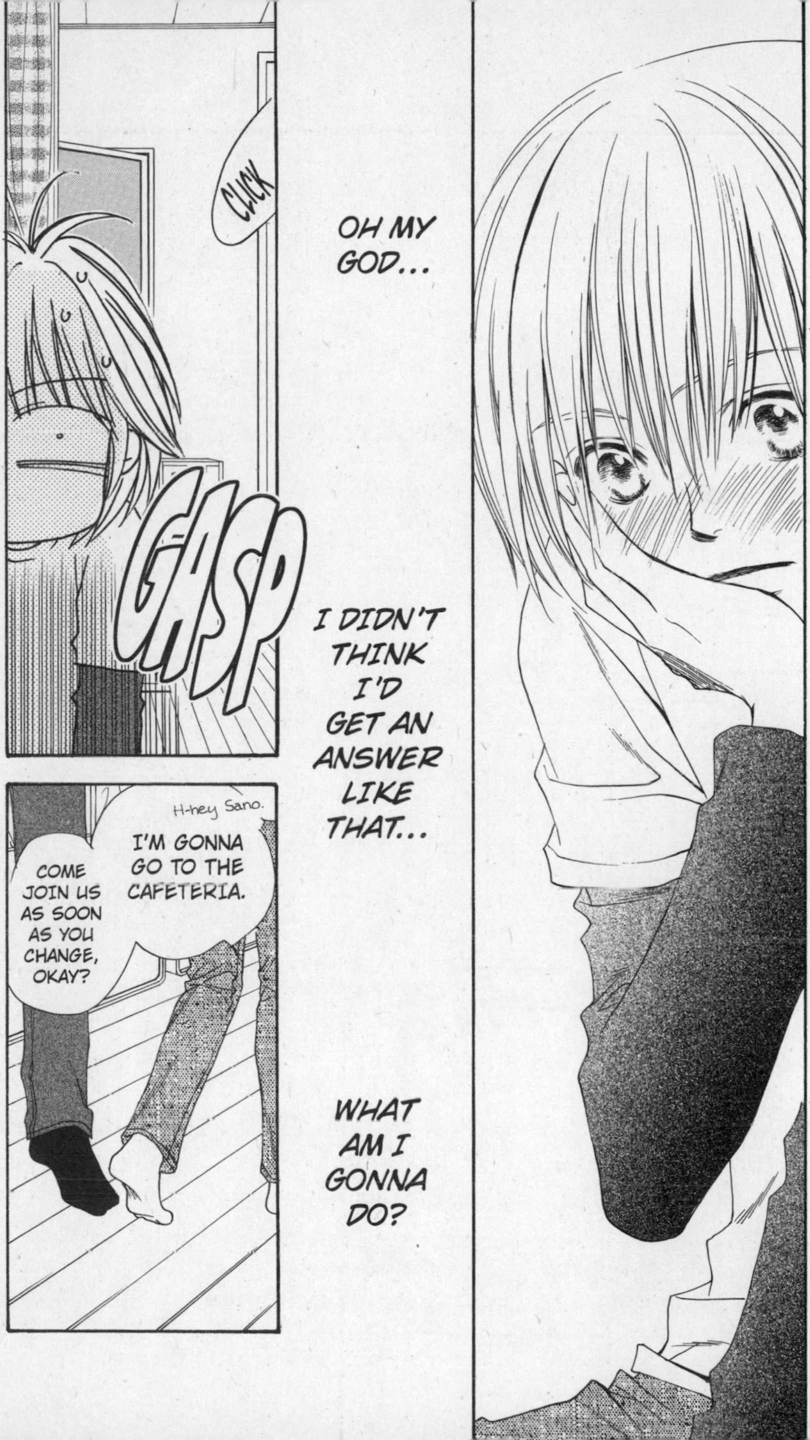
OH MY GOD...
I DIDN'T THINK I'D GET AN ANSWER LIKE THAT...
WHAT AM I GONNA DO?
CLICK
GASP
H-hey Sano.
I'M GONNA GO TO THE CAFETERIA.
COME JOIN US AS SOON AS YOU CHANGE, OKAY?

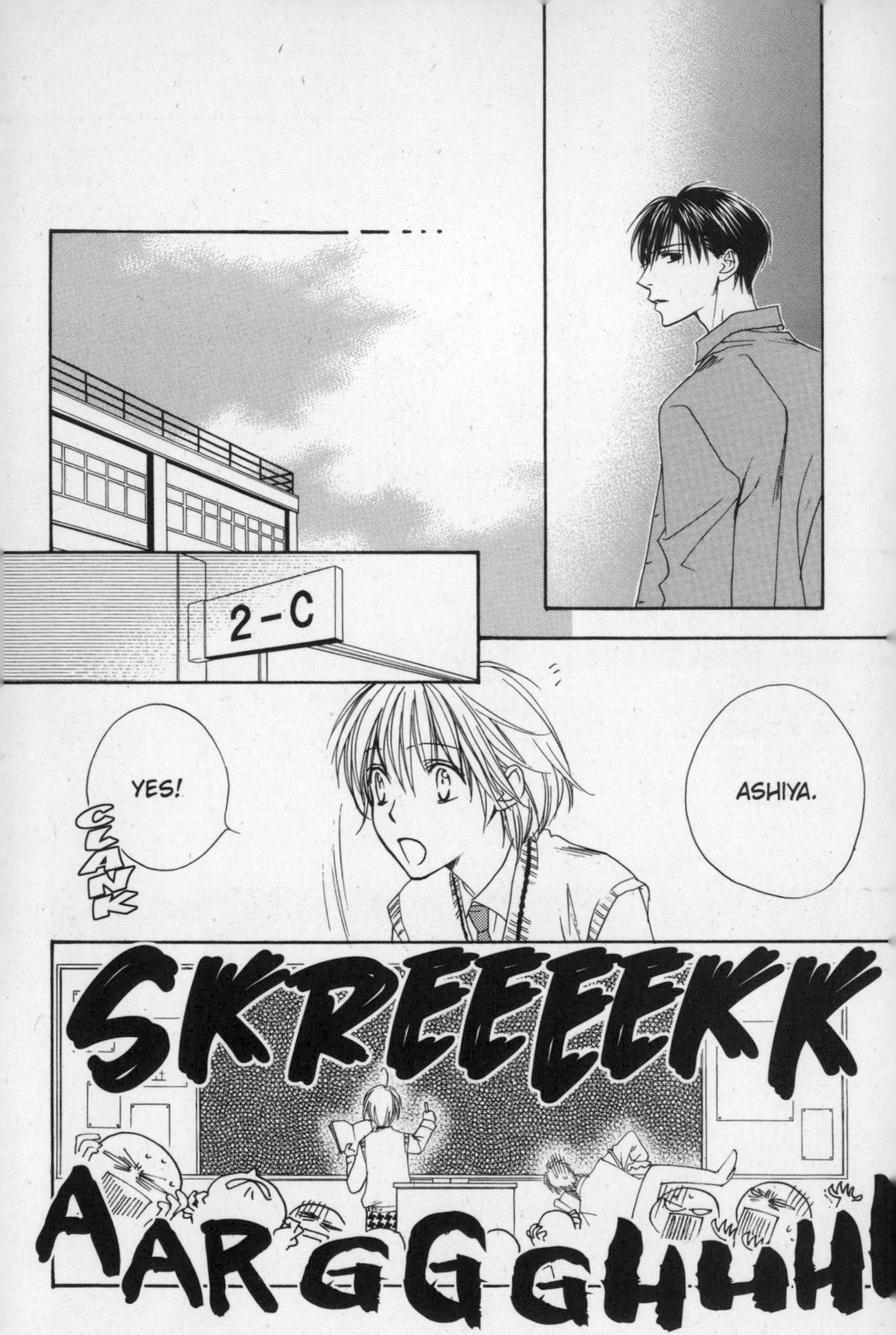
2-C
ASHIYA.
YES!
CLANK
SKREEEEKK
AARGGGHHH

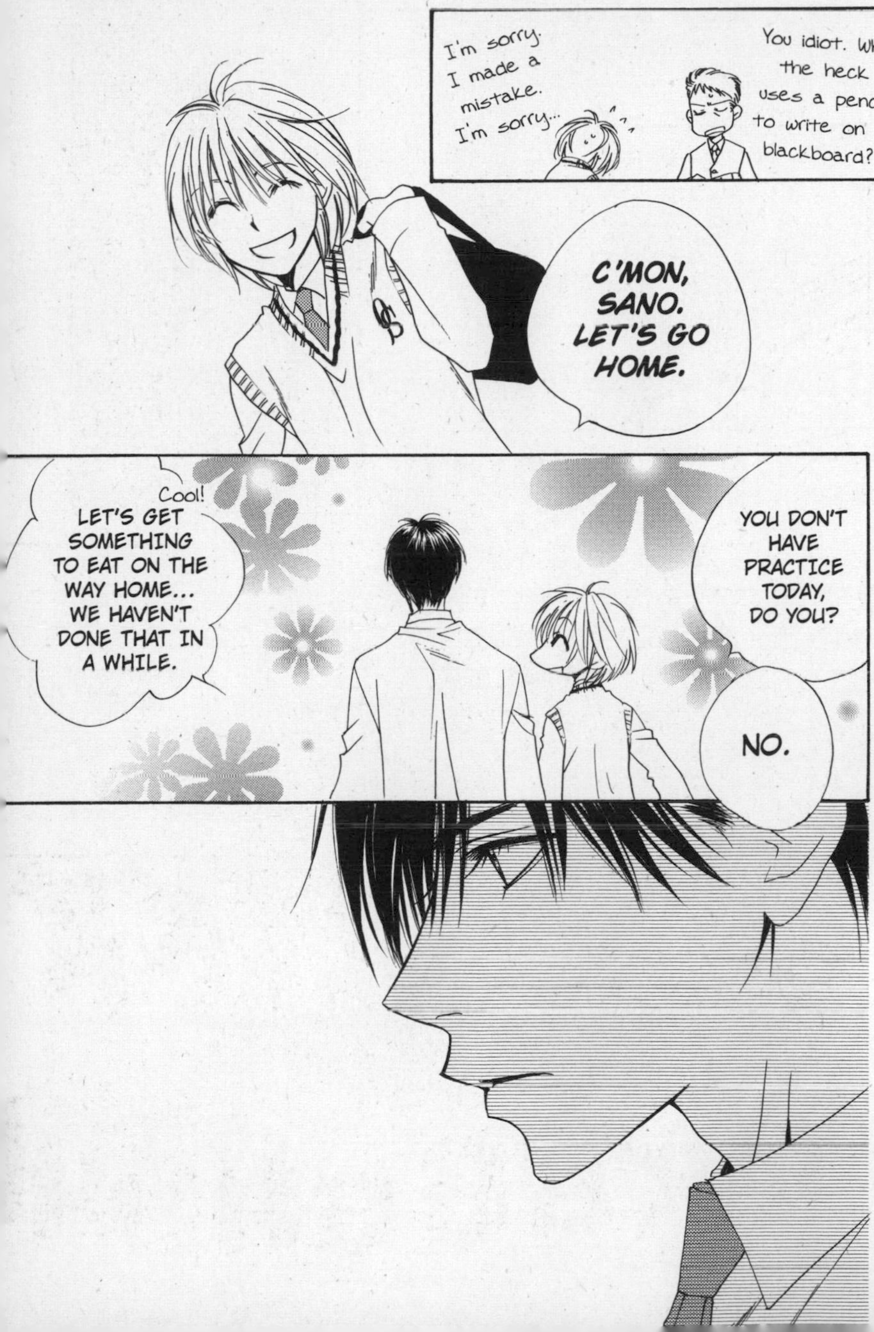
You idiot. Who the heck uses a pencil to write on a blackboard?
I'm sorry. I made a mistake. I'm sorry...
C'MON, SANO. LET'S GO HOME.
YOU DON'T HAVE PRACTICE TODAY, DO YOU?
NO.
Cool!
LET'S GET SOMETHING TO EAT ON THE WAY HOME... WE HAVEN'T DONE THAT IN A WHILE.

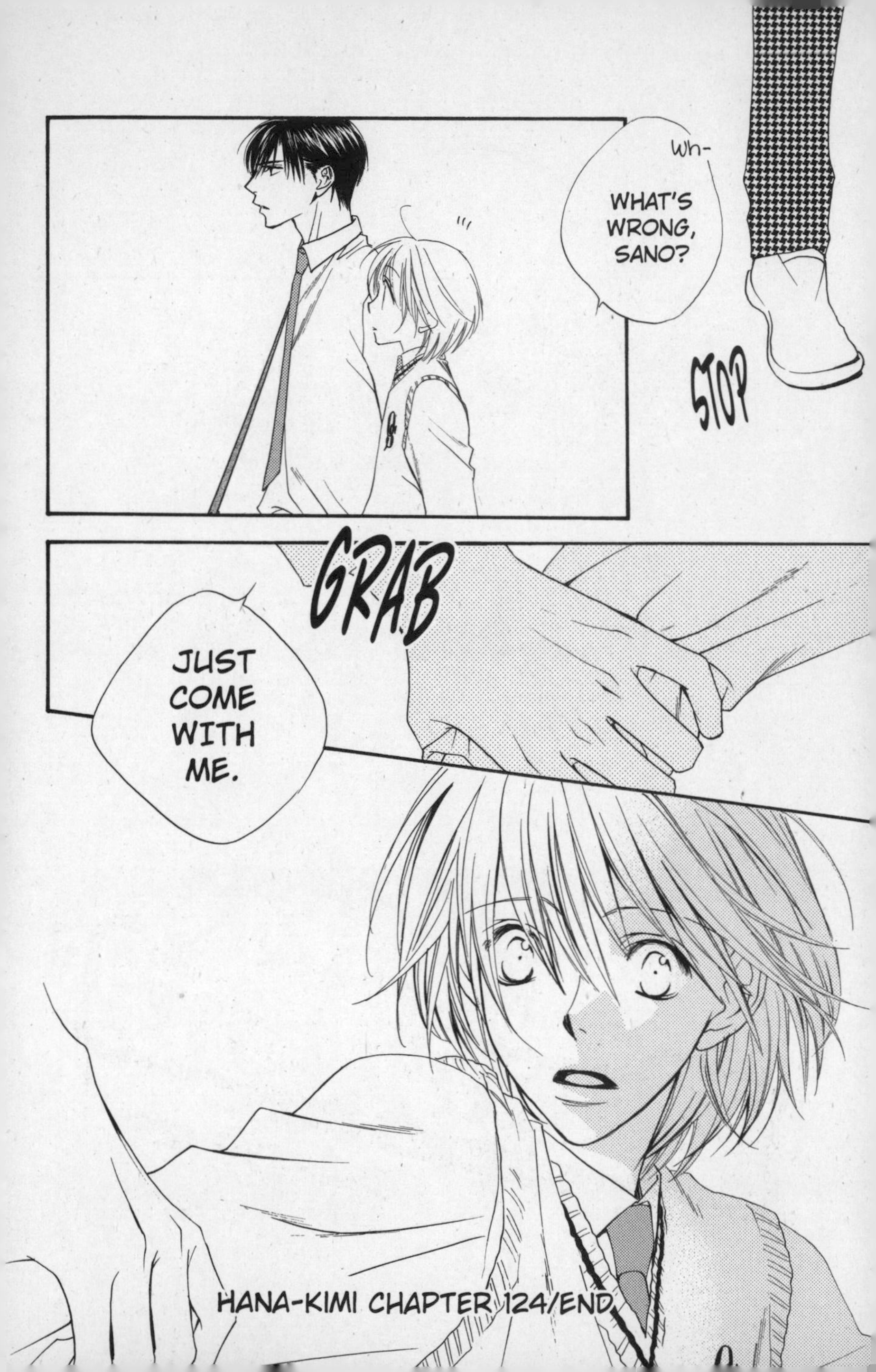
STOP
Wh-
WHAT'S WRONG, SANO?
GRAB
JUST COME WITH ME.
HANA-KIMI CHAPTER 124/END

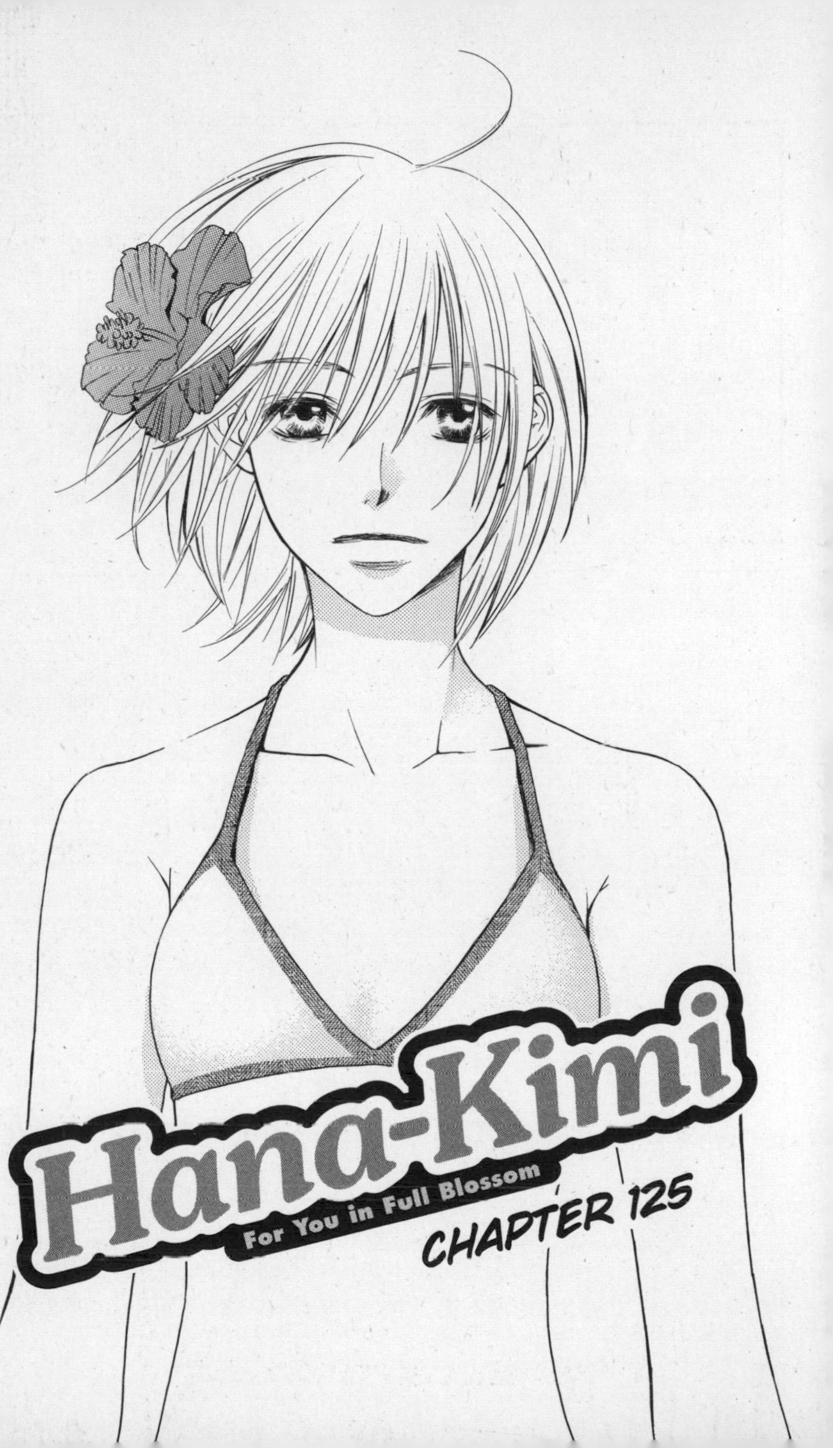
Hana-Kimi
For You in Full Blossom
CHAPTER 125

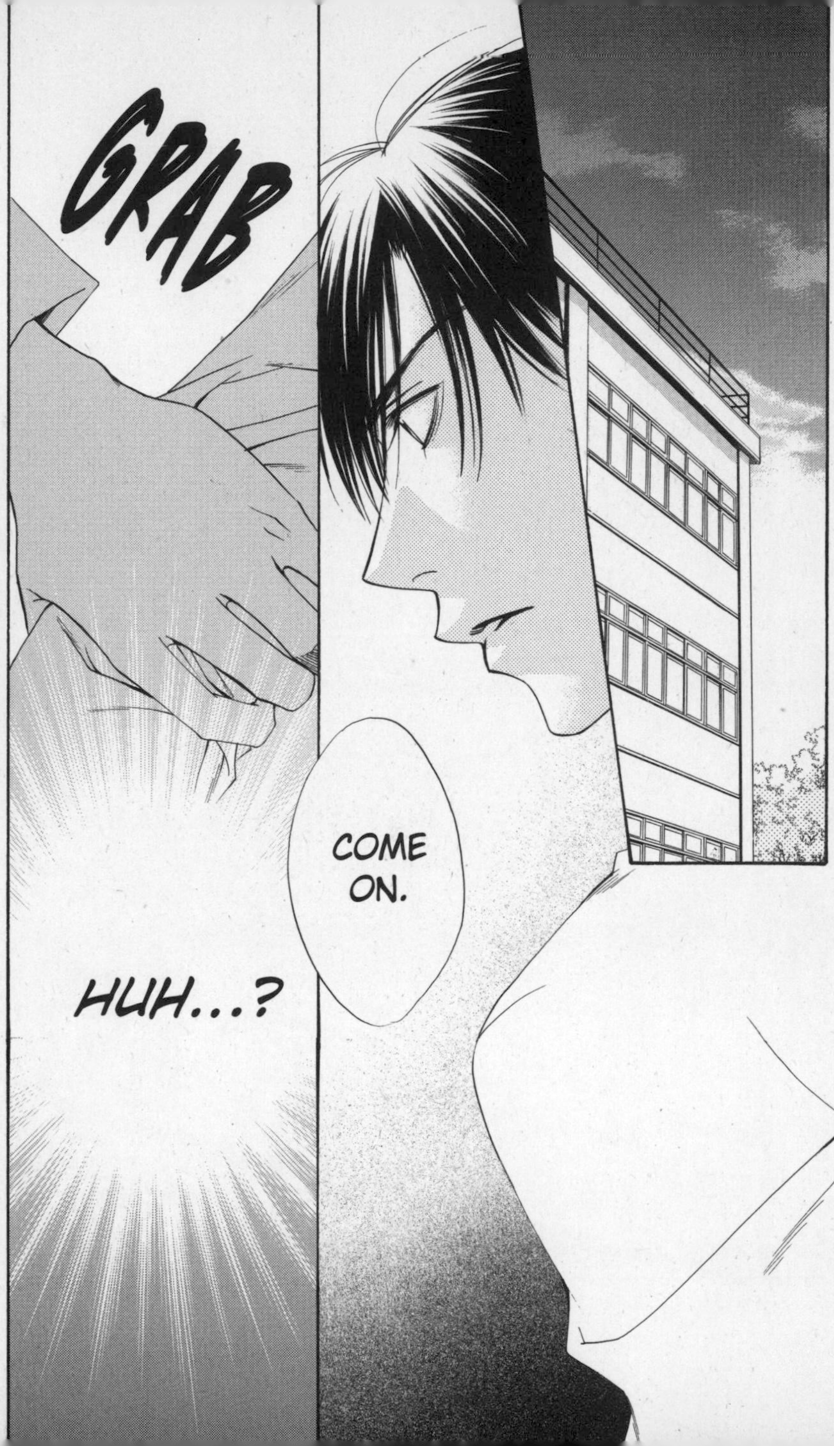
COME ON.
GRAB
HUH...?

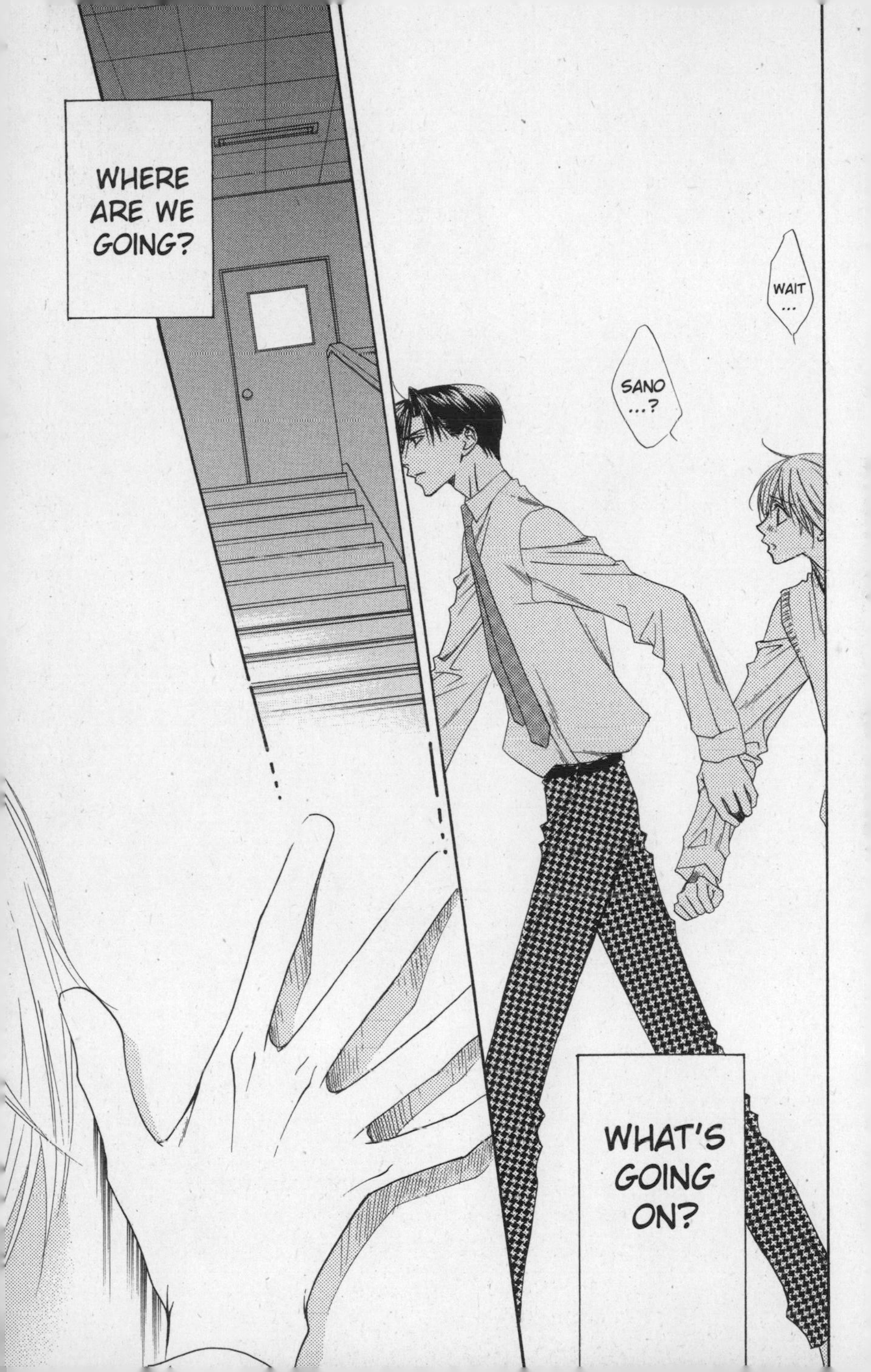
WAIT ...
SANO ...?
WHAT'S GOING ON?
WHERE ARE WE GOING?

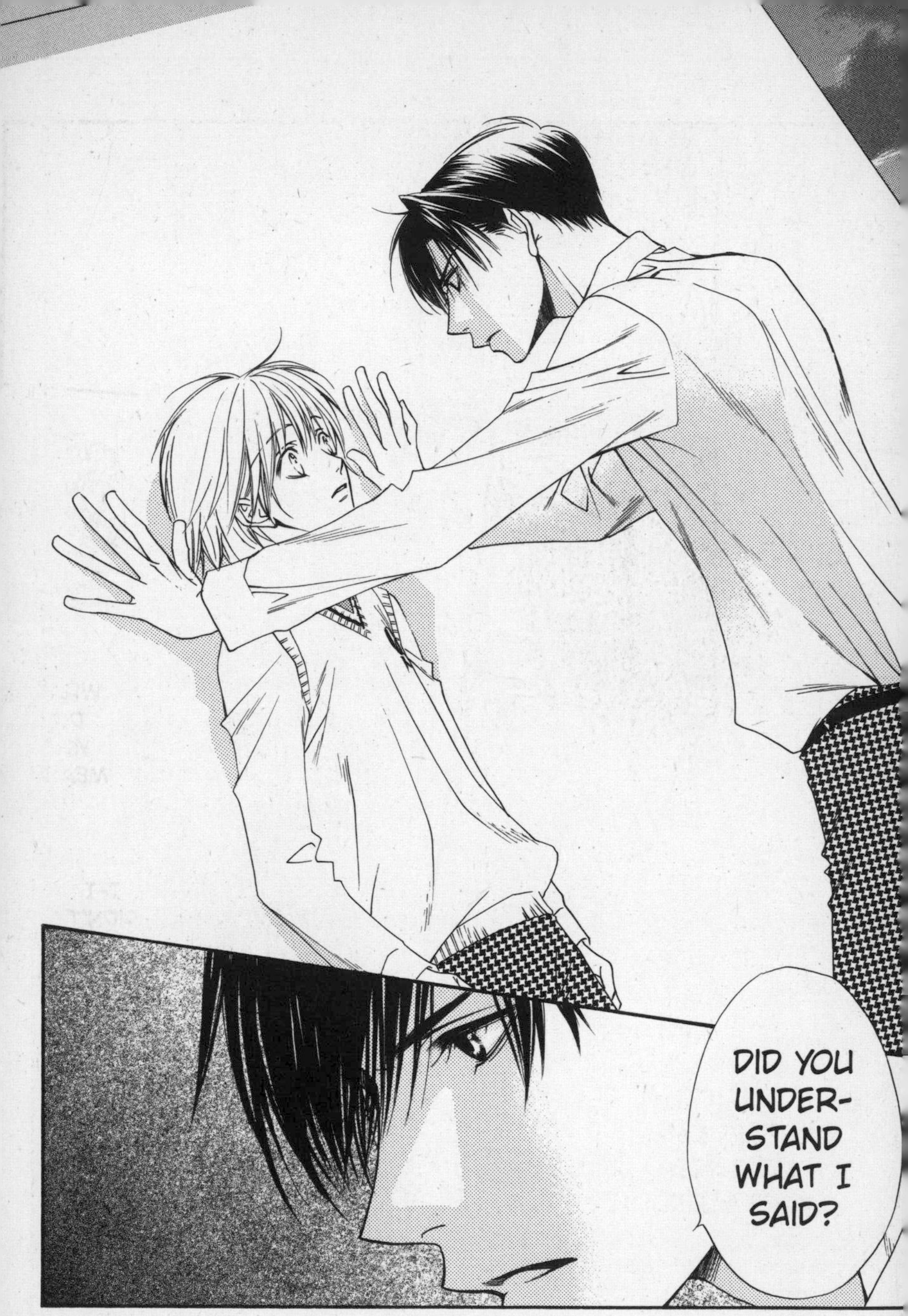
DID YOU UNDER-STAND WHAT I SAID?

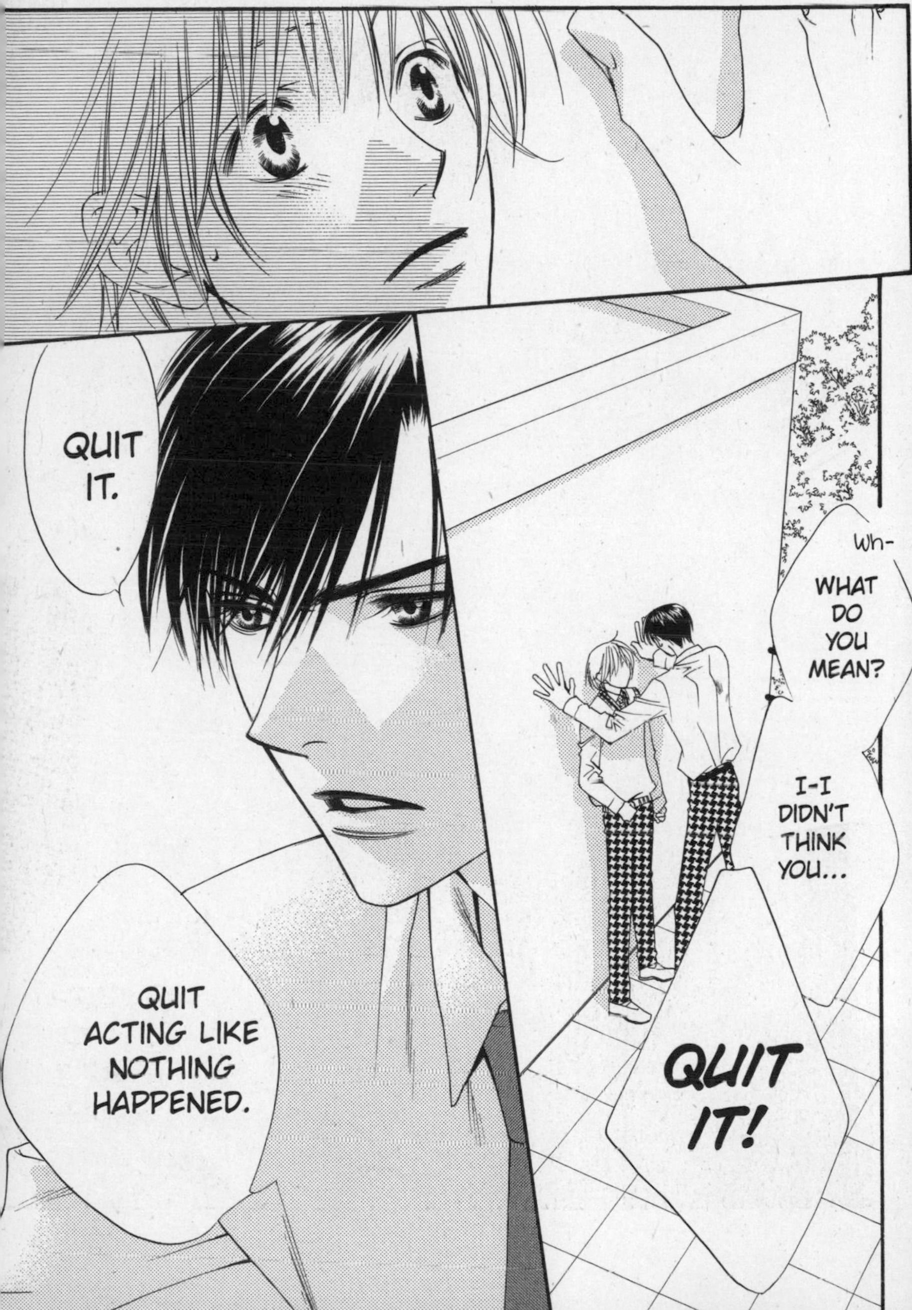
Wh- WHAT DO YOU MEAN?
I-I DIDN'T THINK YOU...
QUIT IT!
QUIT IT.
QUIT ACTING LIKE NOTHING HAPPENED.

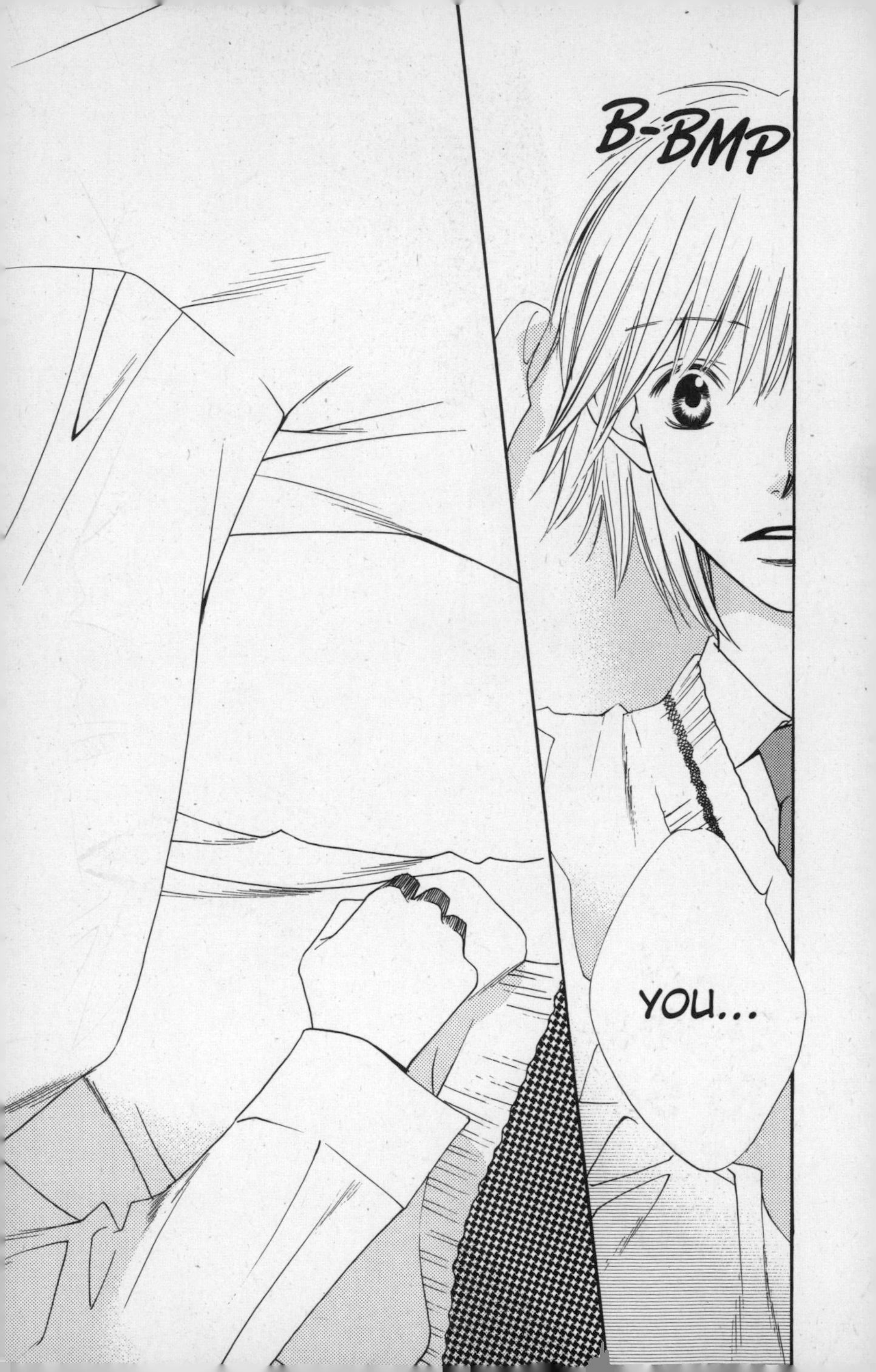
B-BMP
YOU...

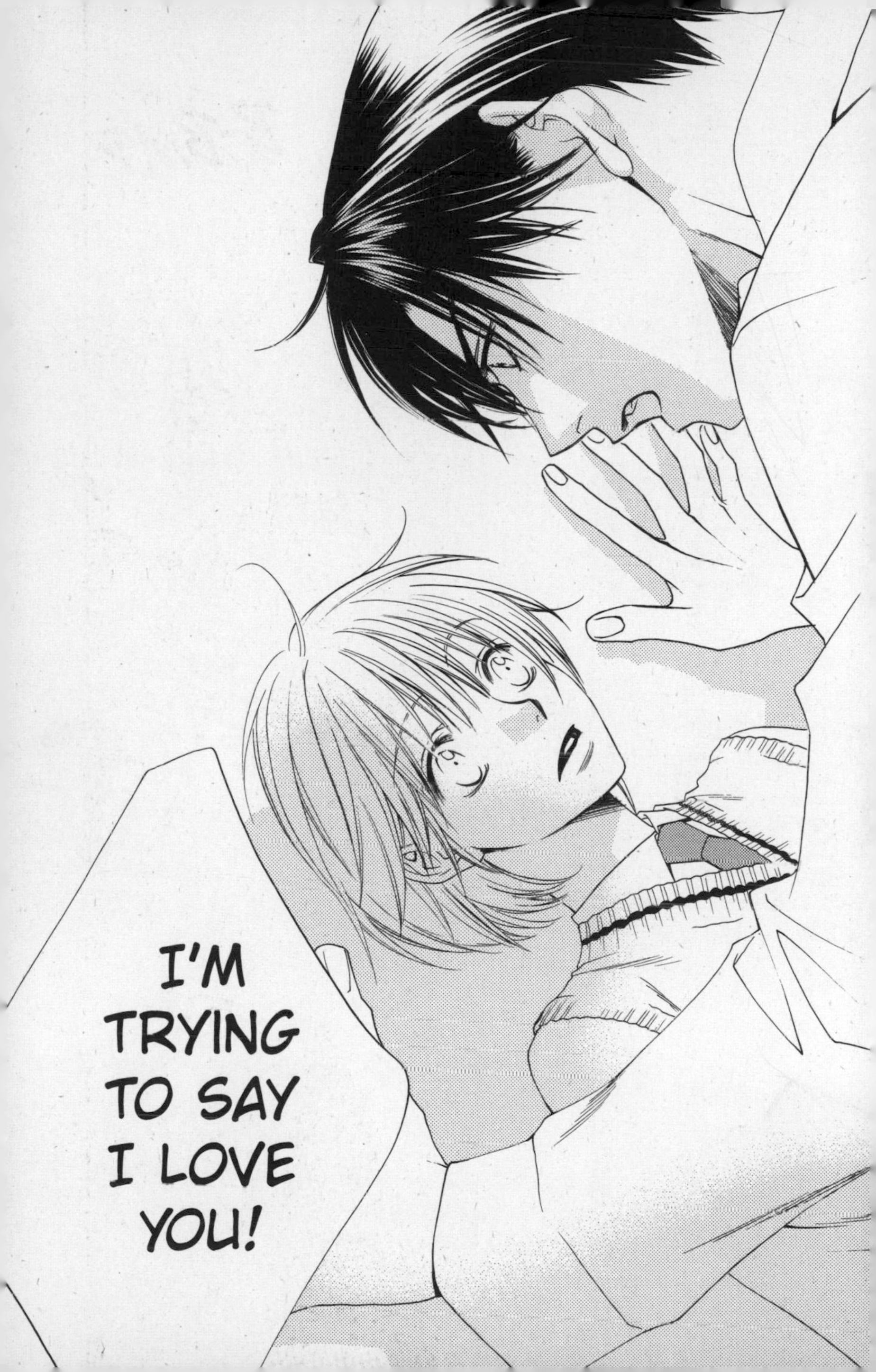
I'M TRYING TO SAY I LOVE YOU!

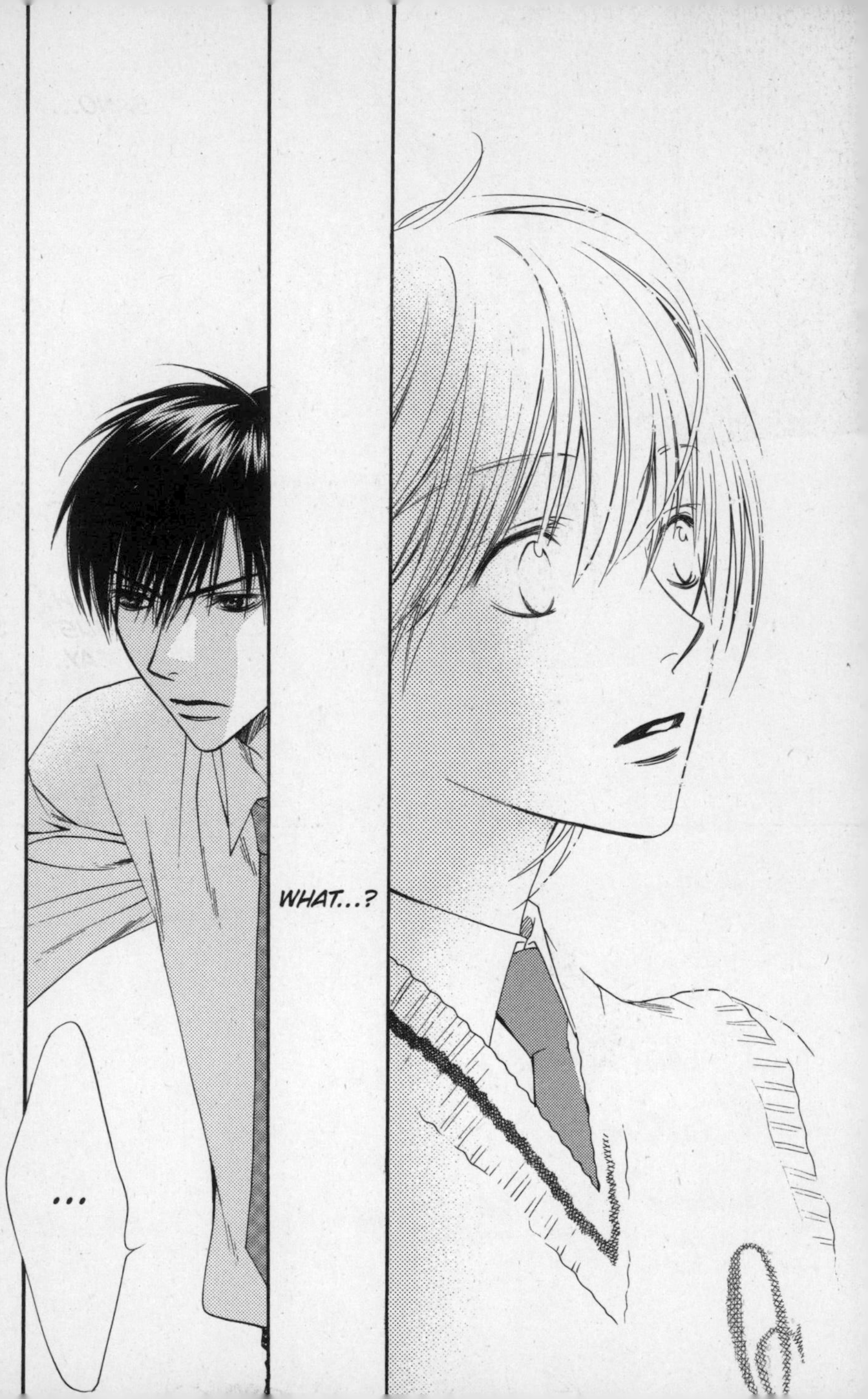
WHAT...?
...

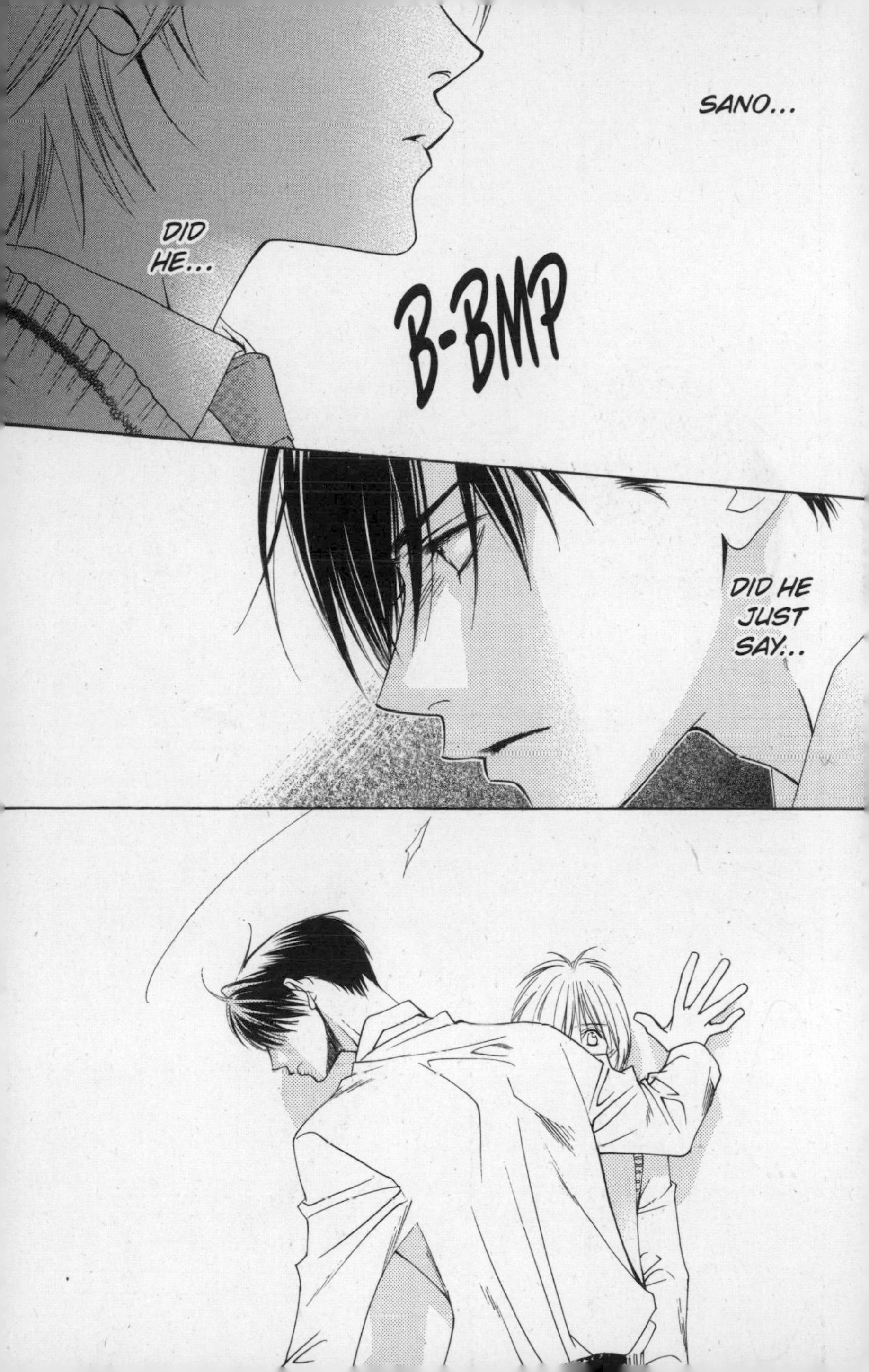
SANO...
DID HE...
B-BMP
DID HE JUST SAY...

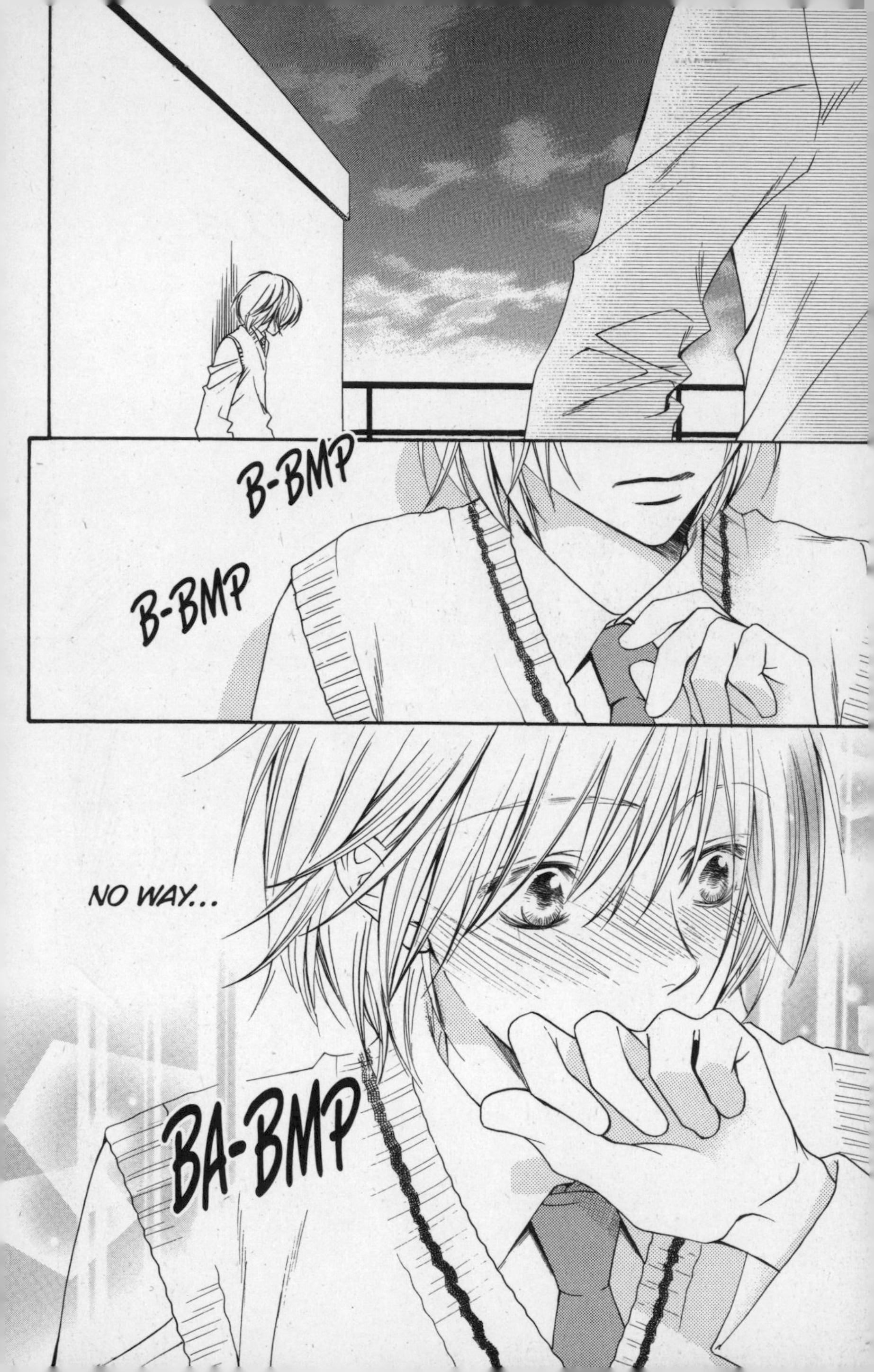
B-BMP
B-BMP
NO WAY...
BA-BMP

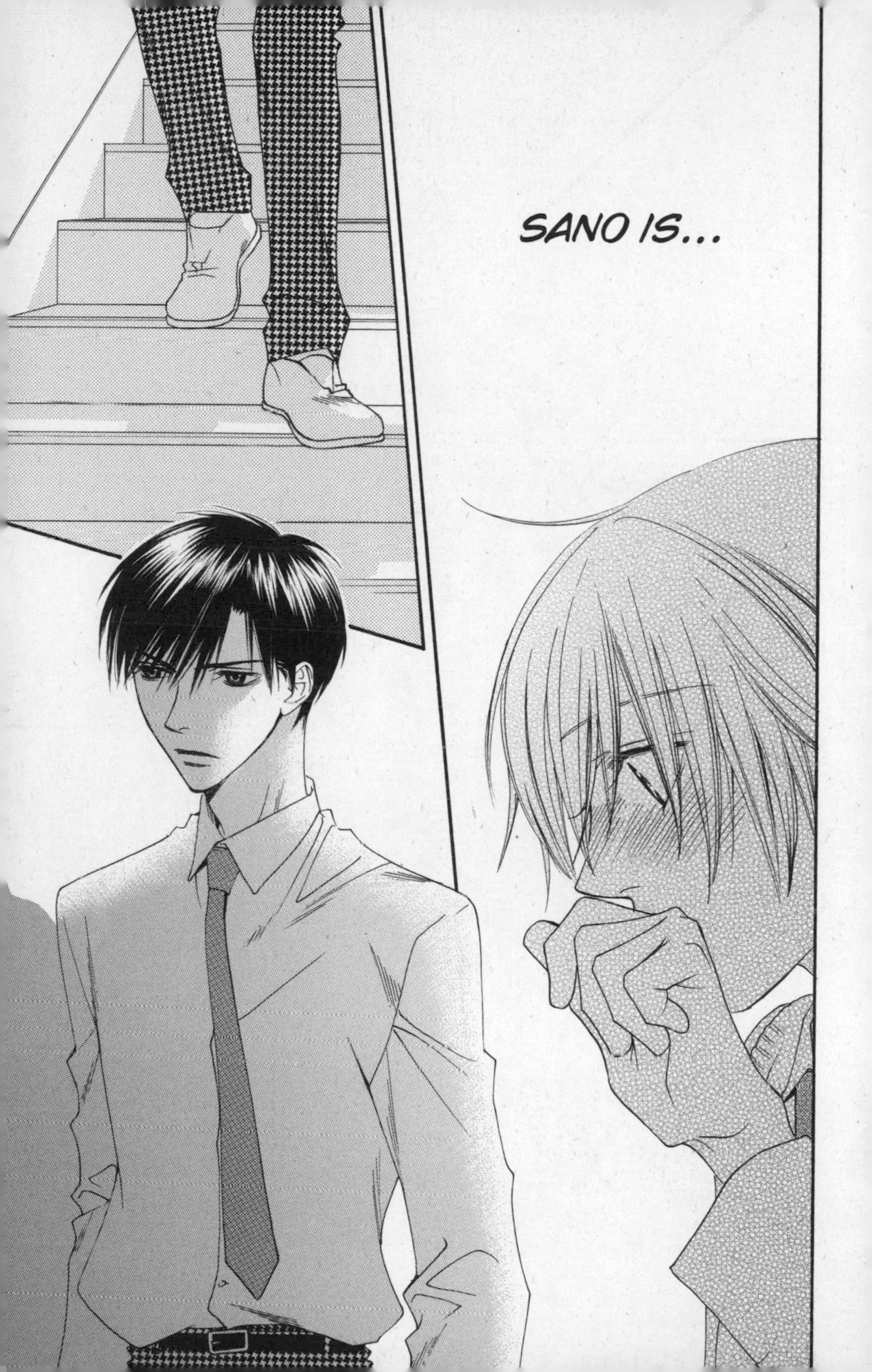
SANO IS...

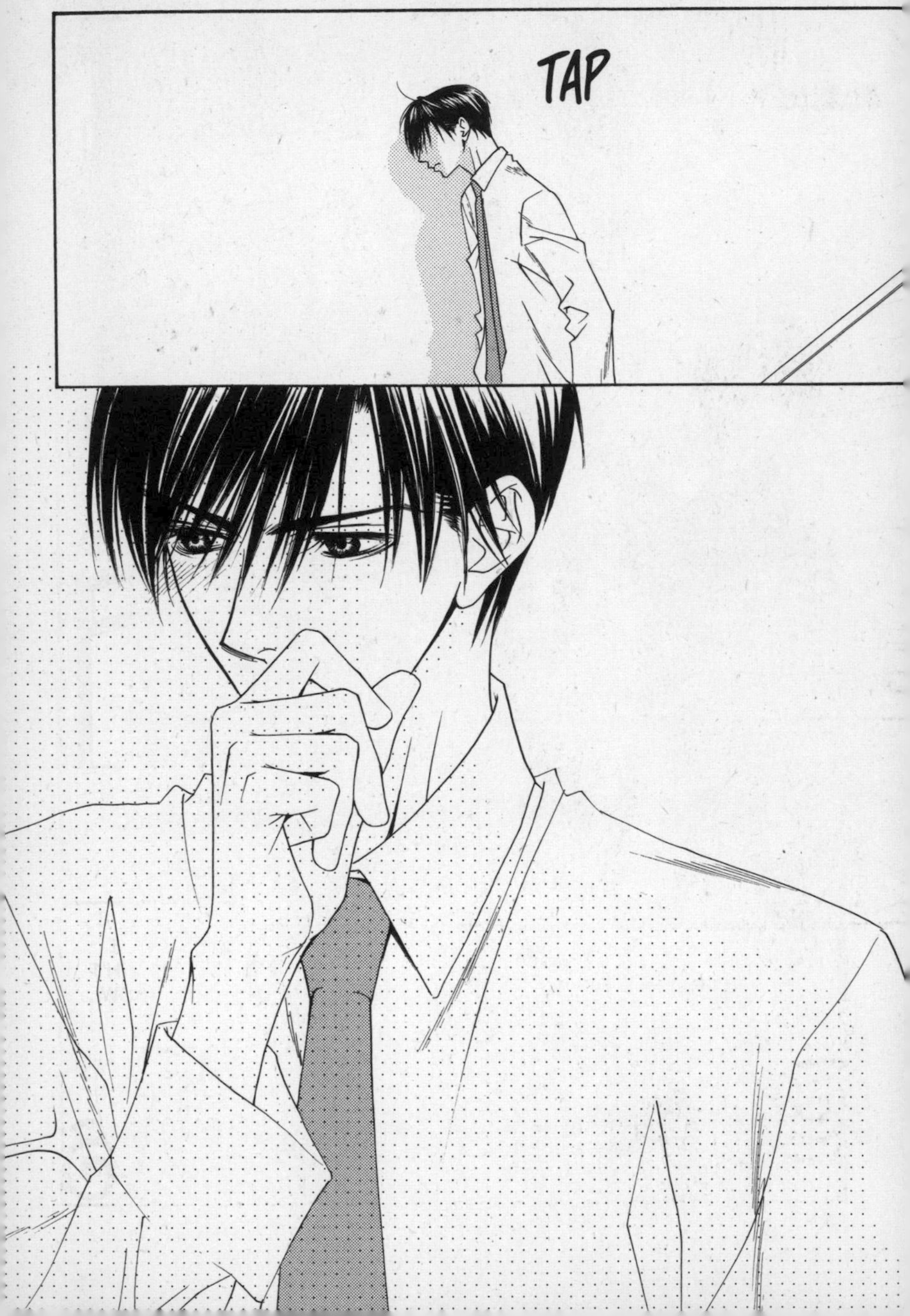
TAP

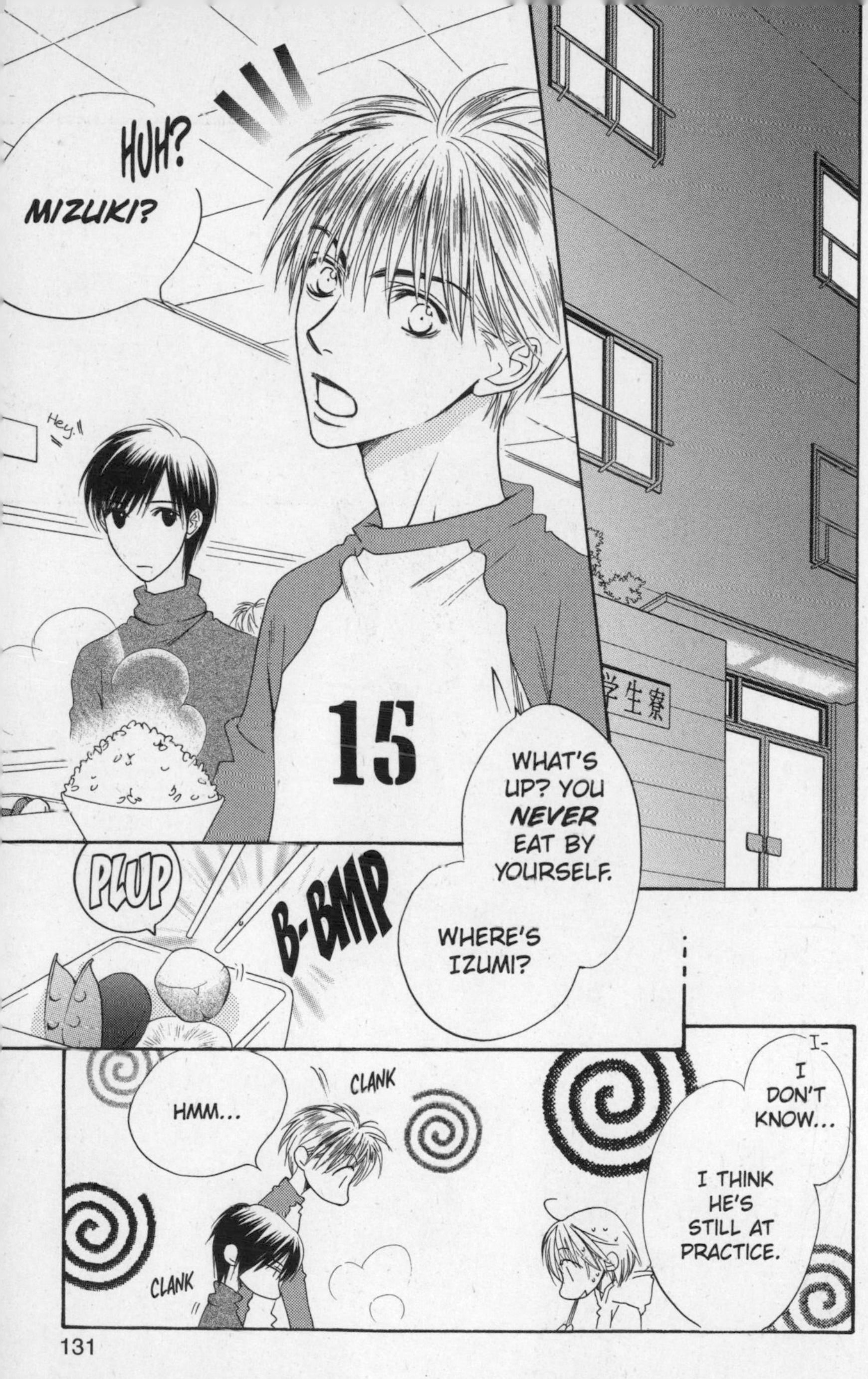
HUH?
MIZUKI?
Hey.
学生寮
WHAT'S UP? YOU NEVER EAT BY YOURSELF.
WHERE'S IZUMI?
B-BMP
PLUP
I- I DON'T KNOW...
I THINK HE'S STILL AT PRACTICE.
CLANK
HMM...
CLANK

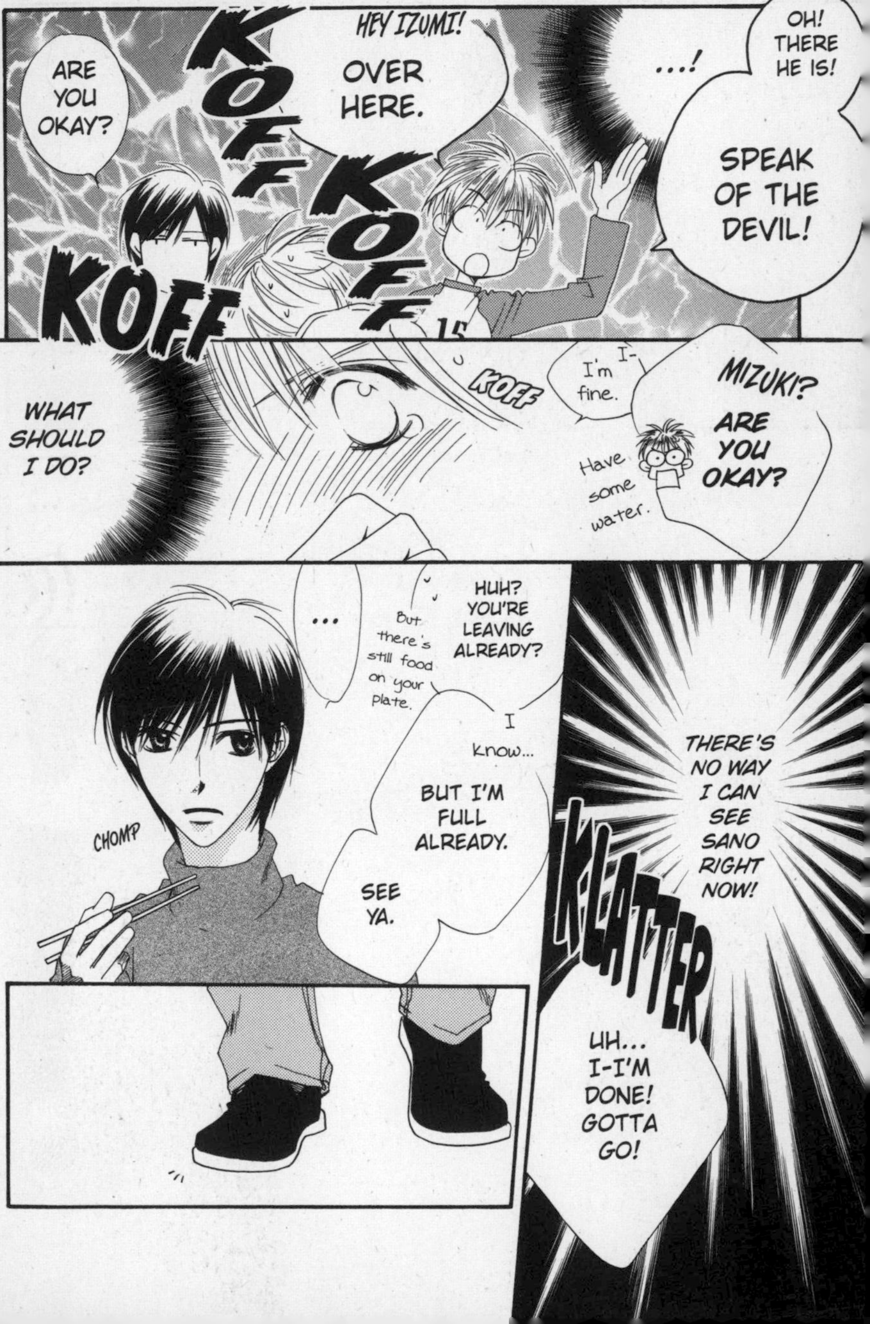
OH! THERE HE IS!
SPEAK OF THE DEVIL!
...!
HEY IZUMI!
OVER HERE.
KOFF KOFF
KOFF
ARE YOU OKAY?
KOFF
MIZUKI? ARE YOU OKAY?
Have some water.
I- I'm fine.
KOFF
WHAT SHOULD I DO?
THERE'S NO WAY I CAN SEE SANO RIGHT NOW!
KLATTER
UH... I-I'M DONE! GOTTA GO!
HUH? YOU'RE LEAVING ALREADY?
But there's still food on your plate.
...
I know...
BUT I'M FULL ALREADY.
SEE YA.
CHOMP

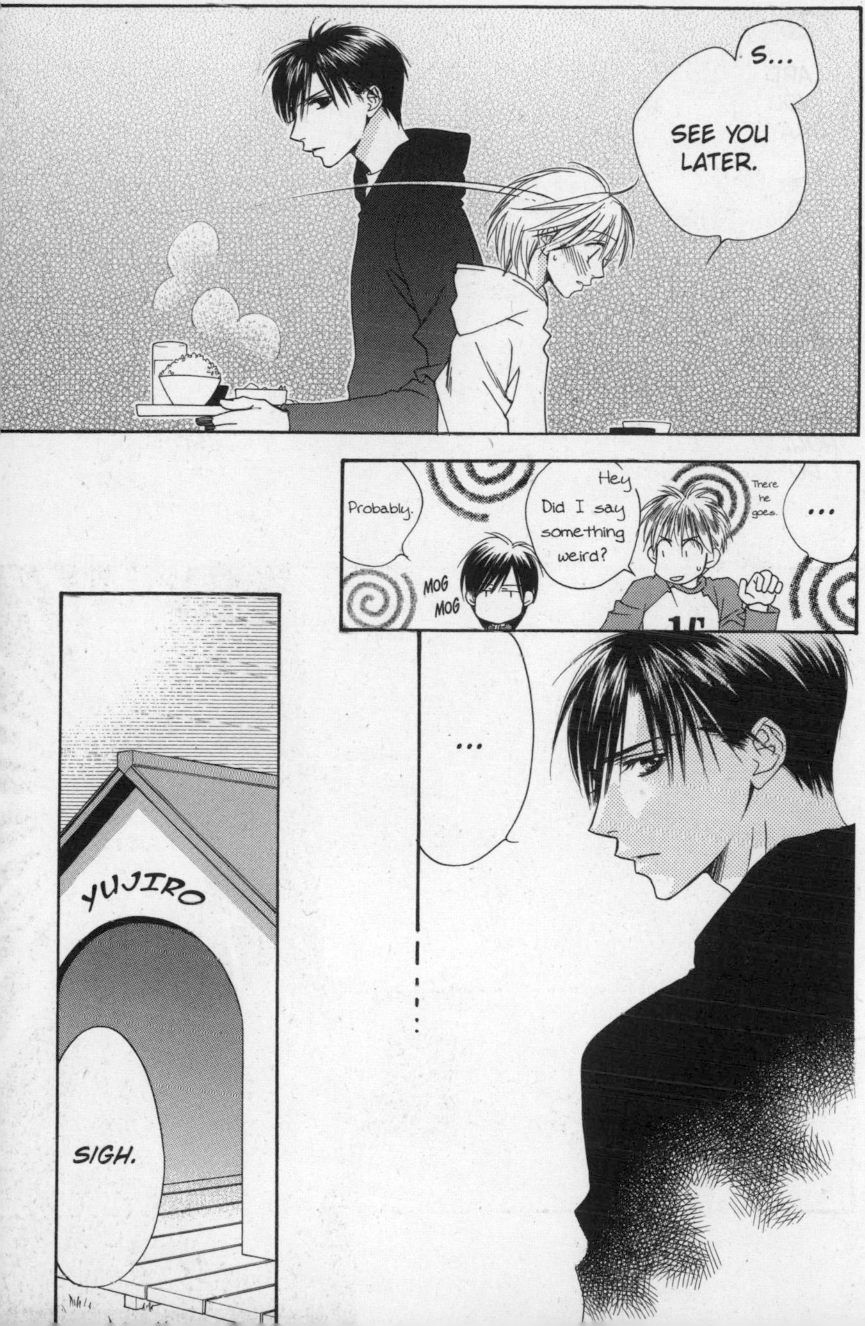
S...
SEE YOU LATER.
...
There he goes.
Hey
Did I say something weird?
MOG MOG
Probably.
...
YUJIRO
SIGH.

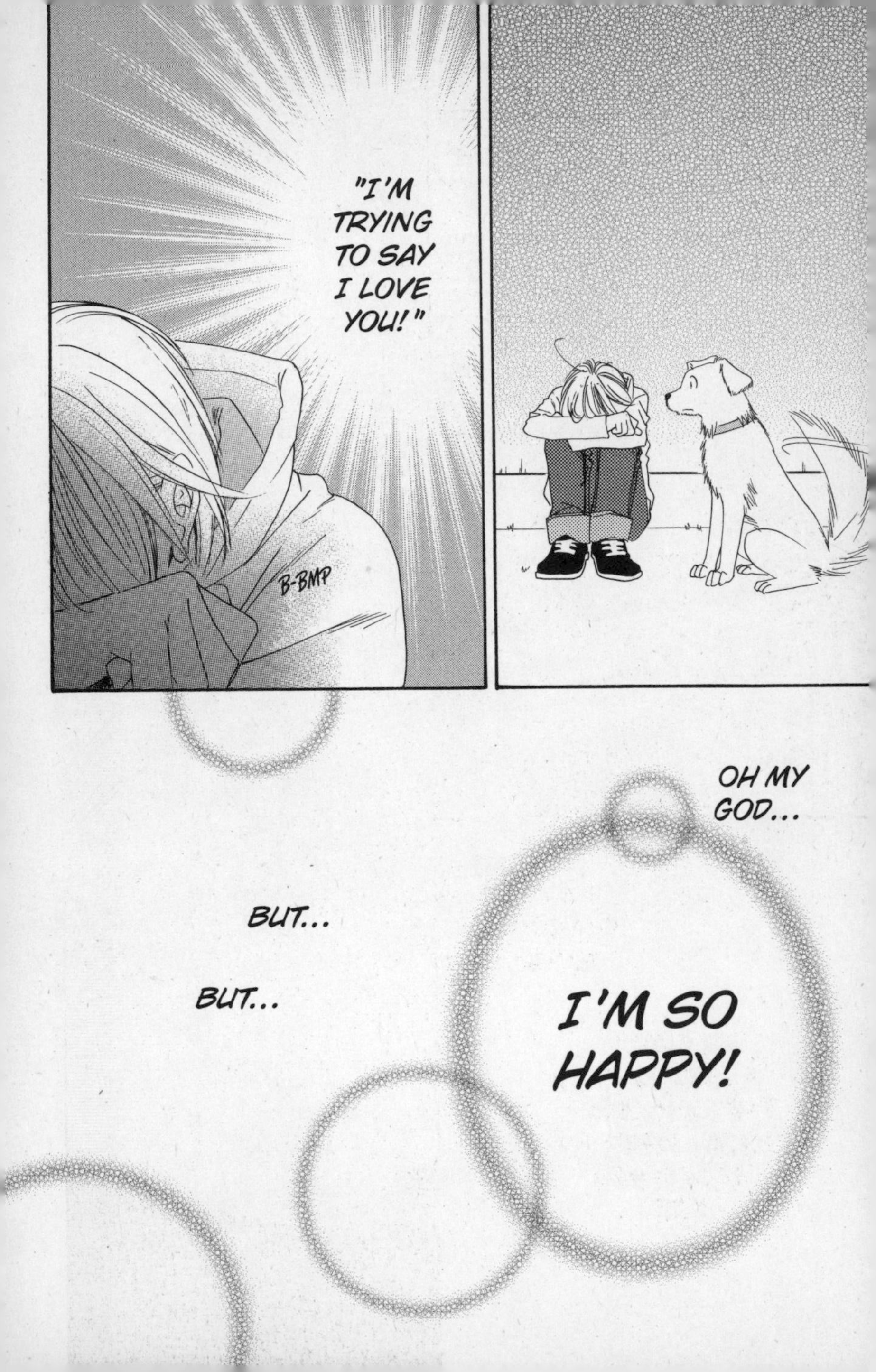
"I'M TRYING TO SAY I LOVE YOU!"
B-BMP
OH MY GOD...
I'M SO HAPPY!
BUT...
BUT...

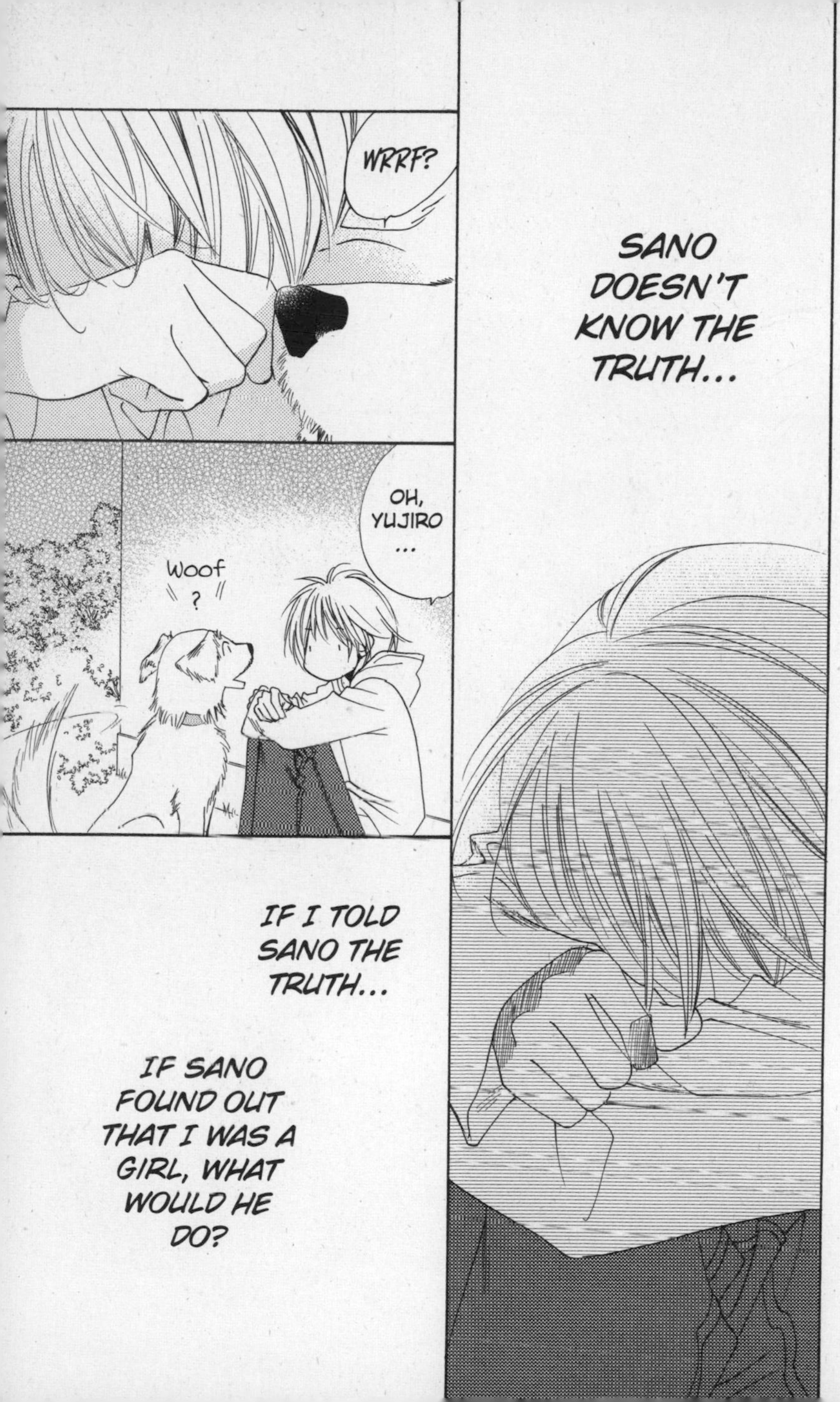
SANO DOESN'T KNOW THE TRUTH...
WRRF?
OH, YUJIRO ...
Woof ?
IF I TOLD SANO THE TRUTH...
IF SANO FOUND OUT THAT I WAS A GIRL, WHAT WOULD HE DO?

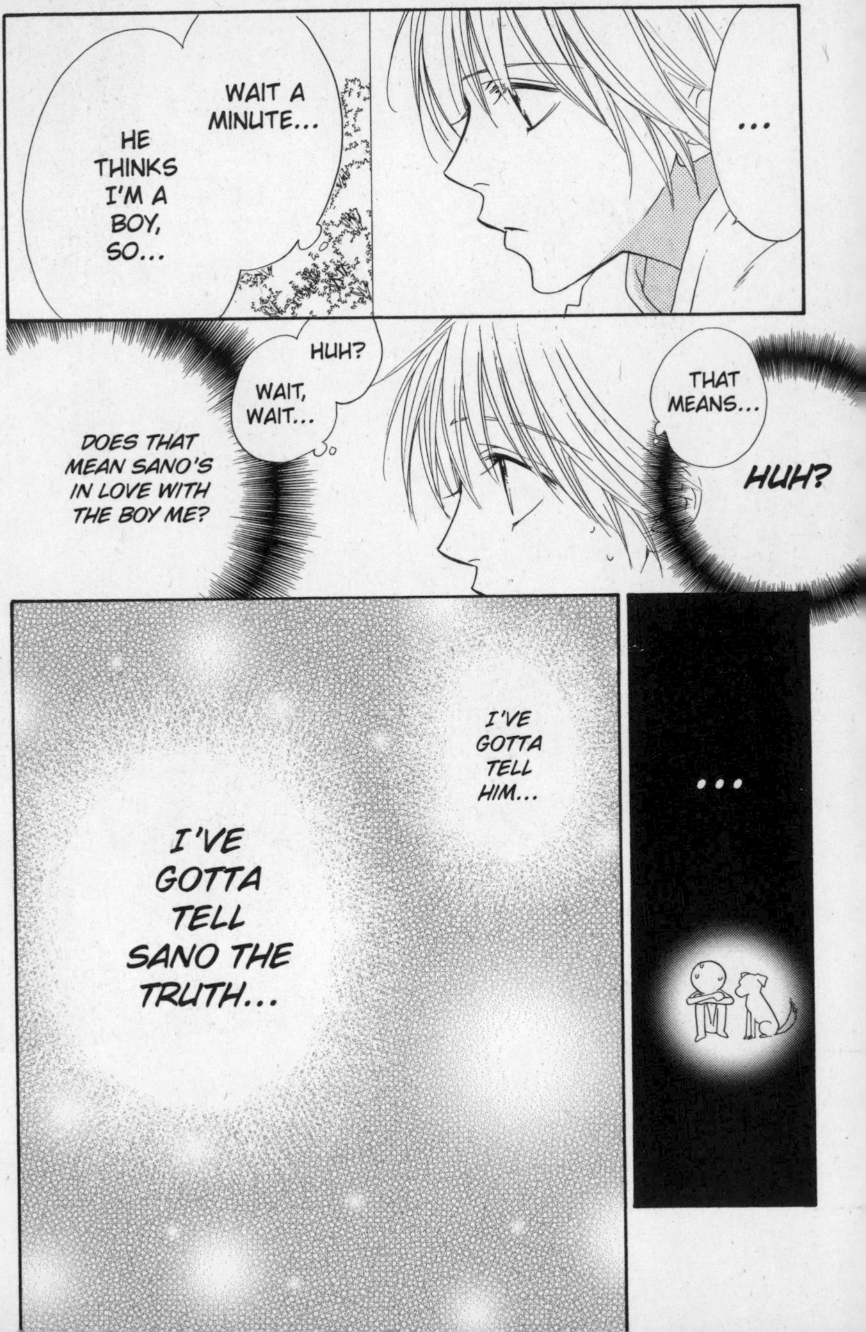
...
WAIT A MINUTE...
HE THINKS I'M A BOY, SO...
THAT MEANS...
HUH?
HUH?
WAIT, WAIT...
DOES THAT MEAN SANO'S IN LOVE WITH THE BOY ME?
...
I'VE GOTTA TELL HIM...
I'VE GOTTA TELL SANO THE TRUTH...

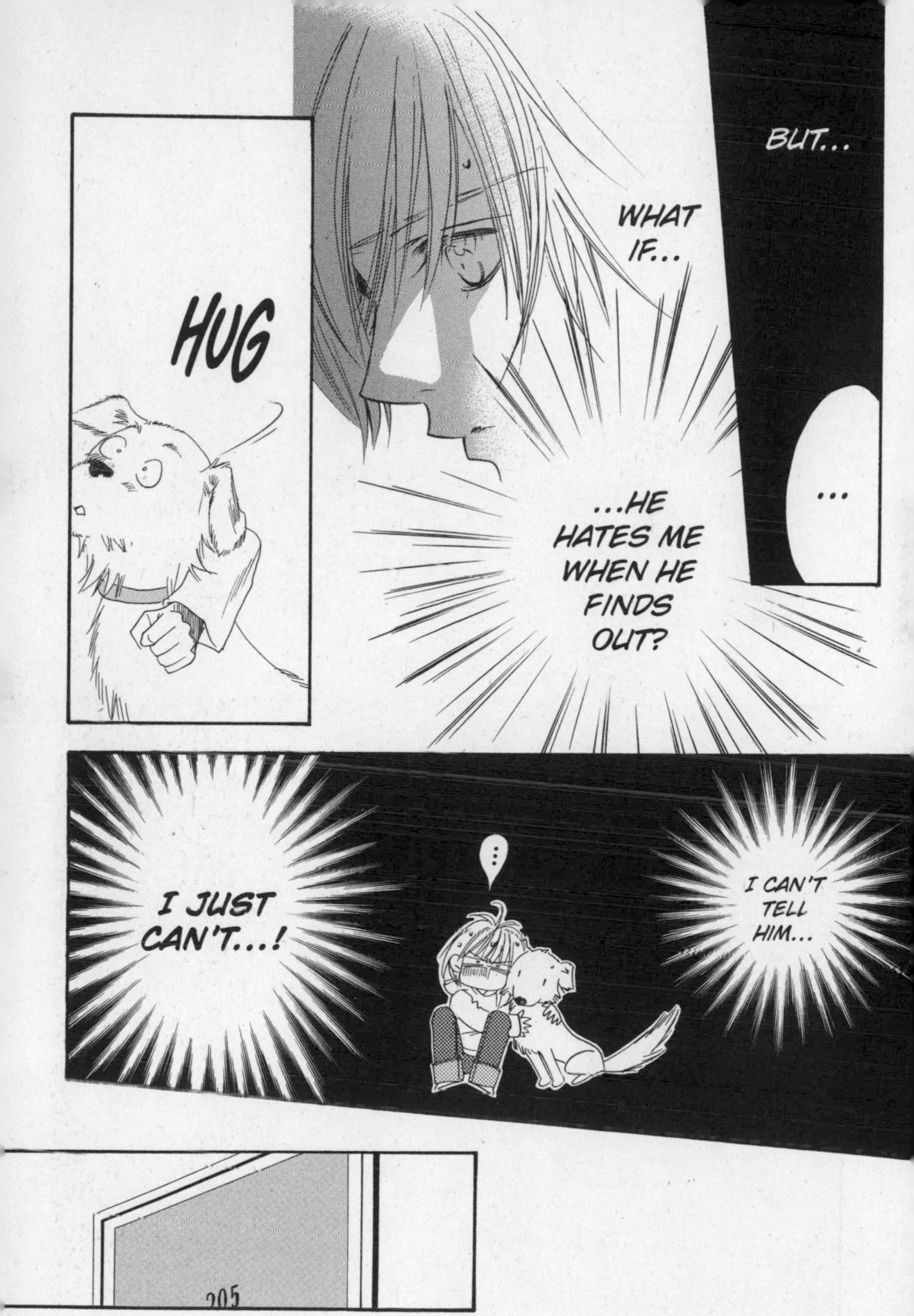
BUT...
...
WHAT IF...
...HE HATES ME WHEN HE FINDS OUT?
HUG
I CAN'T TELL HIM...
...
I JUST CAN'T...!

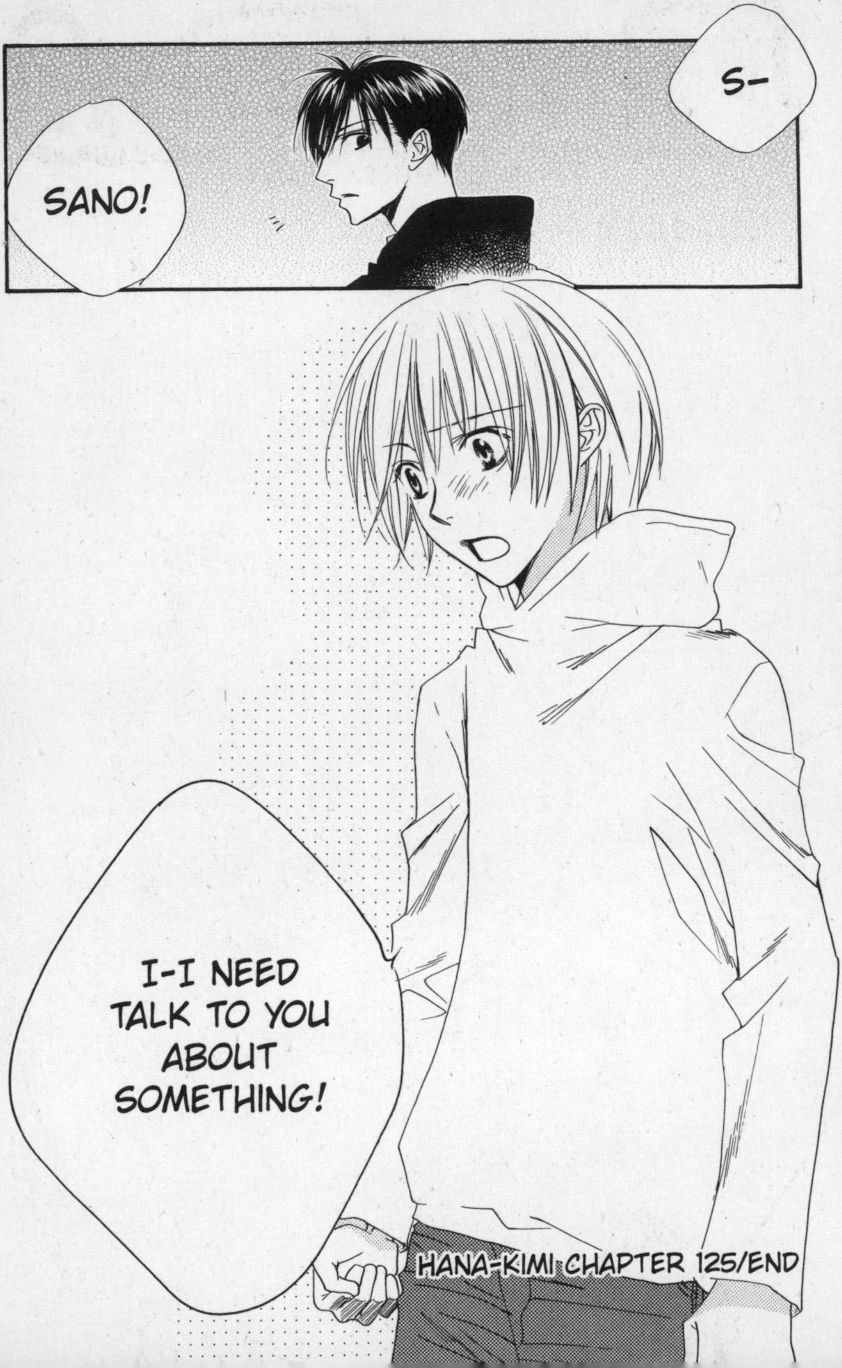
S–
SANO!
I-I NEED TALK TO YOU ABOUT SOMETHING!
HANA-KIMI CHAPTER 125/END

Hana-Kimi

For You in Full Blossom

CHAPTER 126

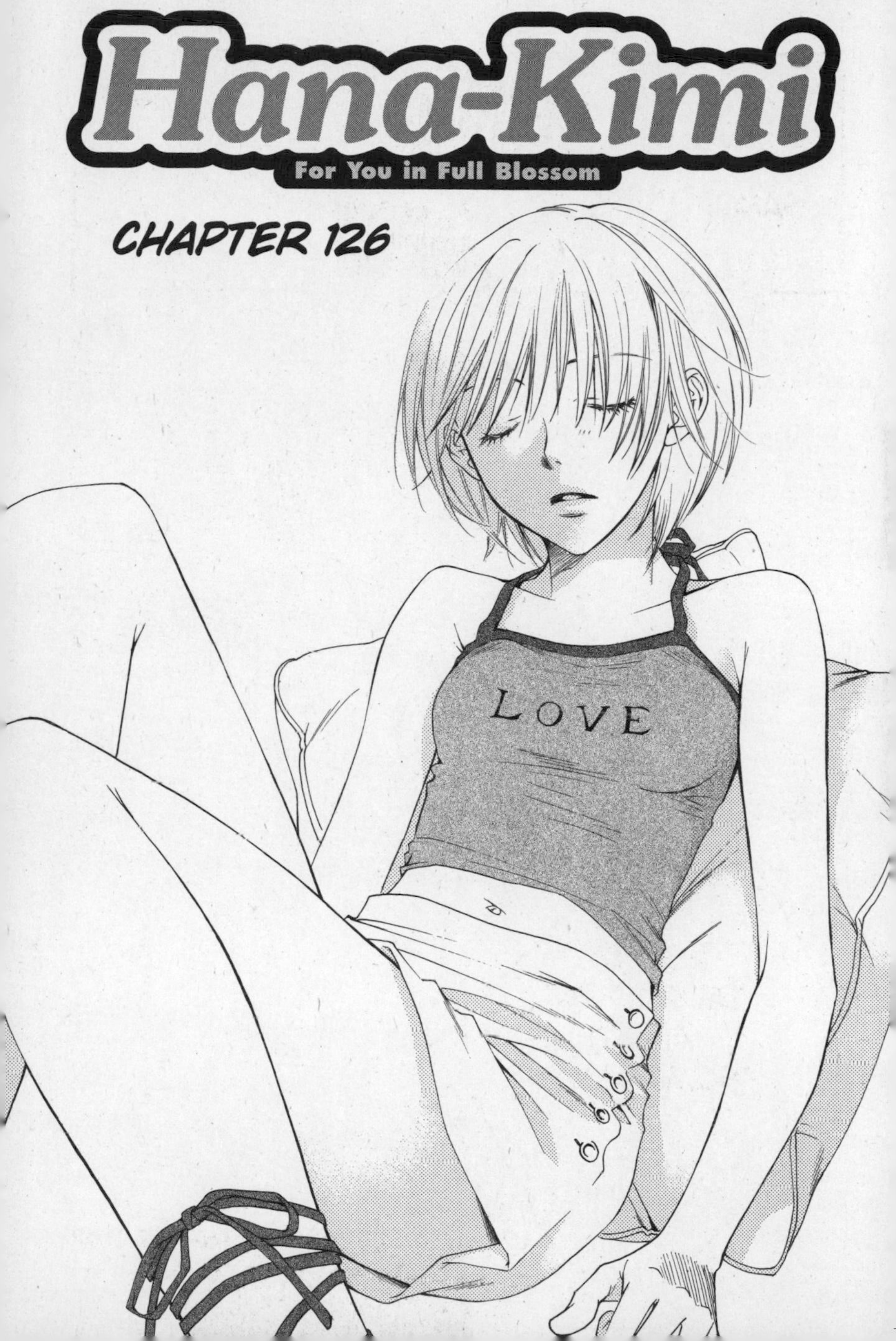
LOVE

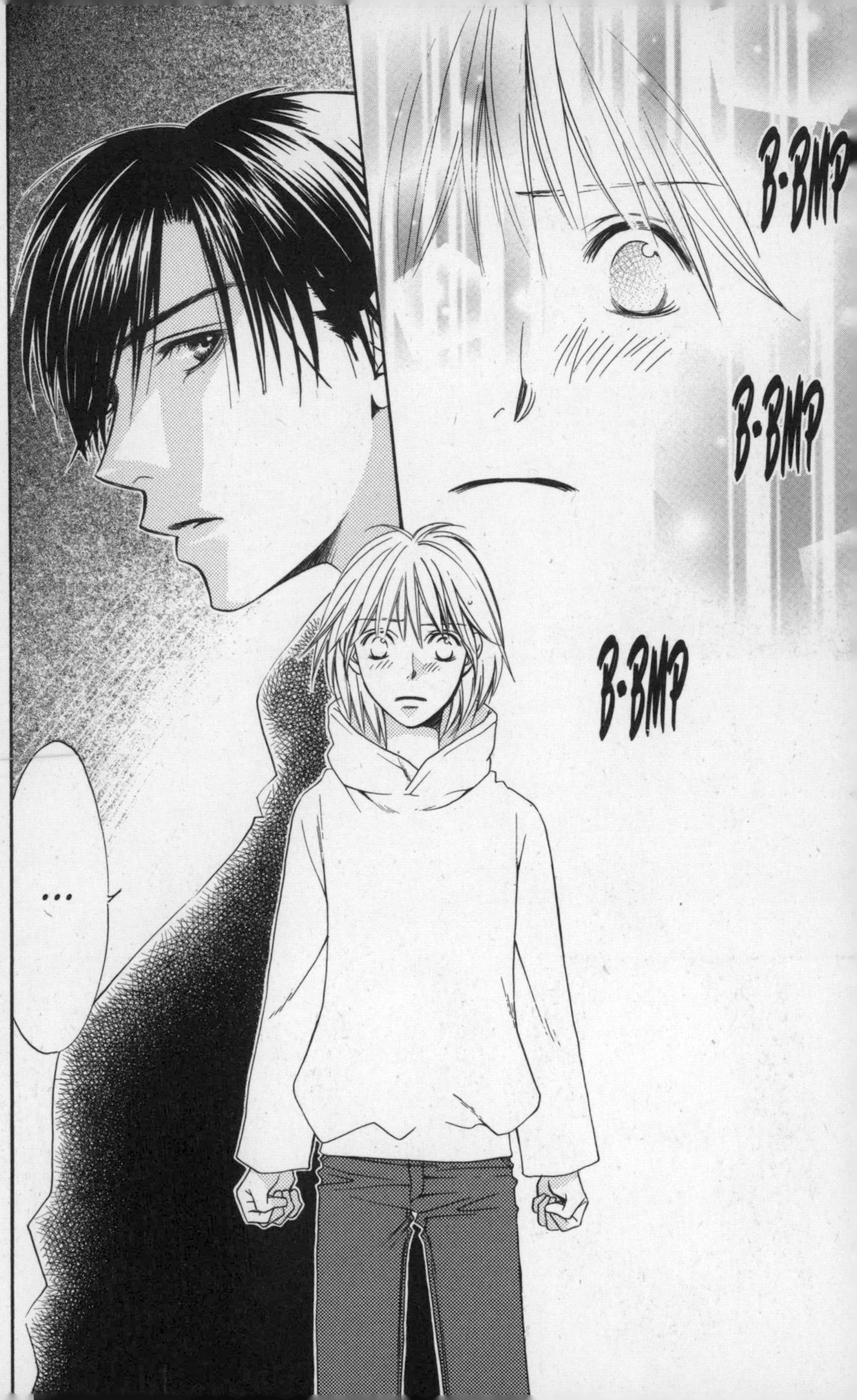
B-BMP
B-BMP
B-BMP
...

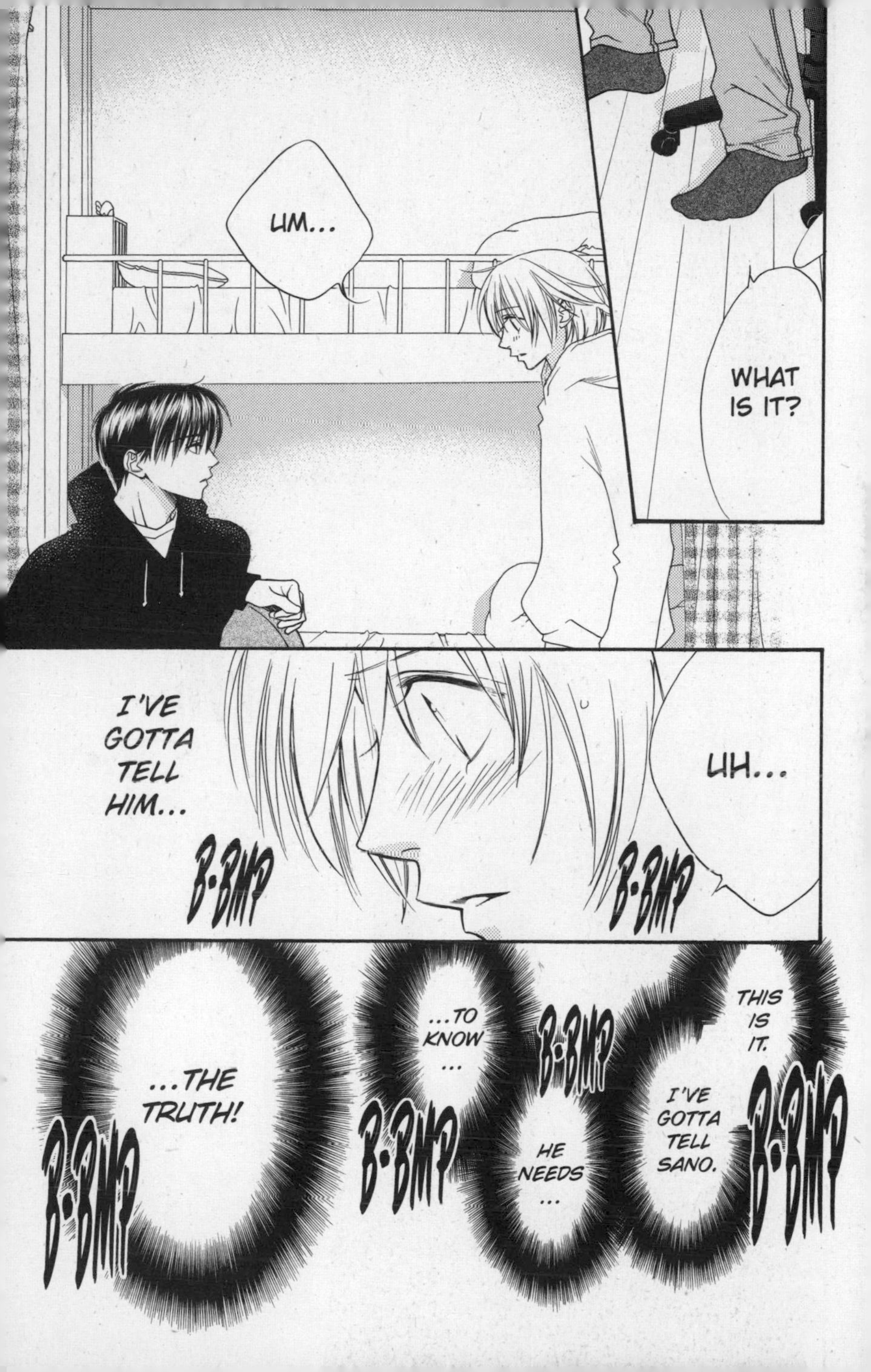
UM...
WHAT IS IT?
UH...
I'VE GOTTA TELL HIM...
B-BMP
B-BMP
THIS IS IT.
I'VE GOTTA TELL SANO.
B-BMP
HE NEEDS...
...TO KNOW...
B-BMP
B-BMP
...THE TRUTH!
B-BMP

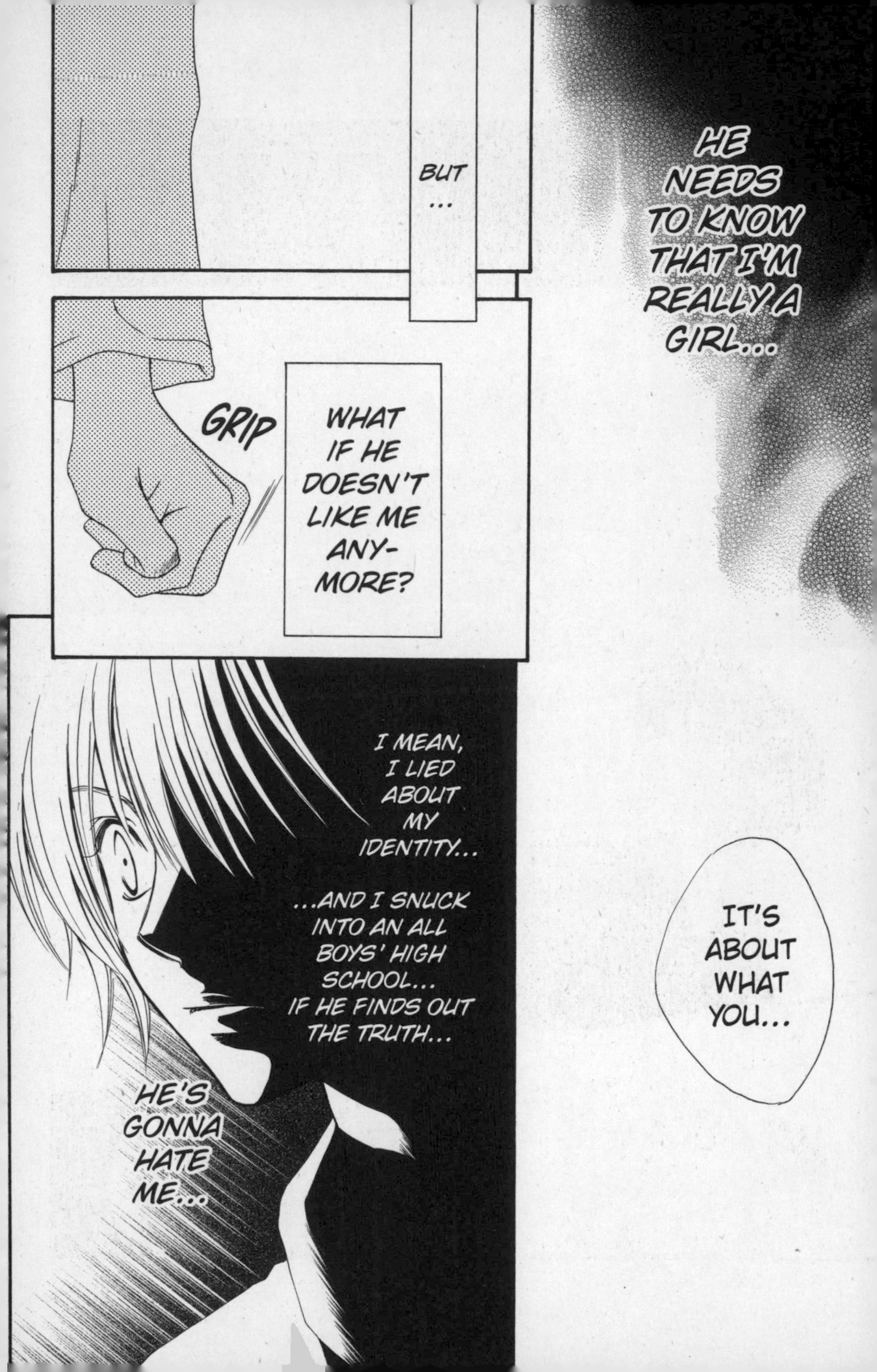
HE NEEDS TO KNOW THAT I'M REALLY A GIRL...
IT'S ABOUT WHAT YOU...
BUT...
GRIP
WHAT IF HE DOESN'T LIKE ME ANY-MORE?
I MEAN, I LIED ABOUT MY IDENTITY...
...AND I SNUCK INTO AN ALL BOYS' HIGH SCHOOL... IF HE FINDS OUT THE TRUTH...
HE'S GONNA HATE ME...

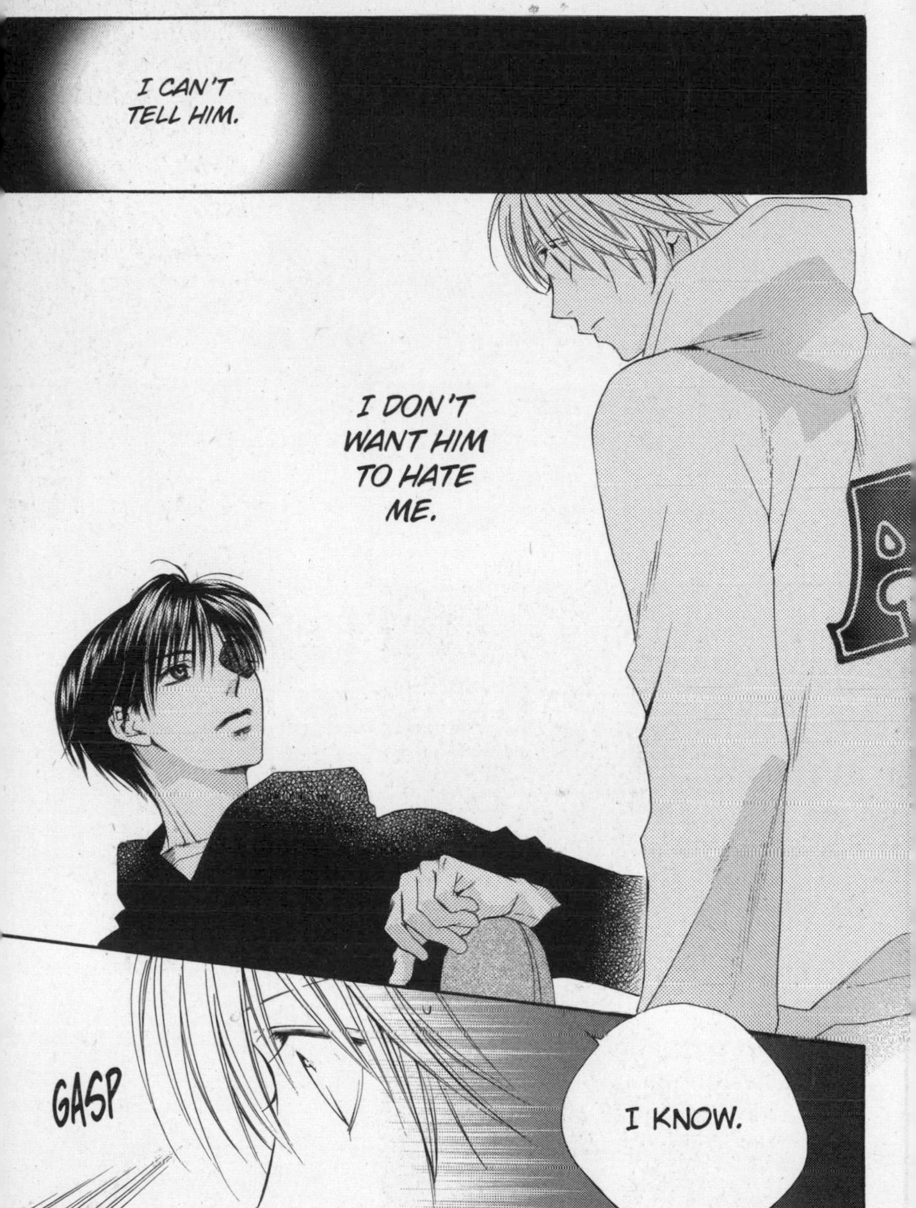
I CAN'T TELL HIM.
I DON'T WANT HIM TO HATE ME.
I KNOW.
GASP

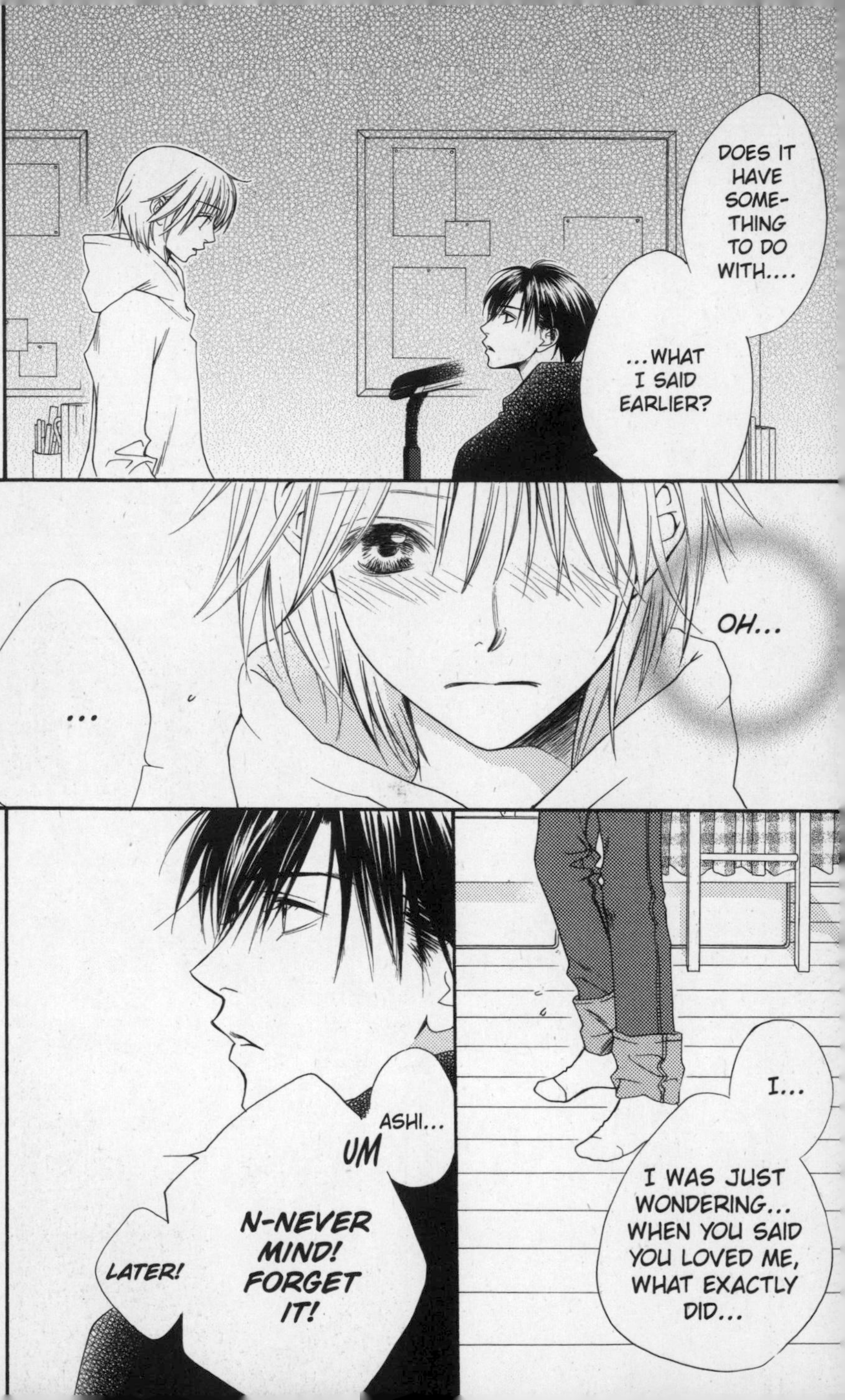
DOES IT HAVE SOME-THING TO DO WITH....
...WHAT I SAID EARLIER?
OH...
...
I...
I WAS JUST WONDERING... WHEN YOU SAID YOU LOVED ME, WHAT EXACTLY DID...
ASHI...
UM
N-NEVER MIND! FORGET IT!
LATER!

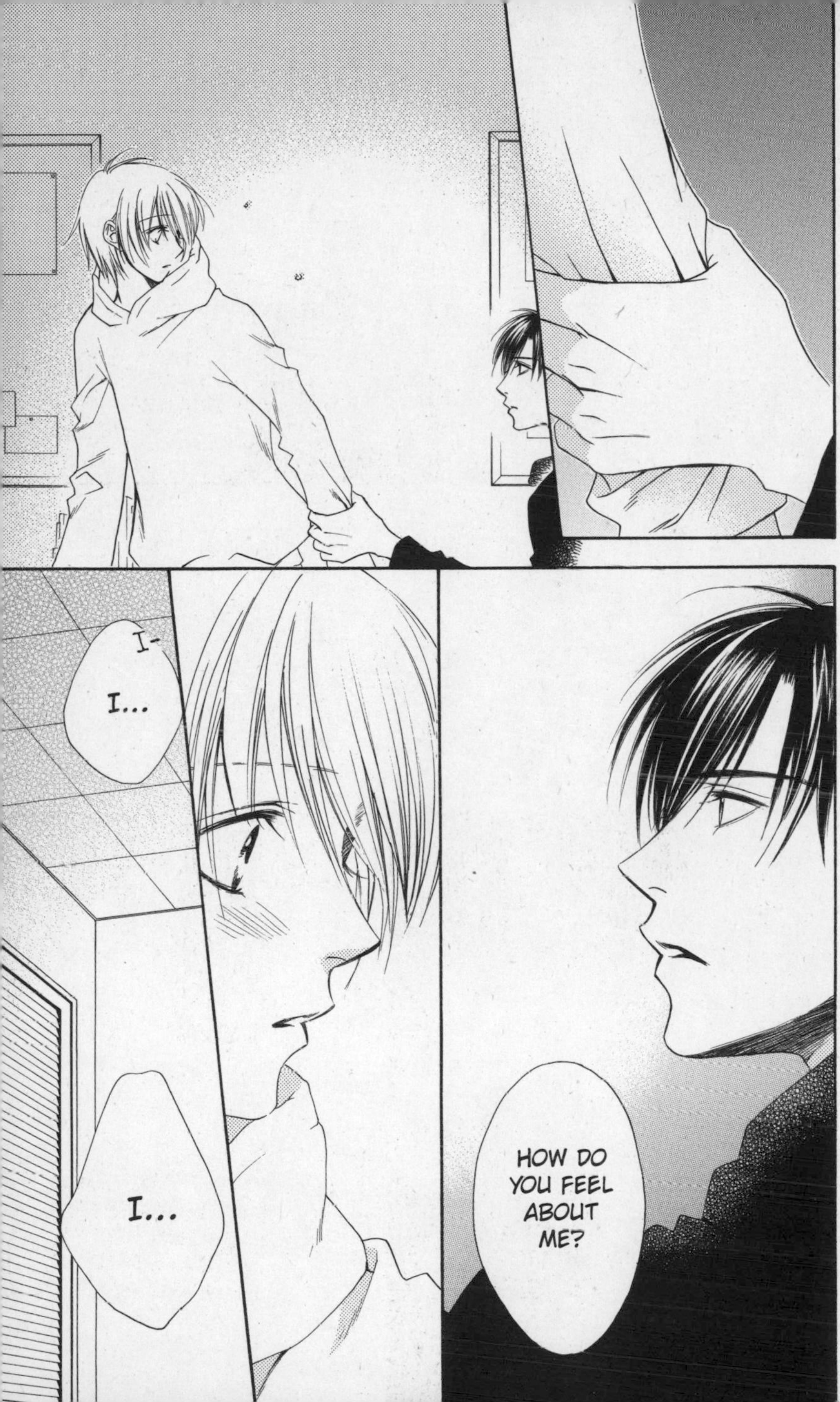
HOW DO YOU FEEL ABOUT ME?
I- I...
I...

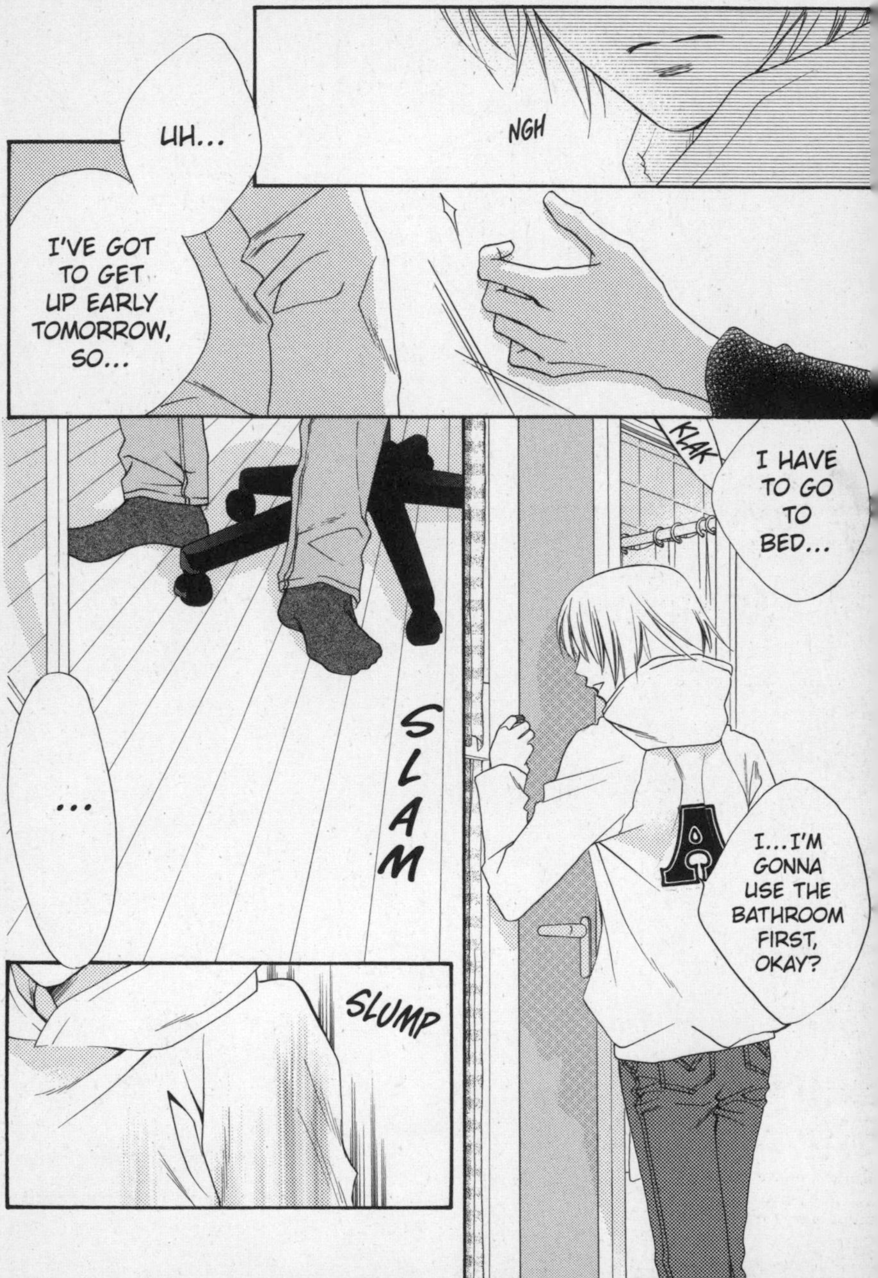
NGH
UH...
I'VE GOT TO GET UP EARLY TOMORROW, SO...
KLAK
I HAVE TO GO TO BED...
I...I'M GONNA USE THE BATHROOM FIRST, OKAY?
SLAM
...
SLUMP

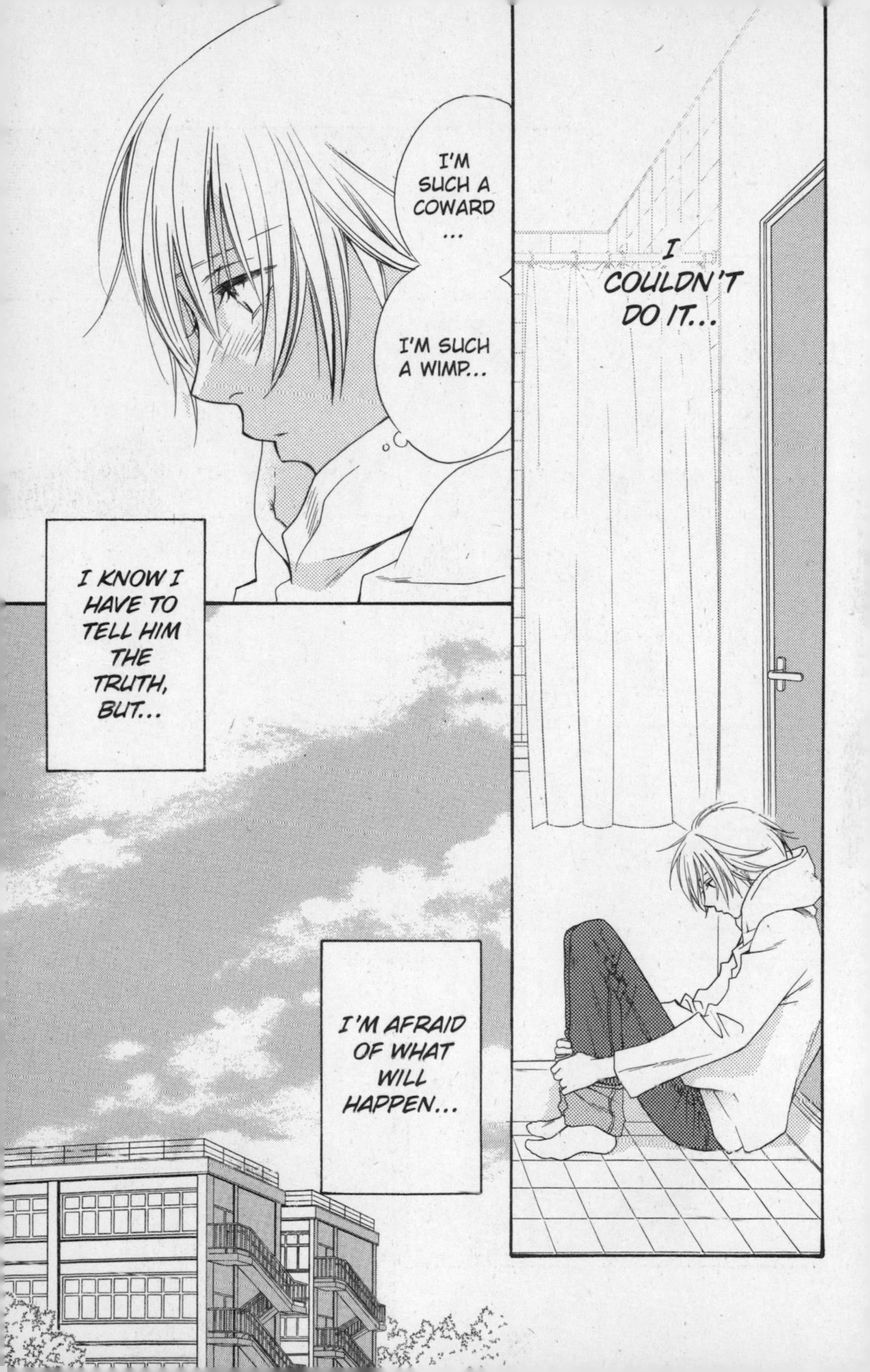
I COULDN'T DO IT...
I'M SUCH A COWARD ...
I'M SUCH A WIMP...
I KNOW I HAVE TO TELL HIM THE TRUTH, BUT...
I'M AFRAID OF WHAT WILL HAPPEN...

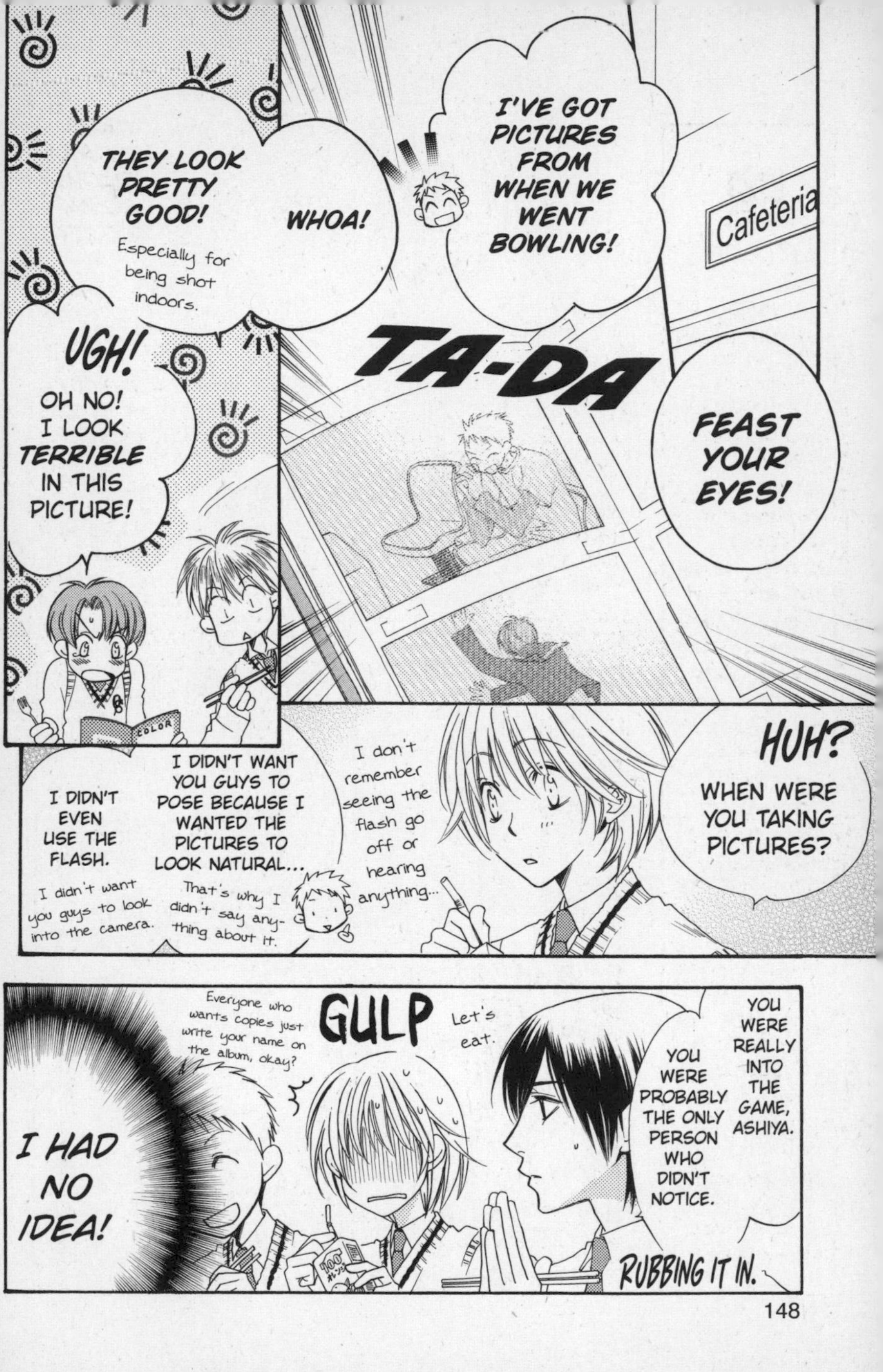
I'VE GOT PICTURES FROM WHEN WE WENT BOWLING!
Cafeteria
TA-DA
FEAST YOUR EYES!
WHOA!
THEY LOOK PRETTY GOOD!
Especially for being shot indoors.
UGH!
OH NO! I LOOK TERRIBLE IN THIS PICTURE!
COLOR
HUH?
WHEN WERE YOU TAKING PICTURES?
I don't remember seeing the flash go off or hearing anything...
I DIDN'T WANT YOU GUYS TO POSE BECAUSE I WANTED THE PICTURES TO LOOK NATURAL...
That's why I didn't say anything about it.
I DIDN'T EVEN USE THE FLASH.
I didn't want you guys to look into the camera.
YOU WERE REALLY INTO THE GAME, ASHIYA.
YOU WERE PROBABLY THE ONLY PERSON WHO DIDN'T NOTICE.
RUBBING IT IN.
Let's eat.
GULP
Everyone who wants copies just write your name on the album, okay?
I HAD NO IDEA!

映

MOVIE

"PIRATES OF THE CARIBBEAN"

I went to see "Pirates of the Caribbean." Just having Johnny Depp as the star was good enough for me, but on top of that, Orlando Bloom was his costar! Thank you, god! I liked Orlando, who played a gorgeous elf in the Lord of the Rings, but Johnny Depp's character really won me over. He was so cool! Every time I go to Tokyo Disneyland, the first ride I go on is always "Pirates of the Caribbean." It was exciting to see some of the scenes from the ride in the movie.

↙ Sometimes I ride "Pirates of the Caribbean" when I enter the park, and again before I leave...that's how much I love it.

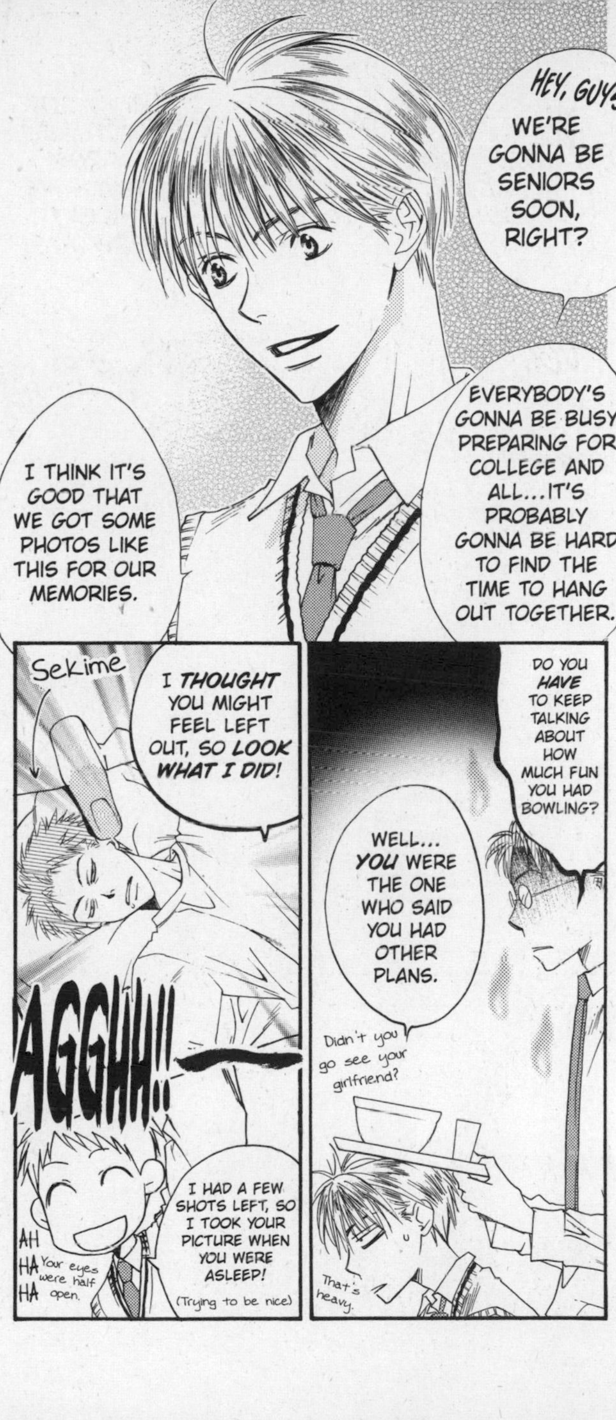
HEY, GUYS. WE'RE GONNA BE SENIORS SOON, RIGHT?
EVERYBODY'S GONNA BE BUSY PREPARING FOR COLLEGE AND ALL...IT'S PROBABLY GONNA BE HARD TO FIND THE TIME TO HANG OUT TOGETHER.
I THINK IT'S GOOD THAT WE GOT SOME PHOTOS LIKE THIS FOR OUR MEMORIES.
DO YOU HAVE TO KEEP TALKING ABOUT HOW MUCH FUN YOU HAD BOWLING?
WELL... YOU WERE THE ONE WHO SAID YOU HAD OTHER PLANS.
Didn't you go see your girlfriend?
That's heavy.
Sekime
I THOUGHT YOU MIGHT FEEL LEFT OUT, SO LOOK WHAT I DID!
AGGHH!!
I HAD A FEW SHOTS LEFT, SO I TOOK YOUR PICTURE WHEN YOU WERE ASLEEP!
AH HA HA
Your eyes were half open.
(Trying to be nice)

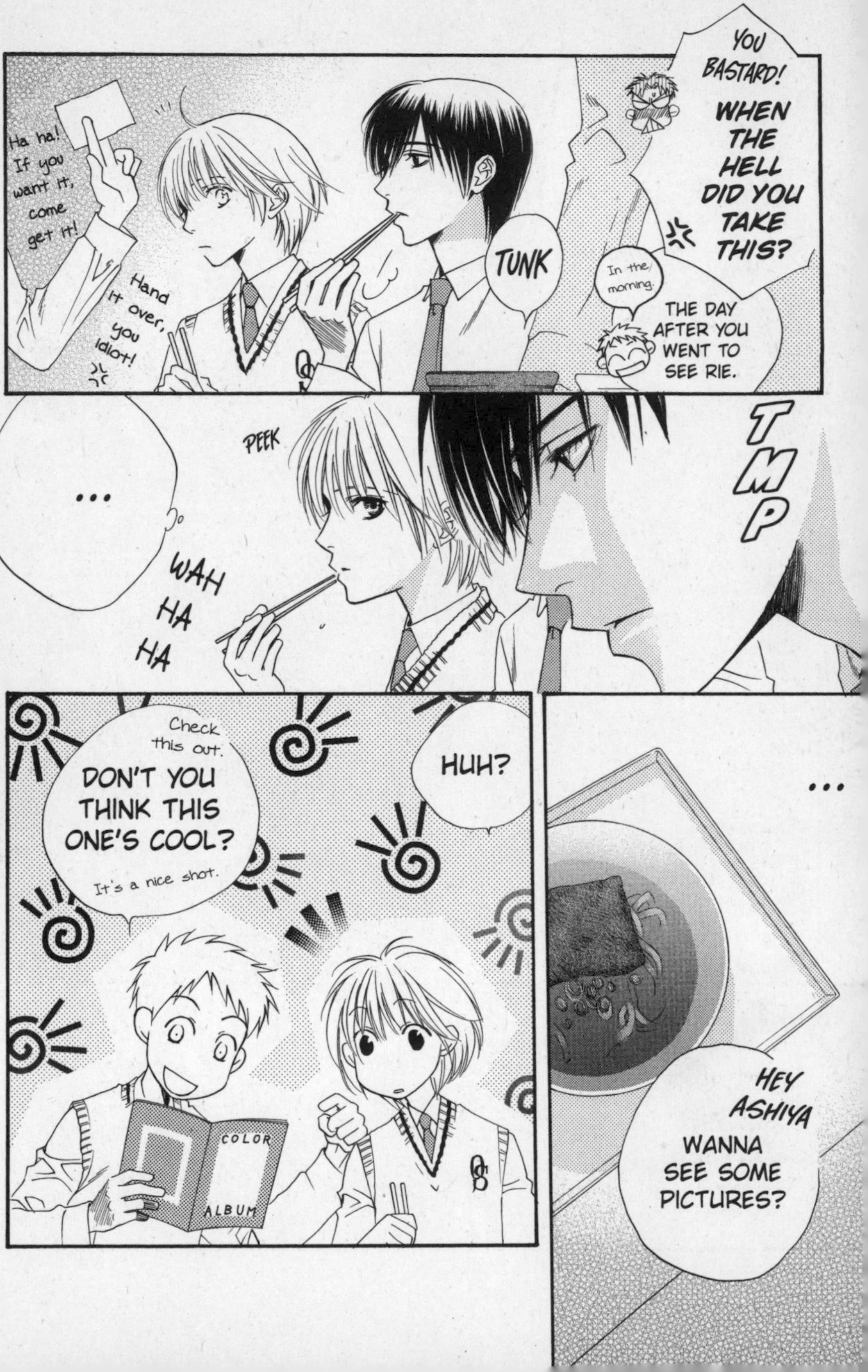
YOU BASTARD! WHEN THE HELL DID YOU TAKE THIS?
In the morning.
THE DAY AFTER YOU WENT TO SEE RIE.
TUNK
Ha ha! If you want it, come get it!
Hand it over, you idiot!
TMP
PEEK
...
WAH HA HA
...
HEY ASHIYA
WANNA SEE SOME PICTURES?
HUH?
Check this out.
DON'T YOU THINK THIS ONE'S COOL?
It's a nice shot.
COLOR
ALBUM

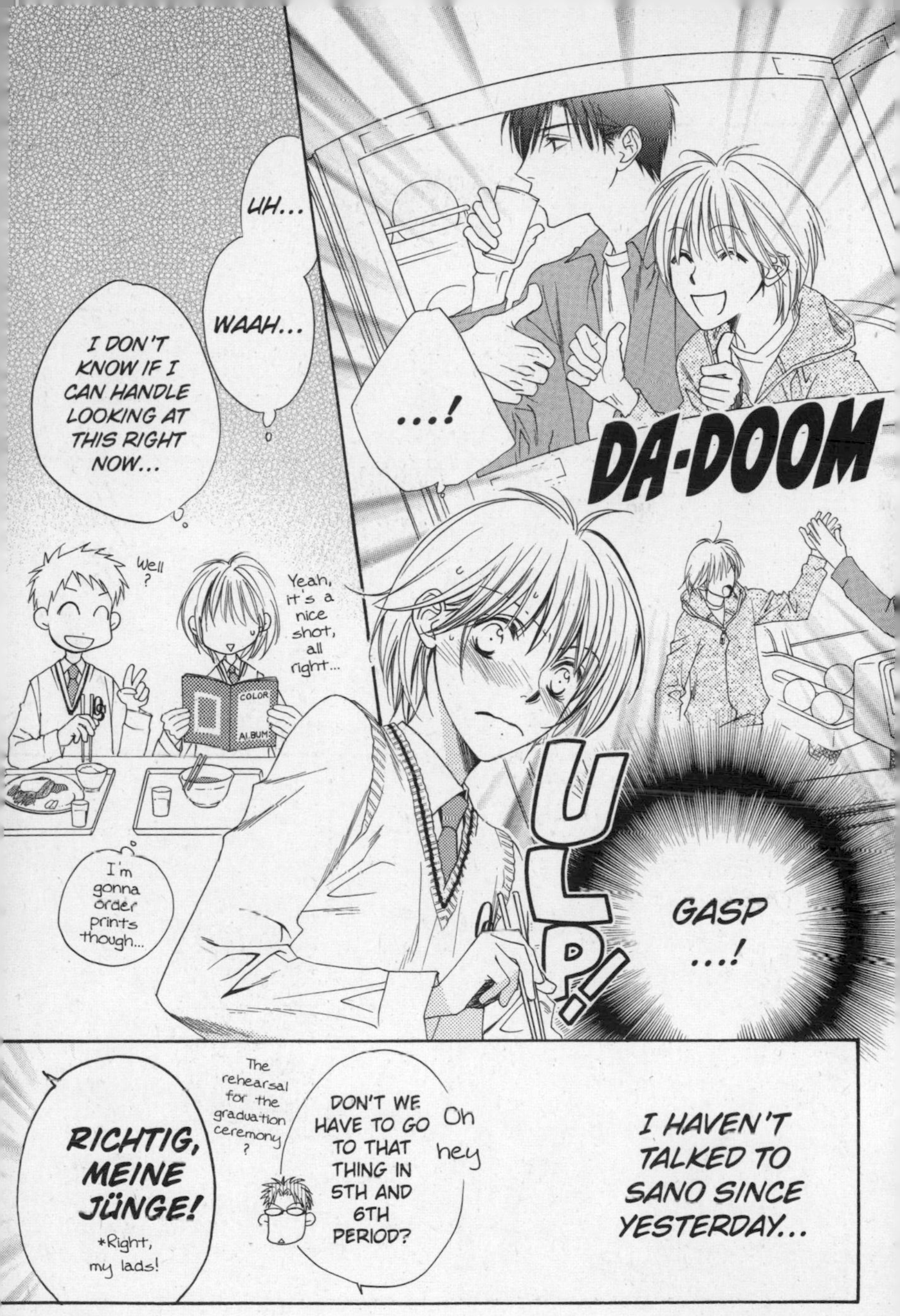
...!
DA-DOOM
GASP ...!
ULP!
UH...
WAAH...
I DON'T KNOW IF I CAN HANDLE LOOKING AT THIS RIGHT NOW...
Well?
Yeah, it's a nice shot, all right...
COLOR ALBUM
I'm gonna order prints though...
I HAVEN'T TALKED TO SANO SINCE YESTERDAY...
Oh hey
DON'T WE HAVE TO GO TO THAT THING IN 5TH AND 6TH PERIOD?
The rehearsal for the graduation ceremony?
RICHTIG, MEINE JÜNGE!
*Right, my lads!

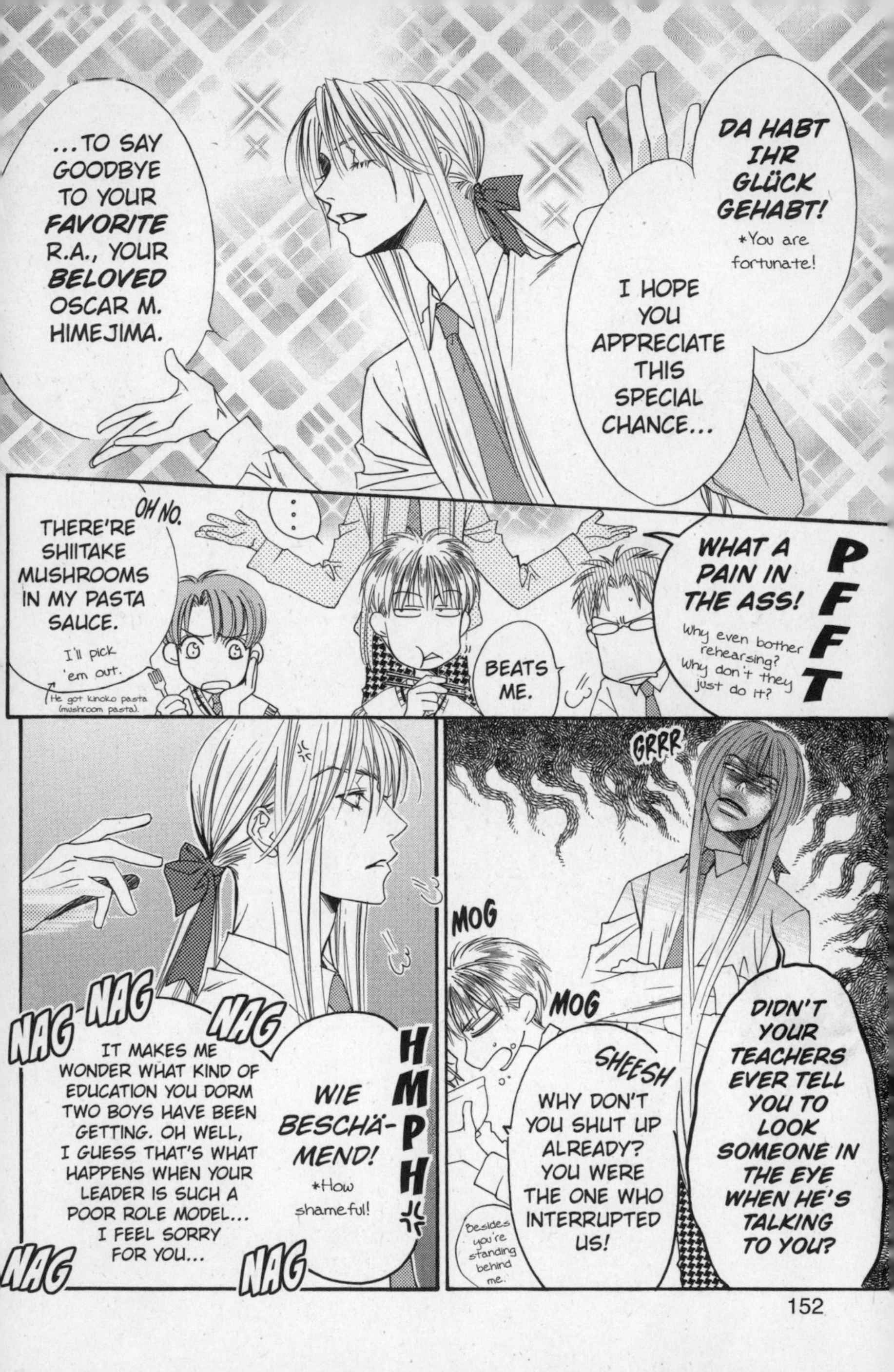
DA HABT IHR GLÜCK GEHABT!
*You are fortunate!
I HOPE YOU APPRECIATE THIS SPECIAL CHANCE...
...TO SAY GOODBYE TO YOUR FAVORITE R.A., YOUR BELOVED OSCAR M. HIMEJIMA.
WHAT A PAIN IN THE ASS!
PFFT
Why even bother rehearsing? Why don't they just do it?
BEATS ME.
...
OH NO.
THERE'RE SHIITAKE MUSHROOMS IN MY PASTA SAUCE.
I'll pick 'em out.
He got kinoko pasta (mushroom pasta).
GRRR
DIDN'T YOUR TEACHERS EVER TELL YOU TO LOOK SOMEONE IN THE EYE WHEN HE'S TALKING TO YOU?
SHEESH
WHY DON'T YOU SHUT UP ALREADY? YOU WERE THE ONE WHO INTERRUPTED US!
Besides you're standing behind me.
MOG
MOG
HMPH
WIE BESCHÄMEND!
*How shameful!
NAG-NAG
NAG
IT MAKES ME WONDER WHAT KIND OF EDUCATION YOU DORM TWO BOYS HAVE BEEN GETTING. OH WELL, I GUESS THAT'S WHAT HAPPENS WHEN YOUR LEADER IS SUCH A POOR ROLE MODEL... I FEEL SORRY FOR YOU...
NAG
NAG

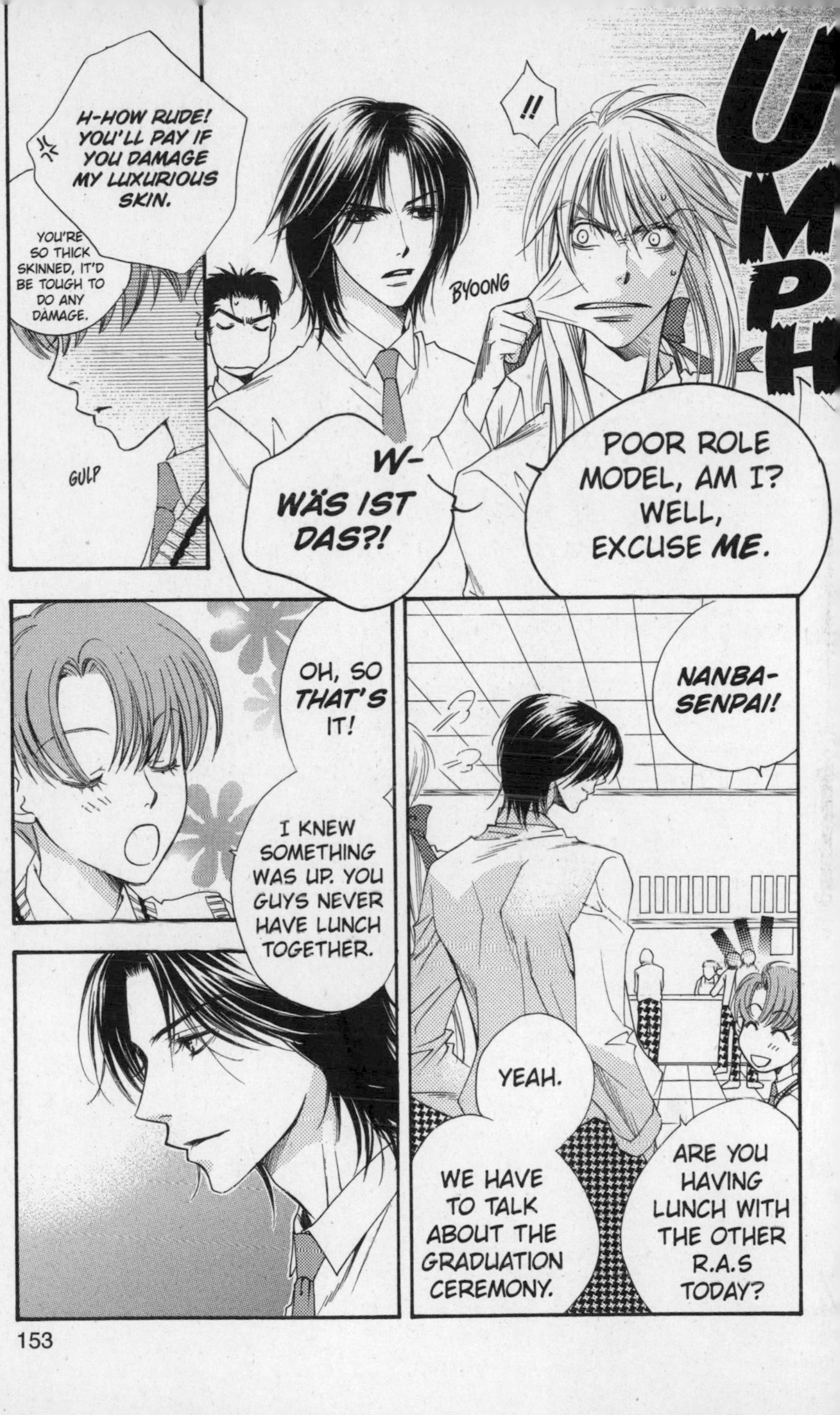
UMPH
!!
BYOONG
POOR ROLE MODEL, AM I? WELL, EXCUSE ME.
W- WÄS IST DAS?!
H-HOW RUDE! YOU'LL PAY IF YOU DAMAGE MY LUXURIOUS SKIN.
YOU'RE SO THICK SKINNED, IT'D BE TOUGH TO DO ANY DAMAGE.
GULP
NANBA-SENPAI!
ARE YOU HAVING LUNCH WITH THE OTHER R.A.S TODAY?
YEAH.
WE HAVE TO TALK ABOUT THE GRADUATION CEREMONY.
OH, SO THAT'S IT!
I KNEW SOMETHING WAS UP. YOU GUYS NEVER HAVE LUNCH TOGETHER.

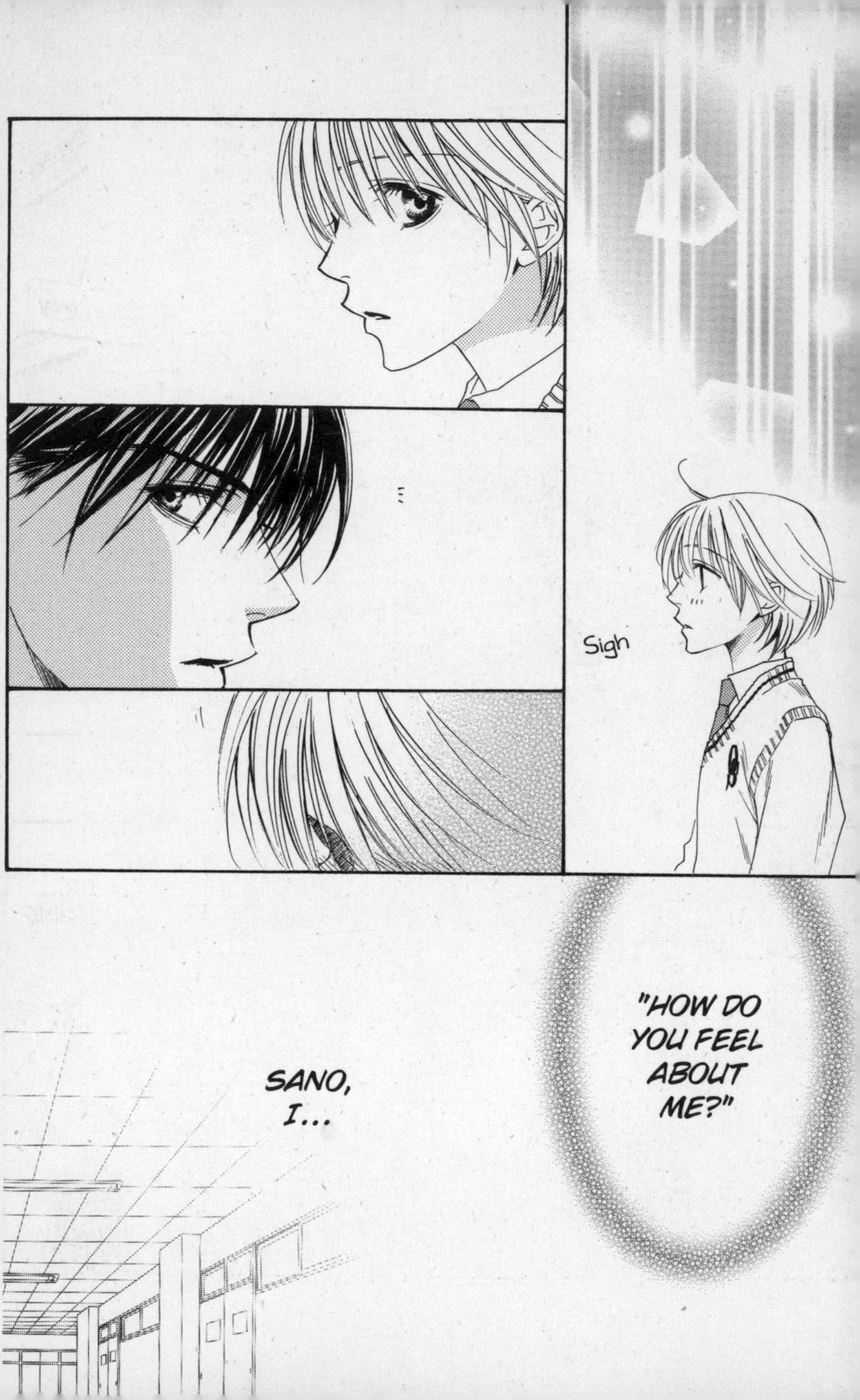
Sigh
"HOW DO YOU FEEL ABOUT ME?"
SANO, I...

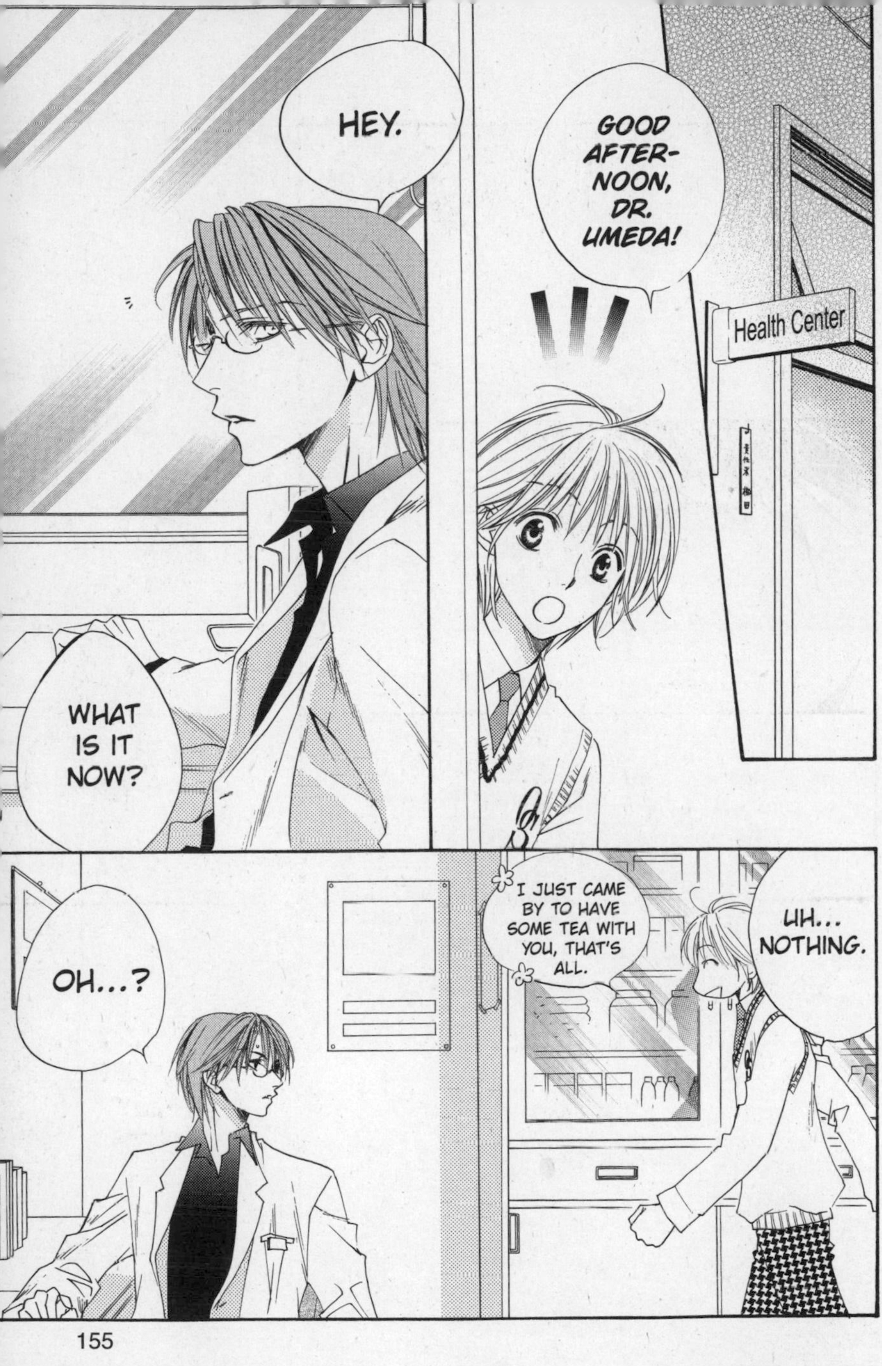
GOOD AFTER-NOON, DR. UMEDA!
Health Center
HEY.
WHAT IS IT NOW?
UH... NOTHING.
I JUST CAME BY TO HAVE SOME TEA WITH YOU, THAT'S ALL.
OH...?

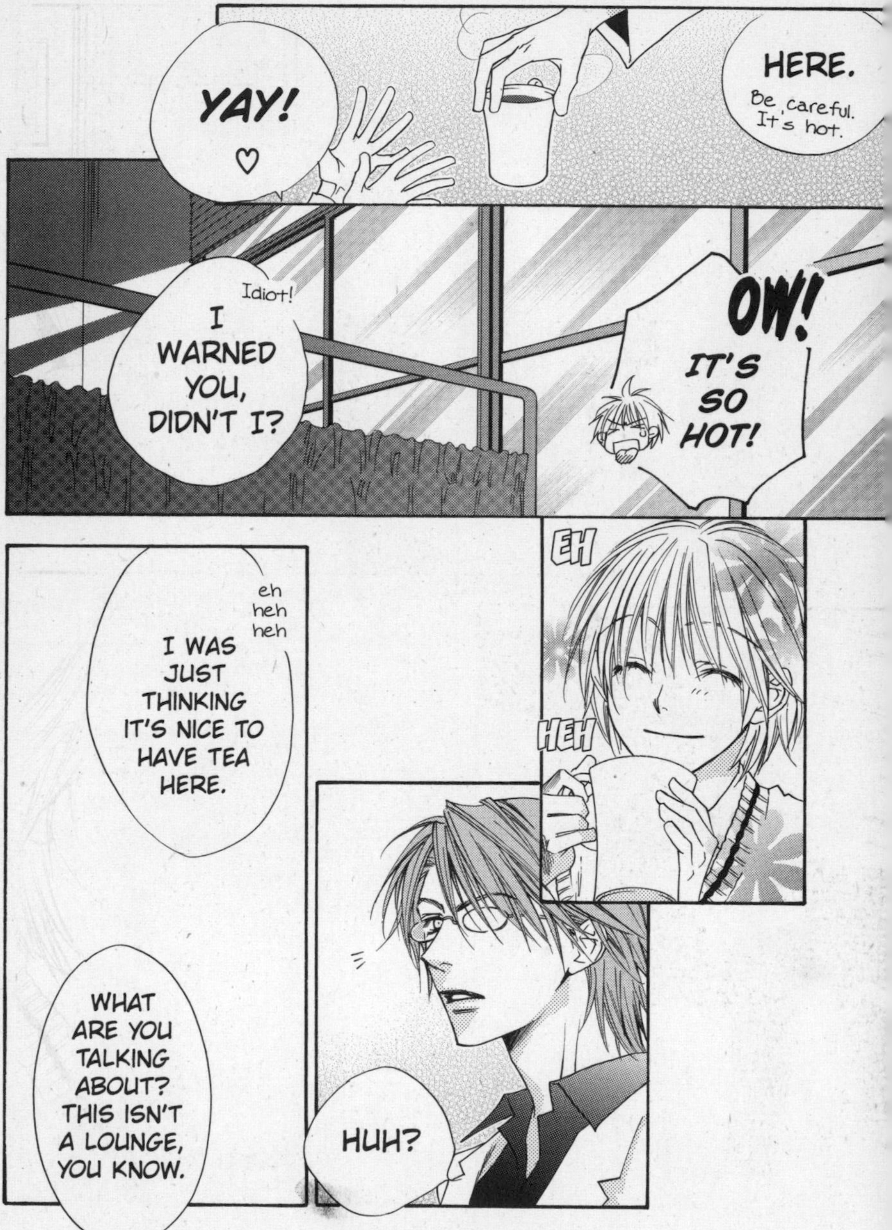
HERE.
Be careful. It's hot.
YAY! ♡
OW! IT'S SO HOT!
Idiot!
I WARNED YOU, DIDN'T I?
EH HEH
eh heh heh
I WAS JUST THINKING IT'S NICE TO HAVE TEA HERE.
HUH?
WHAT ARE YOU TALKING ABOUT? THIS ISN'T A LOUNGE, YOU KNOW.

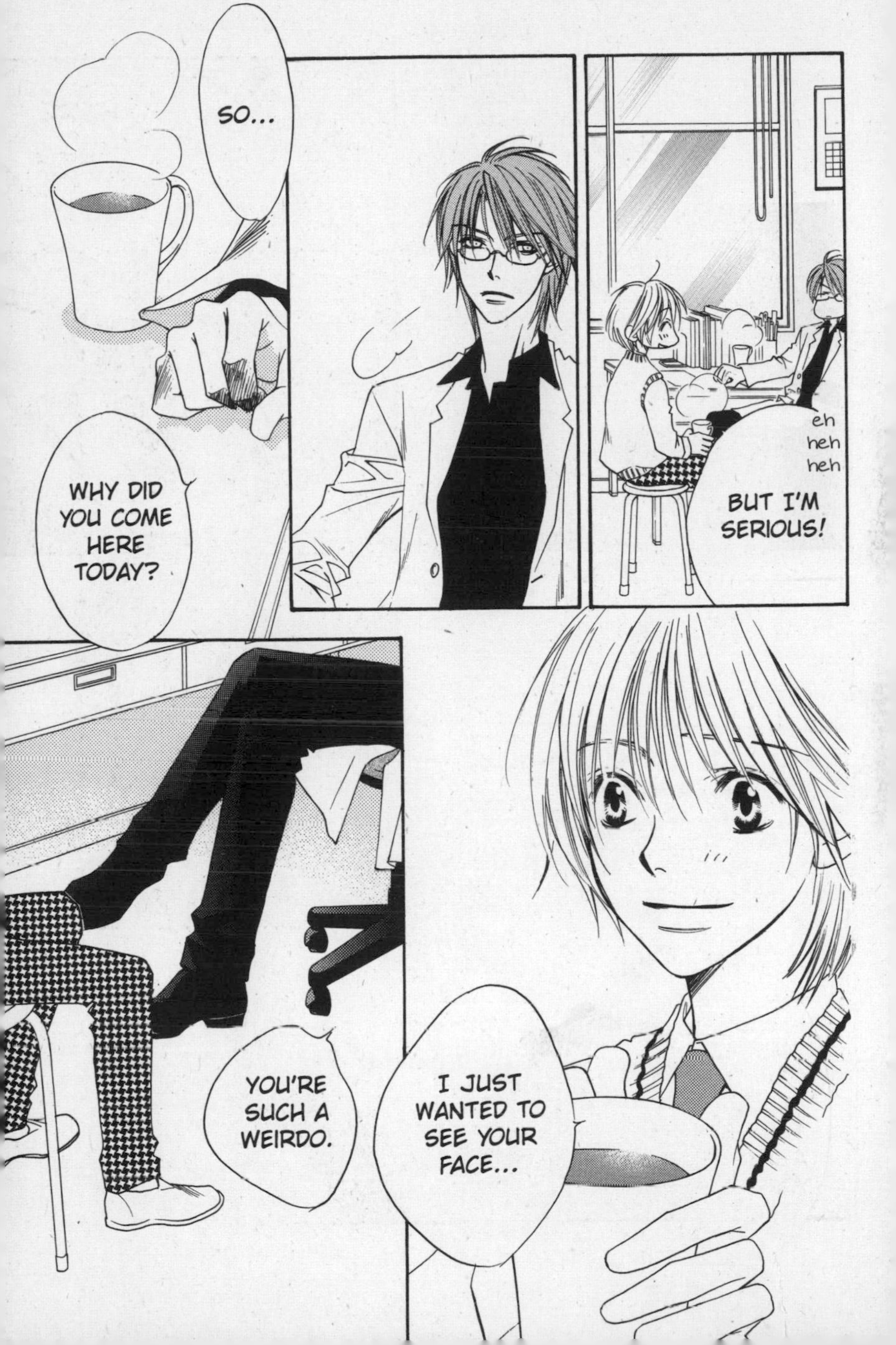
eh heh heh
BUT I'M SERIOUS!
SO...
WHY DID YOU COME HERE TODAY?
I JUST WANTED TO SEE YOUR FACE...
YOU'RE SUCH A WEIRDO.

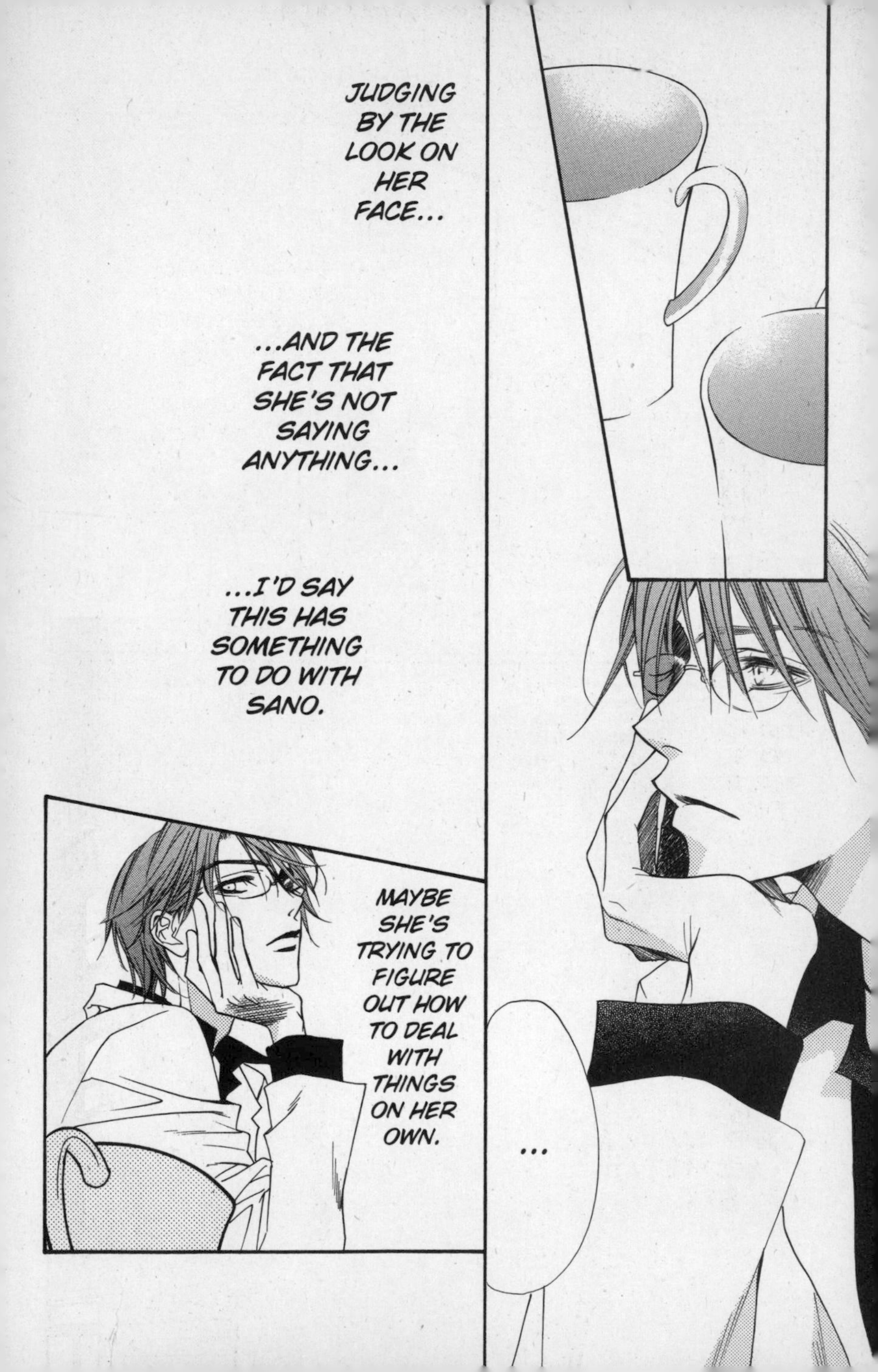
...
JUDGING BY THE LOOK ON HER FACE...
...AND THE FACT THAT SHE'S NOT SAYING ANYTHING...
...I'D SAY THIS HAS SOMETHING TO DO WITH SANO.
MAYBE SHE'S TRYING TO FIGURE OUT HOW TO DEAL WITH THINGS ON HER OWN.

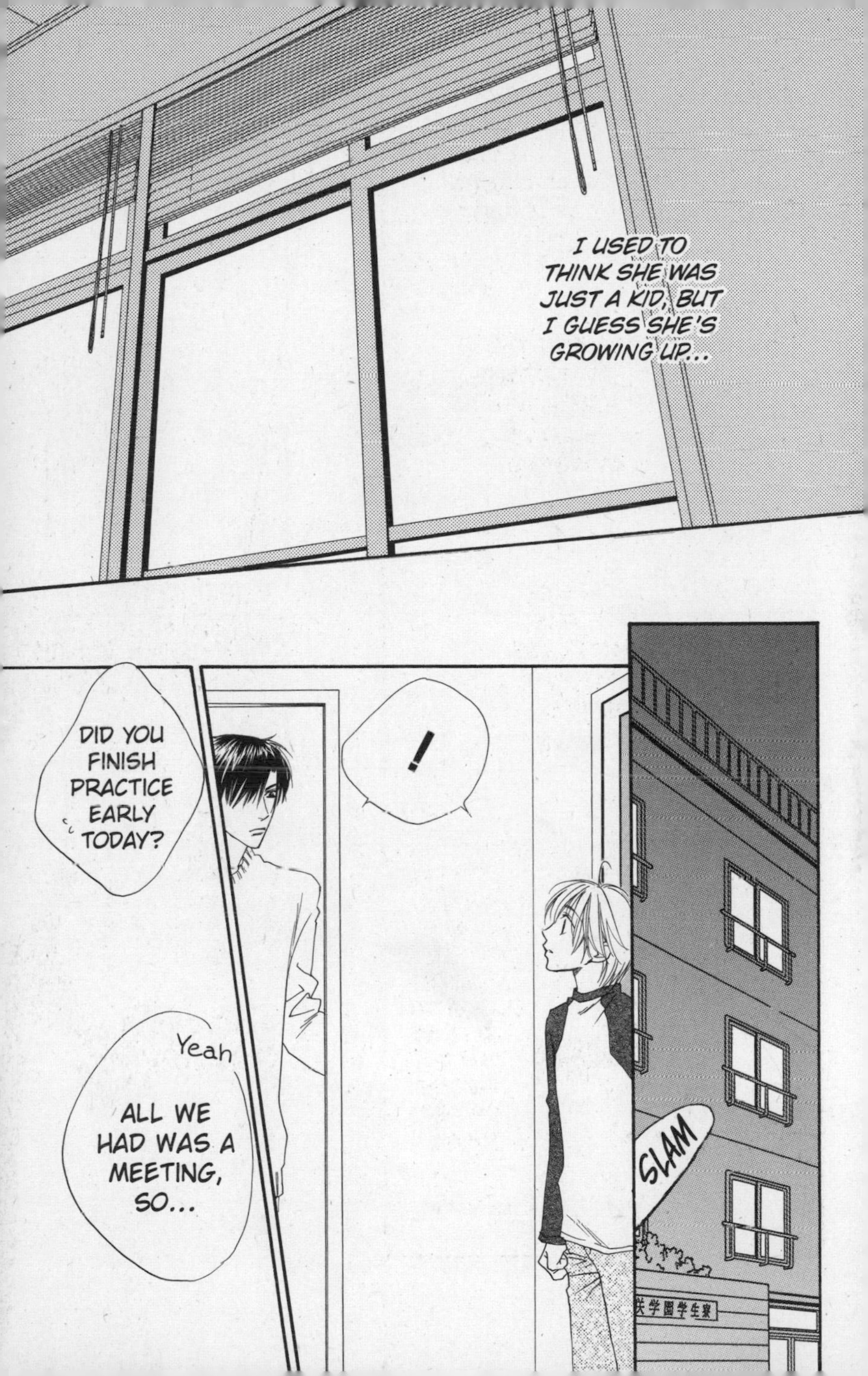
I USED TO THINK SHE WAS JUST A KID, BUT I GUESS SHE'S GROWING UP...
SLAM
!
DID YOU FINISH PRACTICE EARLY TODAY?
Yeah
ALL WE HAD WAS A MEETING, SO...

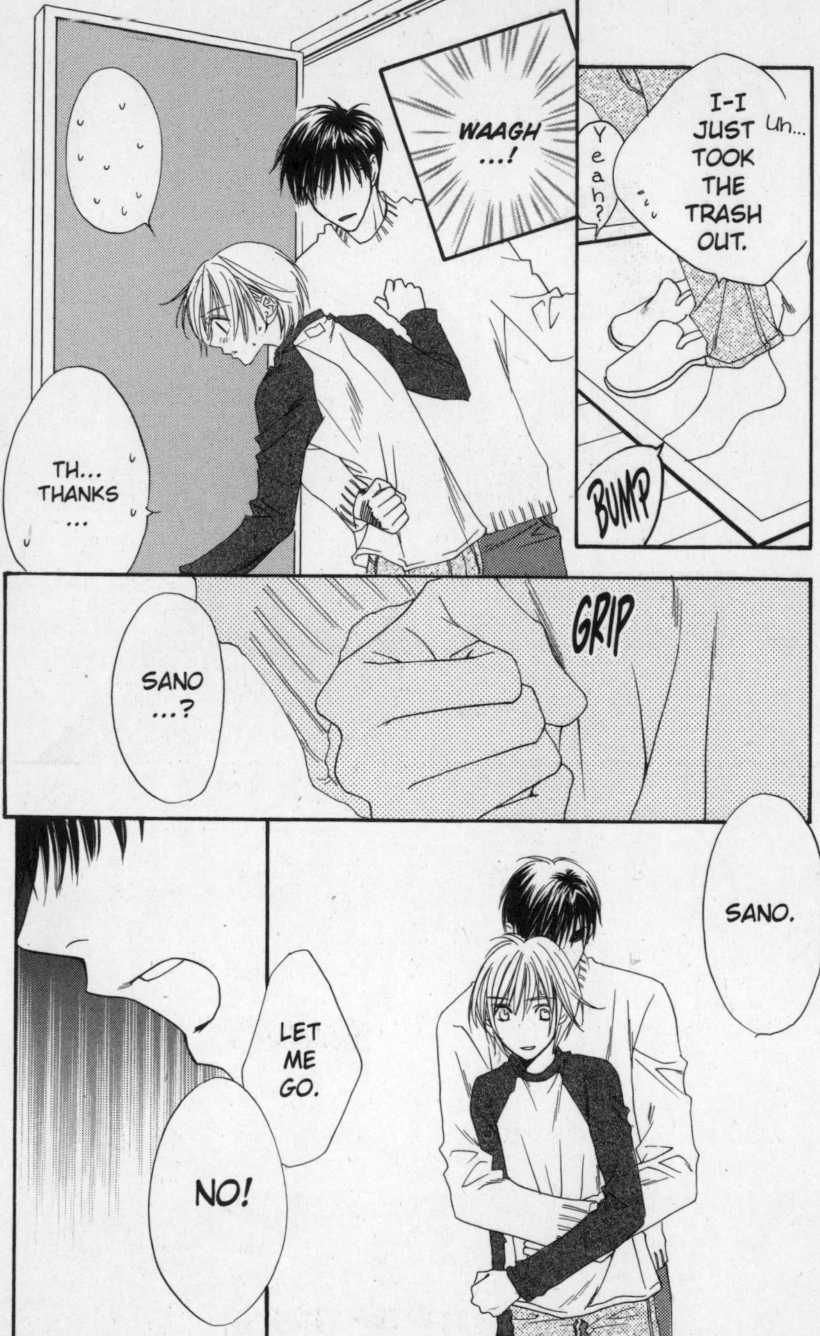
Uh...
I-I JUST TOOK THE TRASH OUT.
Yeah?
BUMP
WAAGH ...!
TH... THANKS ...
GRIP
SANO ...?
SANO.
LET ME GO.
NO!

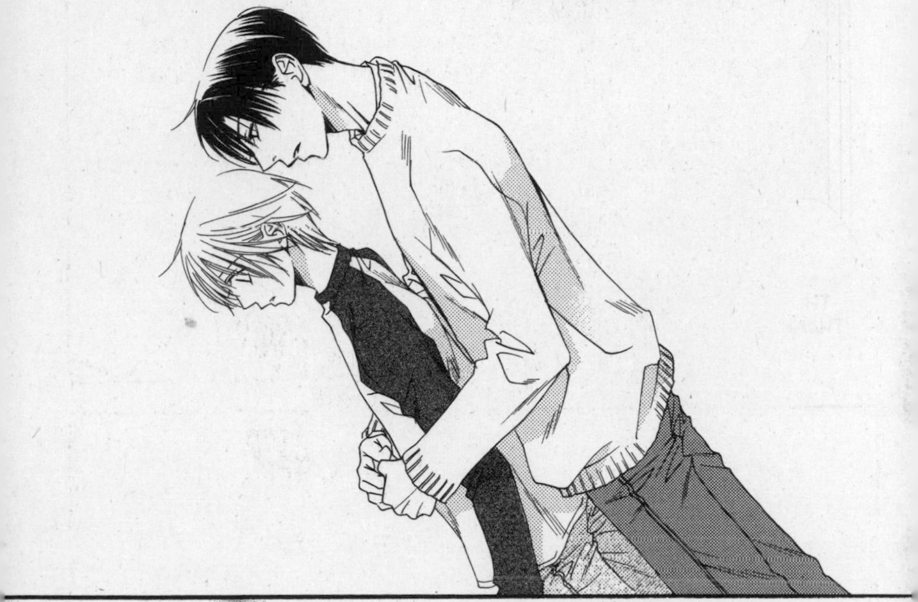

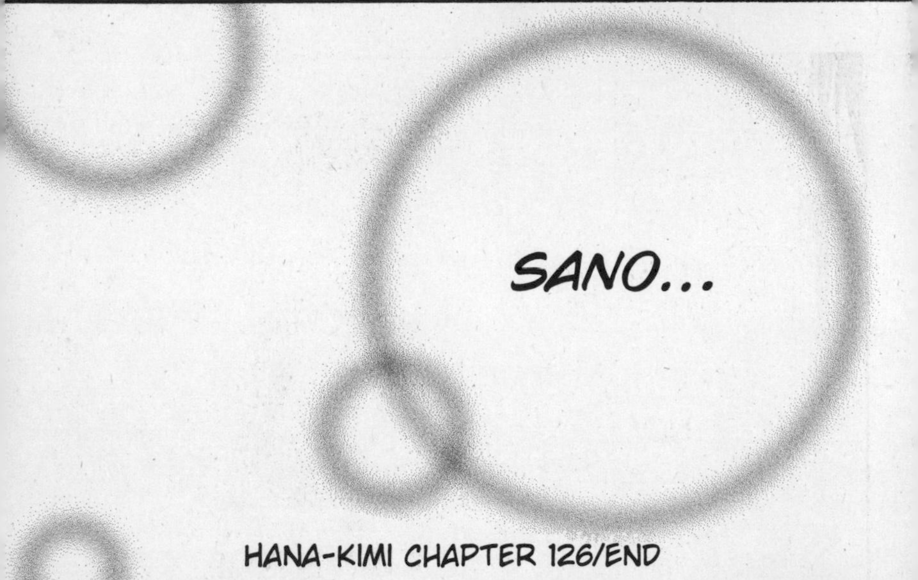
SANO...

HANA-KIMI CHAPTER 126/END

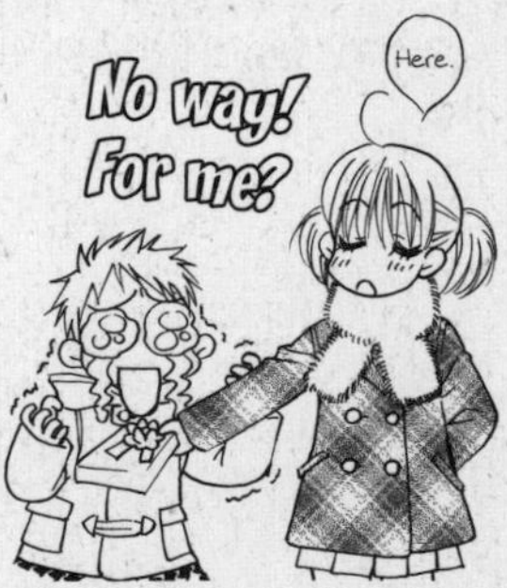
Here.
No way! For me?

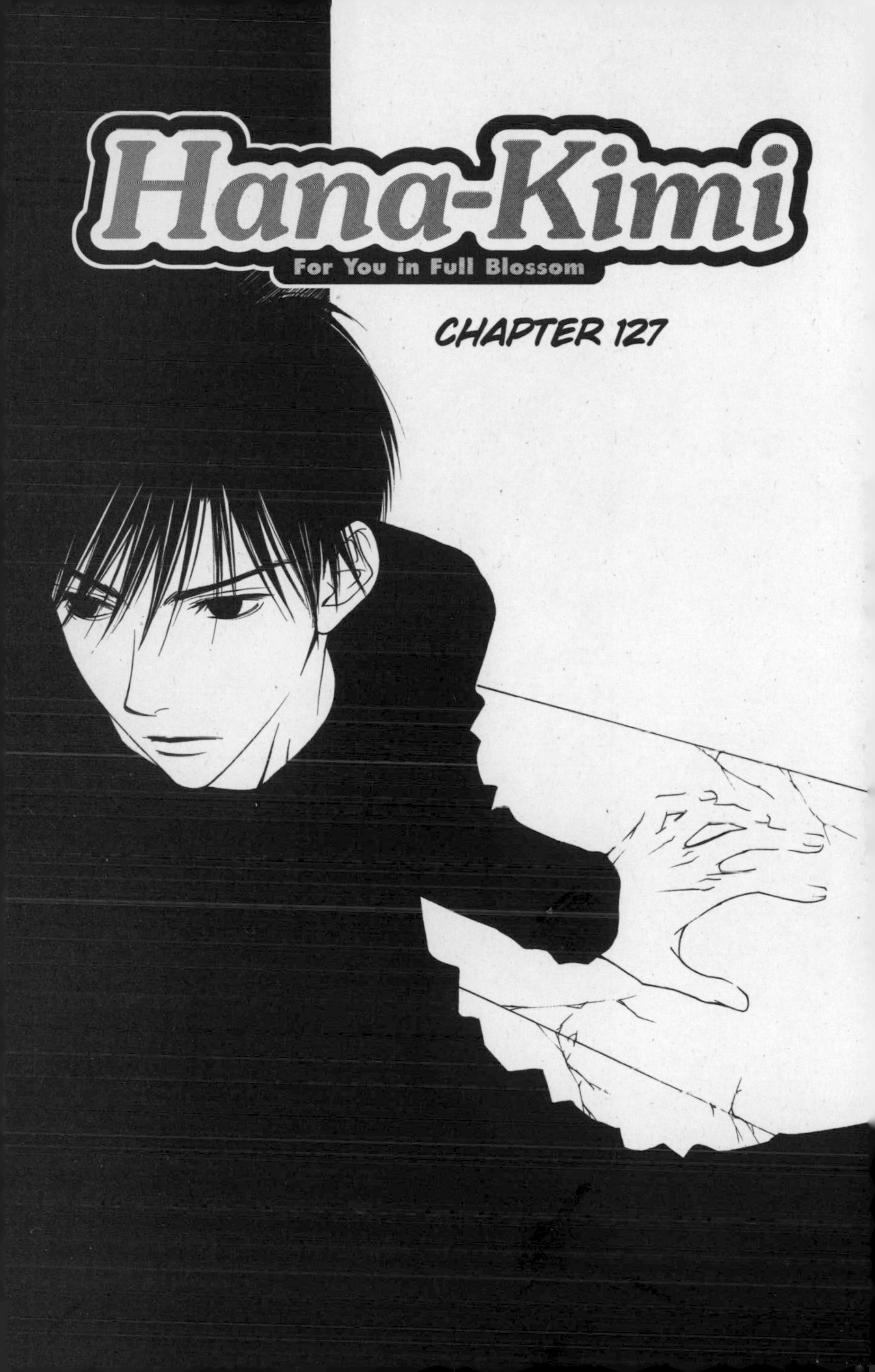
Hana-Kimi
For You in Full Blossom
CHAPTER 127

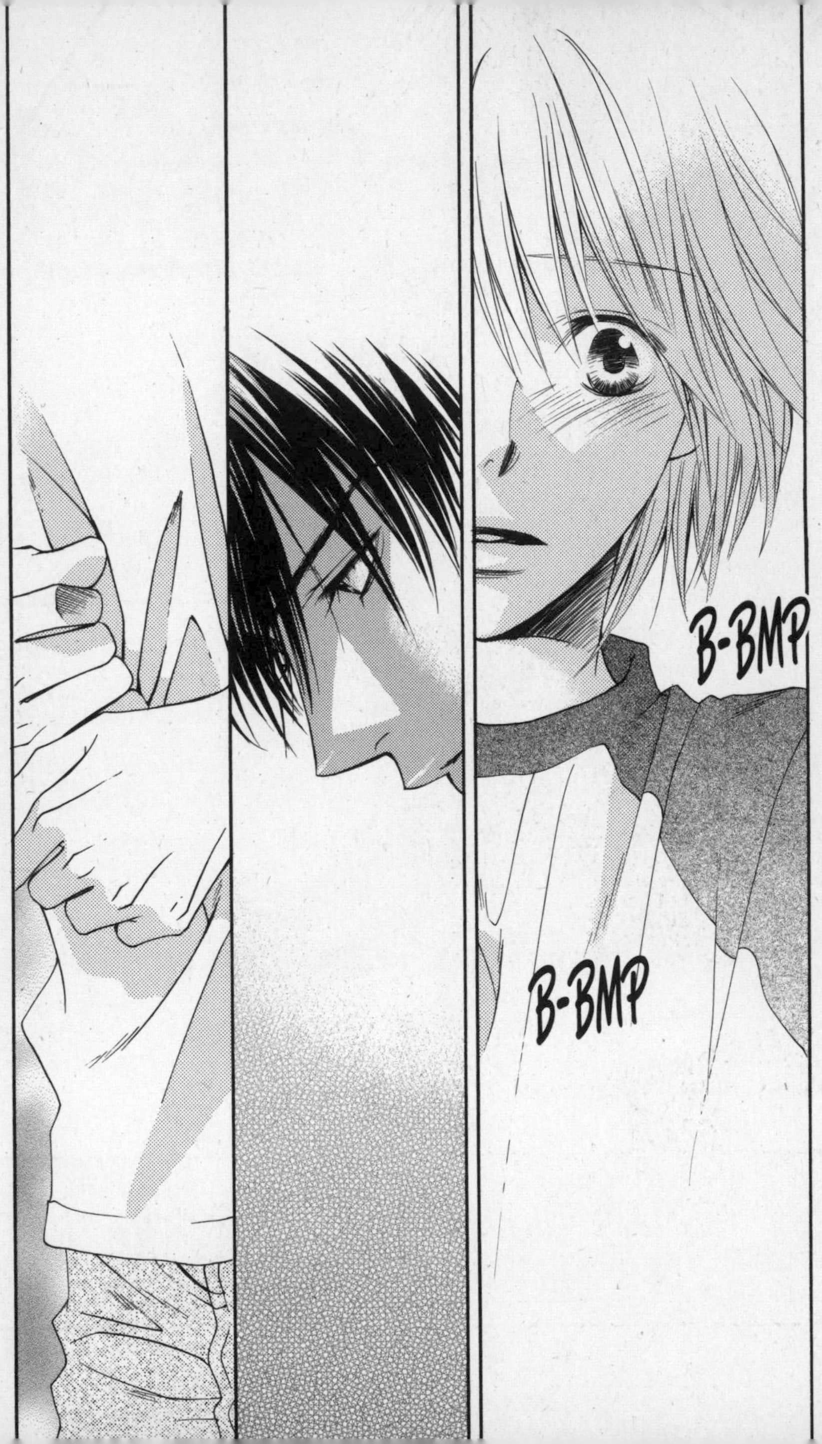
B-BMP
B-BMP

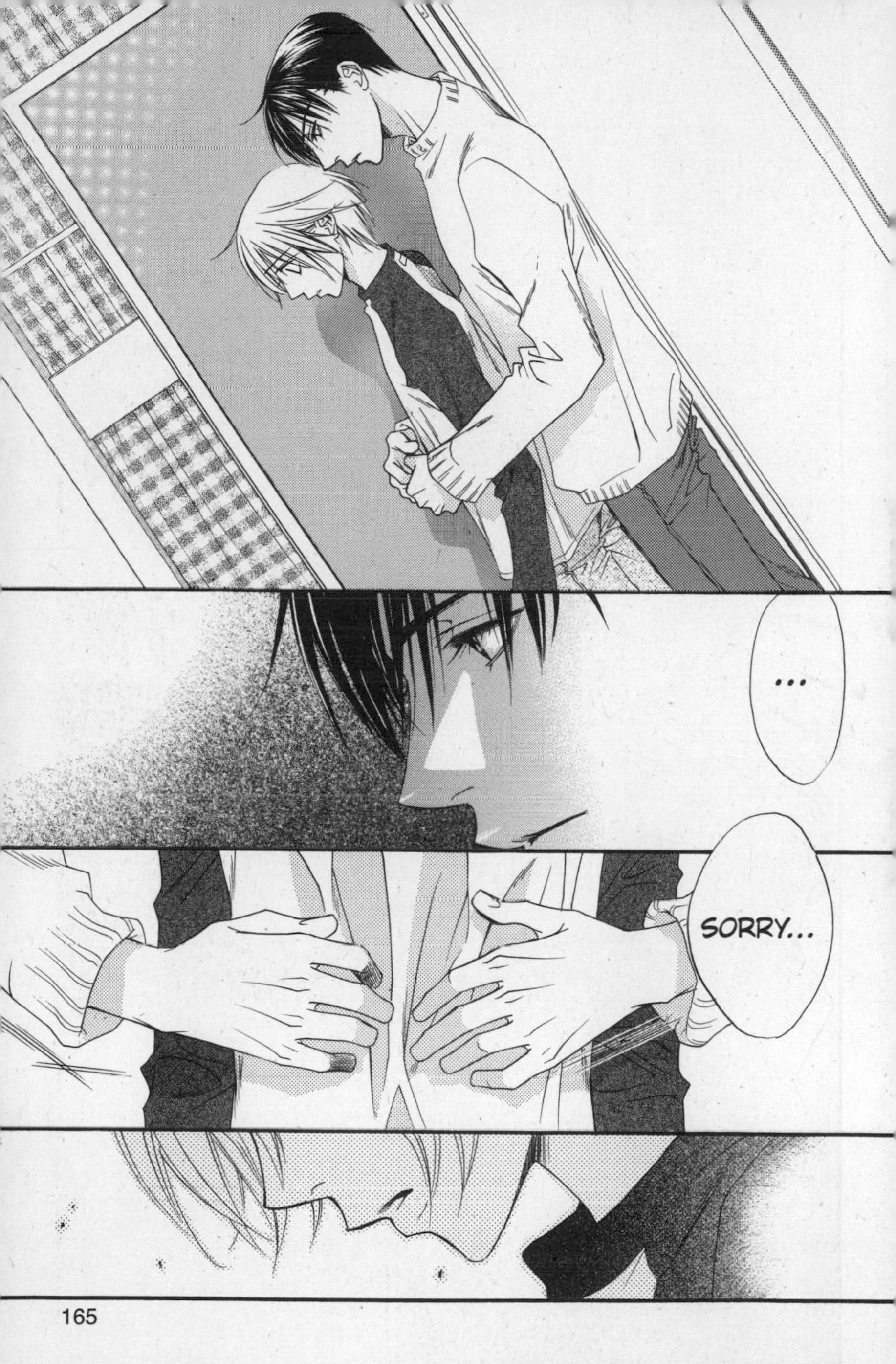
...
SORRY...

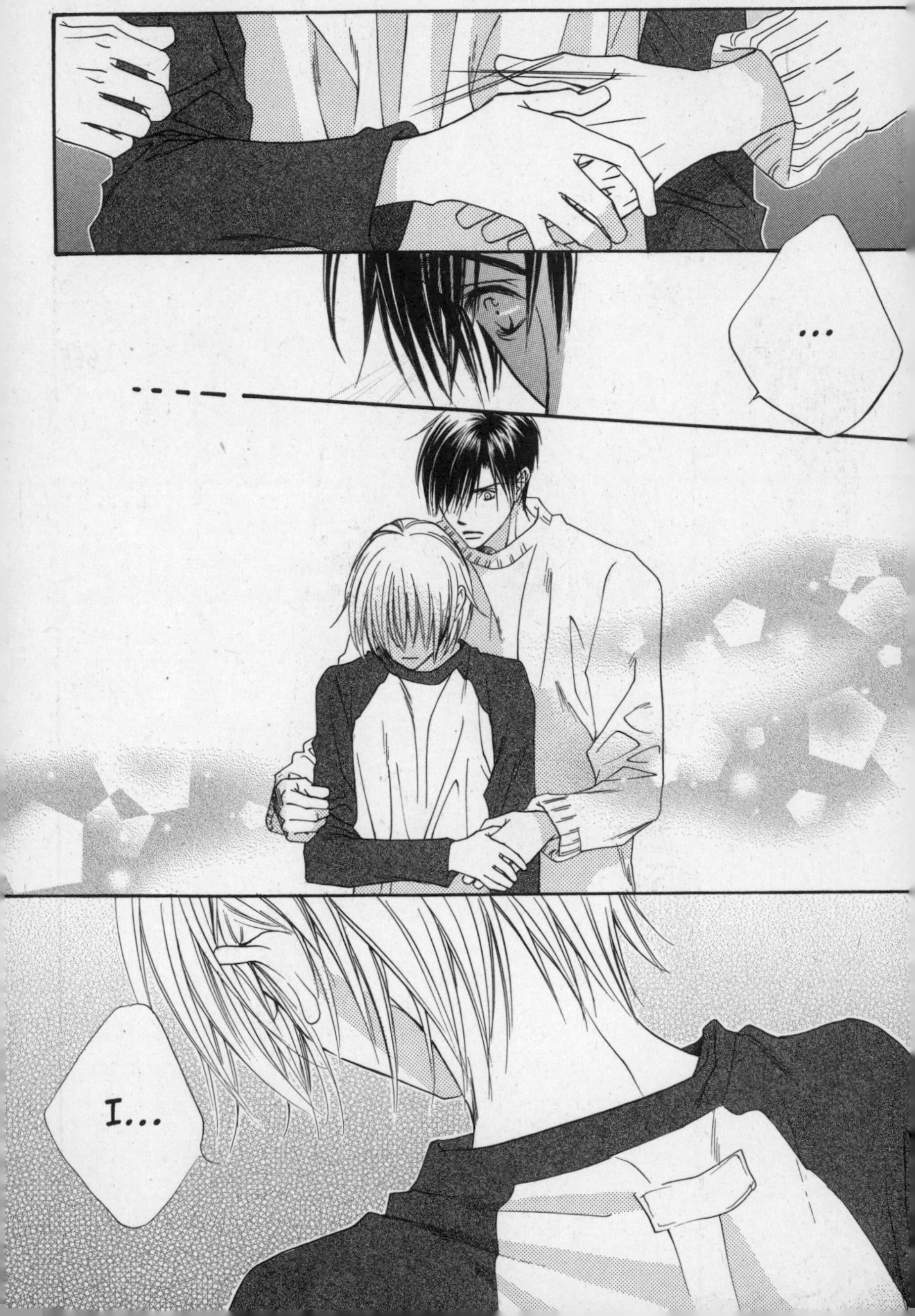
...
I...

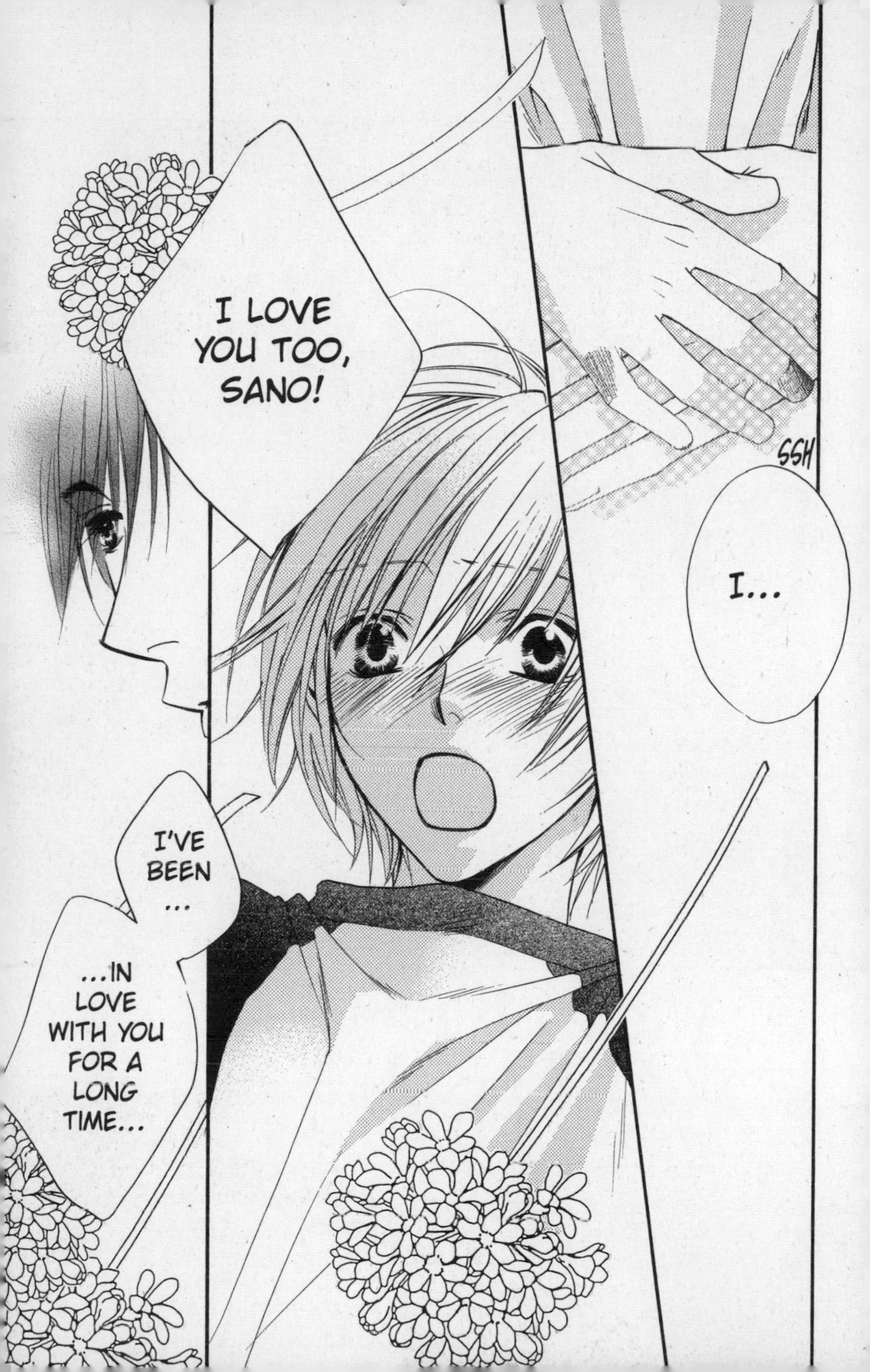
SSH
I...
I LOVE YOU TOO, SANO!
I'VE BEEN ...
...IN LOVE WITH YOU FOR A LONG TIME...

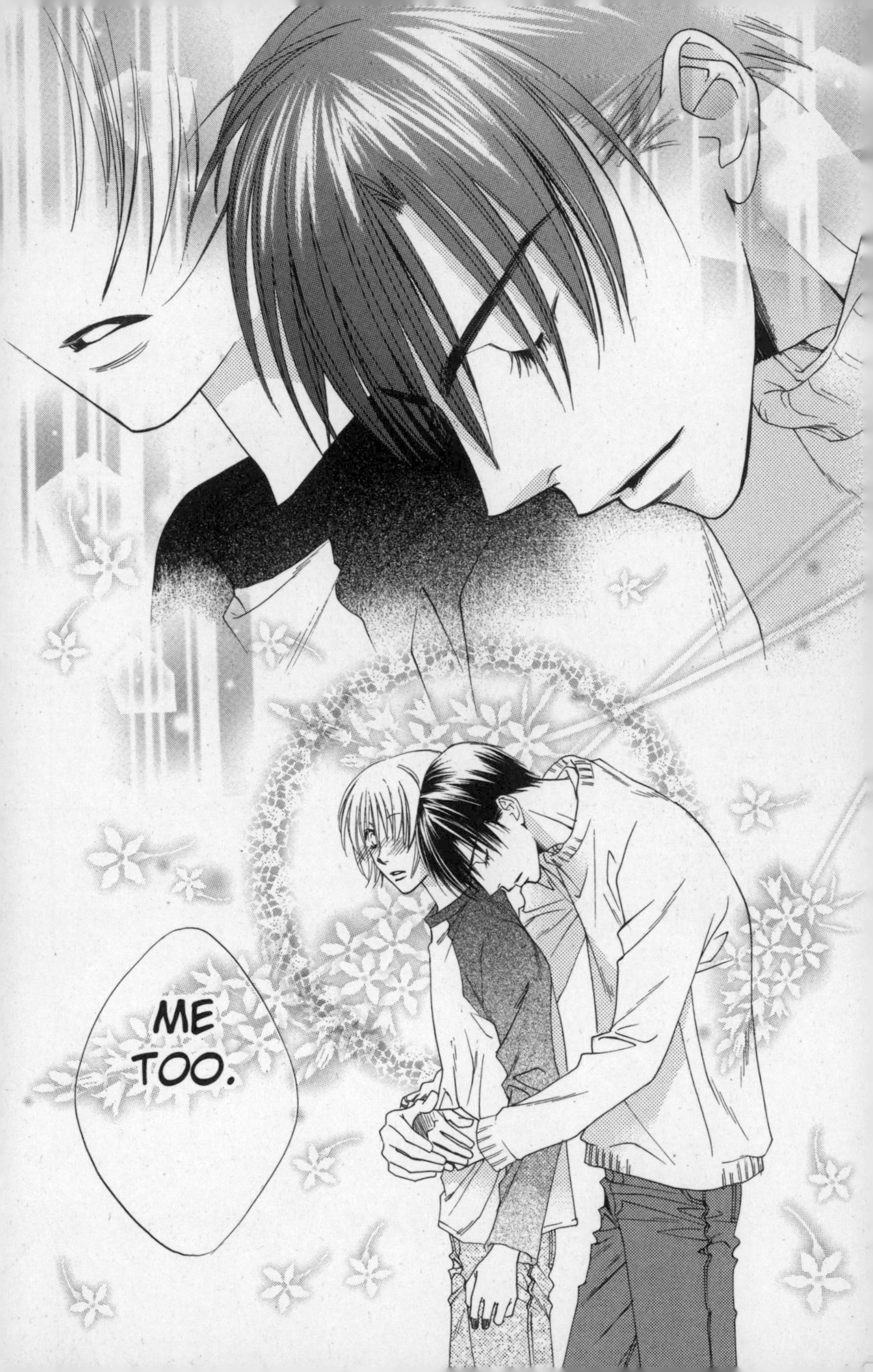
ME TOO.